Prentice Hall
GRAMMAR AND COMPOSITION

SERIES CONSULTANTS

Grade 6
Joleen Johnson
Curriculum Writer, Office of
Secondary Instruction
San Bernardino City Unified Schools
San Bernardino, California

Grade 7
Ellen G. Manhire
English Consultant Coordinator
Fresno, California

Grade 8
Elizabeth A. Nace
Supervisor, Language Arts
Akron, Ohio

Grade 9
Jerry Reynolds
Supervisor, Language Arts
Rochester, Minnesota

Grade 10
Marlene Corbett
Chairperson, Department of English
Charlotte, North Carolina

Grade 11
Gilbert Hunt
Chairperson, Department of English
Manchester, Connecticut

Grade 12
Margherite LaPota
Curriculum Specialist
Tulsa, Oklahoma

CRITIC READERS

Hugh B. Cassell
Jefferson County Public Schools
Louisville, KY

Mary Demarest
St. Mary's Dominican High School
New Orleans, LA

Judy Luehm Junecko
Leesburg High School
Leesburg, FL

Ruth E. Loeffler
Norman High School
Norman, OK

D. Gay Masters
Salem-Keizer Public Schools
Salem, OR

Laura Moyer
Gloversville High School
Gloversville, NY

Avis Satterfield
Virgil I. Grissom High School
Huntsville, AL

Bonnie Scott
St. Augustine High School
St. Augustine, FL

Margie M. Spencer
S. R. Butler High School
Huntsville, AL

Jeanne Bussiere-Stephens
Phillips Academy
Andover, MA

Marvin Zimmerman
Little Rock School District
Little Rock, AR

George Comer
Gary Public Schools
Gary, IN

Prentice Hall

GRAMMAR AND COMPOSITION

SERIES AUTHORS

Gary Forlini **Senior Author**
Pelham High School, Pelham, New York

Mary Beth Bauer Harris County Department of Education,
Houston, Texas

Lawrence Biener Locust Valley Junior-Senior High School,
Locust Valley, New York

Linda Capo Pelham Junior High School,
Pelham, New York

Karen Moore Kenyon Saratoga High School,
Saratoga, California

Darla H. Shaw Ridgefield School System,
Ridgefield, Connecticut

Zenobia Verner University of Houston,
Houston, Texas

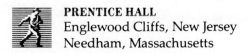

PRENTICE HALL
Englewood Cliffs, New Jersey
Needham, Massachusetts

SUPPLEMENTARY MATERIALS

Annotated Teacher's Edition
Teacher's Resource Book
Computer Exercise Bank
Writing Model Transparencies

Acknowledgments: page 911

PRENTICE HALL **Grammar and Composition**
Fourth Edition

ISBN 0-13-711870-8

10 9 8 7 6 5 4 3

PRENTICE HALL
A Division of Simon & Schuster
Englewood Cliffs, New Jersey 07632

Contents

Grammar   Usage   Mechanics

6

II Usage

8

Composition and Allied Skills

IV Composition–The Writer's Techniques

13 The Writing Process

14

16

VIII Speaking and Listening

Chapter 1

The Parts of Speech

Every word in the English language can be assigned to one of the eight categories, called the *parts of speech* that are shown in the following chart.

THE EIGHT PARTS OF SPEECH		
nouns	adjectives	prepositions
pronouns	adverbs	conjunctions
verbs		interjection

The meaning of a word and the way it is used in a sentence determines its part of speech. This chapter discusses each of the eight parts of speech.

1.1 Nouns and Pronouns

Nouns are the labels that are given to the people, places, and things about which human beings communicate. Pronouns are words that take the place of nouns, replacing them in sentences.

Nouns

Nouns constitute the largest of the parts of speech categories.

A noun is the name of a person, place, or thing.

Determining which words name *people* or *places* usually presents no problems.

PERSON: woman, cousin, pilot, Mr. Lopez, Aunt Margaret

PLACE: university, Main Street, desert, Chesapeake Bay, Ohio

The classification *thing*, however, is as ambiguous as the word itself. It encompasses visible things, ideas, actions, conditions, and qualities.

VISIBLE THINGS: shark, wheat, refrigerator

IDEAS: abolition, militarism, evolution

ACTIONS: dispute, construction, communication

CONDITIONS: fear, loneliness, ownership

QUALITIES: integrity, assurance, vulgarity

Knowing the endings often found on nouns can sometimes aid in identifying them. Some of the most common noun suffixes are *-dom, -ics, -ion, ism, -ment, -ness,* and *-ship*.

EXAMPLES: freedom   entertainment
           aeronautics shyness
           frustration leadership
           socialism

Concrete and Abstract Nouns. Nouns are sometimes grouped according to the characteristics of the things they name. A *concrete* noun names something that you can physically see, touch, taste, hear, or smell. An *abstract* noun names something that is nonphysical, that you cannot readily perceive through any of your five senses.

Concrete Nouns	Abstract Nouns
pitchfork	nationalism
garlic	era
critic	career
bruise	immortality

Singular and Plural Nouns. Nouns can indicate number. *Singular* nouns name one person, place, or thing. *Plural* nouns name more than one. Most plural nouns are formed by the addition of *-s* or *-es* to the singular form. Some plural nouns, however, are formed irregularly and must be memorized. (See Section 27.2 for rules governing the formation of plural nouns.)

SINGULAR NOUNS	
Regular	**Irregular**
valley	mouse
lash	ox
sky	nucleus
PLURAL NOUNS	
valleys	mice
lashes	oxen
skies	nuclei

Collective Nouns. Nouns that name *groups* of people or things are called *collective nouns.* Although a collective noun looks singular, its meaning may be either singular or plural depending on how you use it in a sentence. (See Section 8.1 for rules governing the use of collective nouns in sentences.)

COLLECTIVE NOUNS	
council	orchestra
delegation	team
entourage	troop

Compound Nouns. A noun that is composed of two or more words acting as a single unit is called a *compound noun.* For example, the noun *milk* and the noun *snake* can act together to name a particular animal—a *milk snake.* Compound nouns are usually entered in the dictionary because they name something other than what the individual words suggest. An expression such as *milk bottle,* on the other hand, is not generally considered a compound noun because it means nothing more than what the two words suggest: "a bottle for milk."

Compound nouns may appear in three forms: as separate words, as hyphenated words, or as combined words.

COMPOUND NOUNS	
Separated	crab grass, player piano, snake dance
Hyphenated	jack-in-the-box, light-year, sister-in-law
Combined	dragonfly, eardrum, starfish

If you are in doubt about the spelling of a compound noun, check a dictionary. If you cannot find the expression, write it as separate words.

Common and Proper Nouns. All nouns can be categorized as either common or proper. A *common noun* names any one of a class of people, places, or things. A *proper noun* names a specific person, place, or thing.

Common Nouns	Proper Nouns
playwright	Lillian Hellman, Bernard Shaw
island	Maui, Sicily
building	World Trade Towers, Taj Mahal

As you can see from these examples, proper nouns are always capitalized, whereas common nouns are not. (See Section 11.1 for rules on capitalization.)

A *noun of direct address*—the name of a person you are directly talking to—is always proper, as is a family title before a personal name.

COMMON NOUN: My *aunt* is a taxi driver.

DIRECT ADDRESS: Please tell us, *Dad*, about your trip to Peru.

FAMILY TITLE: For many years *Uncle* David has lived in Iowa.

EXERCISE A: Identifying the Types of Nouns. Copy the following list of nouns. Then identify each according to whether it (1) names a person, place, or thing, (2) is concrete or abstract, (3) is singular or plural, (4) is collective, (5) is compound, and (6) is common or proper.

EXAMPLE: pleasure

(1) thing, (2) abstract, (3) singular, (4) not collective, (5) not compound, (6) common

1. jump suit	11. stitches
2. tomato	12. flock
3. giraffes	13. White House
4. San Francisco	14. umbrella
5. monkey wrenches	15. ugliness
6. Lord Peter Wimsey	16. life preservers
7. herd	17. jack-in-the-pulpit
8. privileges	18. terrorism
9. hope	19. Pearl Harbor
10. Davis Cup	20. sundial

EXERCISE B: Recognizing Compound Nouns. If an expression is in the dictionary, write *compound* and give a brief definition. If an expression is not in the dictionary, simply define the expression from common knowledge.

EXAMPLE: word of honor

compound   solemn promise; oath

1. rain check	6. storm warning
2. rain puddle	7. storm window
3. scarlet fever	8. dog days
4. scarlet glow	9. dog tag
5. scarlet ribbon	10. dog bone

Pronouns

Pronouns help people avoid awkward repetition of nouns.

Pronouns are words that stand for nouns or for words that take the place of nouns.

In the examples below, the italicized words are pronouns. The arrows point to the words that the pronouns stand for.

EXAMPLES: Jan and Ken went to the dance. *They* thought *it* was the best so far this year.

Swimming the Hellespont is a difficult feat. *It* was

accomplished by Lord Byron when *he* was in *his* early thirties.

24

The words that the arrows point to in the examples are called *antecedents*.

Antecedents are nouns (or words that take the place of nouns) for which pronouns stand.

Although an antecedent usually precedes its pronoun, it can also follow the pronoun.

EXAMPLE: After *their* performance, the actors went to a party.

There are several kinds of pronouns in English. Most have antecedents; a few do not. The rest of this section will describe the different kinds of pronouns and discuss their antecedents.

Personal Pronouns. Personal pronouns are used to refer to particular people, places, and things.

Personal pronouns are used to refer to (1) the person speaking, (2) the person spoken to, or (3) the person, place, or thing spoken about.

All of the personal pronouns are listed in the following chart. First-person pronouns refer to the person speaking, second-person pronouns refer to the person spoken to, and third-person pronouns refer to the person, place, or thing spoken about. The personal pronouns in the chart that are italicized are sometimes called *possessive pronouns*.

PERSONAL PRONOUNS		
	Singular	**Plural**
First Person	I, me *my, mine*	we, us *our, ours*
Second Person	you *your, yours*	you *your, yours,*
Third Person	he, she, it him, her *his, her, hers,* *its*	they, them *their, theirs*

The antecedent of a personal pronoun may or may not be clearly stated. In the following examples, only the last sentence, which has a third-person pronoun, has a stated anteced-ent. In the first two examples, the antecedents are implied.

FIRST PERSON: *We* practiced a rousing march for the parade.

SECOND PERSON: *You* must submit *your* application soon.

THIRD PERSON: The blue-birds built *their* nest in the hedge.

Reflexive and Intensive Pronouns. Reflexive and inten-sive pronouns have the same form—both end in *-self* or *-selves*. Their form is the same, but their functions differ.

Reflexive pronouns are used to add information to a sentence by pointing back to a noun or pronoun near the beginning of the sentence.

Intensive pronouns are used simply to add em-phasis to a noun or pronoun.

The eight reflexive and intensive pronouns are formed from personal pronouns.

REFLEXIVE AND INTENSIVE PRONOUNS		
	Singular	**Plural**
First Person	myself	ourselves
Second Person	yourself	yourselves
Third Person	himself, herself, itself	themselves

A reflexive pronoun adds essential information to a sen-tence. An intensive pronoun, however, can usually be removed from the sentence without changing the sentence's basic meaning.

REFLEXIVE: Cats clean *themselves* carefully after each meal.

INTENSIVE: You *yourself* agreed that the house needs painting.

Demonstrative Pronouns. These pronouns are used to point out nouns.

A demonstrative pronoun is used to point out a specific person, place, or thing.

There are four demonstrative pronouns.

DEMONSTRATIVE PRONOUNS	
Singular	**Plural**
this, that	these, those

Demonstrative pronouns may be located before or after their antecedents.

BEFORE: *That* is an ambulance siren.

AFTER: A box of old photographs and my guitar—*these* were all I had been able to salvage from the fire.

Relative Pronouns. These pronouns are used to relate a subordinate clause to another word in the same sentence. (See Section 3.3 for more information about relative pronouns and subordinate clauses.)

A relative pronoun is used to begin a subordinate clause and relate it to another idea in the sentence.

There are five relative pronouns.

RELATIVE PRONOUNS				
that	which	who	whom	whose

As the following sentences show, the antecedent for a relative pronoun is located in another clause of the sentence. Each relative pronoun links the information in a subordinate clause to a word in an independent clause.

Independent Clauses	Subordinate Clauses
We began reading *The Cyclops,*	*which* is a play by Euripides.
I wish to thank Leonard Cook	to *whom* we are grateful.
The show focused on people	*whose* talent is extraordinary.

Interrogative Pronouns. These pronouns are used to ask questions.

An interrogative pronoun is used to begin a direct or indirect question.

The five interrogative pronouns are listed in the following chart.

INTERROGATIVE PRONOUNS				
what	which	who	whom	whose

The antecedent for an interrogative pronoun may not always be known, as the first of the following examples illustrates.

DIRECT QUESTION: *What* fell from that ledge?

INDIRECT QUESTION: He had two problems. I asked *which* needed to be solved first.

Indefinite Pronouns. Very similar in function to nouns, indefinite pronouns do not require specific antecedents. Sometimes, however, indefinite pronouns may have specific antecedents.

Indefinite pronouns are used to refer to persons, places, or things, often without specifying which ones.

The following chart lists the most commonly used indefinite pronouns.

INDEFINITE PRONOUNS				
Singular			**Plural**	**Singular or Plural**
another	everyone	nothing	both	all
anybody	everything	one	few	any
anyone	little	other	many	more
anything	much	somebody	others	most
each	neither	someone	several	none
either	nobody	something		some
everybody	no one			such

NO SPECIFIC ANTECEDENT: *Nobody* was required to clean up, but *many* offered to assist.

SPECIFIC ANTECEDENT: I bought new book covers, but *none* was the right size for this huge volume.

EXERCISE C: Recognizing Antecedents. Write each underlined pronoun and its antecedent. If a pronoun does not have an antecedent, write *none* after the pronoun.

EXAMPLE: Scott turned in his report before it was due.

   his   (Scott)   it   (report)

1. Jo herself has had clairvoyant experiences at various times in her life.
2. The troops trudged through the thick forest. Their throats were parched and they yearned for some refreshment.
3. I think nothing is worse than a steak that is well-done.
4. All of the graduating seniors must pass proficiency tests. Those who fail will not receive a diploma.
5. Pollution hung in a thick cloud over the city. Its debilitating effects caused the schools to cancel their sports events.
6. Amy Lowell is a particularly fine poet. Everyone should read at least one of her poems.
7. It is inspirational to me to read stories of people who have overcome severe handicaps and gone on to lead successful lives.
8. Listening attentively is a valuable skill. Students should train themselves to do it effectively.
9. I asked Marcia what she meant by her mysterious remark.
10. Both of the actors gave superior performances. They captured the hearts of their audience.

EXERCISE D: Identifying the Different Types of Pronouns. Identify each underlined pronoun as *personal, reflexive, intensive, demonstrative, relative, interrogative,* or *indefinite.*

EXAMPLE: Television critics worry about its effect on viewers.

   personal

When over 130,000,000 television viewers turned on (1) their sets to watch *Roots,* (2) few had any idea (3) that (4) this was the beginning of a new television era. Today, docudramas with (5) their colorful dramatizations of historical events make up a substantial portion of (6) each of the networks' programming. But even as American viewers treat (7) themselves to these television triumphs, there are (8) those (9) who denounce (10) them. Critics contend that docudramas mix fact with fiction without telling (11) those (12) who watch (13) them of this. The critics pose some disturbing questions: (14) Who verifies the historical accuracy of these tales? Are the networks doing a disservice by allowing the public to dupe (15) themselves into believing that these distorted accounts are true? (6) Others contend that the critics overstate the seriousness of the problem and insult the viewer (17) who is intelligent enough to distinguish reality from fiction. Nevertheless, the disquieting questions remain. When (18) we realize that the average television set is on for more than six hours a day, we (19) ourselves must ponder the impact these shows may be exerting on us. If we do not, (20) whose version of past events will later fill our textbooks—the Hollywood producers' or the true historians'?

DEVELOPING WRITING SKILLS: Writing Sentences with Different Kinds of Nouns and Pronouns. Use the following instructions to write five sentences of your own.

EXAMPLE: Write a sentence containing a proper noun and a relative pronoun.

My friend hiked the whole length of the Appalachian Trail, which stretches from Georgia to Maine.

1. Write a sentence containing a concrete noun and a personal pronoun.
2. Write a sentence containing an abstract noun and an interrogative pronoun followed by the word *of.*
3. Write a sentence containing a compound noun and a demonstrative pronoun followed by the word *is.*
4. Write a sentence containing a proper noun and a reflexive pronoun.
5. Write a sentence containing a plural noun and an indefinite pronoun followed by the word *in.*

Verbs 1.2

Every complete sentence contains at least one verb, which may consist of as many as four words.

A verb is a word or group of words that expresses time while showing an action, a condition, or the fact that something exists.

In the sentence *The dog raced across the field,* the verb *raced* expresses action. In the sentence *The silk felt slippery to my touch,* the verb *felt* shows a condition. In the sentence *The peacock is in the tree,* the verb *is* simply shows that something exists.

Verbs have a major effect on *syntax*—that is, the way words are put together and related to one another in sentences. Because of this effect, verbs are generally divided into two main categories: *action verbs* and *linking verbs*.

Action Verbs and Linking Verbs

Action verbs, as their name suggests, express either physical or mental action—that is, what someone or something does, did, or will do. Linking verbs serve a more passive function, expressing a condition. Verbs used as linking verbs may also be used simply to show that something exists.

Action Verbs. Action verbs make up the majority of English verbs.

An action verb tells what action someone or something is performing.

ACTION VERBS: The dancer *will attempt* a daring leap.

The kettle *whistled* incessantly.

In the first example, the verb tells what the dancer will do; in the second example, the verb tells what the kettle did. The person or thing that performs the action is called the *subject* of the verb. *Dancer* is the subject of *will attempt. Kettle* is the subject of *whistled.*

Action verbs can also tell what mental actions are being performed, as the two examples at the top of the next page illustrate.

31

MENTAL ACTION: I *considered* my decision carefully.

She *remembered* none of the answers.

Linking Verbs. Instead of expressing action, a linking verb expresses a subject's condition by linking the subject to another word in the sentence.

A linking verb connects its subject with a word generally found near the end of the sentence.

LINKING VERBS: Richard Howard *is* a poet.

Jennifer *was* a senior.

An oral recommendation *should be* sufficient.

I *am being* unkind.

The verb *be* is the most common linking verb. Study the many forms of this verb, in the following chart.

THE FORMS OF *BE*			
am	am being	can be	have been
are	are being	could be	has been
is	is being	may be	had been
was	was being	might be	could have been
were	were being	must be	may have been
		shall be	might have been
		should be	shall have been
		will be	should have been
		would be	will have been
			would have been

When the forms of *be* act as linking verbs, they express the condition of the subject. Sometimes, however, they may merely express existence, usually by working with other words to show where the subject is located.

EXAMPLES: The key *is* in the lock.

The photographer *will be* here soon.

Other verbs can also function as linking verbs. The chart at the top of the next page lists these verbs.

OTHER LINKING VERBS		
appear	look	sound
become	remain	stay
feel	seem	taste
grow	smell	turn

EXAMPLES: After lunch she *became* sleepy.

The bride *looked* radiant.

Most of these verbs can also serve as action verbs. To determine the function of such a verb, insert *am, are,* or *is* in its place. If the resulting sentence makes sense while linking two words, then the verb is serving as a linking verb.

LINKING VERB: The man *looks* busy. (The man *is* busy.)

ACTION VERB: The man *looked* for a taxi.

EXERCISE A: Identifying Action and Linking Verbs. Identify each of the underlined verbs in the following sentences as either an *action verb* or a *linking verb*.

EXAMPLE: The apple pie <u>smells</u> delicious.

linking verb

1. We <u>stayed</u> at charming roadside inns throughout our travels in England.
2. The inexperienced actor's mannerisms <u>seemed</u> rehearsed and unnatural.
3. Following in the family tradition, Elizabeth <u>became</u> a pharmacist.
4. The trail <u>looked</u> perilous to the novice hikers.
5. Brussels sprouts <u>taste</u> bitter to me.
6. The cat <u>appeared</u> from behind the woodshed.
7. I <u>tasted</u> a hint of basil in the soup we were served.
8. The canvas on the lawn chair <u>grew</u> pale after being exposed to the sun.
9. The people in the odd-looking contraption <u>stayed</u> calm in spite of the crowd's laughter.
10. The leaves of the maple tree <u>turn</u> a vibrant shade of red in the fall.

Transitive and Intransitive Verbs

All verbs can be described as either *transitive* or *intransitive*, depending on whether they transfer action to another word in a sentence.

A verb is transitive if it directs action toward someone or something named in the same sentence.

A verb is intransitive if it does not direct action toward someone or something named in the same sentence.

The word toward which a transitive verb directs its action is called the *object* of the verb. Intransitive verbs never have objects. You can determine whether a verb has an object and is thus transitive by asking *Whom?* or *What?* after the verb. (See Section 2.3 for more about objects of verbs.)

TRANSITIVE: He *wrote* a novel. (Wrote *what? Answer:* novel)

The doctor *examined* the patient. (Examined *whom? Answer:* patient)

INTRANSITIVE: The birds *flew* south. (Flew *what? Answer:* none)

She *sings* for the Metropolitan Opera. (Sings *what? Answer:* none)

Notice in the examples that the action of the transitive verbs is done *to* something. The writing is done to the novel, the examining is done to the patient. The action of the intransitive verbs, however, is just done. Nothing receives it.

Linking verbs, which do not express action, are always intransitive. Most action verbs, however, can be either transitive or intransitive, depending on their use in a sentence. Some are either always transitive or always intransitive.

TRANSITIVE OR INTRANSITIVE: The jocky *exercised* the horse.

I *exercise* at the health spa.

ALWAYS TRANSITIVE: A stone wall *encloses* the garden.

ALWAYS INTRANSITIVE: They *cringed* in fear.

34

EXERCISE B: Identifying Transitive and Intransitive Verbs. Write the verbs in the following sentences and label each as *transitive* or *intransitive.*

EXAMPLE: We arrived in time for dinner.

arrived (intransitive)

1. The wind buffeted the frail sapling.
2. At midnight the weary politician conceded the election.
3. I was there on Tuesday.
4. The glider soared beside the majestic cliffs.
5. I made an appointment with the dentist.
6. The visitors noticed the new landscaping around our home.
7. The agile squirrel scampered up to the top of the tall tree.
8. The oil spill polluted the local beaches.
9. After his vacation the President appeared rested.
10. The gymnast balanced carefully on the beam.

Verb Phrases

When a verb consists of more than one word, it is called a *verb phrase*.

A verb phrase is a verb with one, two, or three helping verbs before it.

Helping verbs, also known as *auxiliary verbs* or *auxiliaries,* add meaning to other verbs. Some helping verbs change the time expressed by the key verb. Others, such as *should* and *might,* are used to indicate obligation, possibility, ability, or permission.

SINGLE VERBS: The firm *employed* a new secretary today.

VERB PHRASES: The firm *will employ* a new secretary today.

The firm *should have employed* a new secretary today.

A new secretary *might have been employed* by the firm today.

Any of the forms of the verb *be* that are listed on page 32 can be used as helping verbs, as can the words in the chart at the top of the next page.

HELPING VERBS OTHER THAN *BE*					
do	have	shall	will	can	may
does	has	should	would	could	might
did	had				must

Verb phrases are often interrupted by other words. To find the complete verb in a sentence, locate the key verb first; then, check for helping verbs that may precede it.

INTERRUPTED VERB PHRASES: The firm *will* probably not *hire* a secretary today.

Should the firm *hire* a secretary?

EXERCISE C: Using Verb Phrases. Complete each of the following sentences with an appropriate verb phrase that includes the verb in parentheses.

EXAMPLE: _____ you _____ any of her stories? (read)

Have you read any of her stories?

1. The American Kennel Club _____ _____ dogs into working dogs, sporting dogs, nonsporting dogs, hounds, terriers, and toys. (classified)
2. Euclid _____ _____ _____ the Father of Geometry. (called)
3. The profits from the song "God Bless America" by Irving Berlin _____ _____ to the Scouts. (donated)
4. Next year, professional golfers _____ _____ in at least four big tournaments. (participate)
5. _____ India and Nepal _____ _____ _____ to put their flags atop Mount Everest? (permitted)
6. A person in the Navy with the rank of fleet admiral _____ _____ five stars. (attained)
7. The Jean Hersholt Humanitarian Award _____ always _____ at the Academy Awards. (presented)
8. Liberty Island, home of the Statue of Liberty, _____ formerly _____ as Bedloe's Island. (known)
9. We _____ _____ a new astrological year in March. (begin)
10. Readers _____ long _____ _____ by the eighty-four Perry Mason novels by Erle Stanley Gardner. (entertained)

DEVELOPING WRITING SKILLS: Writing Sentences with Different Kinds of Verbs. Use each of the following verbs in a sentence of your own, following the directions in parentheses.

EXAMPLE: feel (as a linking verb)

   She feels pleased about her grade.

1. taste (as an action verb)
2. taste (as a linking verb)
3. climb (as a transitive verb)
4. climb (as an intransitive verb)
5. prevent (with three helping verbs)

Adjectives and Adverbs 1.3

Adjectives and adverbs are the two parts of speech known as *modifiers*—that is, they slightly change the meaning of other words by adding description or by making them more precise.

Adjectives

An adjective qualifies the meaning of a noun or pronoun by providing information about its appearance, location, and so on.

An adjective is a word used to describe a noun or pronoun or to give it a more specific meaning.

An adjective can answer four questions about a noun or pronoun: *What kind? Which one? How many?* and *How much?*

EXAMPLES: *Green* fields (*What kind* of fields?)

   the *left* window (*Which* window?)

   six lobsters (*How many* lobsters?)

   extensive rainfall (*How much* rainfall?)

When an adjective modifies a noun, it usually precedes the noun. Occasionally, though, the adjective may follow the noun.

EXAMPLES: The banjo teacher was *tactful* about my talent.

   I considered the teacher *tactful*.

37

An adjective that modifies a pronoun usually follows it. Sometimes, however, the adjective may precede the pronoun.

AFTER: They were *brokenhearted* by the verdict.

BEFORE: *Brokenhearted* by the verdict, they started an appeal.

More than one adjective may modify a single noun or pronoun.

EXAMPLE: We elected *a competent, enthusiastic* official.

Articles. Three common *adjectives—a, an,* and *the*—are known as *articles. A* and *an* are called *indefinite articles* because they refer to any one of a class of nouns. *The* refers to a specific noun and, therefore, is called the *definite article.*

INDEFINITE: *a* dictator   *an* outrage

DEFINITE: *the* tarantula

Nouns Used as Adjectives. Words that are usually nouns sometimes act as adjectives. In this case, the noun answers *What kind?* or *Which one?* about another noun.

NOUNS USED AS ADJECTIVES	
pencil *pencil* sharpener	mail *mail* clerk

Proper Adjectives. Adjectives can also be proper. Proper adjectives are proper nouns used as adjectives or adjectives formed from proper nouns. They usually begin with capitals.

Proper Nouns	Proper Adjectives
Monday	*Monday* morning
San Francisco	*San Francisco* streets
Chaucer	*Chaucerian* scholar
Denmark	*Danish* porcelain

Compound Adjectives. Adjectives can be compound. Most are hyphenated; others are combined or are separate words.

HYPHENATED: *ready-made* clothes, *mail-order* catalogs

COMBINED: *crossword* puzzle, *warmhearted* invitation

SEPARATED: *West German* embassy

Pronouns Used as Adjectives. Certain pronouns can also function as adjectives. The seven personal pronouns, known as either *possessive adjectives* or *possessive pronouns,* fill two capacities in a sentence. They act as pronouns because they have antecedents. They also act as adjectives because they modify nouns by answering *Which one?* The other pronouns become adjectives instead of pronouns when they stand before nouns and answer the questions *Which one?*

PRONOUNS USED AS ADJECTIVES	
Possessive Adjectives	
my, your, his, her, its, our, their	ANTECEDENT The committee gave *its* report.
Demonstrative Adjectives	
this, that, these, those	*This* pen and *these* books are Al's.
Interrogative Adjectives	
which, what, whose	*Which* orchard do you own?
Indefinite Adjectives	
Used with singular nouns: another, each, either, little, much, neither, one	*Each* cruiser flew a flag.
Used with plural nouns: both, few, many, several	*Several* choirs competed for top honors.
Used with singular or plural nouns: all, any, more, most, other, some	Buy *any* record that you want. We appreciate *any* donations

39

Verbs Used as Adjectives. Verbs used as adjectives usually end in *-ing* or *-ed* and are called *participles.*

VERBS USED AS ADJECTIVES	
I picked up the *crying* baby.	They were *enlightened* parents.

Nouns, pronouns, and verbs function as adjectives only when they modify other nouns or pronouns. The following examples show how their function in a sentence can shift.

	Regular Function	As an Adjective
Noun	The *deck* of the boat tilted.	I sat in the *deck* chair.
Pronoun	*This* was an idyllic life.	*This* life was idyllic.
Verb	I *waxed* the table.	The *waxed* table shone.

Order of Adjectives. When two or more adjectives are used before a noun, they are usually in a recognizable order, beginning with an article and ending with the noun.

TYPICAL ORDER OF ADJECTIVES	
Article or pronoun used as an adjective	a or your
Size	large
Age	old
Color	green
Participle	hand-blown
Proper adjective	French
Noun used as an adjective	wine
Noun	bottle

Though variations are possible, the general pattern will usually hold true. An article will always be first; a noun used as an adjective will always come directly before the noun.

40

EXERCISE A: Identifying Adjectives. Copy each under-lined noun or pronoun in the following paragraph and write all of the adjectives, if any, that modify it. Be prepared to point out any nouns, pronouns, or verbs used as adjectives.

EXAMPLE: Collections of great art treasures have been pre-served in many <u>places</u> around the world.

places—many

Dresden, an East German (1) <u>city</u>, houses some of the great-est art (2) <u>treasures</u> in the world. From the sixteenth (3) <u>century</u> to the eighteenth century, the Saxon (4) <u>electors</u> collected art from the four (5) <u>corners</u> of the globe and brought them to this (6) <u>location</u>. Though the Saxon (7) <u>reign</u> was short-lived, the treasures have not been; most (8) <u>pieces</u> even survived the Allied (9) <u>bombing</u> during World War II. Today, the public can view delicate Oriental (10) <u>porcelain</u> and sen-sitive, moving (11) <u>paintings</u> of great (12) <u>artists</u>. The Green Vault holds precious (13) <u>metals</u> and jewels, the work of the best European (14) <u>artisans</u>. One display contains shining dia-mond boot (15) <u>buckles</u> and jeweled shirt (16) <u>buttons</u>. To es-timate the (17) <u>value</u> of these (18) <u>treasures</u> would prove vir-tually impossible; (19) <u>many</u> are priceless. For example, at one auction, eight Meissen china (20) <u>pieces</u> sold for $313,720.

EXERCISE B: Putting Adjectives in Order. Put the adjec-tives following each underlined noun in the proper order and write the entire phrase on your paper.

EXAMPLE: <u>jacket</u>—down-filled, new, winter, a

a new down-filled winter jacket.

1. <u>sports car</u>—British, that, small, red
2. <u>road</u>—dirt, a, winding, narrow
3. <u>vase</u>—lovely, this, hand-painted, Japanese
4. <u>insects</u>—flying, iridescent, many
5. <u>coin</u>—bronze, ancient, the, Roman
6. <u>mouse</u>—field, frightened, the, brown, tiny
7. <u>shirt</u>—green, the, silk
8. <u>kitten</u>—Siamese, blue-eyed, little, a
9. <u>library</u>—red, new, brick, our
10. <u>stories</u>—mystery, exciting, several

41

EXERCISE C: Using Adjectives. Pick one of the following items and use adjectives to describe it imaginatively in five or six sentences. Try to be original; do not start with such words as "It looks like . . ." or "It was . . . ."

A character from literature   The aftermath of a disaster
A national landmark   A piece of art

Adverbs

Adverbs, like adjectives, describe other words or make other words more specific.

An adverb is a word that modifies a verb, an adjective, or another adverb.

When an adverb modifies a verb, it will answer any of the following questions: *Where? When? In what manner?* or *To what extent?* An adverb answers only one question, however, when modifying an adjective or another verb: *To what extent?* Because it specifies the degree or intensity of the modified adjective or adverb, such an adverb is often called an *intensifier.*

As the following charts show, the position of an adverb in relation to the word it modifies can vary in a sentence. If the adverb modifies a verb, it may precede or follow it or even interrupt a verb phrase. Normally, adverbs modifying adjectives and adverbs will immediately precede the word they modify.

ADVERBS	
Adverbs Modifying Verbs	
Where?	**When?**
Inflation zoomed *upward.*	She *never* cleaned the room.
The jurors remained *there.*	*Later,* we toured the museum.
In what manner?	**To what extent?**
He *officially* announced it.	His temper was *still* boiling.
She was *graciously* helping.	He *always* did it right.

Adverbs Modifying Adjectives	Adverbs Modifying Adverbs
To what extent?	To what extent?
The solution was *quite* logical.	He worked *very* competently.
It was an *extremely* sour lemon.	I am *not* completely finished.

Adverbs as Parts of Verbs. Some verbs require an adverb to complete their meaning. Adverbs used this way are considered part of the verb. An adverb functioning as an integral part of a verb does not answer the usual questions for adverbs.

EXAMPLE: The car *backed up* along the curb.

Nouns Functioning as Adverbs. Several nouns can function as adverbs that answer the question *Where?* or *When?* Some of these words are *home, yesterday, today, tomorrow, mornings, afternoons, evenings, nights, week, month,* and *year.*

NOUNS USED AS ADVERBS	
Nouns	As Adverbs
Evenings are restful times.	I work *evenings.* (Work *when?*)
My *home* is miles from here.	Let's head *home.* (Head *where?*)

Adverb or Adjective? Adverbs usually have different forms from adjectives and thus are easily identified. Many adverbs are, in fact, formed by the addition of *-ly* to an adjective.

ADJECTIVE: Our professor looked *pensive.*

ADVERB: The professor looked at her notes *pensively.*

Some adjectives, however, also end in *-ly.* Therefore, you cannot assume that every word ending in *-ly* is an adverb.

ADJECTIVES: an *ugly* scene

a *nightly* jaunt

Some adjectives and adverbs even share the same form. You can determine the part of speech of such words by checking

43

their function in the sentence. An adverb will modify a verb, adjective, or adverb; an adjective will modify a noun or pronoun.

ADVERB: The concert ran *late*.

ADJECTIVE: We enjoyed the *late* dinners in Spain.

EXERCISE D: Identifying Adverbs. Each of the following sentences contains from one to four adverbs. Write each adverb and then write the word or words that it modifies.

EXAMPLE: We sailed the boat all afternoon.

all   (afternoon)   afternoon   (sailed)

1. Yesterday, the architects sketchily explained the plans they have for the office building.
2. A southerly storm approached quickly, drenching the area with an extremely heavy downpour.
3. Almost apologetically, she presented her handmade gift.
4. The roller coaster crazily raced up and down before it eventually released its dizzy passengers.
5. Her ghastly pallor was attributed to the extremely long illness from which she had recently recovered.
6. My hand jerked involuntarily, and my glass crashed violently against the floor.
7. The delivery person apparently found my note but did not read it.
8. Though it was an uphill battle, I was extremely happy with the final product.
9. His manly physique certainly helped him win the role in the repertory's newest production.
10. He often prattles continuously and monotonously.

EXERCISE E: Adding Adverbs to Sentences. Copy the following sentences, adding at least one adverb to each. If necessary, change the wording of the sentence, but do not use the same adverb more than once.

EXAMPLE: Most people have seen the figure of Uncle Sam.

Most people have often seen the figure of Uncle Sam.

44

(1) Since the War of 1812, the symbol of Uncle Sam has characterized the American government. (2) This famous symbol came from the initials that were stamped on barrels of salted meat by a United States Army meat inspector. (3) Citizens in New York and Vermont liked the nickname and began to use it. (4) Uncle Sam achieved fame in 1813 when he was pictured in a Troy, New York, newspaper. (5) By 1830 Uncle Sam had donned his familiar, splashy costume of stars and stripes. (6) A clown dressed as Uncle Sam delighted crowds during the 1800's and helped to popularize the costume. (7) In 1813 most newspaper cartoonists depicted Uncle Sam as a young man. (8) By 1917 he had grown older. (9) On a poster that was used during the First World War, Uncle Sam pointed his wrinkled finger at the young men across the United States and declared, "I want you." (10) Congress made Uncle Sam an official national symbol in 1961.

DEVELOPING WRITING SKILLS: Writing Sentences with Adjectives and Adverbs. The underlined word in each of the following sentences is either an adjective or an adverb. If the word is an adjective, write a sentence of your own in which you use it as an adverb. If the word is an adverb, write a sentence using it as an adjective.

EXAMPLE: A center fielder on a baseball team should be a <u>fast</u> runner.

He should not drive so fast along this narrow, twisting roadway.

1. The <u>straight</u> ribbon of freeway led across the vast expanse of desert.
2. The shovel bit <u>deep</u> into the black soil.
3. I solved the <u>hard</u> algebra problem quite easily.
4. The flagman motioned the car <u>right</u>.
5. The building jutted <u>high</u> into the sky.
6. I left at six for an <u>early</u> appointment.
7. The boy consumed <u>more</u> spaghetti.
8. The vise on the workbench will hold the wood <u>tight</u> until the glue dries.
9. She performed <u>well</u> on her driver's examination.
10. We visited him <u>daily</u> in the hospital.

1.4 Prepositions, Conjunctions, and Interjections

Two of the final three parts of speech—prepositions and conjunctions—function in sentences as connectors. *Prepositions* express relationships between words or ideas, whereas *conjunctions* join words, groups of words, or even entire sentences. The last part of speech, *interjections,* functions by itself, independent of other words in a sentence.

Prepositions

Prepositions make it possible to show relationships between words. The relationships shown may involve, for example, location, direction, time, cause, or possession.

A preposition relates the noun or pronoun that appears with it to another word in the sentence.

Study the following chart so that you can recognize all prepositions on sight. Notice that some prepositions are *compound*—that is, they are made up of more than one word.

PREPOSITIONS			
aboard	aside from	by means of	in spite of
about	as of	concerning	instead of
above	at	considering	into
according to	atop	despite	in view of
across from	barring	down	like
across	because of	during	near
after	before	except	nearby
against	behind	for	next to
ahead of	below	from	of
along	beneath	in	off
alongside	beside	in addition to	on
along with	besides	in back of	on account of
amid	between	in front of	onto
among	beyond	in place of	on top of
apart from	but	in regard to	opposite
around	by	inside	out

out of	regarding	to	unto
outside	round	together with	up
over	since	toward	upon
owing to	through	under	with
past	throughout	underneath	within
prior to	till	until	without

See how the prepositions relate the italicized words below.

LOCATION: The brush fire *burned* atop the *hill*.
PREP

DIRECTION: The brush fire *burned* toward our *campsite*.
PREP

TIME: The fire *burned* for three *days*.
PREP

CAUSE: The brush fire *started* because of *carelessness*.
PREP

POSSESSION: *Smoke* from the *fire* could be seen for miles.
PREP

Prepositional Phrases. A preposition is always part of a *prepositional phrase.*

A prepositional phrase is a group of words that includes a preposition and a noun or pronoun.

The noun or pronoun with a preposition is called the *object of the preposition.* Objects may have one or more modifiers. A prepositional phrase may also have more than one object.

EXAMPLES: I walked slightly *ahead of her.*
OBJ

The shampoo bottle *on the shelf* was almost empty.
OBJ

We were adopted *by a lovable, brown-eyed puppy.*
OBJ

Our new house is located *near stores and schools.*
OBJ OBJ

In some questions, prepositional phrases are broken up.

EXAMPLES: *What* were we talking *about*?
OBJ PREP

Where did this come *from*?
OBJ PREP

See Section 3.1 for more about prepositional phrases.

Preposition or Adverb? Since prepositions and adverbs occasionally take the same form, they may be difficult to tell apart. Words that can function in either role included *around, before, behind, down, in, off, on, out, over,* and *up.* To determine the part of speech of these words, see if an object accompanies the word. If so, the word is used as a preposition.

OBJ

PREPOSITION: The child ran *down the hill*.

ADVERB: The flag was *down*.

EXERCISE A: Identifying Prepositional Phrases. Write the prepositional phrases from the following paragraph and circle each preposition.

EXAMPLE: During my vaction I discovered the exciting sport of cross-country skiing.

⟨During⟩ my vacation ⟨of⟩ cross-country skiing

(1) The thrill of cross-country skiing is infecting people around the globe.   (2) The sport originated across the Atlantic Ocean in the Scandinavian countries and was brought to the United States by Scandinavian settlers. (3) According to recent figures, more than two million people are now cross-country skiers. (4) Cross-country skiers can compete for prizes in races held around the world. (5) A Norwegian race, the Birkenbeiner, honors two skiers who heroically carried a Norwegian prince to safety amid a civil war in the early thirteenth century. (6) The skiers were called "birch legs" or "birkenbeiner" because of the birch that they wrapped around their legs for warmth. (7) Californians hold the Snowshoe Thompson Race, named after a mail carrier. (8) By means of cross-country skiing, this man regularly carried the mail ninety miles through the Sierras. (9) The most popular cross-country race, however, is probably the one in Sweden called the Vasaloppet. (10) Ten thousand people gather every year for this competition.

EXERCISE B: Distinguishing Between Prepositions and Adverbs. Identify the underlined word in each sentence as either a *preposition* or an *adverb*. If the word is a preposition, write its object on your paper as well.

48

EXAMPLE: They are waiting <u>near</u> the door.

preposition   door

1. A college student shinnied <u>up</u> the flagpole.
2. The sun went <u>down</u> behind the hill.
3. The lights were mistakenly left <u>on</u> overnight.
4. When she went <u>away</u>, we left as well.
5. The elephant suddenly turned <u>around</u> and charged.
6. We remained <u>behind</u> after the others had left.
7. A button on my blazer fell <u>off</u>.
8. A valley lies <u>below</u> the sea.
9. The antique chair was <u>in</u> good condition.
10. For dinner the couple went <u>out</u> and had a leisurely meal.

EXERCISE C: Using Prepositional Phrases. Copy the following sentences, adding a prepositional phrase that provides the information requested in the parentheses. The last two sentences require the addition of more than one prepositional phrase.

EXAMPLE: We went to the soccer game.   (time)

We went to the soccer game after school.

1. I longingly watched the sailing vessels.   (location)
2. We postponed the soccer match.   (cause)
3. The snow level topped three feet.   (time)
4. The pungent odor assailed my senses.   (possession)
5. Monorails provide transportation.   (location)
6. Several motel rooms were burglarized.   (time)
7. The hound retrieved the fallen duck.   (location)
8. We won the championship.   (cause)
9. The bats flew erratically.   (time, duration)
10. The house had no electricity.   (location, cause)

Conjunctions

Conjunctions are the words that join other words within sentences.

A conjunction is a word used to connect other words or groups of words.

There are three main kinds of conjunctions: *coordinating, correlative,* and *subordinating.* Sometimes a kind of adverb, the *conjunctive adverb,* is also considered a conjunction.

Coordinating Conjunctions. The seven coordinating conjunctions are used to connect similar parts of speech or groups of words of equal grammatical weight.

COORDINATING CONJUNCTIONS						
and	but	for	nor	or	so	yet

WITH NOUNS AND PRONOUNS: Inge *and* I attended the lecture.

WITH VERBS: Our dog whined *and* scratched at the door.

WITH ADJECTIVES: The steak was tender, large, *yet* tasteless.

WITH ADVERBS: The man responded quickly *but* incorrectly.

WITH PREPOSITIONAL PHRASES: I will go to Greece *or* to Spain.

WITH SUBORDINATE IDEAS: The agency said that jobs were available *but* that qualified personnel to fill them were not.

WITH COMPLETE IDEAS: He seemed distressed, *so* we discussed his problem.

Correlative Conjunctions. Working in pairs, the five correlative conjunctions join elements of equal grammatical weight in sentences in much the same manner as coordinating conjunctions do.

CORRELATIVE CONJUNCTIONS		
both . . . and	either . . . or	neither . . . nor
not only . . . but also	whether . . . or	

WITH NOUNS: *Both* the employers *and* the employees agree.

WITH NOUNS AND PRONOUNS: Call *either* Ed *or* me if you need help.

WITH ADJECTIVES: The rain was *not only* heavy *but also* cold.

WITH PREPOSITIONAL PHRASES: Put the check *either* in the drawer *or* beside the telephone.

WITH COMPLETE IDEAS: *Neither* did the swelling go down *nor* did the pain subside.

50

Subordinating Conjunctions. Subordinating conjunctions join two complete ideas by making one of the ideas subordinate to or dependent upon the other.

SUBORDINATING CONJUNCTIONS			
after	because	lest	till
although	before	now that	unless
as	even if	provided	until
as if	even though	since	when
as long as	how	so that	whenever
as much as	if	than	where
as soon as	inasmuch as	that	wherever
as though	in order that	though	while

The subordinate idea in a sentence always begins with a subordinating conjunction and makes up what is known as a *subordinate clause*. (See Section 3.3 for more information about clauses.) A subordinate clause may either follow or precede the main idea in a sentence.

EXAMPLES: The referees watched carefully *lest* they miss a key play.
MAIN IDEA · SUBORDINATE IDEA

Although the fumigator sprayed, the termites remained.
SUBORDINATE IDEA · MAIN IDEA

When trying to identify subordinating conjunctions, remember that some of these conjunctions can also function as prepositions or adverbs. *After, before, since, till,* and *until* often act as prepositions; *after, before, when,* and *where* often act as adverbs.

SUBORDINATING CONJUNCTION: *After* the billboards were removed, the area's natural beauty was restored.

PREPOSITION: The main course was served *after* the salad.

ADVERB: The parade began at noon and ended an hour *after*.

Conjunctive Adverbs. Conjunctive adverbs act as transitions between complete ideas by indicating comparisons, contrasts, results, and other relationships. The chart on the next page lists the most common conjunctive adverbs.

51

CONJUNCTIVE ADVERBS		
accordingly	finally	nevertheless
again	furthermore	otherwise
also	however	then
besides	indeed	therefore
consequently	moreover	thus

As shown in the following examples, punctuation is usually required both before and after conjunctive adverbs. (See Sections 12.2 and 12.3 for a more thorough discussion of the punctuation of conjunctive adverbs.)

EXAMPLES: The doctor did help my back problem; *however*, I still experience occasional pain.

The earthquake damaged the wall structure. *Moreover*, it broke some water pipes.

My hay fever grew worse. I, *nevertheless*, refused to remain inside.

EXERCISE D: Identifying Conjunctions in Sentences. Write the conjunction in each sentence and identify it as *coordinating, correlative,* or *subordinating.*

EXAMPLE: I could not decide whether your answer was right or wrong.

whether   or   (correlative)

1. The physics instructor explained the theory, but I did not understand it.
2. Roger is significantly taller than Doug is.
3. You should eat salads since they are good for your digestion.
4. I checked several banquet facilities before I finally chose this one.
5. Unless you reform, you will be dismissed.
6. I burned my tongue, for the soup was still too hot to eat.
7. Whenever the shepherd gave the order, the dog began to round up strays.
8. Not only can you do some packing, but you can also carry out some boxes.

9. Persimmons and pumpkins can be used to make excellent spice cookies.
10. Now that the harvest is behind them, the farmers can relax.

EXERCISE E: Distinguishing Between Subordinating Conjunctions, Prepositions, and Adverbs. Identify each underlined word as a *subordinating conjunction, preposition,* or *adverb.*

EXAMPLE: Before we planted seeds, we fertilized the garden.

             subordinating conjunction

1. Shirley rented a typewriter until the end of the month.
2. Where do you keep the silverware?
3. They bought more exotic fish after they had experimented with goldfish.
4. My relatives had toured Europe four times before.
5. You should see Maine, where the thick forests come right to the ocean's edge.
6. When did the school board vote on that issue?
7. I haven't skied since last February.
8. Louis stayed on board till the final warning bell forced him to leave.
9. We refinanced the house because we needed money.
10. We had dinner before the performance.

EXERCISE F: Using Conjunctive Adverbs. Write the following pairs of sentences, adding appropriate conjunctive adverbs.

EXAMPLE: Many scholars believe that Homer wrote *The Iliad* and *The Odyssey*. Some scholars claim that he never existed.

           Many scholars believe that Homer wrote *The Iliad* and *The Odyssey*. Some scholars, however, claim that he never existed.

1. The mythological gods had unearthly powers. They possessed many human frailties.
2. One of the most common themes in mythology is love. Many stories tell of lovers' betrayals, loyalties, and jealousies.

3. Aphrodite refused Zeus' love. He gave her hand in marriage to his son Hephaestus.
4. Hera, wife of Zeus, has been called mythology's most jealous wife. She spied on all of Zeus' actions.
5. Other gods participated in dramatic adventures. They often fought in battles against huge odds.
6. Hercules captured the Cretan bull. He was well-known for his great strength.
7. Hades ruled the underworld. He was not a totally evil creature.
8. Upon his death Sisyphus was condemned to roll a stone up a hill in Hades. The stone always rolled back down.
9. The winged horse Pegasus has become a symbol of poetic inspiration. A constellation is named after him.
10. Phidias, a Greek, was inspired to sculpt the statue of Olympian Zeus. He is perhaps even better known for his statue of Athena.

Interjections

Interjections express motion. Unlike most words, they have no grammatical connection to other words in a sentence.

An interjection is a word that expresses feeling or emotion and functions independently of a sentence.

Interjections can express a variety of sentiments, such as happiness, fear, anger, pain, surprise, sorrow, exhaustion, or hesitation.

SOME COMMON INTERJECTIONS				
ah	dear	hey	ouch	well
aha	goodness	hurray	psst	whew
alas	gracious	oh	tsk	wow

Exclamation marks or commas usually set off an interjection from the rest of the sentence, as the following examples show.

EXAMPLES: *Ouch!* That bee sting throbs.

Goodness, if you don't leave now, you will be late!

54

EXERCISE G: Using Interjections. Write five sentences containing interjections that express the following general emotions. Underline the interjections in your sentences.

EXAMPLE: surprise

<u>Oh</u>, what was that noise?

1. indecision   4. exhaustion
2. sorrow   5. fear
3. urgency

DEVELOPING WRITING SKILLS: Using Prepositions and Conjunctions in Sentences. Follow the instructions to write five sentences of your own.

EXAMPLE: Write a sentence containing a subordinate conjunction.

When you have finished reading that book, may I borrow it?

1. Write a sentence containing two prepositions.
2. Write a sentence containing two coordinating conjunctions.
3. Write a sentence containing one preposition and one correlative conjunction.
4. Write a sentence containing two prepositions and one subordinating conjunction.
5. Write a sentence containing one coordinating conjunction and one subordinating conjunction.

Reviewing Parts of Speech 1.5

Words are flexible, often serving as one part of speech in one sentence and as another part of speech in another. To assume, therefore, that once a word is identified as a noun it is always a noun will lead to confusion.

Words as Different Parts of Speech

A word's part of speech should be determined only by the way it is used in a sentence.

How a word is used in a sentence determines its part of speech.

Notice, for example, the many functions of the word *outside*.

AS A NOUN: The *outside* of the house desperately needs painting now.

AS AN ADJECTIVE: It was an *outside* chance, but I took it anyway.

AS AN ADVERB: The children played *outside*.

AS A PREPOSITION: We went sightseeing *outside* the city boundaries.

The following chart suggests questions to ask yourself when you are trying to identify a word's part of speech in a sentence.

Parts of Speech	Questions to Ask Yourself	Examples
Noun	Does the word name a person, place, or thing?	The *chancellor* at *Harvard University* carried the *mace*.
Pronoun	Does the word stand for a noun?	*You* lent *most* of *them* to *me*.
Verb	Does the word tell what someone or something did?	I *duplicated* the notes.
	Does the word link one word with another word that identifies or describes it?	The flag *was* colorful. She *sounded* sincere.
	Does the word merely show that something exists?	The plane *will be* there.
Adjective	Does the word tell what kind, which one, how many, or how much?	A *few singing* telegrams were ordered.

Parts of Speech	Questions to Ask Yourself	Examples
Adverb	Does the word tell where, when, in what manner, or to what extent?	This elevator goes *up*. We perform *next*. Talk *very softly*. The brooch was *certainly* exquisite.
Preposition	Is the word part of a phrase that includes a noun or pronoun?	*Beyond our hedge* wild brush grows *in abundance*.
Conjunction	Does the word connect other words in the sentence?	*Because* the time changed, *both* you *and* I arrived late; *however*, the group waited.
Interjection	Does the word express emotion and function independently of the sentence?	*Oh*, report about 7:00; *well*, maybe that is too early.

EXERCISE A: Identifying Parts of Speech. Identify the part of speech of each underlined word.

EXAMPLE: <u>Smile</u> at the baby and you will get a <u>smile</u> in return.
           verb   noun

1. We were <u>bowling</u> with a borrowed <u>bowling</u> ball.
2. I went <u>early</u> to catch the <u>early</u> bus.
3. <u>Many</u> of us felt that there were <u>many</u> injustices in that particular law.
4. <u>Well</u>, I think I will do <u>well</u> on the upcoming examination.
5. Put that package <u>down</u> and come <u>down</u> the steps.
6. I <u>left</u> the store and turned <u>left</u>.
7. <u>Goodness</u>, I really like to see such <u>goodness</u> praised.
8. <u>Post</u> this notice on that <u>post</u>.
9. We wanted <u>neither</u> of the choices offered, but <u>neither</u> Jim nor I was in a position to bargain.
10. We called in a <u>carpet</u> cleaner to clean our dirty living room <u>carpet</u>.

EXERCISE B: More Work with Parts of Speech. Identify the part of speech of each underlined word.

EXAMPLE: Vincent Van Gogh was a <u>talented</u> artist.

        adjective

   (1) <u>Some</u> say that creative minds are (2) <u>restless</u> minds, and (3) <u>when</u> they speak of Vincent Van Gogh, (4) <u>they</u> may well be right. As a young child, (5) <u>Vincent</u> was not (6) <u>very</u> well-behaved and (7) <u>often</u> turned (8) <u>upon</u> himself. He started school rather late, (9) <u>but</u>, dissatisfied with the system, he eventually dropped out. Vincent started drawing at age eight, impressing his (10) <u>family</u> with his clever sketches. While he pursued his art career during the course of his life, he (11) <u>was</u> supported by his brother, Theo. (12) <u>Restlessly</u>, he sought his own style but was influenced largely by (13) <u>the</u> impressionist painters. It was not (14) <u>until</u> 1885 that a painting of his, *The Potato Eaters,* received (15) <u>popular</u> acclaim. But (16) <u>alas</u>, even (17) <u>recognition</u> did (18) <u>not</u> satisfy (19) <u>him</u>. Consequently, he experienced severe (20) <u>mental</u> disturbances (21) <u>and</u> at one point (22) <u>entered</u> a sanitarium. Vincent Van Gogh (23) <u>could</u> not seem to escape the depression (24) <u>that</u> gripped him, and thus in 1890, this talented painter (25) <u>committed</u> suicide.

DEVELOPING WRITING SKILLS: Using Words as Different Parts of Speech. Write ten sentences of your own using the following words as indicated.

EXAMPLE: Use <u>garden</u> as a noun.

        You have a well-kept vegetable garden.

1. Use <u>sleep</u> as a verb.
2. Use <u>sleep</u> as a noun.
3. Use <u>several</u> as a pronoun.
4. Use <u>several</u> as an adjective.
5. Use <u>game</u> as a noun.
6. Use <u>game</u> as an adjective.
7. Use <u>by</u> as an adverb.
8. Use <u>by</u> as a preposition.
9. Use <u>dear</u> as an adjective.
10. Use <u>dear</u> as an interjection.

58

Skills Review and Writing Workshop

The Parts of Speech

CHECKING YOUR SKILLS

Identify the part of speech of each underlined word.

For more than 100 years, beginning with the (1) growth of manufacturing in the (2) United States, children as young as ten were put to work in factories. (3) Most of these (4) children were forced to leave school and to work up to twelve hours a day for as little as 35¢ an hour. (5) Their parents had little choice (6) but to send them to work. Their own wages (7) were so low that children's incomes were essential (8) to (9) family survival. Many (10) progressive states enacted child labor laws during the early years of the twentieth century. It wasn't (11) until 1938, however, that the U.S. Supreme Court (12) upheld a federal law setting (13) limits on child labor. (14) Alas, during the intervening years, (15) many thousands of children were deprived of an education. They were also denied a (16) carefree and healthful childhood. (17) Unfortunately, protection of children under the federal Fair Labor Standards Act is not (18) absolute. Since the law does not cover farm workers, many young children are (19) still performing hard labor at minimal wages for at least (20) part of each year.

USING GRAMMAR SKILLS IN WRITING
Reporting a Special Event

TV news writers must use the parts of speech correctly so the news is effectively presented. Imagine you are a TV news writer and write a news story by following the steps below.

Prewriting: Select a news event. Think about the purpose of the event, the accompanying activities, and the outcome.

Writing: Begin with a brief overview of the event. Summarize the topics discussed, problems resolved, or actions taken.

Revising: Make sure that you have used all parts of speech correctly. After you have revised, proofread carefully.

2

Basic Sentence Parts and Patterns

When infants first begin to speak, they utter a single word to convey their needs. Later, children begin to compose sentences containing both a subject and an action. By the age of four or five, most children have become familiar with the basic sentence patterns. With time, their sentences take on greater complexity and sophistication. In studying a language, it often helps to view it as a child learns it—looking first at the basic parts of sentences and then using that knowledge to examine more difficult sentence patterns. This chapter will focus on how parts of speech are combined to form sentences.

2.1 Subjects and Verbs

Language is the tool with which people shape their ideas and communicate them to others. For the communication to be meaningful, a speaker or writer must choose appropriate words and put them in an order that the listener or reader can follow and understand. Unfortunately, many things can interfere with this process. A writer, for example, may use words that a reader does not understand. The resulting breakdown in communication is easily repaired if the reader takes the time to use a dictionary. But if the writer fails to put the words in an understandable order, the reader most likely will become hopelessly confused.

In any language, the basic order of words that expresses meaning is the sentence. In English, every sentence has two essential parts, a *complete subject* and a *complete predicate,* which in turn comprise other parts. Being aware of these parts and of how they are related can help you in your speaking and writing to avoid unintentionally letting the order of your words get in the way of your ideas.

Complete Subjects and Predicates

A group of words in English is considered a sentence when it has two parts, either clearly stated or implied.

A sentence is a group of words with two main parts: a complete subject and a complete predicate. Together, these parts express a complete thought.

The complete subject contains the noun, pronoun, or group of words acting as a noun, plus their modifiers, that tells *who* or *what* the sentence is about. Located in the complete predicate is the verb or verb phrase, plus any modifiers and complements, that tells what the complete subject *does* or *is.* (See Section 2.3 for more information about complements.) The length of a complete subject and predicate can vary greatly.

Complete Subjects	Complete Predicates
Flowers	bloom.
A bell-clanging street car	moved through the intersection.
A souffle or quiche	is a delicious main dish.
The candidate's pragmatic approach to fiscal problems	impressed the voters attending the rally last Thursday.

In some sentences, a portion of the predicate may precede the complete subject. In the following example, *at midnight* modifies *ate.*

COMPLETE   COMPLETE SUBJECT   PREDICATE

EXAMPLE: At midnight the weary tourists ate their dinner.

Recognizing Complete Subjects and Complete Predicates. Copy the following paragraph, drawing a vertical line between each complete subject and complete predicate. Some sentences may require more than one line.

EXAMPLE: The gently rocking boat|lulled us to sleep.

(1) Morning came quickly. (2) Long before sunrise, the alarm clock rang. (3) Sluggishly, we dragged ourselves from a restful sleep. (4) At five o'clock we left the dock. (5) We were sailing out of the bay on a yacht equipped with every convenience. (6) From bow to stern, the boat measured forty feet. (7) During the night, a fog had crept in. (8) It greatly limited visibility and made the air cold. (9) Sophisticated directional equipment led us through the fog. (10) Inside the cabin we were warm, dry, and eager to begin deep-sea fishing.

Fragments

When either the complete subject or complete predicate is missing, the resulting group of words does not constitute a sentence. Instead, it is called a *fragment,* which is usually considered an error in writing.

A fragment is a group of words that does not express a complete thought.

You can correct a fragment by adding the missing parts.

Fragments	Complete Sentences
People with respiratory ailments. (Complete predicate missing)	People with respiratory ailments *should avoid smog-ridden cities.* (Complete predicate added)
Always lasts twelve hours in the tropics. (Complete subject missing)	*Night* always lasts twelve hours in the tropics. (Complete subject added)
In the new concert hall. (Complete subject and complete predicate missing)	*Minor adjustments* in the new concert hall *improved the acoustics.* (Complete predicate and rest of complete subject added)

In conversations, fragments usually do not present a problem since repetition, tone of voice, gestures, and facial expressions all help to communicate meaning. In writing, however, fragments should be avoided since the reader is alone with the words on the page and cannot go to the writer for clarification. An exception, of course, is writing that represents speech, such as the dialogue in a play or short story. Even then, fragments must be used carefully so that the reader can follow the flow of ideas.

Another exception in writing is the occasional use of *elliptical sentences,* in which the missing word or words can be easily understood.

ELLIPTICAL SENTENCES: Until later.

Why such a sad face?

See Section 4.1 for more information about fragments and how to correct them.

EXERCISE B: Locating and Correcting Sentence Fragments. Decide whether each item is a sentence or a fragment. If it is a sentence, write *sentence.* If it is a fragment, rewrite it to make it a sentence.

EXAMPLE: In spite of her painful sprained ankle.

She finished the race in spite of her painful sprained ankle.

1. His mother, a gentle, yet strong woman.
2. Stepped from the boat after a rugged trip across the Atlantic.
3. Diane dipped her doughnut into her milk before taking a bite.
4. Into the sky filled with dark thunderclouds.
5. The car's hood, hot from the sun's rays.
6. Sat around the campfire, roasting marshmallows.
7. The spider wove a beautiful, yet deadly web.
8. An old alligator with its thick, bumpy hide and enormous jaws.
9. My traveling companion carried a lightweight suitcase aboard the plane.
10. Under the weight of numerous responsibilities.

Simple Subjects and Predicates

When all modifiers and complements are removed from a complete subject and complete predicate, an essential word or group of words remains in each. These essential elements, called the *simple subject* and *simple predicate,* are the core around which sentences are developed.

The simple subject is the essential noun, pronoun, or group of words acting as a noun that cannot be left out of the complete subject.

The simple predicate is the essential verb or verb phrase that cannot be left out of the complete predicate.

The following chart shows simple subjects underlined once and simple predicates underlined twice. Notice how any remaining words either modify the simple subject and simple predicate or help to complete the meaning of the sentence.

SIMPLE SUBJECTS AND SIMPLE PREDICATES	
Complete Subjects	**Complete Predicates**
Small pocket <u>calculators</u>	<u>fit</u> nicely into coat pockets.
<u>Ronald Reagan</u>	<u>starred</u> in many films in his early career.
<u>Pictures</u> of Saturn	<u>have</u> certainly <u>revealed</u> much about the planet.

Notice in the last example that the simple subject is *pictures*, not *Saturn,* which is the object of the preposition *of.* Objects of prepositions never function as simple subjects. In this same example, notice also that the simple predicate is a verb phrase interrupted by an adverb.

NOTE ABOUT TERMINOLOGY: From now on in this text, the term *subject* will be used to refer to a simple subject, and the term *verb* will be used to refer to a simple predicate. Whenever subjects and verbs need to be indicated in examples, subjects will be underlined once and verbs will be underlined twice.

Locating Subjects and Verbs. You can employ either of two methods for locating subjects and verbs in sentences to help you check your own writing and avoid fragments. The first method involves locating the subject first. Ask, "What word tells what this sentence is about?" Once you have the answer—in other words, the subject—then ask, "What did the subject do?" This gives you the verb.

Some people, however, prefer to find the verb first. In this case, ask first, "What is the action verb or linking verb in the sentence?" This question should give you the verb. Then ask, "Who or what?" before it. The resulting word or words will be the subject.

Watch these methods applied to the following example.

EXAMPLE: African termites build huge mud castles up to twenty feet high.

To find the subject, first ask, "What word tells what this sentence is about?"

ANSWER: termites (*Termites* is the subject.)

Then ask, "What did the termites do?"

ANSWER: build (*Build* is the verb.)

To find the verb first, ask, "What is the action verb or linking verb in this sentence?"

ANSWER: build (*Build* is an action verb.)

Then ask, "Who or what build?"

ANSWER: termites (*Termites* is the subject.)

Sometimes, a sentence contains numerous modifiers, making isolation of the subject and verb very difficult. Simplify these sentences by mentally crossing out adjectives, adverbs, and prepositional phrases.

EXAMPLE: The business of home computers should grow extensively in the next ten years.

With the skeletal sentence that remains, you can easily use one of the two methods just introduced to determine the subject and verb. (See Sections 2.2, 3.3, and 3.4 for information about subjects and verbs in more complicated sentences.)

More Than One Subject or Verb. So far, the examples in this section have contained only one subject and one verb. Sometimes, however, a sentence may contain a *compound subject* or *compound verb.*

A compound subject is two or more subjects that have the same verb and are joined by a conjunction such as *and* or *or.*

EXAMPLES: The <u>train</u> and <u>car</u> <u>collided</u> at the intersection.

<u>Nickels</u>, <u>dimes</u>, or <u>quarters</u> <u>are used</u> in these meters.

Like subjects, verbs can be compound.

A compound verb is two or more verbs that have the same subject and are joined by a conjunction such as *and* or *or.*

EXAMPLES: <u>I</u> neither <u>saw</u> them nor <u>overheard</u> them.

<u>Most</u> of the passengers <u>had left</u> the ship and <u>begun</u> to explore the city.

Some sentences may contain both a compound subject and a compound verb.

EXAMPLE: The private <u>plane</u> and the <u>airliner</u> <u>flew</u> too close, <u>touched</u> wing tips, and almost <u>crashed</u>.

EXERCISE C: Identifying Subjects and Verbs. Copy each of the following sentences, drawing a vertical line between the complete subject and complete predicate. Then, underline each subject once and each verb twice.

EXAMPLE: The <u>state</u> with the most people | <u>is</u> California.

1. Some apes have been taught signs for words.
2. Rebecca Latimer Felton was the first woman to serve as a United States Senator.
3. Many of the current television programs are airing sensitive, controversial issues.
4. Members of the Coast Guard rescued the passengers of the sinking ocean liner.

5. A glittering Monte Carlo lures the wealthy to its port.
6. The behavior of sharks has been studied by biologists.
7. Intricate ironwork decorated the outside of the stately New Orleans home.
8. People in stressful situations will often show symptoms of fatigue.
9. The pyramids in Egypt have attracted tourists for thousands of years.
10. New York is the setting for many pieces of American literature.

EXERCISE D: Locating Compound Subjects and Compound Verbs. Write the parts of each compound subject and compound verb. Note that some sentences may have both.

EXAMPLE: The babies kicked their feet and gurgled at each other.

kicked   gurgled

1. The rod and reel stood in the corner ready for use.
2. We headed south for a mile and then turned east.
3. Either George Burns or Bob Hope would get my vote for best comedian.
4. Shoppers and salespersons felt the tension of the holidays and snapped at one another.
5. Both Sara and Blythe liked the story "The Lie" by Kurt Vonnegut, Jr.
6. The talented circus troupe balanced on high wires and swung from trapezes.
7. She stared at the problem and speculated on its answer.
8. Neither the Alaskan cruise nor the tour of English inns had tickets still available.
9. Both bees and hummingbirds gather nectar and pollinate flowers.
10. We built, sanded, and stained those tables.

DEVELOPING WRITING SKILLS: Developing Sentences from Subjects and Verbs. Write five sentences using the directions on the next page. Make sure each of the sentences is complete. Use adjectives, adverbs, prepositional phrases, and conjunctions where appropriate.

EXAMPLE: compound subject + *are*
            Both Steve and Jim are on the honor roll.

1. *fields* + verb phrase
2. compound subject + *were driven*
3. *President-elect* + compound verb
4. compound subject + *surfed and swam*
5. *accountant and lawyer* + verb phrase

2.2 Subjects in Different Kinds of Sentences

Finding subjects and verbs enables you to check your sentences for logic, clarity, and completeness. Most often, the subject will precede the verb. Sometimes, however, the subject will assume another position when the purpose of the sentence changes. This section will explain the four functions of English sentences and examine the positions subjects can hold.

The Four Functions of Sentences

All complete sentences contain a subject and verb, but not all sentences function in the same way. In English all sentences can be classified according to one of four functions: *declarative, interrogative, imperative,* and *exclamatory.*

A *declarative* sentence, the most common sentence in English, is used to express facts and opinions.

A declarative sentence states an idea and ends with a period.

EXAMPLES: Different wild flowers grow in different regions of the United States.

            Most people do not enjoy taking risks.

To pose a question, an *interrogative* sentence is used.

An interrogative sentence asks a question and ends with a question mark.

EXAMPLES: What harm did the delay cause?

            Who designed the Guggenheim Museum?

Demands or requests are conveyed through *imperative* sentences.

An imperative sentence gives an order or direction and ends with a period or exclamation mark.

When an imperative sentence expresses force or emotion, an exclamation mark rather than a period may be placed at the end of the sentence. Notice also that although most imperative sentences have an understood *you* as the subject, an order phrased like a question may have a stated subject.

EXAMPLES: Call the insurance agent, please.

Watch out for that car!

Would you please stop that!

The last type of sentence, the *exclamatory* sentence, is always used to convey strong emotion.

An exclamatory sentence conveys emotion and ends with an exclamation mark.

As the first two of the following examples show, declarative and interrogative sentences are classified as exclamatory sentences when their primary purpose is to express strong emotion. Other sentences such as the last of the following examples, a sentence with an understood subject and verb, are purely exclamatory.

EXAMPLES: The new baby just arrived!   (declarative)

Isn't her voice magnificent!   (interrogative)

Perfect!

EXERCISE A: Identifying the Four Functions of Sentences. Identify each sentence as *declarative, interrogative, imperative,* or *exclamatory.* Then write the end mark for each sentence.

EXAMPLE: As I ran down the street, I heard someone call to me

declarative .

(1) "Hey, you (2) Slow down for a minute (3) I bet you haven't had breakfast yet (4) Here—how about some granola muffins"

(5) I stopped in surprise as the garbage collector lobbed two packages of English muffins at me

(6) "Do you know how much perfectly good bread they throw away there" (7) He gestured to the grocery store that backed my apartment complex (8) "I always collect it and give it out to my friends along the route (9) Is there anything else that I can get you"

(10) This dark-haired, beardless Santa Claus reached into the cabin of his truck (11) Two loaves of cinnamon raisin bread appeared

(12) "Do you mean they give you all of this for free"

(13) "Actually, I pull it out of their trash bins before I dump them (14) It is perfectly good, though—just a day or two old"

(15) I had to admit that the bread in my hand looked no different from the plastic-wrapped bread that lined the grocery shelves (16) I capitulated

(17) "Hey, this is neat (18) I have never eaten bread from a trash can before, but I'll give it a try (19) I run almost every day so maybe I will see you again soon"

(20) "Look for me (21) I don't always have this much loot, but whatever I've got, it's yours (22) And tell your neighbors"

(23) He flashed me a smile and pointed upwards (24) "Don't you think we have a lot to be thankful for"

(25) I waved goodbye with the raisin bread

EXERCISE B: Writing Sentences with Different Functions.

Write a sentence for each number in the following chart. Be sure that you use the subject indicated at the left and the function indicated at the top. For example, the first sentence should be a *declarative* sentence about *television*.

	Declarative	Interrogative	Imperative	Exclamatory
Television	1	2		
Politics			3	4
Trivia	5			6
Basketball		7	8	
Subways	9			10

Hard-to-Find Subjects

The position of a subject in relation to its verb may vary according to the function of the sentence. Some subjects, therefore, are more difficult to find than others.

Subjects in Declarative Sentences. In most declarative sentences the subject precedes the verb. This subject-verb order is the normal pattern for declarative sentences. There are, however, two exceptions: sentences beginning with *there* or *here* and sentences that are inverted for emphasis.

When *there* or *here* begins a declarative sentence, it is often erroneously identified as the subject.

The subject of a sentence is never *there* or *here*.

These words usually serve as adverbs that modify the verb by explaining *where*. The most effective technique for making the subjects visible in these kinds of sentences is to rearrange the sentence in your mind so that *there* or *here* comes after the verb. If *there* sounds awkward after the verb, it is an *expletive,* a device used merely to get the sentence started. In this case simply drop *there* from the sentence when you rearrange it.

Sentences Beginning with *There* or *Here*	Sentences Rearranged with Subject Before Verb
There <u>are</u> my prize <u>orchids</u>.	My prize <u>orchids</u> <u>are</u> there.
Here <u>is</u> your <u>ticket</u> to the concert.	Your <u>ticket</u> to the concert <u>is</u> here.
There <u>were</u> <u>funds</u> available.	<u>Funds</u> <u>were</u> available.

Occasionally, sentences beginning with *there* or *here* may be in normal word order with the subjects before the verbs.

EXAMPLE: Here <u>you</u> <u>are</u>.

Sentences inverted for emphasis also vary from the regular subject-verb pattern of declarative sentences. In such sentences the subject is deliberately positioned at the end of the sentences to focus attention on it.

71

In some declarative sentences, the subject follows the verb in order to receive greater emphasis.

Often prepositional phrases begin such inverted sentences. Mentally shifting the words at the beginning of the sentence to the middle or to the end makes the subject easier to detect.

Sentences Inverted for Emphasis	Sentences Rephrased with Subject Before Verb
Deep into the cavernous hole <u>went</u> the <u>miners</u>.	The <u>miners</u> <u>went</u> deep into the cavernous hole.
Around my head <u>buzzed</u> the most persistent <u>fly</u>.	The most persistent <u>fly</u> <u>buzzed</u> around my head.

Subjects in Interrogative Sentences. Many interrogative sentences follow the usual subject-verb order, making the subject easy to identify.

EXAMPLE: What television <u>shows</u> <u>have</u> the best ratings?

Almost as often, however, an inversion occurs, changing the subject's location within the sentence.

In interrogative sentences, the subject often follows the verb.

Inverted interrogative sentences will commonly begin with a verb, a helping verb, or one of the following words: *how, what, when, where, which, who, whose,* or *why.* When looking for the subject in these sentences, mentally change the interrogative sentence into a declarative sentence, as the following examples illustrate.

Questions	Rephrased Questions
<u>Is</u> the <u>coffee</u> ready?	The <u>coffee</u> <u>is</u> ready.
<u>Will</u> <u>you</u> <u>prepare</u> the monthly statements?	<u>You</u> <u>will prepare</u> the monthly statements.
How <u>should</u> this <u>line</u> <u>be read</u>?	This <u>line</u> <u>should be read</u> how.

Subjects in Imperative Sentences. Subjects in imperative sentences are usually implied, not specifically stated.

In imperative sentences, the subject is understood to be *you*.

In the chart below, the left side shows imperative sentences in which the subjects are implied. The right side shows the positions where the understood subjects logically occur.

Imperative Sentences	With Understood *You* Added
Wait for the delivery person, please.	[You] wait for the delivery person, please.
In an earthquake, crawl under a study table.	In an earthquake, [you] crawl under a sturdy table.
Carolyn, turn down that stereo.	Carolyn, [you] turn down that stereo.

In the last example in the chart, the person to whom the sentence is addressed is named. However, *Carolyn,* a noun of direct address, does not function as the subject of the sentence. The subject is still understood to be *you.*

Subjects in Exclamatory Sentences. In exclamatory sentences subjects may come after verbs or be missing entirely.

In an exclamatory sentence, the subject may come after the verb or may be understood.

The same technique employed to find subjects in interrogative sentences can be used to find the subject in many exclamatory sentences.

REVERSED ORDER: What else could I have done! (I could have done what else.)

Can this be real! (This can be real.)

Some exclamatory sentences may be so elliptical that both the subject *and* the verb are implied. For such sentences as these, common sense and context serve as your best guides for determining the unstated subject and verb.

Exclamatory Sentences with Understood Subjects and Verbs	With Understood Parts Added
Quick!	[<u>You</u> <u>come</u> here] quick!
Air!	[<u>I</u> <u>need</u>] air!

EXERCISE C: Locating Hard-to-Find Subjects. Write the subject and verb in each sentence. Include in parentheses any words that are understood or implied. Underline each subject once and each verb twice.

EXAMPLE: Here is my report.

<u>report</u> <u>is</u>

1. On the table lay the unopened letter.
2. Are you planning to go to the Macy's Thanksgiving Day Parade this year?
3. Through the speakers came the wonderful sound of blues artist B.B. King.
4. There are thousands of foster children in America ready for adoption.
5. Does John Denver typify a country singer or a ballad singer?
6. More benefits!
7. Where did you buy that granola?
8. Here are some tips on fly casting.
9. Remember to call me.
10. Was Henry Hudson Dutch or British?
11. Help!
12. Lead us in the Pledge of Allegiance, please.
13. There is his social security check.
14. Where could I go?
15. Are teenagers adequately preparing themselves to become leaders of society?
16. Over the mountains trudged the weary but determined pioneers.
17. After dinner, finish your homework.
18. There are real rattlesnake roundups in Texas.
19. Oxygen!
20. How much did the first televisions cost?

DEVELOPING WRITING SKILLS: Writing Different Kinds of Sentences with Hard-to-Find Subjects. Follow the instructions to write ten sentences with hard-to-find subjects.

1. Write a declarative sentence beginning with *there* or *here* used as an adverb.
2. Write a declarative sentence beginning with *there* as an expletive.
3. Write a declarative sentence with an inverted order.
4. Write an interrogative sentence beginning with a verb.
5. Write an interrogative sentence beginning with a helping verb.
6. Write an interrogative sentence beginning with *how, what, when, where, which, who, whose,* or *why.*
7. Write an imperative sentence with an understood *you.*
8. Write an exclamatory sentence with an inverted order.
9. Write an exclamatory sentence phrased like a question.
10. Write an exclamatory sentence with both the subject and the verb implied.

Complements 2.3

Some sentences are complete with just a subject and a verb or with a subject, verb, and modifiers, as in *The ointment stung* or *The burn ointment stung momentarily.*

The meaning of many sentences, however, depends on additional words to finish the idea begun by the subject and verb. For example, *Mr. Potter continuously mislays . . .* or *My novelette is . . .* remain confusing and incomplete even though each has a subject and verb. To complete the meaning of the predicate parts of those sentences, a writer must add *complements:* for example, *Mr. Potter continuously mislays his glasses* or *My novelette is a satire.*

A complement is a word or group of words that completes the meaning of the predicate of a sentence.

There are five different kinds of complements in English: *direct objects, indirect objects, objective complements, predicate nominatives,* and *predicate adjectives.* The first three occur in

75

sentences with transitive action verbs, while the last two, often grouped together as *subject complements,* are found only with linking verbs. (See Section 1.2 for more information about action and linking verbs.)

Direct Objects

Direct objects, the most common of the five types of complements, complete the meaning of action verbs by telling who or what receives the action.

A direct object is a noun, pronoun, or group of words acting as a noun that receives the action of a transitive verb.

EXAMPLES: I <u>leased</u> a small beach bun$\overset{\text{DO}}{\text{ga}}$low.

<u>Mud</u> and <u>leaves</u> <u>clogged</u> the gu$\overset{\text{DO}}{\text{tt}}$ers.

To determine the direct object of a sentence, ask *Whom?* or *What?* after an action verb. If the sentence offers no answer, the action verb is intransitive and there is no direct object in the sentence.

EXAMPLES: The <u>curator</u> of the museum <u>led</u> the $\overset{\text{DO}}{\text{tour}}$. (Led *what? Answer:* tour)

The <u>employer</u> <u>reprimanded</u> her $\overset{\text{DO}}{\text{secretary}}$. (Reprimanded *whom? Answer:* secretary)

Her <u>voice</u> <u>echoed</u> in the halls. (Echoed *what? Answer:* none; the verb is intransitive)

In some inverted questions, the direct object may appear before the verb. Rephrase such questions as statements in normal word order to locate the direct objects.

INVERTED QUESTION: Which $\overset{\text{DO}}{\text{dessert}}$ <u>should</u> I <u>order</u>?

REWORDED AS A STATEMENT: I <u>should order</u> which $\overset{\text{DO}}{\text{dessert}}$.

76

Keep alert for sentences with more than one direct object, called a *compound direct object.* If a sentence contains a compound direct object, asking *Whom?* or *What?* after the action verb will yield two or more answers.

EXAMPLES: The <u>model</u> <u>wore</u> brown pants and a tweed blazer.
                                                 DO   DO

The <u>Pilgrims</u> <u>ate</u> wild turkey, nuts, and corn on the
                              DO   DO   DO

first Thanksgiving.

In the last example, *Thanksgiving* is the object of the preposition *on.* An object of a preposition is never a direct object.

EXERCISE A: Recognizing Direct Objects. Write the direct object in each sentence, including all parts of any compound direct objects.

EXAMPLE: Sometimes, artists find inspiration for their work in
                     a particular place.

                     inspiration

(1) Georgia O'Keeffe spent her early years in the Midwest. (2) Later, she studied art in Chicago and New York. (3) From 1912 to 1914, she supervised art teachers in the public schools in Amarillo, Texas. (4) From 1916 to 1918, she directed the art professors at a college in Canyon, Texas. (5) In New York O'Keeffe later married Alfred Stieglitz, a famous American photographer. (6) Stieglitz displayed O'Keeffe's paintings in his art gallery. (7) The desert had inspired O'Keeffe. (8) She earned fame for her paintings of the Southwest. (9) Many of the paintings contain rocks, animal bones, and flowers. (10) From 1949 O'Keeffe made her permanent home near Taos, New Mexico.

Indirect Objects

Indirect objects are found in sentences with direct objects.

An indirect object is a noun or pronoun that appears with a direct object and names the person or thing something is given to or done for.

77

Indirect objects are common with such verbs as *ask, bring, buy, give, lend, make, promise, show, teach, tell,* and *write.*

EXAMPLES: I <u>promised</u> Kelly a bicycle on his birthday.

EXAMPLES: I <u>promised</u> Kelly a bicycle on his birthday.

The <u>judge gave</u> the jury instructions.

Like direct objects, indirect objects can be compound.

EXAMPLE: I <u>showed</u> my father and mother my poem.

When locating the indirect object in a sentence, first make sure the sentence contains a direct object. Then ask yourself one of these questions after the verb and direct object: *To or for whom?* or *To or for what?*

EXAMPLES: The <u>teacher</u> <u>taught</u> our class public speaking.
(Taught speaking *to whom? Answer:* class)

We <u>made</u> the couch a slipcover. (Made slipcover *for what? Answer:* couch)

To avoid confusing an indirect object with a direct object, always remember to ask the right questions in the correct order. First, ask *Whom?* or *What?* after the verb to find the direct object. If the sentence contains a direct object then ask *To or for whom?* or *To or for what?* after the verb and direct object to find the indirect object.

EXAMPLE: Pat <u>gave</u> Doug a tremendous hug. (Gave *what? Answer:* hug) (Gave hug *to whom? Answer:* Doug)

Remember also that an indirect object almost always sits squarely between the verb and direct object. In a sentence in normal word order, it will never follow the direct object nor will it ever be the object of the preposition *to* or *for.*

EXAMPLES: <u>Maria</u> <u>sent</u> her picture to me.

<u>Maria</u> <u>sent</u> me her picture.

78

In the first sentence at the bottom of the previous page, *to me* is a prepositional phrase that follows the direct object. Only when the preposition is dropped from the sentence and the *me* precedes the direct object does *me* function as an indirect object.

EXERCISE B: Recognizing Indirect Objects. Write the underlined words in each sentence and identify each as a *direct object, indirect object,* or *object of a preposition.*

EXAMPLE: Frank gave his <u>friends</u> <u>vegetables</u> from his garden.

        friends (indirect object)   vegetables (direct object)

1. They bought the <u>condominium</u> for their <u>daughter</u>.
2. The university granted the incoming <u>freshman</u> a four-year <u>scholarship</u>.
3. The builder showed the prospective <u>owners</u> some special <u>additions</u> to the house.
4. Beverly Sills sang an <u>aria</u> at the charity <u>ball</u>.
5. Mrs. Phelps taught <u>piano</u> in her <u>home</u>.
6. Eric told his young <u>campers</u> a harrowing bedtime <u>tale</u>.
7. Aunt Harriet described our complete family <u>tree</u> to <u>me</u>.
8. When did they deliver the dining room <u>set</u> to <u>you</u>?
9. Our club made <u>ice cream</u> for the old-fashioned <u>picnic</u>.
10. I ordered <u>you</u> a sweater from the <u>catalog</u>.

Objective Complements

While an indirect object almost always comes before a direct object, an *objective complement* will almost always follow a direct object. As its name implies, the objective complement "complements" or adds to the meaning of the direct object.

An objective complement is an adjective or noun that appears with a direct object and describes or renames it.

A sentence containing an objective complement may at first glance seem to have two direct objects. Identifying an objective complement is simplified when you know they occur only with such verbs as *appoint, call, consider, declare, elect, judge, label, make, name, select,* or *think.*

79

EXAMPLES: The <u>producers</u> of the movie <u>declared</u> it successful.
$\overset{\text{DO}}{}$ $\overset{\text{OC}}{}$

The <u>President</u> <u>made</u> him an ambassador.
$\overset{\text{DO}}{}$ $\overset{\text{OC}}{}$

<u>History</u> <u>judged</u> Abraham Lincoln a fine President.
$\overset{\text{DO}}{}$ $\overset{\text{OC}}{}$

Like other sentence parts, objective complements can be compound.

EXAMPLE: I <u>called</u> Dave a very talented swimmer and a brilliant
$\overset{\text{DO}}{}$ $\overset{\text{OC}}{}$

lawyer.
$\overset{\text{OC}}{}$

To determine whether a word is an objective complement, say the verb and direct object, and then ask *What?*

EXAMPLE: The <u>committee</u> <u>declared</u> the chairman incompetent.
$\overset{\text{DO}}{}$ $\overset{\text{OC}}{}$

(Declared chairman *what? Answer:* incompetent)

EXERCISE C: Using Objective Complements. Add an objective complement of the type indicated to each of the following sentences.

EXAMPLE: The judges selected that entry <u>(noun)</u>.

The judges selected that entry the winner.

1. We named our new puppy <u>(noun)</u>.
2. The board considered the company's new president <u>(adjective)</u>.
3. Unanimously, all my friends in the class appointed me <u>(noun)</u>.
4. The editor of the high-school magazine appointed Janet <u>(noun)</u>.
5. The neighborhood children think my yard <u>(noun)</u>.
6. Our organization elected Terry <u>(noun)</u>.
7. The new living room curtains make the room <u>(adjective)</u> and <u>(adjective)</u>.
8. They named the twins <u>(noun)</u> and <u>(noun)</u>.
9. The builders made the housing development <u>(noun)</u>.
10. A court judged the defendant <u>(adjective)</u>.

80

Subject Complements

Linking verbs require *subject complements* to complete their meaning.

A subject complement is a noun, pronoun, or adjective that appears with a linking verb and tells something about the subject of the sentence.

Predicate Nominatives. The subject and the predicate nominative refer to the same person, place, or thing.

A predicate nominative is a noun or pronoun that appears with a linking verb and renames, identifies, or explains the subject of a sentence.

The last example has a compound predicate nominative.

EXAMPLES: Ann Pace <u>became</u> a geologist for an oil company.

The <u>winner</u> <u>is</u> you.

Merlin Olsen <u>is</u> an actor and former football player.

Predicate Adjectives. As the label indicates, a predicate adjective is not a noun or a pronoun but an adjective.

A predicate adjective is an adjective that appears with a linking verb and describes the subject of the sentence.

A predicate adjective refers to the subject by describing it in much the same way any adjective modifies a noun or pronoun.

EXAMPLES: Your <u>reasoning</u> <u>seems</u> logical.

The <u>melody</u> <u>sounded</u> light and cheerful.

EXERCISE D: Identifying Subject Complements. Write the subject complement or subject complements in each sentence. Then identify each as a *predicate nominative* or *predicate adjective*.

EXAMPLE: Jean should become a successful college student.

            student   (predicate nominative)

1. After my course in astronomy, I became an avid stargazer.
2. The rainclouds appeared distant yet forbidding.
3. The unruly child grew belligerent and then sullen.
4. Those plants to the left are a hybrid.
5. Paul Revere was a silversmith and a maker of dentures.
6. My quilted comforter felt warm and soft against my skin.
7. The air was sweet with the scent of apple blossoms.
8. She is both a competent doctor and a devoted mother.
9. The juice tasted bitter and warm.
10. The vast lawns of the country estate were a vivid green.

DEVELOPING WRITING SKILLS: Using Complements in Your Own Writing. Write two sentences to illustrate each of the complements introduced in this section: *direct objects, indirect objects, objective complements, predicate nominatives,* and *predicate adjectives.* Underline each subject once and each verb twice. Label the complements.

EXAMPLE: <u>Karen</u> <u><u>felt</u></u> proud of her success.
                   PA

2.4 Basic Sentence Patterns

The simplest pattern for an English sentence is the subject followed by an intransitive verb. "A taxi is coming" is in the S-V pattern. This section reviews the five other basic sentence patterns used for sentences with complements and those used for inverted sentences.

Five Basic Patterns with Complements

Sentences with complements follow set patterns.

In the English language, subjects, verbs, and complements follow five basic sentence patterns.

Except as predicate adjectives or objective complements, adjectives are never part of a sentence's basic pattern. Nor are adverbs, conjunctions, interjections, or prepositional phrases, which add details to or connections between the sentence parts. As you study, mentally eliminate these additional words to see the skeleton of the sentences clearly.

The Three Patterns with Transitive Verbs. A sentence with a transitive action verb will include at least one complement: a direct object. A sentence with a direct object may also contain an indirect object or an objective complement.

SENTENCE PATTERNS WITH TRANSITIVE VERBS	
Patterns	**Examples**
S-AV-DO	She recklessly <u>hit</u> the brakes. [DO] Voraciously, <u>Edgar</u> <u>ate</u> the fresh salmon. [DO]
S-AV-IO-DO	I <u>tipped</u> the waiter [IO] five dollars. [DO] We <u>bought</u> our boat [IO] a new tachometer. [DO]
S-AV-DO-OC	We <u>named</u> our dog [DO] Major. [OC] They <u>judged</u> the movie [DO] appropriate for us. [OC]

The Two Patterns with Linking Verbs. A linking verb will always link the subject of the sentence with a subject complement. The subject complement will be either a predicate nominative or a predicate adjective.

SENTENCE PATTERNS WITH LINKING VERBS	
Patterns	**Examples**
S-LV-PN	That <u>gentleman</u> <u>is</u> a foreign diplomat. [PN] <u>Success</u> in business <u>was</u> her goal. [PN]

	PA
S-LV-PA	My gas <u>bill</u> <u><u>was</u></u> outrageous.

The <u>field</u> <u><u>grew</u></u> barren from overuse.

Patterns with Compound Sentence Parts. Any of these basic sentence patterns can be expanded by making one or more of its parts compound. Such simple expansions can add variety and style to your writing.

SOME BASIC SENTENCE PATTERNS WITH COMPOUND PARTS

Patterns	Examples
S-S-V	The <u>timekeeper</u> and the <u>referee</u> <u><u>talked</u></u> on the sideline.
S-AV-DO-DO	The <u>driver</u> <u><u>ran</u></u> a stop sign and a red light.
S-LV-LV-PN	My <u>aunt</u> <u><u>was</u></u> and still <u><u>is</u></u> a fine seamstress.
S-AV-DO-AV-DO-OC	The <u>storekeeper</u> <u><u>left</u></u> the shop and <u><u>appointed</u></u> me manager in her absence.

EXERCISE A: Identifying Basic Sentence Patterns. Write each sentence, underlining the subject once, underlining the verb twice, and circling each complement. Then write the pattern of each sentence, using the abbreviations in the chart.

EXAMPLE: Both <u>kittens</u> <u><u>seem</u></u> (friendly) and (playful.)

S-LV-PA-PA

1. Resoundingly, I hit the blacktop and skinned my knees on the rough surface.
2. The retired couple made gardening their full-time occupation.
3. We talked for hours and hours.
4. For such a small restaurant, the menu appeared extensive.

84

5. The treasurer and a secretary embezzled thousands from the company.
6. Its strong rhythm and fine sound won the band many enthusiastic reviews.
7. He dived into the water and emerged two minutes later.
8. The actress flashed her smile and waved a gloved hand at the admiring crowd.
9. The picture on the rubber stamp became my trademark for all my correspondence.
10. After questioning, the suspect no longer seemed defensive and evasive.

Inverted Patterns

Inverted sentences also follow a number of set patterns.

In an inverted sentence pattern, the subject is never first.

Questions in particular are likely to follow inverted patterns.
Patterns in Inverted Questions. Although some questions are not inverted, most are. In an inverted question, the subject often follows the verb or appears between a helping verb and the verb. Complements usually follow the verb and the subject, but a direct object may sometimes come before the verb.

Patterns	Examples
V-S	<u>Was</u> <u>Jennifer</u> at field hockey practice today?
	Why <u>was</u> <u>Dan</u> here?
HV-S-V	<u>Must</u> <u>you</u> <u>work</u> so hard?
	Why <u>were</u> <u>they</u> <u>shouting</u>?
HV-S-V-COMP	<u>Does</u> <u>Mark</u> <u>write</u> $\overset{\text{DO}}{\text{poetry}}$?
HV-S-V-COMP-COMP	<u>Did</u> <u>Kathleen</u> <u>give</u> $\overset{\text{IO}}{\text{them}}$ $\overset{\text{DO}}{\text{directions}}$?
COMP-HV-S-V	Which $\overset{\text{DO}}{\text{recipe}}$ <u>did</u> <u>you</u> <u>follow</u>?

| | DO | IO |
COMP-HV-S-V-COMP   Which book <u>did</u> <u>Richard</u> <u>loan</u> you?

PN
V-S-COMP   <u>Were</u> <u>they</u> members of the band?

PA
<u>Was</u> <u>Laura</u> angry?

Patterns in Sentences Beginning with *There* or *Here*. Most sentences beginning with *there* or *here* are inverted. The subject follows the verb.

Pattern	Example
V-S	There <u>is</u> my <u>mother</u>.

Patterns Inverted for Emphasis. When a sentence is inverted to emphasize a subject, the subject follows the verb. When a sentence is inverted to emphasize a complement, the complement appears near the beginning of the sentence, before the subject and the verb.

Patterns	Examples
V-S	Over the treetops <u>rose</u> the red <u>kite</u>.
COMP-S-V	What despair <u>I</u> <u>felt</u>! (DO)
COMP-S-V-COMP	What inspiration <u>you</u> <u>gave</u> us! (DO / IO)
COMP-S-V	What a concert <u>that</u> <u>was</u>! (PN)
COMP-V-S	How happy <u>was</u> that <u>sound</u>. (PA)

Like the five basic sentence patterns with complements, inverted sentence patterns may be expanded by making one or more of their parts compound.

DO   DO
EXAMPLE: Which skirt and sweater <u>did</u> <u>you</u> <u>wear</u> to the party?

86

EXERCISE B: Identifying Inverted Patterns. Write the sentences, underlining the subjects once, underlining the verbs twice, and circling the complements. Then identify the sentence patterns, using the abbreviations in the charts.

EXAMPLE: Has Michael told you that story?

HV-S-V-COMP-COMP

1. Has Kevin left yet?
2. Here is Linda now.
3. Which award did you receive?
4. What a day we had!
5. Were Susan and Bob late for the meeting?
6. What good children they are.
7. Did Mr. Holland give the class a test yesterday?
8. Were your friends at the party?
9. In the basket slept four tiny kittens.
10. Was Judy the soloist at the concert?

DEVELOPING WRITING SKILLS: Writing Sentences in a Variety of Patterns. Use each pattern in a sentence of your own. Then underline each subject once, underline each verb twice, and circle each complement.

EXAMPLE: S-AV-IO-IO-DO

We gave Mark and Liz a surprise party.

1. S-LV-PN	6. HV-S-V
2. S-AV-DO-OC	7. COMP-S-V
3. S-AV-DO-DO	8. COMP-V-S
4. S-AV-IO-DO	9. HV-S-V-COMP-COMP
5. S-LV-PA	10. V-S-COMP

Diagraming Basic Sentence Parts 2.5

A pictorial representation of a sentence is called a diagram. Just as a map can help a driver understand directions, so a diagram can help you visualize a sentence's structure. This section will explain the traditional rules for diagraming the basic sentence patterns that were covered in this chapter.

Subjects, Verbs, and Modifiers

To diagram a subject and a verb, draw a horizontal line and place the subject on the left and the verb on the right. Separate the two with a vertical line.

EXAMPLE: Malcolm should have volunteered.

Malcolm	should have volunteered

Adjectives and adverbs sit on slanted lines beneath the words they modify.

EXAMPLE: The very large bird glided surprisingly gracefully.

When the subject of an imperative sentence is understood to be *you,* place it in parentheses on the main line. Inverted sentences in which the subject follows the verb are also diagramed in the regular subject-verb order. The capital letter shows which word begins the sentence.

EXAMPLES: Call home soon.   Has Regina telephoned yet?

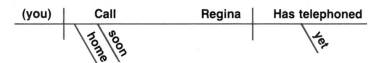

Rearrange a sentence beginning with *there* or *here* so that the subject comes first. Then, if *there* or *here* functions as an adverb, diagram it below the verb. If *there* functions as an expletive, place it on a horizontal line above the subject. Use the position of an expletive for interjections and nouns of direct address also. Diagrams illustrating these types of sentences are shown at the top of the next page.

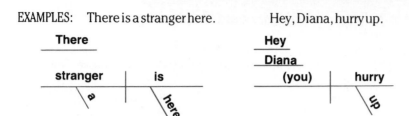

EXAMPLES: There is a stranger here.   Hey, Diana, hurry up.

EXERCISE A: Diagraming Subjects, Verbs, and Modifers. Correctly diagram each sentence.

1. The giant python slithered silently.
2. Her extremely high fever finally dropped.
3. Is my notebook here?
4. My, there goes one expensive automobile.
5. Leslie, do not dawdle.

Adding Conjunctions

Conjunctions are generally shown in a diagram on a dotted line between the words which they connect. In the example presented below, conjunctions join both adjectives and adverbs.

EXAMPLE: The long and difficult report was read quickly but not easily.

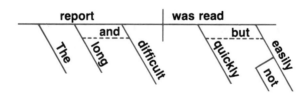

Conjunctions connecting compound subjects and compound verbs are also placed on dotted lines drawn between the words which they connect. In the example on the next page, the horizontal line of the diagram is split so each of the compound parts appears on a line of its own. Notice how correlative conjunctions and helping verbs shared by more than one verb are placed. If each part of the compound verb had its

89

own helping verb, each would be placed on the line with its own verb.

EXAMPLE: Both you and I must pack today and move out tomorrow.

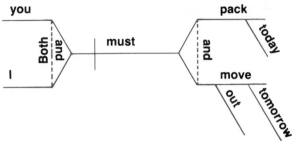

As the above example shows, modifiers in sentences that contain compound parts are carefully positioned with the individual words that they modify. If a word modifies an entire compound element, as illustrated in the following example, the modifier is positioned beneath the main line of the diagram.

EXAMPLE: Yesterday, the campers and counselors swam and fished.

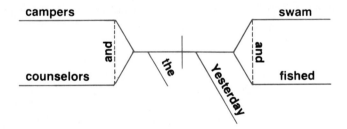

EXERCISE B: Diagraming Sentences with Conjunctions.
Correctly diagram each sentence.

1. The tiny tugboat and the gigantic cruiser steamed away.
2. The horses neighed nervously and shied away.
3. Her letter, scented and pink, arrived today.
4. Today, both Darrin and Peter have continuously memorized and rehearsed.
5. Neither Luis nor Mary have arrived yet.

Complements

Since complements complete the meaning of a verb, they are diagramed on the predicate side of the sentence. Direct objects sit on the same line as the subject and verb and are separated from the verb by a short vertical line. Indirect objects are placed on a horizontal line extending from a slanted line directly below the verb.

EXAMPLES: I sliced the cheese.   Dick bought us a wok.

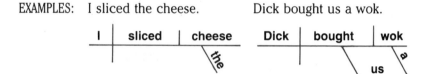

An objective complement is placed right after a direct object. A short slanted line pointing toward the direct object separates it from the rest of the sentence.

EXAMPLE: The supervisor named Lee division manager.

Subject complements are also placed on the main line, separated from the linking verb by a short line that slants back toward the subject and verb.

EXAMPLES: Margarita is a soprano.   The dirt road was bumpy.

Compound complements are diagramed by splitting the lines on which they appear. Conjunctions are placed on dotted lines drawn between the words they connect.

EXAMPLE: We gave our grandmother and grandfather airplane

tickets and money.

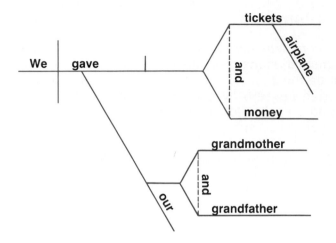

EXERCISE C: Diagraming Complements. Correctly diagram each sentence.

1. My old scrapbook held old snapshots and other mementos.
2. The group gave Kirk and Nat an elaborate map and some instructions.
3. His monthly salary was meager and inadequate.
4. My parents consider me an excellent driver.
5. Tammy is my sister and a good friend.

DEVELOPING WRITING SKILLS: Writing and Diagraming Sentences. Use the following patterns to write five sentences of your own. Then correctly diagram each sentence. Keep your sentences simple but be sure to include appropriate adjectives and adverbs.

EXAMPLE: S-AV-DO-AV-DO

　　　　　Rose peeled apples and baked a pie.

1. S-V	6. S-AV-IO-IO-DO
2. S-V-V	7. S-AV-DO-OC
3. S-AV-DO	8. S-LV-PN
4. S-AV-DO-DO	9. S-S-LV-PA-PA
5. S-AV-IO-DO	10. HV-S-V-COMP

Skills Review and Writing Workshop

Basic Sentence Parts and Patterns

CHECKING YOUR SKILLS

Identify each of the underlined sentence parts as a *subject, verb, direct object, indirect object, objective complement, predicate nominative,* or *predicate adjective.*

(1) William Randolph Hearst was born in 1863. (2) He became a newspaper (3) publisher. Hearst's parents owned (4) interests in silver mines. (5) They gave (6) him vast (7) sums of money to invest in his newspaper empire. In the early twentieth century, Hearst (8) established (9) newspapers in San Francisco, New York, Chicago, and other large cities. He sought the (10) support of labor unions and other groups with grievances against the established order. Hearst (11) advocated (12) yellow journalism, a newspaper style that emphasized sensationalism at the expense of news. In Hearst's newspapers appeared sensational crime and vice (13) stories, human interest (14) features, (15) pictures, and (16) cartoons. The content of the newspapers was (17) popular with the mass of readers, and by 1935 Hearst had built the world's largest newspaper publishing (18) empire. Even critics (19) considered Hearst a (20) master of American journalism.

USING GRAMMAR SKILLS IN WRITING
Evaluating an Activity

Imagine you are to evaluate the activities of a club or community group. Follow the steps to write your evaluation.

Prewriting: Think about the major benefits of the group. Consider which aspects of the group could be improved.

Writing: Start with your overall evaluation. Then discuss possible improvements. Describe how your participation in the group has affected or influenced you.

Revising: When you revise, make sure you have used a variety of sentence patterns. Then proofread carefully.

3

Phrases and Clauses

A proficient writer approaches language in much the same way that a sculptor approaches clay. Using their skills and imagination, they interact with the formless material to try to shape it into a work that will express their thoughts and personality. The previous chapters in this unit have discussed the essential materials at a writer's command: the parts of speech and the basic English sentence patterns. This chapter will describe the other kinds of elements that writers can use to expand the basic patterns and to achieve a greater range of expression.

3.1 Prepositional Phrases and Appositives

When one-word adjectives and adverbs cannot convey all of the details and relationships that a writer needs to express, the writer can often use a structure known as a *phrase* to express the precise idea.

A phrase is a group of words, without a subject and verb, that functions in a sentence as one part of speech.

Two common types of phrases that are used to add to the meaning of sentences are *prepositional phrases* and *appositive phrases*.

Prepositional Phrases

As shown in Section 1.4, prepositional phrases contain a preposition and a noun or pronoun called the object of the preposition. The object may have modifiers and be compound.

EXAMPLES: PREP   OBJ OF PREP
on the freshly pressed white jacket

PREP   OBJ OF PREP   OBJ OF PREP
beside the driftwood and seaweed

Prepositional phrases modify adjectives or adverbs and are called either *adjective phrases* or *adverb phrases.*

Adjective Phrases. Like adjectives, adjective phrases modify nouns and pronouns.

An adjective phrase is a prepositional phrase that modifies a noun or pronoun by telling what kind or which one.

Adjective phrases can modify any sentence part occupied by a noun or pronoun.

EXAMPLES: S
An etching *of a medieval battlement* sold quickly.
(*What kind* of etching?)

DO
My aunt has a fear *of bugs.* (*What kind* of fear?)

IO
I sent my friend *in Iowa* a card. (*Which* friend?)

PN   OBJ OF PREP
Joe Lewis was a boxer *with an impressive number of wins.* (*What kind* of boxer? *What kind* of number?)

More than one adjective phrase may modify the same word.

EXAMPLE: Water the plants *with pink flowers in the den.*

Adverb Phrases. Like adverbs, adverb phrases modify verbs, adjectives, and other adverbs.

An adverb phrase is a prepositional phrase that modifies a verb, adjective, or adverb by pointing out where, when, in what manner, or to what extent.

95

When modifying a verb, an adverb phrase may come before or after the modified word.

MODIFYING A VERB: *In Central Park* you can ride horse-drawn carriages. (Can ride *where?*)

The volcano rumbled *in the early morning hours.* (Rumbled *when?*)

I consumed the sundae *in short order.* (Consumed *in what manner?*)

Except for one section, the lawn was mowed. (Was mowed *to what extent?*)

MODIFYING AN ADJECTIVE: I am angry *with you.* (Angry *to what extent?*)

MODIFYING AN ADVERB: The shovel bit deep *into the earth.* (Deep *to what extent?*)

As with adjective phrases, more than one adverb phrase can modify the same word.

EXAMPLE: *Before breakfast,* the smell of bacon drifted *into my bedroom.* (Drifted *when?* Drifted *where?*)

EXERCISE A: Identifying Adjective and Adverb Phrases.
Write the prepositional phrases in the following paragraph. Then identify each prepositional phrase as *adjective* or *adverb*.

EXAMPLE: The idea of beauty is not identical in all cultures.

of beauty   (adjective)   in all cultures   (adverb)

(1) The many cultures of the world have different conceptions of physical beauty. (2) In China at one time young girls had their feet bound so that they measured only three or four inches. (3) In some societies today, pins and plugs are inserted through the nose, lips, and ears. (4) In some Eskimo areas of North America, bones are worn through the lips whereas among the aborigines of Australia, they are worn through the septum of the nose. (5) People of other cultures decorate their bodies with lace-like patterned bumps. (6) The Nuba of Sudan rub mud into small cuts, producing intricate

patterns of scars. (7) In parts of Burma, women with long necks are deemed attractive. (8) About their necks the women, therefore, wear increasing numbers of brass spirals. (9) In several Asian societies, people stain their teeth with betel juice because white teeth are thought ugly. (10) Western cultures have also had their share of unusual beauty habits: Corsets, hair dyeing, tattooing, and earpiercing are just a few.

Appositives and Appositive Phrases

To *appose* means "to place near or next to." Appositives and appositive phrases are words placed next to nouns and pronouns to provide additional information.

Appositives. When you name something and then immediately rename it to give further information, you are using an appositive.

An appositive is a noun or pronoun placed next to another noun or pronoun to identify, rename, or explain it.

EXAMPLES: My dog, *a pointer*, stood silently alert.

She did not care for his hobby, *running.*

These examples show appositives set off by commas. Commas are used only when the appositive contains *nonessential* (or *nonrestrictive*) material—that is, material that can be removed from the sentence without altering its meaning. If the material is *essential* (or *restrictive*), no commas are used.

EXAMPLE: My friend *Marilyn* broke her collarbone.

At first I thought the city *Chicago* was confusing.

See Section 12.2 for more about punctuating appositives.

Appositive Phrases. When an appositive is accompanied by one or more modifiers it becomes a phrase.

An appositive phrase is a noun or pronoun with modifiers placed next to a noun or pronoun to add information and details.

One-word adjectives, adjective phrases, or other groups of words acting as adjectives can modify an appositive.

EXAMPLE: The linebacker, *a quick, strong senior from Texas,* tackled the quarterback.

Appositives and appositive phrases can accompany nouns and pronouns occupying any part within a sentence.

WITH A SUBJECT: My jacket, *a windbreaker,* fits well.

WITH A DIRECT OBJECT: I bought a book, *an international atlas.*

WITH AN INDIRECT OBJECT: The man gave his wife, *his partner for ten years,* a beautiful opal ring.

WITH AN OBJECTIVE
COMPLEMENT: I called the canary Caruso, *the name of a famous operatic tenor.*

WITH A PREDICATE NOMINATIVE: She is an actress, *an Academy Award winner.*

WITH THE OBJECT OF A PREPOSITION: In a shady area, *a grove of spruce,* I ate my lunch.

To set up contrasts, appositives and appositive phrases may begin with the word *not.*

EXAMPLE: You should leave at seven o'clock, *not eight o'clock.*

Appositives and appositive phrases can be compound.

EXAMPLE: The family—*Trapp, his wife, and his children*—escaped from Austria during World War II.

Use appositives and appositive phrases to tighten your sentences. Often, two sentences can be combined by turning the information in one sentence into an appositive.

TWO SENTENCES: The fruit was picked. The fruit was sun-ripened pears.

SENTENCE WITH APOSITIVE PHRASE: The fruit, *sun-ripened pears,* was picked.

3.1 Prepositional Phrases and Appositives

EXERCISE B: Identifying Appositives and Appositive Phrases. Write each appositive or appositive phrase.

EXAMPLE: Carrots, a good source of vitamin A, were served.

a good source of vitamin A

1. We saw *The Nutcracker Suite,* this year's holiday ballet.
2. His companion, a large dog, followed him everywhere.
3. She was elected president, the company's highest position.
4. We strolled along the beach, two miles of clean sand.
5. I gave my great uncle—a lovable old man—a present.
6. He handed the bellhop his luggage, an old knapsack.
7. They gave my cousin Susan an award for attendance.
8. They went to Brazil, the largest country in South America.
9. The yak, a long-haired wild ox, is found in Tibet.
10. On the wall hung a painting, a portrait of my grandmother.

EXERCISE C: Using Appositives and Appositive Phrases to Combine Sentences. Combine each pair of sentences by turning one into an appositive or appositive phrase.

EXAMPLE: Washington, D. C., is fascinating. It is our capital.

Washington, D. C., our capital, is fascinating.

1. The city of Washington, D.C., was designed by Major Pierre Charles L'Enfant. He was a French architect and engineer.
2. Tourists flock to Washington, D.C. It is a beautiful city with historic significance.
3. The white marble Capitol has a large dome on top. The Capitol is the building where Congress meets.
4. Many visit the White House. It is the President's residence.
5. The Washington Monument is on the Mall. It is an obelisk.
6. The Jefferson Memorial is a replica of the Pantheon in Rome. This memorial overlooks the Potomac River.
7. The Library of Congress is possibly the world's largest library. It has collections that anyone may use.
8. The National Gallery houses many art treasures. It is one of the largest marble buildings in the world.
9. Many government officials have residences in Georgetown. Georgetown is a fashionable part of Washington, D.C.
10. Each September, the President's Cup Regatta is held on the Potomac River. It is an annual motorboat racing contest.

DEVELOPING WRITING SKILLS: Using Prepositional and Appositive Phrases. Use the following instructions to write five sentences of your own. Then underline the prepositional and appositive phrases in your sentences.

EXAMPLE: Write a sentence about a *friend,* using an appositive phrase.

Jean, <u>my friend from Chicago</u>, will arrive tomorrow.

1. Write a sentence about *cars,* using a prepositional phrase.
2. Write a sentence about *Lincoln,* using an appositive phrase.
3. Write a sentence about *pie,* using two prepositional phrases.
4. Write a sentence about *whales,* using an appositive phrase.
5. Write a sentence about *Mars,* using a prepositional phrase and an appositive phrase.

3.2 Verbals and Verbal Phrases

The word *verb* is part of the grammatical term *verbal.*

A verbal is a word derived from a verb but used as a noun, adjective, or adverb.

Like verbs, verbals may be modified by adverbs and adverb phrases or have complements. A verbal with modifiers or a complement is called a *verbal phrase.* This section will introduce the three kinds of verbals—participles, gerunds, and infinitives—and the phrases that can be formed around them.

Participles and Participial Phrases

Many adjectives are actually verbals known as *participles.*

A participle is a form of a verb that acts as an adjective.

EXAMPLES: A *killing* frost swept through the valley.

A *frightened* doe bounded into the woods.

Forms of Participles. Participles come in three forms: *present participles, past participles,* and *perfect participles.* The next chart shows how each is formed.

100

Kinds of Participles	Forms	Examples
Present Participle	Ends in *-ing*	His *fascinating* responses convinced us. The water shone with *glimmering* phosphorescence.
Past Participle	Usually ends in *-ed,* sometimes *-t, -en,* or another irregular ending	The *extended* table accommodated more people. The *engrossed* secretary didn't hear the phone.
Perfect Participle	Includes *having* or *having been* before a past participle	*Having exercised,* I rested. *Having been asked,* he gave his opinion.

Participles precede or follow the words they modify, answering *Which one?* or *What kind?* as do one-word adjectives.

A verb has a subject and expresses the main action; a participle acting as an adjective describes a noun or pronoun.

Functioning as a Verb	Functioning as a Participle
Her muscles are *aching.*	She rubbed her *aching* muscles.
The employees *respected* their boss.	The *respected* boss had the employees' support.

Participial Phrases. The addition of modifiers and complements to a participle produces a *participial phrase.*

A participial phrase is a participle modified by an adverb or adverb phrase or accompanied by a complement. The entire phrase acts as an adjective.

Examples at the top of the next page show different modifiers and complements that a participial phrase can have.

WITH AN ADVERB: *Burning brightly,* the fire lit up the room.

WITH AN ADVERB PHRASE: The bone *broken in two places* healed.

WITH A DIRECT OBJECT: *Holding the snake,* I felt its cool skin.

A comma usually sets off a participial phrase at the beginning of a sentence. Within the sentence, however, a phrase is set off by commas only if it is *nonessential* to the sentence.

Nonessential Participial Phrase	Essential Participial Phrase
Mr. Sharp, *driving that combine,* owns the farm.	The man *driving that combine* owns the farm.

See Section 12.2 for more information about punctuating participial phrases.

Like appositives, participial phrases can be used to combine the information in two sentences into one sentence.

TWO SENTENCES: The candidate's speech expressed her opinion about several important issues. It convinced many people to vote for her.

COMBINED SENTENCES: The candidate's speech, convincing many people to vote for her, expressed her opinions about several important issues.

The candidate's speech, expressing her opinions about several important issues, convinced many people to vote for her.

Nominative Absolutes. Sometimes, participles occur in phrases that are grammatically separate from the rest of the sentence. These phrases, called *nominative absolutes,* can show time, reason, or circumstance.

A nominative absolute is a noun or pronoun followed by a participle or participial phrase that functions independently of the rest of the sentence.

The following examples show nominative absolutes.

TIME: *Three hours having passed,* $\overset{S}{I}$ $\overset{V}{\underline{decided}}$ to wait no longer.

REASON: *My stomach growling with hunger,* $\overset{S}{I}$ $\overset{V}{\underline{made}}$ a sandwich.

CIRCUMSTANCE: Many $\overset{S}{\underline{students}}$ $\overset{V}{\underline{missed}}$ final exams, *the flu epidemic having struck at the end of the semester.*

The participle *being* is sometimes understood rather than expressed in some nominative absolutes.

EXAMPLE: *The camera [being] out of film,* we had to stop taking pictures.

Do not mistake a nominative absolute for the main subject and verb in a sentence. As a phrase a nominative absolute cannot stand independently as a complete sentence.

EXERCISE A: Recognizing Participles and Participial Phrases.
Write the participle or participial phrase in each sentence. Then label it as *present, past,* or *perfect.*

EXAMPLE: Led by the captain, the team trotted onto the field.

Led by the captain   (past)

1. A scathing attack was delivered by the politician.
2. The wheat swaying in the wind was like waves.
3. The houses ruined by the fire smoldered until the next morning.
4. A giant balloon billowing forth with hot air rose slowly into the sky.
5. At the dance, the reserved girl sat in the shadow behind a large philodendron.
6. The dignitary representing the President will address the Security Council today.
7. Having interviewed several people, the reporter felt ready to write the article.
8. I listened to the crows cawing continuously in the fields.
9. Having been warned, I used a good deal of caution when I approached the guard dog.
10. The document, yellowed with age, contained the information we needed.

EXERCISE B: Writing Participial Phrases. Change each underlined verb into a participial phrase and use it in a sentence of your own.

EXAMPLE: The town of 20,000 inhabitants <u>elected</u> a police chief last month.

The officers elected last year are not living up to their promises.

1. The plane will be <u>delayed</u> for another hour.
2. She was <u>washing</u> her hair when someone knocked.
3. The district attorney's persistent questions <u>badgered</u> the nervous witness.
4. The marathon runner <u>tired</u> too quickly and dropped out.
5. The students have <u>collected</u> clothing for the refugees.
6. Someone had <u>shouted</u> at the dog, and it looked very sad.
7. The woman was <u>satisfying</u> her curiosity with a world tour.
8. We <u>greased</u> the ball bearings, and the skates worked well.
9. Because she had <u>overthrown</u> the base, our team won.
10. They <u>patched</u> the jacket so that the tear was not noticeable.

EXERCISE C: Recognizing Nominative Absolutes. Write each sentence, underlining the subject once, underlining the verb twice, and circling the nominative absolute.

EXAMPLE: Storm clouds appearing overhead, we left the beach.

(Storm clouds appearing overhead,) we <u>left</u> the beach.

1. The critics having liked the movie, we wanted to see it.
2. I read all the travel literature on Canada, my enthusiasm mounting with each brochure.
3. A month having passed with no news, I called our relatives.
4. The case having been settled, the attorneys did not spend long in court.
5. Temperatures over 100° for weeks, many wells went dry.
6. I am looking for a part-time job, my allowance not being large enough to cover my expenses.
7. The dog having awakened us, we escaped the fire unhurt.
8. I could not finish writing the letter on the computer, my last diskette having been filled.
9. The television still on, I fell asleep on the couch.
10. The plants beginning to wilt, she finally watered them.

Gerunds and Gerund Phrases

Verbs ending in -*ing* can be used as nouns called *gerunds.*

A gerund is a form of a verb that acts as a noun.

EXAMPLES: *Vaulting* is my best event in gymnastics.

Swallowing hurt my sore throat.

The Function of Gerunds in Sentences. By themselves gerunds function in sentences like any other nouns.

SOME USES OF GERUNDS IN SENTENCES	
As a Subject	*Striking* is considered a revolutionary tactic in some countries.
As a Direct Object	A successful chef must enjoy *cooking.*
As an Indirect Object	He gives *gardening* all of his attention.
As a Predicate Nominative	Her worst fault is *lying.*
As an Object of a Preposition	Lock the door before *leaving.*
As an Appositive	One field, *engineering,* has an open job market.

To avoid confusing verbs, participles, and gerunds, which all can end in -*ing*, check the word's use in the sentence.

VERB PHRASE: My friends *are traveling* in India.

PARTICIPLE: A *traveling* salesperson came to the door.

GERUND: *Traveling* tires me out.

NOTE ABOUT GERUNDS AND POSSESSIVE PRONOUNS: Only the possessive form of a personal pronoun is appropriate before a gerund.

INCORRECT: We were intrigued by *them pantomiming.*

CORRECT: We were intrigued by *their pantomiming.*

105

Gerund Phrases. A gerund with modifiers or a comple-ment is called a *gerund phrase.*

A gerund phrase is a gerund with modifiers or a complement, all acting together as a noun.

In the following chart, notice the variety of different kinds of modifiers and complements that a gerund phrase can contain.

GERUND PHRASES	
With Adjectives	*His loud, persistent yawning* disrupted the meeting.
With an Adjective Phrase	*Worrying about the deadline* prevented the writer from sleeping.
With an Adverb	I estimated the cost by *calculating quickly.*
With an Adverb Phrase	*Fishing from the pier* is permitted.
With a Direct Object	*Reproducing copies* grows more expensive each year.
With Indirect and Direct Objects	Mr. Roberts suggested *writing them a letter.*

EXERCISE D: Identifying Gerunds and Gerund Phrases. Write the gerund or gerund phrase in each sentence. Then identify its function in the sentence.

EXAMPLE: Taking this shortcut will save time.

Taking this shortcut   (subject)

1. Talking during a test is strictly forbidden in this class.
2. The librarian began cataloging the newest books.
3. His newest hobby, arranging flowers, gives him pleasure.
4. A qualification for applicants is having an art degree.
5. He left almost immediately after a day of teaching.
6. Raking leaves fills many of my afternoons in the fall.
7. In 1980 the U.S. Olympic hockey team gave playing hockey new glamour.
8. Our club proposed giving the patients a Halloween party.

9. By gathering nuts, the squirrel made ready for winter.
10. His special talent is reading people's minds.

Infinitives and Infinitive Phrases

Infinitives, the third type of verbal, can function as three parts of speech.

An infinitive is a form of a verb that generally appears with the word *to* and acts as a noun, adjective, or adverb.

In the first of the following examples, the infinitive is acting as a noun. In the second, it as acting as an adjective.

EXAMPLES: I would like *to sleep.*

Our instructor gave us an assignment *to do.*

Forms of Infinitives. There are two kinds of infinitives—*present infinitives* and *perfect infinitives.*

Kinds of Infinitives	Forms	Examples
Present Infinitive	*To* plus the base form of a verb	I like *to debate.* *To concede* is *to lose.*
Perfect Infinitive	*To have* or *to have been* plus a past participle	I would have liked *to have gone.* *To have been praised* would have sufficed.

Do not mistake prepositional phrases for infinitives. In an infinitive a verb follows the word *to.* In a prepositional phrase beginning with the word *to,* a noun or pronoun follows the word *to.*

INFINITIVES: to boast, to have excelled

PREPOSITIONAL PHRASES: to them, to a friend

Sometimes, infinitives do not include the word *to.* After the verbs *dare, hear, help, let, make, please, see,* and *watch,* the *to* will usually be understood rather than stated.

EXAMPLE: The student helped *teach.*

The Function of Infinitives in Sentences. The flexibility of infinitives enables them to be used in almost any capacity.

INFINITIVES USED AS NOUNS	
As a Subject	*To have cheated* was immoral.
As a Direct Object	Barbara decided *to leave.*
As a Predicate Nominative	Our best protection was *to have been inoculated.*
As an Object of a Preposition	I was about *to speak.*
As an Appositive	Our good intention, *to diet,* disappeared quickly.
INFINITIVES USED AS MODIFIERS	
As an Adjective	The doctor gave me some vitamins *to take.*
As an Adverb	Ice cream is easy *to freeze.*

Infinitive Phrases. When you add modifiers, complements, or subjects, an infinitive becomes an *infinitive phrase.*

An infinitive phrase is an infinitive with modifiers, a complement, or a subject, all acting together as a single part of speech.

Study the following chart to see some of the ways infinitives can be expanded into phrases.

INFINITIVE PHRASES	
With an Adverb	The baby wanted *to wiggle continuously.*
With an Adverb Phrase	I plan *to visit during the afternoon.*
With a Direct Object	The foghorn helped *warn incoming ships.*
With Indirect and Direct Objects	The bank decided *to lend the family the money.*
With a Subject and Complement	The student asked *the college to send a catalog.*

EXERCISE E: Identifying Infinitives and Infinitive Phrases.
Write each infinitive or infinitive phrase. Then identify its part
of speech as a *noun, adjective,* or *adverb.* If the infinitive or
infinitive phrase is used as a noun, further identify its function
as a *subject, direct object, predicate nominative, object of a
preposition,* or *appositive.*

EXAMPLE: We climbed for three hours to reach the campsite.

to reach the campsite   (adverb)

1. To capture the splendor of the scene on film required all
   her photographic skill.
2. The young man had money to burn.
3. To learn about new inventions can be exciting.
4. During the test, Mrs. Linton permitted us to use our
   dictionaries.
5. Diane was next to bat.
6. The decision, to try for the two-point conversion, became
   the turning point in the game.
7. Her financial goal was to earn one million dollars by age
   thirty-two.
8. The person to see about your complaint has left.
9. The city's plans are to build a large convention center and
   hotel complex.
10. To listen carefully is important.

DEVELOPING WRITING SKILLS: Writing Sentences Using Verbals. Change each of the following verbs into the two
kinds of verbals indicated in the chart. Then use each one as
a verbal phrase in a sentence of your own. Underline the verbal phrases in your sentences.

	Participle	Gerund	Infinitive
1. confuse	x		x
2. sail	x	x	
3. achieve	x		x
4. undertake		x	x
5. yearn		x	x

3.3 Clauses

Clauses, like phrases, are groups of related words, but unlike phrases, they have a subject and a verb.

A clause is a group of words with its own subject and verb.

There are two kinds of clauses: *independent* and *subordinate* clauses.

An independent clause has a subject and a verb and can stand by itself as a complete sentence.

All complete sentences must contain at least one independent clause; additional independent or subordinate clauses may be added. *The school will be closed on Friday* is an example of an independent clause. *I ate some crackers, but I was still hungry* is an example of one independent clause added to another. *The house was quiet after the children left for school* is an example of an independent clause followed by a *subordinate clause.* Though *after the children left for school* contains a subject *(children)* and a verb *(left),* the clause cannot stand alone. It becomes meaningful only when joined to the independent clause *The house was quiet.*

A subordinate clause, although it has a subject and a verb, cannot stand by itself as a sentence; it is only part of a sentence.

Subordinate clauses give the writer an important tool since they can add important details to sentences and show relationships between separate ideas. Within sentences, subordinate clauses act as either adjectives, adverbs, or nouns.

Adjective Clauses

Adjective clauses describe, limit, or qualify nouns or pronouns in ways often not possible with one-word adjectives or adjective phrases.

An adjective clause is a subordinate clause that modifies a noun or pronoun by telling what kind or which one.

An adjective clause appears after the noun or pronoun it modifies and usually begins with a relative pronoun *(that, which, who, whom,* or *whose)* or sometimes with a relative adverb (such as *before, since, when, where,* or *why.)*

EXAMPLES: The rug, *which I bought yesterday,* is beige.

I still remember the time *when you broke your arm.*

Essential and Nonessential Adjective Clauses. Like participial and appositive phrases, adjective clauses are punctuated according to whether they add *essential* or *nonessential* information to the sentence.

> **An adjective clause that is not essential to the basic meaning of a sentence is set off by commas. An essential clause is not set off.**

The following chart demonstrates the difference between nonessential and essential clauses. (See Section 12.2 for more information about punctuating adjective clauses.)

Nonessential Adjective Clause	Essential Adjective Clause
The Silk Road, *which led to the riches of China,* was once filled with caravans having many donkeys and camels.	The road *that led to the riches of China* was once filled with caravans having many donkeys and camels.

You can often combine information from two sentences into one by using either a nonessential or an essential adjective clause.

TWO SENTENCES: *Gone with the Wind* is a historical novel about the Civil War years. It was made into a successful movie.

ADJECTIVE CLAUSES: *Gone with the Wind,* which is a historical novel about the Civil War years, was made into a successful movie.

A historical novel about the Civil War years that was made into a successful movie was *Gone with the Wind.*

111

Introductory Words in Adjective Clauses. Relative pronouns and relative adverbs not only begin adjective clauses but also function within the subordinate clause.

Relative pronouns connect adjective clauses to the words they modify and act as subjects, direct objects, objects of prepositions, or adjectives in the clauses.

Relative pronouns act, first, as an introduction to the clause, and, second, as a subject, direct object, object of a preposition, or adjective *within* the clause. The role of the relative pronoun can be determined by isolating the adjective clause from the rest of the sentence and then by identifying its subject and verb. Since adjective clauses are sometimes in inverted order, you may need to rearrange the words mentally.

THE USES OF RELATIVE PRONOUNS WITHIN ADJECTIVE CLAUSES	
As a Subject	*Sentence:* The fish *that was just reeled in* set a record.
	Clause: that was just reeled in
As a Direct Object	*Sentence:* Someone broke the window *that I recently fixed.*
	DO *Reworded clause:* I recently fixed that
As an Object of a Preposition	*Sentence:* This is my aunt *of whom I have spoken.*
	OBJ OF PREP *Reworded clause:* I have spoken of whom
As an Adjective	*Sentence:* I have a friend *whose witty remarks amuse me.*
	Clause: whose witty remarks amuse me

NOTE ABOUT UNDERSTOOD RELATIVE PRONOUNS: In some adjective clauses, the relative pronoun may be understood.

EXAMPLE: The job [*that*] *I am applying for* pays well.

Relative adverbs do not possess the flexibility of relative pronouns. They function only as adverbs within clauses.

THE USE OF RELATIVE ADVERBS WITHIN ADJECTIVE CLAUSES	
As an Adverb	*Sentence:* The inn *where we stayed* was called the Benbow Inn.
	Reworded clause: we stayed where

EXERCISE A: Identifying Adjective Clauses. Write each adjective clause, underlining its subject once and verb twice. Then circle the relative pronoun or relative adverb and identify its function in the clause.

EXAMPLE: I applied to the college that my mother attended.

   (that) my mother attended   (direct object)

1. We visited the Rockies, which have spectacular scenery.
2. The statement that I just made still reflects my position.
3. The man whose groceries I walked off with was upset.
4. Pavarotti, who sings at the Metropolitan Opera, is a tenor.
5. We made reservations at the hotel where we want to stay.
6. The plane which I will take from Atlanta will stop in Dallas.
7. We had six inches of snow the day before you arrived.
8. The couch that I bought converts into a comfortable bed.
9. The nest that a robin built in our tree has two eggs in it.
10. The book on which she had built her reputation was not her best by any means.

EXERCISE B: Punctuating Adjective Clauses. Write each sentence, underlining the adjective clause and adding commas if necessary.

EXAMPLE: We wrote Mr. Gomez who was our coach last year.

   We wrote Mr. Gomez, *who was our coach last year.*

1. Model trains that can carry people have been built.
2. Arthur Ashe who was a successful tennis star spoke to us.
3. I devoured the fruit cake the day it arrived.
4. I joined an organization that raises money for charity.
5. People who work hard for their money appreciate its value.

6. I gave my baby sister who was crying some apple juice.
7. I must paint the front porch which has started to peel.
8. The storm that was approaching us was a hurricane.
9. You would enjoy reading the book I just finished.
10. Many of his constituents agreed with the way that he voted.

Adverb Clauses

An *adverb clause* functions in a sentence in much the same way one-word adverbs and adverb phrases do.

An adverb clause is a subordinate clause that modifies a verb, adjective, adverb, or verbal. It does this by pointing out where, when, in what manner, to what extent, under what condition, or why.

An adverb clause contains a subject and a verb, though not the main subject and verb in the sentence, and begins with a subordinating conjunction. (See Section 1.4 for a list of subordinating conjunctions.) This kind of subordinate clause may modify any word an adverb can.

ADVERB CLAUSES	
Modified Words	**Examples**
Verb	We called *because we were worried about you.*
Adjective	Lee appeared confident *as she took her exams.*
Adverb	The movie ended sooner *than we expected.*
Participle	The radio, blaring *as I attempted to do my studies,* made concentration impossible.
Gerund	I relax by watching television *after I study.*
Infinitive	I wanted to ski *while the snow lasted.*

Adverb clauses can be used to combine two sentences into one and to show relationships between ideas.

114

TWO SENTENCES: Bill Bradley was a basketball star. He became
                  a United States Senator.

COMBINED: Bill Bradley was a basketball star before he be-
            came a United States Senator.

   Sometimes, adverb clauses beginning with *as* or *than* are elliptical—that is, the verb or both the subject and the verb are
understood but not stated.

VERB UNDERSTOOD: I ate as much dessert *as he* [*did*].

SUBJECT AND   The hotel manager had more business
VERB UNDERSTOOD: *than* [*he had*] *rooms.*

   See Section 7.2 for rules about the correct use of pronouns
in elliptical clauses.

EXERCISE C: Identifying Adverb Clauses. Write the adverb clause in each sentence. Then indicate whether it modifies a *verb, adjective, adverb*, or *verbal*.

EXAMPLE: Although rain had been predicted, the sun shone.

           Although rain had been predicted   (verb)

1. She developed laryngitis whenever she caught a cold.
2. Hobbling on crutches while my foot heals is difficult.
3. Our crew rowed faster than our competition did.
4. We checked the stock report when the newspaper came.
5. The wheels of the train, clanging as they moved, occasionally emitted sparks.
6. We hoped to dig the well where the water table was high.
7. The oily streets are as slippery as butter is.
8. The coffee, gurgling as it perked, had a delicious aroma.
9. To wait until a deadline approaches is generally not wise.
10. I went to the library since I needed to do research.

EXERCISE D: Recognizing Elliptical Clauses. Write each
adverb clause, adding in parentheses the understood words.

EXAMPLE: I enjoyed reading this book more than that one.

           than (I did) that one

1. This haircut looks better than the last.
2. Karen Hinton is not as responsible as Millicent Ramat.

115

3. My brother has fewer blond streaks in his hair than red.
4. Aunt Delia helps you more than me.
5. The child for whom I babysat was as good as gold.
6. The last assignment took longer to do than this one.
7. I received more praise for my act than criticism.
8. My new camera takes better pictures than my old one.
9. My parents were as pleased with my grades as I.
10. The speech was more inspirational than informative.

Noun Clauses

The *noun clause* is the third kind of subordinate clause.

A noun clause is a subordinate clause that acts as a noun in a sentence.

As the following chart shows, a noun clause can perform any function in a sentence that any other kind of noun can.

USES OF NOUN CLAUSES IN SENTENCES	
Functions in Sentences	Examples
Subject	*Whatever tools you need* can be found at Ames Hardware.
Direct Object	The dentist treated *whichever patient arrived first.*
Indirect Object	The group sent *whoever requested information* a brochure about seals.
Predicate Nominative	To get rid of this cold is *what I would like.*
Object of a Preposition	I will cut the board to *whatever length you desire.*
Appositive	The students made their request, *that the due date for research papers be extended.*

Noun clauses frequently begin with *that, which, who, whom,* or *whose,* the same words that can begin adjective clauses. Other words that can begin noun clauses are *how, if, what, whatever, when, where, whether, whichever, whoever,* and *whomever*. Besides serving to introduce a noun clause, these words sometimes serve a function within the clause as well.

SOME USES OF INTRODUCTORY WORDS IN NOUN CLAUSES	
Functions in Clauses	**Examples**
Adjective	She could not decide *which flavor of ice cream she wanted.*
Adverb	I do not know *when the paint will dry.*
Subject	*Whoever understands this* should help those who do not.
Direct Object	*Whatever my supervisor advised* I did.
No Function	The gardener said *that we should plant the bulbs now.*

When the word *that* has no function within the clause except to introduce it, it is often omitted.

EXAMPLE: We remembered [*that*] *you wanted to go.*

Since some of the words that introduce noun clauses also introduce adjective and adverb clauses, do not let the introductory word be your only guide to determining the type of clause. Always check the function of the clause in the sentence. With noun clauses, you can also try substituting the words *fact, it, thing,* or *you* for the clause. If the sentence retains its smoothness, the clause is probably a noun clause.

NOUN CLAUSE: I knew *that you would volunteer.* (I knew *it.*)

EXERCISE E: Identifying Noun Clauses. Write each noun clause. Then identify the function of each noun clause as *subject, direct object, indirect object, predicate nominative, object of a preposition,* or *appositive.*

EXAMPLE: A rewarding and interesting career is what everyone wants.

what everyone wants   (predicate nominative)

117

1. The system stifled whatever creativity I might have had.
2. We gave whoever ate at our restaurant an after-dinner mint.
3. Our resolution, that the group be expanded, required money.
4. We found that her loquacity was difficult to bear.
5. Whoever signs this form must sign all other transactions.
6. The tourist inquired about what time the bus was leaving.
7. The store sent whoever had charge accounts a statement.
8. Her fear is that she will be caught in an elevator.
9. Whatever time the baby falls asleep will be his bedtime.
10. Give this verification slip to whoever is at the desk.

EXERCISE F: Identifying Subordinate Clauses. Identify each underlined clause as *adjective, adverb,* or *noun.*

EXAMPLE: I want to be all that I am capable of becoming.
           —Katherine Mansfield

           adjective

1. I have never been hurt by what I have not said.—Calvin Coolidge
2. Nothing is enough for the man to whom enough is too little.—Epicurus
3. There are things that are important beyond all this fiddle. —Marianne Moore
4. It is better to know some of the questions than all of the answers.—James Thurber
5. Whoever seeks to set one race against another seeks to enslave all races.—Franklin D. Roosevelt
6. Those who do not complain are never pitied.—Jane Austen
7. Be charitable before wealth makes thee covetous.—Sir Thomas Browne
8. Life leaps like a geyser for those who drill through the rock of inertia.—Dr. Alexis Carrel
9. The world stands out on either side no wider than the heart is wide.—Edna St. Vincent Millay
10. Never stand begging for that which you have the power to earn.—Miguel de Cervantes

DEVELOPING WRITING SKILLS: Using Subordinate Clauses to Expand Sentences. Complete each sentence, filling in the blank with the kind of clause indicated.

118

EXAMPLE: We gave advice to <u>(noun clause)</u>.

We gave advice to whoever asked for it.

1. <u>(adverb clause)</u>, the Spanish Club will go to Mexico.
2. Our high school band, <u>(adjective clause)</u>, played today.
3. Here is the valuable antique <u>(adjective clause)</u>.
4. We went to the discount store <u>(adverb clause)</u>.
5. <u>(noun clause)</u> is not very important.
6. Her beautiful smile is <u>(noun clause)</u>.
7. <u>(adverb clause)</u>, I plan my wardrobe carefully.
8. Our family will eat <u>(noun clause)</u>.
9. Her uncle lives in a house <u>(adjective clause)</u>.
10. <u>(adverb clause)</u>, I finally abandoned my efforts.

Sentences Classified by Structure 3.4

Sentences may be classified according to the kind and number of clauses they contain.

The Four Structures of Sentences

Different combinations of independent and subordinate clauses form four basic sentence structures.

A simple sentence consists of a single independent clause.

A compound sentence consists of two or more independent clauses joined by a comma and a coordinating conjunction or by a semicolon.

A complex sentence consists of one independent clause and one or more subordinate clauses.

A compound-complex sentence consists of two or more independent clauses and one or more subordinate clauses.

Study the examples of each type of sentence structure in the chart on the next page. Notice that simple sentences can contain compound subjects, compound verbs, or both. Notice also that a subordinate clause may fall between the parts of an independent clause or even within an independent clause.

FOUR STRUCTURES OF SENTENCES

Simple Sentences	I <u>received</u> your letter last week. Either <u>Fran</u> or <u>Dave</u> <u>will sell</u> the tickets. Frightened by the thunder, the <u>dog</u> <u>ran</u> and <u>hid</u>.
Compound Sentences	One <u>group</u> <u>addressed</u> the envelopes, and <u>another</u> <u>sorted</u> them by ZIP code. <u>Spring</u> <u>had arrived</u>; <u>flowers</u> <u>bloomed</u> everywhere.
Complex Sentences	┌────── SUBORDINATE CLAUSE ──────┐ Although the old <u>photograph</u> <u>had faded</u> badly, ┌──── MAIN CLAUSE ────┐ we <u>could</u> still <u>see</u> many details. MAIN ┌── SUBORDINATE CLAUSE The <u>book</u>, which <u>recounts</u> South African history, CLAUSE ⌊SUBORDINATE CLAUSE⌋ <u>is banned</u> in the very nation that <u>it</u> <u>describes</u>. ┌──── MAIN CLAUSE ────┐ SUBORDINATE CLAUSE I <u>will do</u> whatever <u>you</u> <u>say</u>.
Compound-Complex Sentences	INDEPENDENT CLAUSE SUBORDINATE CLAUSE I <u>turned on</u> the heat as soon as <u>we</u> <u>arrived</u>, and INDEPENDENT CLAUSE now the <u>house</u> <u>is</u> warm. SUBORDINATE CLAUSE INDEPENDENT CLAUSE When <u>I</u> <u>left</u> the house, <u>I</u> <u>was</u> extremely anxious, ┌────── INDEPENDENT CLAUSE ──────┐ SUBORDINATE CLAUSE but <u>I</u> <u>knew</u> <u>I</u> <u>would do</u> well on the test.

As you can see in the examples of complex sentences, independent clauses in complex sentences are often called *main clauses* to distinguish them from subordinate clauses. The subject and verb of a main clause are often called the *subject of the sentence* and the *main verb* to distinguish them from the other subjects and verbs that appear in the sentence.

120

EXERCISE: Identifying the Four Structures of Sentences. Identify each sentence as *simple, compound, complex,* or *compound-complex.*

EXAMPLE: Whoever is the last to leave should lock the door.

  complex

1. Neither did the winds die, nor did the unbearable heat subside.
2. The clerk rang up the sale and then wrapped our purchases for us.
3. Though the detectives worked diligently, they could not unravel the mystery.
4. When the network produced the special, the critics gave it mixed reviews.
5. The peninsula—a long, pencil-like projection—was covered with thick vegetation.
6. People who continually complain rarely have many friends.
7. We found the entrance to the turnpike quickly, but then we ran out of gas.
8. The session was for whatever complaints people wanted to air, and the supervisors heard quite an assortment.
9. Leaving the safety of the harbor, we ventured out to sea.
10. The room was stuffy, so I opened the window nearest the chair where I sat.

DEVELOPING WRITING SKILLS: Writing Sentences with Different Structures. Write ten sentences of your own following the structures listed below. Underline each subordinate clause.

1. simple sentence
2. simple sentence with compound subject
3. simple sentence containing an appositive phrase
4. compound sentence with a verbal phrase
5. compound sentence joined by a semicolon
6. complex sentence with an adverb clause
7. complex sentence with a noun clause
8. complex sentence with an adjective and adverb clause
9. compound-complex sentence
10. compound-complex sentence with a noun clause and an adverb clause

3.5 Diagraming Phrases and Clauses

Phrases and clauses are diagramed in different ways to set them apart visually. This section will demonstrate how to diagram a variety of different phrases and clauses.

Prepositional Phrases

Diagram a prepositional phrase beneath the word it modifies. Place an adjective phrase beneath the noun or pronoun it modifies; place an adverb phrase beneath the verb, adjective, or adverb it modifies. Put the preposition on a slanted line and its object on a horizontal line. Place modifiers of the object beneath it on slanted lines. Diagram compound objects of the preposition just as you would other compound sentence parts.

EXAMPLE: The desk *with the faulty leg* is located *in the first row or the second one.*

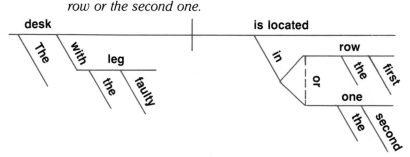

To diagram an adjective phrase that modifies the object of the preposition of another prepositional phrase, study the example on the left. To diagram an adverb phrase that modifies an adjective or an adverb, study the example on the right.

EXAMPLE: The keys are *on the table by the door.* I arrived home late *at night.*

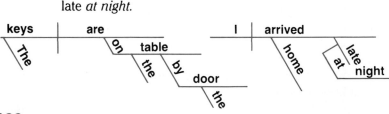

To diagram two prepositional phrases that modify the same word use the following example as a guide.

EXAMPLE: I will meet you *near the door* or *in the auditorium.*

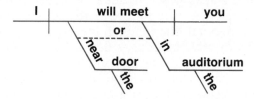

EXERCISE A: Diagraming Prepositional Phrases. Correctly diagram each sentence.

1. On the wall we hung kites of every size and shape.
2. Sleepily, he pressed the alarm button on his clock.
3. Our family piled into the car and headed for the freeway.
4. My friend was sensitive to my needs and fears.
5. With ease the mechanic changed the flat tire on our car.

Appositives and Appositive Phrases

Put an appositive in parentheses following the noun or pronoun it renames. Any modifiers go directly beneath it.

EXAMPLE: Mrs. Rebholtz, *a friend of the family,* will visit us.

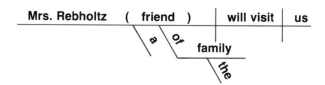

EXERCISE B: Diagraming Appositive Phrases. Correctly diagram each sentence.

1. My home, a small, two-bedroom apartment, is convenient.
2. I gave the bride, a young woman of twenty, a quilt.
3. The organization, a group of parents, wrote letters.
4. We visited Columbia, a town in Missouri.
5. Jurors should report to Judge Bean, a strict but fair guardian of the law.

Verbals and Verbal Phrases

Verbal phrases, which are constructed around participles, gerunds, and infinitives, are never diagramed on a straight line.

Participles and Participial Phrases. Because a participle functions as an adjective, it is placed partly on a slanted line and partly on a horizontal line beneath the noun or pronoun it modifies. Adverbs or adverb phrases that modify it are placed below it. When a participle has a complement, the complement is placed in its normal position, on the horizontal line with the participle, separated from it by a short vertical line.

EXAMPLE: A child *selling candy* came to our house.

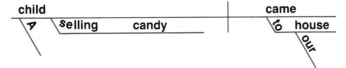

Since it is grammatically separate from the rest of the sentence, a nominative absolute is diagramed in the same way an expletive is.

EXAMPLE: *The meeting concluded for this month,* we left.

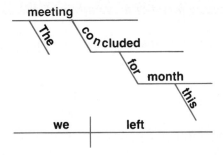

Gerunds and Gerund Phrases. Gerunds can occupy any position in a diagram that a noun can. When they function as subjects, direct objects, predicate nominatives, or appositives, gerunds sit atop a pedestal on a stepped line. Modifiers and complements are diagramed in the usual manner.

EXAMPLE: *Fixing the garbage disposal* required much time.

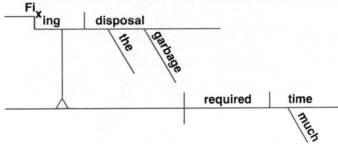

A gerund or gerund phrase functioning as an indirect object or as the object of a preposition goes on a stepped line extending from a slanted line.

EXAMPLE: We bought a small car for *driving around town.*

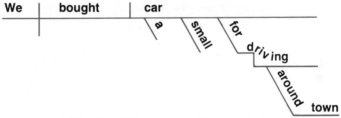

Infinitives and Infinitive Phrases. Since infinitives can be used as nouns, adverbs, or adjectives, there are a variety of ways to diagram them. An infinitive used as a noun sits on a pedestal on a line similar to yet less complex than the line used for a gerund. Modifiers and complements are diagramed in the usual manner.

EXAMPLE: My resolution for the new year is *to exercise daily.*

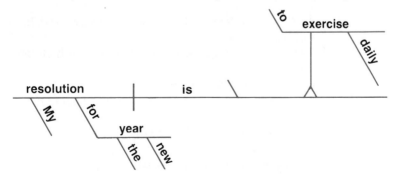

The diagram of an infinitive used as an adjective or adverb looks like the diagram of a prepositional phrase.

EXAMPLE: World War I was supposedly the war *to end all war.*

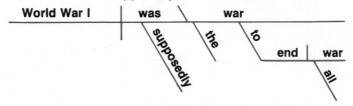

When an infinitive has an understood *to,* indicate the implied word in parentheses. If the infinitive has a subject, extend the left side of the infinitive line and place the subject there.

EXAMPLE: We heard *thunder rumble during the night.*

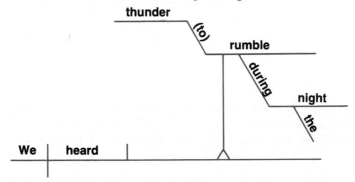

EXERCISE C: Diagraming Verbal Phrases. Correctly diagram each sentence.

1. The students writing feverishly in blue books ignored the entrance of the proctor.
2. Training for a major competitive event leaves an athlete little time for other activities.
3. We were asked to start with the national anthem.
4. Capitalizing on his good fortune, the man bought some property in the area.
5. She served tea tasting of herbs to her guests.
6. Help me tie this bow securely.
7. We had no desire to see that movie again.

126

8. Furnishing oranges and sodas was the responsibility of the team manager.
9. Learning to diagram sentences develops both manual and mental skills.
10. Her worst habit, being tardy, greatly irritated all of her teachers.

Compound, Complex, and Compound-Complex Sentences

All the sentences you have diagramed up to this point have been simple sentences. However, diagraming the other three sentence structures—compound, complex, and compound-complex—involves most of the same rules. The primary difference is that another baseline is added for each additional clause.

Compound Sentences. Each of the independent clauses in a compound sentence is diagramed separately. They are then joined together at the verbs by a dotted step line. The conjunction or semicolon is written on this step line.

EXAMPLE: *I drove for six hours,* and *he slept soundly.*

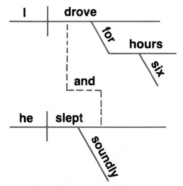

Complex Sentences. Diagraming complex sentences involves knowing how to position each of the three kinds of subordinate clauses in relation to the independent clause. An *adjective clause* is diagramed below the main clause as if it were a separate sentence. A slanted dotted line going from the relative pronoun or relative adverb in the adjective clause to the word the clause modifies joins the two. The position of the relative pronoun changes depending on its function in the adjective clause. In the following example the relative pronoun functions within the subordinate clause as a subject.

EXAMPLE: The car *that sped around the corner* had no headlights.

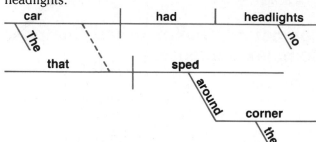

The dotted line must be bent to connect the clauses properly when a relative pronoun acts as either an object of a preposition or an adjective. The dotted line must also be bent when a relative adverb introduces an adjective clause.

EXAMPLE: The person *to whom you spoke* is president of the firm.

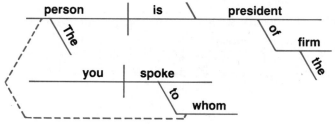

An understood relative pronoun in an adjective clause should be included in parentheses in a diagram.

EXAMPLE: I wrote the letter *I owed to my friend.*

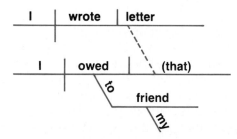

128

An *adverb clause* is diagramed with the subordinating conjunction written on the connecting line. This line should join the verb in the adverb clause to the modified verb, adjective, adverb, or verbal in the main clause.

EXAMPLE: *When the speaker became ill,* the lecture was canceled.

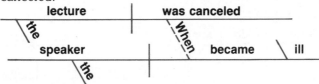

Place in parentheses any understood words in an elliptical adverb clause.

EXAMPLE: Our dog is larger *than yours.*

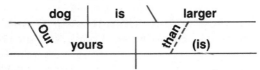

A *noun clause* is placed on a pedestal in the position it occupies within the sentence. The pedestal meets the noun clause at the verb. In the following example, the noun clause is acting as a direct object.

EXAMPLE: I will wear *whatever is clean.*

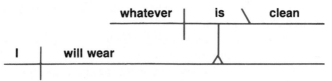

If a noun clause's introductory word has no other function than to introduce the clause, write it alongside the pedestal.

EXAMPLE: Earl said *that you had a birthday.*

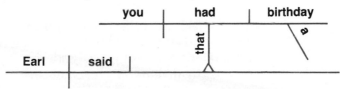

Compound-Complex Sentences. To diagram *compound-complex sentences*, simply combine the skills you learned for diagraming compound and complex sentences.

EXAMPLE: The man *who owned the shop* fixed my typewriter, but he refused to charge me *because the repairs were minor.*

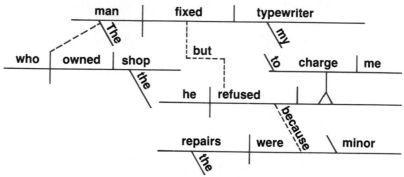

EXERCISE D: Diagraming Compound, Complex, and Compound-Complex Sentences. Correctly diagram each sentence.

1. I ate the sherbet quickly, but it still started to melt.
2. After we finished our errands, we had lunch.
3. We celebrated on the day when the project was complete.
4. Salmon that are spawning know the exact river to which they must return.
5. We must mail this today, or it will not arrive on time.
6. We should stay at whatever place is cheapest; money is scarce at this time.
7. Tracy saw an automobile accident on Tuesday, and now she is driving more carefully.
8. The couple sat inside the warm house while the snow fell.
9. When he noticed a spot on his coat, he took it to the cleaners, but they were unable to remove the spot.
10. The bus that was scheduled to take us had engine problems, so the company sent us another.

DEVELOPING WRITING SKILLS: Writing and Diagraming Various Sentence Structures. Write four sentences: one simple, one compound, one complex, and one compound-complex. Then correctly diagram each sentence.

Skills Review and Writing Workshop

Phrases and Clauses

CHECKING YOUR SKILLS

Identify each underlined phrase as a *prepositional, appositive, participial, gerund,* or *infinitive phrase*. Identify each underlined clause as an *adjective, adverb,* or *noun clause*.

The relationship between Saudi Arabia and the United States is important (1) <u>to both countries</u>. Although there are many reasons (2) <u>for our desire</u> (3) <u>to have good relations with the Saudis</u>, the main reason can be summed up (4) <u>in one word</u>: oil. Since 1938, (5) <u>when oil companies struck oil in Saudi Arabia</u>, our need for a supply (6) <u>of this commodity</u> has governed relations (7) <u>between the two lands</u>. Saudi Arabia, (8) <u>which produces more oil</u> (9) <u>than Texas</u>, uses its profits (10) <u>to import western goods</u>. The Saudis have been quick (11) <u>to modernize their land</u>. They have relied (12) <u>on American expertise</u> in (13) <u>developing their cities</u>. The Saudis, (14) <u>driving imported cars</u>, have begun (15) <u>to modernize their roads</u>. Under their leader, (16) <u>King Fahd</u>, the Saudis do not want to be influenced by western lifestyle. (17) <u>To live comfortably</u>, keeping their traditions, is (18) <u>what the Saudis want</u>. Whether they can insulate themselves (19) <u>from western customs</u> remains (20) <u>to be seen</u>.

USING GRAMMAR SKILLS IN WRITING
Writing Copy for a Book Jacket

Imagine you are a promotional writer. Follow the steps below to write jacket notes conveying your enthusiasm for a book.

Prewriting: Decide which elements you want to discuss.

Writing: Refer to some of the qualities that make this book unique.

Revising: When revising, make sure your phrases and clauses are as varied as possible. Then proofread carefully.

4

Avoiding Sentence Errors

If you know something about the most common errors in writing, you can more effectively eliminate them from your own work as you proofread. This chapter examines common sentence errors and gives guidelines for repairing them.

4.1 Fragments and Run-ons

Hasty writers sometimes omit crucial words, punctuate awkwardly, or leave their thoughts unfinished. These cause two common sentence errors: fragments and run-on sentences.

Fragments

Though fragments may be used purposefully for a stylistic effect, they are generally considered a writing error.

Do not unintentionally capitalize and punctuate phrases, subordinate clauses, or words in a series as if they were complete sentences.

Reading your work aloud and listening to the natural pauses and stops should help you avoid fragments.

Sometimes, to repair a fragment, you can merely connect it to words that come before or after it.

PARTICIPIAL FRAGMENT: Angered by the injustice of the remark.

ADDED TO   *Angered by the injustice of the remark,*
NEARBY SENTENCE: Linda argued with her friend.

PREPOSITIONAL FRAGMENT: With his hand in the cookie jar.

ADDED TO   The four-year-old culprit was caught *with*
NEARBY SENTENCE: *his hand in the cookie jar.*

A fragment containing a pronoun and a participial phrase can often be repaired by dropping the pronoun and adding the participial phrase to a nearby sentence.

PRONOUN AND PARTICIPIAL FRAGMENT: The one waiting nearby.

ADDED TO NEARBY SENTENCE: We boarded the bus *waiting*
                            nearby.

Sometimes, you may need to add missing sentence parts. A noun phrase (a noun with its modifiers), for instance, will need a verb if it is to be used as a subject. If the noun phrase is to be used as a complement, an object of a preposition, or an appositive, it will need both a subject and a verb.

NOUN FRAGMENT: A hurricane with fierce winds and rain.

COMPLETED   *A hurricane with fierce winds and rain* lashed the
SENTENCES: coast.

The weather forecaster predicated *a hurricane with fierce winds and rain.*

The damage from *a hurricane with fierce winds and rain* can be severe.

The storm, *a hurricane with fierce winds and rain,* drove people from their homes.

Notice what missing sentence parts must be added to other types of phrase and clause fragments to make them complete.

NOUN FRAGMENT WITH PARTICIPIAL PHRASE: The food eaten by us.

COMPLETED SENTENCE: *The food* was *eaten by us.*

VERB FRAGMENT: Will be at the rehearsal today.

COMPLETED SENTENCE: I *will be at the rehearsal today.*

PREPOSITIONAL FRAGMENT: On the kitchen table.

COMPLETED SENTENCE: I put the groceries *on the kitchen table.*

133

PARTICIPIAL FRAGMENT: Found under the desk.

COMPLETED SENTENCES: The keys *found under the desk* were mine.
The keys were *found under the desk.*

GERUND FRAGMENT: Reading stories to children.

COMPLETED SENTENCES: *Reading stories to children* can be fun.
She enjoys *reading stories to children.*
He was *reading stories to children.*

INFINITIVE FRAGMENT: To see the job done well.

COMPLETED SENTENCES: *To see the job done well* is my goal.
I expect *to see the job done well.*

ADJECTIVE CLAUSE FRAGMENT: Which was a condensed version.

COMPLETED SENTENCE: I read an abridgment, *which was a condensed version.*

ADVERB CLAUSE FRAGMENT: After the fish tasted our new bait.

COMPLETED SENTENCE: *After the fish tasted our new bait,* we quickly caught our limit.

NOUN CLAUSE FRAGMENT: Whatever our host serves us.

COMPLETED SENTENCE: We will eat *whatever our host serves us.*

If a series of words seems long enough to be a sentence, check to make sure that it contains a subject and a verb *and* expresses a complete thought. It may be a long fragment masquerading as a sentence.

SERIES FRAGMENT: After reading Steinbeck's novel, with its probing look at poverty and greed, in the style so typical of this master storyteller.

COMPLETED SENTENCE: *After reading Steinbeck's novel, with its probing look at poverty and greed, in the style so typical of this master storyteller,* I recommended the book to friends.

EXERCISE A: Identifying and Correcting Fragments. If an item contains one or more complete sentences, write *correct.* If the item contains a fragment, rewrite it to make one or more complete sentences.

134

EXAMPLE: Pleased by the applause of the audience. The violinist played an encore.

Pleased by the applause of the audience, the violinist played an encore.

1. Their faces shining with delight at seeing the movie star.
2. I wanted one thing. To take a long nap.
3. The committee was impressed by this application. Which we received just yesterday.
4. I enjoy working with my hands.
5. Traffic lights flashing erratically as the cars jammed in the intersection, unsure whose turn it was to proceed.
6. The apples cooked. With their sweet juices bubbling away.
7. Just as Mr. Chao said goodbye.
8. Classified ads filled the pages of the newspaper.
9. A report to write and math to do before tomorrow.
10. The silhouettes of the trees against the light of the moon.

Run-ons

A run-on sentence, called a *run-on,* is two or more sentences capitalized and punctuated as if they were one.

Use punctuation, conjunctions, or other means to join or separate the parts of a run-on sentence correctly.

There are two kinds of run-ons: *fused sentences,* which are two or more sentences joined with no punctuation, and *comma splices,* which have two or more sentences separated only by commas rather than by commas and conjunctions.

FUSED SENTENCE: The team pushed forward for the last yard they were inches short.

COMMA SPLICE: Only one package arrived in the mail, the other items never came.

As with fragments, proofreading or reading your work aloud will usually help you find any run-on sentences in your writing. Once found, they can be corrected by adding punctuation and conjunctions or by rewording the sentences. The chart on the next page demonstrates the various methods for correcting run-ons.

FOUR WAYS TO CORRECT RUN-ONS	
With End Marks and Capitals	
Run-on: The sale was in full swing in the store people crowded the aisles.	*Sentence:* The sale was in full swing. In the store people crowded the aisles.
With Commas and Conjunctions	
Run-on: The wrapping paper needed cutting we could not locate the scissors.	*Sentence:* The wrapping paper needed cutting, but we could not locate the scissors.
With Semicolons	
Run-on: Our zoo has acquired many rare animals, for example it now has a pair of pandas.	*Sentence:* Our zoo has acquired many rare animals; for example, it now has a pair of pandas.
By Rewriting	
Run-on: The horse show began late, someone had misplaced the registration forms.	*Sentence:* The horse show began late because someone had misplaced the registration forms. (Changed to complex sentence)
Run-on: We replaced the sparkplugs, the filter was also bad.	*Sentence:* We replaced the sparkplugs and the filter. (Changed to simple sentence with compound direct object)

EXERCISE B: Identifying and Correcting Run-ons. If a sentence is a run-on, correct it. Use each of the four methods for correcting run-ons at least once. If it is correct as written, write *correct.*

EXAMPLE: I want to study genetics it is a developing science.

I want to study genetics, a developing science.

1. I looked down, I saw that the well was apparently dry.
2. We read the Preamble to the Constitution, our group felt anew the power of those words.

3. The boy had trouble with the decimal point when multiplying he always put it in the wrong place.
4. The thermometer broke, the mercury spilled onto the floor.
5. I mislaid my car keys, my house keys were also gone.
6. It is against the law to litter, nevertheless, people do it.
7. Ann threw away the check, but she eventually recovered it.
8. I generally like the climate of the area where I live I do not enjoy the subfreezing temperatures of winter.
9. Everyone should be polite, however many people are rude.
10. I made my own chili to eat it one needs an iron stomach.

DEVELOPING WRITING SKILLS: Avoiding Fragments and Run-ons. Write the paragraph, correcting all fragments and run-ons.

EXAMPLE: Mosquitoes are pests, they are difficult to control.

Mosquitoes are pests that are difficult to control.

(1) Mosquitoes, those nasty little insects whose bites cause our skin to swell and itch. (2) They inhabit every state in the Union and most areas of the world. (3) Actually, the bites should not be considered mere irritants they lead to many deaths every year. (4) These insects transmit many ailments. (5) Temporary insanity, filariasis, and many types of viral and bacterial infections. (6) Of course, mosquitoes must bite to survive, the females need the protein from the blood to produce their eggs. (7) The females weigh one ten-thousandth of an ounce when unfed, they triple that after a single bite. (8) Among nature's greatest achievements, the two intricate pumps inside the female's head. (9) Only one bite is necessary, they draw enough blood to produce seventy-five eggs. (10) Much has been done to halt the growth of mosquitoes, nothing, however, completely eradicates these insects.

Misplaced and Dangling Modifiers 4.2

Careful writers put modifiers as close as possible to the words they modify. When modifiers are misplaced or left dangling in a sentence, the result is often ludicrous, illogical, or confusing. This section will show you methods for correcting misplaced and dangling modifiers.

Misplaced Modifiers

A *misplaced modifier* is placed too far from the modified word.

A misplaced modifier seems to modify the wrong word in the sentence.

Any modifying phrase or clause can be misplaced.

MISPLACED MODIFIERS: A man fell over a rock *running in a race.*

We heard the telephone ring *while watching television.*

Move modifiers closer to the words they modify.

CORRECTED SENTENCES: A man *running in a race* fell over a rock.

While watching television, we heard the telephone ring.

A special misplaced modifier is the *squinting modifier*—a phrase or clause that appears to modify two words at once.

SQUINTING MODIFIER: She heard *upon her arrival* that Lee had resigned.

The phrase *upon her arrival* could modify either the verb *heard* or the verb *had resigned.* Move the phrase so that it clearly modifies one part of the sentence or the other.

CORRECTED SENTENCES: *Upon her arrival* she heard that Lee had resigned.

She heard that Lee had resigned *upon her arrival.*

EXERCISE A: Identifying and Correcting Misplaced Modifiers. Write each sentence, correcting the misplaced modifier.

EXAMPLE: Swinging from the branches, we saw two monkeys.

We saw two monkeys swinging from the branches.

1. We saw the seagulls sitting at the sidewalk cafe.

2. We arranged to have a pizza made by phone.
3. Whirling round and round, we saw our clothes in the drier.
4. The grandfather clock awoke me chiming out the hour.
5. He got up and went out the door taking the laundry.
6. Under the couch, he found the dollar.
7. The young girl ran toward her horse crying with joy.
8. The spaghetti was served to the child smelling of garlic.
9. The buildings on the ground from the plane looked small.
10. Covered with mold, he threw out the cheese.

Dangling Modifiers

With *dangling modifiers* the word that should be modified is missing completely from the sentence.

A dangling modifier seems to modify the wrong word or no word at all because the word it should modify has been omitted from the sentence.

Dangling participial phrases are corrected by adding missing words and making other needed changes. In the example, the *director* did the casting, not the *fine group of actors*.

DANGLING PARTICIPIAL PHRASE: *Casting the play*, a fine group of actors was chosen carefully.

CORRECTED SENTENCE: *Casting the play*, the director carefully chose a fine group of actors.

Dangling infinitive phrases and elliptical clauses can be corrected in the same way. The problem will generally be with the verb rather than a noun or pronoun. However, you will usually need to change a noun or pronoun as well as the verb.

DANGLING INFINITIVE PHRASE: *To go to the game*, seats must be reserved.

CORRECTED SENTENCE: *To go to the game*, you must reserve seats.

DANGLING ELLIPTICAL CLAUSE: *While watching the game*, another goal was made.

CORRECTED SENTENCE: *While watching the game*, we saw another goal made.

A dangling adverb clause may also occur when the antecedent of a pronoun is not clear.

DANGLING
ADVERB CLAUSE: *When she was ninety years old,* Mrs. Smith's granddaughter arranged a surprise party.

CORRECTED
SENTENCE: *When Mrs. Smith was ninety years old,* her granddaughter arranged a surprise party.

EXERCISE B: Identifying and Correcting Dangling Modifiers. If a sentence contains a dangling modifier, rewrite it using one of the techniques described in this section. If a sentence is correct, write *correct.*

EXAMPLE: Having finished the assignment, the hour was late.

Having finished the assignment, I realized how late it was.

1. To eat before the game, dinner must be ready within fifteen minutes.
2. While laughing, the chicken bone stuck in her throat.
3. Checking all the stations, the assembly line was running smoothly.
4. Having lost my hat, I missed the bus I wanted.
5. Falling on the stairs, my jaw was dislocated.
6. To get out of the woods, a compass was used.
7. When they were three years old, the twins' parents took them to Disney World.
8. After eating snacks all day, dinner looked unappetizing.
9. Before presenting it, you must carefully rehearse a speech.
10. Having decorated the cake, it looked like a work of art.

DEVELOPING WRITING SKILLS: Avoiding Misplaced and Dangling Modifiers. Fill in each blank with the kind of phrase or clause indicated, being careful to avoid using any misplaced or dangling modifiers.

EXAMPLE: I still remember the day (adjective clause).

I still remember the day that I started kindergarten.

1. When carving the turkey, (independent clause).
2. (elliptical clause), she devoured the meal.
3. (participial phrase), the jockey rode the horse to victory.

4. To remark on such a trivial matter, (independent clause).
5. (participial phrase), the huge rock threatened the boats in the area.
6. Standing speechless before the group, (independent clause).
7. After leaving the race, (independent clause).
8. (adverb clause), Paula's aunt gave her a family album.
9. (participial phrase), the family explained their destitute circumstances.
10. (elliptical clause), he asked for a receipt.

Faulty Parallelism 4.3

Good writers try to present a series of ideas in similar grammatical structures so that they will read smoothly. If one element in a series is not parallel with the others, the result may be jarring and its meaning may be altered. This section will show you how to correct this error, called *faulty parallelism.*

Recognizing the Correct Use of Parallelism

To present a series of ideas of equal importance, you should use parallel grammatical structures.

Parallelism is the placement of equal ideas in words, phrases, or clauses of similar types.

Parallel grammatical structures may be made up of two or more words of the same part of speech, two or more phrases of the same type, two or more clauses of the same type, or occasionally two or more sentences of the same type.

PARALLEL WORDS: The wrestler looked *strong, fit,* and *agile.*

PARALLEL PHRASES: The greatest pleasure I know is *to do a good action by stealth* and *to have it found out by accident.*—Charles Lamb

PARALLEL CLAUSES: The tennis star *whom I have met* and *whom you saw last Thursday* will speak.

PARALLEL SENTENCES: *It couldn't be, of course. It could never, never be.*—Dorothy Parker

141

Now examine the following paragraph, which begins *A Tale of Two Cities* by Charles Dickens, a novel about the French Revolution. Notice how the parallel structures set up vivid contrasts.

EXAMPLE: It was the best of times, it was the worst of times, it was the age of wisdom, it was the age of foolishness, it was the epoch of belief, it was the epoch of incredulity, it was the season of Light, it was the season of Darkness, it was the spring of hope, it was the winter of despair, we had everything before us, we had nothing before us, we were all going direct to Heaven, we were all going direct the other way—in short, the period was so far like the present period, that some of its noisiest authorities insisted on its being received, for good or for evil, in the superlative degree of comparison only.

EXERCISE A: Recognizing Parallel Structures. Write the parallel structures in the following sentences. Then identify what each is composed of: *words, phrases, clauses,* or *sentences.*

EXAMPLE: We must hope for the best, not for the worst.
        for the best   for the worst (phrases)

1. They know that we will help them and that the price will be quite low.
2. Sarah's cat was Siamese. Tom's dog was Pekinese.
3. Listening carefully and ignoring interruptions are essential in that class.
4. They gave their children love, hope, and attention.
5. The leader shouted his speech from the balcony, leaning out toward the crowd, trying to maintain their interest.
6. Pleasures last awhile. Honors last forever.
7. The presents were hidden behind the curtains, under the couch, and in the old Greek vase.
8. She succeeded because she tried new ideas and because she was not easily ignored.
9. Joel thought the movie shallow, boring, and pointless.
10. He hoped to buy a car without having to spend all of his savings.

142

Correcting Faulty Parallelism

Faulty parallelism occurs when a writer uses unequal grammatical structures to express related ideas.

Correct a sentence containing faulty parallelism by rewriting it so that each parallel idea is expressed in the same grammatical structure.

Faulty parallelism can involve words, phrases, and clauses in series or in comparisons.

Nonparallel Words, Phrases, and Clauses in Series. Always check a series of ideas in your writing for parallelism. If, for example, you begin a series with prepositional phrases, make all the items in the series prepositional phrases.

The following chart presents some nonparallel structures and shows how they can be repaired to restore the smoothness and clarity to the sentence. Notice how coordinating conjunctions (*and, but, or,* and so forth) often join series and can signal you to check the items they connect for parallelism.

CORRECTING FAULTY PARALLELISM IN SERIES	
Nonparallel Structures	**Corrected Sentences**
GERUND GERUND *Planning, drafting,* and NOUN *revision* are three steps in the writing process.	GERUND GERUND *Planning, drafting,* and GERUND *revising* are three steps in the writing process.
INFIN I was appalled *to see her* PHRASE INFIN *manners, to hear her bad* PHRASE PART *language,* and *feeling her* PHRASE *intense animosity.*	INFIN I was appalled *to see her* PHRASE INFIN *manners to hear her bad* PHRASE INFIN *language,* and *to feel her* PHRASE *intense animosity.*
NOUN Some experts feel *that our* CLAUSE *population is too large,* but INDEP CLAUSE *it will diminish.*	NOUN Some experts feel *that our* CLAUSE *population is too large* but NOUN CLAUSE *that it will diminish.*

143

Though correlative conjunctions, such as *both . . . and* or *not only . . . but also,* connect just two related items, writers sometimes include more words than they should with the first part of the conjunction. The result is faulty parallelism.

NONPARALLEL: The student not only *won a National Merit scholarship* but also *a local scholarship.*

CORRECTED: The student won not only *a National Merit scholarship* but also *a local scholarship.*

Nonparallel Words, Phrases, and Clauses in Comparisons. As the old saying goes, you cannot compare apples with oranges. In writing comparisons, you generally should compare a phrase with the same type of phrase and a clause with the same type of clause. Furthermore, you should make sure your ideas themselves, as well as the structures you use to express them, are logically parallel.

CORRECTING FAULTY PARALLELISM IN COMPARISONS	
Nonparallel Structures	**Corrected Sentences**
NOUN Most people prefer *corn* to GERUND PHRASE *eating Brussels sprouts.*	NOUN Most people prefer *corn* to NOUN Brussels sprouts.
PREP PHRASE I left my job *at 7:00 p.m.* PART rather than *stopping work* PHRASE *at 5:00 p.m.*	PREP PHRASE I left my job *at 7:00 p.m.* PREP rather than *at the usual* PHRASE *5:00 p.m.*
S DO *I* delight in foggy *days* as S much as sunny *days* delight DO other *people.*	S DO *I* delight in foggy *days* as S much as other *people* delight DO in sunny *days.*

EXERCISE B: Correcting Faulty Parallelism. Rewrite each sentence to correct the faulty parallelism.

EXAMPLE: She not only plays soccer but also basketball.

She plays not only soccer but also basketball.

144

1. The new employee was lazy, insolent, and often came late.
2. I think the plants did well because they were fertilized rather than because of my talks to them.
3. Ken either will go to the parade or to the Egyptian museum.
4. I hate weeding as much as having shots upsets me.
5. He both wanted to keep his job and to move to the country.
6. Going home is better than to stay here.
7. I would choose reading a book over a television show.
8. His old tennis shoes were dirty, laceless, and smelled.
9. The coach tells me that I bat well, but I field poorly.
10. Laughing together, sharing one another's problems, and to overlook faults—these make true friends.

DEVELOPING WRITING SKILLS: Writing Sentences Containing Parallel Structures. Follow the instructions in parentheses to revise each sentence, making sure the revised sentences contain parallel structures.

EXAMPLE: If you have completed all the assignments, you will do well on the test. (Add another adverb clause.)

If you have completed all the assignments and if you have reviewed your notes carefully, you will do well on the test.

1. Gathering honey, the bees worked diligently. (Add another participial phrase.)
2. I listened to the melody floating through the air. (Add another independent clause.)
3. The writer published a novel. (Add three adjectives.)
4. I love gardening. (Compare gardening to something else.)
5. I will participate in the log rolling contest. (Add two more prepositional phrases.)
6. The parade route headed down Main Street. (Add two more verbs with prepositional phrases.)
7. The knight had to slay the dragon. (Add another verbal phrase.)
8. I was pleased by the game we played. (Add another prepositional phrase that is modified by an adjective clause.)
9. By keeping the thermostat at 68°, we can conserve energy. (Add another verbal phrase.)
10. I prepared the sandwiches for the picnic. (Add two more direct objects.)

4.4 Faulty Coordination

When two or more independent clauses of unequal importance are joined by *and,* the result is *faulty coordination.*

Recognizing Faulty Coordination

To *coordinate* means "to place side by side in equal rank." Two independent clauses that are joined by the coordinating conjunction *and,* therefore, should have equal rank.

Use *and* or other coordinating conjunctions only to connect ideas of equal importance.

The following example shows ideas of equal importance joined by the conjunction *and.*

CORRECT COORDINATION: John dusted, *and* I vacuumed.

Sometimes, however, writers carelessly use *and* to join independent clauses that either should not be joined or should be joined in another way so that the real relationship between the clauses will be clear. The faulty coordination puts all the ideas on the same level of importance even though they logically should not be. (See Section 16.1 for more information about connecting your ideas logically.)

FAULTY COORDINATION: Steam was pouring forth from my car, *and* the gas station attendant said I should have had it checked months ago.

I didn't do well, *and* the race was very easy.

The dog looked ferocious, *and* it was snarling and snapping at me.

Occasionally, writers will also string together so many ideas with *and*'s that the reader is left breathless.

STRINGY SENTENCE: The man who entered the restaurant wore a sport shirt and slacks, *and* he asked for a table, *and* the maitre d' apologetically said the man had to have a tie and jacket, *and* the man became furious and left.

146

EXERCISE A: Recognizing Faulty Coordination. For the six sentences in which *and* is used improperly, write *faulty*. For the sentences in which *and* is used properly, write *correct*.

EXAMPLE: I took the examination, and I passed it.

        correct

1. The spaniel has been snapping and barking at approaching strangers, and her puppies were born last night.
2. Oak trees lined the street, and it was called Grand Avenue.
3. The children jumped into the unheated pool and squealed as they hit the water, and immediately they hopped out and dried themselves off and decided to forgo the swim.
4. The outside of my house wears a fresh coat of paint, and the inside has been newly redecorated.
5. I remembered that I had read the book a long time ago, and I saw the movie last night.
6. My throat felt parched, and the cool drink soothed it.
7. The covered wagon creaked across the plains, and its wheel became mired in mud, and six oxen freed it.
8. You will come, and our family will show you around town.
9. I relaxed while lying in the sun, and soon I fell asleep.
10. I could hardly get the key in the lock, and my fingers were numb from the cold.

Correcting Faulty Coordination

Faulty coordination can be corrected in the following ways.

Correct faulty coordination by putting unrelated ideas into separate sentences or less important ideas into subordinate clauses or phrases.

When faulty coordination occurs in a sentence in which the independent clauses are not closely related, separate the clauses and omit the coordinating conjunction.

FAULTY
COORDINATION: Steam was pouring forth from my car, *and* the gas station attendant said I should have had it checked months ago.

CORRECTION: Steam was pouring forth from my car. The gas station attendant said I should have had it checked months ago.

The second method for correcting faulty coordination involves examining each independent clause. If one is less important or subordinate, turn it into a subordinate clause.

FAULTY COORDINATION: I didn't do well, *and* the race was very easy.

CORRECTED SENTENCE: I didn't do well even though the race was very easy.

The third method involves reducing an unimportant idea to a phrase—that is, changing the compound sentence into a simple sentence. An independent clause that can be reduced to a phrase will often begin with a pronoun and a linking verb, such as *he is* or *it was.* In the following example, notice that the second clause has been turned into a participial phrase.

FAULTY COORDINATION: The dog looked ferocious, *and* it was snarling and snapping at me.

CORRECTED SENTENCE: Snarling and snapping at me, the dog looked ferocious.

Stringy sentences should be broken up and revised using any of the three methods just described. Experiment with a few possibilities before making a choice. Following is one way that the stringy sentence on page 146 can be revised.

REVISION OF
STRINGY SENTENCE: The man who entered the restaurant wore a sport shirt and slacks. When he asked for a table, the maitre d' apologetically said the man had to have a tie and jacket. At that, the man became furious and left.

EXERCISE B: Correcting Faulty Coordination. Rewrite each sentence, correcting the faulty coordination.

EXAMPLE: Learning to parallel park was difficult for me, and I finally mastered the technique.

Although learning to parallel park was difficult for me, I finally mastered the technique.

1. I slowly climbed to the lookout point, and reaching the top provided me with a spectacular view.
2. The car is dented, and it has room for six.

148

3. We watched a special on naturalist John James Audubon, and the organization dedicated to birds is named after him.
4. The truck had a full load, and it slowed down going uphill.
5. We turned on the television, and a commercial promptly showed up, and I turned the channel looking for something better, and commercials were on wherever I turned.
6. Evan has a new wool pullover, and he plans to wear it to the beach where the wind can turn very cold.
7. I walked on my sprained ankle, and it started to rain.
8. Rocky Bleir received a serious injury in Vietnam, and he came back to play football for the Pittsburgh Steelers.
9. She studies astronomy, and this is the science that deals with the stars.
10. The crowds to see the movie were enormous, and we ordered tickets prior to going, and we still sat near the screen and came away with kinks in our necks.

DEVELOPING WRITING SKILLS: Avoiding Faulty Coordination in Sentence Combining. Combine each pair of sentences, avoiding faulty coordination.

EXAMPLE: Gorillas look ferocious. They are really very gentle.

Although gorillas look ferocious, they are really very gentle.

1. I lost the gold charm. It had been a gift from my father.
2. Daydreams invade the day. Nightmares haunt the darkness.
3. Millions of bats inhabit one particular cave. They journey each night to a lake over a hundred miles away.
4. I enjoy thumbing through encyclopedias. They contain fascinating articles.
5. The ice was left out. It melted all over the countertop.
6. The handbook had a soft cloth cover. It was filled with clever ideas and shortcuts for household tasks.
7. The shepherds huddled near the fire. It was their only source of warmth.
8. I use a knapsack for a daylong hike. I switch to a backpack for longer excursions.
9. The Vikings had early settlements in Canada. They left remains that we study today.
10. The man in front of me refused to stop talking during the movie. I asked the management to remove him.

149

Skills Review and Writing Workshop

Avoiding Sentence Errors

CHECKING YOUR SKILLS

Rewrite the paragraph, correcting all sentence errors.

(1) A dramatic social change has taken place in the United States during the last 30 years, the number of two-paycheck families has increased. (2) As a result of the women's movement, high cost of living, and desiring to lead the "good life." (3) Today, more than 60% of families outside the home have two members working. (4) This shift in employment patterns has had significant benefits for women's career growth and income security, it has also created some problems. (5) With two wage earners, American society faced changes in the lifestyle of families. (6) Leaving the home to work in large numbers, some children have not been properly supervised. (7) Industry competing for qualified workers, hired many women and it was not prepared for workers who needed more flexible work hours. (8) Women want their children to have good care while they are at work. (9) They both want professional success and family stability. (10) As a result of these needs, gradual changes in corporate and public policy to accommodate two-paycheck families.

USING GRAMMAR SKILLS IN WRITING
Writing a Press Release

Your writing will not be effective if it contains sentence errors. Imagine you work for a public relations firm and write a press release for a new product following these steps.

Prewriting: Think of a new product and several reasons why consumers should buy it. Does the product have any unique qualities that make it stand out from competing products?

Writing: Describe the product's most important characteristic first. Explain how it is better than competing products. Write your press release so that it stands out.

Revising: Look over your sentences and correct any errors. After you have revised, proofread carefully.

150

UNIT II

Usage

5

Levels of Usage

In the English language, there are two main levels of usage: *standard* and *nonstandard.* Standard English, spoken and written by the majority of educated speakers, is the more uniform of the two. There is little variation in the grammar of standard English between one region of the United States and another, or even between one English-speaking country and another. Differences in the meanings of words are also slight. All that may vary significantly is the way that some words or expressions in the language are pronounced. Nonstandard English, in contrast, is mainly spoken language used by certain social, regional, or ethnic groups. It includes grammatical constructions, vocabulary, and pronunciations that differ from the accepted rules of standard English.

Both standard English and nonstandard English contribute to the overall richness of the language. Each of the levels can communicate effectively for those people who are accustomed to using it. In this chapter, you will learn to identify the factors, such as time, place, and occasion, that determine which level of usage is appropriate.

5.1 The Varieties of English

Both standard and nonstandard English have variations of usage. In this chapter you will study two forms of standard English, both formal and informal, and two forms of nonstandard English, both dialect and slang. You will also learn some of the distinctive characteristics of American English.

Standard English

In the United States, the language used by most educated people is called standard English. Depending on the time, place, and occasion, the level of standard English may be either *formal* or *informal.* The distinction between formal and informal English may be as simple as whether a person says "Please be seated" to an honored guest or "Grab a chair" to a good friend.

Formal English. Serious speaking and writing, such as that found in a President's State of the Union message or a scholarly analysis, usually requires the use of formal English. This is the language of the schools and universities, of government, in legal documents, and of most businesses. At its best it is never stilted or unnecessarily difficult. You will be studying formal English in this unit so that you will have a firm command of it in those circumstances that require you to use the language formally.

Formal English uses traditional standards of correctness. It is characterized by complex sentence structures and an extensive vocabulary.

In the passage of formal English below, the sentence structure is complex but not difficult to understand. Notice the passage contains no contractions or casual expressions.

EXAMPLE: Changes in methods of child rearing are important not only because they contribute to changes in the character of the future citizens of the planet but because making changes in the way children are raised affects the character of those who raise them—parents, teachers, physicians, legislators.
—Margaret Mead

Informal English. Although you will often need to express your ideas in formal English, especially when writing, the kind of language you are most likely to encounter and use in everyday situations is informal Englsh.

This is the kind of language used in newspapers, in advertisements, on television, in personal letters, and in casual conversation.

Informal English is conversational in tone. It uses a smaller vocabulary than formal English and generally shorter sentences.

Informal English often includes contractions and casual expressions. This passage is from a personal letter by Flannery O'Connor. Notice its conversational tone.

EXAMPLE: Me, I just got out of the hospital where I had my middle entered by the surgeons. It was all a howling success from their point of view and one of them is going to write it up for a doctor magazine as you usually don't cut folks with lupus. But the trip in was necessary though nothing turned out malignant and I will soon be restored on turnip green potlicker. Right now I am just killing time and would be mighty proud to see you & Benedict. It's a good time of year to see these parts. Everything is in bloom.—Flannery O'Connor

EXERCISE A: Recognizing Formal and Informal English.
Label each sentence as *formal* or *informal*.

EXAMPLE: Dad said we've got to clean up this mess by noon.

           informal

1. The film, though directed by a novice in the industry, was awarded several of the most prestigious awards.
2. Well, we just couldn't believe that Robby finally arrived.
3. Alarmed by the results of her experiment, the scientist sought to confirm the data with a second experiment.
4. The repeal of the Stamp Act brought unusual rejoicing in America, but the same could not be said for Great Britain.
5. The kids howled with delight as we rode them piggyback around the backyard.
6. Surely you're not going to wear that awful tie!
7. No one foresaw the dire consequences that the legislation would have on the region's ecological balance.
8. The reading of poetry is made more dynamic by speech, for poetry should be heard to be most appreciated.
9. I told them they just couldn't camp out in a vacant lot.
10. The marine, stirred by solemnity of the occasion, proudly saluted his country's flag.

Nonstandard English

The line that divides nonstandard English from informal standard English is a thin one. English is considered nonstandard when it does not follow all the rules of standard English. Two kinds of nonstandard English are *dialect* and *slang*.

Dialect. Dialect is any distinctive pattern of speech whose use is restricted to a specific geographical location or to a specific social or ethnic group. It is considered nonstandard whenever it differs from the standard usage of educated speakers.

A nonstandard dialect is a form of English that makes use of words, pronunciations, and sentence structures not used in standard English.

Dialects develop when people live in isolation. The more isolated they are, the more their dialect will vary from the standard form. As geographical, social, and ethnic barriers disappear between separated peoples, their dialects tend to merge.

The following stanza from the poem "To a Mouse" by Robert Burns is an example of the Scottish dialect of English. Although many of the words and pronunciations are unfamiliar, you should understand the meaning if you read it aloud.

EXAMPLE: Wee, sleekit, cow'rin, tim'rous beastie,
O what a panic's in thy breastie!
Thou need na start awa sae hasty,
Wi' bickering brattle!
I wad be laith to rin an' chase thee
Wi' murd'ring pattle!—Robert Burns

Slang. Slang is made up of words such as *neat* and phrases such as *hang out* that enjoy a usually short-term popularity. Slang generally originates among groups sharing a common social bond or activity, such as among students or rock musicians.

In casual situations such as conversation and letter-writing, slang can be acceptable. It can make language colorful. However, the novelty of slang usually fades quickly and a new word or expression soon takes its place. Slang is not acceptable usage in formal situations.

Slang is a nonstandard form of English that is colorful and expressive but short-lived.

The larger the group and the more closely associated with the mainstream of society, the more likely it is that the group's slang will become part of the standard vocabulary. Most Americans, for example, would recognize a used car dealer's use of the term *cream puff* to mean "a car in excellent condition." On the other hand, the slang words that a group of smugglers might use, almost like secret code words, to shield their activities from the outside world have little chance of becoming standard vocabulary. In the following passage, notice such slang words as *pad, C-note,* and *ace.*

EXAMPLE: Bosie and Jan left Sam's pad in a real hurry once he began to spill his gut. It seems Sam needed a C-note to bribe some prof into changing a flunking grade into an ace.—Rosemary Frost

EXERCISE B: **Recognizing Dialect and Slang.** Label each sentence as *dialect* or *slang.*

EXAMPLE: A wee lad it was peeking o'er the windowsill.

   dialect

1. The cops nabbed the crooks but couldn't find the loot.
2. The kids are just hanging out on the main drag.
3. She's wantin' to learn us readin' and writin' now.
4. The dude rented a far out pad on the other side of town.
5. The groupies decked themselves out and crashed the party.
6. My brother he done finish his work already.
7. They cain't git in unless y'all open the door.
8. The hip place to go is that ragtime joint on the west side.
9. I'll hae no hend wi't all yer shenanigans.
10. It gives me the creeps when he acts like a big shot.

DEVELOPING WRITING SKILLS: Using Varieties of English. Write a paragraph in standard, formal English. Then rewrite it, using nonstandard English that contains dialect or slang.

The History of English 5.2

One way to understand how we use the English language is to study its history. English has a long family history with roots in many lands and many tongues. In this section you will see how our language has gradually changed since its beginning more than fifteen hundred years ago.

Three Periods of Language Growth

The development of the English language is divided into three periods. The first period, known as *Old English,* or Anglo-Saxon, dates from about 450 to 1150 A.D. The second period, *Middle English,* dates from 1150 to 1500. The third period, *Modern English,* dates from 1500 to the present.

The development of the English language is divided into Old English, Middle English, and Modern English.

Old English (450–1150 A.D.). The seeds of the English language were first planted in the British Isles around the middle of the fifth century A.D. Three Germanic tribes, the Angles, the Saxons, and the Jutes, invaded the Isles and drove the native Celtic tribes to the north and west. The Germanic tribes named the island *Englaland* and spoke a language they called *English*.

During the Old English period, the development of the English language was influenced by other languages. In 600 A.D. Roman missionaries came to England and brought with them the Latin language and its Roman alphabet. The Roman alphabet replaced the ancient Runic one. The missionaries also brought new words to the subjects of religion, education, and literature. Nearly half of the words in modern English have come down from the Latin. Following are examples of modern words that have their origin in Latin words.

EXAMPLES: *priest, altar, mass, psalm, temple, memorandum*

Between 750 and 1050 the Vikings invaded parts of England. They, too, contributed words to the English language from their Old Norse language. The two languages resembled each other since they both came from a parent Germanic language.

157

Following are words in modern English derived from Old Norse.

EXAMPLES: *egg, sky, gape, skirt, skin, skull, outlaw, crawl*

By the eleventh century, Old English had developed a grammar that was highly *inflected;* words changed their forms according to their function in a sentence. Nouns had four case endings, verbs had person and number endings, pronouns had a complex system, and adjectives had various endings.

Middle English (1150–1500 A.D.). In 1066 England was invaded by a group known as Normans. The Norman Conquest brought not only their French warriors and kings to England, but also an elaborate culture and an elegant language. French became the language of government and education. It was spoken by the upper classes and in the king's court. However, the working classes continued to speak English.

The following chart compares words of Old-English, working-class origin, with words of French, or upper-class origin.

WORDS OF OLD-ENGLISH AND FRENCH ORIGINS	
Old English	French
folk	baron, nobility
house	mansion, palace, manor
work, live	leisure, fashion, dance
eat, food, meat	feast, beef, jelly, peach

During the Middle English period about ten thousand French words entered the English vocabulary because the upper class and working class had to communicate with one another.

Of the thousand most commonly used words in modern English, nearly sixty-two percent are of Old English origin and were not replaced by French words. These words include some of the most basic words of our lives and, as a result, have survived the significant changes that occurred during the Middle English period.

The French language did not replace English, however. The English kept their language alive, and they changed it radically.

Over many years, they simplified the grammar by abandoning complicated inflectional endings. They gave most nouns simple plurals, and eliminated many difficult irregular verbs. They used word order and structure words such as prepositions to communicate meaning.

In addition to an enlarged vocabulary and a simplification of the grammar, the Middle English period also saw a marked diversification in dialects. Londoners, with their speech influenced by French accents, sounded different from people in the North whose dialect was influenced by years of contact with Old Norse dialects. The regional differences included variations in pronunciation, grammar, and spelling. The following examples show regional variations of the word "love."

EXAMPLES: *loves* (North) *loveth* (South) *lovens* (Midland)

In the fourteenth century, French domination ended and English was re-established as the language of government and culture. A new standard for the English language developed, based on the East Midland dialect, the dialect spoken in London, the nation's capital and its most populous city. It was the center of England's economic, cultural, and intellectual life. The Midland dialect was spoken in the king's court. It was the king's English and was highly imitated. This dialect became the standard in the early development of modern English.

Modern English (1500 to the present). During the Modern English period, four major events changed the English language. They were the *English Renaissance,* the *Great Vowel Shift,* the publication of *Samuel Johnson's dictionary,* and the settlement of America and rise of *American English.*

The English Renaissance was a period of renewed interest in the classical past and a view of the future. Interest in ancient Greece and Rome resulted in thousands of Latin and Greek words entering English between 1550 and 1650. The view toward the future brought about the need to name new concepts. Borrowing from the Latin and Greek, the English coined words such as *progress, calculus, astronomy,* and *equator.*

During this period of trade and exploration, Englishmen used new words to name their goods and information.

EXAMPLES: *violin* (Italy) *gauze* (Gaza)
              calico (India) *tea* (China)

By the late 1500's the *Great Vowel Shift* had occurred in the English language. This shift changed the pronunciation of six vowels and diphthongs in stressed syllables. Vowels took on the sound we hear today. The word pronounced *clay-nuh* in Middle English was now pronounced *clean;* the word pronounced *hoo-suh* was now *house;* the word pronounced *moose* was now *mouse.*

The availability of books increased after the invention of the printing press. Reading created a need to standardize spelling that was not needed when English was mainly a spoken language.

In 1755 *Samuel Johnson's dictionary* set the standard for spelling and syntax that set the basic structure and sound of the English language.

In the 1600's, when the Europeans were colonizing the areas that today comprise the United States, English was but one of many languages spoken. In addition to the languages of the Native Americans, the languages of the Dutch, the French, the Spanish, and the African slaves were also spoken. America's language grew and changed like the nation itself and became a dialect distinct from it parent tongue. That dialect is known as *American English.*

Over several hundred years, American English has become increasingly different from British English. The British pronounce some words in a very different fashion. Americans, for example, pronounce *schedule* with an initial *sk* sound. The British pronounce the word with an initial *sh* sound.

There are also many words and expressions that differ in meaning. Notice in the chart below that the words and expressions used by the British are different from our usage.

American Usage	British Usage
washcloth	face flannel
cookie	biscuit
trash truck	dust cart
flashlight	torch
line	queue
soccer	football
two weeks	fortnight
yard	garden

EXERCISE A: Discovering British Expressions. The British use the following words and expressions with different meanings than Americans do. Look the items up in a dictionary and write the word or expression an American would use.

EXAMPLE: braces   suspenders

1. boot   4. bobby   7. tube   10. flat
2. sweet   5. spanner   8. lorry
3. lift   6. level crossing 9. bonnet

EXERCISE B: Identifying Important Events in the History of the English Language. Label each event or development as pertaining to the Old English, Middle English, or Modern English period. Then briefly describe the importance of each.

EXAMPLE: Norman Conquest

Middle English   entry of French words into English

1. the publication of Samuel Johnson's dictionary
2. the introduction of the Roman alphabet
3. the Great Vowel Shift
4. the invasion of England by the Vikings
5. the end of using inflectional endings in English
6. the proliferation of English dialects
7. the English Renaissance
8. the decline in usage of the Celtic language
9. the simplification of English
10. the East Midland dialect

DEVELOPING WRITING SKILLS: Researching the History of the English Language. Research one of the topics listed, using encyclopedias and books on history and language.

1. How did historical events affect the development of the English language?
2. On what bases have linguists divided English language development into three periods?
3. What changes in the English language resulted from the Great Vowel Shift? How has this affected modern English?

161

Skills Review and Writing Workshop

Levels of Usage

CHECKING YOUR SKILLS

Rewrite the following paragraph into formal English.

(1) After I quit work, I wanted to go to a keen new scifi film at the mall. (2) I'm really into scifi, so I got the guys together. (3) We met at my place, but we didn't have any wheels. (4) Jack and Paul had a gig, so we couldn't count on them. (5) Amy, the whiz kid, said she had to study. (6) She hates farout films anyway, and standing in line bugs her. (7) Finally we decided to go check out the new video shop. (8) It had a lot of real neat stuff, so we hung out there for a while. (9) I thought the evening was going to be the pits, but it turned out okay after all. (10) Still, that Amy gives me a pain; I wish she'd get it together.

USING USAGE SKILLS IN WRITING
Writing a Translation

Nonstandard English is never used in formal writing. Informal English, however, may contain casual expressions. Write a paragraph in nonstandard English. Use slang or dialect, or try to reproduce the distinctive language of your town or neighborhood. Follow the steps below to "translate" the paragraph into standard English.

Prewriting: Decide which style is more appropriate to the subject you have chosen—formal or informal. Underline the words and expressions in your original paragraph that need to be replaced.

Writing: Good translators maintain the spirit of the original version, as well as the content. For example, if your original paragraph is serious, do not make your translation funny. Convey the information and/or emotion in the original as faithfully as you can.

Revising: Check your paragraph for accuracy when you look over the translation. Be sure your English is clear so the meaning is clear. After you have revised, proofread carefully.

Chapter 6

Verb Usage

A solid understanding of verbs and their many uses is necessary in order to speak and write well. Most native speakers of English automatically use the correct verb form when they speak, but there are many grammatical situations that can be tricky.

In this chapter you will study how verbs are formed and how they show time. The chapter will also explain how verbs express facts, commands, and wishes or possibilities and how verbs indicate whether subjects perform or receive action.

Verb Tenses 6.1

Besides expressing actions or conditions, verbs have different *tenses* to indicate when the action or condition occurred.

A tense is a form of a verb that shows the time of an action or condition.

The Six Verb Tenses

There are six tenses that indicate when an action or condition of a verb is, was, or will be in effect. Each of these six tenses has at least two forms.

Each tense has a basic and a progressive form.

The chart at the top of the next page shows the *basic* forms of the six tenses.

THE BASIC FORMS OF THE SIX TENSES	
Present	I *work* as a carpenter's apprentice.
Past	I *worked* five days last week.
Future	I *will work* only two days next week.
Present Perfect	I *have worked* for almost a year now.
Past Perfect	I *had worked* only on weekends until this past month.
Future Perfect	I *will have worked* for one year by the end of this month.

The basic forms of the six tenses are identified simply by their tense names. The progressive forms, however, are identified by their tense names plus the word *progressive*.

Notice in the next chart that all of the progressive forms end in *-ing*.

THE PROGRESSIVE FORMS OF THE SIX TENSES	
Present Progressive	I *am working* right now.
Past Progressive	I *was working* when you called.
Future Progressive	I *will be working* this weekend.
Present Perfect Progressive	I *have been working* harder than usual lately.
Past Perfect Progressive	I *had been working* nights until the new schedule was announced.
Future Perfect Progressive	I *will have been working* on this project a month before it is done.

There is also a third form, the *emphatic,* which exists only for the present and past tenses. The present emphatic is formed with the helping verbs *do* or *does,* depending on the subject. The past emphatic is formed with *did.*

THE EMPHATIC FORMS OF THE PRESENT AND THE PAST	
Present Emphatic	I *do work* harder than you.
Past Emphatic	I *did work* last night.

EXERCISE A: Recognizing Verb Tenses and Their Forms.
Identify the tense of each verb and its form if the form is not basic.

EXAMPLE: We have been running.

         present perfect progressive

1. I did investigate.
2. He was waiting.
3. I had been studying.
4. He will have left.
5. We listened.
6. They have been walking.
7. She will forget.
8. They float.
9. I will have finished.
10. I accept.
11. She was limping.
12. He had been typing.
13. They do understand.
14. I will have been running.
15. You have failed.
16. I am going.
17. She helped.
18. It had disappeared.
19. He will come.
20. We will have decided.

The Four Principal Parts

Each verb in the English language has four principal parts from which all of the tenses are formed.

A verb has four principal parts: the present, the present participle, the past, and the past participle.

The chart below shows the principal parts of two verbs.

THE FOUR PRINCIPAL PARTS			
Present	**Present Participle**	**Past**	**Past Participle**
talk	talking	talked	talked
draw	drawing	drew	drawn

The first principal part is used for the basic forms of the present and future tenses as well as the emphatic forms. The present tense is formed by adding an -s or -es when the subject is *he, she, it,* or a singular noun *(I talk, Mary draws)*. The future tense is formed with the helping verb *will (I will talk, Mary will draw).* The present emphatic is formed with the helping verbs *do* or *does (I do talk, Mary does draw).* The past emphatic is formed with the helping verb *did (I did talk, Mary did draw).*

The second principal part is used with various helping verbs for all six of the progressive forms *(I am talking, Mary was drawing,* and so on).

The third principal part is used to form the past tense *(I talked, Mary drew).*

The fourth principal part is used with helping verbs for the basic forms of the three perfect tenses *(I have talked, Mary had drawn,* and so on).

EXERCISE B: Recognizing Principal Parts. Identify the principal part used to form each verb in Exercise A.

EXAMPLE: We have been running.

present participle

Regular and Irregular Verbs

The way a verb forms its past and past participle determines whether it is classified as *regular* or *irregular.*

Regular Verbs. The majority of verbs are regular; their past and past participles are formed according to a predictable pattern.

A regular verb is one whose past and past participle are formed by adding *-ed* or *-d* to the present form.

The chart on the next page shows the principal parts of three regular verbs. Notice that the past and past participle of each verb are formed in the same way. The helping verb *have* is in parentheses in front of the past participle to remind you that this verb form is considered a past participle only if it used with a helping verb.

Pay particular attention to the spelling. Notice that a final consonant is sometimes doubled to form the present participle (sto*pp*ing) as well as the past and past participle (sto*pp*ed). A final *e* may also be dropped to form the present participle (mana*g*ing).

166

PRINCIPAL PARTS OF REGULAR VERBS			
Present	**Present Participle**	**Past**	**Past Participle**
contend	contending	contended	(have) contended
manage	managing	managed	(have) managed
stop	stopping	stopped	(have) stopped

Irregular Verbs. Although most verbs are regular, many of the most common verbs are irregular.

An irregular verb is one whose past and past participle are not formed by adding -ed or -d to the present form.

The charts that follow group a number of irregular verbs according to common characteristics. The verbs in the first two charts have the same past and past participle. The verbs in the third chart deserve special attention because the past and past participle are formed in a variety of ways.

It is important to master the principal parts of irregular verbs because they often cause usage problems. One common problem is using a principal part that is nonstandard (saying, for example, *knowed* instead of *knew*). A second problem is confusing the past and past participle when they are different (saying "she done" instead of "she did"). A third problem is spelling. Notice that a final consonant may be doubled to form both the present participle (forge*tt*ing) and the past participle (for-go*tt*en). A final *e* may also be dropped to form the present participle (driv*i*ng).

IRREGULAR VERBS WITH THE SAME PRESENT, PAST, AND PAST PARTICIPLE			
Present	**Present Participle**	**Past**	**Past Participle**
bid	bidding	bid	(have) bid
burst	bursting	burst	(have) burst
cost	costing	cost	(have) cost
cut	cutting	cut	(have) cut
hit	hitting	hit	(have) hit
hurt	hurting	hurt	(have) hurt
let	letting	let	(have) let

put	putting	put	(have) put
set	setting	set	(have) set
shut	shutting	shut	(have) shut
split	splitting	split	(have) split
spread	spreading	spread	(have) spread
thrust	thrusting	thrust	(have) thrust

IRREGULAR VERBS WITH THE SAME PAST AND PAST PARTICIPLE

Present	Present Participle	Past	Past Participle
bind	binding	bound	(have) bound
bring	bringing	brought	(have) brought
build	building	built	(have) built
buy	buying	bought	(have) bought
catch	catching	caught	(have) caught
cling	clinging	clung	(have) clung
creep	creeping	crept	(have) crept
fight	fighting	fought	(have) fought
find	finding	found	(have) found
fling	flinging	flung	(have) flung
get	getting	got	(have) got *or* (have) gotten
grind	grinding	ground	(have) ground
hang	hanging	hung	(have) hung
hold	holding	held	(have) held
keep	keeping	kept	(have) kept
lay	laying	laid	(have) laid
lead	leading	led	(have) led
leave	leaving	left	(have) left
lend	lending	lent	(have) lent
lose	losing	lost	(have) lost
pay	paying	paid	(have) paid
say	saying	said	(have) said
seek	seeking	sought	(have) sought
sell	selling	sold	(have) sold
send	sending	sent	(have) sent
shine	shining	shone *or* shined	(have) shone *or* (have) shined
sit	sitting	sat	(have) sat

sleep	sleeping	slept	(have) slept
spend	spending	spent	(have) spent
spin	spinning	spun	(have) spun
stand	standing	stood	(have) stood
stick	sticking	stuck	(have) stuck
sting	stinging	stung	(have) stung
strike	striking	struck	(have) struck
swing	swinging	swung	(have) swung
teach	teaching	taught	(have) taught
win	winning	won	(have) won
wind	winding	wound	(have) wound
wring	wringing	wrung	(have) wrung

IRREGULAR VERBS THAT CHANGE IN OTHER WAYS

Present	Present Participle	Past	Past Participle
arise	arising	arose	(have) arisen
bear	bearing	bore	(have) borne
beat	beating	beat	(have) beaten *or* (have) beat
become	becoming	became	(have) become
begin	beginning	began	(have) begun
bite	biting	bit	(have) bitten
blow	blowing	blew	(have) blown
break	breaking	broke	(have) broken
choose	choosing	chose	(have) chosen
come	coming	came	(have) come
do	doing	did	(have) done
draw	drawing	drew	(have) drawn
drink	drinking	drank	(have) drunk
drive	driving	drove	(have) driven
eat	eating	ate	(have) eaten
fall	falling	fell	(have) fallen
fly	flying	flew	(have) flown
forget	forgetting	forgot	(have) forgotten *or* (have) forgot
freeze	freezing	froze	(have) frozen
give	giving	gave	(have) given
go	going	went	(have) gone
grow	growing	grew	(have) grown

169

know	knowing	knew	(have) known
lie	lying	lay	(have) lain
ride	riding	rode	(have) ridden
ring	ringing	rang	(have) rung
rise	rising	rose	(have) risen
run	running	ran	(have) run
see	seeing	saw	(have) seen
shake	shaking	shook	(have) shaken
shrink	shrinking	shrank	(have) shrunk
sing	singing	sang	(have) sung
sink	sinking	sank	(have) sunk
slay	slaying	slew	(have) slain
speak	speaking	spoke	(have) spoken
spring	springing	sprang	(have) sprung
steal	stealing	stole	(have) stolen
stride	striding	strode	(have) stridden
strive	striving	strove	(have) striven
swear	swearing	swore	(have) sworn
swim	swimming	swam	(have) swum
take	taking	took	(have) taken
tear	tearing	tore	(have) torn
throw	throwing	threw	(have) thrown
wear	wearing	wore	(have) worn
weave	weaving	wove	(have) woven *or* (have) wove
write	writing	wrote	(have) written

When you have a question about the correct form of an irregular verb, consult a dictionary.

EXERCISE C: Learning the Principal Parts of Irregular Verbs. Write the present participle, the past, and the past participle of each verb.

EXAMPLE: become
    becoming became become

1. break	6. lay	11. fight	16. bind
2. put	7. spread	12. eat	17. arise
3. ring	8. tear	13. swing	18. grind
4. teach	9. bite	14. shake	19. shine
5. choose	10. shut	15. sing	20. stride

170

EXERCISE D: Choosing the Correct Forms of Irregular Verbs. Choose the correct form of the verb in parentheses.

1. It must have (creeped, crept) into the house last night.
2. I have (written, wrote) a note for Bob to take to school.
3. The debris had been (flung, flinged) onto the shore.
4. A Dalmatian (sprang, sprung) into the limousine.
5. The apparition supposedly had (ridden, rode) a black horse.
6. I have (come, came) to deliver a message.
7. Carol had (broke, broken) her promise again.
8. He has always (thrown, throwed) a ball very well.
9. The horse had stumbled, (fallen, fell), and thrown its rider to the ground.
10. I have (blowed, blown) all the candles out with one breath.
11. She has (went, gone) into town for the afternoon.
12. He had (eaten, ate) before we went to the game.
13. As the heat intensified, the windows (busted, burst).
14. You have (wore, worn) those jeans all week.
15. You should have (brung, brought) cooler clothes.
16. I (bid, bidded) several times at the auction.
17. The concert (began, begun) before everyone had arrived.
18. She had (tore, torn) a piece of cloth and wrapped his hand.
19. Cristina (sang, sung) alto in the church choir.
20. He had (bore, borne) the pain without a murmur.
21. The icy rain (freezed, froze) on the Eskimos' parkas.
22. Uncle Marty had (gave, given) all the candy away.
23. She had (ran, run) in the relay race last year.
24. Karen (catched, caught) the ball.
25. He had (taken, took) a compass but forgot to consult it.
26. Closing her eyes, Gwen (drank, drunk) the bitter tonic.
27. Carl has (striven, strove) to be the best salesperson.
28. The chimpanzees (swinged, swung) from the branches.
29. Susan (grew, growed) two inches this year.
30. They had (spoken, spoke) out of turn.
31. If I had (knew, known) the meeting would be this unorganized, I wouldn't have come.
32. She (saw, seen) something that made her very angry.
33. He had already (bit, bitten) into the baked Alaska before he realized it was made with shaving cream.
34. In *Les Miserables* the major character was sent to prison because he had (stole, stolen) a loaf of bread.

35. Meg (shook, shaked) the stick in the air to make her point clear to us.
36. Ted was perturbed by his inability to have (growed, grown) a full beard by the week's end.
37. Pat's father had (flew, flown) home from Phoenix to be with his son.
38. Chris has (swore, sworn) never to return to that movie theater again.
39. Helen (winded, wound) a sheet around herself and went to the costume party as a mummy.
40. She had (rose, risen) to speak her mind at the assembly.
41. I (did, done) exactly what I was asked to do.
42. The survivor (clinged, clung) to the rubber rafts.
43. Her wool sweater had (shrank, shrunk) after it was washed the third time.
44. In *Beowulf* the hideous monster Grendel sneaked into the hall and (slayed, slew) the sleeping warriors.
45. She has (driven, drove) the same car for ten years.
46. He (swam, swum) ten laps before climbing slowly out of the pool.
47. She (wrang, wrung) the truth from the suspect by making every imaginable threat.
48. The butler (rang, rung) a tiny crystal dinner bell.
49. A butterfly had (flew, flown) too near the spider's web.
50. Mr. Vance (taught, teached) a health class and four chemistry classes last year.

EXERCISE E: Supplying the Correct Forms of Irregular Verbs. Write the appropriate past or past participle for each verb in parentheses.

EXAMPLE: Around 1500, clockmakers' invention of the mainspring (bring) about a new kind of timepiece—the watch.

brought

   (1) The first watches, about five inches round and three inches thick, were not easily (wear). (2) Some people (hang) them from belts. (3) The wealthy (let) their servants carry around these cumbersome timepieces. (4) Like the clocks of the period, these watches (strike) the hour. (5) However, the wearer never (know) the exact time, for early watches had only

one hand—the hour hand. (6) About 1675 the English (begin) the custom of carrying watches in vest pockets. (7) By 1710 the first wristwatches were being (sell) in Switzerland. (8) But few people (choose) to wear wristwatches until the twentieth century. (9) As late as 1914, Swiss consumers (see) the wristwatch as a passing fad. (10) Today, about eighty million watches are (buy) every year throughout the world.

Verb Conjugation

The *conjugation* of a verb presents all its different forms.

A conjugation is a complete list of the singular and plural forms of a verb in a particular tense.

The singular forms of a verb correspond to the singular personal pronouns *(I, you, he, she, it)*, and the plural forms correspond to the plural personal pronouns *(we, you, they)*.

The charts that follow conjugate the irregular verb *go.* To conjugate a verb, you need the principal parts: the present *(go)*, the present participle *(going)*, the past *(went)*, and the past participle *(gone)*. You also need various helping verbs such as *have, has, will,* and so on.

The chart below conjugates the verb *go* in its basic forms. Notice that only three principal parts—the present, the past, and the past participle—are used to conjugate all six of the basic forms.

CONJUGATION OF THE BASIC FORMS OF *GO*		
Present	**Singular**	**Plural**
First Person	I go	we go
Second Person	you go	you go
Third Person	he, she, it goes	they go
Past		
First Person	I went	we went
Second Person	you went	you went
Third Person	he, she, it went	they went

Future

First Person	I will go	we will go
Second Person	you will go	you will go
Third Person	he, she, it will go	they will go

Present Perfect

First Person	I have gone	we have gone
Second Person	you have gone	you have gone
Third Person	he, she, it has gone	they have gone

Past Perfect

First Person	I had gone	we had gone
Second Person	you had gone	you had gone
Third Person	he, she, it had gone	they had gone

Future Perfect

First Person	I will have gone	we will have gone
Second Person	you will have gone	you will have gone
Third Person	he, she, it will have gone	they will have gone

Only one principal part, the present progressive, is used in conjugating the six progressive forms.

CONJUGATION OF THE PROGRESSIVE FORMS OF GO		
Present Progressive	**Singular**	**Plural**
First Person	I am going	we are going
Second Person	you are going	you are going
Third Person	he, she, it is going	they are going
Past Progressive		
First Person	I was going	we were going
Second Person	you were going	you were going
Third Person	he, she, it was going	they were going

174

Future Progressive

First Person	I will be going	we will be going
Second Person	you will be going	you will be going
Third Person	he, she, it will be going	they will be going

Present Perfect Progressive

First Person	I have been going	we have been going
Second Person	you have been going	you have been going
Third Person	he, she, it has been going	they have been going

Past Perfect Progressive

First Person	I had been going	we had been going
Second Person	you had been going	you had been going
Third Person	he, she, it had been going	they had been going

Future Perfect Progressive

First Person	I will have been going	we will have been going
Second Person	you will have been going	you will have been going
Third Person	he, she, it will have been going	they will have been going

The chart at the top of the next page provides a conjugation of the emphatic forms of *go.* Remember that the emphatic exists only for the present and past tenses.

Notice that only one principal part, the present, is used to conjugate the emphatic forms. Notice also that only three helping verbs—*do, does,* and *did*—are used in the conjugation of the emphatic forms. *Do* and *does* are used for the present emphatic; *did* is used for the past emphatic.

175

CONJUGATION OF THE EMPHATIC FORMS OF *GO*		
Present Emphatic	**Singular**	**Plural**
First Person	I do go	we do go
Second Person	you do go	you do go
Third Person	he, she, it does go	they do go
Past Emphatic		
First Person	I did go	we did go
Second Person	you did go	you did go
Third Person	he, she, it did go	they did go

NOTE ABOUT *BE:* The present participle of *be* is *being*. The past participle is *been*. The present and the past depend on the subject and tense of the verb.

PRESENT:	I am	we are
	you are	you are
	he, she, it is	they are
PAST:	I was	we were
	you were	you were
	he, she, it was	they were
FUTURE:	I will be	we will be
	you will be	you will be
	he, she, it will be	they will be

EXERCISE F: Conjugating Verbs. Conjugate the verbs below in their basic, progressive, and emphatic forms.

1. plan   2. break

DEVELOPING WRITING SKILLS: Using Different Tenses.
Use each verb in a sentence of your own.

EXAMPLE: Future perfect of *finish*
                        I will have finished the project by tomorrow.

176

1. Past perfect of *borrow*
2. Present progressive of *land*
3. Future perfect of *spring*
4. Future perfect progressive of *fly*
5. Present of *burst*
6. Past progressive of *intend*
7. Present of *wear*
8. Past emphatic of *try*
9. Future of *investigate*
10. Present progressive of *swim*
11. Past of *lose*
12. Present emphatic of *surrender*
13. Future of *pierce*
14. Past perfect progressive of *study*
15. Past of *sell*
16. Future perfect progressive of *paint*
17. Future of *exercise*
18. Present perfect of *succeed*
19. Present of *hope*
20. Present emphatic of *wish*

The Correct Use of Tenses 6.2

The basic, progressive, and emphatic forms of the six tenses show time within one of three general categories: present, past, and future. This section will explain how each verb form has a specific use that distinguishes it from the other forms.

Present, Past, and Future Time

Good usage depends on an understanding of how each form works within its general category of time to express meaning.

Uses of Tense in Present Time. Three different forms can be used to express present time.

The three forms of the present tense show present actions or conditions as well as various continuous actions or conditions.

The chart below gives an example of each of these forms.

FORMS EXPRESSING PRESENT TIME	
Present	I draw.
Present Progressive	I am drawing.
Present Emphatic	I do draw.

The main uses of the basic form of the present tense are shown in the chart below.

USES OF THE PRESENT
Present action: The vendor *shouts* to a potential customer.
Present condition: My cold *is* contagious.
Regularly occurring action: They frequently *drive* to New Hampshire.
Regularly occurring condition: This road *is* slippery in winter.
Constant action: Fish *breathe* through gills.
Constant condition: Human beings *are* primates.

The present may also be used to express historical events. This use of the present, called the *historical present,* is occasionally used in narration to make past actions or conditions come to life.

THE HISTORICAL PRESENT
Past action expressed in historical present: The events of July 4, 1776, *bring* to fulfillment the political ideals of the Enlightenment.
Past condition expressed in historical present: After the defeat of Antony and Cleopatra, Octavian *is* the undisputed leader.

A similar use of the present is called the *critical present.* It is most often used to discuss deceased authors and their literary achievements.

THE CRITICAL PRESENT
Action expressed in critical present: Dame Agatha Christie *writes* with a skill that *makes* her stories classics.
Condition expressed in critical present: In addition to his novels, Thomas Hardy *is* the author of eight volumes of poetry.

The present progressive is used to show a continuing action or condition. Notice that the continuing *actions* may be of a long or short duration.

178

USES OF THE PRESENT PROGRESSIVE

Long continuing action: I *am working* on my uncle's farm this summer.

Short continuing action: I *am washing* the dishes.

Continuing condition: Meg *is being* very helpful.

The four main uses of the present emphatic are shown in the next chart.

USES OF THE PRESENT EMPHATIC

Emphasizing a statement: I *do intend* to accept her generous offer.

Denying a contrary assertion: No, he *does* not *have* the keys.

Asking a question: Do you *supply* the equipment?

Making a sentence negative: She *does* not *have* our permission.

Uses of Tense in Past Time. There are seven verb forms that express past actions or conditions.

The seven forms that express past time show actions and conditions beginning in the past.

The following chart provides examples of each of these seven forms.

FORMS EXPRESSING PAST TIME

Past	I drew.
Present Perfect	I have drawn.
Past Perfect	I had drawn.
Past Progressive	I was drawing.
Present Perfect Progressive	I have been drawing.
Past Perfect Progressive	I had been drawing.
Past Emphatic	I did draw.

The uses of the most common form, the past, are shown in the chart at the top of the next page.

USES OF THE PAST
Completed action: They *halted* work on the new bridge.
Completed condition: Several apartments *were* available.

Notice in the chart above that the time of the action or the condition could be changed from indefinite to definite if such words as *last week* or *yesterday* were added to the sentences.

The present perfect, the uses of which are illustrated in the next chart, always expresses indefinite time; such words as *last week* or *yesterday* cannot be added to a verb in the present perfect to make it definite. Notice in the chart that the present perfect can be used to show action or conditions continuing from the past to the present.

USES OF THE PRESENT PERFECT
Completed action (indefinite time): They *have antagonized* us.
Completed condition (indefinite time): I *have been* here before.
Action continuing to present: It *has rained* intermittently for two days now.
Condition continuing to present: I *have felt* tired all day.

The past perfect expresses a past action or condition that took place before another.

USES OF THE PAST PERFECT
Action completed before another past action: Perhaps the nomadic hunters *had drawn* in the dirt before they drew on the cave walls.
Condition completed before another past condition: Rhoda *had been* a photographer until she *became* ill.

The uses of the three progressive forms that express past time are shown in the chart at the top of the next page. Notice that the present perfect progressive and the past perfect progressive are used only to show continuing actions, not conditions.

180

USES OF THE PROGRESSIVE FORMS THAT EXPRESS PAST TIME	
Past Progressive	*Long continuing action in the past:* She *was going* to law school that year.
	Short continuing action in the past: I *was talking* to Rose when you tried to call.
	Continuous condition in the past: I *was being* honest when I said I was sorry about the incident.
Present Perfect Progressive	*Action continuing to the present:* Edith *has been adding* more rocks and minerals to her collection.
Past Perfect Progressive	*Continuing action interrupted by another:* He *had been dreaming* of victory until reality became inescapable.

The uses of the past emphatic are shown below.

USES OF THE PAST EMPHATIC
Emphasizing a statement: The cactus *did grow* without any water.
Denying a contrary assertion: But I *did leave* you a message!
Asking a question: When *did* the United States *recognize* China?
Making a sentence negative: He *did* not *read* the memorandum.

Use of Tense in Future Time. There are four forms that can express future time.

The four forms that express future time show future actions or conditions.

The chart below gives example of these four forms.

FORMS EXPRESSING FUTURE TIME	
Future	I will draw.
Future Perfect	I will have drawn.
Future Progressive	I will be drawing.
Future Perfect Progressive	I will have been drawing.

The following chart shows the uses of the future and the future perfect.

USES OF THE FUTURE AND FUTURE PERFECT	
Future	*Future action:* I *will exercise* in the morning.
	Future condition: I *will be* late for dinner.
Future Perfect	*Future action completed before another:* I *will have run* a mile by the time you arrive.
	Future condition completed before another: The orchestra *will have been* on tour for a month before the new concert season begins.

Notice in the next chart that the future progressive and the future perfect progressive are used only to express future actions, not conditions.

USES OF THE PROGRESSIVE FORMS THAT EXPRESS FUTURE TIME	
Future Progressive	*Continuing future action:* Rita *will be studying* all weekend.
Future Perfect Progressive	*Continuous future action completed before another:* Sharon *will have been sculpting* for ten years before she gives her exhibit.

NOTE ABOUT EXPRESSING FUTURE TIME WITH THE PRESENT TENSE: The basic form of the present and the present progressive are often used with other words to express future time.

EXAMPLES: A new restaurant *opens* in town next weekend.

That ship *is sailing* tomorrow for Hawaii.

EXERCISE A: Identifying the Uses of Tense in Present Time. Identify the use of the verb in each sentence, using the labels in the charts on pages 178–181.

1. These tight shoes hurt my feet.
2. Diane is doing remarkably well on her diet.
3. Tolstoy is the author of many short stories.

4. The sky is becoming overcast.
5. Halley's comet returns every seventy-six years.
6. I am sometimes forgetful.
7. A flight from Chicago does arrive this afternoon.
8. Jim is in Detroit.
9. My father is building a log cabin in the mountains.
10. Carolyn reads at least one novel a week.

EXERCISE B: Using Tense in Past Time. Write the indicated form of each verb in parentheses.

1. I (ask—*past*) you to deliver these packages.
2. Our school (adopt—*present perfect*) the honor system.
3. The students (discuss—*past progressive*) the new film.
4. His hair (be—*present perfect*) white for many years.
5. Alexander Dumas (write—*past perfect*) plays before he began writing *The Three Musketeers.*
6. John (study—*present perfect progressive*) more diligently this semester.
7. The angry customer (insist—*past emphatic*) on a refund.
8. Someone (leave—*past perfect*) a package on his desk.
9. Ricky (travel—*present perfect*) throughout Europe.
10. Joan (find—*past*) the keys behind the desk.

EXERCISE C: Using Tense in Future Time. Choose the correct verb in parentheses to complete each sentence.

1. By nightfall I (will have planted, will have been planting) over a hundred disease-resistant elms.
2. I (will be, will have been) disappointed if all my friends are away for the summer.
3. If Ms. Ramon teaches this class, her enthusiasm (will motivate, will have motivated) the students.
4. No pets (will have been allowed, will be allowed) in this new condominium.
5. Ginger (will be, will have been) in Brazil next summer.
6. Soon they (will be exploring, will have been exploring) the coast of Antarctica for nearly a month.
7. Tomorrow I (will fly, will have flown) to London.
8. By the time we stop, we (will have been driving, will be driving) over ten hours.

9. The coach told us that we (will practice, will have practiced) on Sunday.
10. The polls can not say for sure who (will have won, will win) the election.

Sequence of Tenses

A sentence with more than one verb must be consistent in its time sequence.

When showing a sequence of events, do not shift tenses unnecessarily.

It is, however, sometimes necessary to shift tenses, especially when a sentence is complex or compound-complex. The tense of the main verb often determines the tense of the subordinate verb. Moreover, the form of a participle or infinitive often depends on the tense of the main verb in the sentence.

Verbs in Subordinate Clauses. Frequently it is necessary to look at the tense of the main verb in a sentence before deciding the tense of the verb in the subordinate clause.

The tense of a verb in a subordinate clause should follow logically from the tense of the main verb.

As you study the combinations of tenses in the charts that follow, notice that the choice of tenses affects the logical relationship between the events that are being expressed. Some combinations indicate that the events are *simultaneous*—meaning that they occur at the same time. Other combinations indicate that the events are *sequential*—meaning that one event occurs before or after the other.

SEQUENCE OF TENSES		
MAIN VERB IN PRESENT		
Main Verb	**Subordinate Verb**	**Meaning**
I *understand* . . .	PRESENT that he *writes* novels. PRESENT PROG that he *is writing* a novel.	Simultaneous events: All events occur in present time.

184

	PRESENT EMPH that he *does write* novels.	
I *understand* . . .	PAST that he *wrote* a novel. PRESENT PERF that he *has written* a novel. PAST PERF that he *had written* a novel. PAST PROG that he *was writing* a novel. PRESENT PERF PROG that he *has been writing* a novel. PAST PERF PROG that he *had been writing* a novel. PAST EMPH that he *did write* a novel.	Sequential events: The writing comes before the understanding.
I *understand* . . .	FUTURE that he *will write* a novel. FUTURE PERF that he *will have* *written* a novel. FUTURE PROG that he *will be writing* a novel. FUTURE PERF PROG that he *will have been* *writing* a novel.	Sequential events: The understanding comes before the writing.

MAIN VERB IN PAST

	PAST that he *wrote* a novel. PAST PROG that he *was writing* a novel	Simultaneous events: All events take place in past time.
I *understood* . . .		

	PAST EMPH that he *did write* a novel.	
I *understood* . . .	PAST PERF that he *had written* a novel. PAST PERF PROG that he *had been writing* a novel.	Sequential events: The writing came before the understanding.
MAIN VERB IN FUTURE		
I *will understand* . . .	PRESENT if he *writes* a novel. PRESENT PROG if he *is writing* a novel. PRESENT EMPH if he *does write* a novel.	Simultaneous events: All events take place in future time.
I *will understand* . . .	PAST if he *wrote* a novel. PRESENT PERF if he *has written* a novel. PRESENT PERF PROG if he *has been writing* a novel. PAST EMPH if he *did write* a novel.	Sequential events: The writing comes before the understanding.

When the main verb in a sentence is in one of the perfect or progressive forms, the verb in the subordinate clause will usually be in the present or past tense. The chart at the top of the next page indicates which forms of a main verb usually require a subordinate verb in the present and which forms of a main verb usually require a subordinate verb in the past.

There are, however, exceptions to this generalization. Therefore, instead of relying on hard-and-fast rules, you should rely on the meaning of the sentence to determine the tense of the verb in the subordinate clause. The tense of the subordinate verb should always follow logically from the tense of the verb in the main clause.

186

If the Main Verb Is . . .	Then the Subordinate Verb Should Usually Be . . .
Present Progressive Present Perfect Progressive Future Perfect Future Progressive Future Perfect Progressive	Present
Present Perfect Past Progressive Past Perfect Past Perfect Progressive	Past

EXAMPLES: They *are studying* hard before they *take* the test.
PRESENT PROG   PRESENT

I *have been studying* because exams *begin* soon.
PRESENT PERF PROG   PRESENT

They *will have arrived* by the time we *finish*.
FUTURE PERF   PRESENT

She *will be wearing* a cast until the fracture *heals*.
FUTURE PROG   PRESENT

I *will have been driving* two days before I *arrive*.
FUTURE PERF PROG   PRESENT

He *has cashed* the check that he *received*.
PRESENT PERF   PAST

She *was dressing* casually wherever she *went*.
PAST PROG   PAST

The cows *had sensed* the rain before it *began*.
PAST PERF   PAST

She *had been watering* the plants when we *were* away.
PAST PERF PROG   PAST

Rather than memorizing rules for the sequence of tenses, learn to rely on logic as you construct your own sentences.

NOTE ABOUT *WOULD HAVE:* In a subordinate clause beginning with *if*, do not repeat the helping verbs *would have* when the main verb also contains *would have*. As you can see from the examples, the verb in the subordinate clause should be changed to the past perfect.

EXAMPLE: If he *would have cooked* the leg of lamb properly, it *would have been* pink and juicy rather than black and burnt.

If he *had cooked* the leg of lamb properly, it *would have been* pink and juicy rather than black and burnt.

Time Sequence with Participles and Infinitives. Frequently the form of a participle or infinitive determines whether the events are simultaneous or sequential. Participles can be present *(seeing)*, past *(seen)*, or perfect *(having seen)*. Infinitives can be present *(to see)* or perfect *(to have seen)*.

The form of a participle or infinitive should set up a logical time sequence in relation to a verb in the same clause or sentence.

To show simultaneous events, you will generally need to use the present participle or the present infinitive, whether the main verb is present, past, or future.

SIMULTANEOUS EVENTS	
In Present Time	PRESENT PRESENT *Seeing* the results, she *laughs.* PRESENT PRESENT He *needs to confirm* the results.
In Past Time	PRESENT PAST *Seeing* the results, she *laughed.* PAST PRESENT He *needed to confirm* the results.
In Future Time	PRESENT FUTURE *Seeing* the results, she *will laugh.* FUTURE PRESENT He *will need to confirm* the results.

To show sequential events, you will generally need to use the perfect form of the participle or the infinitive, regardless of the tense of the main verb.

188

SEQUENTIAL EVENTS	
In Present Time	PERFECT PRESENT PROG *Having seen* the results, she *is laughing.* (The seeing comes before the laughing.)
	PRESENT PERFECT He *is* fortunate *to have worked* with you. (The working comes before the being fortunate.)
In Past Time	PERFECT PAST *Having seen* the results, she *laughed.* (The seeing came before the laughing.)
	PAST PERFECT He *was* fortunate *to have worked* with you. (The working came before the being fortunate.)
Spanning Past and Future Time	PERFECT FUTURE *Having seen* her work, I *will recommend* her. (The seeing comes before the recommending.)
	FUTURE PERFECT He *will be* fortunate *to have worked* with you. (The working comes before the being fortunate.)

EXERCISE D: Using the Correct Forms of Subordinate Verbs, Participles, and Infinitives. Rewrite each sentence, following the instructions in parentheses.

1. Our captain chose John for the team. (Add a phrase containing the perfect participle of *see.*)
2. Eventually he wrote to his congresswoman. (Add a subordinate clause containing the past perfect of *try.*)
3. My plan is that I will leave before the evening train departs. (Change *will leave* to a perfect infinitive.)
4. She is afraid. (Add a subordinate clause containing the present perfect of *hear.*)
5. Joel liked watching the storm clouds gather. (Change *watching* to a present infinitive.)
6. The ballerina retired gracefully. (Add a phrase containing the perfect participle of *dance.*)
7. Lisa is working industriously at her new job as a law clerk in the city. (Add a subordinate clause containing the present of *earn.*)

8. She was glad she had gained experience in the field of electronics. (Change *gained* to a perfect infinitive.)
9. The conductor listened to the cacophony in angry silence. (Add a phrase containing the perfect participle of *expect*.)
10. You will notice the difference. (Add a subordinate clause containing the present perfect of *observe*.)

EXERCISE E: Correcting Errors in Tense. Rewrite the following paragraph, correcting unnecessary shifts in tense.

(1) General Custer was not quite the honorable soldier that some historians would like us to have believed. (2) Shortly after he returned to duty after years of suspension from the army—the army has found him guilty of abandoning his men and having deserters shot without trials—he and General Elliott lead their troops against a Cheyenne village. (3) When it has become clear that the warriors would retaliate, Custer retreated, not waiting for Elliott and Elliott's soldiers who, as a result, will all die. (4) Just before the end of his life, Custer was receiving permission to explore the possibility of establishing a military post in the Black Hills. (5) The Northern Plains tribes were owning the territory, which according to rumor is rich in gold. (6) With him Custer takes geologists who did find this precious metal. (7) Soon after, hordes of prospectors have invaded the land, violating the treaty. (8) The Indians had objected and the government was sending soldiers, supposedly to force the miners' departure. (9) However, both miners and soldiers remained on the land, and in 1876 Custer is disobeying orders by taking on a scouting venture the Seventh Cavalry, which is under the command of another general, and a reporter who was supposed to be making Custer a newspaper hero. (10) The rest is common knowledge; Custer has led his troops to a bloody defeat at Little Big Horn.

Modifiers That Help Clarify Tense

The time expressed by a verb can often be clarified by adverbs such as *always* or *frequently* and phrases such as *last week* or *now and then*.

Use modifiers when they can help clarify tense.

EXAMPLES: We walk to school *every day.*

My brothers cut the grass *once a week.*

EXERCISE F: Using Modifiers to Improve Meaning. Rewrite each sentence by adding a modifier that indicates time.

1. My father is going on a business trip.
2. Sally has invited us to come to her party.
3. Our camping trips are very exciting.
4. The study showed that everyone needs a vacation.
5. The climate in this part of the country is very cold.
6. My sister cuts the grass.
7. Jim cleaned out the garage.
8. Elderly people get colds in the summer.
9. Mr. Walsh walks his dog past my house.
10. My grandparents come to visit us.

DEVELOPING WRITING SKILLS: Using the Correct Tense in Your Writing. Begin or complete each sentence with your own words.

1. We were aware that _____.
2. Having announced the results, the teacher _____.
3. _____, the victors celebrated in style.
4. He would have taken your advice if _____.
5. By the time she gets here, _____.
6. Having heard the arguments, the judge _____.
7. Hearing her name called, Beth _____.
8. _____, everyone resumed work.
9. We finished our homework only after _____.
10. Watching the fireworks, he _____.

The Subjunctive Mood 6.3

There are three *moods* or ways in which a verb can express an action or condition: indicative, imperative, and subjunctive. The *indicative* mood, the most common, is used to make factual statements ("Karl *is* helpful.") and to ask questions ("*Is* Karl helpful?"). The imperative mood is limited to sentences that give orders or directions ("*Be* helpful."). This section will focus on the correct uses of the subjunctive mood.

The Correct Use of the Subjunctive Mood

There are two important differences between verbs in the subjunctive mood and those in the indicative mood. First, in the present tense, third-person singular verbs in the subjunctive mood do not have the usual *-s* or *-es* ending. Second, the subjunctive mood of *be* in the present tense is *be,* and in the past tense it is *were,* regardless of the subject.

Indicative Mood	Subjunctive Mood
He *listens* to me.	I suggest that he *listen* to me.
They *are* ready.	He insists that they *be* ready.
She *was* impatient.	If she *were* impatient, she would not be suited for this work.

There are two general uses of the subjunctive mood.

Use the subjunctive mood (1) in clauses beginning with *if* or *that* to express an idea contrary to fact or (2) in clauses beginning with *that* to express a request, a demand, or a proposal.

To use the subjunctive mood correctly, you must remember to check the *if* and *that* clauses in your sentences.

Expressing Ideas Contrary to Fact. Ideas contrary to fact are most commonly expressed as wishes or conditions. Using the subjunctive mood in these situations helps to show that the idea expressed is not now true and may never be true.

EXAMPLE: He wishes that he *were* more likable.

One impossible condition of employment was that she *be* ready to travel at any time.

He talks about art as if he *were* an expert.

Expressing Requests, Demands, and Proposals. Even though this use of the subjunctive suggests that the ideas expressed are not now true, it indicates that they could or should be true in the future. Most verbs that make a request, a demand, or a proposal are usually followed by a *that* clause, which will generally contain a verb in the subjunctive mood.

VERBS OFTEN FOLLOWED BY *THAT* CLAUSES WITH SUBJUNCTIVE VERBS			
ask	insist	prefer	request
demand	move	propose	require
determine	order	recommend	suggest

REQUEST: She requests that we *be* on time for the test.

DEMAND: It is required that each student *wear* a uniform.

PROPOSAL: He proposed that a motion *be* made to adjourn.

EXERCISE A: Using the Subjunctive Mood. Rewrite each sentence, changing the verb that should be in the subjunctive mood to the subjunctive mood.

EXAMPLE: She wished that she was rich.

She wished that she were rich.

1. He wishes that he was a few inches taller.
2. The judge insists that the reporter remains outside.
3. I prefer that she waits in the lobby.
4. They stared at me as if I was a ghost.
5. If I was offended, I would certainly not be smiling.
6. He does not merely ask that a student attends his class.
7. Adam reacted as if he was being paid a compliment.
8. Every blouse on the rack looked as if it was second-hand.
9. I move that the minutes from the meeting are read.
10. It is necessary that you are more patient.

Auxiliary Verbs That Help Express the Subjunctive Mood

Since certain helping verbs suggest conditions contrary to fact, they can often be used in place of the subjunctive mood.

Could, would, or *should* can be used to help a verb express the subjunctive mood.

The sentences on the left in the chart on the next page have the usual subjunctive form of the verb *be: were.* The sentences on the right have been reworded with *could, would,* and *should.*

THE SUBJUNCTIVE MOOD EXPRESSED THROUGH AUXILIARY VERBS	
If the future *were* clear, we'd act decisively.	If the future *could* be clear, we'd act decisively.
If someone *were* to escort her, she would go.	If someone *would* escort her, she would go.
If you *were* to move, would you write to me?	If you *should* move, would you write to me?

EXERCISE B: **Using Auxiliary Verbs to Express the Subjunctive Mood.** Rewrite each sentence, using an auxiliary verb to express the subjunctive mood.

EXAMPLE: He demanded that the ransom be paid.

He demanded that the ransom should be paid.

1. If you were less messy, I would not need to work so hard.
2. This meeting would run more smoothly if he were friendlier.
3. She wishes that Kate were relaxed and comfortable.
4. If Noreen were to invite you, would you attend?
5. The house would be warmer if you were to heat it better.
6. I would go to the library if I were to get home earlier.
7. The car would run better if you were to adjust the engine.
8. If Raul were to get up earlier, he would not be late.
9. I could see more clearly if I were to clean my glasses.
10. If you were to get the job, I would drive you to work.

DEVELOPING WRITING SKILLS: **Writing Sentences Using the Subjunctive Mood.** Write a sentence using each item, making sure each sentence contains a verb in the subjunctive mood.

1. require that   3. as if
2. I suggest   4. that she be

6.4 Voice

This section discusses a characteristic of verbs called *voice*.

Voice is the form of a verb that shows whether the subject is performing the action.

In English there are two voices: *active* and *passive.* Only action verbs can indicate voice; linking verbs can not.

Active and Passive Voice

If the subject of a verb performs the action, the verb is active; if the subject receives the action, the verb is passive.

Active Voice. Any action verb can be in the active voice. The action verb may be transitive (that is, it may have a direct object) or intransitive (without a direct object).

A verb is active if its subject performs the action.

In both examples below, the subjects perform the action. In the first example, the verb *manipulated* is transitive; *strings* is the direct object which receives the action. In the second example, the verb *gathered* is intransitive; it has no direct object.

ACTIVE VOICE: The puppeteer *manipulated* the strings.

Dead leaves *gathered* in the garden.

Passive Voice. Most action verbs can also be passive.

A verb is passive if its action is performed upon the subject.

In the following examples, the subjects are the receivers of the action. The first example names the performer, the puppeteer, but *puppeteer* is now the object of the preposition *by* instead of the subject. In the second example, no performer of the action is mentioned.

PASSIVE VOICE: The strings *were manipulated* by the puppeteer.

The dead leaves *were gathered* into large bags.

A passive verb is always a verb phrase made from a form of *be* plus the past participle of a transitive verb. The tense of the helping verb *be* determines the tense of a passive verb. The chart on the next page provides a short conjugation in the pas-

195

sive voice of the verb *believe* in the three moods. Notice in the chart that there are only two progressive forms and no emphatic form.

THE VERB *BELIEVE* IN THE PASSIVE VOICE	
Present Indicative	he is believed
Past Indicative	he was believed
Future Indicative	he will be believed
Present Perfect Indicative	he has been believed
Past Perfect Indicative	he had been believed
Future Perfect Indicative	he will have been believed
Present Progressive Indicative	he is being believed
Past Progressive Indicative	he was being believed
Present Imperative	(you) be believed
Present Subjunctive	(if) he be believed
Past Subjunctive	(if) he were believed

EXERCISE A: Distinguishing Between the Active and Passive Voice. Identify each verb as *active* or *passive*.

1. The winning essays were selected for their originality and lucidity.
2. Our bread truck delivers as quickly as possible.
3. Murphy has been chosen for the task.
4. Carefully he removed the glass from the picture window.
5. They prepared for any eventuality.
6. Fry the eggs on one side only.
7. The last sentence in the contract has been reworded.
8. Formal gowns will be worn at the dance.
9. My reflection stared back at me from the mirror.
10. The dog was being rewarded for his quick response.
11. She threw a handful of herbs into the pot.
12. Hundreds of applications were received.
13. His numerous complaints are being ignored.
14. These pants have shrunk at least two sizes.
15. A single guppy energetically swam around the large tank.
16. Pools of water were lying beneath the broken spouts.
17. The tigers will have been fed by noon.

196

18. Kay's seeming indifference is misconstrued by her friends.
19. They discussed their views with the President.
20. A cold compress was quickly applied to the wound.

EXERCISE B: Forming the Tenses of Passive Verbs.
Conjugate each verb in the passive voice, using the first eight entries in the chart on page 196 as your model.

1. deliver (with *it*)
2. praise (with *you*)
3. nominate (with *I*)
4. alert (with *they*)

Using Active and Passive Voice

As soon as you can distinguish between the active and passive voice, you can use this knowledge to improve your own writing. Most good writers prefer the active to the passive voice.

Use the active voice whenever possible.

The active voice is usually more direct and economical. The first sentence below is shorter and more direct than the other.

ACTIVE VOICE: Debbie *repaired* the dripping faucet.

PASSIVE VOICE: The dripping faucet *was repaired* by Debbie.

The passive voice has two important uses in English.

Use the passive voice to emphasize the receiver of an action rather than the performer of an action.

Use the passive voice to point out the receiver of an action whenever the performer is not important or not easily identified.

RECEIVER EMPHASIZED: Lori *was mystified* by the message.

PERFORMER UNKNOWN: A ransom note *was tacked* to the door.

PERFORMER UNIMPORTANT: The potholes *will be repaired* soon.

EXERCISE C: Using the Active Voice. Rewrite each of the ten sentences in Exercise A that have verbs in the passive voice. Change or add words as necessary in order to put each verb into the active voice.

EXERCISE D: Correcting Unnecessary Use of the Passive Voice. Rewrite the following paragraph, changing at least five uses of the passive to active.

(1) He had no time left to wonder why he had forced himself to take a course in public speaking. (2) The summation of the student whose name alphabetically preceded his own was listened to by Ben, standing in the wings of the auditorium. (3) The necessary organizational skills had been given to Ben by three months of practice in the classroom. (4) But today the old symptoms of fear returned. (5) Now, without waiting for his name to be called, Ben walked onto the stage. (6) The neatly written index cards were carefully placed on the podium's solid wooden surface, the microphone was adjusted, and he looked out at the sea of faces. (7) A few minutes later, when his speech was concluded, Ben gathered his notes and prepared to walk from the stage. (8) He thought he was being reproached by the audience through their absolute silence. (9) Then the clapping was begun by one person, and suddenly he was washed by waves of applause. (10) Lingering at the podium for a moment, Ben allowed himself to receive their recognition.

DEVELOPING WRITING SKILLS: Using the Active and Passive Voice in Writing. Describe an incident in which you forced yourself to do something that you were afraid to do. Include two appropriate sentences using the passive voice correctly. Make sure all the other sentences use the active voice.

198

Skills Review and Writing Workshop

Verb Usage

CHECKING YOUR SKILLS

Rewrite the following paragraph correcting all errors in verb usage. Use the active voice throughout.

(1) If you is overweight, you have probably try many diets. (2) No doubt you will have lose and gained many pounds. (3) You could try some of these suggestions if they appealed to you. (4) Pills should not be took. (5) You will be losing weight if you changed your eating habits. (6) Words that will have been avoided are words like MORE. (7) I am supposed to be dieting last week. (8) My friend have been dieting all month. (9) If you was to walk an hour a day, you can lose 30 pounds a year. (10) Being told to clean your plate will not always be the best advice.

USING USAGE SKILLS IN WRITING
Writing the History of a Vehicle.

The skillful writer must use verbs effectively when moving from past time to present time, or to future time. Compare a present-day vehicle with one that might bring children to school 100 years from now.

Prewriting: Think about the way your future vehicle will travel, how it will look, the number of passengers it will hold, and who will operate it.

Writing: Point out the differences between vehicles used now and the future vehicle. Keep in mind that some of the good features of present-day buses, cars, and planes might be lost. Remember that a new product is not necessarily better in every way.

Revising: Check the verbs in your paragraph. Be sure they are grammatically correct and that the majority are in the active voice. Use the check lists on pages 167–170 and the dictionary to check irregular verbs. After you have revised, proofread carefully.

Chapter **7**

Pronoun Usage

At one time in the English language, both nouns and pronouns changed form according to their use in a sentence. For example, the form that a noun would have as a subject was different from the form it would have as a direct object. Today, English relies more on the order of words than on changes in form to indicate a word's use.

Some words, however, still change form to indicate their use. It is pronouns that change form most often. In this chapter you will study the various forms of pronouns and their uses.

7.1 Case

The only parts of speech that have *case* are nouns and pronouns.

Case is the form of a noun or pronoun that indicates its use in a sentence.

The Three Cases

Both nouns and pronouns have three cases, each of which has its own distinctive uses.

The three cases are the nominative, the objective, and the possessive.

The uses of the three cases are listed in the chart at the top of the next page.

200

Case	Use in Sentence
Nominative	Subject of a Verb, Predicate Nominative, or Nominative Absolute
Objective	Direct Object, Indirect Object, Object of a Preposition, Object of a Verbal, or Subject of an Infinitive
Possessive	To Show Ownership

Nouns generally pose no difficulty since they change form only to show possession.

NOMINATIVE: The *clock* had been broken for years.

OBJECTIVE: We tried to fix the *clock*.

POSSESSIVE: The *clock's* hands could not be repaired.

In the first sentence, *clock* is nominative because it is the subject of the verb. In the second sentence, *clock* is objective because it is the object of the infinitive *to fix*. The form changes only in the possessive case when an *'s* is added.

Notice in the following chart that personal pronouns often have different forms for all three cases.

Nominative	Objective	Possessive
I	me	my, mine
you	you	your, yours
he, she, it	him, her, it	his, her, hers, its
we	us	our, ours
they	them	their, theirs

EXERCISE A: Identifying Case. Write the case of each underlined pronoun. Then write its use.

EXAMPLE: The letter was addressed to *me*.

objective (object of a preposition)

1. *My* parents are strict and never waver in their decisions.
2. My friends and I gave *him* a pet snake.
3. His most receptive listeners were *we* and they.
4. Mrs. Stapleton gave *us* an interesting assignment.

5. The company has decided to hire *her.*
6. Visiting the botanical gardens was *his* idea.
7. Their references establish *them* as good credit risks.
8. The caretaker and his wife's cottage was empty, *they* apparently having departed without notice.
9. I will send *them* a map to our new house.
10. This restaurant will not let *us* enter without jackets.
11. The prettiest garden is *theirs.*
12. *You* must accept my apology.
13. *Yours* is not the best answer nor is it the worst.
14. The school awarded *her* a scholarship.
15. The only one who qualified was *she.*
16. *Their* assimilation into the new culture was very quick.
17. Without hesitating, *she* answered all of the questions.
18. The elevator ride left *me* with an upset stomach.
19. *He* dazzled the audience with his magical feats.
20. No one knew how *they* had got inside the building.

The Nominative Case

The nominative case is used when a personal pronoun acts in one of three ways.

Use the nominative case for the subject of a verb, for a predicate nominative, and for the pronoun in a nominative absolute.

These three uses are illustrated in the chart below.

NOMINATIVE PRONOUNS	
As the Subject of a Verb	*I* will paint the ceiling while *she* sands the woodwork.
As a Predicate Nominative	The winners were *he* and *she.*
In a Nominative Absolute	*She* having finished her speech, the audience stood and applauded.

Informal Use of the Predicate Nominative. Formal usage requires that a nominative pronoun follow a linking verb. In informal situations, however, the objective case is often used instead.

INFORMAL: It was *me* who requested the explanation.

FORMAL: It was *I* who requested the explanation.

Nominative Pronouns in Compounds. Be sure that a pronoun used as part of a compound subject or compound predicate nominative is in the nominative case. Check yourself by mentally rewording the sentence.

COMPOUND
SUBJECT: The plumber and *I* inspected the sink.
   (*I* inspected the sink.)

   Her brother and *she* made the dessert.
   (*She* made the dessert.)

COMPOUND
PREDICATE
NOMINATIVE: The fastest eaters were Rudy and *he*.
   (Rudy and *he* were the fastest eaters.)

   Most hurt by the slander were Lin and *I*.
   (Lin and *I* were most hurt by the slander.)

Nominative Pronouns with Appositives. When a pronoun used as a subject or predicate nominative is followed by a noun in apposition, make sure the pronoun is in the nominative case.

SUBJECT: *We* environmentalists are willing to take a stand.

PREDICATE NOMINATIVE: The winners were *we* seniors.

EXERCISE B: Identifying Pronouns in the Nominative Case. Choose the pronoun in the nominative case to complete each sentence. Then write the use of the pronoun.

EXAMPLE: The driver of the car was (he, him).

   he (predicate nominative)

1. Reggie and (she, her) will pay the bill.
2. I think (he, him) will be the best judge.
3. Her complexion shone with good health, (she, her) having thrived in the cold climate.
4. Cautiously, Grace and (them, they) crossed the street.
5. History will prove that the best president was (him, he).
6. (We, Us) taxpayers will have to pay for this project.
7. Never was there a better gymnast than (him, he).
8. The teacher said that he and (I, me) will count the votes.
9. Kevin and (I, me) are going to Maine this weekend.
10. (We, Us) entrepreneurs appreciate the risks in the venture.

EXERCISE C: Using Pronouns in the Nominative Case.
Write a nominative pronoun to complete each sentence. Then write the use of the pronoun.

1. Pat and _____ shoveled the snow from the sidewalk.
2. Did Francisco and _____ organize the block party?
3. The oldest members of the family are grandfather and _____ .
4. People knew J. P. Morgan was a philanthropist, _____ having endowed the Pierpont Morgan Library.
5. _____ are the leading publishers of children's literature.
6. Before signing, _____ read the small print carefully.
7. The worst archers at the field trials were Gary and _____ .
8. Late for a meeting, _____ quickly hailed a taxi.
9. The most diligent students are Edith and _____ .
10. Jacques serves braised veal that _____ gourmets appreciate.

The Objective Case

Objective pronouns are used for any kind of object in a sentence as well as for subjects of infinitives.

Use the objective case for the object of any verb, preposition, or verbal or for the subject of an infinitive.

The chart below illustrates the uses of objective pronouns.

OBJECTIVE PRONOUNS	
Direct Object	A piece of plaster hit *him* on the head.
Indirect Object	My uncle sent *me* a lace fan from Spain.
Object of Preposition	Three little children sat in front of *us* during the ceremony.
Object of Participle	The sharks following *them* were very menacing.
Object of Gerund	Answering *you* will be difficult.
Object of Infinitive	I am obligated to help *her* with the paper work.
Subject of Infinitive	The firm wanted *her* to audit its records.

Objective Pronouns in Compounds. As with the nominative case, errors with objective pronouns most often occur in compounds. To check yourself, mentally remove the other part of the compound.

EXAMPLES: Cracking ice floes warned Burt and *him*.
(Cracking ice floes warned *him*.)

Sally told my cousin and *me* everything.
(Sally told *me* everything.)

Take special care to use the objective case after the preposition *between*.

INCORRECT: This argument is just between you and *I*.

CORRECT: This argument is just between you and *me*.

Objective Pronouns with Appositives. When a pronoun used as an object or as the subject of an infinitive is followed by a noun in apposition, remember to use the objective case.

EXAMPLES: The test intimidated *us* students.

She bought *us* amazed nieces a boa constrictor.

The expedition is exciting for *us* astronauts.

EXERCISE D: Identifying Pronouns in the Objective Case. Choose the pronoun in the objective case to complete each sentence. Then write the use of the pronoun.

1. Asking (him, he) for a raise will not be easy.
2. Africa's diamond mines provide work for (they, them).
3. They make (us, we) waiters wear uniforms.
4. The guilt haunting (him, he) was unrelenting.
5. The librarian gave (us, we) boys invaluable help.
6. I forgot to inform (her, she) of her legal rights.
7. The landscape challenged (we, us) backpackers.
8. A low flying bat gave Lynn and (I, me) a moment of panic.
9. Our sister always wanted (us, we) to take her with us.
10. The fear paralyzing Marion and (I, me) was irrational.

EXERCISE E: Using Pronouns in the Objective Case. Write an objective pronoun to complete each sentence. Then write the use of the pronoun.

205

1. The ferry took my friends and _____ across the river.
2. We have to show _____ that we are eager to cooperate.
3. The airport near _____ was closed during the storm.
4. Stop persecuting _____ because their ways are not yours.
5. The manager gave _____ an application to complete.
6. The problems facing Dan and _____ can be solved.
7. John's rapid calculations always astounded _____.
8. You cannot obtain pedigree papers for your dogs without registering _____.
9. I bought this book for you and _____.
10. Mother wanted Ann and _____ to give the boys lessons.

The Possessive Case

Although errors are less common in the possessive case than they are in the other two cases, you should take care to use the possessive case before gerunds.

Use the possessive case before gerunds.

EXAMPLES: *Your* meandering about the topic is confusing.

We objected to *his* insinuating that we were lazy.

Ms. Malin insists on *our* attending every class.

Another mistake to avoid is using an apostrophe with possessive pronouns, which already show ownership. Spelling such as *our's, their's,* and *your's* is incorrect. In addition, do not confuse a possessive pronoun with a contraction.

POSSESSIVE PRONOUNS: The book had lost *its* cover.

The students cast *their* votes.

CONTRACTIONS: *It's* not likely that he will return.

They're the only ones who voted.

EXERCISE F: Using Pronouns in the Possessive Case.
Choose the correct word in each set of parentheses.

1. The car's noise made (its, it's) approach easy to detect.
2. (Their, They're) experience makes them valuable employees.
3. (Your, You're) light tap on the door wasn't heard by us.

4. This house has been well maintained, and (its, it's) in a desirable location.
5. Steep losses precipitated (me, my) selling the business.
6. The winning ticket is (yours, your's).
7. Frightened by (him, his) raving, I edged toward the door.
8. (Hers, Her's) is a radically new approach.
9. They dislike (your, you) meddling in these matters.
10. (Your, You're) invited to attend the premier.

DEVELOPING WRITING SKILLS: Writing Sentences with Nominative, Objective, and Possessive Pronouns. Use the following instructions to write five sentences of your own.

1. Use *us* as the subject of an infinitive.
2. Use *my* before a gerund.
3. Use *yours and ours* as the compound subject of a verb.
4. Use *she* as part of a nominative absolute construction.
5. Use *he and I* as a compound predicate nominative.

Special Problems with Pronouns 7.2

Choosing the correct form of a pronoun is not always a matter of choosing the form that sounds correct. For example, would it be correct to say, "John is smarter than *me*"? Though the sentence may sound correct to you, it is incorrect because an objective pronoun has been used when a nominative pronoun is needed.

This section will discuss the proper uses of *who* and *whom* and the use of pronouns in clauses where some of the words are omitted but understood.

Using *Who* and *Whom* Correctly

In order to use the correct form of *who* and *whom* and the related forms *whoever* and *whomever* you need to know how the pronoun is used in a sentence. If you determine the pronoun's use, you can determine the appropriate case.

Learn to recognize the various cases of *who* and *whom* and to use them correctly in sentences.

The chart shows the forms and uses of these pronouns.

Case	Pronouns	Use in Sentence
Nominative	who, whoever	Subject of a Verb Predicate Nominative
Objective	whom, whomever	Direct Object Object of a Verbal Object of a Preposition Subject of an Infinitive
Possessive	whose, whosever	To Show Ownership

NOTE ABOUT *WHOSE:* Do not confuse the possessive pronoun *whose* with the contraction *who's,* which means "who is" or "who has."

POSSESSIVE PRONOUN: *Whose* umbrella is this?

CONTRACTION: *Who's* taken my umbrella?

The nominative and objective cases are the real source of problems. Get into the habit of analyzing the structure of your sentences when you use these pronouns. There are two kinds of sentences in which these pronouns can appear.

In Direct Questions. *Who* is the correct form when the pronoun is the subject of a simple question. *Whom* is the correct form when the pronoun is the direct object, object of a verbal, or object of a preposition. A question in the normal subject-verb order will always correctly begin with *who.*

EXAMPLE: *Who* wants a free ticket to the game?

A question in inverted order will never correctly begin with *who.* To see if you should use *whom* instead of *who,* reword the question as a statement. If you change the order of the words, you often find that you need to use *whom.*

EXAMPLES: *Whom* were you discussing?
(You were discussing *whom.*)

Whom did you hope to see at the party?
(You did hope to see *whom* at the party.)

Whom did you receive a letter from?
(You did receive a letter from *whom.*)

208

In Complex Sentences. Choosing the correct case of *who* and *whom* is easier if you remember that the pronoun's use within the subordinate clause determines its case.

EXAMPLE: They screened *whoever* applied for the scholarship.

In the preceding example, the pronoun appears to be the direct object of *screened*. A closer look at the pronoun's position, however, reveals that it is the subject of the subordinate clause *whoever applied for the scholarship*. Thus, the nominative form *whoever* is correct. The entire subordinate clause is the direct object of the sentence.

Follow these steps to see if the case of a pronoun in a subordinate clause is correct. First, isolate the subordinate clause. (If the complex sentence is a question, rearrange it in normal subject-verb order.) Second, if the subordinate clause itself is inverted, rearrange the words in their usual order. Finally, determine the pronoun's use within the subordinate clause.

EXAMPLE: *Who* may I say is calling?

   Reworded sentence: I may say *who* is calling

   Subordinate clause: who is calling

   Use of pronoun: subject of verb *is calling*

   Case for subject of a verb: nominative *(who)*

EXAMPLE: Is the tall man the one *whom* they suspect?

   Subordinate clause: whom they suspect

   Reworded clause: they suspect *whom*

   Use of pronoun: direct object of *suspect*

   Case for direct object: objective *(whom)*

EXAMPLE: The recluse chased away *whomever* his dog barked at.

   Subordinate clause: whomever his dog barked at

   Reworded clause: his dog barked at *whomever*

   Use of pronoun: object of preposition *at*

   Case for object of preposition: objective *(whomever)*

Determining Case in Subordinate Clauses with Parenthetical Expressions. Sometimes subordinate clauses are interrupted by parenthetical expressions, such as *I think, we believe,* or *they say.* These extra words have no effect on the appropriate case of *who* and *whom.*

EXAMPLES: The independent candidate is the one *who*, experts predict, will win the election.

The independent candidate is the one *whom*, experts predict, the voters will elect.

NOTE ABOUT *WHOM* AND *WHOMEVER* IN INFORMAL ENGLISH: *Whom* and *whomever* are now used less frequently in informal English, especially when the object of a preposition is separated from its preposition. When the pronoun directly follows the preposition, it is still customary to use the objective case.

INFORMAL: *Who* did you receive a letter from?

FORMAL AND INFORMAL: From *whom* did you receive a letter?

EXERCISE A: Using *Who* and *Whom* Correctly in Questions. Choose the correct pronoun in each sentence.

1. (Who, Whom) volunteered to take the children to the park?
2. (Who, Whom) did Elizabeth Bennett ultimately marry?
3. (Who, Whom) did they blame?
4. (Who, Whom) did she expect to find at home?
5. To (who, whom) should I direct my question?
6. (Who, Whom) was the last to leave the classroom?
7. (Who, Whom) are you asking to the dance Saturday?
8. From (who, whom) are you expecting a call?
9. (Who, Whom) is the manager of this store?
10. (Who, Whom) did the President appoint as the ambassador?

EXERCISE B: Using *Who* and *Whom* Correctly in Clauses.
Write the subordinate clause in each sentence. Then indicate how the form of *who* or *whom* is used.

EXAMPLE: She wants to know who will be coming.

who will be coming   (subject)

1. I don't know who won the election yesterday.
2. You should always respond to whoever challenges your honesty.
3. His pranks are played only on people whom he likes.
4. Anyone who likes tennis will also like this game.

210

5. Mercury was the god who, I think, carried messages.
6. I would like to thank whoever sent the anonymous gift.
7. Your brusque manner annoys whomever you approach.
8. That young man is a talented gymnast whom I admire.
9. It is Matthew who plays lead guitar in the band.
10. We will help whoever applies for financial aid.

Pronouns in Elliptical Clauses

An *elliptical clause* is one in which some words are omitted but still understood. The word *are,* for example, is omitted in the elliptical clause *than you* at the end of the sentence "I am older than you." Errors in pronoun usage can easily be made when an elliptical clause is used in making a comparison. In such a sentence, either the subject, verb, or both can be understood.

In elliptical clauses beginning with *than* or *as,* use the form of the pronoun that you would use if the clause were fully stated.

The case of the pronoun depends on whether the omitted words belong after or before the pronoun. The omitted words in the examples below are supplied in brackets.

WORDS LEFT OUT AFTER PRONOUN: Ray is as dedicated as *he.*
Ray is as dedicated as he [is].

WORDS LEFT OUT BEFORE PRONOUN: You gave Lewis more than *me.*
You gave Lewis more than [you gave] me.

To determine the correct pronoun for an elliptical clause, first mentally add the missing words. If the understood words come after the pronoun, choose a nominative pronoun. If the understood words come before the pronoun, choose an objective pronoun.

As you can see in examples below, the case of the pronoun can sometimes change the entire meaning of the sentence.

NOMINATIVE PRONOUN: He liked her more than *I.*
He liked her more than I [did].

OBJECTIVE PRONOUN: He liked her more than *me.*
He liked her more than [he liked] me.

211

To choose a pronoun in an elliptical clause, follow the steps outlined in the chart below.

CHOOSING A PRONOUN IN ELLIPTICAL CLAUSES
1. Consider the choices of pronouns: nominative or objective.
2. Mentally complete the elliptical clause.
3. Base your choice on what you find.

EXERCISE C: Identifying the Correct Pronoun in Elliptical Clauses. Rewrite each sentence, choosing one of the pronouns in parentheses and completing the elliptical clause.

EXAMPLE: They have a larger house than (we, us).

They have a larger house than we do.

1. You are less skilled in gymnastics than (she, her).
2. Carla works as hard as (we, us).
3. My friend enjoyed your company more than (I, me).
4. These chores are more of a bother to me than to (he, him).
5. Henry bought more presents than (I, me).
6. This wholesale company is as reliable as (they, them).
7. He works longer hours than (she, her).
8. Bob Dylan is a better performer than (he, him).
9. I encouraged him more than (she, her).
10. Grace was as awkward in social situations as (he, him).

EXERCISE D: Using the Correct Pronoun in Elliptical Clauses. Rewrite each sentence, choosing an appropriate pronoun and completing the elliptical clause.

1. Her sister is as likable as _____.
2. Eileen is far more patient than _____.
3. Annie and her brother are better musicians than _____.
4. He has been less successful than _____.
5. No one else is as mistrustful as _____.
6. Alfred is as interested in astronomy as _____.
7. She was happier at the news of the birth than _____.
8. He needs more free time than _____.
9. Our team has won more games than _____.
10. William is as likely to win as _____.

212

**DEVELOPING WRITING SKILLS: Writing Sentences with
Who, Whom, and Elliptical Clauses.** Use each item in a sentence of your own.

1. more than me
2. as happy as he
3. better than she
4. less than he
5. whom

6. whoever
7. less honest than she
8. more than us
9. as wise as they
10. as well as them

Skills Review and Writing Workshop

Pronoun Usage

CHECKING YOUR SKILLS

Rewrite the following paragraph correcting all pronoun errors.

(1) Joe is the one whose doing the cooking. (2) Because of him complaining, Jack and me chopped all the onions. (3) You and him insisted on us fixing the salad. (4) Whom did you say would make the pudding? (5) That bowl isn't your's. Its our's. (6) Sally cooks as well as him, just between you and I. (7) Jack will help whomever peels potatoes. (8) Who did you say wanted to hire Sally to work in they're kitchen? (9) Jack and myself are taking lessons from Jan. (10) No one cooks better than her.

USING USAGE SKILLS IN WRITING
Writing a Review of a Meal

A good writer must know the correct uses of pronouns in order to write clearly. Imagine you have just eaten a delicious (or not so delicious) meal in a restaurant. Follow the steps below to write about that experience. Be sure to use first person.

Prewriting: You may want to invent your eating experience. You may want to describe a real meal. Make a list of the topics you want to discuss. A restaurant critic would include food, environment, and service.

Writing: A simple statement that the food was poor (or delicious) is not enough. Begin with the appetizer. Describe what you ate why you thought it was good (or bad) and how the dish might be improved. Do the same for the main course and dessert. Discuss the quality of the service and the general atmosphere of the restaurant.

Revising: Go over your work to be sure your pronouns are in the correct case. Improve your sentences. After you have revised, proofread carefully.

Chapter 8

Agreement

If you play a musical instrument, you know how one sour note can ruin an entire performance. Success depends on making all the notes flow harmoniously. The same principle applies to the sentences you write. All the parts of a sentence should work together in harmony. One ungrammatical or illogical word can sound like a sour note and jar a reader or listener. Grammatical *agreement* refers to the harmony that parts of a sentence must have.

In this chapter you will study subject and verb agreement as well as pronoun and antecedent agreement.

Subject and Verb Agreement 8.1

In order to make a subject and a verb agree with each other, you must make sure that both are *singular* or that both are *plural.* This section will focus on distinguishing between singular and plural subjects and singular and plural verb forms.

The Number of Nouns, Pronouns, and Verbs

In grammar the idea of *number* indicates if a word is singular or plural. Only three parts of speech indicate number: nouns, pronouns, and verbs.

Number refers to the two forms of a word: singular and plural. Singular words indicate one; plural words indicate more than one.

Recognizing most nouns as either singular or plural is seldom a problem. Most nouns form their plurals simply by adding *-s* or *-es*. Some, such as *mouse* or *ox*, form their plurals irregularly: *mice, oxen.*

Many pronouns have different forms to indicate their number. The chart below shows the different forms of personal pronouns.

PERSONAL PRONOUNS		
Singular	**Plural**	**Singular or Plural**
I	we	you
he, she, it	they	

The grammatical number of verbs is sometimes more difficult to determine. The form of many verbs can be either singular or plural, depending on the subject. Notice that the verb forms *see* and *have seen* are considered singular if used with a singular subject and plural if used with a plural subject.

SINGULAR: I *see.*   I *have seen.*

PLURAL: We *see.*   We *have seen.*

There are some verb forms that can be only singular. The personal pronouns *he, she,* and *it* and all singular nouns have special forms in the present tense and the present perfect tense that are always singular.

ALWAYS SINGULAR: He *sees.*   He *has seen.*

The verb *be* has special forms that are used only with certain singular subjects. In the present tense, the pronoun *I* has its own form. *He, she, it,* and singular nouns also have their own singular form of *be.*

ALWAYS SINGULAR: I *am.*   He *is.*

All singular subjects except *you* share the same verb form in the past tense of *be.*

ALWAYS SINGULAR: I *was.*   He *was.*

The chart at the top of the next page shows those verb forms that are always singular and those that can be singular or plural, depending on the subject.

216

VERBS	
Always Singular	**Singular or Plural**
(he, Jane) sees	(I, you, we, they) see
(he, Jane) has seen	(I, you, we, they) have seen
(I) am (he, Jane) is	(you, we, they) are
(I, he, Jane) was	(you, we, they) were

A verb form will always be singular if it has had an *-s* or *-es* added to it or if it includes the words *has, am, is,* or *was.* The number of any other verb form depends on its subject.

EXERCISE A: Determining the Number of Nouns, Pronouns, and Verbs. Identify each item as *singular, plural,* or *both.*

EXAMPLES: explodes

            singular

1. volcano	6. bakes	11. ivy	16. meteorite
2. speaks	7. is	12. are	17. has fallen
3. am	8. they	13. vitamins	18. was skating
4. puddles	9. behave	14. will be	19. have
5. you	10. memories	15. tells	20. tried

Singular and Plural Subjects

Two general rules of subject and verb agreement cover all of the more specific rules.

A singular subject must have a singular verb.

A plural subject must have a plural verb.

In the following examples, subjects are underlined once, verbs twice.

SINGULAR SUBJECT AND VERB: Jeremy craves affection.

                            She was being coy.

PLURAL SUBJECT AND VERB: These boys crave affection.

                            They were being coy.

Intervening Phrases and Clauses. When a sentence contains a phrase or clause that separates the subject from its verb, simply ignore the intervening group of words when you check for agreement.

A phrase or clause that interrupts a subject and its verb does not affect subject-verb agreement.

In the first example below, the singular subject, *decision,* agrees with a singular verb, *is,* despite the intervening phrase. In the second example, the plural subject, *families,* agrees with a plural verb, *require,* despite the intervening clause.

EXAMPLES: The <u>decision</u> of the legislators <u>is</u> upsetting to many people.

The <u>families</u> whose town was flooded during the hurricane <u>require</u> temporary shelter.

Intervening parenthetical expressions, such as those beginning with *as well as, in addition to, in spite of,* or *including,* also have no effect on the agreement of the subject and its verb.

EXAMPLE: Your <u>information</u>, in addition to the data gathered by the computer, <u>is helping</u> to solve the scheduling problem.

Relative Pronouns as Subjects. When *who, which,* or *that* acts as the subject in a subordinate clause, its verb will be singular or plural depending on the number of the antecedent.

The antecedent of a relative pronoun determines its agreement with a verb.

In the first example below, the antecedent of *who* is *one;* therefore, the singular verb *has* is used. In the second example, the antecedent of *who* is *candidates;* therefore, the plural verb *have* is used.

EXAMPLES: Chuck is the only one of those candidates <u>who</u> <u>has</u> prior experience in government.

Chuck is just one of several candidates <u>who</u> <u>have</u> prior experience in government.

218

EXERCISE B: Making Subjects Agree with Their Verbs.
Choose the verb in parentheses that agrees with the subject of each sentence.

1. Her powerful grip (results, result) from much exercising.
2. A gravel driveway (provides, provide) better traction.
3. Dark blue (goes, go) well with most other colors.
4. Seen through a microscope, the snowflake's lacy pattern (fills, fill) us with wonder.
5. They sometimes (provokes, provoke) me to anger.
6. Minor headaches (indicates, indicate) stress.
7. His cellar (hides, hide) a dreadful secret.
8. Most kitchen countertops (is, are) laminated plastic.
9. These wallpaper designs (is, are) reproduced in miniature.
10. Australia (was, were) the original home of this wombat.

EXERCISE C: Making Separated Subjects and Verbs Agree. Choose the verb in parentheses that agrees with the subject of each sentence.

1. Acupuncture, a medical procedure that comes to us from the Chinese, (is, are) receiving greater attention.
2. In the park a crumbling pavilion used for concerts (evokes, evoke) memories of the past.
3. Turpentine, derived from coniferous trees, (is, are) used to clean messy paint spills.
4. This casserole, which is made with beef and various vegetables, (serves, serve) six people.
5. Her only piece of jewelry, an unusual pendant made with tiny seashells, (is, are) hanging from her neck.
6. This daguerreotype, as well as those on the far wall, (was, were) among the first ever made.
7. These easy exercises, along with the one described in that book, (is, are) designed to relax you.
8. During this crisis, his ability to deal with problems (seems, seem) to be crumbling.
9. The houses built on the beach (needs, need) repairs.
10. Dairy products, such as cream or butter, (causes, cause) food to spoil quickly in warm weather.
11. Senior citizens from all over the country (has, have) come here to protest the rising cost of living.

219

12. The wax pears, arranged in a bowl, (fools, fool) many people.
13. Ants carrying tiny burdens on their backs (struggles, struggle) back to the colony.
14. My uncle, who is as eccentric as anyone you might know, (talks, talk) incessantly.
15. A fledgling with two anxious parents (has, have) been trying to return to the nest all morning.
16. The debate to be shown on several television stations this evening (is, are) worth seeing.
17. The total, equaling the money in the cash register plus the credit slips, (is, are) two thousand dollars exactly.
18. Walter's mule, a mean animal that bites anyone who comes too close, always (brays, bray) a warning.
19. This slice of bread with mold growing on its sides (was, were) lying in the bottom of the bread drawer.
20. A bear with two cubs (has, have) been seen nearby.

EXERCISE D: Making Relative Pronouns Agree with Their Verbs. Choose the verb in parentheses that agrees with the subject of each subordinate clause.

1. These games of chance, which often (costs, cost) players a fortune, will be investigated by the district attorney.
2. Brandy is the only one out of the twenty dogs in the obedience class that (ignores, ignore) every command.
3. The orchestra will play a new medley of songs that (appeals, appeal) to most audiences.
4. Jeanette is the strongest of the survivors who (was, were) trapped in the cave.
5. This is one of those practical jokes that (hurts, hurt) everyone involved.
6. Buy some outfits that (makes, make) you look slim.
7. Only a basic understanding of the sciences that (is, are) taught in junior high school is needed for this course.
8. One of the chemicals that (was, were) found in the river comes from two different sources.
9. Dr. Cooper is one of those rare general practitioners who willingly (makes, make) house calls.
10. The collection of poems, which (was, were) not favorably reviewed, won two awards nevertheless.

Compound Subjects

Different rules of agreement apply when the words *or, nor,* or *and* are used to join two or more subjects.

Singular Subjects Joined by *Or* or *Nor*. When two singular subjects are joined by *or* or *nor,* use a singular verb.

Two or more singular subjects joined by *or* or *nor* must have a singular verb.

EXAMPLE: Either <u>green</u> or <u>blue</u> <u>is</u> suitable for the background.

Plural Subjects Joined by *Or* or *Nor*. A compound consisting of plural subjects requires a plural verb.

Two or more plural subjects joined by *or* or *nor* must have a plural verb.

EXAMPLE: Neither the <u>paints</u> nor the <u>brushes</u> <u>are</u> in the studio.

Subjects of Mixed Number Joined by *Or* or *Nor*. If a compound subject consists of a singular subject and a plural subject, determining the number of the verb is more difficult.

If one or more singular subjects are joined to one or more plural subjects by *or* or *nor,* the subject closest to the verb determines agreement.

EXAMPLES: Either a <u>lantern</u> or <u>candles</u> <u>are used</u> on the porch.

Either <u>candles</u> or a <u>lantern</u> <u>is used</u> on the porch.

Subjects Joined by *And*. A single rule applies to most situations in which *and* joins two or more subjects.

A compound subject joined by *and* is generally plural and must have a plural verb.

Whether the parts of the compound subject are all singular, all plural, or mixed in number, the conjunction *and* usually acts as a plus sign and indicates the need for a plural verb.

EXAMPLES: A <u>lantern</u> and a <u>candle</u> <u>are used</u> on the porch.

<u>Candles</u> and <u>lanterns</u> <u>are used</u> on the porch.

<u>Candles</u> and a <u>lantern</u> <u>are used</u> on the porch.

Exceptions occur when the parts of the compound subject equal one thing and when the word *each* or *every* is used before a compound subject. Each of these situations requires a singular verb.

EXAMPLES: <u>Bread</u> and <u>butter</u> <u>was</u> all they offered us.

Every <u>chart</u> and <u>diagram</u> <u>was drawn</u> with precision.

EXERCISE E: Making Compound Subjects Agree with Their Verbs. Choose the verb in parentheses that agrees with the subject of each sentence.

1. Each crack and crevice (was, were) filled with cement.
2. The many days of waiting and weeks of uncertainty (has, have) kept Miriam in an anxious state.
3. Several dented helmets and a few shattered swords (was, were) found strewn across the ancient battlefield.
4. Glass, wood, tile, or other materials (is, are) used to create beautiful mosaics.
5. Coal or wood (is, are) burned in this stove.
6. Probably neither Jupiter nor the other outer planets (is, are) capable of sustaining life.
7. A hammer and a screwdriver (is, are) all you will need.
8. Thrilling rides and an exciting midway (draws, draw) people to the annual fair.
9. Neither threats nor coaxing (causes, cause) Art to be swayed from a decision.
10. Ham and eggs (is, are) my favorite breakfast.
11. Several household utensils and a bronze cauldron (has, have) been recovered from the burial mound.
12. Neither redwoods nor giant sequoias (grows, grow) in this part of the country.
13. The cost of the eye examination and the price of new glasses (was, were) paid for by my parents.
14. Leather coats or down jackets (is, are) being worn this year.
15. Every table and chair in this house (was, were) built by my great-grandfather.
16. A book or a magazine (helps, help) to pass the time spent on the bus.
17. Both the children and their nanny (was, were) exhausted.

18. Either expertly applied paint or varnish (has, have) given a professional look to these wooden dressers.
19. Either the elevator or the escalators (takes, take) you there.
20. Beside the fireplace two calico cats and a spotted dog (was, were) waiting for our return.

Confusing Subjects

Certain confusing subjects require special attention.

Hard-to-Find Subjects. If a subject comes after its verb, you must still make sure they agree in number.

A subject that comes after its verb must still agree with it in number.

If a subject comes after its verb, the sentence is said to be inverted. Check the agreement of the subject and verb by mentally putting the sentence in the usual subject-verb order.

EXAMPLE: Under the hen's wing <u>was</u> a tiny <u>chick</u>.

(A tiny chick was under the hen's wing.)

Which magazines <u>does</u> <u>he</u> <u>buy</u>?

(He does buy which magazines.)

There <u>are</u> no more <u>days</u> in this year.

(No more days are in this year.)

NOTE ABOUT *THERE'S* AND *HERE'S:* A common mistake is the misuse of *there's* and *here's,* contractions for *there is* and *here is.* They must agree with singular subjects.

INCORRECT: Here'<u>s</u> <u>Ann</u> and <u>Tanya</u> now, both ready to leave for the snow slopes as soon as possible.

CORRECT: Here <u>are</u> <u>Ann</u> and <u>Tanya</u> now, both ready to leave for the snow slopes as soon as possible.

Subjects of Linking Verbs. Another agreement problem involves linking verbs and predicate nominatives.

A linking verb must agree with its subject, regardless of the number of its predicate nominative.

In the first example below, the plural subject *rockets* requires the plural verb *were*, even though the predicate nominative *(signal)* is singular. In the second example, the singular subject *signal* requires the singular verb *was*, even though the predicate nominative *(rockets)* is plural.

EXAMPLES: Rockets <u>were</u> the signal to begin the battle.

The <u>signal</u> to begin the battle <u>was</u> rockets.

Collective Nouns. Collective nouns—words such as *jury, family,* or *committee*—name groups of persons or things. They may be either singular or plural, depending on the meaning.

A collective noun takes a singular verb when the group it names acts as a single unit.

A collective noun takes a plural verb when the group it names act as individuals with different points of view.

SINGULAR: The <u>team</u> <u>has won</u> every game.

A <u>flock</u> of starlings <u>is flying</u> overhead.

PLURAL: The <u>team</u> <u>are quarreling</u> in the locker room.

The <u>flock</u> of starlings <u>jostle</u> one another as they race
for the pieces of bread.

One collective noun, *number,* deserves special attention. When used with *the, number* is always singular; when used with *a, number* is always plural.

SINGULAR: The <u>number</u> of whooping cranes <u>has been
increasing</u>.

PLURAL: A <u>number</u> of whooping cranes <u>have been reared</u>
successfully by sandhill cranes.

Plural-Looking Nouns. Nouns that look plural but are actually singular can also cause agreement problems.

Nouns that are plural in form but singular in meaning agree with singular verbs.

Some of these nouns name branches of knowledge: *acoustics, aesthetics, civics, economics, gymnastics, mathematics,*

224

physics, politics, and *social studies.* Others are singular in meaning because, like collective nouns, they name single units: *macaroni* (one dish consisting of many pieces of pasta); *measles, mumps,* and *rickets* (one disease); and so on.

SINGULAR: <u>Mathematics</u> <u>is</u> my most difficult subject.

Measles <u>threatens</u> unborn babies.

Some of these words are especially tricky. When *ethics* and *politics,* for example, name characteristics or qualities rather than branches of knowledge, their meanings are plural. Similarly, such words as *eyeglasses, pliers, scissors,* and *trousers* generally take plural verbs although they name single items.

PLURAL: Nina's <u>ethics</u> <u>are adjusted</u> to fit any occasion.

Jack's <u>politics</u> <u>were</u> not our concern.

The <u>scissors</u> <u>are</u> in the sewing box.

Indefinite Pronouns. Some indefinite pronouns are always singular, including those that end in *-one (anyone, everyone, someone),* those that end in *-body (anybody, everybody, somebody),* and those that imply one *(each, either).* Others are always plural: *both, few, many, others,* and *several.*

Singular indefinite pronouns take singular verbs.

Plural indefinite pronouns take plural verbs.

ALWAYS SINGULAR: Almost <u>everyone</u> <u>likes</u> his music.

<u>Everybody</u> <u>is expected</u> to be here on time.

<u>Neither</u> of the dresses <u>looks</u> good on you.

ALWAYS PLURAL: <u>Both</u> of these shoes <u>squeak</u>.

<u>Many</u> in the class <u>excel</u> in writing.

<u>Others</u> <u>overlook</u> the difficulties.

Some indefinite pronouns can be either singular or plural, depending on the antecedent.

The pronouns *all, any, more, most, none,* and *some* usually take a singular verb if the antecedent is singular and a plural verb if it is plural.

225

In the first example, the antecedent of *most* is *pie,* a singular noun; *most* is singular. In the second, the antecedent of *most* is *hinges,* a plural noun; *most* is also plural.

SINGULAR: <u>Most</u> of the pie <u>was eaten</u>.

PLURAL: <u>Most</u> of the hinges <u>have been oiled</u>.

Titles. The titles of books and other works of art can be misleading if they sound plural or consist of many words.

A title is singular and must have a singular verb.

EXAMPLES: <u>*Dr. Jekyll and Mr. Hyde*</u> <u>is</u> a psychological thriller.

<u>*The Bunner Sisters*</u> <u>is</u> a novel by Edith Wharton.

Amounts and Measurements. Amounts and measurements usually express single units.

A noun expressing an amount or measurement is usually singular and requires a singular verb.

In the first three examples below, the subjects agree with singular verbs. *Twenty-five cents* is a single sum of money; *four tablespoons* is a single measurement; and *three fourths* is one part of a whole. In the last example, however, *half* refers to many individual items and is therefore plural.

EXAMPLES: <u>Twenty-five cents</u> <u>starts</u> the dryer.

<u>Four tablespoons</u> of salt <u>has made</u> the soup inedible.

<u>Three fourths</u> of that nation <u>is impoverished</u>.

<u>Half</u> of the brochures <u>were mailed</u> yesterday.

EXERCISE F: Making Confusing Subjects Agree with Their Verbs. Choose the item in parentheses that agrees with the subject of each sentence.

1. Here (is, are) the options for your consideration.
2. Our swimming team (is, are) likely to win the competition.
3. *The Virginians* (is, are) a novel by William Thackeray.
4. His tactics at first (seems, seem) to be self-serving.
5. The herd of cattle (is, are) milling about aimlessly.

6. His mumbled apology and its obvious insincerity (was, were) my reason for disliking him.
7. Two gallons of whitewash (is, are) all that we need.
8. The black trousers (is, are) more appropriate.
9. Economics (is, are) my sister's major in college.
10. Her broken eyeglasses (was, were) lying on the ground.
11. Virginia Woolf's *The Waves* (is, are) an unusual novel.
12. A swarm of killer bees (is, are) advancing northward.
13. A good idea for raising money (is, are) having everyone demonstrate a craft and having people sign up for lessons.
14. Twenty dollars (includes, include) the price of breakfast.
15. At the beginning of the play, a group of girls (enters, enter) all carrying letters.
16. To and fro in their narrow cage (paces, pace) the lions.
17. All of his change (was, were) tossed onto the table.
18. At this moment few (remains, remain) in the room.
19. The clergy (is, are) divided over minor issues in doctrine.
20. Measles (is, are) sometimes a dangerous disease.
21. His faltering steps (was, were) the first sign of recovery.
22. Half of the hamsters (was, were) rejected by their mother.
23. Any of these furnaces (does, do) a good job of heating.
24. A number of quails (is, are) hiding in the underbrush.
25. Some of the bananas (has, have) rotted.

DEVELOPING WRITING SKILLS: Applying the Rules of Subject and Verb Agreement. Use each item at the beginning of a sentence, followed by the verb *is* or the verb *are.*

1. neither of the boys
2. the audience
3. two dollars
4. biogcnetics
5. next to the desk
6. each of the club members
7. most of the cement
8. spaghetti and meatballs
9. either she or her parents
10. some of the children

Pronoun and Antecedent 8.2 Agreement

Like a subject and its verb, a pronoun and its antecedent must agree. An antecedent is the word or group of words for which the pronoun stands.

Agreement Between Personal Pronouns and Antecedents

While a subject and verb must agree simply in number, a personal pronoun and its antecedent must agree in three ways.

A personal pronoun must agree with its antecedent in number, person, and gender.

The *number* of a pronoun indicates if it is singular or plural. *Person* refers to a pronoun's ability to indicate either the person speaking (first person); the person spoken to (second person); or the person, place, or thing spoken about (third person). *Gender* is the characteristic of nouns and pronouns that indicates whether the word is *masculine* (referring to males); *feminine* (referring to females); or *neuter* (referring to neither males nor females).

The only pronouns that indicate gender are third-person singular personal pronouns.

GENDER OF THIRD-PERSON SINGULAR PRONOUNS		
Masculine	**Feminine**	**Neuter**
he, him, his	she, her, hers	it, its

In the example below, the pronoun *his* agrees with its antecedent, *Kevin,* in number (both are singular), in person (both are third person), and in gender (both are masculine).

EXAMPLE: *Kevin* is very generous with *his* money.

Agreement in Number. When an antecedent is compound, making the pronoun agree can be a problem. Keep the following three rules in mind to determine the number of compound antecedents.

Use a singular personal pronoun with two or more singular antecedents joined by *or* or *nor*.

EXAMPLE: Either *Craig* or *Todd* will bring *his* stereo.

Use a plural personal pronoun with two or more antecedents joined by *and*.

EXAMPLE: *Melissa* and *I* are studying for *our* examinations.

228

An exception occurs when a distinction must be made between individual and joint ownership. If individual ownership is intended, use a singular pronoun to refer to a compound antecedent. If joint ownership is intended, use a plural pronoun.

SINGULAR: *Nat* and *Cecily* were reluctant to bring *her* dog. (Cecily owns the dog.)

PLURAL: *Nat* and *Cecily* were reluctant to bring *their* dog. (Both Nat and Cecily own the dog.)

SINGULAR: Neither my *brother* nor my *father* let me use *his* car. (The brother and father each own a car.)

PLURAL: Neither my *brother* nor my *father* let me use *their* car. (The brother and father own the same car.)

The third rule applies to compound antecedents whose parts are mixed in number.

Use a plural personal pronoun if any part of a compound antecedent joined by *or* or *nor* is plural.

PLURAL: When the *boys* or their *sister* comes home, give *them* this message.

Agreement in Person and Gender. Unnecessary shifts in person or gender spoil pronoun-antecedent agreement.

When dealing with pronoun-antecedent agreement, take care not to shift either person or gender.

SHIFT IN PERSON: *Mike* is attending the state university because *you* pay less tuition there.

CORRECT: *Mike* is attending the state university because *he* pays less tuition there.

SHIFT IN GENDER: The *horse* threw *its* head back and stood on *his* hind legs.

CORRECT: The *horse* threw *its* head back and stood on *its* hind legs.

Generic Masculine Pronouns. A masculine pronoun that refers to a singular antecedent whose gender is unknown is said to be *generic,* meaning that it applies to both masculine and feminine genders. Although the generic masculine pro-

229

noun is the traditional standard usage, many writers prefer to rephrase the sentence.

When gender is not specified, use the masculine or rewrite the sentence.

EXAMPLES: Any *person* can learn to ski if *he* tries.

Any *person* who tries can learn to ski.

People can learn to ski if *they* try.

EXERCISE A: Making Personal Pronouns Agree with Their Antecedents. Write an appropriate personal pronoun to complete each sentence.

1. Boris and Leo improved _____ act by constant practice.
2. If the dark blue paint or the pale yellow is not oil-based, don't use _____.
3. Neither the bed nor the rugs retained _____ new look.
4. All the participants showed _____ appreciation.
5. Neither Mark nor Sam brought _____ radio to the game.
6. Lincoln is Nebraska's capital and Omaha is _____ largest city.
7. My parents gave me _____ permission to go on the trip.
8. Andy and Lois sold several acres of _____ joint property.
9. Either Wanda or Wendy left _____ scarf in the car.
10. Ms. Stone and _____ secretary attended the convention.

EXERCISE B: Avoiding Shifts in Person and Gender. Rewrite each sentence, correcting the unnecessary shift in person or gender.

EXAMPLE: With mischief in his eyes, the baby hid its rattle.

With mischief in his eyes, the baby hid his rattle.

1. Each girl must submit their report before leaving.
2. Those hikers will soon realize that you cannot walk for miles in shoes meant for dress wear.
3. The welders wear goggles so that your eyes will be shielded from the sparks.
4. Trying to protect its calf, the cow disregarded her own safety as the coyotes approaches.
5. We learned in chemistry that you should often try again.

230

6. The students want to know what you should bring to class on Monday.
7. As hurricane Donna swept along the predicted path, it left destruction in her wake.
8. All the team members learned that you have to practice hard to win.
9. That nation has strengthened its economy, and now she has solid social programs.
10. We all knew which bus you had to take to the city.

Agreement with Indefinite Pronouns

When an indefinite pronoun such as *each, one,* or *several* is the antecedent of a personal pronoun, both pronouns must agree. Errors are rare when both pronouns are plural.

Use a plural personal pronoun when the antecedent is a plural indefinite pronoun.

EXAMPLE: *All* of the students left *their* books in the library.

A similar rule applies when both pronouns are singular.

Use a singular personal pronoun when the antecedent is a singular indefinite pronoun.

An intervening phrase or clause does not affect agreement in number between a personal pronoun and its antecedent. Notice in the first example below that the antecedent of *its* is *either* (a singular pronoun), not *bears*. In the second example, notice that while the gender of the personal pronoun *(her)* is determined by other words in the sentence, the number of the personal pronoun is determined by the singular antecedent *(one).*

EXAMPLES: *Either* of the bears will perform for *its* trainer.

   One of the women was reluctant to volunteer more of *her* time.

If other words in the sentence do not indicate gender, you may use the generic masculine pronoun or you may rephrase the sentence.

EXAMPLES: *Each* of the politicians gave *his* opinion.

   All of the politicians gave *their* opinions.

For those indefinite pronouns that can be either singular or plural *(all, any, more, most, none,* and *some),* agreement depends on the number of the indefinite pronoun's antecedent. In the first example below, the antecedent of *some* is *meat,* a singular noun. In the second example, the antecedent of *some* is *workers,* a plural noun.

EXAMPLES: *Some* of the meat had lost *its* flavor.

                Some of the workers disliked *their* jobs.

Sometimes, strict grammatical agreement may result in an illogical sentence. In the example below, *neither* is a singular antecedent in agreement with *it;* logic, however, calls for a plural personal pronoun.

ILLOGICAL: Because *neither* of the windows would budge, we had to leave *it* open.

CORRECT: Because *neither* of the windows would budge, we had to leave *them* open.

NOTE ABOUT *EVERYBODY* AND *EVERYONE:* In informal situations, the plural personal pronoun *their* is often used to refer to the singular indefinite pronouns *everybody* and *everyone.* In formal writing, however, the generic *his* or a rephrasing of the sentence is still preferred.

INFORMAL: *Everyone* can contribute *their* ideas for the show.

FORMAL: *Everyone* can contribute *his* ideas for the show.

FORMAL AND INFORMAL: *Everyone* can contribute ideas for the show.

EXERCISE C: Making Personal Pronouns Agree with Indefinite Pronouns. Choose the correct pronoun in each sentence.

1. Each of the men raised (his, their) arms to the crowd.
2. All of the paints will keep (its, their) color for years.
3. Both of the boys will complete (his, their) assignments.
4. Many who heard the thunder thought (he, they) would outwit the storm.
5. Either of the actresses will do (her, their) best.
6. Prior to living in the dormitory, each of the girls had tried living in (her, their) own apartment.

232

7. Several of the photographs had lost (its, their) finish.
8. Few of the items in the store seemed worth (its, their) price.
9. If everybody rushes toward you at once, avoid (him, them) by stepping aside.
10. Most of the girls like (her, their) new swimming coach.
11. While neither of the apples looked ripe, we had no choice but to eat (it, them).
12. All of those who spoke seemed unwilling to state (his, their) honest opinions.
13. Each of the boys looked out for (his, their) buddy.
14. Only one of the girls had (her, their) hair cut.
15. Some of the students voiced (his, their) discontent at the meeting last night.
16. Most of the teachers gave (his, their) consent.
17. Each of my uncles volunteered (his, their) time.
18. All of the patrons wanted (his, their) money back when the play was cancelled.
19. Not one of the boys took (his, their) nap this afternoon.
20. Surprisingly, neither of these wigs, with (its, their) unnatural colors, looked strange on Phil.

Agreement with Reflexive Pronouns

Reflexive pronouns—those ending in *-self* or *-selves*—should be used only to refer to a word appearing earlier in the sentence, as in "Our *parents* treated *themselves* to a vacation."

A reflexive pronoun must agree with an antecedent that is clearly stated.

Do not use a reflexive pronoun if a personal pronoun can logically be used instead. In the example below, *myself* has no antecedent. The personal pronoun *me* should be used instead.

POOR: The hard work was done by Leslie and *myself.*

CORRECT: The hard work was done by Leslie and *me.*

EXERCISE D: Using Reflexive Pronouns Correctly. Rewrite each sentence, correcting the misused reflexive pronoun.

1. Scott and myself were the first ones to arrive.
2. To whom other than herself should the award be given?

3. Mary and Jean forgot to invite John and myself.
4. Andrea and himself were the most popular couple there.
5. The only person who can convince them is yourself.
6. Carmen looked at themselves in the photograph.
7. May Jerry and myself have a piece of your pizza?
8. Who besides yourself can stay late today?
9. The person who has the best batting average is himself.
10. The teacher and herself will hand out the books.

DEVELOPING WRITING SKILLS: Making Pronouns and Antecedents Agree. Write a sentence for each item below, using each item as the antecedent of a personal pronoun.

1. lamb	5. guests and we	8. actress
2. neither	6. Heather or Claire	9. most
3. nation	7. Jacob	10. pilots
4. few	and his brothers	

8.3 Special Problems with Pronoun Agreement

Pronouns whose antecedents are vague, ambiguous, or too distant can cloud the meaning of a sentence. This section will show you how to correct these special problems if they should arise in your writing.

Vague Pronoun References

For the meaning of a sentence to be clear, the antecedent of any pronoun needs to be clearly stated or understood.

A pronoun requires an antecedent that is either clearly stated or clearly understood.

Antecedents for *Which, This, That,* and *These*. The pronouns *which, this, that,* and *these* are often used incorrectly to refer to a vague or overly general idea.

The pronouns *which, this, that,* and *these* should not be used to refer to a vague or overly general idea.

234

In the following sentence it is impossible to point to exactly what the pronoun *this* stands for.

VAGUE
REFERENCE:
Mr. Winter, our host, insisted that his wife did nothing well. Mrs. Winter contended that she was one of a long line of excellent equestrians. *This* ruined the entire meal for all of us.

"This what?" a reader might ask. The answer is not stated nor is it clearly understood. You can correct such vague, overly general references by turning the pronoun into an adjective that modifies a specific noun or by revising the sentence to eliminate the vague pronoun.

CORRECT:
Mr. Winter, our host, insisted that his wife did nothing well. Mrs. Winter contended that she was one of a long line of excellent equestrians. *This argument* ruined the entire meal for all of us.

Mr. Winter's insistence that his wife did nothing well and Mrs. Winter's contention that she was one of a long line of excellent equestrians ruined the entire meal for all of us.

Antecedents for *It, They,* and *You.* The personal pronouns *it, they,* and *you* must also have clearly stated antecedents.

The personal pronouns *it, they,* and *you* should not be used with vague antecedents.

Errors with these pronouns can be corrected either by replacing the pronoun with a specific noun or rewriting the sentence to eliminate the imprecise pronoun.

In the example below, the pronoun *it* has no clearly stated antecedent. The pronoun should be replaced with a precise noun or the sentence should be rephrased in order to eliminate the pronoun altogether.

VAGUE REFERENCE:
I am having a tooth extracted. The dentist said that I will hardly feel *it*.

CORRECT:
I am having a tooth extracted. The dentist said that I will hardly feel the *extraction.*

The dentist said that I will hardly feel having my tooth extracted.

235

In the next example, the pronoun *they* is used without an accurate antecedent.

VAGUE REFERENCE: I was a fan of Brenda Starr for years before *they* revealed the identity of her mystery man.

CORRECT: I was a fan of Brenda Starr for years before the *cartoonist* revealed the identity of her mystery man.

I was a fan of Brenda Starr for years before the identity of her mystery man was revealed.

A somewhat different problem occurs when the personal pronoun *you* is misused. The use of *you* is valid only when it refers directly to the reader or listener.

In the first example below, *you* is vague and should be replaced with another pronoun, such as *one* or *I*. In the second example, *you* is not appropriate unless the reader or speaker lived in the time described.

VAGUE REFERENCE: The gathering was so somber *you* dared not speak.

CORRECT: The gathering was so somber *one* dared not speak.

VAGUE REFERENCE: Before homes had modern plumbing, *you* had to pump water from a well.

CORRECT: Before homes had modern plumbing, *people* had to pump water from a well.

NOTE ABOUT *IT:* In a number of idiomatic expressions, *it* is used correctly without an antecedent. In phrases such as *"It* is dark," *"It* is time," and *"It* is raining," the idiomatic use of *it* is accepted as formal standard English.

EXERCISE A: Correcting Vague Pronoun References.
Rewrite the sentences below, correcting the vague pronouns.

EXAMPLE: Sue heard that they had discovered a new fuel.

Sue heard that scientists had discovered a new fuel.

1. To stake a claim on the frontier, you had to live there.
2. We grumbled about the work done on the house because they left the roof open and the floor warped.
3. Cal always wore a neatly pressed handkerchief in his vest pocket and a pin on his lapel. That made him feel rich.

4. During the weather forecast they predicted sunny skies and cool temperatures for the rest of the week.
5. I quickly shifted to a more neutral topic, and this prevented the inevitable argument over politics.
6. She wore a sweater over her blouse and a vest over the sweater. That was too bulky.
7. Valery is self-disciplined and energetic. These will be useful throughout life.
8. Ross writes articles for the sports section of our school newspaper, and this makes him well-known at the games.
9. We are adding to our small ranch, and it should help everyone feel less cramped.
10. After waxing his new car, Jack polished the chrome and cleaned the interior. This became a monthly project.
11. Nellie has always been aloof and quiet. These have alienated her from her peers.
12. When my father spoke angrily, you listened.
13. Near the East River in New York City you can see the United Nations Headquarters.
14. George was too busy and involved with his own work, which was his way of ignoring people.
15. When we stayed in Massachusetts, they told us to visit Walden's Pond.
16. Egyptian priests were generally taught to read hieroglyphics, and you would often learn to write them too.
17. Unless translators know the different dialects you cannot render current South American literature into English.
18. As gusts blew the tumbleweeds across the prairie, they seemed playful.
19. Two of my brothers run for the track team, which is a sport that teaches discipline.
20. Our tour guide gave us background information on Rainier National Park and the Grand Coulee Dam. That impressed us.

Ambiguous Pronoun References

A pronoun is *ambiguous* if it can refer to more than one possible antecedent.

A pronoun should never refer to more than one antecedent.

If a pronoun has more than one possible antecedent, the meaning of the sentence will be unclear.

Personal Pronouns with Two or More Antecedents. A personal pronoun's antecedent should be unmistakable.

A personal pronoun should always be tied to a single, obvious antecedent.

In the example below, the pronoun *he* is confusing because it can refer to either *Sam* or *Steve.*

AMBIGUOUS REFERENCE: Sam told Steve that *he* needed a vacation.

CORRECT: Sam told Steve that Steve needed a vacation.

While talking to Steve, Sam said that he himself needed a vacation.

Ambiguous Repetition of Personal Pronouns. Sometimes repetition of the same pronoun within a sentence can create confusion.

Do not repeat a personal pronoun in a sentence if it can refer each time to a different antecedent.

In the example below, the second use of *she* is unclear. The sentence needs to be rephrased to clarify the meaning.

AMBIGUOUS REFERENCE: Janet shouted to Kelly when *she* saw that *she* was about to be splashed by a bus.

CORRECT: Janet shouted to Kelly when *she* saw that *Kelly* was about to be splashed by a bus.

Janet shouted to Kelly when *Janet* saw that *she herself* was about to be splashed by a bus.

EXERCISE B: Correcting Ambiguous Pronoun References. Rewrite the following sentences, correcting the ambiguous pronoun references.

1. The stewardess told the woman that she would ask someone to help her find the missing luggage.
2. This bonsai is growing in a container that discourages root growth, but it still seems too small.
3. Stephanie asked Betty Jane if she could help with the cooking.

4. While Barney wheeled his small son around the park, he was very contented.
5. Jon was forced to take a detour onto a country road, and it seemed to lead nowhere.
6. You would never have known that Suzanne had inherited a vast fortune from her mother. She was a very shrewd woman.
7. Craig informed Harry that he would have to leave soon.
8. The waitress served us slices of warm bread and gave us the menus. We buttered and ate them immediately.
9. This recipe for quiche is my favorite. It is easy to follow, and it tastes wonderful if it is followed exactly.
10. Our weekend guests promised to return to our lodge next summer and bring additional vacationers, but they never came.

Avoiding Distant Pronoun References

A final rule for pronoun references applies to situations in which the pronoun's antecedent is too remote.

A personal pronoun should always be close enough to its antecedent to prevent confusion.

A distant pronoun reference can be corrected by moving the pronoun closer to its antecedent or by changing the pronoun to a noun.

DISTANT REFERENCE: Two chickens moved about in the doorway. On the porch, an old rocker creaked slightly back and forth. *They* pecked aimlessly at the floor.

CORRECT: As the two chickens moved about in the doorway, *they* pecked aimlessly at the floor. On the porch, an old rocker creaked slightly back and forth.

Two chickens moved about in the doorway. On the porch, an old rocker creaked slightly back and forth. The *chickens* pecked aimlessly at the floor.

EXERCISE C: Correcting Distant Pronoun References. Rewrite the following sentences, correcting the distant pronoun references.

239

1. Nick traced his finger over the obscured letters on the grave marker. For many years the grasses and weeds had grown in this cemetery where he and his dog had gone today for a walk. He mused over the patience of the person who had carved them, without benefit of modern tools.
2. The barker, his voice rising above the clamor, begged the crowds to see the amazing tattooed man. Tommy felt for his last dollar and hesitated briefly. Drawn by his promise of a once-in-a-lifetime thrill, Tommy held out the money.
3. In many stories by Ray Bradbury, the Martians are described as gentle, highly intelligent creatures who are destroyed by people from earth. They are written so skillfully that readers truly feel they have entered another world.
4. Not far from the shore, a small sailboat seemed motionless, its mast like a needle. Red and white buoys dotted the horizon. There was no one on it to unfurl the sail.
5. We plunged our hands into the huge mound of popcorn. Before us on the screen were the faces of the men, women, and children starving in Africa. Once it was gone, we guiltily put the box under the seat.
6. Muffins fresh from the oven filled wicker baskets. Jars of homemade jam, the fruit glistening along the glass sides, made our mouths water. Their smell filled the room.
7. The meeting had gone badly, Mr. Snelling reflected, as he loosened his tie. He had forgotten to bring his notes, and he felt that he was not dressed appropriately. It had been given to him by his daughter and was a conservative brown.
8. Swimming helplessly in the cistern, the mouse searched for a way to escape. Located in the basement, it had been built to hold water during the dry season.
9. As Jacob looked down from the helicopter, he could see the village he had known most of his life. Then it circled several times and began the descent.
10. Her lungs ached from holding her breath. Thick smoke poured under the door as she irrationally groped for her glasses. Soon they would involuntarily expand, seeking air.

DEVELOPING WRITING SKILLS: Avoiding Special Problems with Pronouns. Write five sentences comparing two of your favorite relatives. Make sure that each pronoun you use has a clearly stated antecedent.

Skills Review and Writing Workshop

Agreement

CHECKING YOUR SKILLS

Rewrite the following paragraph correcting all errors in subject-verb and pronoun-antecedent agreement.

(1) Many folk remedies for health, while not scientific, seems to work. (2) One family thinks that garlic tea cure colds. (3) There are another family that recommend mint tea. (4) However, everyone I know think neither garlic nor mint are effective. (5) Each of my aunts dose themselves with a different remedy when she has an upset stomach. (6) A book called *Mailbag of Natural Remedies* list many home remedies. (7) Bacon and eggs are not recommended for ulcers. (8) Neither Juliette nor Katherine likes their cold pill. (9) The two brothers and their sister is now taking cod liver oil. (10) Either Trudy or Joan can make catnip tea if they try.

USING USAGE SKILLS IN WRITING

Writing a Movie Review

Writers who want their opinions to be clear and meaningful must follow the rules of agreement. A movie review usually presents specific information about the film, the people in it, and the people who made it. Follow the directions below to write a movie review.

Prewriting: Select a movie you enjoyed or disliked. Give clear reasons for your opinion. Organize your reasons into categories such as plot, acting, directing, setting.

Writing: You might begin by describing something in the movie you loved or disliked. State your opinion. Substantiate your opinion with examples. You could end your review with a brief conclusion that summarizes what you have said.

Revising: Make sure your nouns and pronouns agree with your verbs. Check your review for other grammatical errors. After you have revised, proofread carefully.

Chapter 9

Adjective and Adverb Usage

You have probably noticed that adjectives and adverbs change form, especially in comparisons. You might say, for example, "The Amazon River is *longer* than the Mississippi, but the Nile is the *longest* of the three." The adjective's form depends on whether two things are being compared or more than two things are being compared.

This chapter will show you how to form various adjectives and adverbs and how to avoid some specific errors that often occur in comparisons.

9.1 Degrees of Comparison

In the English language there are three *degrees,* or forms, of most adjectives and adverbs that are used in comparisons.

Most adjectives and adverbs have different forms to show degrees of comparison.

Recognizing Degrees of Comparison

In order to write effective comparisons, you first need to know the three degrees.

The three degrees of comparison are the positive, the comparative, and the superlative.

In the following chart both kinds of modifiers are shown in each of the three degrees. Notice the three different ways that the words change form: (1) with *-er* and *-est*, (2) with *more* and *most*, and (3) with entirely different words.

DEGREES OF ADJECTIVES		
Positive	**Comparative**	**Superlative**
slow	slower	slowest
disagreeable	more disagreeable	most disagreeable
good	better	best
DEGREES OF ADVERBS		
slowly	more slowly	most slowly
disagreeably	more disagreeably	most disagreeably
well	better	best

EXERCISE A: Recognizing Positive, Comparative, and Superlative Degrees. Identify the degree of each underlined modifier.

EXAMPLE: My uncle was <u>more generous</u> than I expected.

          comparative

1. This chair is <u>more comfortable</u> than that one.
2. Andrew wore his <u>good</u> suit to the celebration.
3. His was the <u>most concerned</u> voice she had heard.
4. Jan <u>deftly</u> flipped the pancake in the air.
5. Your <u>best</u> decision should be made after you rest.
6. Max is <u>more determined</u> when the odds are against him.
7. These pears will ripen <u>more quickly</u> if the sun hits them.
8. The cat's claws were <u>swiftly</u> unsheathed.
9. Please let me try on the <u>smallest</u> size.
10. I was <u>more disappointed</u> by his attitude than by his failure.

Regular Forms

Just as there are both regular and irregular verbs, adjectives and adverbs can be either regular or irregular. The number of syllables in regular modifiers determines how they form their degrees.

Modifiers of One and Two Syllables. The first of two rules applies to modifiers of one or two syllables.

Use -*er* or *more* to form the comparative degree and -*est* and *most* to form the superlative degree of most one- and two-syllable modifiers.

The more common method for forming the comparative and superlative degrees of one- and two-syllable modifiers is to add -*er* and -*est* to the positive degree rather than to use *more* and *most*.

EXAMPLES:	tiny	tinier	tiniest
	blue	bluer	bluest
	smart	smarter	smartest
	funny	funnier	funniest

More and *most* are used with certain modifiers of one and two syllables when adding -*er* and -*est* would sound awkward.

EXAMPLES:	brisk	more brisk	most brisk
	spiteful	more spiteful	most spiteful
	charming	more charming	most charming

All adverbs that end in -*ly* form their comparative and superlative degrees with *more* and *most* regardless of the number of syllables.

EXAMPLES:	curtly	more curtly	most curtly
	shrewdly	more shrewdly	most shrewdly

Modifiers of More Than Two Syllables. For modifiers of three or more syllables, forming the comparative and superlative degrees is easy.

Use *more* and *most* to form the comparative and superlative degrees of all modifiers with three or more syllables.

EXAMPLES:	beautiful	more beautiful	most beautiful
	superfluous	more superfluous	most superfluous
	delectable	more delectable	most delectable

NOTE ABOUT COMPARISONS WITH *LESS* AND *LEAST:* Meaning the opposite of *more* and *most, less* and *least* can be used to form another version of the comparative and superlative degrees of most modifiers.

EXAMPLES: soft   less soft   least soft

appetizing   less appetizing   least appetizing

graciously   less graciously   least graciously

EXERCISE B: Forming Regular Comparative and Superlative Degrees. Write the comparative and superlative form of each modifier.

EXAMPLE: wise

wiser, wisest

1. lucky	11. rapid	21. shocking
2. pleasing	12. rapidly	22. delightful
3. soon	13. tasty	23. stunning
4. strange	14. wide	24. carefully
5. thick	15. green	25. short
6. pretentious	16. safely	
7. heavily	17. cold	
8. fond	18. hopeful	
9. clever	19. hard	
10. curly	20. proudly	

Irregular Forms

Because several adjectives and adverbs form their comparative and superlative degrees in unpredictable ways, it is necessary to memorize them.

The irregular comparative and superlative forms of certain adjectives and adverbs must be memorized.

As you read the following chart, separate the irregular modifiers that cause problems for you from the ones you already use correctly. Then study and memorize them. Notice that some of the modifiers differ only in the positive degree. *Bad, badly,* and *ill,* for example, all have the same comparative and superlative forms *(worse, worst).*

IRREGULAR MODIFIERS		
Positive	**Comparative**	**Superlative**
bad	worse	worst
badly	worse	worst
far (distance)	farther	farthest
far (extent)	further	furthest
good	better	best
ill	worse	worst
late	later	last *or* latest
little (amount)	less	least
many	more	most
much	more	most
well	better	best

NOTE ABOUT *BAD* AND *BADLY:* *Bad* is an adjective; *badly* is an adverb. *Bad* can *not* be used as an adverb after an action verb. Notice in the example that it is used correctly as an adjective after a linking verb.

INCORRECT: The children behaved *bad* last night.

CORRECT: The children felt *bad* last night.

Badly is used correctly as an adverb after an action verb, not a linking verb.

INCORRECT: The children felt *badly* last night.

CORRECT: The children behaved *badly* last night.

NOTE ABOUT *GOOD* AND *WELL:* *Good* is an adjective; *well* can be either an adjective or adverb. Like *bad, good* can *not* be used as an adverb after an action verb. It is used correctly as an adjective after a linking verb.

INCORRECT: The children behaved *good* last night.

CORRECT: The children felt *good* last night.

Well is usually an adverb and, like *badly,* can be used after an action verb.

CORRECT: The children behaved *well* last night.

246

Well is an adjective when it refers to satisfactory conditions or a person's health. In these situations, it can be used after a linking verb.

CORRECT: All is *well* at home.

The children felt *well* after their naps.

EXERCISE C: Forming Irregular Comparative and Superlative Degrees. Write the appropriate form of the underlined modifier to complete each sentence.

EXAMPLE: The film is good, but the book is _____.

better

1. The old line of cars is selling <u>well</u>, but we hope the new line will sell even _____.
2. We drove <u>far</u> to reach a gas station and even _____ to reach a restaurant.
3. El Paso is <u>farther</u> from here than Laredo, but Amarillo is the _____ of the three.
4. Jan looks <u>better</u> in blue than in red, but she looks _____ in green.
5. Joe has <u>little</u> patience for board games and even _____ for word games.
6. Connie has <u>much</u> interest in physics and even _____ in chemistry.
7. The scientist pursued her research quite <u>far</u> last year, but she intends to pursue it even _____ this year.
8. There were <u>many</u> guests at Sam's party, but there were _____ at Roxanne's.
9. I still feel <u>ill</u> this morning, but I felt _____ last night after dinner.
10. George arrived <u>late</u>, but Walter arrived even _____.

DEVELOPING WRITING SKILLS: Using Adjectives and Adverbs to Make Comparisons. Write a sentence with each word in the degree indicated.

EXAMPLE: nervous—comparative

Penelope was more nervous after the test than she was before the test.

247

1. clear—superlative
2. trustworthy—comparative
3. alert—positive
4. good—superlative
5. bad—positive
6. badly—superlative
7. far—positive
8. malicious—comparative
9. windy—comparative
10. secretive—superlative
11. good—comparative
12. far—superlative
13. likely—superlative
14. late—comparative
15. much—comparative
16. shrewd—comparative
17. calmly—superlative
18. pleasing—comparative
19. reasonable—superlative
20. well—positive

9.2 Clear Comparisons

Once you know how to form regular and irregular adjectives and adverbs, you can work on eliminating problems with comparisons. In this section, you will learn the proper uses of the comparative and superlative degrees. You will also learn how to avoid making illogical comparisons.

Using Comparative and Superlative Degrees

One basic rule with two parts covers the correct use of comparative and superlative forms.

Use the comparative degree to compare two persons, places, or things. Use the superlative degree to compare three or more persons, places, or things.

As the following examples illustrate, there need not be any obvious reference to specific numbers when you make a comparison. The number of items being compared is often indicated in the context of the sentence.

COMPARATIVE: Orange will be *more conspicuous* than blue.

I am *less talented* than Sheila.

This weekend was *more hectic* than the last.

SUPERLATIVE: Orange is the *most conspicuous* color of all.

I am the *least talented* person for this work.

This was the *most hectic* weekend we have had.

The superlative degree can sometimes be used solely for emphasis, without indicating any specific comparison. This usage, however, is more acceptable in informal English than it is in formal English.

EXAMPLES: The movie is *most exciting*.

Our decision is *most definitely* final.

NOTE ABOUT DOUBLE COMPARISONS: A *double comparison* is a usage error caused by using both *-er* and *more* or both *-est* and *most* to form a regular modifier. A double comparison can also be caused by adding any of these to an irregular modifier.

INCORRECT: This is the *most happiest* day of my life.

My cold is *worser* today than it was yesterday.

CORRECT: This is the *happiest* day of my life.

My cold is *worse* today than it was yesterday.

EXERCISE A: Using the Comparative and Superlative Forms Correctly. Choose the correct comparative or superlative form in each sentence.

1. Abe is (nicer, nicest) than his friend Hal.
2. Which of your parents is (more likely, most likely) to drive us to school tomorrow?
3. The movie was much (worse, worst) than we were told.
4. Carolyn is the (younger, youngest) of the four daughters.
5. Which of the two campsites is (farther, farthest)?
6. Jim's plan is (more viable, most viable) than Kay's plan.
7. Suzie is (better, best) at chess than Robert.
8. Edgar is the (better, best) player on the basketball team.
9. The noise in our classroom was (louder, loudest) than the noise in the classroom next to us.
10. Carla is clearly the (brighter, brightest) of the twins.

EXERCISE B: Supplying the Comparative and Superlative Degrees. Write the appropriate comparative or superlative degree of the modifier in parentheses.

EXAMPLE: Winston is the (funny) student in our class.

funniest

1. This road will be (muddy) after the snow melts.
2. He has the (good) record on the team.
3. Your reasoning would be (clear) if you would think through the problem slowly.
4. Wear a (warm) coat and leave the other in the closet.
5. My grades in art history were (good) this semester than last semester.
6. Randy is the (old) of the three boys.
7. Brad is (much) eager to participate than I am.
8. Snow is (heavy) than usual after a rainfall.
9. Josh is (susceptible) to colds than his brother is.
10. The problem is (much) serious than you thought.

Logical Comparisons

In order to write logical comparisons, you must make sure you do not unintentionally compare unrelated items or something with itself.

Balanced Comparisons. If two or more things being compared are not of a similar kind, the comparison may be illogical and even ridiculous.

Make sure that your sentences compare only items of a similar kind.

In the following unbalanced examples, the sentences illogically compare dissimilar things: *Message* cannot be compared to *post card;* an idea cannot be compared to *Monica;* and *plants* in a greenhouse cannot be compared to an entire *greenhouse.*

UNBALANCED: A *message* conveyed by telephone is more private than a *post card*.

BALANCED: A *message* conveyed by telephone is more private than *one* written on a post card.

UNBALANCED: Bud's *idea* is less original than *Monica.*

BALANCED: Bud's *idea* is less original than *Monica's.*

UNBALANCED: The *plants* in this greenhouse are lusher than the *greenhouse* down the road.

BALANCED: The *plants* in this greenhouse are lusher than *those* in the greenhouse down the road.

Other and *Else* in Comparisons. Another kind of illogical comparison results when something is unintentionally compared to itself.

When comparing one of a group with the rest of the group, make sure that your sentence contains the word *other* or the word *else*.

In the first example below, *the Grand Canyon,* which is one of the national parks, cannot be compared to all national parks. Adding *other* excludes the Grand Canyon from the rest of the national parks. In the second example, *the new member* cannot be compared to all the members on the team because the new member is one of those people. Adding *else* excludes the new member from the rest of the group.

ILLOGICAL: We thought the Grand Canyon was *more beautiful than any* national park we visited.

LOGICAL: We thought the Grand Canyon was *more beautiful than any other* national park we visited.

ILLOGICAL: Corey runs *better than anyone* on the team.

LOGICAL: Corey runs *better than anyone else* on the team.

EXERCISE C: Making Balanced Comparisons. Rewrite each sentence, correcting the unbalanced sentence.

EXAMPLE: Shelly's voice is better than Ted.

Shelly's voice is better than Ted's.

1. Duane's work on the blackboard is more legible than Linda.
2. The conditions in the eye of a hurricane are calmer than the perimeter.
3. Feeding the seals is more fun than the alligators.
4. A moose's antlers are bigger than a deer.
5. The spots on a serval are similar to a bobcat.
6. Contact with poison ivy can hurt as much as poison oak.
7. Jonathan's term paper is longer than Richard.
8. The floats in this year's parade are fewer than last year.
9. Listening to music is more relaxing than a television show.
10. The water in the Great Lakes is purer than they were a decade ago.

251

EXERCISE D: Using *Other* and *Else* in Comparisons. Rewrite each sentence, correcting the illogical comparison.

1. Arnold's report on the history of humanism was more fascinating than anyone's.
2. The village parson was more respected than any person who lived there.
3. Dora steered her canoe through the rapids with a skill greater than that of any of the contestants.
4. Ask Marge to check the records because she is more thorough than anyone.
5. Rosalie, the winner of five consecutive magic contests, could perform more tricks than anyone we ever saw.
6. That dog barks more than any in this neighborhood.
7. Ted invited Carla to the party because she was friendlier than anyone.
8. When the bell rings, this hallway is more crowded than any in the school.
9. I like chocolate more than any candy.
10. Ask Jim to carry the box because he is stronger than anyone in the class.

Absolute Modifiers

A few modifiers cannot be used in comparisons because they are *absolute* in meaning—that is, their meanings are entirely contained in the positive degree. If, for example, one vase is *priceless,* another vase can not be *more priceless.*

Avoid using absolute modifiers illogically in comparisons.

Among the most common absolute modifiers are the words *dead, entirely, eternal, fatal, final, identical, infinite, mortal, opposite, perfect,* and *unique.* Rather than use words such as these in comparisons, you should try to find similar words whose meanings are not absolute.

ILLOGICAL: This truth is *more eternal* than any other.

LOGICAL: This truth is *more enduring* than any other.

ILLOGICAL: Your thesis is *more unique* than anyone else's.

LOGICAL: Your thesis is *more original* than anyone else's.

Many idiomatic expressions, however, use absolute modifiers correctly in comparisons.

EXAMPLES: You couldn't be *more right*.

The *squarer* compartment accommodates more luggage.

Although such expressions are considered standard English, you can usually find a word that better expresses your meaning.

EXERCISE E: Avoiding Absolute Modifiers in Comparisons. Rewrite each sentence, correcting the illogical comparison.

1. His report was more complete than mine.
2. My Aunt Jane's solution was more perfect than my Uncle Walter's.
3. This step is more irrevocable than the last one.
4. Julie was more overwhelmed with math homework than Keith was.
5. We wanted a painting that was less unique than Aunt Mary's.
6. They finally found a route that led straighter to their destination.
7. These two white kittens are more identical than those two black ones.
8. Her decision was more opposite mine than his was.
9. A coral snake's venom is more fatal than a rattlesnake's.
10. The flowers I picked are less dead than the ones you picked.

DEVELOPING WRITING SKILLS: Writing Effective Comparisons. Use the following instructions to write five sentences of your own.

1. Compare the difference between two domestic animals.
2. Compare three units of measurement.
3. Compare one profession with another.
4. Compare three actors or actresses.
5. Compare a contemporary author's novel with a deceased author's novel.

Skills Review and Writing Workshop

Adjective and Adverb Use

CHECKING YOUR SKILLS

Rewrite the paragraph, correcting all adjective and adverb errors.

(1) Some of the most unique sculptures in medieval European churches are hidden. (2) The sculptures, called misericords (seats of mercy), are more interesting. (3) These most beautiful sculptures are found under the hinged choir stall seats. (4) Attached under the seats are small ledges with carved supports to hold them on safer. (5) Medieval monks had to stand for more long hours during church services than we do. (6) When the seats were raised, the oldest monks, or those who felt badly, could perch on the ledge, yet appear to stand. (7) Because the supports were hidden, the carvers took them less serious, so the supports have more unusual subject matter. (8) The carvers created graphically representations of ordinary life. (9) Looking at these sculptures, you can understand medieval life best. (10) They give us greatest knowledge about the lives of those people.

USING YOUR SKILLS IN WRITING
Writing a Comparison to Convince

Imagine that a friend must choose which record to buy: one by your favorite singer or one by a singer whom you dislike. Compare the two and convince your friend there is only one choice.

Prewriting: Decide which aspects of the recording you are going to compare: voice, delivery, style, material, backup. Take notes on your ideas.

Writing: State why you prefer one performer over the other. Then compare and contrast the two performers point by point, using details to support your opinion.

Rewriting: Read over your comparison to be sure you have used comparatives correctly and used adjectives and adverbs effectively. Check the list of irregular modifiers on page 246. After you have revised, proofread carefully.

10

Miscellaneous Problems in Usage

Many small problems that can spoil the clarity of your speaking or writing do not fall into any of the broad categories of usage that were covered in preceding chapters. Some of these problems involve distinctions between standard and nonstandard usage. Others involve similar spellings or meanings. The next two sections are intended to help you improve your mastery of the small details that contribute to effective speaking and writing.

Negative Sentences 10.1

In today's English a clause usually needs just one negative word to convey a negative idea. More than one negative word can be redundant and confusing.

Recognizing Double Negatives

A clause containing two negative words when only one is needed is said to contain a *double negative*.

Do not write sentences with double negatives.

The chart below provides examples of double negatives and the two ways of correcting each double negative.

CORRECTING DOUBLE NEGATIVES	
Double Negatives	**Corrections**
Janet *wouldn't* do *nothing*.	Janet *wouldn't* do anything. Janet would do *nothing*.
Nobody here wants *no* trouble.	*Nobody* here wants any trouble. We want *no* trouble.
I *don't never* go there.	I *don't* ever go there. I *never* go there.

Sentences containing more than one clause can correctly contain more than one negative word. Each clause, however, usually contains no more than one negative word.

EXAMPLE: Since we *didn't* remember to mail the invitations, *no-body* came to the party.

EXERCISE A: Avoiding Double Negatives. Choose the word in parentheses that makes each sentence negative without forming a double negative.

1. We don't have (no, any) tickets for tonight's concert.
2. Carlos won't (ever, never) make that mistake again.
3. Don't hide the keys (nowhere, anywhere) obvious.
4. The witness had seen (no one, anyone) suspicious.
5. The professor wouldn't accept (no, any) late papers.
6. Since it hadn't snowed, we (could, couldn't) go skiing.
7. Wendy was (nowhere, anywhere) near the tree when it fell.
8. Because of his fever, Ricky couldn't do (any, no) work.
9. Marlene wouldn't accept help from (no one, anyone).
10. I didn't see (no, any) shooting star last night.

Forming Negative Sentences Correctly

A negative sentence can be formed correctly in one of three ways.

256

Using One Negative Word. The most common way to form a negative sentence is to use a single negative word, such as *never, no, nobody, nothing, nowhere, not,* or the contraction *-n't* added to a helping verb.

Do not use two negative words in the same clause.

DOUBLE NEGATIVE: The store *doesn't* accept *no* credit cards.

CORRECT: The store *doesn't* accept any credit cards.

The store accepts *no* credit cards.

Using *But* in a Negative Sense. When *but* is used as an adverb, it will often have a negative sense. If so, it should not be accompanied by another negative word.

Do not use *but* in its negative sense with another negative.

DOUBLE NEGATIVE: He *wasn't but* a child at the time.

CORRECT: He was *but* a child at the time.

He was only a child at the time.

Using *Barely, Hardly,* and *Scarcely.* Each of these words also makes a sentence negative.

Do not use *barely, hardly,* or *scarcely* with another negative word.

DOUBLE NEGATIVE: She *wasn't barely* able to tell us who called.

CORRECT: She was *barely* able to tell us who called.

DOUBLE NEGATIVE: I *couldn't hardly* endure the pain.

CORRECT: I could *hardly* endure the pain.

DOUBLE NEGATIVE: He *didn't scarcely* have time to dress.

CORRECT: He *scarcely* had time to dress.

EXERCISE B: Avoiding Problems with Negatives. Rewrite each of the sentences to eliminate the double negatives.

1. Phil never did nothing to antagonize the crew members.
2. You should not drive that car nowhere without snow tires.
3. Nobody knew none of the answers on the exam.
4. I can't find my address book nowhere.

257

5. No one never saw the bear tracking us.
6. Never mix no chlorine bleach with ammonia.
7. Norman won't repeat nothing told to him confidentially.
8. She didn't tell nobody about her visit to the city.
9. Nobody in our community never realized water was a precious resource until there wasn't enough.
10. None of us never forgot an important date in our family.

EXERCISE C: Correcting Double Negatives. Eliminate the error in each of the following phrases and expand the corrected phrase into a sentence of your own.

1. wouldn't hardly try
2. wasn't nobody there
3. couldn't scarcely walk
4. shouldn't never impose
5. weren't but a few
6. isn't barely tolerable
7. nothing won't hurt
8. didn't want no pity
9. hadn't none left
10. not asked nobody

Understatement

Occasionally a speaker or writer may want to imply a positive idea without actually stating it. This indirect method is called *understatement*. Understatement may be used to minimize the importance of an idea, or, conversely, to emphasize its importance.

Understatement can be achieved by using a negative word and a word with a negative prefix.

EXAMPLES: Such accidents are *scarcely unavoidable*.

This phenomenon *isn't* entirely *inexplicable*.

EXERCISE D: Using Understatement. Rewrite each sentence, using understatement.

1. Interruptions from inquisitive children were frequent.
2. The price for this dime store trinket is estimable.
3. I am impressed by your fluency in Russian.
4. The price of the ring is important.
5. Taking some time for yourself is essential.
6. Jill acts decisively on crucial matters.

258

7. Her opinion is relevant.
8. Tad is certainly a conformist.
9. His prose style was pleasing.
10. Considering the barbaric manners of his guests, I think Bob's conduct was honorable.

DEVELOPING WRITING SKILLS: Writing Negative Sentences. Use each item in a negative sentence of your own.

1. not appreciated
2. can see nothing
3. never bothered
4. not unintelligent
5. barely recognizable

6. has hardly begun
7. but two possibilities
8. scarcely noticed
9. not displeased
10. isn't unlikely

One Hundred Common Usage 10.2 Problems

This section provides an alphabetical list of one hundred usage problems that can cause problems in writing and speaking.

Solving Usage Problems

To make the best use of this gathering of usage problems, first read each problem. As you read, note the items that need your special attention.

Study the items in this glossary, paying particular attention to similar meanings and spellings.

You may also use this section as a reference tool. Once you are familiar with the contents, you can refer to individual words as you need them in your work.

(1) a, an. The article *a* is used before consonant sounds; *an*, before vowel sounds. Words beginning with *h, o,* or *u* may have either a consonant sound or a vowel sound.

CONSONANT SOUNDS: a *h*istory lesson (*h*-sound)

a *o*ne-way street (*w*-sound)

a *u*niversal human right (*y*-sound)

VOWEL SOUNDS: an *h*onest day's work (no *h*-sound)

an *o*pen door (*o*-sound)

an *u*nearthly howl (*u*-sound)

(2) accept, except   *Accept,* a verb, means "to receive." *Except,* a preposition, means "leaving out" or "other than."

VERB: I *accept* your challenge to a debate.

PREPOSITION: Everyone came to the picnic *except* her.

(3) accuse, allege   *Accuse* means "to blame" or "to bring a charge against." *Allege* means "to claim something that has not been proved."

EXAMPLES: We mistakenly *accused* an innocent bystander.

They *allege* that their employer ignored regulations.

(4) adapt, adopt   *Adapt,* a verb, means "to change." *Adopt,* also a verb, means "to take as one's own."

EXAMPLES: We *adapted* our sleeping habits to the short Arctic days.

They *adopted* the homeless waif.

(5) advice, advise   *Advice* is a noun meaning "an opinion." *Advise* is a verb meaning "to give an opinion to."

NOUN: I need your *advice*.

VERB: Hikers are *advised* to take along a canteen of water.

(6) affect, effect   *Affect* is almost always a verb meaning "to influence." *Effect,* usually a noun, means "result." Occasionally, *effect* is a verb meaning "to bring about" or "to cause."

VERB: The years spent in the mines *affected* his lungs.

NOUN: One *effect* of her travels was a new open-mindedness.

VERB: His administration *effected* changes in foreign policy.

(7) aggravate   *Aggravate* means "to make worse." Avoid using this word to mean "to annoy."

LESS ACCEPTABLE: He was *aggravated* by their rude manners.

PREFERRED: Scratching will only *aggravate* the mosquito bite.

(8) ain't   *Ain't,* originally a contraction of *am not,* is not considered acceptable standard English. Avoid using it in all writing and speaking.

NONSTANDARD: He *ain't* come home yet.

CORRECT: He *hasn't* come home yet.

(9) allot, a lot, alot   *Allot,* a verb, means "to divide in parts" or "to give out in shares." *A lot* is an informal expression meaning "a great many" or "a great amount." Avoid using it in formal writing. *Alot* is a nonstandard spelling and should never be used.

VERB: The funds were *allotted* equally among the researchers.

NONSTANDARD: She has *alot* of relatives.

INFORMAL: She has *a lot* of relatives.

FORMAL: She has *many* relatives.

(10) all ready, already   *All ready* is an expression functioning as an adjective and meaning "ready." *Already* is an adverb meaning "by or before this time" or "even now."

ADJECTIVE: I am *all ready* to listen to your report.

ADVERB: I have *already* made a decision.

(11) all right, alright   *Alright* is a nonstandard spelling. Always use the two-word form in your writing.

NONSTANDARD: Whatever you decide is *alright* with me.

CORRECT: Whatever you decide is *all right* with me.

(12) all together, altogether   *All together* means "all at once." *Altogether* means "completely" or "in all."

EXAMPLES: We will march *all together* in the rally.

You are *altogether* mistaken about his motive.

(13) A.M., P.M.   *A.M.* refers to hours before noon; *P.M.,* to hours after noon. Do not spell out numbers when you use these abbreviations, and do not use such phrases as "in the morning" or "in the afternoon" with them.

INCORRECT: The train arrives at *ten A.M. in the morning.*

CORRECT: The train arrives at *10:00 A.M.*

(14) among, between *Among* and *between* are both prepositions. *Among* always implies three or more. *Between* is generally used with just two things.

EXAMPLES: There is a feeling of discontent *among* the citizens.

                Juan got *between* Carlos and me.

(15) amount, number Use *amount* with quantities that cannot be counted. Use *number* with things that can be counted.

EXAMPLES: a small *amount* of cream, a large *amount* of profit

                a *number* of empty bottles, a *number* of books

(16) anxious *Anxious* means "worried," "uneasy," or "fearful." Do not use it as a substitute for *eager.*

AMBIGUOUS: I am always *anxious* to meet new people.

CLEAR: I am always *eager* to meet new people.

        I am always *anxious* about meeting new people for the first time.

(17) anyone, any one, everyone, every one *Anyone* and *everyone* mean "any person" and "every person." *Any one* means "any single person (or thing)," and *every one* means "every single person (or thing)."

EXAMPLES: *Anyone* may come to the meeting.

                Any one of these students could be elected.

                Everyone complained about the service.

                Every one of the dishes was broken.

(18) anyway, anywhere, everywhere, nowhere, somewhere These adverbs should never end in *-s.*

NONSTANDARD: It may rain, but we will go hiking *anyways.*

CORRECT: It may rain, but we will go hiking *anyway.*

(19) as Do not use this conjunction to mean "because" or "since."

LESS ACCEPTABLE: We stayed home, *as* our mother was sick, and prepared dinner.

PREFERRED: We stayed home, *since* our mother was sick, and prepared dinner.

262

(20) as to   *As to* is awkward. Replace it with *about.*

NONSTANDARD: Scientists have several theories *as to* how the continents were formed.

CORRECT: Scientists have several theories *about* how the continents were formed.

(21) at   Do not use *at* after *where.* Simply eliminate it.

NONSTANDARD: Do you know where the bus station is *at?*

CORRECT: Do you know where the bus station is?

(22) at about   Avoid using *at* with *about.* Simply eliminate *at* or *about.*

LESS ACCEPTABLE: We arrived *at about* lunch time.

PREFERRED: We arrived *at* lunch time.

We arrived *about* lunch time.

(23) awful, awfully   *Awful* is used informally to mean "extremely bad." *Awfully* is used informally to mean "very." Both modifiers are overused and should be replaced with more descriptive words. In formal writing, *awful* should be used only to mean "inspiring fear."

INFORMAL: He looked *awful* after the operation.

BETTER: He looked *pale and defeated* after the operation.

INFORMAL: I am *awfully* tired.

BETTER: I am *exhausted.*

FORMAL: He felt penitent in the *awful* presence of the king.

(24) awhile, a while   *Awhile* is an adverb, which in itself means "for a while." *A while* is an article and a noun and is usually used after the preposition *for.*

ADVERB: Rest *awhile* before you leave.

NOUN: Stay for *a while* and keep me company.

(25) beat, win   *Beat* means "to overcome (an opponent)." *Win* means "to achieve victory in." Do not use *win* in place of *beat.*

NONSTANDARD: The Dodgers *won* the Yankees in the World Series.

CORRECT: The Dodgers *beat* the Yankees in the World Series.

263

(26) because Do not use *because* after *the reason*. Say "The reason is ... that" or reword the sentence.

NONSTANDARD: *The reason* we left is *because* we got tired.

CORRECT: *The reason* we left is *that* we got tired.

We left *because* we got tired.

(27) being as, being that Avoid using either expression. Use *since* or *because* instead.

NONSTANDARD: *Being that* (or *as*) the tide was high, we left.

CORRECT: *Since* (or *Because*) the tide was high, we left.

(28) beside, besides As prepositions, these two words have different meanings and cannot be interchanged. *Beside* means "at the side of" or "close to." *Besides* means "in addition to."

EXAMPLES: The athletic field is *beside* the school.

Who *besides* you will come to the play?

(29) blond, blonde These two words originally came from French, in which *blond* refers to males and *blonde* to females. Although many writers continue to make this distinction in English, *blond* may correctly be used to refer to either gender.

INCORRECT: My brother is a *blonde*.

CORRECT: My brother is a *blond*.

Harriet is the *blond* (or *blonde*) standing at the top of the stairs.

(30) bring, take *Bring* means "to carry from a distant place to a nearer one." *Take* means the opposite: "to carry from a near place to a more distant place."

EXAMPLES: Please *bring* your paper to me.

Will you *take* the dog to the veterinarian?

(31) bunch *Bunch* means "a number of things of the same kind." Avoid using this word to mean "group."

LESS ACCEPTABLE: A *bunch* of us went downtown.

PREFERRED: A *group* of us went downtown.

She bought a *bunch* of grapes.

(32) burst, bust, busted   *Burst* is the standard present, past, and past participle of the verb *burst. Bust* and *busted* are nonstandard forms.

NONSTANDARD: I will *bust* if I take one more bite.

He shouldn't have *busted* the blister.

CORRECT: I will *burst* if I take one more bite.

He shouldn't have *burst* the blister.

(33) but what   Do not use *but what.* Instead, use *that.*

NONSTANDARD: I don't doubt *but what* I will win.

CORRECT: I don't doubt *that* I will win.

(34) can, may   *Use can* to mean "to have the ability to." Use *may* to mean "to have permission to" or "to be possible or likely to."

ABILITY: This scale *can* register up to five hundred pounds.

PERMISSION: Yes, you *may* leave.

POSSIBILITY: It *may* rain today.

(35) can't help but   This is a nonstandard expression. Use *can't help* plus a gerund instead.

NONSTANDARD: I *can't help but* wonder why you did not call this morning.

CORRECT: I *can't help wondering* why you did not call this morning.

(36) clipped words   Avoid using clipped or shortened words, such as *gym, phone,* and *photo,* in formal writing.

INFORMAL: The plans for a new *gym* were approved.

The *phone* has been out of order all day.

FORMAL: The plans for a new *gymnasium* were approved.

The *telephone* has been out of order all day.

(37) condemn, condone   *Condemn* means "to express strong disapproval of." *Condone* means "to pardon or overlook."

EXAMPLES: They *condemned* him for his neglect of the baby.

I cannot *condone* such cruelty.

(38) continual, continuous   *Continual* means "occurring again and again in succession." *Continuous* means "occurring without interruption."

EXAMPLES: His *continual* coffee breaks caused his dismissal.

His *continuous* absence caused his dismissal.

(39) different from, different than   *Different from* is preferred.

LESS ACCEPTABLE: Your concept of fun is *different than* mine.

PREFERRED: Your concept of fun is *different from* mine.

(40) doesn't, don't   Do not use *don't* with third-person singular subjects. Use *doesn't* instead.

NONSTANDARD: He *don't* like heights.

My watch *doesn't* keep accurate time.

(41) done   *Done* is the past participle of the verb *do*. It should always follow a helping verb.

NONSTANDARD: She always *done* well in school.

CORRECT: She *has* always *done* well in school.

(42) dove   *Dove,* a past tense of *dive,* is considered unacceptable by many speakers and writers. Use *dived* instead.

LESS ACCEPTABLE: He *dove* into the ice-cold water.

PREFERRED: He *dived* into the ice-cold water.

(43) due to   *Due to* means "caused by" and should be used only when the words *caused by* can logically be substituted.

NONSTANDARD: She became blind *due to* a freak accident.

CORRECT: Her blindness was *due to* a freak accident.

(44) due to the fact that   Replace this wordy expression with *since* or *because.*

LESS ACCEPTABLE: *Due to the fact that* he was undernourished, he easily became sick.

PREFERRED: *Since* he was undernourished, he easily became sick.

266

(45) each other, one another *Each other* and *one another* are usually interchangeable. At times, however, *each other* is more logically used in reference to only two; *one another,* in reference to more than two.

EXAMPLES: We should be kind to *each other* (or *one another*).

As the couple walked, they held *each other's* hand.

In our large family, we make every effort to be considerate of *one another's* privacy.

(46) emigrate, immigrate *Emigrate* means "to leave a country for a new residency." *Immigrate* means "to enter a country to establish a residency."

EXAMPLES: During the Potato Famine, many Irish people *emigrated* from Ireland.

Many Irish people *immigrated* to the United States.

(47) enthused, enthusiastic *Enthused* is nonstandard. Replace it with *enthusiastic.*

NONSTANDARD: All of us are *enthused* about the new science project.

CORRECT: All of us are *enthusiastic* about the project.

(48) farther, further *Farther* refers to distance. *Further* means "additional" or "to a greater degree or extent."

EXAMPLES: The sun is much *farther* from us than the moon.

We want *further* information from the committee about the new proposals.

(49) fewer, less Use *fewer* with things that can be counted. Use *less* with qualities and quantities that can not be counted.

EXAMPLES: *fewer* complaints, *fewer* problems, *fewer* diseases

less coffee, *less* incentive, *less* trouble

(50) former, latter *Former* refers to the first of two previously mentioned items. *Latter* refers to the second of the two.

EXAMPLE: The box contained hollyhocks and sweet williams. The *former* we planted along the wall; the *latter* we thought would be more suited for the rock garden.

(51) get, got, gotten These forms of the verb *get* are acceptable in standard English, but whenever possible it is best to find a more specific word.

INFORMAL: *get* a license, *got* wealthier, to have *gotten* fame

BETTER: *obtain* a license, *acquired* greater wealth, to have *achieved* fame

(52) gone, went *Gone* is the past participle of *go* and should be used as a verb only with a helping verb. *Went* is the past of *go* and is never used with a helping verb.

NONSTANDARD: Hilda *gone* to see her sister in Iowa.

Bob *could have went* to any college he wanted to.

CORRECT: Hilda *has gone* to see her sister in Iowa.

Hilda *went* to see her sister in Iowa.

Bob *could have gone* to any college he wanted to.

(53) good, lovely, nice Whenever possible, replace these weak and overused words with a more specific adjective.

WEAK: *good* description, *lovely* vacation, *nice* taste

BETTER: *clear* description, *exotic* vacation, *refined* taste

(54) hanged, hung Use *hanged* to mean "executed." Use *hung* to mean "suspended."

EXAMPLES: The revolutionary council *hanged* the ministers of former government.

Two beautiful spider plants *hung* from the high ceiling in the kitchen.

(55) healthful, healthy Things are *healthful;* people are *healthy.*

LESS ACCEPTABLE: Bean sprouts are *healthy* in any diet.

PREFERRED: Bean sprouts are *healthful* in any diet.

(56) if, whether These two subordinate conjunctions are interchangeable. When using *whether,* it is not necessary to include *or not* after it.

EXAMPLE: We wonder *if* (or *whether*) Joel will meet us for practice after school.

(57) in, into *In* refers to position. *Into* suggests motion.

POSITION: Each piece of silverware is *in* the correct place.

MOTION: Put all of the silverware *into* the drawer.

(58) irregardless Avoid this word. Use *regardless*.

NONSTANDARD: *Irregardless* of your advice, I voted for Bob.

CORRECT: *Regardless* of your advice, I voted for Bob.

(59) judicial, judicious *Judicial* means "relating to the administration of justice." *Judicious* means "showing wisdom."

EXAMPLES: The Supreme Court is our highest *judicial* tribunal.

Her *judicious* decision was applauded by all.

(60) just When *just* is used as an adverb meaning "no more than," it should be placed right before the word it modifies.

LESS ACCEPTABLE: Just mow the back yard, not the front.

PREFERRED: Mow just the back yard, not the front.

(61) kind of, sort of Do not use *kind of* and *sort of* to mean "rather" or "somewhat."

NONSTANDARD: You look *kind of* pale.

CORRECT: You look *somewhat* pale.

(62) kind of a, sort of a Do not use *a* after *kind of* and *sort of.*

NONSTANDARD: Which *kind of a* dressing do you want?

CORRECT: Which *kind of* dressing do you want?

In addition, avoid such expressions as "this kind of books" or "these sorts of examination." If *kind* or *sort* is singular, the object of the preposition *of* should also be singular. If *kind* or *sort* is plural, make sure the object is plural too.

NONSTANDARD: this *kind* of books

these *sorts* of examination

CORRECT: this *kind* of book

these *sorts* of examinations

(63) lay, lie   *Lay* means "to put or set (something) down." Its principal parts—*lay, laying, laid,* and *laid*—are usually followed by a direct object. *Lie* means "to recline." Its principal parts—*lie, lying, lay,* and *lain*—are never followed by a direct object.

LAY: *Lay* your books on the desk.

They are *laying* the carpet tomorrow morning.

He gently *laid* the eggs in the basket.

She had *laid* forty slate slabs to form the foundation of the walkway.

LIE: *Lie* down for an hour and rest.

The children are *lying* on the floor.

After I became tired, I *lay* down and rested.

The dog has *lain* there all afternoon.

(64) learn, teach   *Learn* means "to acquire knowledge." *Teach* means "to give knowledge to."

EXAMPLES: Helen Keller *learned* the word "water."

Anne Sullivan *taught* Helen the word "water."

(65) leave, let   *Leave* means "to allow to remain." *Let* means "to permit."

NONSTANDARD: *Leave* me do this by myself.

Let the parakeet alone!

CORRECT: *Let* me do this by myself.

Leave the parakeet alone!

(66) like   *Like* is a preposition and should not be used in place of the conjunction *as.*

NONSTANDARD: He is crafty *like* a fox is crafty.

CORRECT: He is crafty *as* a fox is crafty.

He is crafty *like* a fox.

(67) loose, lose   *Loose* is usually an adjective or part of such idioms as *cut loose, turn loose,* or *break loose. Lose* is always a verb, generally meaning "to miss from one's possession."

EXAMPLES: The door hinge was *loose.*

The goat broke *loose* from the pen.

Don't *lose* this telephone number.

(68) mad   In formal usage, the adjective *mad* means "insane." Used informally, *mad* means "angry."

INFORMAL: I am *mad* at you for ignoring me.

FORMAL: Jane Eyre learned that Rochester's wife was *mad.*

(69) maybe, may be   *Maybe* is an adverb meaning "perhaps." *May be* is a helping verb and a verb.

ADVERB: *Maybe* I can investigate this matter myself.

VERB: You *may be* right.

(70) of   Do not use *of* after a helping verb such as *should, would, could,* or *must.* Use *have* instead. Do not use *of* after *outside, inside, off,* and *atop.* Simply eliminate it.

NONSTANDARD: He *must of* remembered he had a date.

CORRECT: He *must have* remembered he had a date.

LESS ACCEPTABLE: He fell *off of* the stool.

PREFERRED: He fell *off* the stool.

(71) OK, O.K., okay   In informal writing, *OK, O.K.,* and *okay* are acceptably used to mean "all right." Do not use either the abbreviations or *okay* in formal writing, however.

INFORMAL: This architect's blueprint looks *okay.*

FORMAL: This architect's blueprint looks *flawless.*

(72) only   *Only* should be placed in front of the word it logically modifies.

EXAMPLES: *Only* Steve bought a balloon. (No one else bought a balloon.)

Steve bought *only* a balloon. (Steve bought nothing else.)

(73) ought   Never use *ought* with *have* or *had.* Simply eliminate *have* or *had.*

NONSTANDARD: The washing machine *had ought* to work now.

CORRECT: The washing machine *ought* to work now.

271

(74) outside of   Do not use this expression to mean "besides" or "except."

NONSTANDARD: No one came to the party *outside of* Dinah.

CORRECT: No one came to the party *except* Dinah.

(75) parameter   This word is correctly used only in mathematical contexts, in which it designates a variable. Do not use *parameter* to mean "boundary," "limit," "scope," "detail," and so on.

LESS ACCEPTABLE: These are the *parameters* of the problem.

PREFERRED: These are the *limits* of the problem.

(76) persecute, prosecute   *Persecute* means "to subject to ill treatment." *Prosecute* means "to bring a lawsuit against."

EXAMPLES: He was *persecuted* for his religious beliefs.

Jack is being *prosecuted* for libel.

(77) plurals that do not end in -s.   The plurals of certain nouns from Greek and Latin are formed as they were in their original languages. Words such as *criteria, media,* and *phenomena* are plural and should not be treated as if they were singular *(criterion, medium, phenomenon).*

INCORRECT: *That criteria* for selecting a winner *is* unfair.

CORRECT: *Those criteria* for selecting a winner *are* unfair.

INCORRECT: The mass *media is* responsible for the fast and accurate distribution of information.

CORRECT: The mass *media are* responsible for the fast and accurate distribution of information.

(78) poorly   *Poorly* is used informally to mean "ill." Avoid this use in formal situations.

INFORMAL: Grandmother is feeling *poorly*.

FORMAL: Grandmother is feeling *ill.*

(79) precede, proceed   *Precede* means "to go before." *Proceed* means "to move or go forward."

EXAMPLES: The *preceding* paragraph introduced the topic.

Proceed to the next step.

(80) principal, principle   As an adjective, *principal* means "most important" or "chief"; as a noun, it means "a person who has controlling authority." *Principle,* always a noun, means "a fundamental law."

ADJECTIVE: His *principal* goal is to make money.

NOUN: Mr. Clark is the school's *principal.*

NOUN: "Thou shalt not kill" is a *principle* of many religions.

(81) raise, rise   *Raise* usually takes a direct object. *Rise* never takes a direct object.

EXAMPLES: *Raise* the flag at dawn.

Smoke *rises* from the chimneys every morning.

(82) real   *Real* means "authentic." The use of *real* to mean "very" or "really" should be avoided in formal writing.

INFORMAL: Dwight was *real* discouraged.

FORMAL: Dwight was *very* discouraged.

(83) says   *Says* should not be substituted for *said.*

NONSTANDARD: Then she *says* to me, "Be quiet!"

CORRECT: Then she *said* to me, "Be quiet!"

(84) seen   *Seen* is a past participle and can be used as a verb only with a helping verb.

NONSTANDARD: I *seen* this movie before.

CORRECT: I *have seen* this movie before.

(85) set, sit   *Set* means "to put (something) in a certain place." Its principal parts—*set, setting, set,* and *set*—are usually followed by a direct object. *Sit* means "to be seated." Its principal parts—*sit, sitting, sat,* and *sat*—are never followed by a direct object.

EXAMPLES: *Set* the chair in this corner.

Sit in a chair before you buy it.

(86) shape   The meaning of *shape* is "spatial form." In formal writing, avoid using *shape* to mean "condition."

INFORMAL: The driver of the car is in serious *shape.*

FORMAL: The driver of the car is in serious *condition.*

273

(87) slow, slowly   Although *slow* can now be used as either an adjective or an adverb, careful writers use it as an adjective. *Slowly* is preferred as the adverb.

LESS ACCEPTABLE: Crawl *slow* along this ledge.

PREFERRED: Crawl *slowly* along this ledge.

(88) so   *So* is a coordinating conjunction. It should be avoided when you mean "so that."

LESS ACCEPTABLE: Move over *so* I can sit down.

PREFERRED: Move over *so that* I can sit down.

(89) take and   This is a nonstandard expression. Eliminate it entirely.

NONSTANDARD: *Take and* put these flowers in a vase.

CORRECT: Put these flowers in a vase.

(90) than, then   *Than* is used in comparisons. Do not confuse it with the adverb *then,* which usually refers to time.

EXAMPLES: A pig is smarter *than* most dogs.

First put the onions in, and *then* add the mushrooms.

(91) that, which, who   *That* refers to people or things; *which* refers only to things; *who* refers only to people.

EXAMPLES: I forgot the key *that* (or *which*) opens this door.

She is an actress *that (or who)* will do very well in the role of Lady Macbeth.

(92) their, there, they're   *Their,* a possessive pronoun, always modifies a noun. *There* can be used either as an expletive at the beginning of a sentence or as an adverb. *They're* is a contraction of *they are.*

PRONOUN: The frightened cattled milled around *their* pen.

EXPLETIVE: *There* can be no room for error.

ADVERB: *There* are the recently excavated artifacts.

CONTRACTION: I hope *they're* not serious.

(93) them, them there, these here, this here, that there   *Them* is always a personal pronoun, never an adjective. When a sentence calls for an adjective, use *these* or *those*

274

in place of either *them* or *them there*. To correct a sentence containing *these here, this here*, and *that there*, simply leave out *here* and *there*.

NONSTANDARD: *Them* flowers certainly look pretty.

CORRECT: *These* flowers certainly look pretty.

NONSTANDARD: *This here* knife needs sharpening.

CORRECT: *This* knife needs sharpening.

(94) till, until   These words are interchangeable. Be careful, however, of spelling. *Till* should not be spelled *til* or *'til; until* always ends in one *l*.

EXAMPLE: The children played *till* (or *until*) it was dark.

(95) to, too, two   *To,* a preposition, begins a prepositional phrase or an infinitive. *Too,* an adverb, modifies adjectives and other adverbs. *Two* is a number.

PREPOSITION: *to* a concert, *to* the attic

INFINITIVE: *to* think, *to* understand

ADVERB: *too* quiet, *too awkwardly*

NUMBER: *two* cents, *two* umbrellas

(96) unique   *Unique* means "one of a kind." It should not be used to mean "odd," "interesting," or "unusual." Since the word means "one of a kind," such expressions as *most unique, very unique,* and *extremely unique* are illogical.

ILLOGICAL: He enjoys a *most unique* life style.

CORRECT: He enjoys a *unique* life style.

(97) want in, want out   These are nonstandard expressions for "want to come in," "want to enter," "want to leave," or "want to get out." *Want* should also not be used before other prepositions such as *down, off,* or *up*.

NONSTANDARD: The dog is scratching at the door because he *wants in.*

CORRECT: The dog is scratching at the door because he *wants to come in.*

NONSTANDARD: I *want down* from this horse.

CORRECT: I *want to get down* from this horse.

(98) ways *Ways* is plural. Do not use it after the article *a*. Use instead the singular form *way*.

NONSTANDARD: I have *a* considerable *ways* to drive yet.

CORRECT: I have *a* considerable *way* to drive yet.

(99) when, where Do not use *when* or *where* directly after a linking verb. Do not use *where* as a substitute for *that*.

NONSTANDARD: A good memory *was when* my dad gave me a pony.

An automat *is where* food is dispensed by machines.

I read *where* old coins are a good investment.

CORRECT: A good memory is of being given a pony by my dad.

An automat is a cafeteria *where* food is dispensed by machines.

I read *that* old coins are a good investment.

(100) -wise Avoid using this suffix to create new words for a particular situation.

LESS ACCEPTABLE: *Energywise*, this freezer is very efficient.

PREFERRED: This freezer is very *energy-efficient*.

EXERCISE A: Avoiding Usage Problems 1–10. Choose the correct expression to complete each sentence.

1. What (affect, effect) did her speech have on you?
2. They should have (all ready, already) left by now.
3. Jim (ain't, isn't) capable of doing that stunt.
4. Everyone (accept, except) me was dressed in black.
5. You can do (alot, much) to improve yourself.
6. A speck of dust can (aggravate, annoy) an inflamed eye.
7. His (advice, advise) should be ignored.
8. Mr. Rodgers is clearly (a, an) honorable man.
9. He tried to (adapt, adopt) a philosophy of nonviolence.
10. The teacher was (aggravated, annoyed) by the noise.
11. One (affect, effect) of the change was increased profit.
12. The ice cream is (all ready, already) to be served.
13. I (accept, except) your proposal.
14. The report (accuses, alleges) negligence by the retailer.

15. How should the committee (a lot, alot, allot) the money?
16. She (accused, alleged) him of trying to evade the issue.
17. The insulin (affected, effected) an immediate improvement.
18. He (advices, advises) her not to take aspirin.
19. The pioneers (adapted, adopted) to a hostile environment.
20. We heard (a, an) haunting melody in the background.

EXERCISE B: Avoiding Usage Problems 11–20. Choose the correct expression to complete each sentence.

1. My keys must be (somewhere, somewheres) here.
2. We should shout the cheer (all together, altogether).
3. One black orchid grew (among, between) many white ones.
4. You look (all right, alright) without any mascara.
5. She feels (anxious, eager) about the colt's injured leg.
6. Despite the economic predictions, I remain an optimist (anyway, anyways).
7. School is dismissed at 3:00 (P.M., P.M. in the afternoon).
8. (Any one, Anyone) of these tools will do the job.
9. I haven't seen Jenny (anywhere, anywheres).
10. An enormous (amount, number) of garbage was piled up.
11. Becky and Jim were (all together, altogether) exhausted after the marathon dance.
12. We have no clues (as to, about) how the car crashed.
13. We were late (as, because) we ran out of gas.
14. Ask (anyone, any one) for assistance.
15. Willy was (anxious, eager) to help his neighbors.
16. It is not (all right, alright) for you to barge in here.
17. Be at the door by 10:00 (A.M., A.M. in the morning).
18. I left the windows open (as, since) no rain was forecast.
19. There should be no strife (among, between) you and me.
20. A large (amount, number) of complaints were received.

EXERCISE C: Avoiding Usage Problems 21–30. Choose the correct expression to complete each sentence.

1. She is (awfully, very) frightened in crowded elevators.
2. As a child, my father was (blond, blonde).
3. Listen to this record for (a while, awhile).
4. Do you know where the children (are, are at)?
5. The reason the cat ran is (because, that) a dog came.

6. I (beat, won) her at a game of handball.
7. (Being that, Since) they expected death at the hands of the Romans, the people of Masada killed themselves.
8. Please (bring, take) that hammer to me.
9. Be at the house (at about, at) five o'clock.
10. (The reason my grandmother lives with us now is, My grandmother lives with us now) because she was lonely.
11. (Beside, Besides) Japan and Germany, what other countries made up the Axis Powers?
12. I look (bad, awful) in shades of purple.
13. (Bring, Take) these overdue books back to the library.
14. The telegram arrived (at about, about) noon.
15. Marlene keeps a kerosene lamp (beside, besides) the door.
16. Karen and Eric are (blonds, blondes).
17. I made a wrong turn and don't know where I (am, am at).
18. Try to (beat, win) the other team if you can.
19. Stay (a while, awhile) and tell us about your new job.
20. We went to the movies (being as, since) we were bored.

EXERCISE D: Avoiding Usage Problems 31–40. Choose the correct expression to complete each sentence.

1. My new computer (can, may) do more than my old one.
2. We (can't help but admire, can't help admiring) her grace.
3. The soap bubbles will (burst, bust) upon contact.
4. I take umbrage at your offensive (ad, advertisement) in yesterday's paper.
5. The (continual, continuous) noise of trains rumbling past his house every half hour kept him awake.
6. Join our (bunch, group) if you enjoy good conversation.
7. The courts can not (condemn, condone) his brutality.
8. She has little doubt (but what, that) her son is qualified.
9. In my previous letter to your firm, I requested that the (phones, telephones) be repaired promptly.
10. The American Standard System is (different from, different than) the Metric System.
11. His music (doesn't, don't) appeal to me very much.
12. I don't doubt (but what, that) she is correct.
13. My typewriter (doesn't, don't) work as well as yours.
14. Rome was (different from, different than) what she expected.
15. I (can't help but regret, can't help regretting) his remark.

16. The flower girl carried a (bunch, group) of daisies.
17. After seeing how much I wanted to ride the tractor, he said that I (can, may) learn how to drive it.
18. The dictator was universally (condemned, condoned) for his ruthless treatment of dissidents.
19. Olivia (burst, busted) out of the den.
20. (Continual, Continuous) walking from dawn until dusk raised blisters on their feet.

EXERCISE E: Avoiding Usage Problems 41–50. Choose the correct expression to complete each sentence.

1. I was nervous when I (dived, dove) into the pool.
2. Thousands of Cubans have (emigrated, immigrated) to this country.
3. She was very (enthused, enthusiastic) about the race.
4. (Due to, Because of) an unavoidable delay, the results of the poll can't be given until next week.
5. We visited New York and Boston. The (former, latter) is the home of the United Nations and the Statue of Liberty.
6. He sometimes (done, has done) work for us in the past.
7. (Farther, Further) suggestions will be appreciated.
8. (Because of, Due to) a heavy rainfall, this expressway has been temporarily closed.
9. I (did, done) better in this class because I cared.
10. Put (fewer, less) water in the soup next time.
11. Tomorrow we must drive a little (farther, further).
12. (Due to the fact that, Since) the air conditioner isn't working, everyone should wear light clothing.
13. I bought a skirt and a blouse, but the sleeves of the (former, latter) were much too short.
14. (Fewer, Less) nails are needed for this type of paneling.
15. The children (dived, dove) into the pile of leaves.
16. Abigail (done, has done) was she promised to do.
17. The starving victims of political revolution (emigrated, immigrated) from Cambodia.
18. I will be forced to buy a new car (because, due to the fact that) my old car's transmission is beyond repair.
19. We (dived, dove) headfirst into the inviting water.
20. Everyone at the meeting was (enthusiastic, enthused) about the plans for a new auditorium.

279

EXERCISE F: Avoiding Usage Problems 51–60. Choose the correct expression to complete each sentence.

1. Eugene is a (nice, friendly) person.
2. Colorful lanterns were (hanged, hung) from the beams.
3. Sandra (got, earned) the respect of the class.
4. (Irregardless, Regardless) of the choppy water, Matt guided the boat beyond the buoys.
5. These figurines belong (in, into) the curio cabinet.
6. I wish Claudia had (gone, went) with us to the beach.
7. Sunshine is (healthy, healthful) because it is a source of vitamin D.
8. Neither parent will (get, obtain) custody of the children.
9. Let's go (in, into) this famous restaurant.
10. We were confident that the administrator would make a (judicial, judicious) decision.
11. They have a (lovely, close) relationship after thirty years of marriage.
12. The children (gone, have gone) to the park this afternoon.
13. (Just take, Take just) a little more time on this.
14. Mary has been very (healthy, healthful) all winter.
15. The boy had (gotten, climbed) to the top of the tree.
16. He gave a (good, detailed) account of his expenditures.
17. There (just was, was just) one thing left to do.
18. He (hanged, hung) his coat on the peg in the hall.
19. What are the responsibilities of the (judicial, judicious) branch of the government?
20. I'll be there, (regardless, irregardless) of the date.

EXERCISE G: Avoiding Usage Problems 61–70. Choose the correct expression to complete each sentence.

1. He (learned, taught) us how to check the oil in the car.
2. (Lie, Lay) the baby on the scales.
3. There (may be, maybe) a hidden clause in the contract.
4. The sun looks (kind of, somewhat) reddish as it sets.
5. A (lose, loose) knot was tied around his wrists.
6. She preened herself (as, like) a peacock would.
7. What (kind of, kinds of) insects are these?
8. Some of the tribe must (of, have) settled in this valley.
9. (Leave, Let) the hors d'oeuvres alone!

10. Let me (lose, loose) from these shackles.
11. (Lie, Lay) down on the couch until your dizziness passes.
12. I would (of, have) come sooner had I known you were ill.
13. I hope I don't (lose, loose) my job in the warehouse.
14. What (sort of, sort of a) jacket do you want to buy?
15. I'm (sort of, rather) reluctant to criticize Paul's work.
16. (May be, Maybe) you will listen to me now.
17. Please (leave, let) me stay as your apprentice.
18. The teacher (learned, taught) the class phonics.
19. His lunatic ravings convinced everyone that he was (angry, mad).
20. I had just (laid, lain) down when the telephone rang.

EXERCISE H: Avoiding Usage Problems 71–80. Choose the correct expression to complete each sentence.

1. There (had ought, ought) to be a law against this.
2. Strange phenomena (has, have) been reported at the house.
3. The developers discussed the (parameters, details) of the new housing project.
4. (Only admit, Admit only) those who have a ticket.
5. Belinda is feeling (ill, poorly) today.
6. Mr. President, will the hostages be (okay, safe)?
7. Everyone (outside of, except) Geoffrey wore a heavy coat.
8. She (hadn't ought, ought not) to talk loudly.
9. It is against my (principals, principles) to harm anyone.
10. The Puritans had been (persecuted, prosecuted) for their supposedly heretical beliefs.
11. (Besides, Outside of) the excellent service, there is nothing to recommend this hotel.
12. The landscaper's plan showed the (parameters, boundaries) of the garden.
13. The queen is feeling (ill, poorly).
14. The (principal, principle) delivered the speech.
15. Scrutinize the (preceding, proceeding) paragraph for errors.
16. The (principal, principle) actor in the film is British.
17. Book publishing in many ways is the least modernized (media, medium).
18. Excuse me, Sir Robert, is everything (satisfactory, okay)?
19. Shall we (precede, proceed) to examine the evidence?
20. He will be (persecuted, prosecuted) for forgery.

EXERCISE I: Avoiding Usage Problems 81–90. Choose the correct expression to complete each sentence.

1. (Set, Sit) here where we can talk undisturbed.
2. He is in poor (shape, condition) after the accident.
3. A frog is larger (than, then) a toad.
4. We were (real, very) sad to learn of her decision.
5. I jumped when she (says, said) to me, "There's a spider on your shoulder."
6. We walked (slow, slowly) along the avenue.
7. Rodney promised to apologize, but then he (says, said) he wouldn't.
8. (Take and leave, Leave) these folders on John's desk.
9. We will (raise, rise) corn next summer.
10. We took a nap (so, so that) we wouldn't be tired later.
11. We rounded up the stray calves and (than, then) headed back to camp.
12. (Set, Sit) this heavy trunk somewhere in the hall.
13. Stand in the light (so, so that) I can take your picture.
14. The plastic flowers looked (real, very) pretty.
15. Please (raise, rise) when your name is called.
16. Virgil laughed and (said, says), "Impossible!"
17. (Slow, Slowly) the wind and rain eroded the soil.
18. The (condition, shape) of the box is rectangular.
19. The bread will (raise, rise) as the yeast ferments.
20. She (took and handed, handed) the money to the cashier.

EXERCISE J: Avoiding Usage Problems 91–100. Choose the correct expression to complete each sentence.

1. (Their, They're) version of handball is jai alai.
2. I have a long (ways, way) to walk before I reach home.
3. The beggar (which, who) always stood at the gate was not there today.
4. A trash can is (the place where, where) the refuse belongs.
5. I (want out, want to get out) of this situation.
6. (Moneywise, In financial matters), she is very shrewd.
7. These roses won't grow well (til, till) they've been pruned.
8. Sarah's approach to a potential customer is (very unique, unusual).
9. (There, They're) the best acrobatic team in the world.

10. Use (too, two) gallons of paint for the living room.
11. Rhonda drove a great (way, ways) just to see you.
12. He (wants in, wants to come in) to escape the furious mob.
13. (Them there, Those) hairless dogs won't live for a week in this cold climate.
14. We want (to, two) perfect our accounting system.
15. The apartment won't be available ('til, until) the first of the month.
16. Some people think that the third time a person goes under the water is (the time, when) he or she will sink.
17. That numismatist told me that this old coin is (very unique, unique).
18. We were bothered by (to, too) many interferences.
19. Jocelyn is very active (sportswise, in sports).
20. (Their, There) are no two fingerprints alike.

EXERCISE K: Correcting Usage Problems. Rewrite each sentence, correcting the error in usage.

1. Anyone of these tablecloths will look fine.
2. Everything is alright now that your father is home.
3. Outside of Ginny, no one was interested in going to the beach for the afternoon.
4. The skeleton of a reptile is different than the skeleton of a mammal.
5. Moira considers it a honor to have been chosen to speak first at the assembly.
6. The pond should of been stocked with fish.
7. Everyone accept Dinah spent the hot day sitting on the veranda.
8. Relax for awhile and your headache will disappear.
9. Take and deliver these newspapers to your customers.
10. His flight was delayed due to thick fog.
11. There ain't any way he can earn that much money before the end of the summer.
12. In order to use this play at our school, we will have to adopt it considerably.
13. The children found shells everywheres they looked.
14. Throw your quarter in the basket of the toll booth.
15. The children were anxious to open their presents on Christmas morning.

16. You should not bust in without knocking first.
17. A startled bullfrog dove off the lily pad.
18. Stir the soup with that there wooden spoon.
19. The reporters asked there questions rapidly since the President was about to leave.
20. The captain of our team had several ideas as to how we can improve our playing.
21. A week after the operation, she was all together recovered.
22. Her singing was effected by a sinus condition.
23. Please take your own ice skates when you come.
24. Clarence can't help but speak slowly and carefully.
25. She adviced us to buy fresh vegetables if possible.
26. Your statement don't answer my question.
27. Who beside Maurice will help us?
28. Even if it does look cloudy, let's go to the zoo anyways.
29. Melanie slipped and fell off of the step.
30. I don't doubt but what Kim is always arguing with them.
31. The kitten wants out.
32. The boys worked slow building their fort.
33. Some of us need farther explanation.
34. The guests were aggravated by their host's irritating remarks about their taste.
35. The insurance company alleged her of being an arsonist.
36. The children were already for bed.
37. Dad's arthritis is making him feel poorly today.
38. Baked potatoes contain less calories than french fries.
39. We saw a bunch of pelicans diving for food.
40. Irregardless of his bad disposition, he is still a competent teacher.
41. Bill seems alright in spite of his narrow escape.
42. The tourists wandered between the trees in the orchard, marveling at the spring blossoms.
43. Will you please lie the money on the kitchen table?
44. We need a larger amount of actors if we want to perform this play.
45. Has anyone of the letters we sent been returned?
46. Where is this town's post office at?
47. The plane will arrive at 8:00 P.M. in the evening.
48. We hanged the picture over the living room sofa.
49. I hope he doesn't loose the money before he arrives.
50. She really should of given us a better explanation.

DEVELOPING WRITING SKILLS: Using the Correct Expressions in Your Own Writing. Use each expression in a sentence of your own.

1. condone
2. principle
3. let
4. raise
5. bunch
6. lie
7. further
8. just
9. ought
10. accept
11. prosecute
12. mad
13. done
14. set
15. immigrate
16. former . . . latter
17. all ready
18. adapt
19. gone
20. except

Skills Review and Writing Workshop

Miscellaneous Problems in Usage

CHECKING YOUR SKILLS

Rewrite the paragraph, correcting the errors in usage.

(1) Perhaps the most important defense butterflies have is there high reproductive rate. (2) By the end of their lifetimes, most females will have lain up to 1,000 eggs. (3) Some butterflies also have chemical defenses, which allow them to take and secrete poisonous substances. (4) Others have sharp hairs, which can effect the skin of enemies. (5) Another of the principle defenses of the butterfly is its coloring. (6) For example, moths who rest in open spaces during the day are colored to match the environment. (7) Being that the colors of their bodies are those of grass, bark, and leaves, they are nearly invisible. (8) Another kind of moth with drab-colored front wings has bright-colored hind wings, and the former can be raised suddenly to startle predators. (9) Beside having the usual defenses, the tiger moth can make a high-pitched noise. (10) These are some of the ways butterflies have adopted to their potentially dangerous environment.

USING USAGE SKILLS IN WRITING
Writing a Press Release

Imagine that you will run for public office. Write a press release announcing your decision, following the steps below.

Prewriting: Make an outline of the information you should include in your announcement. List your opinions on questions of national or local importance, depending on the office you are running for.

Writing: State your candidacy and mention past experiences and achievements that qualify you for the office. Give your stand on important issues and on your plans to implement your candidacy.

Revising: Go over your work, eliminating any usage errors and unnecessary words or material and tightening your structure. After you have revised, proofread carefully.

11

Capitalization and Abbreviation

The goal of every writer should be to write clearly in a style that is both personal and effective. Before achieving this goal, however, a writer must master the mechanics of writing. The word *mechanics* refers to the technical part of constructing sentences. A writer who has mastered the mechanics of writing uses capital letters and abbreviations properly and punctuates many different kinds of sentences correctly.

This chapter presents rules for the use of capital letters and abbreviations. These rules have developed over the years to help people write material so that others can readily understand their meaning. You are probably already familiar with the restricted use of capital letters to signal only certain important words. You may also already use abbreviations in certain situations. Studying the rules in this chapter can help you perfect your writing skill.

11.1 Capitalization

Capitalization signals the beginning of a sentence or points out certain words within a sentence.

To capitalize means to begin a word with a capital letter.

Capitals for First Words

Always capitalize the first word in all types of sentences.

Capitalize the first words in declarative, interrogative, imperative, and exclamatory sentences.

DECLARATIVE: A piece of art often reflects the times in which an artist lives.

INTERROGATIVE: Do you find contemporary art difficult to interpret at times?

IMPERATIVE: Look around you, for art is everywhere.

EXCLAMATORY: That Impressionist painting is magnificent!

Interjections and incomplete questions are also capitalized.

Capitalize the first word in interjections and incomplete questions.

INTERJECTIONS: Oh!   Awful!

INCOMPLETE QUESTIONS: Why not?   When?

If a quotation is a complete sentence, it should also begin with a capital.

Capitalize the first word in a quotation if the quotation is a complete sentence.

EXAMPLES: The instructor began by saying, "Music is a way of painting a picture with melodies."

"To play effectively, you must truly understand the piece you are playing," the professor continued.

"You must practice every day," he emphatically stated. "Nothing is more important than practice."

"If one hears bad music," Oscar Wilde once observed, "it is one's duty to drown it by one's conversation."

The first two examples above show quotations that consist of one sentence each. The third example shows a quotation that consists of two sentences. Notice that the first word of each sentence is capitalized. The last example consists of one sentence that is interrupted by a "he said/she said" expression. Only the first word of the sentence that has been interrupted is capitalized.

When only a portion of a sentence is quoted, do not capitalize the first word unless it is the first word in the sentence in which it is included.

EXAMPLE: As Dostoyevsky advocated, an artist needs to paint what exists around him or her, for art should always be a means of "responding to human needs."

If a sentence follows a colon, it should also be capitalized. The first word of a list of words or phrases following a colon, however, should not be capitalized.

Capitalize the first word after a colon if the word begins a complete sentence.

COMPLETE SENTENCE: She made one point over and over: The painting is more lasting than the artist.

LIST OF WORDS OR PHRASES: I saw some famous art work at the Dresden exhibit: lovely ivory carvings, beautiful paintings, and a magnificent armor display.

Poetry should always be written as the poet intended it to be. In most poetry the first word in each line is capitalized even if it does not begin a new sentence.

Capitalize the first word in each line of most poetry.

EXAMPLE: I mind where we parted in yon shady glen,
On the steep, steep side of Ben Lomond,
Where the deep purple hue the Highland hills we view,
And the moon coming out in the gloamy.
—Lady John Scott

NOTE ABOUT *I* AND *O:* You should always capitalize the pronoun *I* and the interjection *O* even in the middle of a sentence.

EXAMPLES: Father and I agreed on a plan.
"Long fed on boundless hopes, race of man,
How angrily thou spurn'st all simpler fare!"
—Matthew Arnold

Do not capitalize the interjection *oh,* however, unless it occurs at the beginning of a sentence.

290

Colons and capitals are also used in formal resolutions that state the subjects of debates, legislative decisions, and acts.

Capitalize the first word after a colon in a formal resolution.

EXAMPLE: Resolved: That the Senior Class hold a car wash next Saturday to raise money for new band uniforms.

EXERCISE A: Capitalizing First Words. Copy each of the following items, capitalizing the appropriate words.

EXAMPLE: drive carefully.

Drive carefully.

1. "your explanation," said the teacher, "is difficult to accept."
2. i lived with visions from my company,
   instead of men and women, years ago,
   and found them gentle mates, nor thought to know
   a sweeter music than they played on me.
                    —Elizabeth Barrett Browning
3. resolved: that the state legislature increase the school year by three days.
4. the candidate expressed his anger: he could not believe the allegations of the opposing party.
5. remember the line, "o blithe spirit!"
6. i wonder, oh, i wonder, how she will ever get over her grief.
7. how much?
8. how many times have you visited Texas and New Mexico?
9. The mayor said, "we are honored to have you visit our city."
10. oh! this is dreadful!

Capitals for Proper Nouns

Nouns, as you know, name people, places, and things. They are classified as either common or proper. Proper nouns, which name specific examples of people, places, or things, require capitalization.

Capitalize all proper nouns.

COMMON NOUNS: judge, town, clock, sister, ship, violin, sailors, states, apples

PROPER NOUNS: Judge Alexander P. Stevens, Patricia Davis, Cape Cod, Broadway, Denmark, Mississippi Valley, *Newsweek, Air Force 1, Harmony in Red*

As you can see from the preceding examples, there are several categories of proper nouns. One category is names.

Capitalize each part of a person's full name.

EXAMPLES: Felicia A. Burton, G.T. Schmidt, Luis Teresina

Surnames sometimes consist of several parts. Capitalize both parts of surnames beginning with *Mc, O',* or *St.*

EXAMPLES: McNamara, O'Sullivan, St. John

If, however, surnames begin with *de, D', la, le, Mac, van,* or *von,* spelling may differ. To ensure accuracy, ask for the correct spelling.

EXAMPLES: D'Ambrosio or de Ambrosio or Dambrosio

Van Fleet or van Fleet or Vanfleet

The proper names of animals should also be capitalized.

EXAMPLES: Lad, a dog   Flicka, a horse

Proper nouns referring to particular places must also be capitalized. Many of them consist of more than one word and a few contain articles, prepositions, and conjunctions. Articles, prepositions, and conjunctions are not usually capitalized.

Capitalize geographical and place names.

Following are examples of geographical and place names.

GEOGRAPHICAL AND PLACE NAMES	
Streets	Fulton Street, Linden Boulevard
Boroughs, Towns, and Cities	Brooklyn, Houston, Los Angeles
Counties, States, and Provinces	Orange County, Arizona, British Columbia
Nations and Continents	Zimbabwe, the United States of America, Europe, South America

Mountains	Mount McKinley, Atlas Mountains
Valleys and Deserts	Shenandoah Valley, Sahara Desert
Islands and Peninsulas	Canary Islands, Sinai Peninsula
Sections of a Country	the Southwest, New England
Scenic Spots	Olympic National Park, the Colosseum, the Continental Divide
Rivers and Falls	Amazon River, Bridalveil Falls
Lakes and Bays	Lake Huron, Rangeley Lake, Hudson Bay
Seas and Oceans	Adriatic Sea, Pacific Ocean
Celestial Bodies	Saturn, Halley's Comet
Monuments and Memorials	Washington Monument, Arlington National Cemetery, the Alamo
Buildings	Carnegie Hall, City Hall
School and Meeting Rooms	Laboratory C, Room 14, the Oval Office

NOTE ABOUT CAPITALIZING DIRECTIONS: Words indicating direction can be used in two ways: to name a section of a country and to give travel directions. These words are capitalized only when they refer to a section of a country.

EXAMPLES: Urban areas of the *Northeast* face many problems.

We traveled two miles *west* and one mile *south*.

NOTE ABOUT CELESTIAL BODIES: Do not capitalize *moon* and *sun*, as you do the names of other celestial bodies. Capitalize *earth* only when you refer to it as one of the planets. Do not capitalize *earth* when it is preceded by the word *the*.

EXAMPLE: The *moon* is in orbit around the *earth*, and the *earth* is in orbit around the *sun*.

NOTE ABOUT CAPITALIZING *THEATER, HOTEL, COLLEGE,* AND SIMILAR WORDS: Do not capitalize words such as *theater, hotel, college, room,* and so forth unless the word is part of the proper name.

EXAMPLES: They plan to attend *college* next fall.

They plan to go to *Sam Houston State College*.

Capitals are also used with words referring to historical periods, events, documents, dates, and holidays.

Capitalize the names of specific events and periods of time.

SPECIFIC EVENTS AND TIMES	
Historical Periods	the Renaissance, the Mesozoic Era
Historical Events	World War II, the Russian Revolution, Battle of King's Mountain, Rio de Janeiro Conference, Trail of Tears
Documents	the Magna Charta, Declaration of Independence
Days and Months	Tuesday, Fridays, July 20, the third week in April
Holidays and Religious Days	Easter, Father's Day, Martin Luther King Day, Hanukkah, St. Valentine's Day
Special Events	Berkshire Music Festival, the Rose Bowl, Eastern States Exhibition

NOTE ABOUT THE SEASONS: Do not capitalize any reference you make to the seasons.

EXAMPLE: In late *spring* we plant tomatoes in our garden.

References to groups of all kinds are also capitalized. These include organizations, government bodies, races, nationalities, languages spoken by different nationalities, and religions.

Capitalize the names of various organizations, government bodies, political parties, races, nationalities, languages, and religious references.

VARIOUS GROUPS	
Clubs	Kennedy High School Stamp Club, Rotary, New York Athletic Club, Knights of Columbus
Organizations	the Salvation Army, American Medical Association, Veterans of Foreign Wars

294

Institutions	National Museum of Art, the Boston Symphony, John Hopkins Hospital
Schools	Adlai E. Stevenson High School, Stanford University, Rensselaer Polytechnic Institute
Businesses	Allied Chemical Corporation, International Coins and Currency, Inc., Prentice-Hall Canada, Inc.
Government Bodies	the Senate, House of Lords, Nuclear Regulatory Commission, Federal Deposit Insurance Corporation, Army of the Potomac
Political Parties	Republican Party, Liberal Party, the Democrats
Races	Mongoloid, Negro, Caucasian
Nationalities	American, Canadian, Mexican, German, Israeli, Chinese, Mexican, Swiss, Congolese
Languages	English, French, Spanish, Italian, Polish, Swahili, Hindi
Religious References	*Christianity:* God, the Lord, the Father, the Holy Spirit, the Bible, the New Testament, the Holy Father *Judaism:* God, the Lord, the Prophets, the Torah, the Talmud *Islam:* Allah, the Prophets, the Koran, Mohammed, Muslims *Hinduism:* Brahma, the Bhagavad-Gita, the Vedas *Buddhism:* the Buddha, Mahayana, Hinayana

NOTE ABOUT PRONOUN REFERENCES: When you use pronouns to refer to the Judeo-Christian deity they should always be capitalized.

EXAMPLE: I prayed for His help.

When referring to ancient mythology, you should not capitalize the word *god* or *goddess.* The names of the gods and goddesses, however, are capitalized.

EXAMPLES: the *gods* of ancient Greece

the Roman *god* Mars

Finally, three more categories of proper nouns also require capitalization. Study the rule and the examples in the following chart.

Capitalize the names of awards, the names of specific types of air, sea, space, and land craft, and brand names.

OTHER IMPORTANT PROPER NOUNS	
Awards	Nobel Peace Prize, Father of the Year, Pulitzer Prize, Stanley Cup, Oscar, Arista
Specific Air, Sea, Space, and Land Craft	a Boeing 727, *S.S. Columbia, Viking I,* Metroliner
Brand Names	Kellogg's Special K, Kleenex

EXERCISE B: Using Capitals for Proper Nouns. Copy each sentence that needs capitals, adding the necessary capitals. If a sentence needs no further capitalization, write *correct.*

EXAMPLE: The most powerful god of the early greeks was zeus.

The most powerful god of the early Greeks was Zeus.

1. The army of the cumberland operated mainly in the states of georgia, tennessee, and kentucky during the civil war.
2. He speaks three languages: spanish, french, and italian.
3. In the course on comparative religions, we studied the old testament, the new testament, and the koran.
4. My teacher insists that we read the declaration of independence, the constitution, and the bill of rights.
5. Our trip to washington included visits to the lincoln memorial and the tomb of the unknown soldier.
6. Bolivia, located in the central part of south america, is separated from the pacific ocean by chile and peru.
7. My sister received a new york state regents scholarship and a westinghouse science award.
8. Of all the methods of travel, I prefer flying on a lockheed tristar.
9. For science I prepared a chart illustrating the different positions of the big dipper.

10. The culver city art league meets the second monday of every month.
11. The prom at longfellow high school will be on friday, june 17.
12. School begins the day after labor day, and our first holiday is rosh hashana in late september.
13. Much to our surprise, no poet received a national book award this year.
14. Now that we have learned so much about the moon, I wonder how long it will take to get new information about the sun.
15. Marie, who was the leader of arista in high school, was recently elected to phi beta kappa in college.
16. If you have a complaint about your mercury cougar, I suggest you write to the customer relations department of ford motor company in dearborn, michigan.
17. One meeting will be held in conference room b, and the other will be held in conference room 5 in the basement.
18. We saw works by picasso at the museum of modern art.
19. Several of my classmates are sending college applications to northwestern university and to the university of chicago.
20. President during the era of good feeling was james monroe.

Capitals for Proper Adjectives

A proper adjective is an adjective formed from a proper noun or a proper noun used as an adjective. Most proper adjectives require capitalization.

Capitalize most proper adjectives.

PROPER ADJECTIVES
FORMED FROM PROPER NOUNS: American, Elizabethan, Biblical, Chinese

PROPER NOUNS
USED AS ADJECTIVES: a Chicago accent, a March day, a Eugene O'Neill play

Some proper adjectives are no longer capitalized, however.

Do not capitalize certain frequently used proper adjectives.

EXAMPLES: pasteurized milk, turkish towel, french toast, herculean effort, venetian blinds, quixotic quest

297

Brand names used with common nouns are capitalized according to the following rule.

Capitalize a brand name used as an adjective, but do not capitalize the common noun it modifies.

EXAMPLES: Westinghouse refrigerator, Levi jeans

When two proper adjectives are used with one common noun, be guided by the following rule.

Do not capitalize a common noun used with two proper adjectives.

Compare the examples in the following chart. Notice in each case that a common noun used with two or more proper adjectives is not capitalized.

One Proper Adjective	Two or More Proper Adjectives
Conservative Party	Conservative and Liberal parties
Main Street	Main, Welch, and Macopin streets
Mississippi River	Mississippi and Missouri rivers

The last two rules about capitalization with proper adjectives concern proper adjectives to which prefixes have been attached and proper adjectives hyphenated in other ways.

Do not capitalize prefixes attached to proper adjectives unless the prefix refers to a nationality.

EXAMPLES: pro-English   Franco-Prussian

all-American   Anglo-American

Notice that the prefixes in the examples on the left are not capitalized. Those in the examples on the right are capitalized because they refer to nationalities.

Occasionally, you will come across a proper adjective hyphenated in another way.

In a hyphenated adjective, capitalize only the proper adjective.

EXAMPLE: Swedish-speaking immigrant

298

EXERCISE C: Using Capitals for Proper Adjectives. Copy each item that is capitalized incorrectly, making the necessary changes. If an item is already capitalized properly, write *correct.*

EXAMPLE: a brazilian diplomat

a Brazilian diplomat

1. french fries
2. bible study
3. First and Second Avenues
4. Japanese people
5. Anglo-American group
6. lake Erie
7. pasteurized milk
8. himalayan village
9. Ford Automobile
10. a herculean task
11. pro-american poster
12. Lake placid
13. a Shakespearean Play
14. Greek-Speaking secretary
15. an Anglo-french treaty
16. singapore monsoon
17. Spanish-speaking delegate
18. a Canadian coin
19. a boeing 747
20. a Turkish Towel

Capitals for Titles

The titles of people and things must also be capitalized correctly. The following rules will guide you in the correct use of capitals for titles.

Capitalize titles of people and titles of works.

Titles of People. Various types of titles refer to people.

Capitalize a person's title when it is used with the person's name or when it is used in direct address.

WITH A PROPER NAME: Governor Wilson addressed the state legislature.

IN DIRECT ADDRESS: Doctor, will you discuss my symptoms again?

IN A GENERAL REFERENCE: Have you ever met the mayor of our city?

The following chart illustrates the capitalization of a number of different titles. Notice the treatment of prefixes and suffixes.

TITLES OF PEOPLE	
Commonly Used Titles	Sir, Madam, Doctor, Professor, Father, Reverend, Rabbi, Sister, Archbishop, Sergeant, Governor, Senator, Ambassador
Abbreviated Titles	*Before names:* Mr., Mrs., Dr., Prof. *After names:* Jr., Sr., Ph.D., Esq.
Compound Titles	Commander in Chief, Vice President, Secretary of Defense, Lieutenant Governor
Titles with Prefixes or Suffixes	Mayor-elect Ross ex-Senator Norman

Always capitalize titles for certain high-ranking officials.

Capitalize the titles of certain high government officials even when the titles are not used with a proper name or in direct address.

Titles that are always capitalized include those of the President, Vice President, and Chief Justice of the United States, as well as that of the Queen of England.

EXAMPLE: The Chief Justice was appointed by the President.

As a sign of respect, you may also capitalize other titles used without names.

EXAMPLE: The General has served the country well.

Frequently, people refer to their relatives by their titles. These references follow the next rule.

Capitalize titles showing family relationships when they refer to a specific person, unless they are preceded by a possessive noun or pronoun.

WITH THE PERSON'S NAME: Aunt Liz speaks two languages.

IN DIRECT ADDRESS: I'm glad you're coming for lunch, Grandma.

REFERRING TO A SPECIFIC PERSON: Will Father fix it for me?

WITH A POSSESSIVE NOUN: George's mother will meet us.

WITH A POSSESSIVE PRONOUN: My aunt Sue has moved to Iowa.

300

Capitalizing Things. You should also capitalize the titles and subtitles of various works.

Capitalize the first word and all other key words in the titles of books, periodicals, poems, stories, plays, paintings, and other works of art.

Notice in the following chart that none of the articles *(a, an,* and *the)* are capitalized unless they are used as the first word of a title or subtitle. Because conjunctions and prepositions are not considered key words, they also are not capitalized unless they are the first word of the title or subtitle or contain more than four letters.

TITLES OF WORKS	
Books	*Profiles in Courage* *The United States: A History of the Republic*
Periodicals	*The Wall Street Journal* *Newsweek*
Poems	*"To a Prize Bird"* *"The Rime of the Ancient Mariner"*
Stories	*"The Red-Headed League"* *"The Two Bottles of Relish"*
Plays	*On Borrowed Time* *Joan of Lorraine*
Paintings	*Woman with the Blue Veil* *Still Life with Basket of Apples*
Music	*"This Land Is Your Land"* *Carmen*

You must also be sure to capitalize the title of a course of study when it is a language or when the title is followed by a number.

Capitalize titles of courses when the courses are language courses or when they are followed by a number.

WITH CAPITALS: Spanish, Sociology I, English 2
WITHOUT CAPITALS: biology, algebra, homemaking

EXERCISE D: Using Capitals with Titles of People and Things. Copy the following sentences, capitalizing the titles correctly. Underline any words that are printed in italics.

EXAMPLE: Three performances of *fiddler on the roof* will be given by our school next spring.

Three performance of <u>Fiddler on the Roof</u> will be given by our school next spring.

1. Phillip Whitney, m.d., and professor Raul Alvarado are the featured speakers at this evening's meeting.
2. Yesterday morning, captain Stanzione reprimanded private Mathews.
3. Our guest was mayor-elect Sanderson.
4. I registered for psychology 1, french, and geology.
5. May I tell grandfather about our summer vacation plans now, mother?
6. We have been informed that governor Brandon will arrive at noon to meet with the president.
7. Have you read the book *lee's lieutenants* by Douglas South-all Freeman?
8. Two of Diego Rivera's finest paintings are *man and machinery* and *betrayal of cuernavaca*.
9. My cousin Margaret and I enjoy the poetry of Emily Dickinson, especially "success is counted sweetest."
10. I often find myself humming the tune of the song "you are the sunshine of my life," which was written by Stevie Wonder.

Capitals in Letters

Capital letters are also required in parts of personal letters and business letters.

Capitalize the first word and all nouns in letter salutations and the first word in letter closings.

SALUTATIONS: Dear Eric,   Dear Sirs:
CLOSINGS: With love,   Yours truly,

EXERCISE E: Using Capitals in a Business Letter. Copy the following letter, adding all the necessary capitals.

302

43 berry hill lane
cornwall, new york 12518
november 5, 1986

director of admissions
fairleigh dickinson university
1000 river road
teaneck, new jersey 07666

dear director:

after speaking with my college adviser, i may be interested in enrolling in the college of business administration at fairleigh dickinson university in september of next year.

would you please send me your catalog for the college of business administration? i am also interested in your admission requirements and details of the financial aid package provided by the university.

since i live some distance from teaneck, i would also like information about on-campus housing or housing in the area.

thank you very much for your assistance.

yours truly,
elizabeth green

DEVELOPING WRITING SKILLS: Using Capitalization Rules in Original Sentences.

Use the following directions to write twenty sentences of your own, using capitals wherever necessary.

1. Write a sentence in which you name the title of a book and its author. Underline the title.
2. Write a sentence in which you mention the name of the governor of your state.
3. Write a sentence in which you give someone directions. Use words such as *east, northwest, south,* and so on.
4. Write a sentence about your favorite professional athletic team.
5. Write a sentence about a person who speaks two or more languages. Name the languages.
6. Write a sentence about a famous historic site that you have visited or would like to visit.
7. Write a sentence about two oceans that border the United States.

8. Write a sentence naming one of your favorite record albums. Underline the name of the album.
9. Write a sentence in which you mention both your junior and senior high school by name.
10. Write a sentence that includes a direct quotation.
11. Write a sentence about a famous battle or treaty.
12. Write a sentence in which you mention a theater, museum, or other cultural building by name.
13. Write a sentence naming a special sports event.
14. Write a sentence in which you mention three different states you have visited or would like to visit.
15. Write a sentence in which you give the date of your birth.
16. Write a sentence about a product. Use the brand name in your sentence.
17. Write two sentences. Have the second sentence explain the first one. Then join the two sentences with a colon.
18. Write a sentence describing a characteristic you particularly like in a relative. Use both the relative's name and a title indicating his or her relationship to you.
19. Write a sentence naming a book you have read recently. Underline the title of the book.
20. Write a sentence naming your three favorite courses.

11.2 Abbreviation

Abbreviations have been around a long time. They can be traced back to the time when artisans chiseled messages on stone tablets and scribes wrote religious texts on parchment. Using abbreviations helped these people save time and space.

To abbreviate means to shorten an existing word or phrase.

Today, thousands of abbreviations exist in the English language. This section presents the conventions governing the use of many abbreviations you may want to use in your writing. Study and review the rules in the section carefully so you will know which abbreviations can be used in formal writing and which should be reserved for informal situations such as writing lists and notes. The rules, examples, and charts in this section will also guide you in forming different types of abbreviations correctly.

304

Names and Titles of People

A number of rules govern the use of abbreviations for names and titles. The first concerns the abbreviation of people's names.

People's Names. The first time you use a person's name in formal writing, it should be written out in full. In lists or notes, initials may be used in place of the given name.

> **Use a person's full given name in formal writing, unless the person uses initials as part of his or her formal name.**

EXAMPLE: Alice Higgins is a well-known newspaper columnist.

Additional references to the same person may be made in different ways. You may, for example, use just the last name with a title. Or you may use the last name alone.

FIRST REFERENCE: Alice Higgins, the well-known newspaper columnist, will address the twelfth grade.

LATER REFERENCES: Miss Higgins will speak about preparing for a career in journalism.

Higgins will respond to questions after her address.

People's Titles. The titles of people are often abbreviated. First, consider the category of social titles that appear before the proper names of people.

> **Abbreviations of social titles before a proper name begin with a capital letter and end with a period.**

SOCIAL TITLES: Mr., Messrs. (plural of Mr.), Mrs. Mme. (Madame or Madam), Mmes. (plural of Mrs. or Mme.)

Social titles are usually abbreviated. There are, however, two exceptions. *Miss* is not an abbreviation, so it does not end with a period. *Ms.,* which may be used with a proper name to refer to either a single or married woman, is written as if it were an abbreviation for a word, but it is not.

Remember to use abbreviations of social titles only when they are followed by proper names.

USED INCORRECTLY:	The Mrs. is not at home.
USED CORRECTLY:	Mrs. Connolly and Mr. Irving were our class advisors.
	Mmes. Johnson and Stack worked long hours to make the book sale a success.

Sometimes you may wish to use professional, religious, political, or military titles in your writing.

Abbreviations of other titles used before proper names also begin with a capital letter and end with a period.

The abbreviations for some common titles of position and rank appear below. Others may be found in a dictionary.

ABBREVIATIONS OF COMMON TITLES			
Professional		**Religious**	
Dr.	Doctor	Rev.	Reverend
Atty.	Attorney	Fr.	Father
Prof.	Professor	Sr.	Sister
Hon.	Honorable	Br.	Brother
Political		**Military**	
Pres.	President	Pvt.	Private
Sen.	Senator	Sgt.	Sergeant
Rep.	Representative	Capt.	Captain
Gov.	Governor	Lt. Col.	Lieutenant Colonel
Amb.	Ambassador	Maj. Gen.	Major General
Sec.	Secretary	Ens.	Ensign
Treas.	Treasurer	Cmdr.	Commander
Supt.	Superintendent	Vice Adm.	Vice Admiral
Com.	Commissioner	Adm.	Admiral

When you use the full name of an individual in formal writing, you may abbreviate the titles that appear in the chart.

EXAMPLES: Rep. Martin L. Willis is running for reelection.

Prof. Lisa Baxter met with the teachers.

Do not abbreviate the titles in the preceding chart, however, when they are used only with a person's surname.

INCORRECT: Gov. Barrett proposed this piece of legislation.

CORRECT: Governor Barrett proposed this legislation.

INCORRECT: I told Prof. Willard about the experiment.

CORRECT: I told Professor Willard about the experiment.

The abbreviation *Dr.* is an exception. It is often used in front of only a surname.

EXAMPLE: Dr. Rinehart works at the clinic on Thursday.

When you wish to establish the educational qualifications of a person in your writing, you may use an abbreviation of an academic degree, which will generally follow the person's name.

Abbreviations of titles after a name start with a capital letter and end with a period.

The following chart presents the most common abbreviations of academic degrees.

ABBREVIATIONS OF ACADEMIC DEGREES			
B.A. (or A.B.)	Bachelor of Arts	M.S.W.	Master of Social Work
B.S. (or S.B.)	Bachelor of Science	R.N.	Registered Nurse
M.A. (or A.M.)	Master of Arts	M.D.	Doctor of Medicine
M.S. (or S.M.)	Master of Science	D.D.S.	Doctor of Dental Surgery
M.B.A.	Master of Business Administration	Esq.	Esquire (lawyer)
		LL.D.	Doctor of Laws
M.F.A.	Master of Fine Arts	D.D.	Doctor of Divinity
		Ed.D.	Doctor of Education
		Ph.D.	Doctor of Philosophy

EXAMPLES: I suggested Steven R. Gregg, Ed.D., as a consultant.

Lucy Gordon, M.B.A., was hired for the position.

Never use both a title before a person's name and an academic degree after the person's name.

INCORRECT: Prof. Anne Stevenson, Ph.D., recently retired.

CORRECT: Prof. Anne Stevenson recently retired.

Anne Stevenson, Ph.D., recently retired.

Two other common titles, *Jr.* and *Sr.*, are also placed after the full name of a person and set off with commas.

EXAMPLES: John R. Wiggins, Sr., is now ninety years of age.

Andrew Barretta, Jr., will graduate next month.

EXERCISE A: Using Titles Correctly in Sentences. Rewrite each sentence that needs correction, making the necessary changes. If a sentence needs no changes, write *correct.*

EXAMPLE: Prof. Michael Nino, Ph.D., wrote an interesting book.

Michael Nino, Ph.D., wrote an interesting book.

1. Will you ask Lt. Green to check the roster?
2. Miss. Fern Ralston has enrolled in Wheatley College.
3. Arthur Stevens Jr. hopes to succeed his father.
4. I know that Dr. Homenick, M.D., is an excellent physician.
5. Ph.D. Linda Wong will teach at Rutgers this year.
6. Mr. and Mrs. Rinaldo volunteered to organize the awards ceremony.
7. Will you ask Sec. Maxwell to join us?
8. Mary Montini, our Rep., introduced an important resolution.
9. Has M.D. Boris Knopf been named director of the hospital?
10. I spoke to Arnold Webber, d.d.s., only yesterday on the phone.

EXERCISE B: Using Abbreviated Titles in Original Sentences. Write formal sentences of your own using each of the following abbreviated titles.

EXAMPLE: Jr.

Ken Hutchinson, Jr., was chosen for the job.

1. Messrs.
2. Ph.D.
3. Sr.
4. R.N.
5. Maj. Gen.
6. Gov.
7. Dr.
8. Mme.
9. Ens.
10. M.D.

Geographical Terms

In your writing you will sometimes need to refer to a geographical location. The following rules will help you decide when to use abbreviations for these references.

Almost all abbreviations for geographical locations should be reserved for informal writing situations.

Abbreviations for geographical terms before or after a proper noun begin with a capital letter and end with a period.

The following chart lists some common geographical terms and their abbreviations. Use them primarily in addresses, lists, and note-taking situations. Avoid them in formal writing.

COMMON GEOGRAPHICAL ABBREVIATIONS			
Apt.	Apartment	Natl.	National
Ave.	Avenue	Pen.	Peninsula
Bldg.	Building	Pk.	Park, Peak
Blk.	Block	Prov.	Province
Blvd.	Boulevard	Pt.	Point
Co.	County	Rd.	Road
Dist.	District	Rte.	Route
Dr.	Drive	Sq.	Square
Ft.	Fort	St.	Street
Is.	Island	Terr.	Territory
Mt.	Mountain, Mount		

There are two sets of abbreviations for states. The traditional form of abbreviation is a shortening of the state name, capitalized at the beginning and ending with a period. This form, incidentally, does not have abbreviations for Alaska, Hawaii, Iowa, and Utah.

The United States Postal Service developed a new system of abbreviations for states. Each abbreviation consists of two capital letters and no periods. The Postal Service wants you to use them when you address mail. Include the postal ZIP number immediately after the abbreviation.

Traditional abbreviations for states begin with a capital and end with a period. Postal Service abbreviations are all capitals with no periods.

The following chart shows both types of state abbreviations.

STATE ABBREVIATIONS					
State	Tradi-tional	Postal Service	State	Tradi-tional	Postal Service
Alabama	Ala.	AL	Montana	Mont.	MT
Alaska	Alaska	AK	Nebraska	Nebr.	NB
Arizona	Ariz.	AZ	Nevada	Nev.	NV
Arkansas	Ark.	AR	New Hampshire	N.H.	NH
California	Calif.	CA	New Jersey	N.J.	NJ
Colorado	Colo.	CO	New Mexico	N.Mex.	NM
Connecticut	Conn.	CT	New York	N.Y.	NY
Delaware	Del.	DE	North Carolina	N.C.	NC
Florida	Fla.	FL	North Dakota	N.Dak.	ND
Georgia	Ga.	GA	Ohio	O.	OH
Hawaii	Hawaii	HI	Oklahoma	Okla.	OK
Idaho	Ida.	ID	Oregon	Ore.	OR
Illinois	Ill.	IL	Pennsylvania	Pa.	PA
Indiana	Ind.	IN	Rhode Island	R.I.	RI
Iowa	Iowa	IA	South Carolina	S.C.	SC
Kansas	Kans.	KS	South Dakota	S.Dak.	SD
Kentucky	Ky.	KY	Tennessee	Tenn.	TN
Louisiana	La.	LA	Texas	Tex.	TX
Maine	Me.	ME	Utah	Utah	UT
Maryland	Md.	MD	Vermont	Vt.	VT
Massachusetts	Mass.	MA	Virginia	Va.	VA
Michigan	Mich.	MI	Washington	Wash.	WA
Minnesota	Minn.	MN	West Virginia	W.Va.	WV
Mississippi	Miss.	MS	Wisconsin	Wis.	WI
Missouri	Mo.	MO	Wyoming	Wyo.	WY

NOTE ABOUT D.C.: The traditional abbreviation for the District of Columbia is *D.C.*; the Postal Service abbreviation is *DC.* Use the traditional abbreviation in formal writing whenever it follows the word *Washington*.

EXAMPLE: Have you visited Washington, D.C.?

EXERCISE C: Identifying Geographical Abbreviations. Write the meaning of each of the following abbreviations.

EXAMPLE: Prov.

         Province

1. TX	6. Apt.	11. N.H.	16. N.C.
2. Mt.	7. DC	12. CA	17. St.
3. Terr.	8. Natl.	13. Co.	18. Conn.
4. Ave.	9. Rd.	14. Del.	19. Pk.
5. MI	10. WI	15. Is.	20. Rte.

Time, Measurements, and Numbers

Abbreviations are often used for time and measurements. There are also a number of rules for the use of numbers.

Time References. The abbreviations for time spans are not used in formal writing but are useful in informal situations.

Abbreviations for clocked time begin with small letters; those for days of the week and months begin with capitals. All three end with periods.

CLOCKED TIME:	sec. second(s)	hr. hour(s)	
	min. minute(s)	yr. year(s)	

DAYS OF THE WEEK:	Mon.	Monday	Fri.	Friday
	Tues.	Tuesday	Sat.	Saturday
	Wed.	Wednesday	Sun.	Sunday
	Thurs.	Thursday		

MONTHS OF THE YEAR:	Jan.	January	July	July
	Feb.	February	Aug.	August
	Mar.	March	Sept.	September
	Apr.	April	Oct.	October
	May	May	Nov.	November
	June	June	Dec.	December

Unlike the preceding abbreviations, *A.M.* and *P.M.* and *B.C.* and *A.D.* may be used in both formal and informal writing.

Abbreviations of time before noon and after noon are formed with either capital letters followed by periods or small letters followed by periods.

EXAMPLES: A.M. or a.m. (*ante meridiem*, before noon)

P.M. or p.m. (*post meridiem*, after noon)

Use *A.M.* or *P.M.* in your writing only when you use numerals to refer to the time of day.

EXAMPLES: We started climbing the mountain at 5:30 a.m.

We reached the summit at four in the afternoon.

Avoid using words such as morning or evening with the abbreviations *A.M.* or *P.M.* Using both the words and the abbreviations results in redundant expressions.

REDUNDANT EXPRESSION: At 3:30 p.m. this afternoon, we had a thunderstorm.

BETTER: At 3:30 p.m. we had a thunderstorm.

At 3:30 this afternoon, we had a thunderstorm.

B.C. and *A.D.*, are used with historical dates.

EXAMPLES: B.C. (before Christ)

A.D. (*anno Domini*, in the year of the Lord)

These abbreviations are generally used with numerals. The letters *B.C.* always follow the numerals; *A.D.* may either follow or precede the numerals.

Abbreviations for historical dates before and after the birth of Christ require capital letters followed by periods.

EXAMPLES: The ruins were dated at about 50 B.C.

In A.D. 110, barbarian hordes began crossing the mountains and invading the small settlements.

When neither *B.C.* nor *A.D.* is used with a historical date, the reader will assume that *A.D.* is intended.

312

EXAMPLE: A severe drought struck the region in the middle of
           the sixth century.

If you wanted to use *A.D.* in the example above, you would
place it after the word *century.*

Measurements. You will find abbreviations for measurements used often in science, mathematics, homemaking, and
industrial arts. In formal, nontechnical writing, you should
avoid all except those for temperature. Furthermore, none of
them should ever be used (even informally) without numbers.

**For the abbreviations of traditional measure-
ments use small letters and periods. For metric
measurements use small letters and no periods.**

The following chart presents some of the most commonly
used traditional measurements.

ABBREVIATIONS OF TRADITIONAL MEASUREMENTS					
in.	inch(es)	tsp.	teaspoon(s)	pt.	pint(s)
ft.	foot, feet	tbsp.	tablespoon(s)	qt.	quart(s)
yd.	yard(s)	oz.	ounce(s)	gal.	gallon(s)
mi.	mile(s)	lb.	pound(s)	F.	Fahrenheit

Notice that the abbreviation *F.* for *Fahrenheit* is an exception
to the rule. It is capitalized.

Metric measurements are used extensively throughout the
world. You will benefit by learning the most frequently used
metric measurements and their abbreviations. Then, you can
consult dictionaries or other references, which contain complete lists of metric measurements.

ABBREVIATIONS OF METRIC MEASUREMENTS					
mm	millimeter(s)	mL	milliliter(s)	mg	milligram(s)
cm	centimeter(s)	cL	centiliter(s)	cg	centigram(s)
m	meter(s)	L	liter(s)	g	gram(s)
km	kilometer(s)	kL	kiloliter(s)	C	Celsius

Notice that the abbreviations for both *liter* and *Celsius* are
exceptions to the rule. They are both capitalized.

Numbers. In your writing, you will often have to decide whether to spell out numbers or to use numerals.

In formal writing spell out numbers or amounts of less than one hundred and any other numbers that can be written in one or two words.

EXAMPLES: We counted twenty-three squirrels in the park today.

The band had 137 members.

Whenever a number appears at the beginning of a sentence, it should be spelled out. Often, it is better to reword the sentence so the number appears in some other position.

Spell out all numbers found at the beginning of sentences.

ACCEPTABLE: Three hundred forty people applauded the actors.

BETTER: The audience of 340 people applauded the actors.

Certain types of numbers, on the other hand, are almost always written in numerals.

Use numerals when referring to fractions, decimals, and percentages or when writing addresses or dates.

Remember to place these figures within a sentence to avoid having to write them out at the beginning of the sentence.

FRACTION: The new baby weighed 7½ pounds.

DECIMAL: An inch is approximately equal to 2.54 centimeters.

PERCENTAGE: They estimated that Australia has 26 percent of the world's aluminum reserves.

ADDRESS: The office is located at 46 Union Street.

DATE: The meeting will be held on March 25.

EXERCISE D: Abbreviating Time, Measurements, and Numbers. Rewrite each item using numerals and abbreviations correctly.

EXAMPLE: One hundred fifty before Christ

150 B.C.

1. six grams
2. eight millimeters
3. two tablespoons
4. three and a half miles
5. nineteen hundred in the year of the Lord
6. six feet
7. two inches
8. four-and-one-tenth ounces
9. six after noon
10. The address is fifty-three Main Street.

Latin Expressions

Writers often use Latin abbreviations in footnotes and bibliographic references. You may use them in your note-taking.

Use small letters and periods for most abbreviations of Latin expressions.

The following chart offers a selection of frequently used Latin phrases and their abbreviations.

ABBREVIATIONS FROM LATIN		
Abbreviation	**Latin Phrase**	**Meaning**
ad inf.	ad infinitum	to infinity
c., ca., or circ.	circa	about (used with dates)
e.g.	exempli gratia	for example
et al.	et alii	and others
etc.	et cetera	and so forth
ex lib.	ex libris	from the books (of)
ex off.	ex officio	officially; by the virtue of one's office
f.		and the following (page or line)
ff.		and the following (pages or lines)
ib. or ibid.	ibidem	in the same place
i.e.	id est	that is
in loc. cit.	in loco citato	in the place cited
n.b. or N.B.	nota bene	note well; take notice
non seq.	non sequitur	it does not follow

per an.	per annum	by the year
pro tem.	pro tempore	for the time; temporarily
viz.	videlicet	to wit; namely
vs.	versus	against
v.v.	vice versa	the order being changed

Most of these abbreviations are set off with commas in writing. This is because the English words that would replace them in formal writing would be set off this way.

EXAMPLE: Grandfather rambled on about many of his interests, e.g., politics, cattle raising, bronco busting, and fishing.

Marie is now considering several professions, viz., medicine, law, and public relations.

EXERCISE E: Identifying Latin Phrases. Write the English words for the following Latin abbreviations.

EXAMPLE: vs.

against

1. e.g.   3. viz.   5. pro tem.   7. ibid.   9. etc.
2. f.   4. i.e.   6. n.b.   8. non seq.   10. et al.

Business and Government Groups

Some businesses abbreviate the final word in their titles.

An abbreviated word in a business name begins with a capital letter and ends with a period.

BUSINESS ABBREVIATIONS: Co. (Company)   Inc. (Incorporated)

Bros. (Brothers)   Ltd. (Limited)

In formal writing only *Inc.* and *Ltd.* are generally abbreviated.

Sometimes organizations, especially large ones, are referred to by abbreviations formed from the first letter of each word in the organization's name. Businesses, labor unions, government agencies, and other groups may abbreviate their names in this manner.

316

Use all capitals and no periods to abbreviate names whose abbreviations are pronounced letter by letter as if they were words.

The following chart lists some of the organizations that use this type of abbreviation.

ABBREVIATIONS FOR ORGANIZATIONS		
Business Firms	CBS	Columbia Broadcasting System
	UPI	United Press International
	RCA	Radio Corporation of America
Labor Unions	ILGWU	International Ladies Garment Workers Union
	AFL-CIO	American Federation of Labor and Congress of Industrial Organizations
	UMW	United Mine Workers
Government Agencies	FDA	Food and Drug Administration
	IRS	Internal Revenue Service
	VA	Veterans Administration
Other Groups	NAACP	National Association for the Advancement of Colored People
	AAUW	American Association of University Women
	YMCA	Young Men's Christian Association

These abbreviations may be used in all types of writing. It is generally best, however, to give the complete names of less familiar items first and then to enclose the abbreviation in parentheses following the name. After that, the reader will know what the abbreviation means, and the abbreviation may be used alone.

EXAMPLE: The Nuclear Regulatory Commission (NRC) is responsible for licensing nuclear power plants in the United States. The NRC also sets safety standards for the nuclear power industry.

An acronym is a word formed from the first letter or letters of a group of words and then pronounced as a word. Some organizations use acronyms to abbreviate their names.

Use all capital letters and no periods for acronyms that form names.

ACRONYMS: VISTA   Volunteers in Service to America

OPEC   Organization of Petroleum Exporting Countries

Acronyms that may not be recognized by your audience are usually used only after the complete name of the organization has been used once followed by the acronym in parentheses.

EXAMPLE: The North Atlantic Treaty Organization (NATO) was organized in 1949. The members of NATO agreed to settle disputes among themselves by peaceful means, to develop their capacity to resist an armed attack by others, and to consider an armed attack upon any member as an attack upon them all.

EXERCISE F: Abbreviating Names of Organizations. Write the abbreviation for each of the following.

EXAMPLE: Organization of Petroleum Exporting Countries

OPEC

1. Food and Drug Administration
2. Smith Brothers
3. United Press International
4. United Nations
5. Fulton Rugs, Incorporated
6. Internal Revenue Service
7. Federal Bureau of Investigation
8. Volunteers in Service to America
9. North Atlantic Treaty Organization
10. Nuclear Regulatory Commission

Other Common Abbreviations

You may see many of the abbreviations in the following chart in your reading or in the business world.

Study other commonly used abbreviations until you are familiar with them.

318

OTHER COMMONLY USED ABBREVIATIONS

anon.	anonymous	FM	frequency modulation
approx.	approximately	fwd.	forward
assoc.	associate or association	gloss.	glossary
assn.	association	gov. or govt.	government
aux. or auxil.	auxiliary	G.P.O.	General Post Office
A.W.O.L.	absent without leave	Gr.	Greek, Grecian
bibliog.	bibliography	grad.	graduate, graduated
bkt.	basket	hdqrs.	headquarters
bu.	bushel	hi-fi	high fidelity
bull.	bulletin	hosp.	hospital
b.v.	book value	ht.	height
bx(s).	box(es)	ill. or illus.	illustrated
cap.	capital letter	incl.	including, inclusive
CB	citizens band	intro.	introductory, introduction
ch. or chap.	chapter	ital.	italics
C.O.D.	cash on delivery	j.g.	junior grade
dept.	department	k. or kt.	karat or carat
disc.	discount	L.	left
doz.	dozen(s)	mdse.	merchandise
ea.	each	meas.	measure
ed.	edition, editor, edited	mfg.	manufacture
EDT	Eastern Daylight Time	mgr.	manager
equiv.	equivalent	misc.	miscellaneous
est.	established	mkt.	market
EST	Eastern Standard Time	M.O.	money-order
ext.	extra, exterior	m.p.h.	miles per hour
fac.	facsimile	mtge.	mortgage
fict.	fiction	Myth. or mythol.	mythology or mythological

No.	number	recd.	received
P. & L.	profit and loss	ref.	reference, referee
paren.	parenthesis	rhet.	rhetorical, rhetoric
Pat.Off.	Patent Office	rm(s).	ream(s)
pc(s).	piece(s)	r.p.m.	revolutions per minute
pg.	page		
pkg.	package	R.S.V.P.	please reply
poet.	poetical, poetry	sc.	scene
POW	prisoner of war	sp.	spelling, species, specimen
pp.	pages		
prop.	proprietor	spec.	special, specific
pr(s).	pair(s)	SRO	standing room only
pseud.	pseudonym	SST	supersonic transport
pub.	published, publisher	treas.	treasury, treasurer
		vol.	volume
pvt.	private	wkly.	weekly
R.	right	wt.	weight

EXERCISE G: Identifying Common Abbreviations. Write the meaning of each of the following abbreviations.

EXAMPLE: SST

supersonic transport

1. bxs.   3. C.O.D.   5. hosp.   7. m.p.h.   9. pseud.
2. cap.   4. ea.   6. ht.   8. pp.   10. sc.

DEVELOPING WRITING SKILLS: Using Abbreviations in Sentences. Following the rules in this section for using abbreviations, write ten formal sentences of your own. Include an example of each of the following types of abbreviation.

1. a social title
2. a military title
3. an academic degree
4. time after noon
5. year before the birth of Christ
6. an address
7. a percent
8. a business name
9. a government agency
10. an acronym

320

Skills Review and Writing Workshop

Capitalization and Abbreviation

CHECKING YOUR SKILLS

Rewrite the following paragraph, correcting all capitalization and abbreviation errors. Write the complete form of those words that should not be abbreviated in formal writing.

(1) My brother Bill was accepted at penn state u. (2) He looked forward to starting his first semester right after labor day. (3) Since he'd spent the Summer at lake tahoe, CA, he planned to fly back home on Aug. 25, '85, arriving at Kennedy international airport at 8:45 p.m. in the evening. (4) He booked reservations on a boeing 747. (5) Then, at the last minute he changed his plans. (6) A friend was driving to his home in the east in his new ford and bill went with him. (7) They stopped at a holiday inn and best western motel along the way. (8) Bill spent two days with his friend's family in baltimore, md. and then took the amtrak train to N.Y. (9) Our parents drove in from Long Isl. to pick him up. (10) He was glad to get back to our house on river rd in roslyn even if just for a few days.

USING MECHANICS SKILLS IN WRITING
Writing a Letter to Your Senator

To be a good writer you must use capital letters and abbreviations correctly. Imagine you are the president of a political action group writing to your senator about a national issue. Follow the steps below to write an effective letter.

Prewriting: List the important points you want to cover in your letter. If you want to mention a particular bill, be sure to get its correct number.

Writing: Be concise. Your senator is a busy person. Bolster your position with facts and strong supporting arguments.

Revising: Are your arguments convincing? Have you used capital letters and abbreviations where appropriate? After you have revised, proofread carefully.

Chapter 12

Punctuation

Commas, quotation marks, and periods—all these punctuation marks are visual signs, signals that help a reader understand a writer's intentions. Why are certain words in a passage underlined or italicized? Why has a writer enclosed a particular word in brackets? The reader who understands the rules of punctuation will know.

To understand the rules of punctuation and to punctuate correctly yourself, it is necessary to have a thorough knowledge of the elements of sentence structure. You should be able to recognize an appositive, a participial phrase, items in a series, and a complex or compound sentence. Each of these elements—and many others—is punctuated in a specific way.

This chapter presents the major rules of punctuation that are so important to effective writing.

12.1 End Marks

End marks include the period, the question mark, and the exclamation mark. They are used mainly to conclude sentences. The period and the question mark are also used in several special situations.

Basic Uses of End Marks

To conclude sentences correctly you must know whether to use a period, a question mark, or an exclamation mark. First, look at the rules governing the use of the period.

The Period. The period is the end mark used most often.

Use a period to end a declarative sentence, a mild imperative, and an indirect question.

A declarative sentence is a statement of fact or opinion. An imperative sentence gives a command or a direction. Imperative sentences often begin with a verb. An indirect question restates a question within a declarative sentence.

STATEMENT OF FACT: Joyce Kilmer wrote a poem about trees.

STATEMENT OF OPINION: I believe we did the right thing.

COMMAND: Finish your homework before you go out.

DIRECTION: Turn left at the second traffic light.

INDIRECT QUESTION: I asked him where he had learned to ski.

The Question Mark. Direct questions, often in inverted word order, require a question mark at the end.

Use a question mark to end an interrogative sentence, an incomplete question, or a statement intended as a question.

INTERROGATIVE SENTENCES: Have you changed your opinion?

Which country will you visit next?

INCOMPLETE QUESTIONS: Why ? How much?

STATEMENTS INTENDED   This clock runs on batteries?
AS QUESTIONS: We're going to have spaghetti?

Statements intended as questions should not be used too often. It is often better to rephrase them as direct questions.

STATEMENT INTENDED AS A QUESTION: You agree?

REPHRASED AS A DIRECT QUESTION: Do you agree?

The Exclamation Mark. An exclamation mark is intended for emphasis. It calls attention to an exclamatory sentence, an imperative sentence, or an interjection. Exclamation marks should be used sparingly. Reserve them for those occasions when you want to indicate strong emotion in a dramatic way.

Use an exclamation mark to end an exclamatory sentence, a forceful imperative, or an interjection expressing strong emotion.

323

EXCLAMATORY SENTENCES: His admission of guilt shocked us!

That sunset is magnificent!

IMPERATIVE SENTENCES: Never try that trick again!

Come here quickly!

An interjection can be used with either a comma or an exclamation mark. An exclamation mark increases the emphasis.

WITH A COMMA: Oh, she is usually on time.

WITH AN EXCLAMATION MARK: Oh! I am amazed!

EXERCISE A: Using End Marks. Copy each item and punctuate it properly.

EXAMPLE: I bought milk on my way home from school

I bought milk on my way home from school.

1. Whew What a scare that was
2. How many times have you tried to win a race
3. Fowler's book on English usage is a very useful reference book
4. This new model runs on diesel fuel
5. Watch out for that car
6. She asked if I had achieved my goal
7. He took that course last year
8. Benjamin Franklin, an American Renaissance man, was a statesman, scientist, inventor, and author
9. What You expect this panel to believe that
10. Choose the building materials for the new fence carefully

Other Uses of End Marks

Most abbreviations end with a period.

Use a period to end most abbreviations.

If you do not know whether a period is required after a particular abbreviation, refer to Section 11.2 on abbreviations.

ABBREVIATIONS WITH PERIODS: in. Dr. etc. Sr. C.O.D. a.m. D.D.S. Ave. Mrs. Tex. Co. B.C.

ABBREVIATIONS WITHOUT PERIODS: FBI mm NASA TX

When an abbreviation ending with a period is found at the end of a sentence, do not add another period as an end mark.

INCORRECT: The speaker will be Adam Martin, Jr..

CORRECT: The speaker will be Adam Martin, Jr.

If an end mark other than a period is required, however, you must add the end mark.

EXAMPLE: Is the speaker Adam Martin, Jr.?

Periods are also used after numbers and letters in outlines.

Use a period after numbers and letters in outlines.

EXAMPLE: I. Maintaining your pet's health
       A. Diet
         1. For a puppy
         2. For a mature dog
       B. Exercise
       C. Cleanliness
       D. Preventing accidents

If you wish to use a fact that you cannot verify, a question mark within parentheses can be used to show uncertainty. Use it, however, only when the fact cannot be verified.

Use a question mark in parentheses (?) after a fact or statistic to show its uncertainty.

EXAMPLE: Mohammed was born in 570 (?) A.D.

EXERCISE B: Using End Marks in Other Situations. Copy each item that needs punctuation, adding the necessary end marks. Indicate uncertainty about any years. If an item does not need any additional end marks, write *correct.*

EXAMPLE: Mrs Jackson offered to bake cookies for the party.

    Mrs. Jackson offered to bake cookies for the party.

1. Confucius, who died in 470 BC, was a philosopher.
2. Are more space flights being planned by NASA?
3. The tiny toad was 15 mm long.
4. The calendar page gave the following date: Oct 26.

325

5. The package was addressed to Mr Luis Ramirez, 23 Grove St, St Paul, Minn.
6. At 10:30 PM the baby finally fell asleep.
7. I Vitamin A
    A. Sources
        1 Milk, butter, eggs
        2 Green and yellow vegetables
    B. Value
        1 Preserves health of skin
        2 Preserves health of mucous membranes
8. His train is due to arrive on Sat, Apr 17, at 8 am.
9. Jeanette Rankin was the first woman elected to the US Congress.
10. The book was written by historian Arthur Schlesinger, Jr.

DEVELOPING WRITING SKILLS: Using End Marks Correctly in Your Own Writing. Choose a topic and write a paragraph about it. Use each of the end marks correctly.

12.2 Commas

This section presents the rules governing the use of commas. To use commas correctly, you must have a thorough knowledge of sentence structure. Studying this section can help you master the rules governing the use of commas and, at the same time, serve as a review of some basic elements of sentence structure.

Commas That Separate Basic Elements

Commas are used to separate certain basic elements in sentences. These include independent clauses in compound sentences, items in a series, and coordinate adjectives. First, consider commas used to separate independent clauses.

Compound Sentences. Two or more independent clauses properly joined and punctuated form a compound sentence. The independent clauses are often joined by coordinate conjunctions: *and, but, for, nor, or, so,* and *yet.* Commas are then used to separate the independent clauses.

Use a comma before the conjunction to separate two or more independent clauses in a compound sentence.

EXAMPLES: My cousin travels all over the United States each summer, but my brother prefers to stay at home.

My brother prefers to stay at home.

The baseball team has played well so far, and the team hopes to win the last game of the season.

Remember to use both a comma and a coordinate conjunction in a compound sentence. Using only a comma would result in a run-on sentence.

Notice also that the ideas in both of the independent clauses in each of the preceding examples are related. Do not construct a compound sentence from two unrelated clauses.

Finally, do not confuse a compound sentence with a simple sentence that has a compound verb.

SIMPLE SENTENCE   David brought his car in for repairs
WITH A COMPOUND VERB: and waited for it for three hours.

COMPOUND SENTENCE: David brought his car in for repairs, and he waited for it for three hours.

Items in a Series. A series consists of three or more words, phrases, or subordinate clauses of a similar kind.

Use commas to separate three or more words, phrases, or clauses in a series.

WORDS IN A SERIES: Flounder, scrod, bluefish, and mackerel are all in season.

Her performance was flawless, exciting, and inspiring.

PHRASES IN A SERIES: I reached the station as the train pulled in by running at first, walking part way, and limping the final steps.

To check the accuracy of the experiment, we took four readings: at dawn, at noon, at dusk, and at midnight.

SUBORDINATE   The report stressed that light was inade-
CLAUSES IN A SERIES: quate, that the machines lacked safety guards, and that the ventilation system was poor.

327

Notice that the number of commas in each of the preceding series is one fewer than the number of items in the series. If there are three items in a series, two commas are used; if there are four items in a series, three commas are used; and so on.

An alternate style calls for omitting the last comma before the conjunction. Such a style, while correct, does occasionally lead to confusion. The use of the final comma, on the other hand, is always clear.

CONFUSING: We enjoyed the sparkling waves, cool ocean breezes and sunshine.

ALWAYS CLEAR: We enjoyed the sparkling waves, cool ocean breezes, and sunshine.

When conjunctions are used to separate all the items in a series, no commas are needed.

EXAMPLE: We ate hot dogs and baked beans and potato salad.

You should also avoid placing commas before items such as *salt and pepper* that are paired so often that they are thought of as one item.

EXAMPLE: I put the bread, salt and pepper, and napkins away.

Coordinate Adjectives. Sometimes two or more adjectives are used together. *Coordinate adjectives,* adjectives equal in rank, are separated by commas.

Use commas to separate adjectives of equal rank.

COORDINATE ADJECTIVES: a dark, dismal hallway

a tall, attractive, young woman

An adjective is equal in rank to another if the word *and* can be inserted between them without changing the meaning of the sentence. Another way to test whether or not adjectives are coordinate is to reverse their order. If the sentence still sounds correct, they are of equal rank. Testing the examples above shows that the adjectives are indeed coordinate.

If you cannot place the word *and* between adjectives or reverse their order without changing the meaning of the sentence, they are called *cumulative adjectives.* Do not use a comma between cumulative adjectives.

328

Do not use commas to separate adjectives that must stay in a specific order.

CUMULATIVE ADJECTIVES: a new winter coat

many successful people

EXERCISE A: Punctuating Simple and Compound Sentences. Copy only the compound sentences, adding the necessary commas. If a sentence is not compound, write *correct*.

EXAMPLE: I shoveled snow all morning and now I am tired.

I shoveled snow all morning, and now I am tired.

1. My mother and father arrived on time but we had to wait for the other relatives.
2. Our family traveled to Canada last summer and hopes to visit parts of Europe next year.
3. Leslie will graduate from high school this June and several of her other friends will graduate with her but her best friend will not graduate until next year.
4. These customers want their merchandise delivered today or they plan to cancel their orders.
5. We want to do some shopping and then go to a movie.
6. Our car needs a complete tuneup for it has been over six months since it has had one.
7. We neither wanted their assistance now nor would we accept it at some future time.
8. Mother baked three peach pies and froze them for the picnic.
9. Join us at the meeting this evening for it promises to be dramatic and exciting.
10. The sun rose early and shone until the afternoon shower.
11. Max will study art in Paris this summer and hopes to get a scholarship to the Sorbonne for next year.
12. Slim has excellent manners and he always impresses parents.
13. For my report I finished reading a biography of George Eliot and I am about to start one about Charles Dickens.
14. This sentence has two full independent clauses but the other has a compound verb.
15. The ambassador will arrive on the last flight tonight or he will be on an early flight tomorrow morning.

16. Our hockey team arrived early in Greenvale and waited for more than an hour for its bus.
17. I called my parents and told them not to wait up for me.
18. We will take the exam on Friday and should have our grades next week.
19. Ann and Dorothy have been accepted at the same college and plan to be roommates next year.
20. Will you work this summer or vacation with your parents?

EXERCISE B: Punctuating Items in a Series and Coordinate Adjectives. Copy each sentence that needs commas, adding the necessary commas. For any sentences that do not need commas, write *correct.*

EXAMPLE: I cleaned my closet my desk and my room.

I cleaned my closet, my desk, and my room.

1. The leader of the rock group was a friendly attractive youth.
2. Fresh fruit green vegetables lean meat and grain products were part of her diet.
3. She wore her new blue jeans.
4. Our advisor planned the trip chartered the bus and arranged the hotel reservations.
5. A well-planned thoughtful speech followed the introduction.
6. Battles were fought in New Jersey New York Pennsylvania Delaware and Virginia during the Revolutionary War.
7. These hardy plants grow equally well in window boxes in home gardens and in open fields.
8. The survey of the city showed that many buildings were abandoned that many small businesses had closed and that the streets needed repair.
9. For Christmas I bought Father a pair of soft pigskin gloves.
10. The vessel slipped into port on a rainy moonless night.

Commas That Set Off Added Elements

Many individual words, phrases, and clauses also need to be set off with commas. These include introductory material, parenthetical expressions, and nonessential material. First, consider introductory material.

330

Introductory Material. This material consists of words, phrases, or clauses that appear at the beginning of a sentence.

Use a comma after an introductory word, phrase, or clause.

The following examples show what types of introductory material should be set off with commas.

INTRODUCTORY WORDS:	Yes, we do expect to hear from them soon.
	No, there has been no response.
	Well, I was definitely surprised by her question.
NOUNS OF DIRECT ADDRESS:	Barry, will you attend the meeting?
COMMON EXPRESSIONS:	Of course, come to the game with us.
INTRODUCTORY ADVERBS:	Hurriedly, they gathered up their books and papers.
	Patiently, the children's mother explained it to them again.
PREPOSITIONAL PHRASES (of four or more words):	In the shade of the maple tree, a family of raccoons lived.
	After the difficult exam, we were all exhausted.
PARTICIPIAL PHRASES:	Moving slowly, she approached the injured puppy.
	Seated next to each other in the auditorium, we introduced ourselves and started to chat.
INFINITIVE PHRASES:	To choose the right book, I consulted the card catalog.
	To finish my work on time, I will have to work through lunch.
ADVERBIAL CLAUSES:	When she asked for permission to go, she was sure it would be denied.
	If you collect coins, you may be interested in this one.

Only one comma should be used after two prepositional phrases or a compound participial or infinitive phrase.

EXAMPLES: In the pocket of his old jeans, he found the key.

Lost in the woods and frightened by the darkness, the campers huddled together near the fire.

To choose the correct word and to spell correctly, I often consult the dictionary.

Occasionally, you may also need to use a comma with a short prepositional phrase to prevent confusion.

CLEAR: In the morning we ate breakfast at a diner.

CONFUSING: In the rain drops seeped through the window frame.

CLEAR: In the rain, drops seeped through the window frame.

Parenthetical Expressions. The second type of material that needs to be set off with commas is made up of parenthetical expressions. Parenthetical expressions are words or phrases that interrupt the flow of a sentence.

Use commas to set off parenthetical expressions.

The following examples show various types of parenthetical expressions. Notice that they may come at the end of a sentence or in the middle. When a parenthetical expression appears in the middle of a sentence, two commas are needed to set it off from the rest of the sentence.

NOUNS OF DIRECT ADDRESS: Will you have lunch with us, Ted?

I wonder, Dr. Green, if I have any cavities?

CONJUNCTIVE ADVERBS: The tickets were all sold a week before the concert, however.

We could not, therefore, buy one.

COMMON EXPRESSIONS: I listened to the teacher's explanation as carefully as anyone else, I think.

He gave us, in fact, all the information we required.

CONTRASTING EXPRESSIONS: Tom is seventeen, not eighteen.

Lisa's acting ability, not her attractiveness, got her the lead in the school play.

332

Nonessential Material. Finally, consider the need for commas with nonessential material. Appositives, participial phrases, and adjective clauses can be either essential or nonessential. (The terms *restrictive* and *nonrestrictive* are also used to refer to these two kinds of materials.) Essential material, which is necessary to the meaning of a sentence, is not set off with commas.

ESSENTIAL APPOSITIVE:	The singer *Diana Ross* is also an actress.
ESSENTIAL PARTICIPIAL PHRASE:	The woman *buying the tomatoes* is my mother.
ESSENTIAL ADJECTIVE CLAUSE:	The report *that the committee will consider today* was prepared by members of the first-aid squad.

The preceding examples illustrate three kinds of essential elements. In the first example, the appositive *Diana Ross* identifies the specific singer. In the next example, the participial phrase *buying the tomatoes* identifies the specific woman. In the last example, the adjective clause *that the committee will consider today* identifies the specific report. Because they limit or restrict identification to the person or thing described in the appositive, participial phrase, or adjective clause, these items are all essential. They cannot be removed without changing the meaning of the sentences, so they require no commas.

Nonessential elements also provide information, but that information is not essential to the meaning of the sentence. Because nonessential elements do not alter the meaning and are not necessary for purposes of identification, they require commas to set them off.

Use commas to set off nonessential expressions.

NONESSENTIAL APPOSITIVE:	Diana Ross**,** *the singer***,** is also an actress.
NONESSENTIAL PARTICIPIAL PHRASE:	My mother**,** *buying the apples***,** is an excellent cook.
NONESSENTIAL ADJECTIVE CLAUSE:	The first-aid squad's report**,** *which the committee will consider today***,** took six months to prepare.

333

The nonessential elements in the preceding examples are interesting, but they are not necessary to the main ideas in the sentences. *Diana Ross, my mother,* and *the first-aid squad's report* clearly identify the items under discussion. The nonessential elements, therefore, are set off with commas.

EXERCISE C: Setting Off Introductory Material. Copy each sentence that needs commas, adding the necessary commas. If a sentence needs no commas, write *correct.*

EXAMPLE: Finally the plane taxied down the runway.

Finally, the plane taxied down the runway.

1. To practice my speech I rehearsed it in front of a mirror.
2. Cautioned by her mother and warned by her friends Betsy drove slowly through the busy intersection.
3. At the supermarket checkout counters always seem to have long lines.
4. In the kitchen we packed provisions for our camping trip.
5. If the weather is pleasant we hope to attend a concert in the park tonight.
6. George will you help at the bazaar on Saturday?
7. Of course the judge will punish the offenders.
8. Weakened by the storm the battered merchant ship limped into port two weeks late.
9. Delightedly Steve opened the door and greeted his cousins.
10. No I never thought I would have a chance to win first prize.

EXERCISE D: Setting Off Parenthetical Expressions. Copy the following sentences, inserting any commas needed to set off parenthetical expressions.

EXAMPLE: You look best I think in bright colors.

You look best, I think, in bright colors.

1. There are five houses on that street now not the two you remember.
2. You must nevertheless do the assignments.
3. Professor Watkins is I believe one of the top economic experts in the country.
4. Have you been able to find the information Miss Regan?
5. Most of us were surprised in fact by his unusual frankness.

6. His irresponsible behavior not his lack of ability caused his problems.
7. It seems to me however that he should have asked me first.
8. The results we hope will be beneficial to everyone.
9. You know Mrs. Grey we will do whatever we can to help.
10. Please be ready therefore to present your report on Friday.

EXERCISE E: Distinguishing Between Essential and Nonessential Material. Copy each sentence that needs commas, adding the necessary commas. If a sentence contains essential material, write *correct.*

EXAMPLE: Sissy Spacek a talented actress stars in that film.

Sissy Spacek, a talented actress, stars in that film.

1. The surf cresting against the sea wall damaged a number of summer cottages.
2. O'Hare Airport which is one of the busiest airports in the world has severe traffic problems.
3. The building chosen for rehabilitation was on our block.
4. Dr. Stevenson whom you heard lecture last week will speak again today.
5. Heinrich Schliemann who unearthed the ruins at Troy and Mycenae wanted to excavate the Minoan ruins on Crete.
6. I recognized the road that you described in your letter.
7. The three little boys playing near the fence all live on the next street.
8. The Interstate Commerce Commission which was authorized by Congress in 1887 has the power to regulate commerce among the states.
9. The original Fort Laramie built by fur traders William Sublette and Robert Campbell was established in 1834 near the junction of the North Platte and Laramie rivers in what is now the state of Wyoming.
10. The two books recommended by our science teacher are available in the library.

Other Uses of the Comma

You will also need to use commas in your writing in other situations.

Geographical Names. Geographical names may have several parts.

When a geographical name is made up of two or more parts, use a comma after each item.

EXAMPLES: My aunt who lives in Houston, Texas, is visiting us.

Vancouver, British Columbia, Canada, is his home.

Dates. Dates may also be made up of several parts.

When a date is made up of two or more parts, use a comma after each item except in the case of a month followed by a day.

EXAMPLES: I graduated from high school on June 16, 1985, and my brother graduated on June 16, 1986.

Friday, August 23, was the day we met.

If dates contain only months and years, you may omit the commas if you wish.

EXAMPLES: In July, 1981, I started my part-time job.

In July 1981 I started my part-time job.

Titles After a Name. Whenever you use a title after the name of a person or a company, you will have to add commas.

When a name is followed by one or more titles, use a comma after the name and after each title.

EXAMPLE: Susan Martini, Ph.D., teaches chemistry.

Addresses. Commas are also necessary in addresses.

Use a comma after each item in an address made up of two or more parts.

EXAMPLE: Send a copy of the report to Mrs. Robert Brooks, 145 River Road, Jacksonville, Florida 32211.

Commas are placed after the name, street, and city in the preceding example. Instead of inserting a comma between the state and the ZIP code, extra space is left between them.

Most commas in an address are unnecessary in a letter or on an envelope or package. A comma is still needed, however, between the city and the state.

336

EXAMPLE: Mrs. Robert Brooks
            145 River Road
            Jacksonville, Florida 32211

Salutations and Closings. Commas are also needed in other parts of letters.

Use a comma after the salutation in a personal letter and after the closing in all letters.

SALUTATIONS: Dear Emily,   Dear Uncle Frank,   My dear Friend,
CLOSINGS: Yours truly,   Sincerely,   Your friend,

Large Numbers. Commas make numbers easier to read.

With numbers of more than three digits, use a comma after every third digit from the right.

EXAMPLES: 3,823 students   205,000 gallons   2,674,970 tons

Do not use commas with ZIP codes, telephone numbers, page numbers, serial numbers, years, or house numbers.

ZIP CODE: 07632   TELEPHONE NUMBER: (805) 555-6224
PAGE NUMBER: 1258   SERIAL NUMBER: 602 988 6768

Elliptical Sentences. In elliptical sentences words that are understood are left out. Commas make them easier to read.

Use a comma to indicate the words left out of an elliptical sentence.

EXAMPLE: Allan did his homework carefully; Fred, carelessly.

The words *did his homework* have been omitted from the second clause of the elliptical sentence. The comma has been inserted in their place, however, so the meaning is still clear.

Direct Quotations. Another use of commas is to indicate where direct quotations begin and end.

Use commas to set off a direct quotation from the rest of a sentence.

EXAMPLES: "You came home late," commented Ann's father.

             She said, "I went to play practice after school."

             "I hope," Ann's father said, "the audience realizes how hard everyone works to make the play a success."

For Clarity. Finally, you may need to use commas to prevent readers from misunderstanding a sentence.

Use a comma to prevent a sentence from being misunderstood.

UNCLEAR: In the reservoir water is stored.
CLEAR: In the reservoir, water is stored.

NOTE ABOUT THE CARELESS USE OF COMMAS: You have now seen many rules governing the use of commas. Studying these rules will help you use commas correctly. Knowing the rules will also help you avoid using unnecessary commas. Because commas appear so frequently in writing, some people are tempted to use them where no commas are required. Be sure you know the reason why you are inserting commas each time you use them.

The following examples illustrate some ways commas may be misused. Avoid making these mistakes in your own writing.

MISUSED WITH AN ADJECTIVE AND NOUN: After a hike I enjoy a cool, refreshing, breeze.

CORRECT: After a hike I enjoy a cool, refreshing breeze.

MISUSED WITH A COMPOUND SUBJECT: During the subway strike, my friend Nancy, and her sister Julia, walked to school every day.

CORRECT: During the subway strike, my friend Nancy and her sister Julia walked to school every day.

MISUSED WITH A COMPOUND VERB: The right fielder leaped as high as he could, and caught the ball.

CORRECT: The right fielder leaped as high as he could and caught the ball.

MISUSED WITH A COMPOUND OBJECT: She bought a jacket with knitted cuffs, and a hood.

CORRECT: She bought a jacket with knitted cuffs and a hood.

MISUSED WITH PHRASES: Reading the letter, and thinking of how he would answer it, Brian did not hear his mother call him.

CORRECT: Reading the letter and thinking of how he would answer it, Brian did not hear his mother call him.

338

MISUSED WITH CLAUSES:	He discussed what nutrients are essential to good health, and which foods will best supply them.
CORRECT:	He discussed what nutrients are essential to good health and which foods will best supply them.

EXERCISE F: Using Commas in Other Situations. Copy the following sentences, inserting the necessary commas.

EXAMPLE: "I hope I made enough sandwiches" Abigail said.

   "I hope I made enough sandwiches," Abigail said.

1. Mail entries by May 30 1986 to Box 5 Troy Iowa 52537.
2. Harold Andre Sr. lives in Santa Barbara California.
3. In 1978 the United States imported 8230000 barrels of oil.
4. In one day 5675 people called the toll-free phone number (800) 555-0220 to pledge money for the charity drive.
5. Jim spent his savings on a new bicycle; Pat on a typewriter.
6. "We'll be late" Virginia worried "unless we hurry."
7. In the dark stairways can prove hazardous.
8. Karen Wilson D.D.S. will open an office in this building.
9. Paul said "On Saturday I will mow the lawn."
10. Montreal Quebec Canada has about 1214300 people.

EXERCISE G: Using Commas in a Social Letter. Copy the following friendly letter, inserting the necessary commas.

736 Williams Avenue
Dayton Ohio 45402
August 5 1981

Dear Margaret

Well after almost six weeks of travel my family and I have returned from our exciting trip to Egypt. Returning to the United States we were struck by the difference in cultures. It felt I think like going from an old world to a new.

Naturally, we saw all the famous sights: the Pyramids and Sphinx at Giza the temples of Karnak and Luxor the Aswan Dam and of course Cairo. Much to my surprise I was fascinated by Cairo the capital city of Egypt. I visited the Egyptian Museum the Cairo Tower Mohammed Ali Mosque and other places.

My mother bought an old expensive bracelet. As if that

weren't enough she also invested in a caftan called a galabias and two brass trays.

I'm looking forward to your visit next week and I'll tell you about the rest of my experiences then.

Affectionately

Brad

DEVELOPING WRITING SKILLS: Using Commas Correctly in Your Own Writing. Write ten original sentences according to the following directions.

1. Write a compound sentence joined by the conjunction *but.*
2. Write a sentence containing a series of three phrases.
3. Write a sentence containing two coordinate adjectives.
4. Write a sentence containing two cumulative adjectives.
5. Write a sentence beginning with a participial phrase.
6. Write a sentence containing a parenthetical expression.
7. Write a sentence containing a nonessential appositive.
8. Write a sentence that includes a direct quotation.
9. Write an elliptical sentence.
10. Write a sentence that requires a comma to prevent misunderstanding.

12.3 Semicolons and Colons

This section presents rules governing the use of semicolons (;) and colons (:). Semicolons can help you establish a relationship between independent clauses. They can also help you avoid confusion in sentences with other internal punctuation. Colons can be used as introductory devices to point ahead to additional information as well as in other special situations.

The Semicolon

Semicolons establish relationships between independent clauses that are closely related in thought and structure.

Use a semicolon to join independent clauses that are not already joined by the conjunction *and, but, for, nor, or, so* or *yet.*

The most common way for writers to join independent clauses is by using a coordinate conjunction and a comma.

EXAMPLE: We explored the attic together**,** and we were amazed at all the useless junk we found there.

When no coordinate conjunction is used, however, closely related independent clauses can be joined with a semicolon.

EXAMPLE: We explored the attic together**;** we were amazed at all the useless junk we found there.

Sometimes, the second independent clause may begin with a conjunctive adverb or a transitional expression. Conjunctive adverbs include such words as *also, furthermore, accordingly, besides, consequently, however, instead, namely, nevertheless, otherwise, similarly, therefore, indeed,* and *thus.* Transitional expressions include *as a result, first, second, at this time, for instance, for example, in fact, on the other hand, that is, in conclusion,* and *finally.*

Use a semicolon to join independent clauses separated by either a conjunctive adverb or a transitional expression.

CONJUNCTIVE ADVERB: We visited seven countries in only two weeks**;** consequently, we missed many interesting historical sites.

TRANSITIONAL EXPRESSION: She never knew his name**;** in fact, she really had no interest in meeting him.

The conjunctive adverb and transitional expression are set off in the second independent clauses by commas because they are introductory expressions in the second independent clauses.

A semicolon is also used to avoid confusion when independent clauses or items in a series already contain commas.

Consider the use of a semicolon to avoid confusion when independent clauses or items in a series already contain commas.

INDEPENDENT CLAUSES: The forest, filled with thick underbrush, seemed impassable**;** and the hungry, tired family slumped to the ground in despair.

ITEMS IN A SERIES: I was convinced that we had won when I heard the music of the band, playing our victory march; the jubilant players, clapping and shouting; and the roar of spectators, rising to their feet.

In the last example, semicolons are used instead of commas to separate the three major parts of the series. Commas are used within each of the major parts to set off nonessential participial phrases. You should also consider the use of semicolons when items in a series contain nonessential appositives or adjective clauses.

EXERCISE A: Using Semicolons. Copy the following sentences, inserting one or more semicolons in each.

EXAMPLE: She skis well in fact, she is the state champion.

             She skis well; in fact, she is the state champion.

1. The committee was unhappy with the decision nevertheless, they understood why it had been made.
2. Jean wanted the position in the firm however, she was disturbed about some of the working conditions.
3. Ben struggled up the steep, rocky hill and when he reached the top, Ben collapsed in a heap on the ground.
4. The clipper ship, battered by the vicious storm, fought a losing battle the main mast, weakened by the winds, broke.
5. We have invited cousin Hank, who is an attorney in Atlanta my friend Betty, who lives next door and Betty's brother, who is home from college for the weekend.
6. I am going to order spaghetti and meatballs, salad, and garlic bread they are my favorite foods.
7. The storm washed out the road therefore, it took us an additional hour to reach the cabin.
8. Bran contains large amounts of fiber nutritionists recommend adding it to our diets.
9. The children had looked forward eagerly to moving however, they were disappointed when they learned that few children lived in their new neighborhood.
10. After studying every night, I felt confident that I would pass the test nevertheless, I still felt slightly nervous.

The Colon

Colons are used in several situations. Primarily, colons serve as introductory devices.

Use a colon before a list of items following an independent clause.

EXAMPLES: As part of our assignment, we had to interview a group of experts: an economist, a scientist, and a business manager.

His travels took him to a number of continents: Africa, Australia, Asia, and South America.

Notice that each list in these examples follows an independent clause. If general terms such as *a group of experts* or *a number of continents* were not used, colons would not be appropriate since you would no longer have independent clauses preceding the lists.

EXAMPLES: As part of our assignment, we had to interview an economist, a scientist, and a business manager.

His travels took him to Africa, Australia, Asia, and South America.

Sometimes an independent clause preceding a list ends in a phrase such as *the following* or *the following items.* These phrases should signal you to use a colon to introduce the list.
Colons also introduce certain kinds of quotations.

Use a colon to introduce a quotation that is formal or lengthy or a quotation that does not contain a "he said/she said" expression.

EXAMPLE: Oliver Wendell Holmes, Jr., wrote this about freedom: "It is only through free debate and free exchange of ideas that government remains responsive to the will of the people and peaceful change is effected."

Dialogue or a casual remark should be introduced by a comma even if it is lengthy. Use the colon if the quotation is formal or has no "he said/she said" expression.

A colon may also be used to introduce a sentence that explains the sentence that precedes it.

Use a colon to introduce a sentence that summarizes or explains the sentence before it.

EXAMPLE: His explanation for being late was believable: He had had a flat tire on the way.

Notice that the complete sentence introduced by the colon starts with a capital letter.

Another item introduced by a colon is a formal appositive that follows an independent clause.

Use a colon to introduce a formal appositive that follows an independent clause.

EXAMPLE: I had finally decided on a career: nursing.

The colon is a stronger punctuation mark than a comma. Using the colon gives more emphasis to the appositive it introduces.

Colons are also used in a variety of other situations.

Use a colon in a number of special writing situations.

The chart shows colons used in special writing situations. Study the examples carefully.

SPECIAL SITUATIONS REQUIRING COLONS	
Numerals Giving the Time	1:30 A.M. 9:15 P.M.
References to Periodicals (Volume Number: Page Number)	*Scientific American* 74:12 *Sports Illustrated* 53:15
Biblical References (Chapter Number: Verse Number)	I Corinthians 13:13 Exodus 14:21
Subtitles of Books and Magazines	*A Field Guide to the Birds:* *Eastern Land and Water Birds*
Salutations in Business Letters	Dear Mrs. Gordon: Dear Sir:
Labels Used to Signal Important Ideas	Danger: These are high-voltage wires.

EXERCISE B: Using Colons. Copy each sentence, adding the necessary colons. Underline any words in italics.

EXAMPLE: The article is in *Discover* 5 11.

The article is in <u>Discover</u> 5:11.

1. The office manager gave us a list of needed supplies paper clips, correction fluid, rubber bands, and brass fasteners.
2. We did not go because of bad weather a raging storm.
3. Warning This product is for external use only.
4. The Boeing 727 taxied to a landing at exactly 7 05 A.M.
5. The full title of Rebecca West's book is *Black Lamb and Grey Falcon A Journey Through Yugoslavia.*
6. Historian Samuel Eliot Morison describes the deaths of both Jefferson and Adams on July 4, 1826 "The lives of Thomas Jefferson and John Adams, the one eighty-three and the other ninety years old, were flickering to a close. Could they live until the Fourth, the fiftieth anniversary of the adoption of that great Declaration for which they were jointly responsible? All America was praying that they would."
7. She recited Matthew 6 14 and 6 15.
8. The coach's explanation was simple and direct The team had decided to try to rebuild by using the younger players.
9. His historical research took him to a number of countries England, Belgium, France, Austria, and Germany.
10. The book you need is called *The Revolution Remembered Eyewitness Accounts of the War for Independence.*

EXERCISE C: Using Semicolons and Colons Correctly.

Copy each sentence, inserting needed semicolons or colons.

EXAMPLE: I have just reread my favorite children's book *Bambi.*

I have just reread my favorite children's book: <u>Bambi</u>.

1. Joanne purchased all the picnic supplies soda, potato chips, frankfurters, chopped meat, rolls, and fresh fruit.
2. The family agreed with the doctor's prognosis nevertheless, they decided to get another doctor's opinion.
3. The United States Postal Service issued an unusually attractive commemorative stamp It depicts General Bernardo de Galvez at the Battle of Mobile in 1780.

4. The first record contains selections from the group's concert the second record is a compilation of old hits.
5. The host was a well-known scientist and author Carl Sagan.
6. The President welcomed the foreign dignitary "The people of the United States welcome you and hope that your visit will be a pleasant and productive one."
7. This is her plan She wants to visit Milan and then Rome.
8. Mary Ellen invited Bill, who enjoyed playing cards Sue,who loved to dance and Glen, who didn't enjoy parties at all.
9. The flight to Ireland left at 11 30 p.m.
10. Six pupils took the state scholarship examination today the rest of the group decided to wait for the next test.

DEVELOPING WRITING SKILLS: Using Semicolons and Colons in Your Own Writing. Write a paragraph. Include semicolons used in two different ways and colons used in three different ways.

12.4 Quotation Marks and Underlining

You will often wish to use direct quotations in your writing, for they can enliven short stories and other works of fiction. Direct quotations, the actual words of a character, provide readers much information about a character, both from what he or she says and from the way he or she speaks.

Direct quotations can also be used to support or refute ideas and arguments in nonfiction. You can quote an expert in a particular field to help prove a point you are trying to make.

This section illustrates ways to write and punctuate direct quotations. It also explains the use of underlining and quotation marks to indicate different types of titles, names, and words.

Quotation Marks for Direct Quotations

There are two ways in which you can cite a person's ideas. One way is to reproduce the person's exact words or thoughts. This is called a *direct quotation*. The other way is to give just the general meaning of the person's words or thoughts. This is called an indirect quotation.

A direct quotation represents a person's exact speech or thoughts and is enclosed in quotation marks [" "].

An indirect quotation reports the general meaning of what a person said or thought and does not require quotation marks.

DIRECT QUOTATION: "If I am elected," said the candidate, "I will sponsor a bill to improve local public transportation."

INDIRECT QUOTATION: The candidate said that she planned to work for improvements in local transportation.

Both types of quotations, direct and indirect, are acceptable when you write. Using a direct quotation when it is possible, however, generally results in more interesting and convincing writing.

To enclose a sentence that is an uninterrupted direct quotation, all you need to do is place double quotation marks around the quotation.

EXAMPLE: "One can live in the shadow of an idea without grasping it."—Elizabeth Bowen

Notice that this quotation begins with a capital letter. The same is true of every complete sentence of quoted material.

You may also quote just part of a sentence directly. When a phrase or a fragment is quoted, enclose the quoted words in quotation marks just as you would with a full sentence. Capitalize the first word of the quote, however, only when it falls at the beginning of the sentence you are writing or when it is a proper noun or a proper adjective that would be capitalized in any case.

EXAMPLES: In one of his essays, Wallace Stegner calls the town dump near his home in Saskatchewan "our poetry and our history."

"Our poetry and our history" is how Wallace Stegner refers to the town dump near his home in Whitemud, Saskatchewan.

Many direct quotations contain not only the actual words of a speaker but also words identifying the speaker. These identifying words or phrases are called "he said/she said" expressions or conversational tags. They include such expressions as *she asked, they replied, my father explained,* and *Jenny shrieked.* The possibilities for conversational tags are almost limitless and depend in your own writing solely on your own inventiveness. Conversational tags, however, have one common characteristic: They are never enclosed in quotation marks.

Conversational tags may appear in various positions in relation to direct quotations. First, consider a conversational tag used as an introductory expression.

Use a comma or colon after an introductory expression.

EXAMPLE: My mother warned, "You're now an adult and must be responsible for your own actions."

If you do not use a conversational tag as your introductory expression or if the introductory conversational tag is very formal in tone, set it off with a colon instead of a comma.

EXAMPLES: Bert rose to his feet: "I nominate Marge Wheatley."

At the end of the meeting, Marge spoke of her willingness to serve: "I hope to lead this class in carrying out many exciting activities."

Conversational tags may also act as concluding expressions.

Use a comma, question mark, or exclamation mark after a quotation followed by a concluding expression.

EXAMPLE: "You're now an adult and must be responsible for your own actions," my mother warned.

Notice above that a comma comes before the closing quotation mark and a period follows the conversational tag.

Finally, you may use a conversational tag to interrupt the words of a direct quotation.

Use a comma after part of a quoted sentence followed by an interrupting expression. Use another comma after the expression.

348

EXAMPLE: "You are now an adult," my mother warned, "and must be responsible for your own actions."

Notice in this example that when a quotation is interrupted by a conversational tag, two sets of quotation marks are used to enclose the quotation and two commas are used to set off the conversational tag.

Sometimes a conversational tag interrupts a quotation several sentences in length.

Use a comma, question mark, or exclamation mark after a quoted sentence that comes before an interrupting expression. Use a period after the expression.

EXAMPLE: "You are now an adult," warned my mother. "You must be responsible for your own actions."

Writers usually use all three of the different positions in which conversational tags may be placed. This helps to add variety.

EXERCISE A: Enclosing Direct Quotations in Quotation Marks. Copy each sentence that needs quotation marks, adding the quotation marks that are needed. The quoted fragment has been underlined to indicate where it begins and ends. If no quotation marks are needed, write *correct.*

EXAMPLE: I had pancakes for breakfast, announced Kathleen.

"I had pancakes for breakfast," announced Kathleen.

1. I am going to take my driver's test today, said Gloria.
2. My father replied, I will be happy to help you.
3. Tell me what happened, I pleaded. I can't bear to be in suspense any longer.
4. The principal asked us if we were on our way to the concert.
5. The bus driver sighed, Don't you have the correct change?
6. The salesclerk told us the price of the piano.
7. I know, she answered. I just heard the news on the radio.
8. My little brother says I am the world's bossiest sister.
9. The judge rapped the gavel: I want order in the courtroom.
10. I am so pleased you can visit us, wrote Joyce. We have all missed you since you moved away.

Other Punctuation Marks
with Quotation Marks

Quotation marks are used with commas, semicolons, colons, and all the end marks. The location of the quotation marks in relation to the different punctuation marks varies. Below are rules to help you place the punctuation marks correctly.

Always place a comma or a period inside the final quotation mark.

EXAMPLES: "Give us just another minute," called Mother.

                Marge said, "We're all ready to leave now."

The rule for the use of semicolons and colons with quotation marks is just the opposite.

Always place a semicolon or colon outside the final quotation mark.

EXAMPLES: We were just informed about his "willingness to serve"; we are all pleased.

                The convention gave her ideas its "strong endorsement": Most of the delegates promised to work for their adoption.

The use of question marks and exclamation marks with quotation marks is slightly more complicated.

Place a question mark or exclamation mark inside the final quotation mark if the end mark is part of the quotation.

EXAMPLES: Larry shouted, "Where is my report?"

                My sister retorted, "I will not be insulted!"

The question mark and exclamation mark in these examples are placed inside the final quotation mark because they apply only to the quoted portion of each sentence.

Place a question mark or exclamation mark outside the final quotation mark if the end mark is not part of the quotation.

EXAMPLES: Did the officer say, "I'll be back soon"?

                We were shocked when he said, "Yes"!

EXERCISE B: **Using Other Punctuation Marks Correctly with Quotations.** Copy the following sentences, adding quotation marks where necessary. Quoted fragments are underlined to show where they begin and end.

EXAMPLE: I am so angry with you! Randy shouted.

"I am so angry with you!" Randy shouted.

1. According to H. L. Mencken, William Jennings Bryan was the national tear duct.
2. Did they ask, What can we do to help?
3. I think you can be whatever you want to be, Father said.
4. Emma Lazarus described the poor people of the world as huddled masses yearning to breathe free.
5. She agreed to work day and night; we never believed her.
6. When she saw the new car, she screamed, Hooray!
7. Oscar Wilde commented about a famous contemporary: Mr. Henry James writes fiction as if it were a painful duty.
8. Is that clear? she asked.
9. In the bottle were his secret ingredients: frog legs, talcum powder, and an old arrowhead.
10. Gertrude Stein gave the following advice to Ernest Hemingway: Remarks are not literature.

Quotation Marks in Special Situations

Special situations requiring quotation marks include dialogues, quotations of more than one paragraph, selected portions of a person's words, or one quotation within another.

Dialogues and Long Quotations. One of the best ways to move the action forward in a short story is by using dialogue, the words of the characters themselves.

There are many ways to write dialogue, but rules must be followed so readers can keep track of who is speaking.

When writing dialogue, begin a new paragraph with each change of speaker.

Read the passage below from *The Pearl* by John Steinbeck through for meaning. Then go back and analyze it line by line.

EXAMPLE: The wind drove off the clouds and skimmed the sky clean and drifted the sand of the country like snow.

Then Juan Tomas, when the evening approached, talked long with his brother. "Where will you go?"

"To the north," said Kino. "I have heard that there are cities in the north."

"Avoid the shore," said Juan Tomas. "They are making a party to search the shore. The men in the city will look for you. Do you still have the pearl?"

"I have it," said Kino. "And I will keep it. I might have given it as a gift, but now it is my misfortune and my life and I will keep it." His eyes were hard and cruel and bitter.

Coyotito whimpered and Juana muttered little magic words over him to make him silent.

"The wind is good," said Juan Tomas. "There will be no tracks."

They left quietly in the dark before the moon had risen.   —John Steinbeck

In reading fiction, take time to analyze what you read. Analyzing different styles can help you improve your own style.

A different rule is followed when a writer uses several consecutive paragraphs of material quoted from the same person.

For quotations longer than a paragraph, put quotation marks at the beginning of each paragraph and at the end of the final paragraph.

EXAMPLE: John McPhee in his book *Giving Good Weight* has written an essay about a canoe trip down the St. John River in northern Maine. He introduces his readers to the river in the following way.

"We have been out here four days now and rain has been falling three. The rain appears to be ending. Breaks of blue are opening in the sky. Sunlight is coming through, and a wind is rising.

"I was not prepared for the St. John River, did not

anticipate its size. I saw it as a narrow trail flowing north, twisting through the balsam and spruce—a small and intimate forest river, something like the Allagash, which is not many miles away. The river I imagined would have been river enough, but the real one, the actual St. John, is awesome and surprising.**"**

Notice that both paragraphs of quoted material begin with quotation marks, but only the last paragraph ends with them.

Ellipsis Marks and Single Quotation Marks. Ellipsis marks (. . .) can be very useful when you want to present only part of a long quotation.

Use three ellipsis marks in a quotation to indicate that words have been omitted.

The examples below show how to use ellipsis marks at the beginning, in the middle, and at the end of a quotation.

AN ENTIRE QUOTATION: "The Black River, which cuts a winding course through southern Missouri's rugged Ozark highlands, lends its name to an area of great natural beauty. Within this expanse are old mines and quarries to explore, fast-running waters to canoe, and wooded trails to ride."
—Suzanne Charlé

ELLIPSIS AT THE BEGINNING: Suzanne Charlé described the Black River area in Missouri as having "**. . .** old mines and quarries to explore, fast-running waters to canoe, and wooded trails to ride."

ELLIPSIS IN THE MIDDLE: Suzanne Charlé wrote, "The Black River **. . .** lends its name to an area of great natural beauty. Within this expanse are old mines and quarries to explore, fast-running waters to canoe, and wooded trails to ride."

ELLIPSIS AT THE END: Suzanne Charlé wrote, "The Black River, which cuts a winding course through southern Missouri's rugged highlands, lends its name to an area of great natural beauty**. . . .**"

Notice in the last example that when a period falls right before an omitted portion of the quotation, it is added along with the ellipsis marks to conclude the sentence.

Another special situation involving quotation marks occurs when a writer wishes to include one quotation within another.

Use single quotation marks for a quotation within a quotation.

EXAMPLES: "I will always remember my grandmother quoting Shelley, 'If winter comes, can spring be far behind?' " Michael commented.

"The doctor said, 'Good news!' " she explained.

Rephrase most sentences with one quotation within another to include the same information in a less complicated way.

EXERCISE C: Writing Original Dialogue. Write one page of original dialogue. Use two different characters and include a few lines of description wherever necessary. Enclose the lines of dialogue in quotation marks. Include enough conversational tags so that there will be no confusion about who is speaking.

EXERCISE D: Punctuating with Ellipsis Marks and Single Quotation Marks. Copy each of the following sentences, inserting double or single quotation marks as required.

EXAMPLE: Eudora Welty described a woman as moving **...** with the balanced heaviness and lightness of a pendulum in a grandfather clock.

Eudora Welty described a woman as moving "**...** with the balanced heaviness and lightness of a pendulum in a grandfather clock."

1. "Then the president turned to us and said, I'm afraid I must decline, and walked from the room."
2. Robert Benchley once jested, I haven't been abroad in so long that I almost speak English without an accent.
3. A quotation from Katherine Mansfield begins, I want, by understanding myself, to understand others. . . .
4. "Later they studied Hamlet's famous soliloquy, which begins, To be, or not to be, that is the question."

354

5. Catherine Drinker Bowen has written: All artists quiver under the lash of adverse criticism. . . . When Beethoven heard that a certain conductor refused to perform one of his symphonies, he went to bed . . . until the symphony was performed.
6. "She asked, How did it happen? and burst into tears."
7. Mark Twain ends his criticism of Scott with these words: . . . He did measureless harm; more real and lasting harm, perhaps, than any other individual that ever wrote.
8. My mother said, I always wanted to sing professionally.
9. About Bernard Shaw, Oscar Wilde said that he . . . hasn't an enemy in the world, and none of his friends like him.
10. "What did he mean when he said, You'll be sorry?"

Underlining and Quotation Marks

Several methods are used to indicate different types of titles in various situations. These methods include italics, underlining, and quotation marks. Books, magazines, and other printed material use *italics,* a slanted type face, to indicate some types of titles. In handwritten or typed material, underlining would be used for those titles. Other titles require quotation marks.

Underlining. Certain titles need to be underlined.

Underline the titles of long written works, of publications that are published as a single work, of shows, and of other works of art.

BOOK: <u>To Kill a Mockingbird</u> is a modern classic.

PLAY: He starred in <u>Long Day's Journey into Night</u>.

MAGAZINE: I read <u>Newsweek</u> to keep up with current events.

NEWSPAPER: She agreed with the story in the Los Angeles <u>Times</u>.

MUSICAL: She went to see <u>Peter Pan</u>.

PAINTING: I saw Chagall's painting <u>The Green Violinist</u>.

NOTE ABOUT NEWSPAPER TITLES: The portion of the title that should be underlined will vary from newspaper to newspaper. <u>The New York Times</u> should always be fully capitalized and underlined. Other papers, however, can usually be treated in one of two ways: the Los Angeles <u>Times</u> or the <u>Los Angeles Times</u>. Unless you know the true name of a paper, choose one of these two forms and use it consistently.

Several other types of titles should also be underlined in handwritten or typed material.

Underline the names of individual air, sea, space, and land craft.

EXAMPLE: My brother served on the aircraft carrier <u>Kitty Hawk</u>.

Underlining is also used for foreign words.

Underline foreign words or phrases not yet accepted into English.

EXAMPLES: The voyage was so rough that they suffered from <u>mal de mer</u> constantly.

Her <u>sturm und drang</u> manner was shocking to those of us who had expected a mild young <u>hausfrau</u>.

Many foreign words and phrases are used so often by English-speaking people that they are now considered to be part of the language. Although these words may often retain their foreign pronunciation, they are no longer underlined or italicized.

NOT UNDERLINED: chili, amour, milieu, lasagna, plaza, gestalt, raconteur, teriyaki, andante, sauna

Consult a dictionary that includes foreign words and phrases if you are in doubt about whether a particular word or phrase should be underlined in your writing.

Numbers, letters, and words used as names for themselves are also underlined or italicized.

Underline numbers, symbols, letters, and words used as names for themselves.

EXAMPLES: Her <u>i</u>'s and her <u>l</u>'s look too much alike.

Is that an <u>8</u> or a <u>6</u>?

Avoid sprinkling your speech with <u>you know</u>.

In addition, you may occasionally wish to use underlining to emphasize a particular word or phrase in your writing.

Underline words that you wish to stress.

EXAMPLE: What a <u>ridiculous</u> situation!

In most cases, you should indicate emphasis not by underlining but by choosing and arranging your words with care. Reserve underlining for use only in special instances.

Quotation Marks. Other titles require quotation marks.

Use quotation marks around the titles of short written works, episodes in a series, songs, and parts of long musical compositions or collections.

EXAMPLES: "Edward, Edward" and "Lord Randal" are two familiar English ballads.

Winifred Welles's essay "The Attic" describes her as a child exploring her grandfather's attic.

Read Chapter 1, "Dialogue and Action," in <u>Understanding Drama</u>.

"The Tell-Tale Heart" is an effective horror tale.

One of the most loved songs of the American people is Woody Guthrie's "This Land Is Your Land."

Titles Without Underlining or Quotation Marks. Religious works require neither underlining nor quotation marks.

Do not underline or place in quotation marks the name of the Bible, its books, divisions, or versions, or other holy scriptures, such as the Koran.

EXAMPLE: She recited the Twenty-Third Psalm.

Other titles needing neither underlining nor quotation marks include various kinds of government documents.

Do not underline or place in quotation marks the titles of government charters, alliances, treaties, acts, statutes, or reports.

EXAMPLE: The Versailles Treaty officially ended World War I.

EXERCISE E: Using Underlining and Quotation Marks. Write correctly the following sentences that require underlining or quotation marks. For items requiring neither, write *correct.*

EXAMPLE: In 1610 at the age of 17, Artemisia Gentileschi cre-
           ated the painting Susanna and the Elders.

           In 1610 at the age of 17, Artemisia Gentileschi cre-
           ated the painting <u>Susanna and the Elders</u>.

1. The French expression le style c'est l'homme was one of her favorite sayings.
2. The train called the Twentieth Century Limited traveled between New York and Chicago.
3. Wilkommen, the opening song in the musical Cabaret, is considered a most effective opening number.
4. I just read the poem Wild Swans by Edna St. Vincent Millay.
5. The New York Times has great political influence.
6. William Dean Howell's The Rise of Silas Lapham is one of the best books I've ever read.
7. The Dictionary of Literary Terms is a fine reference work.
8. The One Hundredth Psalm was read during the service.
9. The play Romeo and Juliet is included in the curriculum.
10. The North Atlantic Treaty Organization is an alliance of European countries that includes the United States.

EXERCISE F: Applying the Rules Governing the Use of Quotation Marks and Underlining. Copy the following sentences, using quotation marks or underlining as necessary.

EXAMPLE: In her poem Spring, Edna St. Vincent Millay asked,
           To what purpose, April, do you return again?

           In her poem "Spring," Edna St. Vincent Millay asked,
           "To what purpose, April, do you return again?"

1. Two of romantic painter John Constable's works are Salisbury Cathedral and Haystacks.
2. Chaucer's Canterbury Tales begins with the following words: When in April the sweet showers fall . . .
3. She had bought, Flannery O'Connor wrote, a new dress for the occasion.
4. In his essay Dunkirk, Winston Churchill describes the most famous retreat in history.
5. What factors led you to that conclusion? she asked.
6. I enjoyed Emily Brontë's novel,Wuthering Heights.
7. Bill continued, Then my sister said, I am going to enlist! and my mother began to cry.

8. In Shakespeare's *Romeo and Juliet*, Romeo sighs, . . . O! that I were a glove upon that hand . . .
9. That's my final offer, he blurted. Take it or leave it.
10. Remember to cross your t's and dot your i's.

DEVELOPING WRITING SKILLS: Using Quotation Marks and Underlining Correctly in Your Own Writing. Write ten original sentences according to the following directions.

1. Write a sentence that contains the name of a movie.
2. Write as a direct quotation some advice you plan to give your grandchildren. Include a conversational tag.
3. Write a sentence containing the name of a song or a poem.
4. Write a sentence naming a local newspaper.
5. Write a sentence containing a foreign word or phrase not yet accepted as part of the English language.
6. Write a sentence containing the title and description of a painting you might create.
7. Write a sentence containing the name of an individual air, sea, space, or land craft.
8. Write a sentence containing the name of a short story or poem you might read to a young child.
9. Write a sentence naming a government document.
10. Write a sentence including a word as a name for itself.

Dashes, Parentheses, and Brackets   12.5

Although they are used infrequently, you should be familiar with the use of dashes (—), parentheses (( )), and brackets ([]) and be able to use them when necessary.

Dashes

The dash is a strong, dramatic punctuation mark. It has specific uses and should not be used as a substitute for the comma, semicolon, or parentheses. Overuse of the dash diminishes its effectiveness. Now consider the proper uses of the dash.

Use dashes to indicate an abrupt change of thought, a dramatic interrupting idea, or a summary statement.

EXAMPLES: The hurricane struck at dawn—to this day survivors gasp as they retell the story.

It was a desperate gamble—she stood little chance of winning—but she took it anyway.

The Browns, the Whittiers, and the Santinos—these neighbors brought food to us during the flood.

Some appositives and modifiers may also be set off with dashes.

Use dashes to set off a nonessential appositive or modifier when it is long, when it is already punctuated, or when you want to be dramatic.

APPOSITIVE: The cause of her illness—a rare virus affecting the nervous system—troubled her doctors.

MODIFIER: The drum major—who wore a white uniform, a gold cape, and gold boots—led the band.

Finally, dashes may set off certain parenthetical expressions.

Use dashes to set off a parenthetical expression when it is long, already punctuated, or especially dramatic.

EXAMPLE: Last Saturday night at the party—have you ever seen so much food?—I danced all evening long.

EXERCISE A: Using the Dash. Add one or two dashes to each of the following sentences.

EXAMPLE: A balanced diet contains all the nutrients proteins, carbohydrates, fats, vitamins, and minerals.

A balanced diet contains all the nutrients—proteins, carbohydrates, fats, vitamins, and minerals.

1. Green, leafy vegetables my favorite is swiss chard provide many important vitamins and minerals.
2. Most vitamin C which is important for healthy bones, teeth, gums, and blood vessels comes from fruits and vegetables.

3. Citrus fruits oranges, grapefruits, lemons, and limes all contain vitamin C.
4. Foods containing fiber for example, vegetables, whole grains, and fruits should be part of a balanced diet.
5. Eggs, milk, cheese, and meat do you realize that we spend more money for meat than for any other food? provide proteins important for good health.
6. Meat, eggs, butter, and cheese all these animal products contain cholesterol.
7. Some people are eating less of foods that contain cholesterol a fatlike, waxy substance that many experts believe contributes to narrowing of the arteries.
8. Some animal products that is, fish, chicken, turkey, and skim milk contain less fat and cholesterol than others.
9. Fruits, raw vegetables, and nuts can be substituted for snacks who could get through a day without a snack? that are high in fat and low in other nutrients.
10. Eating balanced diets can help people to live longer, healthier lives a goal worth striving toward.

Parentheses

Parentheses are occasionally used to set off material within a sentence. Commas are the appropriate punctuation marks to use for this purpose in most cases, especially when the material is short and closely related in meaning to the rest of the sentence. Parentheses, on the other hand, are appropriate in some circumstances.

Use parentheses to set off asides and explanations only when the material is not essential or when it consists of one or more sentences.

EXAMPLES: Her job responsibilities (as she learned within the month) were far greater than she had been told.

Documentary novels (two of the most successful are Dreiser's *An American Tragedy* and Capote's *In Cold Blood*) are fictionalized accounts of events based upon newspaper reports or other documentary evidence.

Parentheses are the strongest separators that writers can use. Although material enclosed in parentheses is not essential to the sentence's meaning, a writer indicates that the material is important and calls attention to it by using parentheses.

Special Uses of Parentheses. Parentheses are also used to enclose numerical information.

> **Use parentheses to set off numerical explanations such as the dates of a person's birth and death and around numbers and letters marking a series.**

EXAMPLES: Mary Mapes Dodge **(**1831–1905**)** is best known for her children's book *Hans Brinker,* written in 1865.

His Portland phone number is **(**303**)** 555-4211.

In the next three years, her research will take her to **(**1**)** Lisbon, Portugal; **(**2**)** Montreal, Canada; **(**3**)** Bucharest, Romania; and **(**4**)** New Delhi, India.

You may choose **(**a**)** tennis, **(**b**)** golf, or **(**c**)** track.

Using Other Punctuation Marks with Parentheses. Four rules govern parentheses used with other marks.

> **When a phrase or declarative sentence interrupts another sentence, do not use an initial capital or end mark inside the parentheses.**

EXAMPLE: Grandfather finally sold his car (we used to love riding in it) to an antique car dealer.

Follow the next rule when you interrupt a sentence with a question or exclamatory sentence in parentheses.

> **When a question or exclamation interrupts another sentence, use both an initial capital and an end mark inside the parentheses.**

EXAMPLES: Alan Alda (Didn't he once play Hawkeye**?**) was an intelligent and articulate guest on the talk show.

Aunt Louise (She is the best cook**!**) cooked dinner.

When you place a sentence in parentheses between two other sentences, use the next rule as a guide in punctuating it.

> **With any sentence that falls between two complete sentences, use both an initial capital and an end mark inside the parentheses.**

362

EXAMPLE: Robert Browning often displayed modern psycholog-
           ical insights. (See "My Last Duchess" as an exam-
           ple.) This tends to be true of many great writers.

Finally, there is a general rule for punctuation that belongs
outside the parentheses.

**In a sentence that includes parentheses, place
any punctuation belonging to the main sentence after the parenthesis.**

EXAMPLE: The union committee agreed to the terms (after
           some deliberation), and they explained the contract
           to the members (with some doubts about their
           reaction).

EXERCISE B: Enclosing Material in Parentheses. Copy
the following items, adding parentheses and capitals where
needed.

EXAMPLE: Mosquitoes how I hate their buzzing! bit us.
           Mosquitoes (How I hate their buzzing!) bit us.

1. Florence Nightingale 1820–1910 is regarded as the founder
   of modern nursing.
2. She served as a nurse during the Crimean War 1854–1856.
3. For dinner we had steak, baked potatoes, and broccoli. I
   have always disliked broccoli. A homemade apple pie was
   served for dessert.
4. Built in 1826, the stone barn a Hancock Shaker Village
   landmark housed fifty-two cows.
5. Estoril we drove there from Lisbon is a popular tourist re-
   sort in Portugal.
6. Mystic Village in Connecticut and Sturbridge Village in Massachusetts have you ever visited cither of them? recreate
   life of an earlier period.
7. Her plan is to create a garden of 1 lilacs, 2 roses, 3 tulips,
   and 4 daffodils.
8. The firm's New Jersey phone number is 201 555–4678.
9. Because of the storm what a blizzard!, school was canceled.
10. When you apply to a college, be sure you send a the com-
    pleted application, b your high school transcript, c your
    SAT scores, d several references, and e the registration fee.

Brackets

Brackets are used to enclose a word or phrase added by a writer to the words of another.

Use brackets to enclose words you insert in quotations when quoting someone else.

EXAMPLES: Crowther ended his review of *Bonnie and Clyde:* "And it leaves an astonished critic wondering just what purpose Mr. Penn and Mr. Beatty think they serve with this strangely antique, sentimental claptrap, which opened yesterday [August 13, 1967]."

Lady Caroline Lamb wrote of Byron, "[He is] mad, bad, and dangerous to know."

The Latin expression *sic* (meaning "thus") is sometimes enclosed in brackets to show that the author of the quoted material has misspelled or mispronounced a word or phrase.

EXAMPLE: As Dogberry said, "Be vigitant [sic], I beseech you."

EXERCISE C: Enclosing Material in Brackets. Copy the following items, inserting the necessary brackets.

EXAMPLE: "The shoulders sic marched down the street."

"The shoulders [sic] marched down the street."

1. Archie Bunker's "ground rules and priorororities sic" are always unreasonable.
2. "Fourscore and seven years ago 87 years, our fathers brought forth on this continent a new nation . . ."
3. "We the people of the United States, in order to form a more perfect Union of the thirteen former colonies, establish justice, insure domestic tranquility, provide for the common defense . . ."
4. "Harry and me [sic] were promoted," boasted the little girl.
5. "I pledge allegiance to the flag of the United States of America and to the republic for which it stands, one nation, under God added in 1954, indivisible, with liberty and justice for all."
6. "No perking sic" was written on the sign at the corner.
7. "The figures sculptures made of ice melted in the heat."

8. "Who won the World Serious sic?" asked the little boy.
9. "It is well-known according to whom? that we will win."
10. "As millions watched on television, Joan Benoit won the first women's marathon in Olympics history 1984."

DEVELOPING WRITING SKILLS: Using Dashes, Parentheses, and Brackets in Your Own Writing. Write ten sentences. Each one should illustrate a rule governing the use of dashes, parentheses, and brackets. Remember to follow the rules governing the use of other punctuation marks with parentheses.

Hyphens and Apostrophes 12.6

As a writer you must know the rules governing the use of hyphens and apostrophes. Although the rules are not difficult, you must carefully study them and the examples that illustrate them to avoid making mistakes.

Hyphens

Hyphens are used to join some words and to divide others. The hyphen (-) resembles the dash (—) but is shorter. In your handwriting you should make your hyphens about half the length of your dashes. In typewriting, one hyphen mark is used for a hyphen, while two hyphen marks are used for a dash.

Writers use hyphens with numbers, word parts, and words.

With Numbers. Hyphens are used to join compound numbers.

Use a hyphen when writing out the numbers *twenty-one* through *ninety-nine*.

EXAMPLES: twenty-eight ounces   fifty-five apartments

Fractions used as adjectives are also hyphenated.

Use a hyphen with fractions used as adjectives.

EXAMPLES: seven-tenths inch   three-quarters finished

A fraction used as a noun is not hyphenated, however.

EXAMPLE: One fourth of the members were present.

365

With Word Parts. In some circumstances a hyphen is used after a prefix.

Use a hyphen after a prefix that is followed by a proper noun or adjective.

EXAMPLES: pre-Renaissance   mid-February   un-American

Prefixes often found before proper nouns or proper adjectives are *ante-, anti-, mid-, post-, pre-, pro-,* and *un-*. Hyphenate them when used with proper nouns or proper adjectives.

Three prefixes and one suffix always call for hyphens.

Use a hyphen in words with the prefixes *all-, ex-, self-* and words with the suffix *-elect*.

EXAMPLES: all-powerful   ex-jockey   self-made
             mayor-elect

With Compound Words. Some compound words are also joined with hyphens.

Use a hyphen to connect two or more words that are used as one word, unless the dictionary gives a contrary spelling.

Although some compound words are written as one word and others are written as two words, many compound words are joined with hyphens. Always consult your dictionary if you are in doubt about the spelling of a compound word.

EXAMPLES: sister-in-law   secretary-treasurer   six-year-olds

In addition, use a hyphen with some compound modifiers.

Use a hyphen to connect a compound modifier before a noun unless it includes a word ending in *-ly* or is a compound proper adjective or compound proper noun acting as an adjective.

EXAMPLES WITH HYPHENS: a well-made pair of jeans
                          the bright-eyed children
                          an up-to-date decision

EXAMPLES WITHOUT HYPHENS: widely distributed information
                             East European languages
                             Red River Valley

366

When compound modifiers follow a noun, they generally do not require the use of hyphens.

EXAMPLE: The jeans were well made.

If your dictionary lists a word as hyphenated, however, it should always be hyphenated.

EXAMPLE: The news was up-to-date.

For Clarity. Sometimes a word or group of words might be misread if a hyphen were not used.

Use a hyphen within a word when a combination of letters might otherwise be confusing.

EXAMPLES: semi-illiterate   re-press (to press again)

You should also use a hyphen to prevent confusion when words may be combined incorrectly.

Use a hyphen between words to keep the reader from combining them erroneously.

EXAMPLES: the special delivery-man   the special-delivery man

To Divide Words at the End of a Line. Although you should try to avoid dividing a word at the end of a line, sometimes you must, using a hyphen to show the division.

If a word must be divided at the end of a line, always divide it between syllables.

Needless to say, this rule tells you that you may never divide a one-syllable word at the end of a line. When you must divide a word of more than one syllable, place the hyphen at the end of the first line as shown in the following example.

EXAMPLE: For some time now, the children had been sending let-
           ters describing their adventures at camp.

The second rule governing the use of hyphens at the ends of lines deals with word parts.

If a word contains word parts, it can almost always be divided between the prefix and the root or the root and the suffix.

However, you must avoid leaving a single letter standing alone.

Do not divide a word so that a single letter or the letters *-ed* stand alone.

INCORRECT: a-bout   scream-ed   toast-y
CORRECT: about   screamed   toasty

Proper nouns or adjectives should not be divided.

Do not divide proper nouns or proper adjectives.

INCORRECT: Fe-licia   Amer-ican
CORRECT: Felicia   American

Finally, there is a rule for words already hyphenated.

Divide a hyphenated word only after the hyphen.

INCORRECT: We are going with my sister and my bro-
             ther-in-law.
CORRECT: We are going with my sister and my brother-
             in-law.

EXERCISE A: Using Hyphens to Join Words. If an item does not need hyphens, write *correct*. If it does, add them.

EXAMPLE: up to date report
           up-to-date report

1. thirty first floor
2. semiinvalid
3. ex Senator
4. self adjusting
5. pro American
6. well intentioned advice
7. South American history
8. greatly exaggerated story
9. two thirds cup
10. all around athlete

EXERCISE B: Using Hyphens at the Ends of Lines. If a word is broken correctly, write *correct*. If not, rewrite it.

EXAMPLE: cur-ed
           cured

1. Span-ish
2. sis-ter-in-law
3. excitem-ent
4. un-usual
5. partici-pation
6. frisk-y
7. re-lease
8. Amer-ican
9. gentle-ness
10. self-inter-est

Apostrophes

Apostrophes are used to form possessives, contractions, and a few special plurals.

Forming Possessives. The following rule tells you how to show possession with singular nouns.

Add an apostrophe and an -s to show the possessive case of most singular nouns.

EXAMPLES:　the wallet of the woman　the woman's wallet

the collar of the dog　the dog's collar

the lines of the actress　the actress's lines

Notice in the last example that even when a singular noun ends in -s the possessive is usually formed by adding an apostrophe and an -s. When the resulting word would be hard to pronounce, however, only an apostrophe is added.

AWKWARD:　I enjoy Keats's poetry

BETTER:　I enjoy Keats' poetry

The possessive case of plural nouns follows two rules.

Add an apostrophe to show the possessive case of plural nouns ending in -s or -es.

EXAMPLES:　the barking of the dogs　the dogs' barking

the color of the leaves　the leaves' color

Some plural nouns do not end in -s or -es.

Add an apostrophe and an -s to show the possessive case of plural nouns that do not end in -s or -es.

EXAMPLES:　the books of the women　the women's books

the grazing lands of oxen　the oxen's grazing lands

When you wish to form the possessive case of a compound noun, follow the next rule.

Add an apostrophe and an -s (or just an apostrophe if the word is a plural ending in -s) to the last word of a compound noun to form the possessive.

NAMES OF BUSINESSES AND ORGANIZATIONS:	the Salvation Army's headquarters
	the Department of the Interior's budget
	the Johnson Associates' clients
TITLES OF RULERS AND LEADERS:	Catherine the Great's victories
	Louis XVI's palace
	the chairman of the board's desk
HYPHENATED COMPOUND NOUNS USED TO DESCRIBE PEOPLE:	my sister-in-law's car
	the secretary-treasurer's idea

Possessive expressions involving time, amounts, and the word *sake* are formed by following the next rule.

To form possessives involving time, amounts, or the word *sake*, use an apostrophe and an *-s* or just an apostrophe if the possessive is plural.

TIME:	a month's vacation	three days' vacation
AMOUNT:	one quarter's worth	two cents' worth
SAKE:	for Heaven's sake	for goodness' sake

Note in the last example that the final *-s* is often dropped in expressions involving the word *sake.*

When you make words possessive, you should also indicate the difference between something owned jointly by two or more people and something owned by individuals.

To show joint ownership, make the final noun possessive. To show individual ownership, make each noun possessive.

JOINT OWNERSHIP: I always enjoyed Bob and Ray's radio show.

INDIVIDUAL OWNERSHIP: Liz's and Meg's coats are hanging here.

You should form the possessive case of any noun when the owner's complete name appears before the apostrophe.

INCORRECT SINGULAR:	Jame's idea
CORRECT SINGULAR:	James's idea
INCORRECT PLURAL:	two girl's books
CORRECT PLURAL:	two girls' books

Forming the possessives of pronouns requires two rules.

Use an apostrophe and an -s with indefinite pronouns to show possession.

EXAMPLES: everyone's time   one another's friends

somebody's umbrella   each other's homework

Notice in two of the examples that you add an apostrophe and an -s only to the last word of a two-word indefinite pronoun to form the possessive.

To form possessives of personal pronouns use another rule.

Do not use an apostrophe with the possessive forms of personal pronouns.

The possessive form of personal pronouns already shows ownership. Pronouns in this form should be left just as they are to show possession.

EXAMPLES: his jazz records   our house

her blue sweater   its tires

their party   whose paper

Be careful not to confuse the contractions *who's, it's,* and *they're* with possessive pronouns. They are contractions for *who is, it is,* and *they are.* Remember also that *whose, its,* and *their* show possession.

PRONOUNS: *Whose* homework is this?

Its tires were all flat.

Their dinner is ready.

CONTRACTIONS: *Who's* at the door?

It's going to rain.

They're going to the beach.

Forming Contractions. Another important use of the apostrophe is in forming contractions. One general rule covers all the different types of contractions.

Use an apostrophe in a contraction to indicate the position of the missing letter or letters.

VERB AND *NOT:* cannot   can't   are not   aren't
              could not   couldn't   will not   won't

PRONOUN AND *WILL:*	he will	he'll	I will	I'll
	you will	you'll	we will	we'll
	she will	she'll	they will	they'll
PRONOUN AND *WOULD:*	she would	she'd	I would	I'd
	he would	he'd	we would	we'd
	you would	you'd	they would	they'd
PRONOUN OR NOUN AND THE VERB *BE:*	you are	you're	I am	I'm
	she is	she's	Jane is	Jane's
	they are	they're		

Notice that one of these contractions changes letters as well as drops them. *Will not* becomes *won't* in contracted form.

Contractions with verbs should be used mainly in informal writing and in dialogue. The same is true for another type of contraction, one for years.

EXAMPLES: the class of '84   the depression of '29

Still another type of contraction is found in poetry.

EXAMPLES: *e'en* (for *even*)   *o'er* (for *over*)

Other contractions represent the abbreviated form of *of the* and *the* as they are written in several different languages.

EXAMPLES: O'Hare   o'clock
            d'Lorenzo   l'Abbé

These letters are most often combined with surnames.

A final use of contractions is for representing individual speaking styles in dialogue. As noted above, you will often want to use contractions with verbs in dialogue. You may also want to approximate a regional dialect or a foreign accent, which may include unusual pronunciations of words or omitted letters.

EXAMPLE: Hi, ol' buddy. How you been feelin'?

Avoid overusing the apostrophe with contractions even in dialogue. Overuse reduces the effectiveness of the apostrophe.

Using Apostrophes for Special Plurals. The following rule presents four other situations in which apostrophes are used.

Use an apostrophe and an -s to write the plurals of numbers, symbols, letters, and words used to name themselves.

EXAMPLES: during the 1860's   *m*'s and *n*'s

your *2*'s and *3*'s   no *if*'s or *maybe*'s

three *?*'s in a row

EXERCISE C: Using Apostrophes. Rewrite each of the following items, following the instructions in parentheses.

EXAMPLE: *t* (Write the plural form.)

t's

1. the typewriter of the man (Put in the possessive case.)
2. two of the clock (Write the contracted form.)
3. the book of James (Put in the possessive case.)
4. 1984 (Write the contracted form.)
5. the house of the Joneses (Put in the possessive case.)
6. the cribs of the babies (Put in the possessive case.)
7. the sports of the women (Put in the possessive case.)
8. the stories of each other (Put in the possessive case.)
9. *12* (Write the plural form, underlining the number.)
10. who is (Write the contracted form.)
11. will not (Write the contracted form.)
12. The sandwich belongs to whom? (Reword, substituting a possessive pronoun for *to whom*.)
13. the advice of the Department of Defense (Put in the possessive case.)
14. the comedy act of Pat and Mike (Put in the possessive case.)
15. they are (Write the contracted form.)
16. the report of someone (Put in the possessive case.)
17. the son of Queen Elizabeth II (Put in the possessive case.)
18. a vacation of two weeks (Put in the possessive case.)
19. the bicycles of Jane and Mike (Put in the possessive case.)
20. the dog's tail (Use a possessive pronoun for *dog's*.)

DEVELOPING WRITING SKILLS: Using the Rules for Hyphens and Apostrophes in Original Sentences. Choose ten different rules from this section. Then write sentences of your own that illustrate each of the rules you have chosen.

Skills Review and Writing Workshop

Punctuation

CHECKING YOUR SKILLS

Rewrite the paragraph, adding all necessary punctuation.

(1) Can you sing the song America the Beautiful (2) It is one of our most patriotic moving and popular songs (3) It was the first patriotic song to have had its words and music written by native born Americans (4) Katherine Lee Bates 1859–1929 a professor of English at Wellesley College in Wellesley Massachusetts wrote the words (5) Published in 1930 after her death Bates book Selected Poems contains the words of America the Beautiful (6) Several years before Bates wrote the words Samuel A Ward had written the melody (7) The melody had been written to accompany a hymn but soon it was used to accompany the poem (8) The majestic stirring melody was well suited to the words therefore they have since been used together (9) The lyrics stress the beautiful varied geographical regions of the United States and the virtues Bates hoped her country would embody—for example, brotherhood self control liberty and nobleness (10) By mentioning it in both the first and last stanzas Bates stressed one virtue in particular brotherhood

USING MECHANICS SKILLS IN WRITING
Writing Dialogue

Imagine you are to write a screenplay based on a novel. Follow the steps to write an effective scene.

Prewriting: Choose a chapter from a novel. Consider that the cast and director must be able to keep track of each character's lines through your correct use of punctuation.

Writing: Convert as much of the chapter as possible into conversation or soliloquy, incorporating the descriptive passages.

Revising: Did you begin a new paragraph with each change of character? Did you use quotation marks in the right places? After you have revised, proofread carefully.

Composition

The Writer's Techniques

13

The Writing Process

The writing process is a series of basic steps leading to organized thought and effective communication with the reader. The clear presentation of your impressions, opinions, logic, or argument depends heavily on the attention you give to each of the steps in the writing process.

There are three main stages that characterize the writing process—prewriting, writing, and revising. Each of these stages is necessary in order to write well.

13.1 Prewriting

The first step in the writing process is prewriting. This is the preparatory stage, in which you generate ideas, choose a topic, determine your audience and purpose, focus on a main idea, develop support for that main idea, and decide how you will organize the support.

Generating Ideas

Generating ideas for a topic begins with thinking. Ask yourself some questions. Is the assignment to write about something historical? Sociological? Are you required to report on a controversial issue? Or can you write on some sport, hobby, or activity that interests you?

The sources for your ideas depend on the nature of the writing assignment. If you are writing about a current or historical

376

issue, newspapers, magazines, books, and television will provide you with ideas on the subject. If, on the other hand, you are describing a personal hobby or activity, you might be your own best source of ideas; that is, you might decide to interview yourself to generate ideas for topics to write about.

To gather ideas for writing topics, scan current periodicals and newspapers for events of interest, and survey your own interests, experiences, and ideas.

There are several techniques you can follow to generate ideas in the prewriting stage.

Interview Yourself. To ascertain topics of interest to you, ask yourself questions modeled on the ones in the chart below.

QUESTIONS FOR INTERVIEWING YOURSELF
1. What hobbies interest me?
2. What are my accomplishments, if any?
3. What special activities do I find rewarding?
4. Do I have a job preference?
5. Where have I traveled? What were my favorite vacations?
6. Who are my friends, and why?
7. What are my goals? What do I hope to achieve?
8. What are my values?

Free Writing. Set aside fifteen minutes and begin writing anything that comes to your mind. Do not stop writing during this time, even if you have to repeat certain words or phrases. Do not worry about unrelated or disjointed thoughts; the most important thing is to keep the thoughts flowing steadily, to free-associate, to try to put down as many fresh ideas as possible. At the end of this exercise, put the paper aside, to be read later; at that time you can decide whether any of your ideas have potential as writing topics.

Journal Writing. A daily record of your feelings, thoughts, impressions, and experiences is an excellent beacon of self-discovery. The recurrence of certain ideas may reveal something about your values or your own philosophy of life that you had not previously articulated. These ideas have excellent possibilities for writing topics.

Reading and Saving. Read pervasively. Actively follow events and issues that capture your interest; clip and file these articles for future reference as source material for writing topics.

Clustering. This is a reducing technique, one that narrows a broad topic into a more manageable one for a writing assignment. The method is similar to creating a tree of ideas. Take, for example, the subject of music. Write it in a circle in the center of your paper. Branch out to other circles in which you have written all the ideas you associate with music, for example, rock, classical, instruments, strings, guitars, soloists, songs, and so forth. From your nucleus word, "music," you have generated a score of ideas, one of which will provide you with a topic narrow enough for a short paper.

Brainstorming. Done singly or in groups, this is a start-up technique in which you jot down every thought you have relating to a particular topic. From the multitude of words on your list, a few will stand out as the grassroots of an idea.

Cueing. Cueing is a form of brainstorming in which you ask the five W's (Who? What? Where? When? Why?) in relation to a topic. These are particularly relevant in writing narratives or descriptions. Below is an example of 5-W cueing used to generate ideas for a narrative essay:

Topic: Writing a self-profile
Who: I
What: A childhood experience
Where: On a trip
When: In formative years
Why: To show self-discovery

Alphabet cueing employs another approach to developing ideas on a topic. If you are asked to write a paper describing an emotion or personal experience, you can begin listing appropriate adjectives corresponding to letters of the alphabet. For example, astounded, annoyed, and argyle might appear under letter A.

Five-sense cueing recreates your response to an experience and is an excellent approach to descriptive writing. Listing all

378

the words you can think of related to that experience under the categories of taste, touch, sight, sound, and smell will produce specific and provocative sensory images vital to effective descriptive writing.

From any one or combination of these seven prewriting techniques, you can tap a large reservoir of ideas for writing topics.

EXERCISE A: Self-Survey. Repond to the questions for interviewing yourself on page 377.

EXERCISE B: Free Writing. Write for fifteen minutes without stopping on one of the following topics. Write anything that enters your mind about the topic. Do not worry about grammar at this point. *Do* include your feelings, opinions, sensory impressions, thoughts, and any facts at your disposal concerning the topics.

a favorite sport	crime
finding a job	school spirit
alcoholism and the family	friendship
memories of a trip	love
the drug culture	graffiti
teenagers and parents	favorite songs

EXERCISE C: Journal Writing. Keep a journal for a two-week period. Enter in it any significant events that are happening, conflicts that have arisen, reflective moments of self-awareness, impressions of a friend, serious implications of a television show or of an action you or someone you know has taken.

EXERCISE D: Brainstorming. Work in a group of four or five classmates. Appoint a note-taker. Brainstorm ideas on what society would be like on Planet Mirth. Include descriptions of food, transportation, government, industry, communications, clothing, and so forth, as well as possible value systems, types of art, and the transmission of culture. Then choose one aspect of life on Planet Mirth and, working alone, write a list of everything you can think of relating to that one aspect.

EXERCISE E: Cueing. Write "invention" at the top of your paper. Then list the 5-W's, leaving four or five lines between each question for your responses. The invention may be real or imagined. Answer each question. Then use alphabet cueing to arrive at a description of the invention.

Choosing and Narrowing the Topic

After generating ideas for a topic, it is usually necessary to narrow a broad topic.

Limit the scope of your topic so that it can be covered in a paper of the assigned length.

You must sufficiently narrow your topic in order to deal with it effectively in a short paper. Suppose you are asked to write a descriptive essay about yourself. Your first reaction might be, "Well, on that subject, I could write a book!" Yet, you are asked to write only an essay. Where would you begin? How much would you include? What facts would you leave out, and why?

A clustering approach is an excellent first step in responding to an assignment. In the example below, note the kinds of ideas that can be generated for the topic of a self-profile.

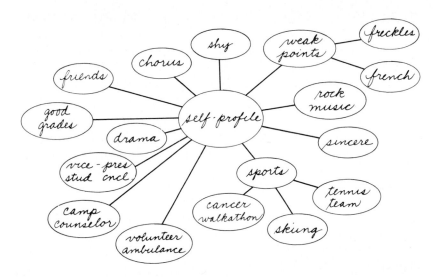

Notice that certain key elements can be gleaned from the cluster and organized conceptually. The student is a member of the Volunteer Ambulance Corps, and he participates in walk-a-thons for the local cancer chapter. Obviously, he is active in community service. At school, he is involved in extra, creative activities such as the chorus and drama club. Also, he demonstrates leadership qualities by taking an active role in the student governing body and taking responsibility for youngsters as a camp counselor.

This student has also noted basic personality traits: In spite of his leadership qualities, he views himself as shy. He prizes sincerity and values his friends.

Several aspects, therefore, emerge from this self-profile: personality, leadership qualities, athletic abilities, citizenship role, and creative talents and interests. Choosing any one, two, or three of these character traits narrows the topic for a self-profile.

EXERCISE F: Narrowing a Topic. Use the clustering technique with one of the topics below.

capital punishment	anarchy	television
freedom	music	natural disasters

Determining Audience and Purpose

Your choice of topic, the vocabulary you use, and the details you include will be influenced both by the audience you are writing for and the purpose of the paper.

Your audience and purpose determine what you write.

The following chart indicates audiences and purposes for topics that have been narrowed from the larger category, the self-profile.

Topic	Audience	Purpose
My Comic Flaw: A Descriptive Essay	Teacher	to inform
Community Service the Hard Way: A Narrative	*Teen News*	to entertain

| Presenting Me: | College Admissions | to persuade |
| A College Profile | Office | |

EXERCISE G: Determining Audience and Purpose. From your cluster in Exercise F, choose one topic that is narrow enough to be developed in a short paper. Identify two possible purposes and their corresponding audiences.

EXAMPLE: Advantages of daycare centers
1. Purpose: to persuade readers of the merits of day-care centers
Audience: working parents; corporations
2. Purpose: to inform readers of the need for funding of the centers
Audience: the voters; the state legislature

Developing a Main Idea and Support

Once you have chosen a topic and identified your purpose and audience, you are ready to present the main idea.

State your main idea in a topic sentence and list the details that support it.

To gather supporting information, impressions, examples, and other details, use any of the prewriting techniques presented under Generating Ideas. To illustrate, consider a main idea from the cluster for a self-profile:

MAIN IDEA (TOPIC SENTENCE):   My leadership experiences make me an ideal applicant for Haverford College.

SUPPORTING DETAILS: 1. Assistant Coach, Drama Club.
2. Counselor at Camp Hiawatha
3. Captain of Freedom High School Varsity Tennis Team
4. Senior Member of Freedom Valley Volunteer Ambulance Corps
5. Vice-President of Student Council

All of these details reinforce the student's persuasive contention that he would be an asset to Haverford College.

382

The final prewriting step involves choosing a way to organize your support. Consider your audience and purpose when you choose a method of organization. If, for example, you were writing directions for someone to follow, you would probably write them in the order in which they should be done. If you were writing a persuasive paper, you might open with your best argument and organize the rest of the paper around that.

Following are common ways of organizing information.

ORGANIZATION OF SUPPORTING INFORMATION	
Chronological order	Information in time sequence
Spatial order	Information arranged according to space relationships
Order of importance	Information arranged from least to most important, or vice versa
Comparison and contrast	Information arranged according to likenesses and differences between two or more subjects
Developmental	Information arranged so that one point leads logically to the next

Here is the list of supporting information for the student's self-profile. It has been arranged in order of importance. The activities that a college admissions officer would probably consider most important are listed first.

1. Vice-President of Student Council
2. Counselor at Camp Hiawatha
3. Senior member of Freedom Valley Volunteer Ambulance Corps
4. Captain of Freedom High School varsity tennis team
5. Assistant Coach of the Drama Club

EXERCISE H: Developing a Main Idea and Support. Choose one of the topics you used in Exercise G. State the main idea you wish to present in a topic sentence. List various ideas you can use to support or develop the main idea. Choose a method of organization and rewrite your list of supporting details according to this method.

DEVELOPING WRITING SKILLS: Prewriting. Develop a self-profile by going through the prewriting stage of the writing process. Begin with a cluster, narrow the topic to three particular character traits, and determine your audience and purpose. For each character trait that you use, state a main idea and list the supporting details. Be sure to save your work for use later.

13.2 Writing

Now that you have selected a topic, identified your purpose and audience, clearly articulated your main idea, and organized supporting notes for it, you are ready to begin writing a first draft.

Writing a First Draft

Writing from your notes generated in the prewriting stage, you create the first, or rough, draft of the composition.

Translate your prewriting notes into sentences and paragraphs; do not worry about grammatical perfection at this point.

During this stage, you are thinking aloud on paper, sometimes changing or reversing your original intent or direction. Note the rough draft of the first paragraph of a self-profile.

> I guess I'm pretty popular. They voted me in as Vice-President of the Student Council. Kids look up to me when a decision has to be made about something. I have a great group of friends. Also, at camp, everyone tries to get into my bunk. I guess I'm pretty much in demand as a counselor. Maybe because I'm fair. Probably I'd be popular on campus at Haverford. I might even wind up president of the freshman class.

The main idea that emerges from this rough draft is that the student considers himself popular. However, the supporting details used to convince Haverford that the student would be a social asset on campus could serve a far better purpose, and that is to emphasize his leadership qualities. A rewritten first draft might look like this:

I'm pretty much a leader at Freedom High. They voted me in as Vice-President of the Student Council. Kids look up to me to make decisions about things like raising money for the senior class trip and the Sweetheart Dance. My friends look up to me, too. At camp, everyone tries to get into my bunk. I'm pretty much in demand as a counselor, probably because I run a good program and I'm fair. I put on shows, campfire nights, canoe races, and I'm in charge of Color War. I would probably be elected to an office at Haverford.

EXERCISE: Writing a First Draft. Write a first draft based on your notes from Exercise H on page 383.

DEVELOPING WRITING SKILLS: Drafting a Self-Profile. Write a first draft based on your notes from Developing Writing Skills on page 384.

Revising 13.3

Even as you write your first draft, you are making revisions in your ideas, changing details to support your main idea. Revising is the refinement of your thoughts and language.

Revising for Sense

Reading your paper for sense is the first step in any revision. Are your paragraphs unified? Are the main ideas supported? The paper's purpose must be logically supported.

REVISING FOR SENSE
1. Is my main idea clear?
2. Have I supported it?
3. Is the paper logical?

EXERCISE A: Revising. Revise the article on page 386 by making sure that the main idea is clearly stated, that it is supported adequately, and that the paper is organized so it makes sense.

It took Christopher Columbus thirty-three days to reach the New World. Five hundred years later, scholars are still debating the exact place where he landed. Some think he landed at San Salvador. That is an island in the Bahamas. There European coins and other artifacts of Columbus's time were found. Columbus's journal described four islands which he listed on his way to what is now known as Cuba. The first one was the island home of the Arawaks. Columbus named it San Salvador. He named the other three Santa Maria, Fernandina, and Isabel. But the British gained control of these islands and all Spanish references to them ceased. Modern cartographers and navigators think he landed at Eleuthera Island, to the north, or at one of the Caicos Islands, to the south. Some historians think he landed at Watlings Island. Some think Cat Island or Rum Cay or Samany Cay. Part of the problem is the loss of Columbus's journal. It was lost in the 16th century. An abridged version was kept by a cleric on board the ship. Historians have relied on this one for their information.

EXERCISE B: Revising a First Draft. Revise your first draft from the exercise on page 385 for sense.

Editing for Word Choice and Sentence Variety

The second step in the revision process is often called editing.

Edit your paper for word choice and sentence variety.

Editing involves asking yourself the questions in the following checklist.

CHECKLIST FOR EDITING
1. Is my language clear and precise?
2. Is there variety in my sentence structure to sustain reader interest?
3. Is the vocabulary appropriate for the intended audience?

A revised rough draft of the student's self-profile follows. Notice that he deleted informal language such as "pretty much"
and "I guess," words that defuse the impact of his leadership
qualities. Note his revisions for sense and order of importance
while stressing his assets to Haverford College.

The Assets I Can Bring to Haverford College

I guess I'm pretty much a leader at Freedom High. They voted
me in as Vice-President of the Student Council. Kids look up to
me to make decisions about things like raising money for the
senior class trip and the Sweetheart Dance. At camp, kids want
me to be their counselor probably because I run a good program
I put on shows, campfire nights, and I'm in charge of Color War.

Being on the Volunteer Ambulance Corps is something I'm very
proud of. A lot of people depend on me. I've even saved lives.
There was an accident on Route 6 one night and and I saved a
woman's life.

I've been captain of Freedom High's Tennis Team for the past
four years. I'm the only player on the team to make the state
championships. We came in second. I train three hours a day,
seven days a week. I do push ups, sit ups, and run.

This year I participated in the cancer walk-a-thon. I walked
ten miles and raised $450.00.

I sing in our school's barbershop quartet. We are very popular
at school assemblies. We sing old favorites everybody knows.

My secret love is acting. I tried out for several drama
productions and made three of them. I played Klinger in our
version of "Mash."

I'm a good student at Freedom High. I made Honor Roll three
years in a row, and I have the highest average in my math class.

EXERCISE C: Revising and Editing. Revise the Sample Student First Draft below for sense and sequence; does it proceed logically and chronologically? Can confusing tenses be eliminated? Can sentences be combined for a smooth flow?

Vacations to Disney World are what I like most. This spring my girlfriend and I went to Disney World. We rented camper space near the park. It has a swimming pool and outdoor barbecue pits. Lots of colored flags are strung up around the campgrounds. It is very cheerful.

There were many attractions at Disney World. One that I look forward to is Space Monster—it's a roller coaster. We had great fun at Disney World, taking in the sights. One night we saw the light parade. The whole sky was lit up. It starts at 9 p.m. We waited hours for the parade to begin. We sat on the curb where the electrical light parade took place. Each year it gets better and better. The excitement of the children is unreal. The last attraction we saw was the fireworks, the sky just lit up with hundreds of colors. It is a fabulous finish to a day filled with memories.

EXERCISE D: Editing. Edit for word choice and sentence variety the paper you revised for Exercise B on page 386.

Proofreading and Publishing

The final step in the writing process is proofreading.

Proofread your paper for mistakes in grammar, spelling, and punctuation.

When you have finished your final version, "publish" it; that is, submit it to the audience that you addressed. In the case of a self-profile, that would be to a college admissions office.

EXERCISE E: Proofreading a Paragraph. Correct the paragraph for any errors in grammar, spelling, or punctuation. If necessary, recopy it neatly.

For city slickers leave collecting in autum is an exhilerating experinece, the leaves fairly obliterate the grounds creating a

388

slipery forrest floor that is often hasardous to walk on. The feiry autumnel colors ilumine the hills injecting ones spirit with the specail joy of being alive. The grey macadam of city streets fade in our memory, it is like an old black and white movie next to 3-D technicolor. The leaves are pointed rounded britle limp jaged conical—each are a collectors delight to be tresured as a momento of a day as natures guest on our return to the cinder-block city.

EXERCISE F: Proofreading a Paper. Proofread the paper you edited for Exercise D on page 388.

DEVELOPING WRITING SKILLS: Revising, Editing, and Proofreading. Revise, edit, and proofread the self-profile you wrote for Developing Writing Skills on page 385.

Finding Your Own Approach 13.4

Now that you have practiced one basic process of planning, writing, and revising a paper, you can experiment with the process. Think about combining and reordering some of the smaller steps to find the process that is most natural for you. This section will give you some suggestions for tailoring the writing process to your own style as well as some hints for handling problems you may encounter as you write.

Adjusting the Steps

One common way to compose and polish papers is to use the steps in the following chart.

PLANNING STEPS
1. Choose a topic.
2. Narrow the topic by focusing on audience and purpose.
3. Write a topic sentence.
4. Develop support through questioning or free-associating.
5. Check support for unity.

6. Choose a logical order for your support.

7. Prepare a rough or modified outline.

WRITING STEPS

1. Follow your modified outline.

2. Compose full sentences for support.

3. Add transitions and main word repetitions.

4. Use other linking devices for coherence.

REVISING STEPS

1. Revise topic sentences that are too general or too narrow.

2. Add supporting information if support is sketchy.

3. Eliminate generalizations, opinions, and repetitions.

4. Eliminate insignificant or extraneous support.

5. Look for more logical arrangements of ideas.

6. Add transitions, repeat main words, and use synonymns, pronouns, bridge ideas, parallelism, and a concluding sentence as necessary.

The basic steps are useful in giving you guidance and direction—a place to begin and methods for proceeding toward a goal. These steps, however, do not always have to be followed in the exact order shown in the chart.

Experiment with the planning, writing, and revising steps to find a process that works well for you.

Writing is not always a linear process, first one step, then the next. Because it is creative, it is sometimes a forward and backward then forward again process. Sometimes you will write with a burst of ideas and energy, and other times you will have to think hard to come up with ideas. No one knows exactly how a person's mind works during the writing process, and each person goes about writing in a slightly different way. One of your challenges should be to discover how you think and write best. By adapting the writing steps you already know, you should be able to find a procedure that is practical for you.

Varying the Planning Steps. Instead of choosing and narrowing a topic, identifying a main idea, and then gathering support, your brainstorming on a general topic might supply supporting details from which a main idea will emerge.

For instance, if you had recently tried canoeing for the first time, you might want to communicate that experience. With this general topic in mind, you might brainstorm as follows:

BRAINSTORMING FOR THE TOPIC CANOEING

—great way to enjoy outdoors

—see hills, forests, and river from a unique perspective

—can be as strenuous as you want—go as many miles as you want in a few hours or many hours

—aluminum canoes—not as tipsy as I expected

—vigorous exercise for arm, shoulder, and back muscles

—cool breeze on the river—especially over the rushing white water

—can float and slide with current

—can beach canoe—picnic and swim

—as a precaution all things in canoe should be waterproof and buoyant

—tie things to canoe so they won't float downstream if canoe tips over

—practice dipping paddle far enough into water to get power

—in summer purple heather, Queen Anne's lace, golden black-eyed susans, lavender thistles on the banks, dense trees covered with shaking leaves, rocky cliffs

—fish jumping, frogs perched on rocks

—ducks sleeping, camouflaged by resemblance to half-wet rocks

—wear shoes that can get wet, hat and clothes that protect you from the hot sun—wear swim suit underneath

—rivers in the summer are warmer, lower, and slower than in the spring—good for learning to paddle a canoe

—in less populated areas, state parks rent canoes on the rivers

—water insects skimming the surface

After you have produced a list of ideas, facts, examples, and details, you can examine your list. You will notice that your list will probably point to one or two main ideas. Most of the items on the list of ideas for canoeing, for example, concentrate on the pleasures of the sport, especially on a river in the summer. Other items on the list refer to equipment and techniques. You could choose to pursue either idea.

Your ideas might lead you to write a paper describing the advantages of summer canoeing to those who have never tried it. Using your list of supporting information, you might write different versions of a main idea.

POSSIBLE MAIN IDEAS: Canoeing on a river in the summer will reward you with good exercise, good views, and outdoor fun.

For exercise, outdoor fun, and a chance to be close to nature, you should try canoeing on a river in the summer.

When you have written a main idea that you like, select the relevant support from your brainstorming sheet, or use the question-and-answer method to develop additional support. Then you can follow the regular steps to evaluate and organize your support before you write a first draft.

Varying the Writing Steps. Armed with a main idea and a list of support, you might decide to evaluate and organize your material *as* you write the first draft, instead of preparing an outline. This method has the advantage of allowing you to capture your ideas when they are fresh. However, you may have to write several drafts to find the best supporting details and a unified organization.

The following chart shows the list of support you might be starting with if you had used the question-and-answer method of brainstorming for support for the topic of canoeing.

QUESTION-AND-ANSWER BRAINSTORMING SHEET
Main Idea: **For exercise, outdoor fun, and a chance to be close to nature, you should try canoeing on a river in the summer.**
Why go canoeing on a river in the summer?
—in summer most rivers are warm, low, and slow   —many state parks rent canoes at this time of year

—calmer and less dangerous than in the spring	—canoeing on a river gives you sense of journeying—rifting with the current takes some of the work out of paddling

What exercise does canoeing provide?

—paddling uses arm, shoulder, and back muscles	—can be as strenuous as you want depending upon how far and how fast you want to go and whether you travel with the current or against it

What outdoor fun can you have canoeing?

—floating and sliding with the current—relaxing —canoe races with friends —can beach canoe—picnic on bank or an island and swim in river	—river bank might have dirt slides into the water and rope swings from trees out into the water —can sunbathe, daydream, or chat as you paddle and float —can race through the white water (rapids)—scary and exciting—better than a ride on a roller coaster at an amusement park

How does canoeing put you close to nature?

—see hills, forests, and rivers from the middle of it all —purple heather, Queen Anne's lace, golden black-eyed susans, lavender thistles on the banks —rocky cliffs	—dense cool trees covered with thousands of shivering leaves —a cool breeze constantly ripples over water —earthy smell —can see fish swimming, frogs squatting on rocks, muskrats searching for food, ducks bobbing on the water, and birds flying about among the trees and bushes along the bank

Your first draft written directly from the support might resemble the following. Notice the ordering of information, the addition of a few ideas not on the list, and the omission of other ideas that were on the list.

First draft   For exercise, outdoor fun, and a chance to be close to nature, you should try canoeing on a river in the summer. In the summer, when rivers are warmer, lower, and slower than in the spring, many state parks rent canoes to groups of people for day trips, and the current on a river takes some of the work out of paddling. As you round each bend, you can see hills, forests, or cliffs on either side of you. From the middle of the river, you can watch banks of flowers, such as purple-tipped heather, creamy Queen Anne's lace, golden black-eyed susans, and lavender thistles slide by. You may also see fish swimming, frogs squatting on rocks, ducks bobbing in the water, and muskrats hunting for food. The breeze rippling over the water will surround you with the earthy smell of moist dirt, dense pine, and leafy trees. As you approach the shallows, where the water rushes over the rocks, you will hear splashing that sounds like waterfalls. When you tire of paddling, you can beach the canoe on some sandy bank, picnic in the shade, or cool off with a swim in the river. Back on the river, you can have canoe races with your friends or shoot the canoe through the rapids. Throughout all this activity, you will be exercising. Paddling uses arm, shoulder, and back muscles. The amount of exercise you get, however, will depend upon how far and how fast you want to go and how much you swim and explore when you are not paddling.

Reading over this first draft, you might decide that it has a dull, disappointing ending. The paper might be stronger if you ended with comments about fun or nature. In fact, when you reexamine your main idea, you see that your reader will expect you to cover exercise first, then fun, and then nature. You could then reorganize according to the developmental order that you now see fits your main idea and support. You might also find some phrases and ideas that are not necessary.

394

After analyzing and marking the first draft of your paper, you should write a second draft showing your rewording of the first draft and the rearrangement of ideas that you consider necessary in order to improve your paper. As you rewrite, improve your paper further by your choice of words, phrases, and transitions.

The paper below is the second draft of the paper that appears on page 394.

Second draft showing reorganization

For exercise, outdoor fun, and a chance to be close to nature, you should try canoeing on a river. In the summer, when the rivers have warmed up and have become more controlled than in the spring, you can paddle quickly or you can drift with the current while you enjoy the scenery unfolding before you. Although the amount of exercise you get will depend upon how far and how fast you want to travel, paddling at any speed will exercise your arm, shoulder, and back muscles. When you tire of paddling or of basking in the sun, you can beach the canoe on some sandy bank and picnic in the shade or take a cooling swim. For pure adventure, you can race canoes with friends or rush through the channels of rapids, dodging rocks, on a ride more exciting than any in an amusement park. Besides providing exercise and fun, canoeing puts you close to nature. Rounding each bend, you can see forests, hills, cliffs, or banks of flowers slide by. On an eastern shore, for example, purple-tipped heather, creamy Queen Anne's lace, golden black-eyed susans, and lavender thistles may line the banks with color. You may also see fish swimming, frogs squatting on shadowed rocks, ducks bobbing on the water, and muskrats hunting for food. The breeze on a river ripples over the water, carrying the earthy smell of moist dirt, the scent of pines, and the hint of fresh, cool air. While floating in deeper water, you can hear the rushing of the water over the rocks in the shallow stretches of the river. The sights, fragrances, and sounds of natural beauty completely surround you.

A draft should be unified, complete, well organized, and smoothly connected before it is recopied as the final version of the paper.

Varying and Revising Steps. Essentially, revising means thinking on paper—adding, deleting, and reorganizing ideas by physically crossing out, circling, and squeezing in different words. You do not have to wait until you have written a first draft in order to begin revising. Instead, try revising your ideas as you work on your prewriting material—topic lists, brainstorming sheets, main ideas, outlines, and so on. Do not be afraid to revise while you are writing. Sometimes, going back to earlier sentences and rewriting them while you are concentrating on the topic leads to smoother paragraphs naturally.

EXERCISE A: Experimenting with Steps in Writing. Choose a topic and write a paragraph. Follow one of the experimental methods for planning, writing, and revising that were discussed in this section. Be sure to show your work for each step. Note whether the approach that you experimented with was helpful or not.

Overcoming Writing Problems

Writers of all ages—students, adults, professionals—can become frustrated when their ideas do not flow freely and when "writer's block" sets in.

Try different techniques to help you begin writing, overcome writing "blocks," and look clearly and critically at your writing.

Writers have used the following techniques to stimulate their thinking and to gain perspective about their work. By experimenting with these techniques, you may find some that work well for you.

Getting Started. Your first problem may be finding a topic when none has been assigned. If you have the freedom to write about anything, be open to all the possibilities from your own experiences and from the world around you. Suggestions in the following chart will show you some ways to locate a topic for writing.

396

SOME METHODS FOR FINDING A TOPIC	
Method	**How It Works**
Taking Action: Carry a pad and pencil with you as you walk around and discover ideas.	—Look around your room for objects such as a poster, postcard, or memento that might spark an idea.
	—Walk around your home. Think about events that have occurred there. Notice unusual features. Think about other people who once lived there and the interests, behavior, and ideas of guests that have visited.
	—Walk around your neighborhood. Look at buildings, landmarks, and vehicles. Study people and think about what might be on their minds, where they might be going, what their interests might be.
Going to Sources: Use a pad and pencil to take notes as you flip through books, magazines, and newspapers at home or the library.	—Leaf through magazines and newspapers for any articles, pictures, or advertisements that might suggest a topic.
	—Browse through bookshelves at home or at the library. Look at titles and contents for a topic.
	—Use the card catalog in the library. Look for subjects such as Astronomy, Boating, Computers, or Crafts that might lead you to interesting topics.

Once you have a list of possible topics for writing, you still may not know which one you want to write about or what you want to say about it. You may need an additional push to get started on choosing and narrowing a topic. The suggestions in the following chart show four different methods that you might use to help you over this hurdle. Two of the methods use thought association and two of the methods employ a head-first approach.

SOME METHODS FOR CHOOSING AND FOCUSING A TOPIC	
Method	**How It Works**
Thought Associations	—Write a general topic on a piece of paper. Time yourself for a minute or so with a clock or timer. Write down as many smaller topics or related ideas as you can. Do not worry about whether or not they all make sense. Then look over the list you have written and select one of the smaller topics as your paragraph topic.
	—Ask someone to read one topic at a time to you, allowing you thirty seconds or a minute to list smaller related ideas for each. Select one of the smaller ideas that you have listed for your topic.
Head-First Approach	—Take a number of possible topics and write each on a different sheet of paper. Beneath each, list all the smaller topics that occur to you. Then see which topic inspires you the most.
	—Begin writing sentences about different topics. Do not worry about the organization or style of what you write. See which topic generates the most ideas.

Overcoming Blocks. Once you have begun writing, you may encounter "writer's block," the point at which you find yourself at a loss for words and ideas. Perhaps you have written only two or three sentences and cannot express the next idea, or perhaps you are more than halfway through the paper. Maybe you have a strong feeling that something has gone awry in your paper. In any event, you can try some of the following methods for "unstopping" your thoughts.

SOME METHODS FOR OVERCOMING BLOCKS	
Method	**How It Works**
Rereading	—Use the sentences you have written so far to help you express the next idea. Reread your sentences and gather momentum for the next sentence. —Concentrate on the last sentence you have written. Certain words may provide a bridge to the next point that needs explaining.
Talking It Over	—Ask someone to listen as you read aloud what you have written so far. Discuss where you intend the paragraph to go from there. —Ask someone to read your writing aloud to you. Listen to your work and frame the next ideas in sentences in your mind.
Going Back to Your Sources	—Reexamine the object or location that suggested your topic. Look at it, think about it, or talk about it with someone. Then, see what ideas occur to you.

—Look again at the book, magazine, or newspaper article that inspired your topic. Review the material, read further, or discuss the ideas with someone. See what new ideas or what direction comes to mind after you have completed these steps.

Gaining Perspective. Sometimes during or after the writing of your first draft, you may feel unsure about what you have written. Because you have been so involved in your writing, you will have to make a special effort to see your work as others do. Looking at your work from a fresh perspective will often enable you to identify any weaknesses in it. Use the suggestions in the following chart to evaluate your work as objectively as possible.

SOME METHODS FOR GAINING PERSPECTIVE	
Method	**How It Works**
Put Your Work Aside	—Put your work down and go on to some other activity. Later, you will return to your writing with a clearer head and immerse yourself in it again by rereading it.
Share Your Writing with Others	—Read your work to an audience of friends or relatives. Ask them to comment on strong points and weaknesses and to offer any suggestions they may have for improvement.
Find an "Editor"	—Ask someone—a friend or relative—to read your work and offer comments and constructive criticism. Discuss ideas for improving selected sentences or the entire paragraph.

400

The rest of this unit and the next one present more opportunities for you to learn about composition and the many forms that it takes. You will usually have a chance to practice applying what you learn in writing of your own. If you refer to this section when you encounter problems in your composition assignments, you should be able to solve many of them without too much difficulty.

EXERCISE B: Preparing to Write. Use the following instructions to choose and narrow a topic.

1. Pretend that you have been told to write a paragraph about some kind of animal. Consult the chart on page 397 and list the specific activities that you could do to get started. Then use one of these activities to find a topic. Write down your topic. Afterwards, write one or two sentences commenting on how the activities helped you.

2. Once you have several possible topics, use two of the ideas in the chart on page 398 to help you narrow the topic.

EXERCISE C: Overcoming a Writing Block. The following paragraphs are incomplete because, in each case, the writer encountered a "block." Choose one of the paragraphs and decide what suggestions you would give the writer to overcome the block. Write three specific activities that the writer could perform to complete the paragraph.

(1) The effects of a dress code on students are often more negative than positive. If the code requires that all must wear identical uniforms, these suits can be depressing. Such a dress code stifles individuality and prevents any possible freedom of choice.

(2) Students should have the opportunity to investigate as many careers as possible while they are still attending school. It is not uncommon for people to be acquainted with only a small number of careers when they are called upon to choose one to pursue themselves. Usually young people are familiar with what their parents or other close relatives do for a living. Students have some experience in watching what sales clerks, teachers, doctors, nurses, and dentists do when they are working.

DEVELOPING WRITING SKILLS: Using Your Own Approach. Choose a general topic, and narrow it until it is appropriate for a paragraph. As you prepare your paragraph, use one of the approaches you learned in this section or one of your own that works well for you. If you have difficulty getting started or if you encounter a "block" of ideas, try any of the suggestions in this section to overcome such problems.

Writing Workshop: The Writing Process

ASSIGNMENT

Topic   Needed Changes in the High School Curriculum

Form and Purpose   An essay that persuades readers of your opinion

Audience   Your local school committee

Length   Five to seven paragraphs

Focus   Develop a thesis statement that argues for substantive changes in the high school curriculum. Then support your thesis with specific facts, examples, details, and reasons. Conclude with a reminder of your thesis and a clincher sentence.

Sources   Books, education periodicals, newspapers, interviews with teachers, administrators, and other students

Prewriting   Decide on specific changes that you will focus on. Then conduct research, take notes, and prepare an outline.

Writing   Use your outline to write your first draft.

Revising   To revise, edit, and proofread your draft, follow the checklist on page 390.

Chapter 14

The Use of Words

Words are building blocks for writing sentences. They represent a writer's ideas, purpose, and attitude; they also create a mood for readers. Therefore, use words that fit exactly the meaning and tone you wish to convey. This chapter points out some of the problems writers encounter in word choice and discusses a variety of methods to avoid these problems. It explores special ways of using words to communicate your thoughts accurately and effectively.

14.1 Using Words Effectively

In this section, you will learn to sharpen your use of words. Using words precisely and choosing strong verbs, nouns, and modifiers express ideas more clearly and forcefully. Also, by avoiding the use of unnecessary or inappropriate words, your writing will become more direct, concise, and unified.

Choosing Precise Words

Using weak verbs, passive constructions, and vague modifiers weakens the impact of your writing. Learn to recognize such colorless or ineffective words and replace them with vivid and specific language whenever possible.

Recognize the difference between bland or in-effective words and strong, colorful language.

Using Action Words. More than any other part of speech, verbs separate forceful writing from weak writing. Action verbs in the active voice enliven your sentences, whereas overuse of linking verbs and passive verbs deadens them.

Use action verbs in the active voice whenever possible to make statements precise and lively.

The following examples show how action verbs can give new force to sentences.

LINKING VERB: Steve's costume *was* frightening to the children.

ACTION VERB: Steve's costume *frightened* the children.

LINKING VERBS: The judges *were* certain that Alvin *was* the winner of the race.

ACTION VERBS: The judges *declared* that Alvin *won* the race.

Sentences may be improved by using verbs that convey strong action. For instance, in some noun/verb/noun constructions, the verb and the second noun can be replaced by a single more vivid verb, as in the following examples.

NOUN/VERB/NOUN: Baron Von Steuben *led* the Continental Army *in drills* at Valley Forge.

    Baron Von Steuben *drilled* the Continental Army at Valley Forge.

NOUN/VERB/NOUN: Heavy rains *caused* a *flood* in our basement.

REVISED: Heavy rains *flooded* our basement.

NOUN/VERB/NOUN: The newspaper *gave* its *endorsement* to the incumbent.

REVISED: The newspaper *endorsed* the incumbent.

Statements also become more vivid and forceful when active rather than passive voice verbs are used. Active voice allows the subject of the sentence to perform an action. Conversely, the subject of a sentence written in passive voice has the action performed on it. Frequently, a change from passive to active voice will increase the impact of your sentence.

405

PASSIVE:	This new driving test *was failed* nine times out of ten.
ACTIVE:	Nine out of every ten people *failed* this new driving test.
PASSIVE:	The sunshine was *filtered* by the fog.
ACTIVE:	The fog *filtered* the sunshine.

Using Specific Words. Sharpen your meaning and attract your readers' attention by using vivid, specific language. When you write, try to use graphic words with crisp, precise meanings rather than bland and general terms that make your writing vague.

Use vivid, specific words to focus descriptions, relate actions, and convey meanings exactly.

Specific concrete words will help you to create a more detailed, well-focused picture. For example, *hamburger cookout, astronomer,* and *split-level house* are more vivid and precise than *meal, scientist,* and *family dwelling.* Similarly, *devoured, assembled,* and *shouted* represent actions more clearly than *ate, did,* and *spoke.* The following sentences show how specific words can improve meaning.

GENERAL:	The batter *pleased* the *crowd* with a *hit* that won the game.
SPECIFIC:	The batter *lifted thousands from their seats* with a *game-winning double.*
GENERAL:	The *leader* vowed to *win* against the enemy.
SPECIFIC:	The *admiral* vowed to *seize the enemy's flagship*.

Choosing the Right Connotations. As you write, you often must choose the right word from several possibilities, frequently from a group of synonyms. Although synonyms have similar literal meanings, called *denotations,* they often have very different shades of meaning or emotional associations called *connotations*. For instance, the words *pleased* and *ecstatic* both denote strong pleasure, yet their connotations are different. You might use *pleased* to describe happiness or some kind of satisfaction, but you would probably choose *ecstatic* to suggest an even more intense and profound feeling, an emotion closer to joy.

Because synonyms do not always bring the same ideas to mind, it is wise to check a dictionary for shades of meaning after you have consulted a thesaurus or dictionary of synonyms. This will help you determine the appropriate connotation for a particular context.

Choose words with the best connotations for your ideas.

In almost any group of synonyms, you will find a whole range of connotations with different tones. The following examples show how synonyms can establish different tones in the same sentence.

FAVORABLE, ADMIRING:	He is a *steadfast* man, and nothing can budge him.
STILL POSITIVE, BUT MOVING TOWARD NEUTRALITY:	He is a *strong-willed* man, and nothing can budge him.
MORE NEGATIVE, SUGGESTING UNREASONABLENESS:	He is an *obstinate* man, and nothing can budge him.
VERY NEGATIVE, SUGGESTING RIDICULE:	He is a *pigheaded* man, and nothing can budge him.

Avoiding Clichés. Clichés, such as "light as a feather" or "clean as a whistle," are worn-out expressions that add a frivolous tone to your sentences. Once these expressions were colorful, but they have faded through overuse and no longer create vivid images in readers' minds. Clichés only function to weaken your writing, making it sound prefabricated and tired.

Replace clichés with fresh, direct words and expressions.

As you see in the following examples, clichés sound dull. You will recognize them easily. Choose fresher, more direct language instead.

CLICHÉ:	Getting the lead in the play put Roberto on cloud nine.
REVISED:	Getting the lead in the play exhilarated Roberto.
CLICHÉ:	The President put his John Hancock on the bill.
REVISED:	The President signed the bill.

407

Using Varied Words. Still another way to add life to your sentences is to use a variety of words instead of overusing any one word in a passage. If you continually repeat one word—for example, one adjective throughout a passage—readers will become distracted by that word. They will notice the repetition of the word and miss your ideas. Notice how the repetition of the word "interesting" saps the meaning from the first of the following passages, while the varied, specific language in the second communicates more information.

Passage with an Overused Word
The many interesting concepts in J.R.R. Tolkien's trilogy *The Lord of the Rings* captured my interest. For example, the magic ring of the title represents some very interesting ideas. The wizard Gandalf, the chief source of truth in the trilogy, gives the hero Frodo an interesting warning about the power of the ring: Anyone who uses the ring's power—even for good—will be inevitably and increasingly corrupted by it.
Passage with Precise Substitutions
The many fascinating concepts in J.R.R. Tolkien's triology *The Lord of the Rings* continue to intrigue me. The magic ring of the title illustrates one of the most thought-provoking ideas. The wizard Gandalf, the chief source of truth in the trilogy, warns the hero Frodo that anyone who uses the ring's power—even for good—will be inevitably and increasingly corrupted by it.

EXERCISE A: Using Action Verbs in the Active Voice. Rewrite each sentence, using an action verb in the active voice.

EXAMPLE: Discarded shopping carts were in front of the super-market entrance.

Discarded shopping carts blocked the supermarket entrance.

1. The passage of the bill was immensely pleasing to the lobbyists.
2. Sunshine was brighter and then was dimmer as clouds passed overhead.

3. Many hardships are suffered by the animals of the Everglades during the dry season.
4. A searing guitar solo was ingeniously played by Jimmy Page.
5. At a science fiction seminar, Isaac Asimov gave a presentation on his theories of time and space.
6. Lucy's interpretation of that incident was upsetting to me.
7. Sociologists took a survey of residents of New City to ascertain income levels.
8. The apartment residents were angry about the owner's mismanagement.
9. Only two questions were missed by me when I took my oral examination.
10. Hundreds of years ago people were of the belief that the sun circled the earth.

EXERCISE B: Choosing Specific Words. Rewrite each sentence, using more specific verbs, nouns, and modifiers. Use your imagination to supply missing details.

EXAMPLE: My teacher strongly recommended that we see the rerun of the Hitchcock movie.

Ms. Faulkner urged us to see the rerun of Hitchcock's *Rear Window*.

1. I have just finished reading a very good novel that takes place during the early years of our country's history.
2. Madge went out west for a while to see things and to have a pleasant change.
3. Michael was happy when he got his report card.
4. The tiny vibrations of the floor were so tiny that had I been even a tiny bit preoccupied I might never have noticed them.
5. Private Robinson saw something move near them and felt strange.
6. Brenda made an attractive garment for herself to wear for a special occasion.
7. The speaker gave her dramatic interpretation.
8. The lazy clouds drifted lazily out over the lake.
9. The fair offered many sources of fun and many kinds of unusual food.
10. The poor weather depressed him.

409

EXERCISE C: Choosing Connotations. Use a dictionary, thesaurus, or dictionary of synonyms to help you write three synonyms for each underlined word. Then circle the one that would work best in the given sentence.

EXAMPLE: Those workers on top of the skyscraper have to move around very <u>carefully</u>.

watchfully   (cautiously)   scrupulously

1. Placed in the care of an adoption agency, the twins <u>asked</u> repeatedly not to be separated.
2. An important aspect of training race horses involves <u>guessing</u> their varied potentials.
3. A yellow car pulled ahead of the others and <u>moved</u> toward the finish line.
4. <u>High-and-mighty</u> remarks by the nation's ambassador earned censure from Security Council members.
5. My uncle bought a quaint rustic cabin <u>ensconced</u> in the White Mountains.
6. Resting in a <u>bad</u> position, the enormous boulder threatened cars that passed on the roadway beneath.
7. Apparently <u>tickled</u> by Joan's answer, Mrs. Caperonis smiled and then proceeded with the lesson.
8. Hoping that she had finally <u>found</u> the source of the problem, Dr. Malone began the complex experiment again.
9. Jasper made the poodle angry so that it began to <u>bark</u>.
10. We just wanted to spend a long, lazy day lying on the beach, <u>perusing</u> the ocean.

Maintaining an Appropriate Tone

Your word choices determine the tone of your sentences, which, like the tone of your voice when you speak, indicates your feelings about your subject and your audience. When you write, your language reveals whether you are approaching your topic seriously or lightly, enthusiastically or coolly. Your language also signals whether you intend to explain, instruct, persuade, or entertain your audience. Make your words sound as if they belong together. By choosing appropriate words, you will accurately convey your attitude toward your subject and audience.

Be aware that a consistent tone can be undermined by several problems. If your tone is interrupted by trite expressions, self-important words, or slang, readers may become confused or irritated. Therefore, you should learn to recognize these problems and avoid them in your writing.

Avoiding Words That May Not Be Understood. Slang is the informal language of a particular social group, while jargon is the specialized vocabulary of a profession or occupation. Both are forms of language with special meanings that may not be generally understood, and both can distort the tone of a passage. Similarly, unnecessary foreign terms can mystify readers who do not understand them. You should replace such language with expressions and explanations that are more widely understood.

Replace slang, jargon, and foreign terms with precise, understandable language.

Slang can vary from day to day, from place to place, and from group to group. Only a small portion of slang becomes a permanent part of the language. Slang appeals to a limited audience, and although it can sound colorful in speech when it is new, it often sounds obsolete and ridiculous in written communication. For these reasons, it is not effective or acceptable in most writing. In addition, slang gives your writing a careless, overly casual tone, as you can see in the following example.

SLANG: We decided to beg off from Mr. Lehman's invitation.

REVISED: We decided to decline Mr. Lehman's invitation.

Like slang, jargon is too specialized a language to be used in formal writing. Each occupation has its own jargon, which usually sounds overly technical to the outsider. If you have to use technical language in your writing, explain your terms carefully.

In the following example, the jargon is easily replaced by a more generally understood expression.

JARGON: Cars whose engines are air-cooled do not require water-retentant coolants.

REVISED: Cars whose engines are air-cooled do not require radiators.

411

Foreign expressions can puzzle your readers even more than slang and jargon. They can be intimidating because they interject an inflated tone into your writing. Substitute English equivalents for such expressions, as in the following revision.

FOREIGN TERM: He had a gift for choosing the *mot juste*.

REVISED: He had a gift for choosing the right word.

Avoiding Self-Important Language. Expressions that sound pompous and self-important distort the tone of your writing and mislead the reader. Self-important language tries to impress the reader with flowery expressions, unnecessarily lengthy words, and complicated structures that sound pretentious. It introduces a falseness and emptiness into your writing; therefore, avoid it.

Replace self-important language with simpler, more direct words.

In the following examples, two different varieties of self-important language—one that is too formal and another that is too ornate—are replaced by simpler, clearer words.

OVERLY FORMAL LANGUAGE: To *become competent* at their *chosen craft*, the *industrious fledgling artisans* worked *feverishly* seven days a week.

REVISED: To *improve their work*, the *young silversmiths labored* seven days a week.

ORNATE LANGUAGE: *Garrulous* waiters attempted to obtain *inordinately generous* tips by acting *obsequious* and *familiar*.

REVISED: *Talkative* waiters tried to get *very large tips* by acting *servile* and *overly friendly*.

Avoiding Euphemisms. Euphemisms are expressions that attempt to cushion the truth. For example, the expression *pass away* is a euphemism for *die;* it softens the impact of the idea of death. The word *detained* is sometimes used as a euphemism for *arrested*. These terms are generally used by people who want to sound nice; unfortunately, they frequently distort what is being said, misleading the reader.

412

Replace euphemisms that make your writing sound insincere with direct language.

In the following sentences, euphemisms are replaced with more direct language.

EUPHEMISM: The representatives of the countries had a *frank exchange of views*.

REVISED: The representatives of the countries had a *disagreement*.

EUPHEMISM: Your room will look neater if you *eliminate the refuse*.

REVISED: Your room will look neater if you *throw out the garbage*.

Avoiding Overly Emotional Language. Emotional language consists of name-calling, extreme modifiers, and other similar expressions. It disrupts the rational tone you should be aiming for in your writing. In addition, it makes you seem insincere and evokes hostility in readers who disagree with you.

Replace overly emotional language with reasonable language.

In the following passage, the overly emotional statements sound angry and immature. Notice that the second passage sounds more reasonable and worthy of the reader's attention.

OVERLY EMOTIONAL LANGUAGE: The City's most recent cutbacks in garbage removal are just another indication of the idiocy and insensitivity of the demagogues who run the government. Conspiring with the tightwad plutocrats who run the banks, these party hacks obviously care nothing about the health and comfort of the beleaguered residents of this city.

REVISED: The City's most recent cutbacks in garbage removal are evidence of what could be a disturbing new policy in this administration. Those responsible for such service cuts seem to be more concerned with satisfying the fiscally-conscious bankers of this city than with safeguarding the health and comfort of the average taxpayer.

EXERCISE D: Eliminating Problems with Tone. Identify the type of problem in each sentence: *slang, jargon, foreign term, self-important language, euphemism,* or *emotional language*. Then rewrite the sentence, correcting the problem.

EXAMPLE: If I am not indisposed at nine o'clock, I'll drive you and your friends to the concert.

Self-important language: If I am not busy at nine o'clock, I'll drive you and your friends to the concert.

1. Because the food in the school cafeteria was poisonously disgusting, most of the students began to bring their own lunches to school.
2. The police apprehended the alleged perpetrator in the act of robbing the jewelry store.
3. Because the head of the committee was *in absentia,* the vote was postponed.
4. Ivy grew over the walls in cascading streams of verdant green, giving visitors a sense of the antiquity of the domicile.
5. Customs officials stopped the car on the Canadian border because the driver had ripped off a tax-free gift shop in New York.
6. Aunt Lilly hired a new household domestic engineer to cook meals for the family and take care of the house.
7. Mr. Edgar Baines, President of the Tallyrand Corporation, elevated to prominence Carmen Miro to begin as Tallyrand's new Director of Corporate Planning.
8. I think the President was a total creep to contradict himself.
9. The lecture was so dull that I crashed right in the middle of it.
10. The airplane taxied down the runway and rose into the azure heavens as easily as a bird.

EXERCISE E: Maintaining an Appropriate Tone. Rewrite the following passage, changing any words not suitable for a general audience unfamiliar with rock groups.

EXAMPLE: The fancy footwork of the group's new song produced good vibes at the concert.

The skillfulness of the group's new song produced good feelings at the concert.

414

(1) Popular since the mid-1960's, the rock band called The Who has wowed 'em from England to Woodstock with their incredibly magical and wondrous special effects and stage shows. (2) They have blasted away the pathetic fools who have tried to compete with them.

(3) The Who came to New York City in 1979 to give one of their finest shows ever. (4) Pete Townsend, lead guitarist, did some really cool jumps and splits. (5) Lead singer Roger Daltrey was at the top of his form as was bassist John Entwhistle. (6) The leading percussional figure of the band had been Keith Moon, but after he passed away in 1977, his duties fell to Keith Jones, who did an outrageous job at the 1979 concert. (7) Dressed to kill, the band hung in there with the flavor of the old days and delivered their coup de grâce with an electrifying version of "Won't Get Fooled Again."

(8) Who concerts are now established musical events, and people of all ages recognize this group. (9) Their popularity since the 1979 concert has not diminished.

Using Words Concisely

When you write, besides choosing precise words and maintaining an appropriate tone, you should try to be concise. Deadwood, redundancy, and wordiness can cause a reader to lose interest in what you have to say. Good writing uses the right number of words for the ideas being expressed.

Recognize when you have used too few words or too many words in your sentences.

Eliminating Deadwood. Nonessential words are called deadwood. These words and phrases fill out sentences without adding meaning. Such padding only confuses and distracts a reader.

Make your writing concise by eliminating nonessential words.

Once you are able to identify deadwood, you can easily eliminate it from your writing. Some deadwood consists of meaningless words. Hedging words, another form of deadwood, are unnecessary qualifiers. Although hedging words may seem safe to use because they are noncommittal, they can lengthen and weaken sentences. The following chart contains words and phrases that are usually deadwood.

DEADWOOD		
Empty Words		
there is (are)	the thing that	of the opinion that
the area of	to the extent that	what I mean is
by way of	it is a fact that	for the reason that
a great deal (of)	in the manner that	due to
the fact that	is the one who is	while at the same time
Hedging Words		
somewhat	it seems (that)	sort of
almost	tends to	kind of
rather	in a way	that might or might not

Eliminating these expressions from your sentences makes your ideas stand out much more sharply. Make certain, however, that the sentences continue to make sense. Occasionally qualifying words, such as almost, are necessary for accuracy. Taking out deadwood may involve rephrasing, as in the examples below.

WITH DEADWOOD: Rains continued for two more days to the extent that they caused major highways to be closed.

CONCISE: Rains continued for two more days causing major highways to be closed.

WITH DEADWOOD: Due to the fact that construction workers are on strike, building plans have halted.

CONCISE: Because construction workers are on strike, building plans have halted.

WITH DEADWOOD: I tend to be made angry when there is a train delay.

CONCISE: Train delays anger me.

416

Avoiding Redundancy. Words that repeat ideas in a sentence are redundant. You can easily identify redundancy by looking for words or phrases that repeat the meaning of other words.

Write concisely by eliminating redundant words, phrases, and clauses.

Notice in the following sentences how redundancy can be eliminated.

REDUNDANT: He used a baseball slightly deformed in shape to create a curve in the pitch. (*Deformed* already refers to shape.)

CONCISE: He used a slightly deformed baseball to create a curve in the pitch.

REDUNDANT: Susan, who is just a beginning horseback rider, over-exaggerates the height of her jumps. (*Exaggerate* means "overstate.")

CONCISE: Susan, who is just a beginning horseback rider, exaggerates the height of her jumps.

REDUNDANT: My friend, who loves to play musical instruments, enjoys playing the guitar, the piano, and the trumpet. (*Enjoys playing* and the rest of the sentence convey a love of playing musical instruments.)

CONCISE: My friend enjoys playing the guitar, the piano, and the trumpet.

Avoiding Wordiness. The words that allow writers to form phrases and clauses can often be eliminated to make sentences more concise. Adjective and adverb clauses, for example, can frequently be reduced to single-word modifiers. Whenever you can shorten or eliminate a lengthy phrase or clause without changing the meaning of the sentence, take the opportunity to do so.

When possible, reduce wordy phrases and clauses to shorter structures.

The chart on the next page shows you how you can tighten sentence structures by reducing wordy structures, including phrases and clauses, into more concise structures.

REDUCING WORDY STRUCTURES	
Wordy Phrase	He spoke from an objective viewpoint.
Concise	He spoke objectively. (Phrase reduced to a single-word modifier.)
Wordy Phrase	Mr. Bloom will send roses to his wife.
Concise	Mr. Bloom will send his wife roses. (Phrase reduced to a noun and modifier.)
Wordy Clause	Michael is an excellent singer, and he is also a member of the orchestra.
Concise	Michael is both an excellent singer and a member of the orchestra. (Clause reduced to part of a compound complement.)
Wordy Clause	At the door was a man who was selling magazines for charity.
Concise	At the door was a man selling magazines for charity. (Clause reduced to a participial phrase.)
Wordy Clause	Nicholas II, who was the czar of Russia, was overthrown during the revolution of 1917.
Concise	Nicholas II, czar of Russia, was overthrown during the revolution of 1917. (Clause reduced to an appositive.)
Wordy Clause	For biology experiments, we need specimens that are fresh.
Concise	For biology experiments, we need fresh specimens. (Clause reduced to a single-word modifier.)

EXERCISE F: Eliminating Deadwood and Redundancy.

Rewrite each sentence, eliminating the unnecessary words and phrases.

EXAMPLE: Phil is a nonstop talker who is saying something all the time.

Phil is a nonstop talker.

1. Wondering thoughtfully about possible punishments, Roberta decided to tell her parents about the fact that she had dented the car.
2. Dr. Sanders, being of the opinion that snakes are extremely dangerous, would rather view them through clear glass that is transparent.
3. Left alone in the vacant, empty classroom, Michele somewhat regretted following her adventurous friends.
4. A hurricane, which may or may not move into our area, is capable of causing extensive damage to our area.
5. Due to the fact that colleges often decide on applicants during the winter, they ask for applications in the fall.
6. At that point in time, Janice thought to herself about dropping physics and adding calculus to her schedule.
7. Pressure will build beneath the pavement to the extent that it will crack the pavement unless a release valve is added to the existing pipes that are there.
8. A large black cloud, enormous in size, testified to the extent of how serious the explosion had been.
9. Rather furious that Ronald was the one who was laughing in class, Mr. Kelton insisted on an apology.
10. At the same time as cars lined up before the open bridge, a string of little tugboats proceeded one after another up the river.

EXERCISE G: Eliminating Wordiness. Shorten the wordy phrases or clauses in each of the following sentences to make each sentence concise.

EXAMPLE: At the entrance was a man who was collecting tickets.

At the entrance was a man collecting tickets.

1. A dangerous reconnaissance mission that was completed by Division 6 earned every man who was participating a service medal.
2. *QB VII,* a novel that was written by Leon Uris, was made into a film.
3. Over the years, termites nested in the foundation, and they slowly ate away wooden supports.
4. Glen Richardson, who was running in the marathon, finished in a time that was respectable.

5. Fillmore's varsity basketball team, which was coached by Mr. Paul Johnson, enjoyed a season that was quite successful.
6. The beaches that are along the Magill south shore have slowly eroded, and this erosion has prompted property owners to demand government action.
7. On stage he wore a cape that was long and black and a mustache shaped like a handlebar.
8. Gregory found his source information, which was in the vertical file and which was listed under the heading "Astronomy."
9. Anyone who is interested in part-time jobs should visit the Youth Employment Service, which is located on the second floor.
10. A possum that was cornered in our basement glared at us in a threatening manner, and it was hissing as we moved closer.

DEVELOPING WRITING SKILLS: Using Words Effectively. Use one of the following suggested topics or think of one of your own, and write a passage of about 150 to 200 words. Be precise in your choice of words, consistent in tone, and concise in the wording of your ideas.

An unforgettable acquaintance
A new insight about a friend
The frustration of a boring job

A special show (play, movie, or television)
Plans for a trip, prank, or tour

14.2 Using Words in Special Ways

When you want to communicate an idea in a way that gives it particular emphasis or to express feelings in a way that truly brings them to life, you can use certain special stylistic devices to help you.

This section explores additional possibilities for word choices. It explains how to use stylistic devices, such as figures of speech, sensory impressions, and symbols. It also encourages you to study professional writing to develop your own use of language.

Using Figures of Speech

Similes, metaphors, personification, and analogies are figures of speech that strengthen your writing by appealing to a reader's imagination.

Using Similes. A *simile* uses the words *like* or *as* to link two different items on the basis of certain shared qualities.

Use similes to emphasize the shared qualities of otherwise dissimilar items.

Notice how the following similes give the reader a new way of looking at the destructive power of a colony of ants and the fragility of a broken umbrella.

SIMILE: Like a wave of brush fires, droves of army ants swept across hundreds of acres of grasslands.

SIMILE: The umbrella turned inside out as limply as a flower.

Using Metaphors. Like a simile, a *metaphor* compares two dissimilar items. However, it draws the comparison by identifying one item completely with another, imaginatively overstating the similarity and equating them: It says one item *is* another. For instance, in the metaphor *The boat was a large white bird on the water,* the reader understands that a comparison has been drawn between the boat's beauty, grace, and ease on the water and the beauty and grace of a bird.

Use metaphors to heighten an imaginative connection between two items.

Metaphors are even more striking figures of speech than similes. They should therefore be used with great selectivity and care. The following sentences include metaphors. Notice how the first one rewords the brush fire/ants simile.

METAPHOR: Droves of army ants swept across hundreds of acres of grasslands, a brush fire that could not be contained.

METAPHOR: Her hair was a bridal veil around her face, shimmering, pale, and still.

Metaphors are imaginative and forceful, so many writers submerge them subtly, in exact, graphic verbs, for instance. A submerged version of the brush fire/ants metaphor follows.

421

SUBMERGED METAPHOR: Droves of army ants scorched the grasslands for miles around.

Using Analogies. An *analogy* is an extended comparison, which develops and explains the various points of similarity between the things compared. Writers often use analogies to relate an unfamiliar experience or set of circumstances to some other condition that will be more familiar to readers.

> **Use analogies to clarify an item, experience, or set of circumstances by likening it point by point to another.**

An analogy usually begins with a simile and then offers some detail and occasionally some narration to illustrate the likeness between two items or experiences. In the following passage, the writer uses an analogy to explain a free fall in terms of a ride in a glass elevator.

ANALOGY: A free fall toward earth is like descending rapidly in a glass elevator. If you lose sight of the structures holding the glass walls, and if you ignore the feel of the floor through your shoes, you will have some sensation of what it is like to float in space, the pull of gravity your only reality.

Using Personification. Personification also works as a kind of metaphor by attributing human qualities to nonhuman things. This figure of speech lends itself readily to humor, but it can also be serious in its emotional impact on a reader.

> **Use personification to endow an inanimate object with human traits for either humorous or vivid effects.**

Personifications can be fun to write, but you should develop them carefully and only for a clearly defined purpose. They can easily sound pretentious and even ridiculous when you want to be serious. The following examples demonstrate the use of personification.

PERSONIFICATION: The welcoming hands of sunlight touched my shoulders, and I looked up.

PERSONIFICATION: The old train wheezed into the station and stopped with a grateful sigh.

EXERCISE A: Writing Similes and Metaphors. Write five similes and five metaphors in sentences, using pairs of items, one from each column. Label the type of comparison that you write.

EXAMPLES: Her *voice* was like a *lifeline* pulling me from unconsciousness. simile

Her *voice* was a *lifeline* pulling me from unconsciousness. metaphor

Her voice pulled me from engulfing unconsciousness. submerged metaphor

face	lifeline
fear	blessing
youth	satin
hands	weapon
air	thirst
beauty	mask
hair	trap
car	monument
friendship	perfume
voice	costume

EXERCISE B: Creating Analogies. Choose one of the following pairs of items or think of a pair of your own. Compare the two items and develop the comparison into an analogy.

1. Studying for an exam—filling a shopping cart quickly
2. A job interview or date—a performance onstage
3. A person you know—some fruit or vegetable
4. Hosting a party—spinning plates
5. Talking to a shy person—running uphill

EXERCISE C: Using Personification. Write five sentences, each containing personification, using an item from the following list in each sentence.

A telephone	A stuffed toy
A skyscraper	Clouds
Waves lapping	A computer
A signpost	A gasoline lamp
A weed	A car rushing

Setting Moods

In descriptive writing, you often want to create a special mood or feeling about a place, person, or series of events. You can do this by using *sensory impressions* or *symbols*.

Using Sensory Impressions. *Sensory impressions* are words that appeal to sight, sound, smell, taste, and touch.

Use sensory impressions to create a mood or recreate a particular experience for your audience.

Words that convey sensory impressions can make a reader remember or imagine specific experiences. The following passage recreates the melancholy feeling and sensations you might have on an autumn night by using details of sight, sound, and touch.

Passage with sensory impressions   The night was coolly lit by a crystalline full moon. As we crunched through the pile of leaves, we cast silver shadows on the ground before us. I shivered as a small sharp wind nipped at my face.

Using Symbols. Within a description you can include a symbol—a person, place, object, or action that the writer invests with significance beyond its literal meaning. Some symbols are natural symbols because of their built-in associations—for example, the sea, the sun, and the change of seasons. But any object can work as a symbol if the writer can convincingly endow it with special meaning.

Endow a concrete thing with symbolic significance to enrich the mood of a passage.

Symbols have more impact if they grow naturally and subtly out of the situation described. The objects that take on deeper meanings should fit into the context of the passage. A writer lays the groundwork for the symbols by establishing a mood from which the symbol's special meaning can develop. In this sense, symbols often work well as concluding effects, culminations of the other details in a passage.

The above description of a fall evening might take on more meaning if words like "small sharp wind" were changed to words like *waning* or *weak*. The passage then becomes a reminder of the passage of time and the inevitability of death.

424

| Passage developing a symbol | The night was coolly lit by a waning crystalline moon. As we crunched slowly through the deep piles of dead leaves, we cast weak shadows on the ground before us. Autumn was almost over. I shivered as a small sharp wind touched my shoulder. |

EXERCISE D: Writing with Sensory Impressions and Symbols. Use one of the following subjects or think of one of your own to write a passage of 150 to 200 words. Include sensory impressions and symbols wherever possible in your passage.

1. The expectations and fears of a young man or woman driving alone to visit a college
2. Your insights or feelings about a family member or friend who has died, or whom you have not seen in a very long time
3. The mood of a bus station or airport very late at night
4. Attitudes and expectations revealed through the items a person is packing for a long-awaited vacation or journey
5. The thought processes of someone who becomes lost, panics, and finally conquers the predicament

Using Professional Models

As you are reading, notice how major writers use various devices to create effective prose. You might want to copy effective passages for future reference, noting the sources of your models.

Study the language used by professional writers to improve your own writing style.

Stephen Crane's *The Red Badge of Courage* contains the following passage. Notice the vividness and precision of the description and its use of figures of speech.

| Metaphor | He became aware that the furnace roar of the battle was growing louder. Great brown clouds had floated to the still heights of air before him. The noise, too, was |
| Submerged metaphor | approaching. The woods filtered men and the fields became dotted.—Stephen Crane |

425

The following passage from "Flowering Judas," by Katherine Anne Porter, illustrates a metaphoric connection between a young woman's clothing and her life.

Precise language
Metaphors

Her knees cling together under sound blue serge, and her round white collar is not purposely nun-like. She wears the uniform of an idea, and has renounced vanities. She has encased herself in a set of principles derived from her early training, leaving no detail of gesture or of personal taste untouched, and for this reason she will not wear lace made on machines. She loves

Submerged metaphor

fine lace, and there is a tiny edge of fluted cobweb on this collar, which is one of twenty precisely alike, folded in blue tissue paper in the upper drawer of her clothes chest—Katherine Anne Porter

The following passage from Nathaniel Hawthorne's *The House of the Seven Gables* employs several devices. Notice how they create a ponderous mood and how the wind becomes a symbol of something ominous in the lives of those in the house.

Personification

Sensory impressions

Symbol

He tried the door, which yielded to his hand, and was flung wide open by a sudden gust of wind that passed, as with a loud sigh, from the outermost portal through all the passages and apartments of the new house. It rustled the silken garments of the ladies, and waved the long curls of the gentlemen's wigs, and shook the window hangers and the curtains of the bedchambers; causing everywhere a singular stir, which yet was more like a hush. A shadow of awe and half-fearful anticipation—nobody knew wherefore nor of what— had all at once fallen over the company.
—Nathaniel Hawthorne

From your study of professional works, you might write a vivid passage that contains sensory impressions, precise language, and a simile like the following.

Sensory impressions

The hot, harsh lights of the acting studio melted decades away from her cunning old face, and she glowed and fattened, growing ageless, beautiful, and

426

Precise
language

Simile

larger than life on the star worship of her students. They paid her to torture them into art. She bellowed at them, pounced on them, and throttled them like an old medicine man trying to wake the dead.

EXERCISE E: Examining a Professional Model. Read the following passage. List the similes, metaphors, personifications, analogies, sensory impressions, and symbols you find.

EXAMPLE: feathery puffs of sweet bloom (sensory impression)

(1) Joel gazed at the girl, not much older than himself. (2) She leaned her cheek against the fiddle. (3) He had never examined a fiddle at all, and when she began to play it she frightened and dismayed him by her almost insect-like motions, the pensive antennae of her arms. (4) And quite clearly, and altogether to his surprise, Joel saw a sight that he had nearly forgotten. (5) Instead of the fire on the hearth, there was a mimosa tree in flower. (6) It was in the little back field at his home in Virginia, and his mother was leading him by the hand. (7) Fragile, delicate, cloudlike, it rose on its pale trunk and spread its long level arms. (8) Among the trembling leaves the feathery puffs of sweet bloom filled the tree like thousands of paradisiacal birds all alighted at an instant. (9) It seemed to be the mimosa tree that lighted the garden, for its brightness and fragrance overlaid all the rest. (10) Out of its graciousness this tree suffered their presence and shed its splendor upon him and his mother. (11) Then the vision was gone.—Eudora Welty.

EXERCISE F: Collecting and Studying Professional Models. Find three passages in professional works with effective words. Copy them and write down each source. Label the devices in each.

DEVELOPING WRITING SKILLS: Using Words in Special Ways. Write a passage of 150 to 300 words on a topic that lends itself to description. Use vivid and specific language, suitable connotations, figures of speech, and words that convey mood. Feel free to use professional models as guides.

Skills Review and Writing Workshop

The Use of Words

CHECKING YOUR SKILLS

Rewrite the following paragraph using active verbs in the active voice. Change ineffective words to make it more precise and consistent in tone.

(1) If present trends continue, the long-popular custom of going to the movies may disappear. (2) More and more people are subscribing to cable TV. (3) Sales of video-cassette players are booming. (4) Sales of popcorn are booming, too. (5) A lot of films are available for home viewing, and special discounts are offered. (6) Also, it has become less expensive to rent a cassette that family and friends can enjoy together than to get tickets to a movie. (7) One major factor in this trend is cost. (8) You now can see popular films of years ago. (9) These old movies are rarely shown in movie theaters. (10) People can watch movies every night, right in their own homes.

USING COMPOSITION SKILLS
Writing Description

A good reporter must know how to write about important events so that readers feel they were on the scene. Follow the steps below to write a description of the rescue of stranded homeowners after a flood or other weather emergency.

Prewriting: Try to envision the scene of the rescue. List the essential information, such as weather conditions, time, and location. Jot down some human interest details, such as reactions of the rescue team and of individual homeowners.

Writing: Set the scene with a topic sentence. Use precise, vivid action language to make your story come alive.

Revising: Have you included important details to help the reader visualize the conditions at the scene? Use the checklist on page 386 to improve your paragraph. After you have revised, proofread carefully.

15

Sentences

Good sentences are more than grammatical units that communicate ideas; they please and interest readers as well. Using varied sentence lengths and structures gives your writing style sophistication and helps to hold the reader's attention. This chapter discusses how you can improve your writing style by varying sentence length, structure, and patterns, and it encourages you to learn from professional writers.

Improving Your Sentences 15.1

Even the most original ideas will lose their impact if they are expressed in monotonous or confusing sentences. The best writing usually mixes long and short sentences and uses a variety of sentence structures. The sentences you write will have flair and pleasing rhythms if you adopt some of the methods for varying sentences discussed in this section.

Sentence Combining

Too many short sentences in a composition create a choppy rhythm. To avoid this, combine sentences to vary their lengths.

Combine short sentences by using compound subjects or verbs; phrases; appositives; or compound, complex, or compound-complex sentences.

METHODS OF COMBINING SENTENCES

Short, Choppy Sentences	Longer, Smoother Sentences
In August, the Grossis hiked in the Sierra Mountains. The Dykes also hike in the Sierra Mountains.	In August, the Grossis and the Dykes hiked in the Sierra Mountains. (Compound subject)
Edna parked the car. She brought packages into the building.	Edna parked the car and brought packages into the building. (Compound verb)
The small dog yapped frantically. It ran away from a large cat.	Yapping frantically, the small dog ran away from a large cat. (Modifying phrase)
Mrs. Kurtz became the new personnel director. She moved her office upstairs.	Mrs. Kurtz, the new personnel director, moved her office upstairs. (Appositive)
The police cars passed, flashing red lights. The fire engines screamed down the boulevard.	The police cars passed, flashing red lights, and the fire engines screamed down the boulevard. (Compound sentence)
He lost his grip on the ladder. He knocked over a can of paint.	When he lost his grip on the ladder, he knocked over a can of paint. (Complex sentence)
The strike continued. Some dock workers continued to appear on picket lines. Others sought new jobs.	While the strike continued, some dock workers continued to appear on picket lines, but others sought new jobs. (Compound-complex sentence)

EXERCISE A: Sentence Combining. Combine each of the following groups of sentences into one longer sentence. Label the method you use *modifying phrase, appositive, compound verb,* and so on.

EXAMPLE: The plane was due to take off. Nick had not come.

Though the plane was due to take off, Nick had not come.   Complex sentence

1. Rust is a popular color. It is often used in home decorating.
2. She had trouble building the fire. A brisk breeze was blowing.
3. Our local newspapers were the *Kensington Chronicle* and the *Orinda Record*. Last year they merged.
4. The dog trotted down the main street. It paused in front of the meat market. It sniffed eagerly.
5. I ran to answer the phone. I slipped on a magazine. I tripped over the coffee table.
6. A canoe came around the bend of the shoreline. The weary campers shouted for help.
7. February was especially cruel that year. Its frigid weather damaged the fruit trees and even the evergreens.
8. Homemade soup bubbled in the big pot. The boys had not eaten since dawn. Now they remembered that.
9. The customs officer opened the suitcase. He saw the toy animals. He smiled.
10. California and Florida both produce citrus. They vie to see who can grow the best oranges.

EXERCISE B: Combining Sentences in a Passage. Rewrite the following passage, combining some of the sentences.

(1) Rose Ann had always lived in the city. (2) Street sounds, crowds, and motion were normal to her. (3) She thought she would never be content anywhere else. (4) Then one summer she drove across the country. (5) She stayed in small inns in little towns. (6) She saw the many different ways Americans live. (7) Today Rose Ann has a new career. (8) She is an innkeeper. (9) Her ten-bedroom inn is on a wooded hill above a lazy river.

Expanding Short Sentences

A series of short, abrupt sentences often sounds awkward.

Eliminate choppy sentences by adding details or by combining ideas.

Sometimes sentences sound abrupt because they include too few details, making them sound plain and uninformative.

431

Short sentences with scanty information can be improved by fleshing them out with details. Modifying words and phrases, appositives, and clauses lengthens these sentences while expanding their ideas. Be sure that the new information is relevant.

The following examples illustrate the different kinds of details that you can add.

LENGTHENING SHORT SENTENCES BY ADDING DETAILS

Short Sentence: The worker hammered tiles onto the roof.

With Adjectives and an Adverb Added	The worker busily hammered fresh, green tiles onto the old roof.
With Prepositional Phrases Added	For nearly an hour, the worker hammered tiles onto the roof of the old barn.
With a Verbal Phrase Added	Defying the searing sun, the worker hammered tiles onto the roof.
With an Appositive Phrase Added	The worker, an ancient ranch hand, hammered tiles onto the roof.
With a Clause Added	Although the summer sun burned down all day, the worker hammered tiles onto the roof.

EXERCISE C: Adding Details. Rewrite each of the following sentences, adding details to make them longer as well as more interesting. Underline and label your additions: modifying phrases, appositives, and so on.

EXAMPLE: The cat meowed.

> PREP. PHRASE   ADJ. ADJ.   ADV.
> *For three hours* the *lost tiger* cat meowed *loudly*
> PREP. PHRASE
> *on our doorstep*.

1. Selma looked at each of her friends.
2. We wore purple caps and gowns.
3. Confusion as well as excitement filled the air.
4. We filed in.
5. He approached the foot of the stage.
6. The audience grew silent.

432

7. Our brothers and sisters looked solemn.
8. Our parents beamed.
9. The principal called the first name.
10. It was hard to believe the day had arrived.

EXERCISE D: Adding Details and Combining Ideas. Rewrite the passage to correct a series of short, choppy sentences. Add details and join ideas to make longer sentences.

(1) The race was over. (2) Sally stumbled to the post. (3) It had been a long five miles. (4) No one had expected her to finish, or even "place." (5) She had shown them. (6) She had worked out for weeks. (7) She had used her training. (8) She had depended on her confidence. (9) She had given all of her energy to this goal. (10) She had now won a personal victory as well as a public one.

Shortening Long Sentences

Long, rambling sentences burden a reader with an overload of ideas. Because too much information is packed into a few sentences, the reader has trouble absorbing the ideas.

Eliminate rambling sentences by separating and regrouping ideas into two or more simpler sentences.

You can improve rambling sentences by dividing them into shorter sentences as in the following chart.

SEPARATING IDEAS IN RAMBLING SENTENCES	
Two Long Compound-Complex Sentences	**Four Shorter Varied Sentences:** **Simple, Compound, Complex, Simple**
Driving on long trips can be physically and mentally fatiguing because for hours drivers must sit in the same position, using the same muscles, and they must	Driving on long trips can be physically and mentally fatiguing. For hours, drivers must sit in the same position, using the same muscles, and they must concentrate on the road. Unless

433

concentrate on the road. Unless they take regular breaks, their leg, back, shoulder, neck, arm, and hand muscles may stiffen or become numb, or even worse, the miles of monotonous macadam can lull their minds to sleep.

they take regular breaks, their leg, back, shoulder, neck, arm, and hand muscles may stiffen or become numb. Even worse, the miles of monotonous macadam can lull their minds to sleep.

Rambling sentences are unusually long compound, complex, or compound-complex sentences. They become easier to follow if they are shortened to sentences with fewer clauses.

Long, rambling sentences can also be improved in another way. Often, when too much information is packed into a few sentences, the ideas sound awkward and confusing. To improve these sentences, you should regroup as well as separate ideas to vary the lengths and to achieve clarity.

The chart shows how a long, rambling sentence can be separated into three shorter ones. Reorganizing as well as separating ideas improves both the rhythm and sense of the passage.

SEPARATING AND REGROUPING IDEAS	
A Long, Rambling Compound-Complex Sentence	**Three Shorter Varied Sentences: Simple, Complex, Complex**
Peter decided to approach the mess in the office, including advertisements, letters, and bills which had accumulated, by first dividing the mail into manageable piles for answering and processing, which Mr. Campbell, his boss, could help him with when he returned, but Peter hoped that he could complete the sorting beforehand.	Peter decided to approach the mess in the office including advertisements, letters, and bills by first dividing the mail into manageable piles. He hoped to complete this sorting before his boss, Mr. Campbell, returned. Then together they could answer the letters and process the bills which had accumulated.

EXERCISE E: Simplifying Long Sentences. Rewrite the following passage by eliminating the rambling sentences. In some of the sentences, separate the thoughts to form sentences with fewer clauses. In others, separate and regroup the ideas. Make sure that the lengths of sentences are varied.

(1) In moving, almost everything that is familiar to a child, except of course members of the family, disappears, leaving the child with a feeling of loss and perhaps without a sense of identity in the new surroundings, and many children at such times attach themselves to certain objects such as a blanket, stuffed animal, or favorite toy, which they have carried with them, because it can serve as a source of comfort and security.
(2) Such attachments can be sensitive stages in a child's development because when the child has become dependent on one particular object, he or she may then resist new things, often holding desperately to the familiar old ones, fearing the type of loss first felt during the move to a new home.

Using Different Sentence Openers and Structures

Although the lengths of sentences may vary, sentences can still sound awkward or monotonous if too many of them have the same kinds of beginnings and structures. For example, a series of sentences all beginning with prepositional phrases may distract a reader. Similarly, a series of compound sentences may sound tedious.

Recognize monotonous writing styles caused by repeating the same sentence openers and sentence structures.

Repeating the same opener in sentence after sentence can create a dull rhythm and can cause a reader to lose interest.

The following passage sounds monotonous because all of the sentences begin in the same way: subject first, then the verb.

Monotonous passage with only subject/ verb openers | Tobias escaped quietly around the corner of the building, but he found that he was not alone. He retreated a few more steps back into the alley as he watched the two figures. They studied a paper and

435

spoke in low voices. The taller one lit a cigarette and looked furtively about him. Tobias held still. He saw the man start and stare toward him through the dusk. Tobias crept backwards down the alley, his eyes never leaving the two men.

A passage can also sound awkward if the writer has overused any particular sentence structure, such as too many complex sentences with adverb clauses, as in the following passage.

Monotonous passage with only complex sentences

As Tobias escaped quietly around the corner of the building, he found that he was not alone. While he retreated a few more steps back into the alley, he watched the two figures study a paper and speak in low voices. When the taller one lit a cigarette, he looked furtively about him. As Tobias held still, he saw the man start and stare toward him through the dusk. When Tobias crept backwards down the alley, his eyes never left the two men.

An effective writing style makes use of varied sentence openers and usually includes some simple, some compound, some complex, and some compound-complex sentences.

Passage with varied sentence openers and structures

As Tobias escaped quietly around the corner of the building, he found that he was not alone. He retreated a few steps back into the alley, and he watched the two figures study a paper as they spoke in low voices. Before long, the taller one lit a cigarette and looked furtively about him. Tobias held still. When he saw the man start and stare toward him, Tobias crept backwards down the alley, his eyes never leaving the two men.

Using Different Sentence Openers. There are many ways to begin sentences to help you achieve a lively sentence style.

Use some of the many options for beginning different sentences in a passage.

In a series of sentences, you should vary your openers. Find the most appropriate sentence beginnings to match your ideas. The following chart shows many of the available possibilities.

436

DIFFERENT WAYS TO BEGIN SENTENCES	
Subject/Verb	Sightseers visited the Great Pyramid.
Adjectives	Worn-out and exhausted, we crawled toward the cave.
Prepositional Phrase	For entertainment, the prince provided clowns and minstrels.
Participial Phrase	Gripping the rope tightly, she completed her ascent to the crow's nest.
Infinitive Phrase	To finish the foundation, we hired a contractor.
Subject with Appositive Phrase	The prophet, a small, withered man, turned to address his assemblage.
Adverb Clause	Before the tide was at its lowest ebb, we returned the rowboats to the boathouse.
One-word Transition	Eventually, light appeared on the horizon.
Transitional Phrase	As a result, the sprinkler system engaged and fire doors closed.
Inverted Order	Within the cloud of galactic dust appeared three huge asteroids.

Using Different Sentence Structures. To achieve sentence variety you should also think about varying the structures of your sentences. Be careful, however, not to let too many words come between the subject and verb of your sentence.

Use some simple, some compound, some complex, and some compound-complex sentences to avoid structural monotony.

Varying length and openers will have some effect upon the structures of your sentences, but you should also specifically check your sentence structures in a passage. Too many sentences of any one structure will stand out awkwardly and detract from your ideas.

In the following passage, the writer has used variety. Notice how different sentence structures enhance the ideas expressed and establish an interesting rhythm.

437

(1) Simple sentence	(1) Snorkeling in tropical waters opens a window on another world. (2) If snorkelers paddle
(2) Complex sentence (Adverb clause)	gently above a coral reef, they will see a colorful garden just below them. (3) Lacy, lavender sea
(3) Compound sentence	fans just like palm fronds wave lazily in the current, and orange, gold, red, and purple coral
(4) Simple sentence	branches up toward the sunlight. (4) Among these underwater trees, fish colored metallic blue, aqua,
(5) Compound-complex sentence	purple, green, orange, yellow, red, and pink drift and flit. (5) When the snorkelers' bubbles and shadows momentarily disturb their world, some of the fish dart to coral caverns, and others swim closer or nibble seaweed nonchalantly.

EXERCISE F: Using Different Sentence Openers. Rewrite the beginning of each sentence below. Use as many different openers as you can, and label the type of opener in each case.

1. Many new houses in the West, in contrast, do not have attics or basements.
2. The child got lost in the crowd at the fair.
3. He sprained his ankle, dashing for a bus.
4. They felt that they could not leave the place until they had fulfilled their obligations.
5. The Red Cross in its Basic First Aid Course teaches three methods to stop bleeding.
6. Mavis was careful not to overwater the begonia to avoid rotting the plant's roots.
7. A six-cylinder engine uses less fuel, not surprisingly, than does one with eight cylinders.
8. The dog, lonely and sad, watched me through the window.
9. Antique jewelry and furniture are smart investments because they appreciate in value rather than depreciate.
10. A faint glimmer appeared through the window.

EXERCISE G: Using Different Sentence Structures. Rewrite the following passage so that it contains simple, compound, complex, and compound-complex sentence structures. In the margin of your paper, identify the structure of each sentence.

(1) I entered the forest as the sun began to set. (2) The shadows were long. (3) I followed a seldom-used path. (4) I felt restless. (5) I had started walking. (6) The forest was cool. (7) The dark branches drooped with the weight of green summer. (8) The leaves fluttered. (9) The brush crackled beneath my feet.

(10) I turned to the left. (11) I walked into a clearing. (12) The grass was short and peppered with dark-colored flowers. (13) I climbed onto a rock. (14) I faced the west. (15) The sun was disappearing into a honey sunset swirl. (16) The clouds shimmered orange. (17) A cool breeze blew the leaves, my hair, and the grass. (18) The sun melted into the trees and soon dropped out of sight. (19) My restlessness was gone. (20) I was at peace.

DEVELOPING WRITING SKILLS: Revising for Variety in Your Sentences. Choose one of the topics that interests you or any other in which you are interested and write a composition of approximately ten sentences. Vary the lengths and use a variety of openers and structures. Then use *three* of the methods that appear below the suggested topics to evaluate the lengths, openers, and structures of your sentences in the short composition you wrote. Revise your sentences to eliminate any weaknesses you discover.

An embarrassing moment	A memorable weather event
Starting over in a new place	Dirtbiking
Handcrafted jewelry	Olympic events

1. Have a reader evaluate whether you have included enough or too much information in each sentence. You may have to flesh out short sentences with more details or break up rambling sentences into simpler groupings of ideas.
2. Read your sentences aloud. If they have a halting, singsong, or faltering rhythm, adjust the lengths, openers, and structures to make the rhythm smooth and pleasing.
3. Identify the opener you used in each sentence. If you used only one or two kinds, rephrase some sentences for variety.
4. Identify the structure of each sentence. Decide whether you have tailored the structure to the idea and whether another structure would be more effective.

15.2 Creating Special Effects

Style is partly determined by the lengths, beginnings, and structures of sentences. It is also determined by how sentences are molded to fit the ideas being expressed. Skilled writers create sentences that please the reader's ear with their rhythm and that suit the ideas. This section explains how to achieve special effects with your sentences by using similar and contrasting patterns, including the effects professional writers achieve by experimenting with their sentences.

Using Different Types of Sentences

When you write sentences in a composition, one of your goals should be to create a variety that holds the reader's interest. Another should be to show your ideas to best advantage. Certain types of sentences—some that you probably use all the time—can highlight your ideas and can affect the speed at which your reader absorbs your ideas.

Consider using different types of sentences to achieve special emphasis for your ideas.

Different types of sentences can be used to achieve emphasis. In a loose sentence, for example, the writer draws the reader's attention to the main idea by placing it first and by placing all modifying phrases and clauses at the end. In a periodic sentence, the writer accents the main idea even more by placing it at the end of the sentence after the modifying phrases and clauses. In a balanced sentence, the writer emphasizes the difference between two or more ideas by using very similar grammatical structures to express them. And in a cumulative sentence, the writer emphasizes the exactness of modifying details by using certain kinds of modifiers and by placing them before, after, or both before and after the main idea. Many of the sentences you write will be loose, periodic, balanced, or cumulative while many others will have some characteristics of more than one of these types of sentences. The following paragraphs introduce each of these types of sentences and discuss their usefulness to you as a writer.

Loose Sentences. A loose sentence follows the common subject-verb-complement order and may conclude with modifying phrases and clauses. A loose sentence can be simple, compound, complex, or compound-complex, but the main idea is always placed at the beginning of the sentence.

Use loose sentences to draw moderate attention to your main ideas.

In a loose sentence the main idea appears first, where the reader immediately notices it. This placement emphasizes the main idea. The details that follow the main idea add information to it.

EXAMPLES: The Great Depression left thousands desperate because their source of income had disappeared overnight and because many banks collapsed. (Main idea—subordinate clause—subordinate clause)

The drought destroyed the area by shriveling the leaves and baking the ground until dust lay everywhere. (Main idea—modifying phrase—subordinate clause)

Because it is natural to think of the main idea first, you will write many loose sentences. They seem logical to both writers and readers. Loose sentences can be read quickly. But you will want to use other types of sentences as well. You should add details at the beginning and in the middle of your loose sentences to give your writing variety.

Periodic Sentences. In a periodic sentence the main idea is presented at the end. The entire main idea can be presented at the end of the sentence, or just the verb and complement, or even just the complement. By beginning with modifying phrases and clauses and by withholding the main idea, the writer builds suspense and raises the reader's expectations.

Use periodic sentences to lead a reader toward a main idea you want to emphasize strongly.

A periodic sentence builds to the main idea, which is revealed at the end for strong impact. The rest of the sentence prepares for the main idea by leading up to it. Placing the main idea at the end of the sentence underscores that idea. The complex sentence, which begins with its subordinate clause and ends with its main clause, is a common example of a periodic sentence. Some other examples follow.

441

EXAMPLES: Abandoning reason and defying fear, the prisoner
            bolted toward the barbed wire fence. (Modifying
            phrases—main idea)

            Her beauty, her talents, and her famous perfor-
            mances—these were the source of her pride and
            power. (Appositives—main idea)

Because a periodic sentence presents a crafted, packaged thought, it can have a dramatic effect. You should use long, intricate periodic sentences only to build to and emphasize a high point. Too many periodic sentences make your writing heavy-handed.

Balanced Sentences. A balanced sentence presents two or more contrasting main ideas using similar grammatical structures. The structural similarity highlights the contrast in the ideas.

Use balanced sentences to emphasize contrasts between two or more main ideas.

A balanced sentence calls attention to its main ideas by presenting them in parallel phrases or clauses. These repetitious grammatical structures set up a rhythm, which makes the ideas stand out. The parts of a balanced sentence are joined by a coordinate conjunction or a semicolon.

EXAMPLES: She appeared sullen and secretive; her twin
            seemed lively and open. (Main idea—main idea)

            The boy had all the money that he wanted but none
            of the love that he needed. (Complement and mod-
            ifying clause—complement and modifying clause)

Like a periodic sentence, a balanced sentence is a well-shaped thought. You can use it to emphasize ideas, to present weighty thoughts with few words, or to make ideas memorable, but you should use balanced sentences infrequently and only to achieve an effect.

Cumulative Sentences. A cumulative sentence is a variation of the loose sentence. It uses details to develop the main idea. A cumulative sentence consists of a main idea or base clause and layers of descriptive detail. These details are added before and after the main idea. The modifying phrases and clauses that add descriptive details are free modifiers, which can be moved around in the sentence or removed entirely.

442

Use cumulative sentences to emphasize modifying details that develop a main idea.

In a cumulative sentence specific modifiers expand a main idea. The modifiers can be adjectives in a series, prepositional phrases, appositives, verbal phrases, nominative absolutes (verbal phrases with their own subjects), adjective clauses, and adverb clauses. Grouped at the beginning and end of sentences, these color modifiers stand out for the reader.

EXAMPLES: The dryer's drum circled monotonously, flinging the towels and sheets, the shirts and jeans against its moving metal walls, the buttons and zippers clicking with every toss. (Main idea—verbal phrase— nominative absolute)

Its tail arching in a gray plume, its paws clutching an acorn, the squirrel watched us, poised and ready to run. (Nominative absolute—nominative absolute—main idea—adjectives in a series)

As the bus pulled up, a gust of air blasted the curb, stirring up dust, leaves, and scraps in a dirty whirlpool, which stung the eyes of the waiting passengers. (Adverb clause—main idea—verbal phrase— adjective clause)

Cumulative sentences can give your writing a density of detail, particularly when you express action or describe something exactly. They give your writing a varied pace and rhythm that can recreate the movement of the thing you are describing. Use cumulative sentences when you want to elaborate on a main idea and convey exact observations. Interspersing cumulative sentences among the other types makes your writing sophisticated and interesting.

EXERCISE A: Identifying Types of Sentences. Identify each of the following sentences as loose, periodic, balanced, or cumulative.

1. A sloop was loitering in the distance, dropping slowly down with the tide, her sail hanging uselessly against the mast. . . .—Washington Irving

443

2. Let us never negotiate out of fear [but] let us never fear to negotiate.—John F. Kennedy
3. Whenever the rain hangs a gray curtain around the house and pitter-patters on the leaves, I am lulled to sleep.
4. We chose to sit on the far side of the stadium for the big game because that side was in the shade.
5. He was standing there, one hand on his hip, the other holding out at an angle the wooden staff, as tall as he was, to the tip of which clung the soft will-o'-wisp.—Ursula Le Guin
6. The energetic came, eager to put their hands to work; the lazy [came], hoping to live with no work at all.—Eric Sevareid.
7. Sitting at the counter in jeans, dark glasses, and a cowboy hat, which was creased and smudged, was a movie star.
8. He would not have backed into the telephone pole, if the gutters had not been cluttered with broken branches and piles of leaves, if two delivery trucks had not blocked the loading zone, and if he had not been in such a hurry.
9. Their eyes sticking up, exposed and beady, three square-bodied crabs floated along the sand, sideways, like some outer space vehicles exploring the surface of a planet pocked with craters.
10. If the curb had not been cluttered with broken branches and piles of leaves, if two delivery trucks had not blocked the loading zone, and if he had not been in such a hurry, he would not have backed into the telephone pole.

EXERCISE B: Practicing with Different Types of Sentences. Examine magazine articles and short stories to find different types of sentences. Find *two* loose, *two* periodic, *two* balanced, and *two* cumulative sentences. Using them as models, write *two* loose, *two* periodic, *two* balanced, and *two* cumulative sentences. Label each sentence.

Using Different Sentence Patterns

Besides using different types of sentences, you can focus on patterns to make the ideas in your sentences stand out for the reader. Using a series of similar structures to set up a pattern

444

and breaking a pattern by using a different structure are two ways to control and vary the rhythm of your sentences.

Consider using repetition of similar structures and contrast of structures to accentuate your ideas.

Using Structural Similarities. Parallel structures repeat grammatical elements within sentences or within groups of sentences. They set a rhythm, draw the reader's attention to the ideas, and indicate that the ideas belong together.

Use parallel structures within a sentence and in groups of sentences to point out relationships among ideas.

As well as emphasizing contrasting ideas in a balanced sentence, using parallelism with items in a series categorizes the items and intensifies them by adding rhythm through repetition.

Parallelism within sentences	The chimpanzee put on a pair of glasses, hopped up on the desk chair, rolled a piece of paper into the typewriter, turned on the machine, and began typing. (Parallel verbs list the chimpanzee's actions.)
	If you want to go on that trip and if you hope to find a place to stay, you should make your reservations now. (Parallel clauses build intensity and emphasize the warning.)

Parallelism can also create effects in a series of sentences. Two or more consecutive parallel sentences indicate that the ideas are equal or related in some way. The following passage begins with a main idea. The structural similarity of the following three sentences emphasizes that many reasons exist for keeping the medical facility open.

Parallelism within a group of sentences	Residents of the Dalewood district can't afford to allow the Dalewood Medical Clinic to close. No similar facility exists near the residential area. No downtown hospital offers a ready local ambulance. And no other facility could replace the personalized service and treatment that area residents have come to trust.

445

Using Structural Differences. Deliberately breaking a pattern within a sentence or a group of sentences draws the reader's attention to the idea contained in the structural contrast.

Use a contrasting structure to emphasize an idea or to present a concluding thought.

Contrast in length and structure can signal a new idea, an opposing idea, or a final idea. A reader becomes accustomed to the rhythm of similar structures. Breaking the pattern heightens the impact of the new idea through contrast. The example below builds intensity through parallel structures, reaching a climax in the final contrasting structure.

Contrasting structures within a sentence	Angered by the constant yapping of her neighbor's dog, exhausted from too little sleep, and terrified by her friend's disappearance, the old woman sat down on the sofa and cried.

A structural contrast coming at the end of a series of sentences can please or startle a reader and announce a final important idea. The following passage contains a final sentence that breaks the pattern. Its short, direct structure hits the reader with the main idea of the passage.

Ending a passage with a structural contrast	He ran across the slippery grass and disappeared under the ropy curtain of the willow branches. He had spent many hours in this hideout, playing card games, reading, and talking to imaginary friends. He took a deep breath to inhale the scent of the tree and scanned the lawn, the hedges, and the patio until he focused on the waiting car. He would never return.

EXERCISE C: Using Structural Similarities. Write several sentences or a passage in which you use structural similarities to underscore relationships among ideas.

EXERCISE D: Using Structural Differences. Write a passage with a pattern that readers will find appropriate and comfortable. Then break the pattern with a contrasting sentence structure.

Using Professional Models

Professional writers craft their sentences to achieve rhythms, emphasis, and subtly successful patterns. Study sentences they write to develop your own stylistic preferences.

Examine and learn from the kinds of sentences that professional writers use.

When you read, certain sentences and passages will impress you. You may notice the rhythm, the boldness or subtlety of the ideas, or some striking pattern. By analyzing the sentences and patterns, you can gather ideas for your writing.

Notice how the writer of the passage below connects a character and nature by using loosely parallel clauses and then how the writer changes the structure to reflect the character's unhappiness.

Passage with loosely parallel clauses	How dreary the moonlight is! robbed of all its tenderness and repose by the hard driving wind. The trees are harassed by that tossing motion, when they would like to be at rest; the shivering grass makes her quake with sympathetic cold; and the willows by the pool, bent low and white under that invisible harshness, seem agitated and helpless like herself. But she loves the scene the better for its sadness: there is some pity in it. It is not like that hard unfeeling happiness of lovers, flaunting in the eyes of misery.—George Eliot

Notice the variety of sentences and the positioning of ideas and rhythm in this passage.

(1) Cumulative sentence (2) Loose sentence (3) Periodic sentence (4) Short, loose sentence	(1) Sparkling eyes, blond hair, bare little arms and legs—that imp of a Tina darted across the room to open the glass doors of the balcony, her childish laughter escaping in muffled giggles. (2) She had started to turn the knob when a hoarse growl, like that of a wild beast surprised in his lair, quickly stopped her. (3) Petrified with fear, she turned around to stare into the room. (4) Everything was dark.—Adapted from Luigi Pirandello

You might recreate the structures and rhythms of the passage in some of your own writing, as in the following example.

(1) Cumulative sentence
(2) Loose sentence
(3) Periodic sentence
(4) Short, loose sentence

(1) Sneakers pounding on hard flooring, our books clutched tightly for quick flight, we raced for the nearest door to escape the dusk of the locker room and the soap drawing of Coach Barnes decorating the shower, our gasps and chuckles nearly doubling us over. (2) Jay reached the exit while we bobbed nervously behind. (3) Piercing the gloom behind us, a shrill whistle issuing from the faculty room we had just passed caused us to turn in unison. (4) There stood Coach Barnes.

EXERCISE E: Using Models of Professional Writing. Find passages that you have read and enjoyed. Make copies of three passages with striking sentence patterns. Use any of the models to write a passage of your own on any topic. Use the types of sentences that the writer used, and follow a pattern similar to that in the model.

DEVELOPING WRITING SKILLS: Experimenting with Types of Sentences and Patterns for Effects. Write a passage of about ten sentences. Use some loose, balanced, periodic, and cumulative sentences, and try to use parallelism and contrast. Feel free to use professional models.

Skills Review and Writing Workshop

Sentence Style

CHECKING YOUR SKILLS

Revise the following paragraph by improving the short, choppy sentences. Combine sentences where possible and expand others by adding details.

(1) Noise can be dangerous. (2) Most people accept noise as a normal part of life. (3) They can suffer permanent hearing loss from noise. (4) Young people are especially susceptible to ear damage. (5) They like amplified rock music. (6) They like souped-up cars and roaring motorcycles. (7) Noise-caused damage is not only to the ears. (8) Noise can cause blood-vessel damage, headaches, stomach problems, and mental fatigue. (9) We can design quieter products. (10) We can pass stricter laws.

USING COMPOSITION SKILLS
Writing a Trip Report

Business people and community leaders who make field trips to gain information must know how to write brief, well-organized reports. Imagine you have taken a field trip to visit your state legislature. Write an effective, one-paragraph report to present to your class by following the steps below.

Prewriting: Think of the purpose of the trip. List what you learned and experienced. Include possible negative factors. Decide whether you would recommend the trip for other classes.

Writing: Begin your report with an introductory statement. Then write a topic sentence that states your main idea. Follow up with supporting details and your final recommendations.

Revising: Be sure that your sentences are varied in length, structure, and openers and that your sentences are arranged in logical order. Use the checklist on page 386 to polish your paragraph. After you have revised, proofread carefully.

16

Clear Thinking in Writing

Even well-written sentences cannot function alone; they depend on the connections between them. Therefore, you must use transitions and other connecting words, as well as grouping your ideas in logical patterns. This chapter examines words that link ideas logically, pitfalls that weaken logical connections among ideas, and patterns of logical reasoning.

16.1 Connecting Ideas Clearly

Sentences move an idea from the beginning to the end of a passage. As you work through these sentences, use words that will establish logical connections between them. Transitions and coordinating and subordinating words help to make relationships among ideas clearer and guide a reader through your thoughts. This section discusses connecting sentences clearly.

Using Transitions

Because a reader expects to follow your overall idea from sentence to sentence through a passage, you must connect each stage of your thinking clearly with the next.

Use transitions to establish relationships among ideas and to clarify the order of ideas.

You may not need transitions in every sentence, but most passages will need *some* transitions to guide the reader. Without them, a passage sounds clumsy and its ideas can be difficult to follow. In the following passage, the thought is complete, but the sentences sound disjointed and confusing.

Passage without transitions

> Trains and buses take about the same amount of time to travel from one place to another. The rides are very different. Riding on a bus is much like riding in a car. A bus is nothing more than a huge car traveling down the highway with twenty-five back seats. A train chugs and hums in a rhythm all its own. Trains are more contained than buses. Riding on a train is like entering a new world, complete unto itself.

Transitions can help clarify relationships. Adding transitions to the preceding passage sharpens the comparison/contrast and makes it flow more smoothly, as the following passage shows.

Passage with transitions

> Trains and buses take about the same amount of time to travel from one place to another. The rides, however, are very different. First of all, riding on a bus is much like riding in a car. In fact, a bus is nothing more than a huge car traveling down the highway with twenty-five back seats. On the other hand, a train chugs and hums in a rhythm all its own. Furthermore, trains are more self-contained than buses. Riding on a train is like entering a new world, complete unto itself.

Transitions can establish both time relationships and spatial relationships among ideas, as the following chart indicates.

TRANSITIONS GROUPED BY PURPOSE			
Time Relationship		**Spatial Relationship**	
first, second, third	later, now	outside	before
next, last	during	inside	ahead
before	earlier	beyond	beneath
finally	after	here	near
meanwhile	then	behind	above

451

Comparison or Contrast		Cause and Effect	
however	nevertheless	thus	so
yet	in like manner	then	because of
likewise	on the contrary	therefore	on account of
similarly	instead	as a result	since
nonetheless	conversely	accordingly	consequently
Addition		**Emphasis**	
also	second	indeed	in other words
besides	as well	in fact	especially
too	in addition	even	
moreover	furthermore		
Examples			
for instance	as an illustration	that is	also
for example		namely	in particular

The following groups of sentences show ways to connect two thoughts logically with transitions. Notice how transitions clarify the relationship among the ideas.

TIME: The pilot switched on the intercom. *Then* he addressed the passengers.

SPATIAL: Two chicks scratched in the gravel. *Overhead*, the hawk waited.

CONTRAST: Doris hates to sing in public. *Yet* she has a beautiful voice.

RESULT: Water trickled over the sandstone for ages. *Inevitably* it wore the rock away.

ADDITION: Today is the last day to enroll in the crafts course. *Moreover*, we will not offer it again.

EMPHASIS: He knew how to be a brilliant host. *Even* his cats looked happy to see us.

EXAMPLE: She was a regal-looking woman. *In particular*, she carried herself in a queenly way.

EXERCISE A: Adding Transitions. Connect each pair of sentences with a transition. Then state the relationship created.

EXAMPLE: I waited for Hans in the bus station. He walked in looking worried.

              I waited for Hans in the bus station. *Eventually,* he walked in looking worried. (time)

1. We sat dejectedly by the window. Rain poured in torrents.
2. The announcer told fans not to enter the field of play. He instructed youths along the sidelines to take seats.
3. Reacting to soaring prices of gasoline and oil, many people will purchase smaller cars. Some will rebuild older cars and modify them to improve efficiency.
4. An unexpected strike by air traffic controllers kept planes on the ground and caused long delays. My father was unable to attend my brother's graduation.
5. John took the dog for a walk. He left to go to the theater.
6. I was so angry at Angela that I could not speak. I hoped never to speak to her again.
7. The Prime Minister was quite contemptuous of treaties. He never honored them.
8. Prospect Hill's football team has earned considerable public attention. Newton High's team has received a great deal of coverage in the media.
9. Intermissions provide important opportunities for stage managers. They can use the time to oversee costume changes, or they can attend to the change of scenery.
10. Horoscopes have offered intriguing, sometimes astounding, predictions. Little scientific evidence exists to explain why some are accurate.

Using Coordination and Subordination

Coordination and subordination clarify connections between ideas. *Coordination* joins related and equal words, phrases, and clauses within a single sentence. It is especially useful in forming compound sentences. *Subordination* joins unequal but related ideas in clauses within a sentence. It enables you to form complex sentences.

Use coordination and subordination to connect related ideas within sentences.

Coordination and subordination provide logical connections in a passage. Without them, writing is awkward and repetitious; the ideas do not flow smoothly from sentence to sentence.

Passage lacking coordination and subordination	Bikers may find long distance bicycle racing an exhilarating and exhausting sport. It is not meant for the "pleasure biker" either. The preparation for a typical race over a fifty-mile course is grueling. Bikers must build their endurance. They must ride for several hours every day. They must train in all kinds of weather all through the year. These hardships are all accepted in the love of the sport.

With coordinating and subordinating words added, the reader can grasp connections easily, and passage sounds smoother.

Passage with ideas connected using coordination and subordination	Bikers may find long distance bicycle racing an exhilarating and exhausting sport, although it is neither for the beginner nor for the "pleasure biker." The preparation for a typical race over a fifty-mile course is grueling because bikers must build their endurance; they must ride for several hours every day, and they must train in all kinds of weather, all through the year. These hardships are all accepted in the love of the sport.

Coordination. *And, but, or,* and other coordinating conjunctions can join equally important ideas within a sentence, telling the reader that a relationship exists between these ideas.

Use coordinating words to join equal, related ideas in a compound sentence.

The chart on the following page lists the most frequently used methods of coordination: coordinating conjunctions, correlative conjunctions, conjunctive adverbs, and semicolons. Notice that conjunctive adverbs are also transitions. When they join two main clauses in compound sentences, they must be used with semicolons. Semicolons can also be used without conjunctive adverbs to show a close relationship between ideas.

454

COORDINATING DEVICES	
Coordinating Conjunctions	**Correlative Conjunctions**
and but or nor yet so	either . . . or neither . . . nor not only . . . but also
Conjunctive Adverbs (and semicolons)	**Semicolons Alone**
; nevertheless, ; moreover, ; consequently, ; otherwise, ; ; however, ; indeed,	

As you use these words, be aware that they can establish relationships like addition, contrast, and cause and effect. Notice how coordinating words are used in the examples below.

COORDINATING CONJUNCTION: Two hundred people waited patiently, *but* the line would not move.

CORRELATIVE CONJUNCTIONS: *Not only* were the ticket sellers inexperienced and slow, *but* the patrons *also* seemed to be taking their time.

CONJUNCTIVE ADVERB: Ticket holders were warned that seats might not be available to everyone; *therefore,* some people gave up and left.

SEMICOLON ALONE: Many who stayed were disappointed; the tickets ran out early.

Subordination. Rather than giving equal weight to all your ideas, emphasize the main points by putting them in the main clauses, while subordinating the less important ideas by putting them in dependent (adjective or adverb) clauses. This indicates the relative weight of your various ideas and increases the variety and fluidity of your sentences.

Use subordinating words to join ideas in a complex sentence and to clarify the relationships between ideas of unequal importance.

The following chart shows how subordinating words can establish different relationships between ideas.

SUBORDINATING WORDS			
Comparisons		**Addition or Identification**	
as though	just as	that	where
as if	as much as	which	whom
as well as		who	whose
Time Relationships		**Cause and Effect**	
after	until	because	whether
whenever	when	so that	provided that
before	while	in order that	
since	as soon as		
Contrasts			
though	whereas	although	

When you connect ideas with subordination, choose the word that best clarifies the connection. Also, indicate the importance of an idea by making it the main clause and putting details in the adjective or adverb clause, as in the example below. The less important idea is always placed immediately after the subordinating word.

TIME: *As soon as* I entered the room, I smelled something burning.

COMPARISON: The children liked the mime *as much as* the actor.

CONTRAST: *Although* he is hot-tempered, I enjoy his company.

CAUSE: *Because* firetrucks were delayed by traffic, the fire spread to an adjacent building.

IDENTIFICATION: I wrote to my sister, *who* lives on the West Coast.

Correcting Problems with Coordination and Subordination. Do not join too many clauses in a single sentence; *excessive* coordination or subordination confuses a reader. You

456

must also make sure that the clauses go together sensibly; *illogical* coordination or subordination muddles your meaning. Finally, you should not use coordination where subordination would be clearer. *Inappropriate* coordination can weaken the presentation of your ideas.

Use coordination and subordination in moderation, in logical places, and at appropriate times.

Notice how the following passage rambles because of too many *and*'s, *but*'s, and *so*'s, and too many subordinating words that are unnecessary.

Excessive use of coordinating and subordinating words	I sat in the coffee shop *because* I was expecting Carol to meet me, *but* she was late *so* I stirred my coffee mechanically *and* wondered what was keeping Carol, *who* is always prompt, *and* I knew that the shop would soon close, *and so* I walked to a pay phone, where I could call, *because* I was worried.

With appropriate coordinating and subordinating words, the passage is easier to follow and less awkward.

Appropriate coordination and subordination	I sat in the coffee shop expecting Carol to meet me, but she was late. Mechanically, I stirred my coffee and wondered what was keeping her. She is always prompt. Because I knew that the shop would soon close and because by now I was worried, I walked to a pay phone to call her.

In compound sentences, make sure that the ideas are equal and related. Then, choose the appropriate conjunction.

WEAK COORDINATION:	Nobody expected Joe to finish the race, *and* he awed us by winning.
IMPROVED COORDINATION:	Nobody expected Joe to finish the race, *but* he awed us by winning.

Similarly, when you use subordination, set up a precise, logical relationship between the clauses. Your main idea should be in the main clause; your dependent clause should modify the main clause.

ILLOGICAL PLACEMENT:	*Because* her leaps and turns finally reached perfection, she studied under Dame Weston.
LOGICAL PLACEMENT:	Her leaps and turns finally reached perfection *because* she studied under Dame Weston.
ILLOGICAL WORD CHOICE:	Janice received an "A" for the course *since* she had been ill during the term.
LOGICAL WORD CHOICE:	Janice received an "A" for the course *although* she had been ill during the term.

Avoid depending so heavily on coordination that you overlook the opportunity to express relationships through subordination. The compound sentence below does not indicate which idea is more important than the other. By subordinating one clause, a cause and effect relationship is established.

WEAK COORDINATION:	I exercised regularly for a month, *and* I made the tennis team for the first time.
CLEAR SUBORDINATION:	*Because* I exercised regularly for a month, I made the tennis team for the first time.

EXERCISE B: Using Coordination. Rewrite each of the pairs of sentences below, joining equal and related ideas. Underline the coordinating word that you use to connect each pair.

EXAMPLE: Hastings yelled at the top of his lungs. We could not hear him over the sirens.

Hastings yelled at the top of his lungs, <u>but</u> we could not hear him over the sirens.

1. Richard must pitch our team to victory. We will be eliminated from the county championship game.
2. Michele is two inches taller than her mother. She is smaller than her sister.
3. Dr. Martin discovered a new technique for formulating molecules. She was awarded a grant to continue her research.

458

4. Machiavelli urged the princes not to oppress the people. He believed that a prince should do whatever is necessary to retain his power and position.
5. Simon arrived late for the performance and realized that he had forgotten his glasses. He had forgotten his ticket.
6. Henry VIII married Catherine of Aragon. He divorced her to marry Anne Boleyn.
7. Jill walked to the field house. She signed up for the team.
8. Casey must construct a four-foot fence around the pond. A neighbor's child might wander near and fall in.
9. Selfishness is unattractive. It is contagious.
10. Dr. Weiner was thankful and relieved to find a taxi. He tipped the driver handsomely.

EXERCISE C: Using Subordination. Rewrite each pair of sentences, using subordination. Underline the subordinating word in each sentence.

EXAMPLE: My cousin lived in a noisy dorm at the university. He had trouble studying in his room.

My cousin, <u>who</u> lived in a noisy dorm at the university, had trouble studying in his room.

1. The airliner lost altitude rapidly. Passengers panicked.
2. My sister stepped through the door into the darkened room. Everyone jumped out and yelled, "Surprise!"
3. Modern dramas often contain scores of characters. Classical Greek plays included no more than a handful.
4. Thomas could not locate his keys. He became angry with himself.
5. A specialist will treat only a certain set of problems. An internist practices general medicine.
6. The storm had passed and flood waters had receded. Rescue teams flew into the stricken valley.
7. The mayor could not win the party's bid. She was popular with the townspeople.
8. Mature trees can survive almost any weather condition or change. Saplings are much more vulnerable.
9. A quiche can turn out lumpy, or even "fall" in the oven. Use an electric blender to mix your ingredients.
10. We finally could sit down to dinner. The telephone rang.

EXERCISE D: Correcting Problems with Coordination and Subordination. Rewrite the passages to correct excessive, illogical, or inappropriate coordination or subordination.

1. Anthony had reservations for a flight that was going to San Diego, but first he had to catch a bus to Chicago, and since the bus was late, he missed the plane as a result.
2. After you check your gas gauge, start the engine and engage your gears.
3. The sun was brighter on the front of the building, and we decided to take the picture on the front steps.
4. The Pope recognized Petrarch's accomplishments as a poet, but Petrarch was designated "poet laureate."
5. Our teacher assigned us an additional problem until we could have more practice.
6. Since a fuse blew out, Lin joined wires inside the radio.
7. When my brother and I went hiking in the mountains so that we might enjoy ourselves, we wanted to hike fifty miles, but not only did we find the hiking strenuous but also the weather became threatening.
8. The mayor instituted a curfew because we could not leave the house after 10:00 p.m.
9. Kristin was happy that Cynthia had offered to drive her into town, and she was not too sure whether or not to accept because she had planned to collect pond water along her walk so that she could bring paramecium samples to biology class on Monday so she declined though she would have enjoyed Cynthia's company.
10. Our star player was benched for the remainder of the game, and the rest of us managed a slim victory.

Using Logical Order

In addition to using transitions, coordination, and subordination, you can establish logical patterns to direct a reader through a series of ideas in a sentence or passage. Readers recognize the basic patterns of thinking and follow them easily in a single sentence or a series.

Whenever possible, use logical orders to make a series of ideas easier to follow.

A series of events, for example, should be presented in the order in which they occur. Arrange visual details in a clear spatial order. Present the steps in a process in the order a reader would follow to repeat the process. Notice the various orders below.

CHRONOLOGICAL ORDER: The skies darkened; a strong wind blew; rain began to fall; and we ran for cover.

SPATIAL ORDER: The first twenty stories of the building were ordinary gray granite. But as the eye climbed higher, the architecture became increasingly ornate. Strips of shining steel gleamed like icicles on the upper floors. The whole structure narrowed to a tower at the top, trimmed with rainbow arcs piled one on top of another.

ORDER OF IMPORTANCE: To quit smoking, one can chew gum as a substitute, avoid the temptation for "just one," and hold fast to self-discipline.

COMPARISON AND CONTRAST ORDER: Both champions play serve-and-volley tennis and display superb form. What distinguishes them from each other is that one relies on safe, sure strokes, the other prefers variety and change of pace.

EXERCISE E: Establishing Logical Patterns. Choose a logical pattern for each item below and rewrite it. Identify the order you have chosen. You may have to alter the items as you rewrite them.

1. I rose from my desk, finished my homework, and turned on the television.
2. Knowing that his big brother would accompany him to camp, Arnold felt proud, surprised, even glad.
3. On our family's drive across the country last summer, we especially enjoyed Nevada, Pennsylvania, Montana, and Illinois.

4. Edward mixed the ingredients thoroughly, set the pan in the oven, assembled the milk, eggs, flour, and sugar, and poured the batter into a cake pan.
5. A dramatic economic slowdown, a brutal civil war, and foreign censure beset the nation almost immediately.
6. I could not stand my new dorm room. The floors were covered with linoleum of a faded floral pattern; several corners were chipped or upturned. The ceiling needed painting, and a single uncovered light bulb cast a clinical glare over the rest of the room. The walls were painted a sickly green, and the small window lacked shades or blinds.
7. The squirrels darted in ten different directions. We startled them when we opened the cellar door. They looked at us for a split second in nervous alertness.
8. The annual town meeting dealt with topics from the absurdly petty to the issue that frightened most residents. Almost everyone had something to say about the gruesome statistic: One household in three had been robbed or vandalized within the past six months. A few people spoke of the need for street repairs. One elderly gentleman reprimanded the Chief of Police for not finding a lost cat. Several people raised the issue of power shortages, which have caused food to spoil.
9. Finally, he decided to run for office. Months before the primaries, his colleagues in the State House urged James Monroe to become a candidate. He knew that his credentials were sound, and support seemed available. At first he discounted the notion, but slowly the advice of his friends and family began to sound plausible.
10. Skicrafts are engineered to glide over the surface with minimal water resistance. The major difference between skicrafts and Boston whalers lies in their purpose. Boston whalers are engineered for capacity. Designed for speed, skicrafts are excellent for racing. Unlike skicrafts, whalers hold a number of passengers, and their most popular uses are for moderate-speed cruising and for fishing.

DEVELOPING WRITING SKILLS: Checking Your Writing for Logical Connections and Order. Write a passage of 150 to 200 words. Read it carefully with these questions in mind:

Have you linked ideas smoothly from sentence to sentence using transitions? Have you joined clauses containing related ideas with coordinating or subordinating words? Have you used moderate, logical, and appropriate coordination and subordination? Do your items or ideas follow a logical order?

Avoiding Problems in Logic 16.2

Once you begin connecting and organizing ideas within and between sentences confidently, you can use whole patterns of reasoning as you develop ideas. This section explores new ways of presenting ideas that will help you avoid weaknesses in reasoning and examines the work of professional writers to help you gather ideas for your own compositions.

Understanding the Direction of Your Thoughts

In writing, three patterns of reasoning often will provide a logical framework for your ideas: *induction,* which leads from specific information to a general conclusion; *deduction,* which leads from a general truth to a specific instance of it; and *cause and effect.*

Induction. One method of presenting your ideas is the inductive approach.

Use induction by presenting concrete evidence before stating your conclusion or main point.

Induction relies on evidence—facts, statistics, examples—that points to a logical conclusion. If your phone is out of order and your neighbors' phones do not work, you can conclude *inductively* that service in your area is cut off. You cannot prove it because you cannot test every phone in town, but you can be reasonably certain of your conclusion. Induction allows a fair sampling of evidence without total proof.

In writing, you can present evidence and a conclusion reached on the basis of the evidence. The inductive conclusion is a general truth based on specific supporting evidence.

In the following passage, inductive reasoning leads the reader through specific evidence to a general conclusion.

Inductive approach	The students in Room 121 seem to work more briskly at a temperature of 70°F. (21.1°C) than at the temperature of 75°F. (23.9°C) to which they had previously been accustomed. In Room 120, class discussions have become more animated at a room temperature of 65°F. (18.3°C) than they had been at 75°F. (23.9°C). And in Room 113, test scores improved significantly at a daily temperature of 68°F. (20°C). As a result of this evidence, the superintendent of schools has concluded that moderately lower temperatures improve student performance.
Evidence	
Conclusion	

Deduction. Another approach to presenting ideas logically is deductive reasoning. While induction begins with specific cases and leads to principles, deduction begins with principles and leads to specific cases. You use deduction when you apply your knowledge and experience to understanding a new thing. In your life so far, you have observed laws of nature, patterns of behavior, and other general principles that help you to predict what will happen in certain circumstances. For example, you know that the prefix *semi-* means *half*; when you see a new word beginning with *semi-*, you *deduce* that it means a thing that is half of something else.

When using deductive reasoning in your writing, you should begin with an accepted truth that does not need to be proven, then give examples that follow the principle. Finally, you should conclude that the examples represent instances of the general truth.

Use deduction by establishing a general principle and then drawing conclusions about specific examples of that principle.

In the statements that follow on this page and on the next page, a general observation is followed by a specific instance. The conclusion makes a prediction on the basis of the observation.

GENERAL PRINCIPLE: Professional basketball players usually retire well before they reach their fortieth birthdays.

SPECIFIC EXAMPLE: Matt Eliott, a professional basketball player, is thirty-eight years old.

464

CONCLUSION: Therefore, Matt Eliott's career as a professional basketball player is probably nearing its end.

Here are some other examples of deductive method.

GENERAL PRINCIPLE: Oak is a golden brown hardwood with a pronounced grain.

SPECIFIC EXAMPLE: My desk is made of hardwood that is golden brown and has a pronounced grain.

CONCLUSION: My desk is made of oak.

GENERAL PRINCIPLE: Most college teachers who hold the rank of professor have doctorates.

SPECIFIC EXAMPLE: My next door neighbor is a professor at the City University.

CONCLUSION: My next door neighbor probably has a doctorate.

In some cases, a general truth is always and absolutely true; in others, it is true *most* of the time. Be careful to phrase statements as either absolutes or probabilities, depending on the degree of truth you wish to express.

Deductive reasoning is used as the structure of the following passage.

Deductive approach general principle

Specific examples

Conclusions made by applying the general principles to the specific examples

Sound travels at the speed of 1,080 feet per second, a rate much slower than the speed of light. Perhaps the best example of the comparatively slow speed of sound is found during an electrical storm. When the storm is directly overhead, you see a flash of lightning a split second before you hear the thunderclap. When the storm is farther away, there is an even greater gap between the lightning and the thunder. Given the knowledge about the speed of sound and light, you can estimate the distance of the storm by counting the number of seconds between the lightning and the thunder. Since a mile is 5,280 feet, and sound travels at a rate of less than 1,100 feet per second, it takes slightly less than five seconds for the sound of thunder to travel one mile. You can also tell how fast the storm is approaching or moving away by paying attention to changes in the length of time between the lightning flash and the thunderclap.

Cause and Effect. *Cause and effect* is another pattern of reasoning that can establish order among your ideas. By stating that one condition "causes" another and that another condition "causes" still another, you set up a logical pattern.

Use a cause and effect approach by showing the logical cause and effect relationships among your ideas.

Cause and effect reasoning appears most frequently in scientific and historical writing, but is also used in other writing situations, such as the following example.

STATEMENT OF CAUSE AND EFFECT: As a result of the injury that disabled the star quarterback for the first part of the season, our football team got off to a slow start and lost its first four games.

When using cause and effect reasoning, establish clear and convincing connections between the causes and the effects. Remember that something that *precedes* something else does not necessarily *cause* it. Finally, feel free to mention the effect *before* the cause, as in the following example.

EFFECT STATED BEFORE CAUSE: Our football team got off to a slow start this year and lost its first four games largely as a result of the injury that disabled the star quarterback during the first part of the season.

Cause and effect structures can be limited to single sentences or developed throughout several sentences or even throughout an entire passage. Notice how the following passage is developed largely through the use of cause and effect reasoning.

Cause
Effect
Cause
Effect
Whenever I am given time to pose for a photograph, I always end up looking frozen, with glazed eyes and a strained smile. On the other hand, when I am caught in an absolutely candid shot, my mouth is always gaping open and my eyes are closed in mid-blink. The happy medium seems to

466

Cause
Effect

be a shot in which I am given about one second's warning. That second gives me time to shut my mouth and open my eyes, but not enough time to arrange my face into my usual painful grin. I manage to look natural but not uncouth, poised but not rigid.

EXERCISE A: Using Induction. Write a passage of 100 to 500 words using induction to reach one of the following conclusions.

1. Ultimately, people pay for wrongdoings they commit.
2. Any ride in an amusement park will make me ill.
3. Well-trained dogs function as protectors for their owners.
4. Last-minute studying leads to academic dissatisfaction.
5. The police in our neighborhood are reasonable people.

EXERCISE B: Using Deduction. Lead deductively from one of these principles to an example, and conclusions about the example.

1. Liquids freeze if the temperature drops sufficiently.
2. Cleanliness is important to good health.
3. In murder mystery novels, the most obvious suspect is seldom the real murderer.
4. Plants must be raised under the proper conditions if they are to grow.
5. Solids can be made to dissolve more quickly in water if the water is heated.

EXERCISE C: Showing Cause and Effect Relationships. On your paper, rewrite the statements below, connecting causes and effects.

1. The costs of construction have gone up tremendously. Fewer new buildings are being built. The prices of houses are escalating. People are finding it more difficult to buy their own homes. The demand for rental housing is increasing. Rents are rapidly going up.
2. The weather was hot and dry. A camper dropped a hot coal in a pile of leaves. A fire started. There was a high wind. The fire spread to the trees in the forest. The forest was al-

467

most entirely burnt down. Later that year, it rained heavily. Flooding occurred. There were no trees to hold the ground in place. There were many mud slides. A number of houses were swept away.

Identifying Errors in Logic

When you write, you must provide all the information and connections your reader needs. To write clearly you must avoid gaps, pitfalls, and errors in logic.

Contradictions. A *contradiction* is an assertion or observation that makes some other statement questionable. You may fail to choose your words carefully and therefore make a statement that contradicts preceding statements.

The contradiction in the following passage results from the failure to clarify certain details.

Passage with a contradiction

The loudspeaker announced that our plane had developed mechanical trouble and would not leave for Dallas until 6:15 P.M. With almost two hours to wait, we ate a leisurely supper in the cafeteria and then strolled along the arcade, chatting and window shopping. We checked through the security gate with time to spare and took off at 5:30 P.M., almost on time.

The contradiction can be corrected by adding details, as in the passage below.

Passage with consistent information

As we entered the terminal, the loudspeaker announced that our plane had developed mechanical trouble and would not leave for Dallas until 6:15 P.M. With almost two hours to wait, we ate a leisurely supper in the cafeteria and then strolled along the arcade, chatting and window shopping. *At 4:45 the loudspeaker announced that a replacement plane had landed.* We checked through the security gate with time to spare and took off at 5:30 P.M., almost on time.

False Assumptions. When you present a series of ideas, you risk overlooking a point that your reader needs. *You* know

468

what you mean; a reader knows only what you write. You must not overlook steps and information or assume that a few words about a vital idea will convey the full meaning you have in mind.

Avoid false assumptions by clarifying all ideas and giving all information your reader needs to follow your thinking.

A false assumption leaves a gap in the development of ideas, forcing the reader to guess what you had in mind. To avoid this problem, reread your work from the reader's point of view. Pretend that you know nothing about the topic; see if your sentences give you enough information.

In the following passage, a writer left out an important connection, creating a gap in understanding.

Unstated idea   Mr. Jackson was appointed vice president in charge of Marketing at the August meeting of the board of directors. Because of Mr. Jackson's record, board opinion was split evenly, but the president's vote broke the tie, and Mr. Jackson was promoted.

To correct a false assumption, you must add the ideas or information necessary that will enable the reader to make all important mental connections and to comprehend your meaning fully.

In a revision of the passage about Mr. Jackson, the writer has corrected the assumption.

Necessary information provided   Mr. Jackson was appointed vice president in charge of Marketing at the August meeting of the board of directors. *His achievement record, however, raised some doubts about his abilities. During his previous tenure as director of Marketing at the branch office, sales had dropped rather sharply in his area.* Because of Mr. Jackson's record, board opinion was split evenly, but the president's vote broke the tie, and Mr. Jackson was promoted.

Hasty Generalizations. A hasty generalization is an idea that is stated without sufficient information or reasoning to support it. Like false assumptions, hasty generalizations create gaps in logical structure, weakening what you say. Unless you are absolutely certain of your facts, avoid such words as *always, never, all,* and *none*.

Avoid hasty generalizations by stating your points precisely and backing them up with the necessary support.

By definition, a hasty generalization is untrue because it overlooks exceptions. It misrepresents your actual intent by overstating the point you want to make.

To determine if you have written a hasty generalization, ask yourself if the idea is true just as you have stated it. If it is not, add specific details or qualifying words to allow for exceptions.

In the following passage, the statement *Nobody seems to care anymore* is a hasty generalization. There are people who *do* care. Also, the statement adds no helpful information to the passage.

Passage with hasty generalization
What has happened to that old slogan, "Service with a smile"? Nobody seems to care any more. It is very frustrating to bring a television set to a repair shop, to be kept waiting for fifteen minutes, and then to be told impatiently to leave it with no assurance of when it will be ready.

To improve the passage, the hasty generalization can be left out or altered. When you face that choice, try to rewrite. Your generalization may be a vague version of a worthwhile idea that could be expressed in more precise terms.

In the preceding passage, the word *nobody* can be made specific. Also, the phrase *to care* might be rewritten in more concrete terms. Notice in the following example how the revision of a hasty generalization clarifies the whole passage.

Statements made more precise
What has happened to that old slogan, "Service with a smile"? Too many tradespeople seem overworked and resentful. It is very frustrating to bring a television set to a repair shop, to be kept waiting for fifteen minutes, and then to be told impatiently to leave it with no assurance of when it will be ready.

Begging the Question. Begging the question is the term generally used for the logical fallacy of circular reasoning. You "beg the question" or argue in circles when you simply restate the question instead of answering it.

Avoid begging the question by not mistaking restatements of questions for their answers.

Begging the question is most likely to occur when a writer is attempting to use the pattern of cause and effect reasoning. In begging the question, the writer ends up saying something like *I am happy because I am contented* or *He is wealthy because he has a lot of money*. You must answer any question you pose and not simply express it in slightly different language.

The following statement begs the question.

BEGGING THE QUESTION: I like *Star Wars* because it is my favorite movie.

In the preceding statement, the writer has not answered the question. Following is an example of a real reason.

CIRCULAR REASONING ELIMINATED: I like *Star Wars* because it contains exciting adventures, colorful characters, brilliant special effects, and many funny moments.

Non Sequiturs. A non sequitur is an assertion that does not follow from the preceding ideas.

Avoid non sequiturs by making sure that each new idea you present follows logically from the previous ideas.

The following passage contains a statement that simply does not belong in any logical sense. The third sentence is a non sequitur because it is not logically connected to the preceding ideas.

Passage containing a non sequitur   Teenagers who repeatedly fail their courses often become dropouts. They are then less likely to find satisfying work than their classmates who do graduate. My second cousin, who never finished the tenth grade, ended up as a burglar.

The first two statements in the preceding passage may be accurate, but the last sentence does not follow logically.

To correct a non sequitur, you must eliminate it entirely, realizing that it is an unworkable idea. You may, however, replace it with a more reasonable idea, such as the one that follows.

Non sequitur eliminated
Teenagers who repeatedly fail their courses often become dropouts. They are then less likely to find satisfying work than their classmates who do graduate. As a rule, dropouts are eligible for fewer jobs and are also likely to earn less money over a lifetime than high school graduates.

EXERCISE D: Checking the Logic of Ideas. In each of the following items, identify the error in thinking as a false assumption, hasty generalization, non sequitur, or begging the question. If you believe the item to be logical, write correct on your paper.

EXAMPLE: I like tennis because it's my favorite sport.
              begging the question

1. Jerry ran well in the race, but he lost because of what his opponent did to him. Jerry's coach made an official complaint to the Athletic Board, but the Board voted to sustain the other athlete's victory.
2. Statistics show that automobile accidents have increased on Highway 41. Among these accidents are those involving tractor-trailers. My brother-in-law owns a tractor-trailer that he often drives on Highway 41.
3. I always eat a leisurely breakfast on weekends. We were leaving for the museum at nine o'clock Sunday morning, so I only had time for juice and a roll.
4. Cheating is not right because it is immoral.
5. Newspapers always exaggerate stories in order to create sensations and increase their circulation.
6. Senator Allbright voted against that bill because he was opposed to it.
7. The speed limit was lowered to 55 miles per hour in 1973. Ever since the speed limit was changed, traffic fatalities have dropped sharply. It seems reasonable to conclude that there is a connection between slower driving speeds and the decline in highway deaths.

8. I tried to understand why Mary left the city so quickly. Then I remembered what she had said to me about her brother. I realized why she had had to leave in such a hurry.

9. People who trap lobsters do not begin to catch full-grown lobsters in Maine until the second half of the summer. The lobsters hibernate until that time in soft shells and most of the lobsters that turn up in lobster traps are not full sized. The coast of Maine is especially attractive during the second half of the summer.

10. All television commercials insult the intelligence of the viewer. Commercial writers always assume that their audiences are not intelligent, and they always aim their commercials to appeal to the lowest common denominator.

EXERCISE E: Revising for Logic. Take another look at the items in which you found errors in logic in Exercise D. Rewrite them to form logical statements.

EXAMPLE: I like tennis because it is a fast, highly competitive sport.

Using Professional Models

Professional writers often use logical approaches such as induction and deduction to report the facts behind a conclusion or observation or to develop some concept or theory. Examine whether writers use inductive or deductive lines of reasoning, cause and effect arrangements, or some other pattern that seems clear, deliberate, and precise as you read.

Study the specific ways professional writers use logical thinking to find models for your own writing.

Viktor Frankl's book *Man's Search for Meaning,* for example, contains many passages developed through logical thinking. Notice in the following passage that the line of reasoning is deductive.

Main point   Those who know how close the connection is between the state of mind of a man—his courage and hope, or lack of them—and the state of immunity of

Specific example | his body will understand that the sudden loss of hope and courage can have a deadly effect. The ultimate cause of my friend's death was that the expected liberation did not come and he was severely disappointed. This suddenly lowered his body's resistance

Conclusion | against the latent typhus infection. His faith in the future and his will to live had become paralyzed and his body fell victim to illness.—Viktor E. Frankl

In another passage, the author uses an effect-cause arrangement. Notice that a statement of effect is followed by a statement of cause. Then, a statement of effect appears followed by two sentences describing a cause. Finally, the first two effects are summarized in a concluding effect, and the first two causes are summarized in a concluding cause. The passage proceeds logically, allowing the reader to follow a clear mental pattern.

Effect | The camp inmate was frightened of making decisions and of taking any sort of initiative whatsoever.

Cause | This was the result of a strong feeling that fate was one's master, and that one must not try to influence it in any way, but instead let it take its own course. In

Effect | addition, there was a great apathy, which contributed in no small part to the feelings of the prisoner. At

Cause | times, lightning decisions had to be made, decisions which spelled life or death. The prisoner would have preferred to let fate make the choice for him. This escape from commitment was most apparent when a

Concluding effect | prisoner had to make the decision for or against an escape attempt. In those minutes in which he had to make up his mind—and it was always a question of

Concluding cause | minutes—he suffered the tortures of hell. Should he make the attempt to flee? Should he take the risk? —Viktor E. Frankl

If you collect good examples of logical reasoning, you will have a file of models and ideas for your own work.

EXERCISE F: Locating Professional Models. Find books and magazines that contain good models of logical arguments: for example, scientific books, journals, magazines and nonfiction books on social issues. As you skim this material, look for ideas or arguments developed by induction, by deduction, and by cause and effect. Copy three passages that you decide are good examples of clearly logical presentations and label the approaches used. Document your sources, recording author, title, and page number(s).

DEVELOPING WRITING SKILLS: Using a Logical Plan in Your Own Writing. Write a passage of 150 to 300 words. You may need to identify your main idea in one sentence, and you will have to gather information—facts, examples, reasons, and so on—to present your ideas logically. Use an inductive or deductive approach, or arrange your ideas according to a cause-and-effect pattern. Give the reader the information needed to establish all necessary mental connections. Try not to write any hasty generalizations, non sequiturs, or other errors. To help you choose a logical plan, use any of the professional models that you found in Exercise F or that you read in the section.

Skills Review and Writing Workshop

Clear Thinking in Writing

CHECKING YOUR SKILLS

Rewrite the following passage, using a logical order and adding transitions, coordination, and subordination to connect the ideas clearly.

(1) Ana arrived at her house and dashed up the steps as fast as she could. (2) Ana left school as soon as the dismissal bell rang. (3) She did not stop to talk with her friends as she usually did. (4) Ana and her mother were going to fly to San Antonio to visit her grandmother. (5) She ran all the way home. Her mother was standing in the hallway with her coat on. (6) Two suitcases were on the floor next to her. (7) She could hardly wait to spend a whole week at her grandmother's house. (8) Aunts, uncles, and cousins would be coming and going constantly. (9) Her grandmother would cook her favorite dishes. (10) She and her cousins would have wonderful times together.

USING COMPOSITION SKILLS
Writing a Travel Brochure

Imagine that you are writing a travel brochure for a travel agency. Choose a destination and do any research that is necessary about the place. Then follow the steps below to write a description of the trip so that people will want to go on it.

Prewriting: List the places of interest that the trip will include as well as the means of transportation and hotel accommodations that the travelers will use. Arrange the information in a logical order.

Writing: Use vivid language that will make people want to go on the trip. Connect your ideas with transitions and use coordination and subordination to make your writing clear.

Revising: Look over your work and make any changes you can to improve it. After you have revised, proofread carefully.

476

UNIT **V**

Composition
Forms and Process of Writing

17

Paragraphs

This chapter explains the essential features of paragraphs. It also discusses problems to avoid when writing paragraphs. The chapter explores methods of planning, writing, and revising paragraphs, with emphasis on finding your own workable approaches to writing.

17.1 Understanding Paragraphs

The standard paragraph is a unit of writing containing a main idea and sentences elaborating the main idea. All of the sentences in a paragraph should work together in a unified and coherent way. This section explains the way a main idea is expressed in a topic sentence and the kinds of information that are needed to support it. The section also explains how unity and coherence are achieved in a paragraph.

Topic Sentences

The topic sentence indicates to the reader the limits of the paragraph by expressing its main idea. It also suggests the purpose and tone of the paragraph.

Features of Good Topic Sentences. A topic sentence expresses the main idea and defines the scope of the paragraph.

The position of the topic sentence varies from paragraph to paragraph. A topic sentence often comes first in the paragraph to prepare the reader for the supporting ideas that follow. However, it may come after some introductory statements, leading

into the supporting ideas; or it may come after the supporting ideas, ending the paragraph and acting as a summary
statement.

The paragraph below begins with its topic sentence, which
leads to the information that follows.

TOPIC *There are all manner of snows, both cruel and kind.*
SENTENCE There is the snow that falls like needles and drifts in
hard ridges on the dead cornfields, is bitterly cold,
Supporting coming down from the northwest and driving into the
information earth like knives. And there is the snow that people
think of as snow, that actually comes very seldom, but
is the symbol of all snows, the childhood miracle that
remains forever an image larger than all the dreary,
bitter or halfhearted snows that come before and
after.—Josephine Johnson

Unsuitable Topic Sentences. To guide the reader, a topic
sentence must accurately state the paragraph's range of ideas.
If it covers either too much or too little information, the topic
sentence may mislead the reader.

**Recognize topic sentences that are too general
or too narrow and revise them to suit the supporting information.**

A topic sentence that is *too general* (too broad or too vague)
leads the reader to expect more ideas than are actually covered
in the paragraph. In the paragraph about snows, for instance,
a topic sentence such as *There are all manner of snows and
rains* would be too comprehensive as a topic sentence because the reader would expect a discussion of rains, but no
discussion of rains is included in the paragraph.

To correct an overly general topic sentence, eliminate any
words and ideas that exceed the scope of the paragraph. Use
more exact words or include fewer ideas: Limit the main idea
to the supporting information that has been used in the paragraph. For instance, eliminating *rains* from the topic sentence
about snows makes it more appropriate for the rest of the
paragraph.

A weak topic sentence may instead be *too narrow;* that is, it
may fail to express the entire range of ideas in a paragraph. For
example, in the paragraph about snows, a topic sentence such

as *Some types of snows are cruel* would be too narrow because kind snows are also described in the paragraph.

To correct an overly narrow topic sentence, reword it to include the overlooked ideas. If you find it difficult to fit all of your ideas into one sentence, write two, then combine them as you did in Chapter 15. In the paragraph about snows, the topic sentence must include both cruel and kind snows because both of these are discussed in the supporting details.

EXERCISE A: Recognizing Topic Sentences. Locate and copy the topic sentence of each paragraph.

(1) Although determining Congressional seats prompted the first national census, additional uses for the information have multiplied over the decades until the list seems endless. Federal and local agencies, businesses and individuals, all rely on census statistics for important information. The value of the census, according to one official, is not only that it provides statistics but that it breaks them down into very local neighborhoods, sometimes as small as a city block. Thus an orthodontist checks to see if a certain neighborhood has enough children of teeth-straightening age to warrant his setting up practice. A shoestore owner uses census information to decide if he should specialize in running shoes or sensible oxfords. In Minnesota, Boy Scout leaders looked at census information to project how many camps might be needed to accommodate new Scouts.—Adapted from Carol Simons

(2) Everyone was agreed that Lincoln was a homely man. The President himself made jokes about it. He was gawky, and his voice was high-pitched and unimpressive. He cared little about appearances; as often as not his clothes did not fit. He made no pretense to fine family. He was the son of a restless farmer who had wandered from Kentucky, where Lincoln was born, to Illinois, where he spent most of his life. Lincoln was as nearly self-educated and self-made as a man can be. He was a village postmaster for a while, a lawyer, a member of the Illinois legislature at Springfield, an unexceptional member of the House of Representatives in Washington for a single term. Little about his life until the 1850's seems adequate to explain the towering person he became.—*American Literature*

480

(3) Selling talking birds to Octavian (later Emperor Augustus) became a minor industry in Rome. In addition to a talking raven, he bought at least two more birds, a magpie and a parrot that had been trained to salute him. An enterprising cobbler thought to cash in on the trend by training a raven to say the appropriate "Ave, Caesar victor imperator" (Hail, Caesar, victorious leader!), but the bird was painfully slow to learn the prescribed phrase. Many times the cobbler exclaimed in exasperation, "Opera et impensa periit!" (work and money wasted!). When the bird had finally learned his line, the man presented it. The raven performed, but Octavian declined to buy it, explaining that he already had enough birds to salute him. At that point the raven said, "Opera et impensa periit!" Octavian laughed and bought the bird.—Adapted from Peter Muller

EXERCISE B: Correcting Topic Sentences. Identify the weak topic sentence in each of the following paragraphs as too general or too narrow. Then write a revised topic sentence.

(1) Beginners in almost any sport are not ready for competition or independent play without first having proper training and guided practice. Crowding the slopes of ski resorts every year, hundreds—maybe thousands—of novice skiers create more hazards for the competent and experienced by taking to the slopes without adequate training and sometimes without proper-fitting equipment. These ill-prepared beginners usually lose control and veer unexpectedly into the path of other skiers or simply fall in everyone's way. Some beginners may be coordinated and agile, but without guidance and training their abilities are only raw materials, and, on the slopes, they can become dangerous—to themselves and to others.

(2) The American traveler will often choose the airplane to reach his or her destination. The most frequent mode of transport, of course, is the automobile. An extensive road network, including many transcontinental routes, encourages this, and many travelers prefer the independence afforded by motoring, even cross-country. Surprising to some, many people today prefer the leisure of train and bus service, which are viable alternatives for budget travelers. Surely, the quickest way to travel is by jet plane, a popular choice, many times faster than the others, but sometimes financially beyond the reach of people.

481

Support

The topic sentence of a paragraph must be developed by supporting information that sufficiently clarifies and explains the main idea.

Features of Good Supporting Information. Supporting information should be specific. Supporting information should also be complete enough to make the paragraph both understandable and interesting to the reader. You can, however, choose to use several different kinds of information as support within one paragraph.

Supporting information should consist of specific examples, details, facts, reasons, or incidents.

The following chart describes the five basic kinds of information—examples, details, facts, reasons, and incidents—that can be used to develop a main idea.

KINDS OF SUPPORT	
Examples	—provide particular instances of a general idea or principle —offer specific items or ideas as evidence
Details	—present the different parts of a person, place, thing, or idea —offer pieces of description
Facts	—provide concrete, verifiable pieces of information to support an idea —offer accurate evidence, such as statistics and other data
Reasons	—provide explanations, justifications, or causes of the main idea —answer the question *Why?* raised by the topic sentence
Incidents	—relate events to support the topic sentence —illustrate the main idea through a brief story

Some paragraphs use only one basic type of support; others use a combination of basic types. The following paragraph uses both details and facts to support the main idea that is expressed in the topic sentence.

TOPIC
SENTENCE

Details and
facts

The design of the Viking ship remains a marvel and feat of technical skill. The Viking ship astonishes us today with its grace and beauty of line. In its day it astonished because of its strength and flexibility. Long and slim, built of oak, with symmetrical ends, long true keel, and overlapping wood planks molded into the shell shape that allowed the Vikings to land without benefit of harbor in very shallow water, the ship was equipped with a vast painted sail amidships, a side rudder, and as many as thirty-four pairs of oars. With the mast topped with a bronze weather vane and often with a prow sculpture, such a ship must have been a magnificent sight setting forth from the fjords. It was this technological weapon, combined with superb seamanship, that gave the Vikings mastery of the sea.—Adapted from Maureen Green

In the following paragraph the topic sentence has been developed by using an incident. Included in the incident are both facts and details. The paragraph then ends with a concluding statement.

TOPIC
SENTENCE

Incident with
facts and
details

A classic example of a form of propaganda by censorship through doctored information is Bismarck's famous Ems telegram of 1870. The point at issue was whether Leopold of Hohenzollern should succeed to the Spanish throne, a candidature supported by Bismarck and opposed by the French. King William of Prussia and the French ambassador had strolled together in the pleasure garden at Ems discussing the problem, although by this time Leopold, alarmed by the fuss his candidature had aroused, had already resigned it and the threat of war seemed to have been averted. But Bismarck wanted war, and, when William sent a telegram in cipher describing the inoffensive discussion that had taken

483

place at Ems, Bismarck and his colleagues were at first despondent at its unimportant nature. Then the chancellor suddenly saw how he could make use of it to save the situation. By cutting out a few words and sentences and then publishing the abrupt telegram as it was, he could make what had been a fairly polite interview appear as a truculent challenge and a consequent snub. The provocative alterations were made and published, and the press on both sides clamored for war. Thus began the Franco-Prussian War in which 141,000 men were killed.—J.A.C. Brown

Inadequate and Inappropriate Support. Just as a topic sentence must adequately cover the support in a paragraph, the supporting information must develop the topic sentence well.

Recognize and revise inadequate or inappropriate support.

Often, the problem with paragraph development is inadequate support; that is, too little information has been supplied to develop the main idea fully. One or two examples or ideas may not make the main idea clear or convincing, especially if the support is not detailed enough. Notice the incompleteness of the information in the following paragraph.

TOPIC SENTENCE

Inadequate supporting information

The people at a baseball or football game can be part of the entertainment. Eating seems to be the primary interest of some people. They spend much of their time hailing the roving vendors or eating food brought from home. Some viewers become restless when the play slows down and walk up and down the aisles and stairs. All these kinds of spectators add to the flavor of the experience.

The two examples of spectator behavior are too sketchy. The paragraph has not gone into depth to elaborate on the main idea, and therefore it is flat and disappointing.

To improve inadequate support, you should reexamine the topic sentence and reconsider your initial ideas. Additional support can come from ideas mentioned in the topic sentence

484

but overlooked in the paragraph, from further development of existing support, or from thinking up more examples, details, facts, or reasons related to your main idea.

In the paragraph about people watching a game, the reader expects more examples of spectator behavior. The paragraph becomes more convincing when specific details are added and when more examples expand the supporting information.

TOPIC
SENTENCE

Additional
details

Additional
details

Added
examples

The people at a baseball or football game can be part of the entertainment. Eating seems to be the primary interest of some people. They spend much of their time hailing the roving vendors or *munching snacks that they have brought with them.* Some viewers easily become restless when the play slows down and walk up and down the aisles and stairs, *trying the view from other parts of the stadium. In contrast, some fans constantly peer through binoculars zooming in on the action the way the television cameras do. Some viewers imagine that they are Howard Cosell or another well-known sportscaster and give a running commentary on the game to those sitting next to them. Still other fans become so involved in the game that they try to tell the referees or coaches what to do by yelling out their opinions and responses to calls and plays and by jumping up and down.* Although some of these kinds of spectators may be distracting, all of them add to the flavor of the experience.

Another problem with supporting information is that it may be the wrong kind of material. Vague statements, generalizations, and weak opinions are inappropriate support. They take up space without furthering the reader's understanding of the main idea.

The following paragraph illustrates these weaknesses in supporting information.

TOPIC
SENTENCE

Vague
statement

A boating enthusiast, I attend boat shows as frequently as possible but usually find them poorly planned and poorly run, making them tiring, frustrating experiences. Right from the beginning, the show is usually a problem because of the way it is

485

Generalization	set up. I can count on waiting hours just to get in and on waiting even longer to see an individual exhibit. And the worst parts are the so-called "experts" at the exhibits. These people really don't know anything. Often, they are salespeople who say: "This beauty will build your image, let me tell you!" or "This one is the fastest little roughneck on the high seas!"
Weak opinion and generalization	

To revise inappropriate support, approach the paragraph from the reader's perspective and supply precise, convincing information. Replace vague statements with clear, exact language. Restate unsupported generalizations with qualifying words or develop them with specific, concrete information. Eliminate unsupported opinions or back them up with solid facts and examples. Notice how the problems in the preceding paragraph have been corrected in the following version.

TOPIC SENTENCE	A boating enthusiast, I attend boat shows as frequently as possible but usually find them poorly planned and poorly run, making them tiring, frustrating experiences. The problems begin at the door—in a waiting line. Because such shows are seasonal, occurring in most cities once a year, and because they are scheduled for usually no longer than a week in one large building, often a convention center, long lines inevitably form first at the entrance and then later at the individual exhibits inside. Waiting for as long as forty-five minutes to two hours at an exhibit is not uncommon. And, of course, the size of the crowd sharply limits any chance of inspecting a particular craft or of gathering craft specifications from an expert. In fact, worst of all are the "experts" themselves. Often, the men and women in charge at exhibit sites are salespeople, not boating experts or builders. A viewer with serious questions will seldom receive comparative statistics and relevant specifications. Instead, the information one receives is sales promotion: "This beauty will build your image, let me tell you!" or "This one is the fastest little roughneck on the high seas!"
Clear, exact language	
Specific facts and details	
Specific facts and details	
Opinion and generalization supported with facts and examples	

486

EXERCISE C: Recognizing Kinds of Support. Reread each of the paragraphs in Exercise A on pages 480–481, and explain which of the paragraphs is developed mainly by an incident, which of the paragraphs is developed mainly by examples, and which of the paragraphs is developed mainly by details and facts.

EXERCISE D: Identifying and Correcting Weak Support. The first sentence in each of the following paragraphs is the topic sentence, but the supporting information in each paragraph is weak. Identify the weakness. Then strengthen each paragraph, by adding to the information in it and by altering the information to make the paragraph clear and strong.

(1) Many television shows have tried to educate the viewer. Popular for years, *Sesame Street,* a children's show, has taught basic skills and employed real learning methods amid "catchy" situations and engaging characters. A big bird, named appropriately "Big Bird," is one character who teaches everything from numbers to manners. Because this creature is both so lovable and so memorable, children probably have learned his lessons.

(2) To work with children—as a tutor, playground supervisor, baby sitter, or in some other role—you need a warm personality and a firm manner. If you are friendly and interested in them, children will trust you. All children like to be happy, and a smile from you will work every time. If you do not set down ground rules, however, children will take advantage of you. They will test you to see what they can get away with. Children can sometimes be irritating and uncooperative. They can nag you until they get their way, or they can cause trouble just to get your attention.

Unity

All the ideas that are included in a paragraph must relate to each other. The topic sentence should present a main idea. The supporting information should develop that main idea with words that maintain a consistent tone throughout the paragraph.

Unity of Ideas and Tone. A paragraph should be limited to its main idea and its expansion or development. It should also maintain the purpose and tone suggested by its topic sentence. A unified paragraph helps the reader to grasp the main idea by omitting any distracting information and unsuitable words.

A unified paragraph includes only information relevant to the main idea and uses words that are consistent in tone.

In the following paragraph, each piece of information helps to explain the main idea, and all the words in the paragraph maintain an objective and informative tone.

TOPIC
SENTENCE

Paragraph
with unified
ideas and
tone

Sea snakes have some unusual adaptations to their life at sea. For example, their nostrils are equipped with valves that close tightly when they submerge. This snug seal enables some species to dive to 300 feet or more and remain there for hours. The reptile can stay under so long because its single large lung, which stretches from near the throat almost to the tail, functions as an aqualung—a combination of air storage sac and buoyancy regulator. Another marine adaptation is a permeable skin that helps the reptile breathe and avoid the bends, or nitrogen poisoning. Any excess nitrogen simply passes through the skin into the sea. There's even an adaptation to compensate for the difference between the salt content in the reptile's body fluids and its surroundings. Salt can be excreted by a gland in the mouth.—Adapted from Emily and Per Ola D'Aulaire

Disunity of Ideas and Tone. A paragraph will be weakened by information that strays from the main idea or by words that disrupt the tone of the paragraph.

Recognize disunity and correct it by omitting extraneous information and changing unsuitable words.

Disunity of ideas or tone can cause a paragraph to fall apart. If a writer mentions unrelated ideas, the paragraph can become difficult to follow. Or, if a writer elaborates too much on

488

any one piece of supporting evidence, the paragraph can become unbalanced. In either case, the reader may question or lose sight of the main idea. Similarly, if a writer uses casual words in a formal paragraph or uses elevated, technical words in an informal paragraph, the reader will be distracted and unity will be lost.

The unity of the following paragraph is broken both by unrelated ideas and by words that do not fit the overall tone of the paragraph.

TOPIC SENTENCE	In Joan Aiken's novel *Go Saddle the Sea,* the main character, a young boy named Felix, barely escapes death in a series of adventures when he runs away from his grandfather's estate in Villaverde, Spain, in
Too informal a word	search of his *dad's* relatives in England. *Felix's paternal grandfather is a duke of great wealth, but he*
Extraneous information	*does not know that Felix exists and never comes to understand Felix because he is becoming senile.*
Too formal words	First, Felix stumbles into an unseen bog and almost *expires.* Then he is mistakenly accused of robbery and thrown into a *penitentiary.* When he escapes, he becomes lost in the mountains during a storm and is captured by primitive people who try to sacrifice
Extraneous information	him. *Joan Aiken enjoys doing research and likes to put these frightening historical facts into her novels.*
	Finally, Felix reaches the coast of Spain only to book passage on a ship that has a crew of pirates. But with
Too formal a word	the help of a few friends and with his own *intrepidity,* good sense, and determination, Felix survives to achieve his goal.

To revise a paragraph for unity of ideas, evaluate both the topic sentence and the supporting information. Examine each supporting idea against the main idea, eliminating any supporting ideas that do not directly support the main idea or that do not develop other supporting ideas. Sometimes you may have to replace extraneous information with relevant supporting ideas.

To correct disunity of tone, you should change words that draw attention to themselves because they clash with the overall tone of the paragraph. Replace words that sound too folksy or casual, too self-important or elevated, too technical, or too opinionated with words that suit the purpose and tone of the paragraph.

The preceding paragraph can be improved by removing the ideas that stray from the main idea and by substituting appropriate words that suit the explanatory tone of the paragraph, as shown in the following paragraph.

TOPIC
SENTENCE

Unifed paragraph with improved supporting information and word choices

In Joan Aiken's novel *Go Saddle the Sea,* the main character, a young boy named Felix, barely escapes death in a series of adventures when he runs away from his grandfather's estate in Villaverde, Spain, in search of his *father's* relatives in England. First, Felix stumbles into an unseen bog and almost *dies.* Then he is mistakenly accused of robbery and thrown into *jail.* When he escapes, he becomes lost in the mountains during a storm and is captured by primitive people who try to sacrifice him. Finally, he reaches the coast of Spain only to book passage on a ship that has a crew of pirates. But with the help of a few friends and with his *courage,* good sense, and determination, Felix survives to achieve his goal.

EXERCISE E: Recognizing Unity and Disunity. Label each of the paragraphs below and on the following page as either *unified* or *disunified.*

(1) The principal cause of the unpopularity, and ultimately the bankruptcy, of the Hartley specialty stores was the inferior quality of their merchandise. Despite a large selection of appliances priced below many other similar types on the market, the Hartley brands were characterized by lousy construction. A Hartley toaster, for example, contained filaments that easily broke—often during original shipments to the store. Once home, customers would frequently find their new toasters to be total wastes. Discourteous service also marred the Hartley reputation. Specialty stores like Hartley's have trouble competing with the larger department store chains. And perhaps the most notorious example of disappointing merchandise could be found in Hartley's clothing sections. Their low prices could not compensate for incredible tailoring and imperfections in materials used, particularly in suits, shirts, blouses, and dresses.

(2) Ever since Charles Dickens wrote the story *A Christmas Carol,* it has appealed to the hearts and imaginations of readers. Generations of parents have read the story to their children, and both children and older readers have thought about the frightening warnings that change Ebenezer Scrooge. Scrooge is a miser, unable to see beyond his own needs and interests. But through "visitations" by ghosts, he sees visions of the past, present, and future. He discovers the harm his love of money has done to himself and others. *A Christmas Carol* convincingly illustrates the theme that helping others may be the most rewarding thing that a person can do.

EXERCISE F: Achieving Unity of Ideas and Tone. Rewrite the paragraph you identified as disunified in Exercise E. Omit any extraneous information and replace any words that disrupt the tone of the paragraph. You may decide to invent some ideas to replace the extraneous material.

Coherence

In addition to a strong topic sentence, solid supporting information, and unity, an effective paragraph has coherence; that is, the ideas are logically arranged and smoothly connected for the reader.

Using Logical Orders. Supporting information in a paragraph should be arranged in the clearest, most logical order. A number of different orders are possible.

Supporting information should follow a clear logical order, such as order of importance, chronological order, spatial order, comparison-and-contrast order, or developmental order.

Order of importance organizes ideas from least significant to most significant. Order of importance particularly suits persuasive paragraphs in which you are building a case for an opinion. *Chronological order,* or time order, presents events in the order of their occurrence and is useful for relating incidents or explaining how something is done. *Spatial order* arranges details by their locations; it functions well in descriptions.

491

Comparison-and-contrast order organizes details and ideas according to similarities and differences. The paragraph may discuss all the features of one item first and then discuss the comparable features of the second item, or the paragraph may alternate between the items, discussing them feature by feature.

Developmental order, more loose and versatile than these other orders, simply develops out of a particular topic sentence and presents information according to an order mentioned in that topic sentence or according to the writer's logical pattern of thought about the main idea. When other orders do not fit, you can use developmental order.

A paragraph may follow only one of these orders or may use a combination of orders. The following paragraph uses comparison-and-contrast order. The supporting information is compared and contrasted feature by feature; first the crocodile's jaw and the alligator's jaw, then the crocodile's fourth tooth and the alligator's fourth tooth. The crocodile is considered item A; the alligator, item B.

TOPIC SENTENCE Comparison and contrst AB Comparison and contrast AB	In basic physical structure, the crocodile and the alligator have one major distinguishing feature: their teeth. *Both* creatures have teeth, of course, *but* the crocodile's teeth are aligned as the jaws close, *whereas* the alligator's teeth overbite; the upper jaw juts out and over the teeth in the lower jaw. *Both* species have a fourth tooth on each side, measurably larger than the rest; *however,* in the crocodile this tooth fits into a notch in the upper jaw leaving it visible when the mouth is closed, *while* in the alligator this tooth fits into a pit in the upper jaw and is hidden from sight.

Using Transitions and Other Connecting Words. No matter what logical order you use to arrange ideas in a paragraph, you will probably need a few connecting words to link ideas, to underscore the order for the reader, and to make the writing flow smoothly from one sentence to the next.

Transitions, coordinating words, and subordinating words clarify the order of ideas and connect them smoothly.

Transition words (such as *first* and *finally*), coordinating words (such as *but* and *and*), and subordinating words (such as *while* and *until*) all guide the reader by pointing out the connections among ideas. Some connecting words are more useful to highlight one logical order than another, as the following chart shows.

CONNECTING WORDS THAT AID COHERENCE	
Logical Order	**Transitions, Coordinating Words, and Subordinating Words**
Order of Importance	first finally for one reason second most even greater third last greatest next also most significant one (of) even more
Chronological Order	when first later formerly while next finally at last then as soon as meanwhile afterward before now after moments later immediately last soon
Spatial Order	outside inside beyond near overhead beneath under over in the distance ahead in front behind to the left (right)
Comparison and Contrast Order	but besides in addition just as . . . so also yet similarly however but . . . also or in contrast whereas on the contrary like too both on the other hand nor as well as
Developmental Order	also finally along with next furthermore for example therefore thus accordingly for instance as a result indeed consequently another in fact namely and

In the example paragraph on page 492, the words in italics are connecting words that lead from one idea to another.

Use of Repetition, Synonyms, and Consistent Pronouns. Another device for achieving coherence is the deliberate repetition of words that highlight and reinforce the main idea. Using synonyms and consistent pronouns for main words connects ideas while adding variety.

Repetition of main words and the use of synonyms and consistent pronouns also aid coherence.

In the following paragraph, the writer purposely repeats the main word *survivor* through the use of the verb *survived.* However, instead of using *old age* throughout, she substitutes the words *his eighties* and *his middle seventies;* and instead of repeating the name *Miró,* she uses the pronouns *he* and *his.*

TOPIC
SENTENCE

Paragraph
connected by
the repetition
of main
words,
synonyms,
and
pronouns

Joan Miró, well into *his eighties,* is one of the great *survivors.* He has *survived* as a human being: Never has *he* been more alert, more spontaneous, more intense. *He* has *survived* as an upright citizen: In *his middle seventies, he* would put up with hardship and discomfort to manifest *his* solidarity with *his* fellow Catalans who were being persecuted by the Franco government. And *he* has *survived* as an artist: Like Claude Monet, Henri Matisse, Pablo Picasso and Georges Braque, *he* seems to have met *old age* at the door and told it to come back another day.—Rosamond Bernier

Using Parallelism and Concluding Sentences. Parallelism—the use of similar grammatical structures—shows that ideas are similar, related, or equal. A concluding sentence—a final sentence that echoes the main idea, summarizes the details, or adds a closing thought—can also aid coherence.

Parallel structures and a concluding sentence can tie together related ideas in a paragraph.

Both of these devices work in the following paragraph. Most sentences in the support follow a subject/verb/complement pattern to signal their equal importance. Notice, also, how the concluding sentence both summarizes the supporting details and ties them to the main idea expressed in the topic sentence.

494

TOPIC
SENTENCE

Parallelism
in sentences
following a
subject/verb/
complement
pattern

Concluding
sentence

The mountainous area around the southern end of Lake Tahoe in California has lost some of its natural beauty in the last twenty years. Housing developments now dot the ridges and meadows where pine forests once stood. Tall hotels and casinos fringe the lake with commercial activity. Caravans of vehicles creep over the pass that leads to the lake. Traces of smog sometimes taint the once pure and refreshing air. The roaring of chain saws and car, motorcycle, plane, and boat engines echoes off the rocky ridges. And even the trails up the rugged mountains and into the more remote valleys are now traveled by packs of hikers of all ages. *Gradually, civilization with all its sights, smells, and sounds is invading the wilderness.*

Correcting Illogical Order and Poor Connections. Even paragraphs with strong supporting information can be weakened by illogical order or by the absence of transitions and other connecting devices.

Recognize and correct faulty coherence caused by an illogical order of ideas or the absence of connecting devices.

If the ideas in a paragraph skip around haphazardly instead of following a clearly defined order, the paragraph will be confusing and difficult to comprehend. If too few or too many transitions are used, the paragraph may be disjointed or heavy-handed. If the writer has not made good use of other connecting devices, the paragraph may sound elementary or awkward.

The following paragraph discusses two famous baseball players, but the writer has not ordered the supporting information logically or made the writing flow from sentence to sentence.

TOPIC
SENTENCE

Illogical
order

Most baseball fans agree that two of the greatest baseball players of all time are Ty Cobb and Joe DiMaggio. Joe DiMaggio was elected to baseball's Hall of Fame in 1955. With the New York Yankees between 1936 and 1952, Joe became one of the greatest outfielders of all time, and his popularity

No
transitions
between
examples

Unnecessary
repetition of
a name

soared when he set a major league record of hits in fifty-six consecutive games, achieving a lifetime batting average of .325. Ty Cobb set a record for the most base hits while he played ball with the Detroit Tigers from 1905 to 1926. Ty Cobb became famous for base-stealing; in one season, Ty Cobb stole ninety-six bases. Ty knew how to slide with style, and he claimed that by watching the baseman's eyes rather than the ball, he could gauge his landing.

To revise a paragraph for coherence, reexamine the main idea and purpose of the paragraph. Try to arrange supporting information according to a logical order suggested by the topic sentence or by the supporting information itself. Once you have rearranged the material, look for places—movement to a new supporting idea, a change in time or place, or addition of details—that would be clearer and smoother with transitions. Then choose the transition that matches and clarifies the particular ideas. To improve the continuity of the paragraph even more, look for main words that can be repeated or replaced by synonyms or pronouns.

When the paragraph about Ty Cobb and Joe DiMaggio is revised for coherence, the information about Ty Cobb comes first according to the topic sentence and to chronological order. Transitions clarify the arrangement of examples and add smoothness to the paragraph. The use of *he* for *Ty* eliminates the unnecessary repetitions of his name. A bridge idea now forms a transition between the supporting information about Ty Cobb and the supporting information about Joe DiMaggio. Notice, too, that the material about Joe DiMaggio now follows a more logical time order, ending with his election to the Hall of Fame.

TOPIC
SENTENCE

Logical
Order

Transitions
and pronouns

Most baseball players agree that Ty Cobb and Joe DiMaggio are two of the greatest baseball players of all time. *While* Ty Cobb played ball with the Detroit Tigers from 1905 to 1926, he set a record for the most base hits. He *also* became famous for base-stealing; in one season, he stole ninety-six bases. *In addition,* Ty knew how to slide with style. He claimed that by watching the baseman's eyes rather than the ball, he could gauge his landing. *Joe*

Bridge idea   *DiMaggio's record also made him a favorite among fans.* When he played for the New York Yankees between 1936 and 1952, he became one of the greatest outfielders of all time, and his popularity soared when he set a major league record of hits in fifty-six consecutive games. Joe's *other* records and his lifetime batting average of .325 earned him his election to baseball's Hall of Fame in 1955.

EXERCISE G: Achieving Coherence. The following six sentences can be arranged to form a coherent paragraph. Decide on the best order for the sentences by recognizing introductory statements, the topic sentence, and a logical order for the supporting ideas. Write the paragraph so that it is coherent.

1. First, it failed to explain why the different planets travel at different angles and at different speeds in relation to each other and to the sun.
2. French astronomer Pierre de Laplace and German metaphysicist Immanuel Kant maintained that the planets in our solar system were formed from a central nebula.
3. Third, and most obvious to critics of the theory, a planet as massive as Jupiter could not have been spread out as a thin ring of matter surrounding the sun, because it would have been impossible for that thin stream to have contracted into a huge spherical body.
4. Because of three major drawbacks, however, critics of the theory found it incomplete and imperfect.
5. Second, centrifugal force alone would not have the power to propel rings of matter outward into space.
6. According to this theory, as the nebula began to rotate, it threw off rings of matter centrifugally, and each of these rings then contracted gravitationally to form the different planets.

EXERCISE H: Improving Coherence in a Paragraph. The following paragraph contains weaknesses in coherence, such as illogical order in the support, lack of transitions, and other awkward connections. Rewrite the paragraph to improve coherence.

(1) Justin had never been to an art auction before, so he entered the large hall nervously, overly conscious of his presence among so many strangers. (2) Feeling out of place, Justin observed the entrances of others and decided to follow a course of action that he thought would be proper. (3) Justin walked confidently to a reception desk where he saw people signing a guest register. (4) Justin waited a moment behind two women signing their names, and Justin signed his own beneath theirs. (5) Finally, Justin took a seat in the last row, folded his hands in his lap, and waited for the bidding to begin. (6) Before Justin sat down, he walked to the other side of the entrance foyer to a coatroom where Justin hung his raincoat among at least fifty others.

Paragraphs with Special Purposes

In a longer piece of writing, different kinds of paragraphs may develop ideas. Many of these paragraphs contain topic sentences and present supporting information. But a writer may also use paragraphs that do not follow this standard format.

In a standard paragraph, the main idea is explicitly stated by the topic sentence and is clearly supported by sufficient, specific, and relevant information. In some pieces of writing, including newspaper and magazine articles and chapters of books, other kinds of paragraphs are often used in conjunction with the standard ones. Because such paragraphs serve different purposes, they may not have the same features as standard paragraphs, but they do contribute to the unity and coherence of the work as a whole.

Special paragraphs vary in structure from standard paragraphs, but they still help unify the central idea in a longer composition.

Just as a paragraph may contain introductory statements, elaboration of support, transitional statements, and a concluding statement, a longer work may contain introductory, continuing, transitional, and concluding paragraphs.

Introductory Paragraphs. An introductory paragraph may lack a topic sentence or consist of only one sentence. It may

498

also mention ideas without developing them further. Usually, it aims to attract attention and to suggest the point of the work.

An introductory paragraph attracts interest and often points out the main idea of the compositon.

An introductory paragraph eases the reader into the topic that later paragraphs will expand. It should suit the purpose and content of the composition. It may specify the topic and indicate the direction of ideas to follow. Often it focuses on the main point. A long article should have a long introduction, whereas a short article needs only a few sentences of introduction.

The following paragraph presents a lively opinion to intrigue the reader, introduces the topic and offers background information. Then it presents the main point of the essay.

Introductory paragraph   The rich have always liked to assume the costumes of the poor. Take the American language. It is more than a million words wide, and new terms are constantly added to its infinite variety. Yet as the decade starts, the United States vocabulary seems to have shrunk to child size.—Stefan Kanfer

Concluding Paragraphs. Like an introductory paragraph, a concluding one may not have a topic sentence. Its length is proportionate to the whole piece of writing. It ties together information that has come before.

Concentrate on summarizing or tying together ideas as you write concluding paragraphs.

A concluding paragraph builds on preceding paragraphs. It will not develop the thoughts it ties together, and it may not have a topic sentence. Instead, it may begin with a transition and refer to the main point of the entire work or to the ideas in the preceding paragraph. It may summarize all the ideas if the piece of writing is long and complex. It may add a final illustration or bit of information. Because it represents the writer's last chance to say something to the reader, the writer tries to create a memorable concluding paragraph. A quotation, incident, question, or play on words helps to implant the main point in the reader's mind.

The following paragraph ends the essay on language. It has no topic sentence; it rephrases the main point. The last sentence echoes the introductory paragraph found on page 499.

Concluding paragraph   In fact, since its beginning, our native tongue has been maligned and mauled, invaded by foreigners and abused at home. No one has ever succeeded in making it uniform, and no one ever will. But then, as Henry Thoreau observed more than a century ago, "Where shall we look for standard English but to the words of a standard man?" As the '80's begin, Americans and their vernacular can be put down as fractious, infuriating, untidy, overbearing, cacophonous—but never as standard. The United States vocabulary may be dressed in blue jeans and work shirts, yet it cannot disguise one of the country's truest and most unassailable treasures: the American language.—Stefan Kanfer

In addition to introductory and concluding paragraphs, there are two other types of special paragraphs: continuing paragraphs and transitional paragraphs.

Continuing Paragraphs. A continuing paragraph does not contain a topic sentence but continues to develop an earlier idea. It elaborates on an idea in a preceding paragraph. The logical order of the information unifies it. The paragraph aids the unity and coherence of the piece because it builds on and is linked to a paragraph that precedes it.

A continuing paragraph supports the topic sentence of an earlier paragraph through coherent development.

A writer may build on a main idea in a new paragraph rather than lengthening the first one. The additional material receives more emphasis that way, and the first paragraph does not get so long that it loses a reader's attention. A continuing paragraph may begin with a transition that connects it with the preceding one.

The passage on the following page includes a continuing paragraph. The first paragraph is standard and has a topic sentence. The second gives additional examples that develop the topic.

Standard paragraph with a topic sentence
A livelier, more responsive people I have never met. I was hustled, jostled, even threatened by Nigerian citizenry, but so was I gently cared for by strangers when I lay ill. I was turned away from meetings with public officials sensitive about publicity, but I was never turned away from a home.

Continuing paragraph
I saw fights break out over traffic incidents and arguments erupt in grocery lines, but most outspoken confrontations seemed to subside as suddenly as they mounted. Seared by northern heat, parboiled by coastal humidity, feelings seemed ever ready to surface into kindness or violence, charity or self-interest.—Noel Grove

Transitional Paragraphs. A transitional paragraph usually contains only one or two sentences, which bridge or link two other paragraphs. It often contains neither a topic sentence nor developed ideas.

A transitional paragraph acts as a bridge leading readers from one group of ideas to another.

Transitional paragraphs sometimes read as though they could be attached to the preceding or following paragraph. They may be single sentences or even the topic sentence of a following paragraph. The paragraph below follows preceding ones, signals a shift in ideas, and presents the topic sentence for the next paragraph.

Transitional paragraph
Emotion is one thing; efficiency is often quite another. The experience of my friend Anthony Akinduro is a case in point.—Noel Grove

Paragraphs with Implied Topic Sentences. A standard paragraph states a topic sentence. Paragraphs with special purposes, however, only *imply* the main idea, leaving the reader to *infer* what it is. Learn to recognize paragraphs without topic sentences so that you are aware of ideas that are stated indirectly and can draw appropriate conclusions from them.

A paragraph may imply its main idea with supporting information rather than state it directly in a topic sentence.

501

A paragraph may develop an idea without expressing it, only implying it throughout. Some main ideas are so clear that spelling them out makes the paragraphs repetitious or simpleminded. Some writers appeal to readers' imaginations by challenging them to infer the main idea. Sometimes, statement of the main idea might impede the action. Descriptive and narrative paragraphs often imply their main ideas.

The following paragraph makes its point by implication. Even though the topic is not stated, the details create a unified idea. Notice that the paragraph might function as either a transition, continuation, introduction, or conclusion in a longer piece of writing.

Paragraph with an implied main idea	The wind zipped through the frozen weeds in the vacant lot. Three people stood separately, shifting from foot to foot. Three pairs of eyes peered brightly above thick woolen scarves, anxious for a glimpse of the bus in the distance. No one spoke, for the air burned in the nose, the throat, the lungs.

Paragraphs with special purposes work together with standard paragraphs to create unified pieces of writing. Notice that the following example begins with an introductory paragraph that makes some initial comments on the general subject of modern art, setting the tone for the paragraphs that follow. The second paragraph provides a transition between the introductory remarks of the first paragraph and the narrower subject of the third paragraph. The third paragraph, a standard one, presents the main idea to be developed.

Introductory paragraph	Modern art has always liked to speak in a strident voice, and modern American art in particular has sounded its cry over the rooftops of the world. Now that the heroic days are over and many of the giants of modernism have passed into death or decrepitude, some quieter voices are being heard more clearly.
Transitional paragraph	No painter was ever quieter than Milton Avery, who died seventeen years ago, loved, admired, and imitated by his peers but comparatively unknown to the general public. In the inevitable recasting and revising of reputations that is part of

history, his fame has risen steadily, and a major retrospective show at the Whitney Museum of American Art in New York is demonstrating why the unassuming work of this quiet but masterful man has come to rank with the major artistic achievements of his time.

Standard (topic sentence and support)

    Avery's career, like his talent, was quite unlike that of anyone else on the scene. In a time of turbulence and continuous change, he remained faithful to his own vision and his own way of doing things. He belonged to no school, took part in no controversy, did nothing to impose himself on the public, and scraped on just above the poverty line for most of his adult years, working away at the only thing that interested him, which was to record on canvas the harmonies of form and color he saw everywhere.—Adapted from Robert Wernick

EXERCISE I: Recognizing Paragraphs with Special Purposes. Look through magazines and books to locate five special paragraphs: transitional, continuing, introductory, concluding, and one with an implied topic sentence. Copy and label each. Note the writer, title of the source, and page number(s).

DEVELOPING WRITING SKILLS: Using Different Kinds of Paragraphs. Write a composition of 350 to 500 words. Exchange papers with another student, then evaluate the paragraphs using the directions below.

1. Label each paragraph as standard or special.
2. If the paragraph is standard, underline the topic sentence. Evaluate it to be sure it is neither too general or too narrow. Then evaluate the support to be sure it is both adequate and appropriate.
3. If the paragraph has a special purpose, identify what the purpose is. Suggest ways in which the paragraph might serve its function more effectively.
4. Evaluate the overall composition in terms of unified ideas and tone. Suggest improvements, if any are necessary.

503

5. Evaluate the overall composition in terms of coherence. Be able to state the kind(s) of order the writer used, and look for places where transitions might enhance the work.

17.2 Writing a Paragraph

An understanding of the key features of standard paragraphs and of the weaknesses that you should avoid can help you develop effective paragraphs. This section discusses prewriting, writing, and revising steps that will also guide you.

PREWRITING: Exploring Topics

Your first major prewriting step involves selecting a topic and forming a main idea for the paragraph. Your goal in this step is to complete a topic sentence reflecting the purpose of the paragraph and limiting the information to be covered.

Generating Ideas. When you are asked to write a paragraph on a topic of your own choosing, your first task will be to think of possible topics. Using one or more of the techniques that are discussed in Secion 13.1 can help you generate ideas for topics. These techniques include interviewing yourself, free writing, journal writing, reading and saving, clustering, brainstorming, and cueing.

Choosing and Narrowing a Topic. In choosing a topic, you should consider your interests, the information available to support the topic, and whether it is narrow enough to be covered in one paragraph.

Generate general ideas for topics, divide them into smaller ones, and choose a topic that is manageable and appealing.

If the topic you begin with is too general for a single thorough paragraph, narrow the topic by thinking of subcategories or smaller topics under the same general topic. Select the one you can handle well in a paragraph.

The following chart illustrates how the general topic *human biology* can be narrowed to several smaller topics and how a smaller topic can then be divided further.

504

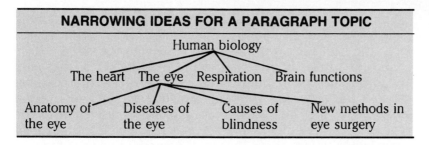

NARROWING IDEAS FOR A PARAGRAPH TOPIC

Human biology

The heart   The eye   Respiration   Brain functions

Anatomy of the eye   Diseases of the eye   Causes of blindness   New methods in eye surgery

You should follow this process of exploring and narrowing a general topic until you can choose a specific topic for your paragraph.

PREWRITING: Focusing on a Main Idea

Once you have a topic, consider the audience for whom you are writing and your purpose as you try to zero in on a main idea.

Consider audience and purpose as you focus a paragraph on a main idea and write a topic sentence.

Asking yourself questions about the topic can lead to possible main ideas. The following chart shows how you can use this process.

QUESTIONS SUGGESTING POSSIBLE MAIN IDEAS	
Paragraph Topic: Anatomy of the Eye	
Questions	**Possible Main Ideas**
What interests me about this topic?	—The eye is less complex than most people realize.
What do I know about the eye's anatomy?	—The eyeball structure has three basic layers, each performing different functions that result in sight.
How does the eye "see"?	—The eye functions very much like a camera.

505

The answers to your questions provide a list of possible main ideas. Examine the list to see which idea interests you most and best suits your own familiarity with the subject.

All of the ideas in the chart would be suitable for a general audience. The first main idea implies a persuasive purpose because it suggests that you will convince your readers of the simplicity of the eye, a task that may take some arguing. The second and third main ideas suggest that you will explain some factual information, the structure and function of the eye.

After you have chosen the main idea, express it in different ways to find the version you like best as a topic sentence. If you chose the second main idea in the preceding chart, your experimental topic sentences might resemble those below.

POSSIBLE TOPIC SENTENCES

Main Idea: The eyeball contains three basic layers, each performing different functions that result in sight.

1. The three basic layers of the eyeball perform different functions that result in vision.

2. The three basic layers of the eye—the sclera, the middle or choroid layer, and the retina—perform specific functions in creating sight.

3. The eyeball consists of three basic layers, which contain the instruments of sight.

You could choose any of these statements to be your topic sentence because they all present the same main idea and have an explanatory purpose. Notice that the wording of the first and third sentences sounds simpler than the wording of the second sentence. You might decide that for an audience unfamiliar with this topic you should save technical terms for the body of the paragraph, where you can explain them. You might then choose the third topic sentence because it gives the main idea the particular focus you would like to have.

EXERCISE A: Finding a Manageable Topic. Choose a general topic that interests you—a musical instrument or a type of clothing, for example—and write it on your paper. Beneath it,

506

list at least four related smaller topics that you might write about in a paragraph. If these smaller topics still seem too broad for a single paragraph, divide them further. Then circle the paragraph topic that appeals to you the most.

EXERCISE B: Choosing a Main Idea and Writing a Topic Sentence. Use the paragraph topic you selected in Exercise A to complete the following instructions.

1. Briefly identify the audience for whom you will write (for example, your friends, your neighborhood, the town council, an editor of a newspaper, and so on).
2. With this audience in mind, write down at least three questions about your topic. Then write down short answers to these questions. Your answers should suggest possible main ideas for the paragraph.
3. Identify the suggested purpose of each main idea.
4. Select the main idea that best suits your knowledge of the topic, your audience, and your purpose.
5. By experimenting with the wording of your main idea, write at least three versions of your topic sentence.
6. Circle the topic sentence that seems most direct, carefully worded, and workable.

PREWRITING: Brainstorming for Support

Once you have a main idea and a topic sentence, you must think of specific information that will support the topic sentence. In this step, you must anticipate your readers' expectations and gather relevant and meaningful support.

Using Creative Methods. When you brainstorm for ideas for a paragraph, think creatively. Rely on your own resources and imagination. Most often, brainstorming will involve carrying on a dialogue with yourself.

Brainstorm for examples, details, facts, reasons, and incidents that will support and develop your main idea.

One method of brainstorming is to free-associate from your main idea. Write down your topic sentence and then list every piece of related information that comes to mind, regardless of whether they are words, phrases, or sentences. Try to write quickly and let one thought spark another. Do not sort your ideas at this stage. If you run out of ideas, reread your topic sentence to start your thoughts flowing again.

The question-and-answer method also works well to provide support for your main idea. To use this method, anticipate questions that your audience might ask after reading your topic sentence. As you think of questions, write them down. Then, answer the questions specifically. Remember that readers might want to know about the meaning of any terms you use.

The chart below illustrates the question-and-answer method.

QUESTION-AND-ANSWER METHOD OF BRAINSTORMING
Topic Sentence: The eyeball consists of three basic layers, which contain the instruments of sight.

What are the basic layers of the eyeball?
—the three basic layers:
    the sclera (outer layer)
    the middle layer (mostly
    the choroid)
    the retina (inner layer)

—eyelids protect from exterior threats
—eye socket cushions the eyeball with fatty tissues and about 6 different muscles

How are these layers instruments of sight?
—the sclera or outer layer has a transparent cornea, which allows light to enter
—the eye socket contains tear glands that keep the eyeball moist
—the middle layer or choroid layer contains blood vessels that nourish the eyeball; also contains the iris and pupil, a hole in the iris which expands and contracts to allow light to pass through a lens

—eyelid muscles react involuntarily to protect the eyeball
—the retina is farthest inside the eyeball and contains nerve cells and light sensitive cells called rods and cones that receive the light, form images, and stimulate the nerve cells, which in turn transmit the images to the brain

508

What other special information pertains to the eyeball?

—the size of the eyeball—
about one inch or 2.5
centimeters in diameter

—the eyeball structure is
similar to the parts of a
camera

—unlike a camera, the eye
cavity contains protective
mechanisms such as
involuntary muscles and
tear glands

Using either method of brainstorming, you will most likely gather too much information for a single paragraph or discover that some of the ideas you have jotted down do not really fit in your paragraph. If you have a long list of supporting information, choose the most useful, significant points. Eliminate any points not relevant to the topic sentence.

Evaluating Support. Once you have a list of supporting information, check the ideas on your list for unity and completeness. Then decide which pieces of information to use, which to eliminate, and which to expand or alter.

Examine all supporting information to eliminate irrelevant or unimportant ideas, to add or expand ideas, or to revise the topic sentence to fit the supporting information.

This step gives you an opportunity to weed out those ideas that do not strengthen your paragraph and perhaps to write down other useful ideas that you may have overlooked. You should read over each item on your list to determine whether it is necessary and helpful to the audience. Cross out those ideas that do not relate to the main idea or directly develop another piece of supporting information. You may have to eliminate repetitious support, or you may find gaps in your supporting material. You should then supply more examples, details, facts, or reasons.

At this point, you may also want to revise your topic sentence to match the supporting information. You may even discover an introductory idea that could affect the wording or placement of the topic sentence.

The topic sentence for the paragraph about the structure of the eyeball might be revised to include a particularly interesting piece of information: physical dimensions.

REVISED TOPIC SENTENCE: The eyeball, *a sphere of about one inch or two and a half centimeters in diameter,* consists of three basic layers, which contain the instruments of sight.

EXERCISE C: Brainstorming for Support. Use the topic sentence that you wrote in Exercise B on page 507. Write the sentence at the top of your paper, and then, beneath it, list as many pieces of supporting information as you can. Use either of two methods—free-association or the question-and-answer method—to find and list appropriate examples, details, facts, reasons, and incidents.

EXERCISE D: Evaluating Your Support. Use your lists of information from Exercise C. On your brainstorming sheet, cross out any pieces of information that you think stray from the main idea or that you find unimportant. Consider adding new information or altering the ideas in your list. Look for any information that could become introductory or concluding ideas. Then reexamine your topic sentence to see if it suits the body of information you have developed for the paragraph. If necessary, revise the topic sentence.

PREWRITING: Organizing Your Support

The next major prewriting step is to find a logical organization for the information you have gathered, so that your ideas appear in an order the reader can easily follow.

Arrange your supporting information in the most logical order.

At this state, reexamine your list of supporting information. Your main idea and list of support may already suggest an appropriate organization, such as order of importance or comparison-and-contrast order. In fact, you may have already jotted down the supporting information in a logical order. If no such order is apparent, try to find a developmental order that presents your ideas naturally and smoothly.

510

Also consider the best position for your topic sentence. Often, you will position the topic sentence early in the paragraph. However, you may want the topic sentence to complete the paragraph, or you may choose to lead into your topic sentence with several introductory ideas.

Your method for achieving an organization will depend on how you work best. For instance, you may rough out a plan for the paragraph on your brainstorming sheet by numbering pieces of support or by drawing circles and arrows. You may write a modified outline by listing your supporting information in the logical order you have chosen to use. Or you may write a more formal topic outline. No matter which method you use to organize your supporting information, you can continue to refine your supporting information by adding, removing, or changing ideas.

For example, a spatial order emerges upon examining the list of information on the structure of the eyeball. This logical order for the paragraph is shown in the following modified outline.

Introductory Ideas About the Eyeball
   1. Rests in skull cavity
   2. Moves with help of different muscles and is kept moist by tear glands
Topic Sentence: The eyeball, a sphere of about one inch or two and a half centimeters in diameter, consists of three basic layers, which contain the instruments of sight.
The Sclera or Outermost Layer
   1. Is the "white" of the eye
   2. Has a transparent cornea, which allows light to enter
The Middle or Choroid Layer Within the Sclera
   1. Contains blood vessels that nourish the eyeball
   2. Contains the iris and pupil, a hole in the iris which expands and contracts to allow light to pass through a lens
The Innermost Layer, or Retina
   1. Contains nerve cells
   2. Contains light-sensitive cells called rods and cones
   3. Is the processing layer; rods and cones receive the light and form images and stimulate nerves cells, which in turn transmit the images to the brain

Concluding Idea Comparing Eyeball and Camera
  1. Resemble each other in structure
  2. Regulate and admit light and focus images on light-sensitive surfaces

EXERCISE E: Organizing Supporting Information. Use the list of supporting information you prepared in Exercises C and D to follow these instructions.

  1. Analyze your topic sentence and your supporting information to determine the most appropriate logical order for the paragraph.
  2. Consider whether you will begin or end the paragraph with your topic sentence or put the topic sentence in the middle after some introductory remarks.
  3. Then organize your paragraph by using numbers or marginal notes on your brainstorming sheet; by writing a modified outline that includes your topic sentence and puts the supporting information in logical order; or by making a topic outline that arranges your supporting information in logical order.

WRITING: Creating a First Draft

The planning you have done up to this point will help you in a number of ways as you write your paragraph. Because you have already worked out most of the paragraph, you will be freer to refine your ideas. As you express your ideas in complete sentences, you can consider the best way to communicate your ideas. You may even change your paragraph as you write by thinking of new, relevant ideas. While your logical order guides you, you can concentrate on making logical connections clear for the reader. And you can also think about the style of your writing.

As you draft your paragraph from your plan or outline, concentrate on connecting your ideas for meaning and flow and on writing interesting, lively sentences.

In addition to following the logical order you have chosen, concentrate on leading the reader along smoothly from idea to idea. Appropriate transitions and coordinating and subordinating words clarify the logical order of your ideas and highlight the relationships among them for the reader. Using repetitions of main words and synonyms and consistent pronouns for main words also ties your ideas together. You may even find parallelism useful in underscoring similarities or a concluding sentence helpful in bringing the entire paragraph to a smooth close.

Varying the rhythm and pattern of your sentences can also help to make your paragraph readable and interesting. As you draft your sentences, consider using sentences of different lengths and beginnings and using a variety of simple, compound, and complex sentences. (For more information on sentence variety, see Sections 15.1 and 15.2.)

Writing on every other line or double spacing and leaving wide margins will give you room to make changes and revisions later.

EXERCISE F: Writing a First Draft. Use your plan or outline from Exercise E to write a first draft of your paragraph. When you are writing, if new ideas that support your main idea or clarify another piece of supporting information occur to you, include them. Try to use transitions and other linking devices to clarify the logical order of your ideas. In addition, try to express your ideas clearly in sentences of different lengths and with different structures.

REVISING: Polishing Your Paragraph

The final state, revising, allows you to look critically at your writing to find errors and to make improvements. You should put your paragraph aside for a while and examine it and revise it when you can view it with some objectivity.

Use a checklist like the following to evaluate all parts of your paragraph and to help you revise.

The checklist on the next page can guide you as you look for weaknesses in the topic sentence, supporting information, unity, coherence, writing style, and the grammar and mechanics of your paragraph.

CHECKLIST FOR REVISING A STANDARD PARAGRAPH

1. Does the topic sentence accurately state the main idea developed in the paragraph or is it too general or too narrow?

2. Does the topic sentence suggest your purpose and suit your intended audience?

3. Does the support contain enough examples, details, facts, reasons, and/or incidents to develop the topic sentence?

4. Can you find any weaknesses among supporting ideas: vague statements, generalizations, or weak opinions?

5. Can you eliminate any extraneous or unimportant information?

6. Does the supporting information follow the most logical order consistently throughout?

7. Have you achieved coherence by using transitions, coordinating and subordinating words, repetitions of main words, synonyms, and consistent pronouns to connect ideas?

8. Could you improve any confusing or awkward places by adding any of the linking devices, parallelism, or a bridge idea?

9. Does the paragraph need a concluding sentence?

10. Do your sentences vary in lengths, openers, and structures?

11. Are the word choices the best you can find for your ideas?

12. Are there any errors in grammar, usage, mechanics, or spelling?

A completed, revised version of the paragraph about the eyeball follows. Transitions—*outermost, within,* and *innermost*—help the reader follow the spatial order. Other transitions—*like a camera* and *then*—tie the paragraph together. Repetition of the main words *eyeball* and *layer* and the use of the pronouns *it* and *its* for the different layers also help to link ideas. Varied sentence structures add to the rhythm of the paragraph.

Introductory ideas

TOPIC SENTENCE

The human eyeball rests in a skull cavity, where it moves with the help of six different muscles and is kept moist by tear glands. The actual eyeball, a sphere of about one inch or two and a half centimeters, consists of three basic layers, which contain the instruments of sight. The outermost layer is called the

Supporting
information
in spatial
order

Concluding
sentence

sclera; this is the "white" of the eye. Through its transparent cornea, a slight bulge in the front of the eye,
light can pass to the interior. Within the sclera is the
middle or choroid layer. This layer contains the blood
vessels that nourish the eyeball, the iris, or colored
part of the eye, and the pupil, a hole in the iris, which
expands and contracts to allow light to reach the eye's
lens and pass through. The innermost layer is the retina, which contains nerve cells and light-sensitive
cells called rods and cones. The retina is the processing layer. It receives the light that has passed through
the other layers, forms images, and stimulates nerve
cells, which in turn transmit the images to the brain.
Like a camera, then, the eyeball with its various layers
regulates and admits light and focuses images on a
light-sensitive surface.

EXERCISE G: Revising Your Paragraph. Reread the first
draft that you wrote in Exercise F. Use the checklist to examine
all features of the paragraph. Make any corrections or changes
on your paper, and then write a good final copy of the
paragraph.

**DEVELOPING WRITING SKILLS: Planning, Writing, and
Revising a Paragraph.** Choose a topic that interests you, and
then carry out all the following steps.

1. Narrow the topic.
2. Find a main idea by considering your audience and
   purpose.
3. Write several versions of your topic sentence expressing
   your main idea.
4. Brainstorm for supporting information and select support
   that is unified and thorough.
5. Organize your supporting information logically.
6. Write a first draft, concentrating on using connecting devices and varying your sentences.
7. Recheck your first draft and use a checklist to help you
   make revisions.
8. Write a good final copy of the paragraph.

Writing Workshop: Paragraphs

ASSIGNMENT 1

Topic Cities of the Future: The Year 3000

Form and Purpose A paragraph that explains and/or describes changes in future cities

Audience Readers of a general science magazine

Length One paragraph

Focus Introduce the topic and main idea in your first sentence. Then describe details about how cities will change by the year 3000.

Sources Books and encyclopedia articles about architecture of the past, present, and future

Prewriting Brainstorm by listing the ways that the cities will change. Number those changes in order of importance, least to most important, and develop a main idea.

Writing Use your notes to write a first draft. Use parallelism in a concluding sentence.

Revising Revise your paper using the checklist on page 514. Concentrate on improving coherence and unity.

ASSIGNMENT 2

Topic   The Strange History of a Food

Form and Purpose   A paragraph that informs and entertains readers

Audience   Readers of a food-history column entitled "Short Order Takeouts" in *Creative Cuisine* magazine

Length   One paragraph

Focus   Identify the food item and state a main idea that indicates why the food has a strange history. Develop a narrative that gives details which support your main idea.

Sources   Cookbooks, encyclopedia articles, food magazines, and interviews with gourmets and chefs

Prewriting   Research the general topic to identify a food story that interests you. Take notes. If you are narrating the story, list the events in chronological order.

Writing   Using your notes, write a first draft. Include only those details that relate directly to your topic sentence.

Revising   The checklist on page 514 will help you focus your revision. Prepare a final draft.

Topics for Writing: Paragraphs

The above photographs invite comparison. If they suggest a writing idea to you, plan and write a comparison and contrast paragraph. If you prefer, choose one of the following comparison topics. Some may have to be narrowed so that they can be adequately covered in a single paragraph.

1. Nuclear Fission and Nuclear Fusion
2. Two Films on the Same General Theme (for example, *Romancing the Stone* and *Raiders of the Lost Ark*)
3. Golf and Hockey
4. Two Political Opponents in a National or State Election
5. Hair Styles as a Reflection of Society: A Look at Two Distinct Periods in History
6. A Modern Abstract Painter and a Modern Realistic Painter
7. Downhill Skiing and Cross-Country Skiing
8. Two Animals That Are Competent Architects and Builders
9. Communism and Democracy
10. The Computer and the Human Mind

18

Kinds of Writing

To become a versatile writer, you should understand the purposes your writing can have. The four basic kinds of writing are *expository,* which explains; *persuasive,* which aims to change reader opinion; *descriptive*, which paints pictures; and *narrative,* which relates series of events. This chapter uses paragraphs as models to discuss these basic kinds of writing because paragraphs are concise units in longer works.

Expository and Persuasive Writing 18.1

Expository writing is informative and varies from scholarly discussions of difficult concepts to practical explanations of matters like first aid and backpacking. When, however, you write to express an opinion, interpret, or argue a course of action, you use persuasive writing.

Expository Writing

The purpose of expository writing is to explain, define, or otherwise provide information to an audience. You write exposition when you prepare a job application, answer a test question, write out a recipe, or direct a friend to your house.

Understanding Expository Writing. Expository writing explains something to an audience. The subject may be a concept, a historical event, a process, or the meaning of a word.

Expository writing is explanatory and informative.

Since it is explanatory, expository writing contains factual, objective, and verifiable information. It does not contain opinions. The following statement of fact is an indisputable matter of public record, whereas the statement of opinion offers a personal judgment, which could be challenged.

STATEMENT OF FACT: The English language is largely hybrid, mixing Anglo-Saxon roots with Latin and French borrowings.

STATEMENT OF OPINION: Because of its largely hybrid nature, the English language is the most versatile and flexible language that exists on earth.

An expository paper states a factual main idea, which can be explained with objective information—examples, details, facts, or incidents. Often, the supporting information can refer to documented sources, such as newspaper accounts, almanacs, encyclopedias, and other historical records.

The explanatory purpose of expository writing should be clear from its informative tone. For very knowledgeable readers, the writer should develop a more detailed explanation and use more advanced language.

Expository paragraph with an explanatory purpose and an informative tone

Hailstones vary greatly in size and shape. They can be as small as a pea or as large as a grapefruit. They can be conical, round, or oblate, dimpled or knobbed with protrusions. The largest stones weigh from one to two pounds and fall at a speed of some 100 miles per hour. People have been reported killed by hailstones in India and a 1977 plane crash in Georgia was attributed to hail. But the greatest damage from hail is to high-value crops such as fruit and vegetables and is caused by small stones that can blanket the ground and occasionally accumulate to a depth of several inches.—John Hallett

In addition to its basic explanatory purpose and informative tone, expository writing may have a secondary purpose and tone. For example, a writer might intend a secondary purpose of defining a term or instructing the reader in some task. The writer might also want to entertain the reader in addition to explaining something. Similarly, expository writing can establish an informative tone while ranging from the serious and formal to the matter-of-fact and informal to the light-hearted and casual. For example, the following discussion of holography—three dimensional photography—both informs and entertains the reader. The paragraph has a casual tone.

Expository paragraph with an entertaining purpose and a casual tone	Essentially each holographic movie display in the Museum of Holography is a transparent, 120-degree, screen-like partition suspended in a smooth semicircle against the wall. A light bulb is fitted at the base against the wall and—presto!—an ethereal embodiment of a personality appears lurking in midair behind the screen. The uncanny motion comes into play as a viewer advances from one side of each display to the other. The speed of action is regulated by the rate at which a viewer walks around the screen. Hence, the viewer has delightful control over whether Joseph Papp appears to recite prose at a ridiculously super-animated pace or a lethargic one.—Adapted from Peggy Sealfon

Prewriting, Writing, and Revising. When you write an expository paper, concentrate on explaining. Focus your topic in a single sentence, gather and organize your supporting information, draft your paragraphs, and revise with the strong and clear intention of communicating information to a particular audience in order to expand that audience's knowledge of your subject.

Focus on explaining the topic to a specific audience as you select the content and language for an expository paper.

The guidelines that are given in the chart on the following page should help you apply what you already know about writing paragraphs to meet the specific requirements of expository writing.

SUGGESTIONS FOR WRITING EXPOSITORY PAPERS

1. Choose a topic that you can explain in just one paper, as well as one that lends itself to a factual treatment.
2. Decide on any secondary purpose and tone.
3. Determine your audience and its knowledge of your topic.
4. Find your main idea and write a statement expressing it.
5. Gather supporting information, and select examples, details, and facts which explain the main idea.
6. Organize your support statements logically for clarity.
7. Concentrate on explaining your purpose as you write.
8. Revise for unity and coherence, and check to see that your tone is objective and informative. (See the checklist for revision on page 514 for additional suggestions.)

EXERCISE A: Understanding Expository Writing. Identify the main idea, the pieces of supporting information, and any secondary purpose and tone in the following paragraphs.

(1) If you are supposed to yawn [onstage], you must learn that the physical reason for yawning is a need for oxygen in the brain. Most of you will open your mouths wide and exhale, and then jump to another action because exhaling felt so peculiar. Instead, you should inhale deeply as you push your jaw down and back until the mouth opens, and you continue to pull the air deeply into your lungs before forcing it up into your head as you exhale. You can create a yawn at will in this way so that your eyes may even water.—Adapted from Uta Hagen

(2) The neutrino is the nearest thing to nothing, being distinguished from the other elementary particles of matter mainly by what it does not have and what it does not do. The traditional theory of the neutrino describes it as a particle without mass and without electric charge. It interacts with matter only through the weakest of the basic forces of nature. The earth moves in a thick soup of neutrinos (there are estimated to be about 100 per cubic centimeter throughout the volume of the universe), but they are such ephemeral particles that they almost never leave any trace of their passage.—*Scientific American*

EXERCISE B: Planning, Writing, and Revising an Expository Paragraph. List five topics suitable for expository writing. Then choose one, and use the suggestions in the chart on page 522 to write an expository paragraph. When revising, refer to the checklist on page 514.

Persuasive Writing

Persuasive writing attempts to persuade the reader to accept the writer's opinion. It appears in editorials, speeches, advertisements, and reviews of films, plays, and books. It is also used in writing that offers interpretations of other works.

Understanding Persuasive Writing. Persuasive writing attempts to change the reader's mind: to make the writer's opinion or interpretation so convincing that the reader agrees with it. In order to accomplish this goal, the persuasive writer must find arguments and language that attract the reader's interest and appeal to his or her reason. An irrational tone can destroy the premise from which your writing begins.

The main features of persuasive writing are a persuasive purpose and a reasonable, convincing tone.

Because persuasive writing attempts to convince the reader to agree with something, it contains statements of opinion, matters of interpretation. The following examples demonstrate the difference between two appropriate and two inappropriate persuasive opinions on which persuasive papers might be based.

SIGNIFICANT OPINION:	Nuclear power presents too great a hazard to public safety to be used as a major energy source.
INSIGNIFICANT OPINION:	I don't like nuclear power.
SUPPORTABLE OPINION:	Of all the American Presidents of the nineteenth century, Abraham Lincoln faced the greatest problems.
UNSUPPORTABLE OPINION:	No other President, past or future, can match Lincoln's greatness.

523

As well as finding significant opinions, readers of persuasive writing look for specific examples, strong evidence, and logical arguments. Clear, relevant information can engage the reader's interest and win consideration of the writer's opinion. Irrelevant information, like an irrational tone, may prevent your reader from accepting your opinion.

When writing persuasively, express your opinions forcefully while respecting opposing views. Firm, reasonable language is more persuasive than emotionally loaded words, which could antagonize readers. Exact, concrete language and relevant comparisons also work to establish credibility and to hold the reader's attention.

The following paragraph, which was written by Barbara Tuchman, argues that the quality of mass market goods has declined in modern times. Notice the historical examples and logical arguments.

Persuasive paragraph with a persuasive purpose and a reasonable tone

In former times, the princely patron had the resources in wealth and power to commission the finest workmanship, materials, and design. Since his motive was generally self-glorification, the result was as beautiful and magnificent as he could command: in crystal and gold and tapestry, in exquisite silks and brocades, in the jewelled and enameled masterpieces of Cellini, the carved staircases of Grinling Gibbons. The decline in quality that has since set in has a good historical reason: The age of privilege is over and civilization has passed into the age of the masses . . . our culture has been taken over by commercialism directed to the mass market and necessarily to mass taste. De Tocqueville stated the problem, already appearing in his time [a century and a half ago], when he wrote: "When only the wealthy had watches they were very good ones; few are now made that are worth much but everyone has one in his pocket."—Adapted from Barbara Tuchman

Persuasive writing varies in the *urgency* of its tone. The writer might simply offer a fresh interpretation, or might spur readers to take action. Tones range from compelling urgency to relaxed chattiness. Notice the casual and amused tone of the following paragraph.

Persuasive paragraph with a humorous tone

Camping out has become so popular among travelers that campgrounds in summer are likely to be simply crawling with people, pets, vehicles, habitats, and implements, all piled onto one prime strip of the Great Outdoors. At a typical crowded campground, the variety of camping styles is in itself a thing of wonder. One family, visible only from the collective waist up, floats about a high pavilion made of canvas and mosquito netting, setting the table for dinner, just as if they had not left the screened porch back home. Only five feet away from them, another group prefers to rough it on the bare ground with a pup tent and campfire, somehow oblivious to the impressive technology of camping equipment that surrounds them. Everything and everybody is crammed into such close quarters that the campground could easily be mistaken for some sort of outdoor convention of recreation equipment vendors, if it were not for the scenic splendor hovering in front of the milling crowd, like a colossal television set.

Prewriting, Writing, and Revising. When you write persuasively, concentrate on presenting a definite opinion and on inducing a reader to accept it. Assume that the reader disagrees with your premise so that you present your argument more forcefully.

Concentrate on defending your opinion to an unsympathetic or apathetic reader in choosing content and language.

Remember to consider any possible opposing arguments, so that you can counter reader objections. Anticipation of opposing arguments helps you to eliminate weak spots in your defense, as the chart below and on the following page demonstrates.

BUILDING YOUR DEFENSE
Main Idea: The privilege of the reporter to protect his or her sources should be waived when such information is crucial to the just outcome of a trial.

525

Argument For	Argument Against	Counter Argument
—the public's right to a just outcome in a trial should take precedence over the reporter's privilege	—rights of reporters are in a different category since they are guaranteed by the Constitution explicitly	—rights of reporters should be waived in the few cases when the court decides that a fair trial requires their information

In order to win your reader to your side, defend your opinion with accurate, specific, and compelling examples, facts, and reasons. The more controversial your opinion, the more carefully you must build your defense.

The following guidelines will help you write persuasive papers, whether highly controversial or merely interpretive.

SUGGESTIONS FOR WRITING PERSUASIVE PAPERS

1. Choose an issue you care about, and determine whether you can support your opinion about it.

2. Decide how controversial the issue is and how intensely you want to convince your reader.

3. Determine your reader's probable response: apathetic, unsympathetic, or strongly opposed.

4. Express your opinion in a main idea that is clear, significant, and supportable.

5. Gather examples, facts, reasons, and incidents to support your opinion. Consider the opposition and list evidence for and against your view.

6. Organize your support logically. For controversial issues, plan to concede one or more points.

7. Write in forceful but reasonable language, using specific, concrete words and logical connections between ideas.

8. Revise by looking for weaknesses in your approach or inconsistencies in tone. (See the checklist for revision on page 514.)

EXERCISE C: Understanding Persuasive Writing. Read the following persuasive paragraphs and identify in each (1) the opinion in the topic sentence, (2) the supporting evidence, and (3) the urgency of the writer's purpose and tone.

(1) In every stage of these oppressions we have petitioned for redress in the most humble terms: our repeated petitions have been answered only by repeated injury. A prince whose character is thus marked by every act which may define a tyrant, is unfit to be the ruler of a free people. Nor have we been wanting in attentions to our British brethren. We have warned them from time to time of attempts by their legislature to extend an unwarrantable jurisdiction over us. We have reminded them of the circumstances of our emigration and settlement here. We have appealed to their native justice and magnanimity, and we have conjured them by the ties of our common kindred to disavow these usurpations, which would inevitably interrupt our connections and correspondence. They too have been deaf to the voice of justice and consanguinity. We must, therefore, acquiesce in the necessity which denounces our separation, and hold them, as we hold the rest of mankind, enemies in war, in peace, friends.—Thomas Jefferson

(2) One of the most insidious and dangerous of the many environmental problems is air pollution, particularly acid precipitation. It is one that simply cannot wait. Sulfur and nitrogen oxides from power and industrial plants are hurled high into the atmosphere. Carried by air currents hundreds of thousands of miles, these particles can be transformed into compounds which contribute to respiratory diseases, sterilize lakes and streams, damage vegetation, and cloud the sky. Accelerating the use of coal for energy to replace oil promises to aggravate already serious situations in the Upper Midwest, Rocky Mountains, Southeast, and New England-Canadian regions. How much more can we take?—Thomas L. Kimball

EXERCISE D: Planning, Writing, and Revising Persuasive Paragraphs. List *five* topics about which you could offer opinions. Select one, and write a persuasive paragraph, using the suggestions in the chart on page 526. If your opinion is controversial, consider opposing arguments and develop counter-arguments. Revise using the checklist on page 514.

DEVELOPING WRITING SKILLS: Writing and Evaluating Expository and Persuasive Paragraphs. Choose one of the following topics, then follow the suggestions in this section to write an expository paper. When you are through writing your first draft, switch to a persuasive tone on the same topic, again, using the suggestions in this section. After both papers are complete, exchange them with another student. Evaluate the other student's papers, identifying any secondary purposes, and suggest improvements, using another color of ink. Revise your own papers, taking into account both the other student's suggestions and the points in the checklist on page 514. Finally, recopy both papers and submit them to your teacher. You may also submit your paragraph to the school newspaper as the basis for a longer article.

Computers	Male and female roles
Criminal justice	Volunteer work that needs to
A sports figure or team	be done in your community
Fast-food restaurants	A concept such as friendship or
A rock group or singer	love

18.2 Descriptive and Narrative Writing

Descriptive and narrative writing are closely related; in fact, narrative writing often contains descriptive elements. Descriptions attempt to create images—pictures that will enable readers to see what you saw as you saw it. Narrations relate a sequence of events in what is commonly considered a story format.

Descriptive Writing

Descriptive writing paints a picture in words that appeal to a reader's senses and imagination. Much of your writing will involve description, ranging from impressions of a vacation spot to a word picture of the structure of a cell.

Understanding Descriptive Writing. Descriptive writing conveys a dominant impression of a topic. The words and details are vivid enough to enable the reader to see the topic as clearly as the writer did.

Descriptive writing communicates a dominant impression using language which appeals to the reader's senses, imagination, and emotions.

The dominant impression may be a quality, characteristic, mood, or feeling that the topic creates. It may be explicitly stated or implied by details and language in the passage.

Descriptive writing should include striking details, such as sizes, colors, and shapes, and exact verbs, concrete nouns, and vivid adjectives. Notice that the following weak description gives a fuzzy picture; the strong one creates a clear image.

WEAK DESCRIPTION: The middle-aged hiker carried a strange collection of things, including binoculars and some pipes.

STRONG DESCRIPTION: The hiker, a man in his late fifties or early sixties, wore a Russian fur cap and carried binoculars and a small knapsack with an umbrella sticking out. Around the back of his belt in little loops hung twelve or more pipes, some of wood, some of horn, and some of ivory.

Effective description also uses sensory impressions and figures of speech. *Sensory impressions* are details that appeal to the sense of sight, smell, hearing, touch, or taste. *Figures of speech*—similes, metaphors, and analogies—help to depict topics clearly. (For a more detailed explanation of sensory impressions and figures of speech, see Section 14.2.)

The specific details, sensory impressions, and imaginative comparisons in a descriptive paragraph should be organized logically. It should be easy for the reader to follow and should clarify the dominant impression the writer wishes to communicate. Many descriptive paragraphs present details in spatial order, such as top to bottom, left to right, or near to far. Other descriptions might be in chronological order.

The following descriptive paragraph by Joan Didion presents a series of images of Bogotá, Colombia. The dominant impression is one of remoteness and aloofness. The details are organized in spatial order, from indoors to outdoors, and in order of importance, leading to the most memorable detail, that of the mountains in the distance.

529

Descriptive
paragraph
creating a
dominant
impression of
aloofness

Of the time I spent in Bogotá I remember mainly images, indelible but difficult to connect. I remember the walls on the second floor of the Museo Nacional, white and cool and lined with portraits of the presidents of Colombia, a great many presidents. I remember the emeralds in shop windows, lying casually in trays, all of them oddly pale at the center, somehow watered, cold at the very heart where one expects the fire. I asked the price of one: "Twenty-thousand American," the woman said, She was reading a booklet called Horoscope: Sagitario and did not look up. I remember walking across Plaza Bolivar, the great square from which all Colombian power emanates, at midafternoon, when men in dark European suits stood talking on the steps of the Capitol and the mountains floated all around, their perspective made fluid by the sun and shadow; I remember the way the mountains dwarfed a deserted Ferris wheel in the Parque Nacional in late afternoon.—Joan Didion

A writer can use descriptive details and language in different ways to produce many different kinds of responses in the reader. Through the selection of particular details, sensory impressions, and certain other words, a writer can create many different moods. In the preceding paragraph, the writer Joan Didion has chosen to emphasize coolness and aloofness. She has emphasized coolness and aloofness by writing about the white walls of the Museo Nacional, the cool emeralds, the deserted Ferris wheel, and the mountains. The writer conveys her fascination with and her detachment from the scene she describes. The paragraph leads a reader to feel resignation and detachment, a mood which arises from the sense of distances and impersonality. She achieves this especially through the use of the image of mountains that are fluid and floating. By choosing different details and language, Joan Didion might have emphasized the city's buzzing life. The paragraph at the top of the next page from Charles Dickens's novel *Little Dorrit* describes another city scene. In this paragraph Dickens has recreated the oppressiveness of a hot Sunday evening in nineteenth-century London, England.

530

Descriptive paragraph creating a mood of gloom and sadness

It was a Sunday evening in London, gloomy, close, and stale. Maddening church bells of all degrees of dissonance, sharp and flat, cracked and clear, fast and slow, made the brick-and-mortar echoes hideous. Melancholy streets in a penitential garb of soot steeped the souls of the people who were condemned to look at them out of windows in dire despondency. In every thoroughfare, up almost every alley, and down almost every turning, some doleful bell was throbbing, jerking, tolling, as if the Plague were in the city and the dead-carts were going round. Everything was bolted and barred that could by possibility furnish relief to an overworked people. Nothing to breathe but streets, streets, streets.—Charles Dickens

Descriptive writing may also have secondary purposes. A description of a car might also serve the purpose of persuading the reader to buy the car. A description might also amuse a reader. For example, a description of a glee club rehearsal might be written in a humorous way by comparing the singers' voices and appearances to some kinds of animals and birds.

The paragraph by zoologist Archie Carr allows non-experts to visualize snakes' "combat dance." Archie Carr's paragraph serves a secondary purpose of informing readers as well as the primary purpose of describing the "combat dance."

Descriptive paragraph that explains with technical description

Another overt piece of snake behavior that rewards a lucky snake-watcher is the combat dance between the males of some species. This is a balletlike posturing by two male snakes, a crossing and recrossing of necks as the two performers raise the foreparts of their bodies high above the ground until they topple over backwards. The routine is punctuated by periods in which the snakes chase each other about at terrific speed. Then the neck crossing is resumed. No biting or constricting or other violence is involved, and the social function of the dance is not clear. Over and above its interest as an arresting instinctive behavior pattern, the occurrence of the ritual in such distantly related animals as pit vipers, rat snakes, and racers is quite extraordinary.—Adapted from Archie Carr

531

Prewriting, Writing, and Revising. Your descriptive papers should make your topic concrete and recognizable. Aim to express your dominant impression through details and vivid language.

Focus on enabling the reader to sense, imagine, and respond emotionally to what you are describing.

Following are guidelines for writing descriptive papers.

SUGGESTIONS FOR WRITING DESCRIPTIVE PAPERS

1. Choose as a topic a person, place, or experience that you know well and can describe with strong impressions.
2. Determine a dominant impression and state it in a topic sentence.
3. Decide a secondary purpose your paragraph might have, such as entertainment or instruction.
4. List as many details, sensory impressions, and comparisons as you can to describe your topic. Use exact and vivid verbs, nouns, and adjectives.
5. Organize your details, impressions, and comparisons in an order which establishes your dominant impression.
6. Appeal to the reader's senses, imagination, and emotions.
7. Revise for vividness and consistency of mood, and make the description as vivid as possible. (See the checklist for revising on page 514.)

EXERCISE A: Understanding Descriptive Paragraphs. Read the following descriptive paragraphs and identify (1) the dominant impression, (2) the details, sensory impressions, or figures of speech, and (3) the mood.

(1) The antique cash register glowed a pale greenish-gold, broken by sullen flecks of green tarnish. Its arching, narrow, decorated front curved gracefully downward to eleven long-stemmed, lotus-headed keys. It seemed to perch lightly and elegantly on the counter, but in truth the thing squatted there, unbudgeable, a dense, implacable weight. It was a product of a

solider time, which lived on in the heavy little machine's solid frame, solid metal, solid wood, solid marble—in all the reassuring substance and solidity that money once could buy.

(2) Myers was the perfect type of rootless municipalized man who finds his pleasures in the handouts or overflow of an industrial civilization. He enjoyed standing on a curbstone, watching parades, the more nondescript the better, the Labor Day parade being his favorite, and next to that a military parade, followed by the commercial parades with floats and girls dressed in costumes; he would even go to Lake Calhoun or Lake Harriet for doll-carriage parades and competitions of children dressed as Indians. He liked bandstands, band concerts, public parks devoid of grass; sky writing attracted him; he was quick to hear of a department-store demonstration where colored bubbles were blown, advertising a soap, to the tune of "I'm Forever Blowing Bubbles," sung by a mellifluous soprano. He collected coupons and tinfoil, bundles of newspaper for the old rag-and-bone man (thus interfering seriously with our school paper drives), free samples of cheese at Donaldson's, free tickets given out by a neighborhood movie house to the first installment of a serial—in all the years we lived with him, we never saw a full-length movie but only those truncated beginnings. He was always weighing himself on penny weighing machines. He seldom left the house except on one of these purposeless errands, or else to go to a ball game, by himself.
—Mary McCarthy

EXERCISE B: Writing Descriptive Paragraphs. List five topics which you could describe in detail. Choose one and write a descriptive paragraph, following the guidelines in the chart on page 532. Revise, using the checklist on page 514.

Narrative Writing

Narrative writing appears in novels and short stories, memoirs, and biographies, but you can find it in all other kinds of writing. You have probably developed some narrative skill by relating experiences and anecdotes in letters and conversations. This section will strengthen those skills.

Understanding Narrative Writing. Narrative writing presents events in chronological order. It involves and entertains through action, details, and sensory impressions.

Narrative writing tells a series of related events in story form and graphic language.

A narrative covers a limited period of time and has a definite beginning, middle, and end. It may be complete in itself or part of a longer piece of writing. In either case, it moves through time; something happens between the opening and closing sentences.

The opening paragraph of a narrative can simply set the scene and start the action. It may state a general truth or main idea that appears at the begining or end of the paragraph. The events in a narrative are usually arranged in chronological order; that is, they move forward in time, telling what happens next.

The writer should involve the reader in what is happening through action verbs, specific nouns, and colorful adjectives. Transitions and other connecting devices make the story flow.

In the following narrative paragraph from a story by Arthur L. Campa, the topic sentence sets the scene and begins the action of this incident. The story is told from the third person partially omniscient point of view so that the reader knows the character's thoughts as well as sees his actions. Notice that the graphic language engages and holds the reader's attention, builds suspense, and makes the reader feel like a witness to the scene.

Narrative paragraph with a third person omniscient narrator	Halfway down the wall the scorpion lost its hold and fell the remaining distance to the earthen floor with a dull thud. Its menacing pincers went up immediately like the horns on a Texas longhorn, as it raised its grayish belly on four pairs of bony legs. José kept his eyes riveted on it and watched every move. Twelve inches of the most vicious spider known lay before him! The scorpion charged. José ran around the table. Again and again the spider raised its lance to deal the fatal blow, but the elusive prey jumped over it. More determined than ever, the scorpion tried to approach José by moving cautiously toward him. More than

once José thought of stepping on the ugly monster, but the thought of touching such a dangerous hard-shelled creature with his bare foot was too revolting. The nocturnal spider snapped its pincers in defiance and made for its prey, poised on the tips of its stout legs. José backed slowly, watching his chance for a spring. Step by step he kept retreating until inadvertently he ran against the wall and stumbled. The scorpion saw its chance and charged, but José resorted to a machicueta, turning over his head with a handspring that cleared him fully six feet across the room. "Caramba!" he exclaimed, "That was too close a call!"
—Arthur L. Campa

Narrative writing can serve secondary purposes, too, making a reader feel depressed, frightened, peaceful, or joyful. It can also amuse, instruct, or persuade.

The following nonfictional narrative by Dorothy Canfield tells how she developed an idea for a story she wrote. The narrative paragraph relates a series of events in order to explain as well as entertain. Notice that it has a first-person narrator and begins with a topic sentence that states a general truth or main idea, which the story then illustrates.

Narrative paragraph with a first person narrator

My story "Flint and Fire" hovered vaguely in a shimmer of general emotion, and then abruptly crystallized itself about a chance phrase and cadence of the voice which pronounced it. One evening, going on a very prosaic errand to a farm-house of our region, I walked along a narrow path through dark pines; beside a brook swollen with melting snow I found the old man I came to see, sitting silent and alone before his blackened small old house. The old man had been for some years desperately unhappy. I had known this, every one knew it. But that evening, played upon as I had been by the stars, the darkness of the pines and the shouting voice of the brook, I suddenly stopped merely knowing it, and felt it. It seemed to me that his misery emanated from him like a soundless wail of anguish. We talked very little, odds and ends of neighborhood gossip, until the old man, shifting his position, drew a long breath and said, "Seems to me I never heard the brook sound

so loud as it has this spring." There came instantly to my mind the recollection that his grandfather had drowned in that brook, and I sat silent, shaken by that thought and by the sound of his voice. And I knew at the same instant that I would try to get that pang of emotion into a story and make other people feel it.
—Adapted from Dorothy Canfield.

Prewriting, Writing, and Revising. When writing a narrative, your concern should be to connect a series of events in graphic language with a consistent point of view.

Make your narration realistic and captivating through action and story-telling language.

The chart gives suggestions for writing lively narratives.

SUGGESTIONS FOR WRITING NARRATIVE PAPERS

1. Choose an idea that you can develop into a series of events in clear, graphic language.
2. Determine the point of view by considering the different narrators you could have.
3. Decide on any secondary purpose, such as to amuse, instruct, or persuade, and any mood you want to convey.
4. Decide on a topic sentence that states a general truth or launches the story. Jot down a version of it.
5. List the events of the story you will relate, keeping in mind the point of view. Jot details, impressions, and language that will make the account realistic.
6. Organize the events in chronological order.
7. As you write, keep a consistent point of view. Involve the reader through graphic language and clear action.
8. Revise for clarity, vividness, and consistency of point of view. (See the checklist for revision on page 514.)

EXERCISE C: Understanding Narrative Paragraphs. Identify the topic sentence; the point of view; the main events; details, sensory impressions, and graphic language; mood; and secondary purposes in the following paragraphs.

536

(1) When my son and I arrived at the pigyard, armed with a small bottle of castor oil and a length of clothesline, the pig had emerged from his house and was standing in the middle of his yard, listlessly. He gave us a slim greeting. I could see that he felt uncomfortable and uncertain. I had brought the clothesline thinking I'd have to tie him (the pig weighed more than a hundred pounds) but we never used it. My son reached down, grabbed both front legs, upset him quickly, and when he opened his mouth to scream I turned the oil into his throat—a pink corrugated area I had never seen before. I had just time to read the label while the neck of the bottle was in his mouth. It said Puretest. The screams, slightly muffled by oil, were pitched in the hysterically high range of pig-sound, as though torture were being carried out, but they didn't last long: it was all over rather suddenly, and his legs released, the pig righted himself.—E.B. White

(2) Jerry dived, shot past the school of underwater swimmers, saw a black wall of rock looming at him, touched it, and bobbed up at once to the surface, where the wall was a low barrier he could see across. There was no one visible; under him, in the water, the dim shapes of the swimmers had disappeared. Then one, and then another of the boys came up on the far side of the barrier of rock, and he understood that they had swum through some gap or hole in it. He plunged down again. He could see nothing through the stinging salt water but the blank rock. When he came up the boys were all on the diving rock, preparing to attempt the feat again. And now, in a panic of failure, he yelled up, in English, "Look at me! Look!" and he began splashing and kicking in the water like a foolish dog. —Doris Lessing.

EXERCISE D: Writing Narrative Paragraphs. List five ideas which you could develop into a story. Choose one and write a narrative paragraph following the suggestions on page 536. Revise according to the checklist on page 514.

DEVELOPING WRITING SKILLS: Writing and Evaluating Descriptive and Narrative Paragraphs. Choose one of the topics that follow or one of your own as the basis for two connected paragraphs of description and narration. First write a paragraph describing some aspect of your topic. Then write a paragraph telling a story about what you have described. Exchange papers with another student and evaluate his or her work. Use your classmate's comments to revise your paper. Then recopy it and submit all your drafts to your teacher. You may decide to extend your work into a full-length narrative. If you do, consider submitting it to your school literary magazine for publication.

A reunion with an old friend

A discovery

A machine that caused problems

The first day of school

A frightening experience with nature

A sports highlight

An experience while moving

Writing Workshop: Kinds of Writing

ASSIGNMENT 1

Topic Description of Something from an Unusual Viewpoint

Form and Purpose A paragraph that describes from a different viewpoint and conveys a dominant impression

Audience Your classmates

Length One paragraph

Focus See the world as an insect, a small animal, or a baby does. Describe a person, place, or thing from that viewpoint. In your description, convey an impression of the subject's awesome size, but do not name the subject.

Sources Personal observation and imagination

Prewriting Choose your viewpoint. Then brainstorm about a subject seen from that viewpoint; list sensory details that convey the dominant impression.

Writing Use your notes to write a first draft. Choose an order that best conveys the dominant impression.

Revising The checklist on page 532 will help you revise. Then read your paragraph aloud to your classmates, who can attempt to identify both the describer and the subject.

ASSIGNMENT 2

Topic   Defending a Historic Act or Belief

Form and Purpose   A paragraph that persuades a reader of the correctness of a historic act or belief

Audience   People with mixed feelings about the act or belief

Length   One paragraph

Focus   State your position in a topic sentence. Develop your position in a reasonable tone by offering supporting facts, examples, and reasons.

Sources   History texts, biographies, television documentaries, newspaper articles, magazine interviews

Prewriting   Select a historic figure who interests you. Research her or his life, and take notes about an act or a belief that you admire.

Writing   Develop a first draft that logically and forcefully defends your position.

Revising   Use the checklist on page 526 to revise your paragraph. Make sure that all the facts, examples, and reasons you included actually support your position.

Topics for Writing: Kinds of Writing

The above piece of art may suggest a writing idea to you. Plan and write about that idea in an expository, persuasive, descriptive, or narrative paragraph. You may prefer to use one of the following topics to develop a paragraph.

1. A Humorous View of Modern Art
2. Hamburgers, Coke Bottles, Soup Cans— The Subjects of Art?
3. A Career as a Commercial Artist
4. Genius or Madness? A Profile of a Famous Artist
5. The Process of Creating a Marble Sculpture
6. Television—Art Form or Artifice?
7. A Good Film Is a "Moving Picture"
8. Explanation and Description of a Particular Style or Movement in Art History (such as Impressionism)
9. The Artistry of the Photographer
10. Filmmaking—Big Business or Art?

19

Essays

An essay is a composition made up of a group of related paragraphs. All of these paragraphs focus on a main point and, together, the paragraphs support and develop the main point.

This chapter discusses the structural features essential to good essays and examines ways in which unity and coherence contribute to the overall presentation of ideas. Steps for planning, writing, and revising standard essays are given also. Finally, the informal essay, which allows experimentation with patterns of organization and style, is presented.

19.1 Understanding Essays

To write essays, you must be able to recognize and understand the features common to any essay. This section explains the parts of an essay and shows how they work together to serve different purposes. It also discusses methods a writer can use to make an essay a unified and coherent piece of writing.

The Parts of an Essay

A standard essay has a number of structural features, each of which has a particular function. The title suggests the topic and main point of the essay. The introduction, or first main part of the essay, further acquaints the reader with the topic, establishes the essay's purpose and tone, and leads into the thesis statement. The thesis statement usually comes at the end of the introduction and defines the main point and scope of the essay. The body, or middle, is the second main part of the essay. It contains two or more well-developed paragraphs, each exploring some aspect of the essay's main point with examples, details, facts, reasons, and incidents. The third and final main part of an essay is the conclusion. It is usually a paragraph at the end, which completes the essay by reminding the reader of the essay's main point. It may include a summary of the ideas in the body of the essay and any final observations or closing remarks. The following diagram illustrates this three-part structure and shows the position of the title and thesis statement.

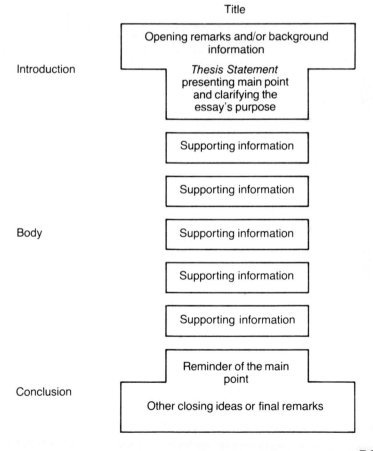

Title

Introduction

Opening remarks and/or background information

Thesis Statement presenting main point and clarifying the essay's purpose

Supporting information

Supporting information

Body

Supporting information

Supporting information

Supporting information

Conclusion

Reminder of the main point

Other closing ideas or final remarks

543

Understanding these structural features will prepare you for planning and writing your own essays.

The Title. A reader gains his or her first impression of an essay from the title. For this reason, a title should grab the reader's attention.

The title of an essay should reflect the main point and purpose of the essay and should capture the reader's interest.

The title should give a preview of the essay. It can reveal the writer's slant or focus on the topic, point up the qualities of the topic, or simply attract reader attention.

No matter how informative the title is, it should not be too long and it should suit the essay's tone. The following chart gives some topics and titles appropriate for them.

SAMPLE TITLES FOR ESSAYS	
Topics	**Titles**
Recent discoveries by archaeologists	"Unearthing New Worlds"
The adventures of skin diving	"Frolicking Among the Fish"
Why the government and people of Australia are worried about the kangaroo population	"Warning: I Brake for Kangaroos"
How to create an herb garden in your own back yard	"Herb Farming at Home"
Ways that new drivers sometimes abuse the rules of the road	"Learning to Keep Your Driver's License"

Introduction with Thesis Statement. The introduction usually consists of a single paragraph, although a long essay may have two or more. The opening statements present the topic and establish the writer's attitude toward the subject and the audience. Most important, the introduction prepares the reader for the thesis statement, which presents the main point and the essay's purpose.

544

The essay's introduction offers opening remarks on the topic and establishes the tone of the essay. It zeroes in on and includes the thesis statement, which states the essay's main point.

The most important sentence in an introduction is the thesis statement because it states the controlling idea or main point. It can also set up a plan for the body of the essay by including subtopics, or divisions of the main point. Thesis statements may be either statements of fact or opinion.

SAMPLE THESIS STATEMENTS		
Thesis Statement	**Purpose**	**Subtopics**
Public libraries in many communities offer special programs for preschoolers, young adults, and adults	To explain	Programs for 1. preschoolers 2. young adults 3. adults
To make an aquarium, buy some equipment, and choose fish that are compatible in a single environment.	To instruct	1. Buying equipment 2. Choosing compatible fish
You should learn to ski.	To persuade	None

This introductory paragraph captures the reader's attention and tells the essay's topic. It sets a serious but friendly tone and guides the reader to the thesis statement, which identifies the main point and indicates an expository purpose.

Introduction to an expository essay

Thesis statement presents a factual main point

In the daytime, we see only one star—our own sun. But when we gaze up into the evening sky, we see thousands and thousands of stars—or suns. From our earthly vantage point, we see few, if any, differences among them. However, according to astronomers, huge differences characterize the millions of suns in the universe. While some are quite similar to our own sun, most are vastly different, particularly in size and temperature.

The following example establishes a different tone and works toward a persuasive purpose. It begins with the writer's personal experience, moves to a statement of the problem, and ends with a proposed response to it. The tone is concerned, casual, and insistent. The thesis statement gives a straightforward opinion and declares a persuasive purpose.

Introduction to a persuasive essay

Thesis statement: opinion and persuasive purpose

After being on the road for just ten minutes one day, I observed the following driving maneuvers: Without warning a van turned right from the left lane, causing the car behind it to jerk to a halt; a station wagon backed up the entire distance of a highway's entrance ramp; a sports car stopped in the middle of a residential street just around a bend while its driver conversed with a pedestrian; and a sedan ran a red light and barely missed the cross traffic. The accident statistics and rising insurance rates confirm what any driver can observe firsthand: The number of negligent drivers is increasing. To combat this menace, our state should institute stricter penalties for negligent driving and moving traffic violations.

The Body Paragraphs. The body paragraphs provide the development of the essay. These make up most of the essay and elaborate on the main point with relevant examples, details, facts, reasons, and incidents. If the thesis statement includes subtopics, the body paragraphs will support and develop each subtopic in order.

The body of an essay contains two or more paragraphs that develop the main point (and any subtopics) with relevant and complete supporting information.

The number of body paragraphs an essay should have depends on the complexity of the thesis statement, the number of subtopics into which the writer divides the main point, and the quantity of available supporting information. Sometimes an essay can have one paragraph for each subtopic. Other times two or more paragraphs will be needed to develop each subtopic. The body paragraphs should always cover the main point thoroughly.

546

The Conclusion. The conclusion, usually no more than one paragraph, wraps up the essay with a reminder of the main point and closing remarks. It leaves the reader satisfied that the topic has been fully explored.

The conclusion of an essay refers to the main point, reminds a reader of the ideas covered, and brings the essay to a satisfying conclusion.

As the writer's final word, the conclusion may summarize, give a last example, or refer to the introduction. It should never repeat whole parts of the essay or start a new topic. The reader should sense the winding down to a close. A final witty or noteworthy sentence can make the essay more memorable for your reader.

All of the key features of an essay should work together to create unity. Notice the six key features of the following essay, and see how each adds to the thought and structure of the whole.

Suns in All Sizes and Colors

Introduction	In the daytime, we see only one star—our own sun. But in the evening sky, we see thousands of stars—or suns. From our earthly vantage point, we see few, if
Thesis statement with two subtopics	any, differences among them. However, according to astronomers, huge differences characterize the millions of suns in the universe. While some are similar to our sun, most are vastly different, particularly in size and temperature.
First body paragraph (develops first subtopic)	Stars range in size from smaller than the earth's diameter to 1,000 times our sun's diameter. The group Alpha Centauri, for example, has a star nearly identical in size to our own. (Actually, scientists calculate the size of this star as 1.1 times that of our sun.) Elsewhere in the universe, Cygnus X-1 had shrunk to a black hole fifteen miles (twenty-five kilometers) across. Our sun, almost one million miles across, dwarfs this tiny star, and is dwarfed in turn by much bigger ones. Betelgeuse, a mere pinpoint in the night sky, is actually a monster about 398 million miles wide (641 million kilometers)—460 times the size of our sun.

Second body paragraph (develops second subtopic)	Just as stars differ greatly in size, so they also vary enormously in temperature. Their surface temperatures can be seen in their light. By passing starlight through color filters and a photometer, or by measuring the spectrum of the light with a spectograph, astronomers can figure out the dominant color and calculate the temperature. Our sun is white/yellow and about 10,000° Fahrenheit (5,500° Celsius). The double star system Capella has two yellow stars with about the same temperature as our sun. Hot stars burn blue, while cool ones have red light. Rigel, a supergiant star with a temperature of 17,000° Fahrenheit (9,400° Celsius), is blue. Sirius B, a dwarf star, is still quite hot at 12,500° Fahrenheit (6,900° Celsius) and emits blue/white light. Red stars have temperatures of less than 5,500° Fahrenheit (3,040° Celsius). Scientists say that our own sun, over the eons, will consume its fuel, cool down, and swell to 100 times its present size. In its old age, it will be a huge red ball in the sky.
Reference to main point	Our sun is only one of the millions of celestial bonfires that are called stars. To reflect the actual state of the universe, the old nursery rhyme would have to read:
Conclusion	Twinkle, twinkle little (medium, giant) star How we wonder *which* you are, Up above the world so high Like a diamond (sapphire/topaz/ruby) in the sky.

EXERCISE A: Identifying Parts of an Essay. Read the following essay on foreign languages written by a student. Then follow the instructions given after the essay.

The Monolingual American

You are in a foreign country and your traveler's checks are stolen. You go to the proper authorities—but they do not speak English. Your luggage is lost in the Paris airport. You complain in English, but the porter stares at you blankly. In a Spanish restaurant, you try to order veal for dinner and are told that you have insulted the waiter. All of these painful episodes can be eliminated by only one thing: knowledge of foreign languages.

This type of verbal faux pas is not limited to ordinary American tourists. Who can forget the Polish people's surprise when Jimmy Carter's interpreter stated that the President was "abandoning" the United States? Mr. Carter's own "Bway-nos Dee-ahs" cannot have endeared him to the Mexican people. Perhaps the worst example of our ignorance of foreign languages was a marketing debacle. General Motors tried in vain to market an economical car, the Nova, in several Latin American countries. Finally someone realized that in Spanish "no va" means "doesn't go."

All of these fiascos and many others underscore Americans' ignorance of foreign languages. The average European student learns two foreign languages. The average American learns none. According to the *Hartford Courant,* less than twenty-five percent of high school students study foreign languages. Our school systems add to the problem. Ninety percent of colleges have dropped language admissions requirements; a quarter of our high schools teach no foreign languages. As a result, nine out of ten Americans comprehend only English. Of those students who have studied another tongue, only seventeen percent use it well.

It is to our advantage to repair this flaw in our educational system. In today's international market, a business person has an edge when speaking a client's language. At home, with the concentrations of Hispanic people in certain areas, a Spanish-speaking professional also enjoys a competitive edge. Ms. Elona Vaisnys of Mount Carmel, a member of the Presidential committee on our foreign language system, said, "You can buy anything anywhere in the world in your own language, but you can't sell."

Americans can no longer assume that everyone speaks English. We are no longer able to demand special treatment. With many high-level technological articles written in German and Russian, the days of "English" supremacy are over. We must realize that foreign languages are vital in international relationships. We must acknowledge what the world has accepted: the importance of learning foreign languages.

1. What is the title of the essay? Is it a good title? Why or why not?

2. How long is the introduction?
3. Is the introduction an effective preparation for the rest of the essay? If so, why? If not, why not?
4. What is the writer's purpose throughout the essay?
5. What audience did the writer seem to have in mind? What tone does the writer establish?
6. What is the thesis statement? What, if any, subtopics does it explicitly mention?
7. How many body paragraphs does the essay have? What is the topic sentence of each body paragraph?
8. List two pieces of supporting information presented in each of the body paragraphs. How does this information help develop the main point of the essay?
9. How long is the conclusion?
10. How does the conclusion remind the reader of the thesis statement? Does the conclusion satisfactorily complete the essay?

Unity and Coherence in Essays

Like any good writing, an essay must be unified and logically ordered from beginning to end. The longer and more complicated a piece of writing is, the more important unity and coherence become to both the writer and the reader. An essay must sustain a focused discussion over many paragraphs. Thus, the qualities of unity and coherence are vital both within an essay's individual paragraphs and throughout the essay as a whole. In a unified essay, all ideas belong together and develop the thesis statement, and the tone is consistent throughout the whole essay. In a coherent essay, all the parts of the essay—every sentence and every paragraph—are arranged in a logical order, and the ideas and information flow smoothly from the introduction to the conclusion.

Overall Unity. Unity in an essay concerns both content and style. All the information included in the essay should be relevant to the main point as it is expressed in the thesis statement. In addition, the writer's attitude toward the subject and the audience, as revealed by the words the writer chooses, must be consistent throughout the whole essay if it is to be unified.

550

An essay has unity if each paragraph is unified and if all the paragraphs support and relate to the thesis statement and to each other.

As the skeleton of ideas, the thesis statement and its subtopics are the main unifiers in an essay. By clearly stating the main point of the essay, the thesis statement guides the writer in choosing significant supporting information. If the writer has the thesis statement in mind at all times, ideas that do not contribute to the main point—that would distract a reader—will appear noticeably out of place. In addition, the subtopics guide the writer to distinguish related information from irrelevant material. Whether the subtopics are stated directly in the thesis statement or chosen after the thesis statement is written, they should be natural divisions, logical categories of the main point, and should relate to each other. If these relationships are strong and clear, by choosing supporting information and developing each subtopic well, the writer will simultaneously develop the thesis statement and stick to the main point. For example, a thesis statement about the efficiency of the Wankel engine suggests four subtopics—the four stages of the power cycle. Each stage and only these stages would be discussed in the body of the essay.

A writer can also use the introduction and conclusion as unifiers. The introduction should narrow the topic to the thesis statement and indicate the essay's scope. By picking up important words or ideas from the introduction, the conclusion can tie together the ideas and information in the essay. The conclusion should imply that the purpose has been accomplished and that the ideas have been treated thoroughly.

Just as all the essay's ideas must be unified, so all the words must create a tone that is consistent from the beginning to the end. The writer must establish and sustain a clear attitude toward the subject and the audience. For example, if the opening paragraph is casual and friendly, the rest of the essay should not shift to a formal, distant tone. Or if the introductory paragraph establishes a matter-of-fact, informative tone, the writer should not offer opinions and personal reactions in the body of the essay. Furthermore, the level of language should not vary. Informal or formal, conversational or scholarly, language should be used consistently in all parts of the essay.

551

Overall Coherence. In addition to having unity, a good essay has coherence. All the information follows a logical order and the essay flows smoothly from idea to idea.

An essay has coherence if the ideas within each paragraph and within the essay as a whole are in logical order and are smoothly connected.

Information in an essay should be logically organized within each paragraph and within the body of the essay as a whole. Ideas in each paragraph and subtopics in the body should follow one of the logical orders: order of importance, chronological order, spatial order, comparison and contrast order, or developmental order. (For more information on logical order, see Section 17.1.) Often the main point and the subtopics—whether they are steps, categories, or arguments—will help determine the best order. Note how a main point and its subtopics can suggest a logical order for the body of an essay.

POSSIBLE ORDER FOR SUBTOPICS	
Subtopics	**Possible Orders**
Three reasons why a proposed law should be defeated	Order of Importance
Rewards that motivated the fifteenth-century Spanish explorers	
Events of an exploration through a cave	Chronological
Stages in the metamorphosis of a caterpillar	
Original structures of Rome's Colosseum	Spatial
Sights along Alaska's Yoho Falls	
Crime statistics in two cities	Comparison and Contrast
Team versus individual sports	
Specific use for common products	Developmental
Effects of radiation poisoning	

Essay Showing Overall Unity and Coherence. An essay about the Wankel engine could be made coherent through its organization and use of transitions. The subtopics, the four stages of the engine's power cycle, could follow chronological and spatial order. Because the essay is explaining a process, the development of each subtopic could also follow chronological and spatial order. The essay could achieve unity as well as coherence by developing each subtopic with information on that particular stage only. In the following excerpt from an essay by a student, notice the transitions in italic type and the other connecting devices that clarify the relationships among ideas within each paragraph as well as from paragraph to paragraph.

Understanding the Wankel Engine

Thomas Edison, the great inventor and scientist, once remarked that "genius is 10% inspiration and 90% perspiration." Perhaps one modern example of this truism can be found in the case of Felix Wankel and his Wankel engine. Wankel's revolutionary engine took him over twenty years to perfect, and it is only now beginning to be recognized and accepted. The major advantage of this engine lies in its light, simple construction. In the Wankel engine, there are only two major parts: an oval, peanut-shaped housing and a three-sided rotor that fits inside it.

Similarly, the engine's operation is simple and can be understood if one follows one of the rotor's three sides at a time. (Realize, though, that the other two faces duplicate these steps.) Basically, the Wankel engine works by drawing in a fresh gasoline-air mixture, compressing it, igniting it, and sweeping the burnt gases out of the engine.

The *beginning* step, drawing in a fresh gasoline-air mixture, is an example of the engine's simplicity. Along one side of the oval housing is an intake port which admits the gasoline-air mixture. As the leading edge of the rotor face rotates in its clockwise motion past the intake port, it feeds the gas-air mixture into the cavity between the rotor face and the housing. The intake continues *until* the trailing edge of the rotor face moves past the port, shutting off the flow.

After the fuel mixture is drawn into the engine, it is *then* compressed. The turning rotor face moves against the almost flat sidewall that is directly opposite the intake port. Due to the unique shape of the rotor and the housing, the volume of the cavity decreases significantly. *As a result,* the fuel mixture contained in it is compressed by a factor of nine. This compression greatly aids the burning of the fuel and increases the engine's efficiency.

However, the most important part of the engine's operation is the ignition of the fuel mixture, for this is the source of the engine's thrust. This phase begins *when* the air-gas mixture is at the point of greatest compression. *At this point,* the spark plug inside the housing fires, igniting the gases. The *resulting* explosion drives the rotor in its clockwise motion.

As a result of the ignition, the gases are used up and must be disposed of. The *final* step, sweeping the used fuel out of the engine, takes care of this process. It is an important step in that it prepares the engine for another cycle. *In this process,* the leading edge moves around the housing *until* it uncovers the exhaust port, which is located adjacent to the intake port. The high-pressure gases are *then* swept out of the engine chamber, and the engine is *now* ready to repeat the process.

Clearly, the Wankel's simplicity seems to be of major importance in today's society. Its lightness is the key to compactness, lower maintenance, and fuel economy. Because of consumers' and auto manufacturers' desire for these qualities, the popularity of the Wankel is rising rapidly. An indication of this trend is found in the words of Dr. David E. Cole, associate professor of mechanical engineering at the University of Michigan: ". . . by 1980 the predominant American auto engine will be a Wankel." Indeed, Felix Wankel deserves commendation for his genius, inspiration, and perspiration in developing such a remarkable product.—Thomas Wu

EXERCISE B: Recognizing Unity and Coherence in an Essay. Reread the student essay above. Then answer the following questions.

1. What is the single, clear main point made in the thesis statement?
2. How are the subtopics related to the main point made in the thesis statement?
3. In what way are the subtopics related to each other?

554

4. What is the tone of the essay? Where, if anywhere, does the tone change?
5. How would you rate the unity of this essay? Where, if anywhere, does the essay become disunified?
6. In what order are the subtopics arranged?
7. Is this order effective? If so, why? If not, why not?
8. What words or phrases act as transitions?
9. What repeated main words and synonyms contribute to the coherence of the essay?
10. Examine one paragraph for coherence. How is it organized? What transitions, repeated main words, and synonyms unify the paragraph? Are pronouns clear and consistent throughout?

DEVELOPING WRITING SKILLS: Analyzing an Essay. Look in anthologies of nonfiction, in magazines, or in special sections of newspapers for a unified, coherent essay. Use the questions in Exercises A and B to analyze the essay and evaluate its unity and coherence.

Writing an Essay 19.2

Now that you are familiar with the structure of a standard essay, you are prepared to create successful essays of your own.

PREWRITING: Planning Your Essay

The initial planning steps are vital to your essay. From generating ideas for topics to choosing and narrowing a topic to writing a sharply defined thesis statement, following a few basic steps can help you throughout the entire writing process.

Generating Ideas and Choosing a Topic. Unless a topic has been assigned to you, you can find topics by using your imagination and exploring your interests, as well as by examining books and other sources of ideas. Using other techniques such as interviewing yourself, free writing, journal writing, clustering, brainstorming, and cueing can help you generate essay topics also. (See Section 13.1 to review these techniques.) Write down possible topics as you think of them.

Use various techniques to generate ideas for essay topics.

Below is an example of brainstorming for an essay topic. While generating possible topics, you might jot down some that are somewhat narrowed already, such as the use of animals in space exploration in the 1960's, early American painters, and popular American myths. As you brainstorm, break down some general topics into smaller ones.

BRAINSTORMING FOR AN ESSAY TOPIC	
The Renaissance —development of Italian art —the expansion of scientific knowledge	*Hockey* —development of the game —how to shoot properly —the importance of a goalie
The use of animals in space exploration of the 1960's	*What to do in the Scottish Highlands*
Student employment —full-time career opportunities —the minimum wage —starting your own service business	—Loch Ness —Scottish castles —surrounding islands (Orkneys, Isle of Skye) *Early American Painters* *Popular American myths*

Once you have a general topic of your own or one that has been assigned to you, be sure that your essay will have a specific point. In other words, narrow your area of interest to a topic that you can discuss satisfactorily in a single essay.

Reduce a general topic to a more specific one that you can cover thoroughly in an essay.

Although you may find that some are narrow enough to be starting points for essays, in most cases you must narrow the idea further in order to be able to cover it. Remember that the broader your topic is, the more superficial your treatment is likely to be; it is always best to define your topic sharply.

Determining Audience, Purpose, and Main Points. Once you have found a topic, you have a starting place. You now need to find a main point—something to say about your topic. This main point is what you will explain, expand, or ar-

556

gue for in your essay. Deciding on your audience can help you sharpen your topic to a main point, as can thinking about your purpose.

Focus on a main point by determining your audience and purpose.

Thinking about the readers with whom you plan to communicate and about your purpose—to explain, persuade, describe, relate events—can guide your selection of a main point. An essay about starting your own service business, for example, could be written for an audience of other students who have had experience with self-employment or for adults who are skeptical about the idea. Or it could be aimed at students who know little about the topic.

Suppose you decide to write for students who are unfamiliar with the concept of starting a business. With this audience in mind, you could ask yourself questions about your topic, to find some possible main points.

Questions	Main Points
What kinds of service businesses can high school students start?	—High school students can start businesses that involve handiwork around the house and yard, special skills such as typing and tutoring, and creative projects such as catering children's parties and recycling.
What are the advantages for high school students of starting a service business?	—The advantages that starting a service business gives you are the opportunity to make more money than in some conventional jobs and flexibility in your working hours.
What single idea do I most want to communicate to the audience?	—Working for yourself is a real alternative to "regular" after-school jobs.

Each of the main points in the chart focuses on some aspect of the topic of students' working for themselves, but each main point suggests a different purpose and emphasis. The first point explains some of the businesses that students can start; its purpose would be expository. The second and third main points, on the other hand, are persuasive; they are both directed toward selling the idea of starting a service business. The second point focuses on the benefits while the third main point merely states an opinion about students' working for themselves.

Writing a Thesis Statement. Any main point can be written as a thesis statement by expressing it as a complete sentence and polishing it. Experiment with the wording of your thesis statement by writing several versions to find the appropriate emphasis for your ideas. One of your potential thesis statements might be preferable because it includes subtopics that could guide your planning for the body of the essay.

If you were writing for an audience unfamiliar with the topic of starting your own service business, you might choose to have a persuasive purpose and to express the second main point as your thesis statement. The chart shows several thesis statements that you might write using the second main point.

POSSIBLE THESIS STATEMENTS

Main Point: The advantages of a service business are the opportunity to make more money than in some conventional jobs and to give you flexible working hours.

1. Working for yourself has the advantages of giving you the opportunity to make more money than you would in some conventional jobs and of giving you flexible working hours.

2. Hang up that gas pump and crumple that grocery bag; become your own boss to make more money and choose your own hours.

3. Starting your own service business can provide lucrative wages and the independence of a flexible work schedule.

4. If you try, you might think of some valuable services you can perform that pay more than some conventional jobs and that give you flexible working hours.

558

Each of these four possible thesis statements has a slightly different meaning and a different tone. The first thesis statement is the most direct and plain, clearly stating the idea of advantages of a service business. The second is the most casual and striking, resembling a high-powered sales pitch. The third thesis statement is direct and slightly more formal than the others, and the fourth includes the idea of valuable services and creative thinking. After considering the four thesis statements in the chart, you might decide that you favor the first thesis statement since it is a straightforward one with a personal tone.

Developing Supporting Information. Having formulated your thesis statement, you can begin planning the rest of the essay. Even though you may still change your thesis statement if you want to at some later point, your present thesis statement can establish the scope and direction of your essay and guide you in your search for supporting information. When you brainstorm for support, keep your purpose and audience in mind.

Brainstorm for examples, details, facts, and reasons to develop your main point.

You can follow at least two methods of brainstorming. In one, you can generate supporting material through a process of free association. You should write your thesis statement at the top of your paper and jot down everything that comes to your mind that might be usable in the development of this main point. Or you might want to use a question-and-answer method, writing down questions that a reader would naturally raise about your main point and then jotting down all the material you know that answers these questions. If your thesis statement contains subtopics, these can be included as part of the questions you ask and can help lead you to appropriate answers.

Whatever method you use for brainstorming, your goal should be to gather as many related examples, details, facts, reasons, and incidents as possible from your own experience, knowledge, and recent reading. If your essay seeks to explain a concept or event, you should gather factual information and give credit to any books, magazines, or newspapers that supply you with relevant material. If your essay is descriptive or narrative, concentrate on specific details, sensory impressions, actions, and events. Your goal at this point in your preparation is quantity; you can refine and screen your ideas once they are down on paper.

The following chart applies the question-and-answer method of brainstorming to gather strong, thorough supporting information. Notice that it makes use of the subtopics in the thesis statement and also incorporates some of the methods for building a defense for an opinion because this is a persuasive essay.

BRAINSTORMING FOR SUPPORTING INFORMATION

Thesis Statement: Working for yourself has the advantages of giving you the opportunity to make more money than you would in some conventional jobs and of giving you flexible working hours.

What are some of the valuable services that high school students can perform that pay more than conventional jobs?

—typing for as much as $.75 a page for about $5.00–$7.50 an hour

—work for older people
 —walking their dogs
 —shoveling snow
 —running errands
 —could pay about $4.00 an hour

—household work for working people
 —cleaning
 —washing windows
 —polishing floors

—tutoring—can charge $4.00–$5.00 an hour, if you're a good tutor

—home improvement projects
 —cleaning eaves
 —painting indoors and outdoors
 —people willing to pay for services they don't have time or skill to do themselves

---

How does running a service business give you flexible hours?

—you can work as much as you want
 —grooming pets

—you can schedule your work around your studying and school activities

---

560

—collecting aluminum cans for recycling
—refinishing furniture
—hauling away trash
—you can work just on weekends
—organizing and publicizing garage sales
—catering children's birthday parties
—you can work only over long weekends or holidays
—bringing in mail, caring for pets, watering lawns
—tutor a few afternoons a week
—offer private classes for children in sports, crafts, piano, or guitar on a few afternoons a week
—teach a few evening classes at a community center in folk dancing, crafts, sewing, weight training
—work when you want

What are some arguments against running your own service business?

—requires a lot of planning, developing customers
—takes advertising
—might require investment in equipment

What are some counter-arguments on the pro side?

—planning pays off
—find contacts in your community through parents' friends and work, through clubs and religious organizations
—free advertising by using bulletin boards at grocery
stores, community centers, local businesses
—neighbors might lend equipment; parents might help in the investment; local hardware stores might rent the equipment reasonably

---

Organizing Your Essay. Once you have a thesis statement and plentiful supporting information, you have the raw materials for your essay. Now you must organize your information, examine it for unity and completeness, and prepare a plan for your writing.

Organize your supporting information into logical subtopics of the thesis statement and then make an outline to guide your writing.

561

Each writer discovers a preferred way of doing the organizing step, but a few guidelines can be helpful. You should identify subtopics, if your thesis statement does not include them. They should be natural categories, steps, divisions, or outgrowths of your main point. Your essay should have two or more subtopics. If your thesis statement does not contain subtopics, you may find, by examining your supporting information, that the material divides logically into two or three groups or parts. Decide which will come first, next, and last. Can your subtopics follow a chronological or spatial organization? A comparison and contrast order? Can you use a developmental order or order of importance? If your essay is persuasive, which subtopic is most convincing? If it is expository, what organization would be most helpful?

The essay on starting your own service business is already partially organized by its thesis statement, which contains subtopics—the two advantages of working for yourself: (1) the jobs and (2) flexible working hours. If you examine the supporting information and consider the persuasive purpose of the essay, you may see another subtopic in which you mention the arguments against the thesis statement and then counter with arguments in favor of it. This way you dispose of negative points first and move on to your important reasons and examples. Thus the essay has three subtopics, one refuting some opposing points, one discussing opportunities to make money, and one discussing flexible working hours. You might decide that flexible hours are more important than money and organize by order of importance.

All your supporting information should be sorted and grouped under an appropriate subtopic and evaluated for unity at the same time. Eliminate pieces of information that do not fit under a subtopic and support the thesis statement. Delete support that is repetitious or vague. To fill gaps, think up additional supporting information so that you cover each subtopic. You can complete this organizing and sorting right on your brainstorming sheet by circling ideas that belong together or by numbering all ideas relating to the first subtopic with *1*'s and all those for the second subtopic with *2*'s and so on.

You may want to revise your thesis statement to reflect important ideas that occurred to you during your organizing. The only other organizing you will need to do is deciding on a logical order for pieces of information under each subtopic. Again, the orders for coherence—order of importance, chronological order, spatial order, comparison and contrast order, and developmental order—can be useful.

The blueprint or rough plan from which you will write your essay should show all of your organizing decisions. Your plan may simply be your brainstorming sheet marked and numbered. It may be a modified outline with subtopics as headings and supporting material listed in logical order under each, or it may be a formal topic outline that shows the relative importance of your supporting information as well as the order.

For the essay on working for yourself, you might write a topic outline like the following. The thesis statement has been revised slightly for smoothness. The first subtopic is organized like a debate with a few of the opposition's arguments admitted and three pro arguments presented. The second and third subtopics are also actually pro arguments, in order of importance. All the material follows developmental order.

Thesis Statement: Working for yourself has advantages. You can make more money than you would in some conventional jobs and you can have flexible working hours.

I. Not difficult to start your own service business
   A. (Con argument) Impractical to start your own business
      1. Takes a great deal of planning
      2. May require some financial investment for advertising and equipment
   B. (Pro argument) Possible to find customers easily
      1. Make contacts through the community
      2. Make contacts through parents and their work
      3. Make contacts through clubs and religious organizations
   C. (Pro argument) Possible to advertise inexpensively
      1. Run one initial ad in newspaper
      2. Place ads free on bulletin boards in stores, businesses, and community centers
   D. (Pro argument) Possible to obtain equipment
      1. Borrow from neighbors
      2. Buy with parents' help
      3. Rent from local stores

II. Making more money than in some conventional jobs
  A. Possible to do household work for working people
    1. Clean houses for $6.00 an hour
    2. Wash windows, polish floors, shampoo rugs
  B. Possible to help out older people
    1. Work for at least $4.00 an hour
    2. Garden, walk dogs, shovel snow, do laundry, shopping, and errands
  C. Possible to do home improvement projects
    1. Receive good wages from people who don't want to pay high professional fees
    2. Paint houses indoors and out
  D. Possible to tutor for $4.00 to $5.00 an hour
  E. Possible to type for $7.50 an hour
    1. Type papers and manuscripts
    2. Make more than an office employee at $3.50 an hour
III. Having flexible working hours
  A. Set own hours to fit school and other activities
  B. Possible to work only on long weekends or holidays by taking care of people's houses, lawns, pets
  C. Possible to work only on weekends
    1. Cater children's birthday parties
    2. Organize and publicize garage sales
  D. Possible to work only on a few afternoons
    1. Tutor
    2. Teach private classes for children
  E. Can work as much as you want doing assorted jobs

Although you can leave your title and conclusion until later, thinking about them at this point can be helpful. Considering different titles can help you firm up the essay's tone. You will want to devise a short, direct title that will interest the reader and suggest the main point. Having some ideas in mind for your conclusion can motivate you as you write.

EXERCISE A: Selecting and Refining Topics for Essays.
Choose one of the following general topics or use one of your own. Beneath the topic, list at least four smaller topics that would narrow the general topic to the scope of a single essay. Then circle the one narrowed topic that you prefer to write about.

Professional sports	A career or college major
The history of a game	Ancestry
	Victims of crimes
A political stand	An extinct or near-extinct species
Amateur photography	of animal
Vitamins or nutrition	
Home computers	

EXERCISE B: Preparing a Thesis Statement. Using the topic you selected in Exercise A, follow these instructions.

1. Briefly describe the audience for whom you are writing.
2. Keeping this audience in mind, write down at least three questions about your topic. Write brief answers that will be possible main points for your essay.
3. Determine the purpose of each possible main point, and choose one that intrigues you and serves your purpose.
4. Phrase this main point in three or four different thesis statements and choose the one you like best.

EXERCISE C: Gathering Supporting Information. Use your thesis statement from Exercise B, and then follow one of the following methods for gathering support.

1. Use free association to list beneath your thesis statement all the supporting information that comes to mind.
2. Write down questions that a reader would expect you to answer about your thesis statement. Then write all the answers—all the examples, details, facts, reasons, and incidents—that you can think of.

EXERCISE D: Ordering Supporting Information. Use your brainstorming sheet from Exercise C to plan the order of ideas for your essay. Follow these steps.

1. Examine your thesis statement and supporting information and identify two or more subtopics.
2. Choose a logical order for these subtopics.
3. Decide the order of information for each subtopic and delete repetitious, irrelevant, or vague information. Add information if necessary to cover each subtopic well.

565

4. Examine your thesis statement and revise it if it no longer exactly fits your ordered and unified supporting information.
5. Finally, show your organizing decisions on your brainstorming sheet, in a modified outline, or in a topic outline.

EXERCISE E: Planning an Introduction, Title, and Conclusion. Using your outline and original list of supporting information, sketch a few ideas for an introduction. Experiment with two or three possible titles for your essay, and list two or three ideas for your conclusion.

WRITING: Creating a First Draft

By the time you write an outline or plan, your preparatory steps are completed. You can now think about writing a first draft of the entire essay in which you should strive for a unified tone and smooth connections among ideas.

Use your outline and notes to write a complete, coherent version of the essay.

When you actually write your draft, use every other line to allow room for revisions or alterations later on. Think about your purpose and audience as you write, and establish and maintain an appropriate and consistent attitude toward your subject and reader. Do you want to sound friendly or scholarly? Formal or informal? Casual or serious? In addition, as you compose sentences, make a deliberate effort to link your ideas smoothly by using transitions, repeating main words, using synonyms for main words, or employing other connecting devices. Vary the length and structure of sentences to make your writing more interesting and to emphasize important ideas. Use precise words, and try to maintain a consistent level of language.

If you were to complete the essay on working for yourself, you might produce a finished version like the following. The marginal comments point out the essay's structure, and some of the transitions are italicized. Notice the repetition of main words and the use of synonyms throughout the essay to link ideas.

Title	Becoming Your Own Boss
Introduction	The thought of part-time work may conjure up images of bussing dishes, pumping gas, bagging groceries, or running a cash register. But there are other ways to make money. You might consider becoming your own employer by painting houses, gardening, or
Thesis statement	tutoring. Working for yourself, you can make more money than in conventional jobs, and you can have flexible hours.
Subtopic 1: arguments against the drawbacks	Some of you might argue that working for yourself takes a great deal of planning and investment. Although these views are valid, the problems are all surmountable. There are various ways you can find customers: through community contacts, friends and business acquaintances, and clubs and religious groups. You can advertise for little money in local newspapers. You can place free ads on bulletin boards in stores, community centers, local businesses, and schools. You will probably find that neighbors will lend you necessary equipment, parents will help with your initial investment, or local stores will rent you equipment reasonably. Sometimes you can get secondhand machines cheaply through want ads. And once set up, a service business provides profitable and convenient work.
Subtopic 2: making more money than in some conventional jobs	By performing useful services, you may find that you earn more than the minimum wage. Many people today pay others to do their household work. Working people, for example, may pay as much as $6.00 an hour for housecleaning. They will pay at least that much for having heavy work done such as window washing, floor polishing, and rug and upholstery shampooing. Older people often pay $4.00 an hour for gardening, dog walking, snow shoveling, or having laundry, shopping, and errands done. Some homeowners lack the interest or skill to do home improvement projects. They would rather pay students to do indoor or outdoor painting than engage a professional service at a higher fee. Others will pay to have odd jobs, such as minor carpentry work, done. If you are a good tutor, you can charge from $4.00 to $5.00 an hour. An accurate typist can

make $7.50 an hour typing papers for college or graduate students or manuscripts for writers or publishers. This is well above the $3.50 an hour a part-time office worker earns.

Subtopic 3: having flexible working hours

The real advantage of running a business might be working when and as much as you want. You can adjust working hours to fit your study time and extracurricular activities. You might work only on long weekends, minding people's houses, collecting their mail, watering their lawns, or caring for pets. You might work on weekends, catering children's birthday parties or running garage sales. If afternoon work suits your schedule, you might tutor on free afternoons or conduct private classes in crafts, sports, or music for children. Or, if you want to work many hours, you might do household jobs for older or working people, groom pets, refinish furniture, type for business people or other students, tailor, or collect cans, newspapers, and bottles for recycling.

Reminder of thesis statement

Conclusion

When you consider working for yourself, you can see that the possibilities for making the most money in the time you have depends on how creative, enterprising, and conscientious you are. You might find your service business so lucrative that you can share it with other students, perhaps by hiring them to work for you, or increase it to full time in the summer. Rather than be discouraged about the part-time job market for students, remember that clerking in a store, flipping hamburgers, and answering phones are not your only choices.

EXERCISE F: Writing the First Draft of an Essay. Use your rough version of your introduction and your plan or outline to write a complete version of your essay, ending with the ideas you listed for your conclusion and any others that come to mind. Try to maintain the tone you set in the introduction and thesis statement by keeping your audience and purpose in mind. As you write, attempt to achieve a fresh, readable style. Use transitions and other connecting devices to clarify your ideas for the reader. Write in complete sentences and double-space or skip every other line.

REVISING: Polishing Your Essay

The revision stage gives you a chance to rethink your ideas and refine your writing.

Check your essay to make any necessary improvements before you make your finished copy.

If possible, set your first draft aside awhile before you revise. After a short interval to gain some objectivity, take a fresh look at your writing. Look for ways to improve the content and organization. Make changes that will improve your essay's clarity, forcefulness, interest, unity, or coherence.

CHECKLIST FOR REVISING A STANDARD ESSAY

1. Is the title appealing and appropriate?
2. Does the introduction arouse interest, provide background information, set a tone, and lead toward the main point?
3. Is the main point clearly stated in the thesis statement?
4. Do the body paragraphs support subtopics of the thesis statement? Is the main idea of each paragraph clear?
5. Have you included enough support—examples, details, facts, reasons, and incidents—to develop each subtopic thoroughly?
6. Are the subtopics arranged in logical order: order of importance, chronological order, spatial order, comparison and contrast order, or developmental order?
7. Is the information within each paragraph arranged logically and connected by transitions and other linking devices?
8. Does the conclusion refer to the main point of the essay?
9. Do your word choices convey the tone you intend? Does the tone remain consistent throughout the essay?
10. Do sentences have varied lengths, openers, and structures?
11. Can you find errors in spelling, grammar, usage, or punctuation? If you are not sure, check a dictionary or the grammar, usage, and mechanics units of this book.
12. Does the essay communicate with your audience and fulfill its purpose?

EXERCISE G: Revising Your Essay. Check for content, organization, language and style. Use the checklist on page 569 for a final review. Change anything that you think requires improvement. Then make and proofread a final copy and submit it to your teacher.

DEVELOPING WRITING SKILLS: Planning, Writing, and Revising an Essay. Choose another essay topic from the list below, or think of one of your own. Refine the topic, develop support, organize, and write a first draft. Use other students as your audience. Exchange completed essays with a classmate and use the checklist to evaluate the other student's work. Improve your essay according to the comments you receive. Then submit a final copy.

Language	Politics
Traffic laws	Beauty
Dancing	Conservation
Comedy	Newscasting
Spectator sports	Insects

19.3 Writing Different Kinds of Essays

This section focuses on three kinds of essays which you may need to write: expository, persuasive, and informal. Expository writing informs readers. Persuasive writing influences the reader's opinion or moves him or her to action. Informal essays are more loosely structured and individual in style.

Writing Expository Essays

When you write to report information, explain functions or operations, define concepts, or instruct, you are writing an expository essay. This type of essay is objective and straightforward and gives concrete factual information.

Understanding Expository Essays. The special features of expository essays are an explanatory purpose and an informative tone. All expository writing communicates facts; it does not express opinions or try to change the reader's opinions.

Expository essays present factual material and have an informative tone.

Expository essays follow the three-part structure of any standard essay, but their thesis statements are clearly explanatory. They present factual statements and objective evidence which bolsters the statements. Notice below that a fact can be observed or verified, while an opinion cannot be.

STATEMENT OF FACT: By 1995, one American in four will be sixty years old or more.

STATEMENT OF OPINION: In another decade, there will be more older Americans than ever before.

The following chart presents three thesis statements suitable for an expository essay. Each one expresses a factual main point that a writer can support with objective material. Each also has a specific purpose, as the second column shows. The last statement includes suggested subtopics.

SAMPLE THESIS STATEMENTS FOR EXPOSITORY ESSAYS		
Thesis Statements	**Purpose**	**Stated Subtopics**
According to historians, sod houses were the creation of hardy, resourceful settlers.	To report	None
Computers are changing the work flow in large offices.	To explain	None
Experiential learning is an asset to college students.	To define	(1) Combines work and study (2) Earns wages and credits

Supporting information serves the explanatory purpose by offering specific examples and details that lead the reader to understand the thesis statement. It can come from your personal experience, reading, or the statements of experts. It should be organized logically under subtopics that focus on the important aspects of the main point.

571

Expository essays employ an informative tone, which indicates that the writer is presenting new knowledge. The tone and language should suit the reader's knowledge or experience. Opinions and careless word choice are flaws in expository essays. The writer should project objective, unemotional attitudes through careful use of language and selection of reliable facts. In the thesis statement above about sod houses, the phrase "According to historians" sets an authoritative tone. Though expository essays can be both serious and humorous, they should all use this informative tone.

Prewriting, Writing, and Revising. For expository essays, follow the same steps you use in writing any essay. Give special attention to your purpose, audience, and tone.

Focus on your explanatory purpose, your audience, and the use of an informative tone as you prepare an expository essay.

Consider topics with which you are familiar, that lend themselves to objective, factual presentations. Decide whether you will report, explain, instruct, or define.

Make sure your thesis statement expresses a fact and not an opinion. It should make your expository purpose clear. For example, this thesis statement shows that the essay will explain the steps in a process: Computers are changing the work flow in large offices.

As you brainstorm for supporting information, think of your purpose and your audience. When writing for less knowledgeable readers, provide background information. For more knowledgeable readers, explore the subject more deeply.

Your thesis statement will help you organize your supporting information. For example, the thesis statement on sod houses suggests chronological order, while the one on experiential learning prepares the reader for comparison and contrast.

As you write, concentrate on explaining your topic to your audience. Move logically through the supporting ideas, giving all the information the reader needs. Use transitions to help the reader follow your explanation.

EXERCISE A: Recognizing the Features of Expository Essays. Read the following expository essay, and answer the questions that follow it.

Soddies—The Homes and Their Builders

What kind of house did American settlers invent? Many people would answer: log houses. But log dwellings were common in northern Europe when emigrants were peopling the New World. So were brick homes, and the clapboard ones we associate with New England.

The one kind of dwelling that was the invention of clever, hard-working American settlers was the sod house of the plains.

The "soddies" who first built these unusual homes of soil were the hardy men and women who thought the seaboard states were getting too crowded. In the second half of the 1800's, they left the cities and established farms and pushed westward beyond the Appalachian Mountains into the unsettled "Indian lands."

In wagons and carts, on horseback and on foot, they traveled to the great prairies. There the government offered them sixty acres of free farm land. To make the land their own forever, homesteaders had only to settle down, make the virgin soil productive, and build permanent houses.

Imagine how homesteading families must have felt when they first caught sight of the vast stretches of waving buffalo grass. Their first thought must have been appreciation for the natural gifts of the bountiful continent and for opportunity. But the second idea must have come quickly: How would they ever build houses? Back East, they had lived in homes of sawed lumber from plentiful forests. Here there was not a tree as far as the eye could see.

The determined farmers used what was available. They hitched up their mules and cut down the sea of tall grass. Then they drove plows over the sod, dense and tough with the matted roots of wild plants. They cut it into strips a foot wide and a half a foot thick. They hacked the strips into manageable "bricks," and laid them end to end, with the shorn grass downward, forming rectangles which outlined their new homes. A second layer of sod pieces went on top, covering the seams of the first row. Loose, damp earth, pushed into the cracks, made the building tight and warm. The back-breaking work went on until the sod walls rose high enough for a man to stand upright.

Then a ridge-pole—prize possession of a settler—went on top, running from one end of the house to the other. If a soddy were well off, he had planks brought from the East and nailed them to the pole, extending the ends over the front and back walls. If not, he made do with tarpaper. Either way, more sod was laid on top of the roof, with the cut grass facing the sky.

A few lucky families had window glass set in scrap lumber frames. Most people used oiled paper or gunnysacks in the window openings. The floors were invariably hard-packed earth. Occasionally, a homesteading woman insisted on the whitewashed inside walls she had had back East.

Soddies were not perfect dwellings. Sometimes the roofs leaked or collapsed under the weight of the sod. Small animals and bugs nested in the grassy roofs and fell into the house. The rooms were dark, because of the expense of real windows.

Nevertheless, soddy farmers could be pleased with their handwork, and soddies grew fiercely proud of their homes. They boasted about the thick walls that kept them cool in summer and warded off strong gales. In winter, a few corncobs in the stove kept them warm. Neither blizzards nor fire could penetrate the foot-thick walls which they themselves had erected.

Some sod houses have stood on the plains for over a century, housing two or three generations. According to one writer, a handful of Americans were still living in sod houses as late as 1970, in the western states.

The surviving sod houses—and the thousands that have crumbled into heaps of mud—are a monument to the strong and independent men and women who undertook the arduous and awesome task of opening the western United States and creating its own architecture.

1. What does the title contribute to the essay? What other title can you suggest?
2. How does the introduction prepare the reader for an expository essay?
3. What is the thesis statement?
4. What are the subtopics developed in the body?
5. In what order are the subtopics arranged? Can you suggest an alternative order?
6. What are two specific pieces of information presented in each body paragraph?
7. What are five instances in which transitions, repetitions of main words, or synonyms help to tie the ideas together?

574

8. How is the concluding paragraph related to the thesis statement? What words and ideas link the introduction and conclusion?
9. How does the last sentence "clinch" the essay?
10. To what extent does the essay fulfill its purpose? What words contribute to the informative tone?

EXERCISE B: Writing an Expository Essay. Narrow one of the following topics to a main point and decide on a purpose and audience. Gather supporting information and organize an essay. Write it and add a title. Revise for good transitions, unity, and informative tone.

How to make croissants	Sanskrit, our mother tongue
World trade before Columbus	
Building Perry's Lake Erie fleet	Folk dancing around the world
Vitamin C and your health	
Raising food without chemicals	The return of Halley's comet

Writing Persuasive Essays

Some of the writing in newspapers—especially on the editorial page—is persuasive. This form is especially lively and interesting. It is often very subjective, but it also contains facts and reasoning in defense of opinions. The following pages highlight the special features of persuasion.

Understanding Persuasive Essays. Persuasive purpose and tone mark this type of essay that seeks to show something in a new light or to persuade readers to act. While the tone varies with the topic and the writer's feelings, it is always reasonable and compelling

Persuasive essays attempt to convince the audience to accept the writer's opinion by presenting reasons and facts reasonably and forcefully.

The thesis statement should reveal the persuasive purpose, reasonable tone, and the opinion that the essay defends. Whereas an expository essay is based on fact, a persuasive one is based on controversy. Notice the following examples. In the

575

first, the writer formed an opinion after studying evidence. The second, an observation with which no one could argue, is not suitable for a persuasive essay.

CONTROVERSIAL STATEMENT: The Central High basketball team will probably be division champs.

FACTUAL STATEMENT: The Central High team goes into the play-offs with ten wins and three losses.

The following chart presents thesis statements for opinions that can be defended and sample subtopics.

SAMPLE THESIS STATEMENTS FOR PERSUASIVE ESSAYS	
Thesis Statements	**Stated Subtopics**
Real estate values on the east coast are depriving families of the pleasure of home ownership.	None
The series "The Jewel in the Crown" is the best dramatization ever to appear on television.	None
Switzerland, neutral in the two world wars, is a military nation.	(1) Universal service (2) Weekly rifle practice (3) Tank traps on roads

Supporting information gives evidence for the essay's opinion. It can be logical reasons or examples, facts, and details, but never unsubstantiated opinions. It should be solid, authoritative, rational, and believable and should appeal even to readers who disagree with you.

The tone should be reasonable but forceful and respectful of opposing views. The language and information should show that you are informed and consider all sides of issues. Avoid emotional language and name-calling that might antagonize readers.

Beyond that, the tone can vary widely to suit the audience and the intensity of purpose. It can be lighthearted, humorous, or serious. You might expect strong opposition or simply want to express an original interpretation of a subject.

Prewriting, Writing, and Revising. When planning, writing, and revising, never lose sight of your goal to persuade the reader. Always keep strong awareness of your audience.

When writing a persuasive essay, focus on convincing your audience with sound evidence presented in a reasonable way.

Focus your topic by deciding what you think and what you want readers to think. A specific, supportable opinion helps.

The support you develop should suit your audience. Decide whether the reader is sympathetic, apathetic, or opposed.

BUILDING STRONG ARGUMENTS FOR A PERSUASIVE ESSAY

Thesis Statement: Seashores, like national parks, should be open to all citizens.		
Evidence For	**Evidence Against**	**Counter Arguments For**
—Beaches are a national, not an individual or municipal resource	—Selling public land rights has historic precedence in the U.S.	—It is not too late to stop the diversion of public land
—Public lands are important for the quality of life of our citizens	—Communities can see to the quality of life of their residents	—People living inland should also have quality of life
—Recreation is a right of all citizens	—Landowners in beach areas are entitled to privacy and order	—Taxes support public lands; all taxpayers should have access to them

Use a list like this to organize, especially when you are convincing readers to endorse a controversial view. Acknowledge the validity of some opposing arguments early in the essay. This *conceding a point* suggests that you are fair-minded and see some right on the opposition side. Always follow up immediately with your own arguments, presenting them forcefully to show that they outweigh opposition views.

In general, order of importance is useful in persuasive writing, even when you use opposing views. It places your best argument last, to clinch your defense. Or begin with the obvious arguments and build to less obvious ones. This takes advantage of the impact of the unexpected.

Begin by capturing interest, not antagonizing. Lead gradually toward the thesis statement. Keep a reasonable, consistent tone, avoiding emotional or loaded language. Imagine that you are speaking to the reader. Finally, rephrase the main point and add an appealing, fitting title.

Revise to make the essay more persuasive, using the checklist on page 569.

EXERCISE C: Recognizing the Features of Persuasive Essays. Read the essay and answer the questions that follow it.

Health: A Matter of Choice

"My grandmother lived to be a hundred. What have I got to worry about?" is the attitude of a friend of mine. Another friend, a junk food addict, claims, "So what if I get sick? I've got insurance." Most bizarre of all is the smoker in my family, who says with a laugh, "By the time I get cancer, they'll have a cure for it." While all these people are optimistic, they are making a fundamental mistake: They are not taking responsibility for their own health. Yet if modern medical wisdom has made anything clear, it is this: Our own choices, our own lifestyles have an impact on our lives—and deaths.

Consider first the myths. Heredity? It is certainly true that heredity plays a role in life span; long-lived families tend to produce long-lived offspring. But there is no way of telling whether any one individual has inherited the particular characteristics that make a difference. Furthermore, since the choices we make can undo that difference, we can waste what nature has given us. Current medicine? No one denies that modern technology has rescued many people who would have died in an earlier era; smallpox, for example, once a major killer, has been eradicated worldwide. Even so, however, some medical thinkers attribute no more than three percent of the decline in the incidence of a disease to medicine. Future medicine? This is the biggest illusion of all, a putting of one's fate in the hands

578

of a genie in a bottle who will grant our wish. Some diseases may, in fact, forever resist human control. And even when new methods are identified, testing, verification, and marketing take years. Are we wise to believe these will be fewer than the years we have?

Counter these myths with the recommendations of the experts. The fact that these recommendations appeal also to common sense make them not one whit less valid.

First, we are told, regular, lifelong activity is essential. The increase in recent years of the number of people jogging, hiking, and joining health clubs attests to a growing awareness of its importance. Not only does regular activity stimulate the body's pulmonary and cardiovascular processes, but recent evidence also suggests it may have other benefits. The brittle bones and bent spine of old age, for example, may be preventable by regular exercise (as well as adequate calcium intake).

Second is the reorientation of diet away from processed foods, fatty meats, and high cholesterol foods to fresh foods, whole grains, and fruits and vegetables. Here, too, the last decade has witnessed profound changes in people's choices, with observable results: A substantial cutback in American consumption of red meat, eggs, whole milk, and butter has contributed to a twenty-five percent decline in coronary heart disease. Fortunately, too, many of the dietary recommendations that decrease the risk of heart disease may also help in the prevention of cancer.

Exercise and diet contribute to health; the third and perhaps most important step means avoiding known causes of death. The warning on the cigarette box is unequivocal: "Cigarette smoking is dangerous to your health." Besides the obvious potential danger of lung cancer, emphysema, or other lung disorders, there are other known results: other kinds of cancers—mouth, esophagus, bladder—heart disease, and ulcers. And the warning about excessive use of alcohol is also clear: an increased risk of acccident, of liver disease, of brain damage.

The overall message shouts to be heard, and fortunately more and more people seem to be hearing it: The responsibility for our own health does not lie in our genes or in the medical establishment, present or future; it lies with us, in our choices. We can say "Yes" to longer, healthier lives by what we do with them now.

1. How is the title appropriate or inappropriate?
2. How does the introduction prepare readers for persuasion?
3. What is the thesis statement?
4. What subtopics are developed in the body of the essay?
5. What order is used? What other order can you suggest?
6. Where are opposing arguments mentioned? Which are conceded?
7. What other arguments—for or against—can you suggest?
8. What transitions, repetitions, and synonyms are used?
9. What words establish a reasonable tone? Do you feel sympathetic or antagonistic toward the writer? Why?
10. How does the final paragraph "clinch" the essay?

EXERCISE D: Planning, Writing, and Revising a Persuasive Essay. Choose one of the following topics or choose one of your own. Then plan, write, and revise a persuasive essay. Keep your purpose and the tone in mind as you write.

The best American novelist	Why you should be elected
The fun of coin collecting	to the student government
Controlling immigration	The best team in the league

Writing Informal Essays

Informal essays are more individual and flexible than other kinds, with greater variation in style and structure.

Understanding Informal Essays. Informal essays cover a wide range of topics: political events, scientific discoveries, or observations. The topic of an informal essay may not appear in the thesis statement or first paragraph; it may be implied. Nevertheless, the writer must care about the topic, know it well, and cover it satisfactorily in the essay.

An informal essay is a short composition that is usually light in tone and personal.

Impressions, experiences, and personal responses distinguish this kind of essay from expository and persuasive ones. Informal essays may also relate to large social issues. Their titles are more fanciful than those for other essays. The first title in the chart pokes fun at childhood memories; the last makes a pun on a title and implies trouble during filming.

TITLES AND TOPICS OF INFORMAL ESSAYS	
Topics of Informal Essays	**Titles of the Essays**
Violin lessons (writer's memories)	"The Noblest Instrument" by Clarence Day
Why young people should consider college (special issue)	"Why Go to College" by Robert M. Hutchins
Process of making the movie *Citizen Kane*	"Raising Kane" by Pauline Kael

Every informal essay needs a controlling idea. It may resemble a standard thesis statement, be spread throughout the essay, or be implied.

Prewriting, Writing, and Revising an Informal Essay. Informal essays should be unified and logical.

Informal essays should be unified in ideas and tone and should be coherent throughout.

The tone and organization may be unique, personal, introspective, casual, or conversational, but it should be consistent and should hold the ideas together. The connecting devices may be woven into the ideas more subtly; they can be repetitions of main words and synonyms, consistent pronouns, and parallelism. Because of these differences, informal essays demand more from readers than standard essays do.

EXERCISE E: Recognizing the Features of Informal Essays. Read the essay and answer the questions that follow it.

Title	The World in a Wall
Background idea and description	The crumbling wall that surrounded the sunken garden alongside the house was a rich hunting ground for me. It was an ancient brick wall that had been plastered over, but now this outer skin was green with moss, bulging and sagging with the damp of many winters. The whole surface was an intricate
Indication of main point: wall seen as world in miniature	map of cracks, some several inches wide, others as fine as hairs. Here and there large pieces had dropped off and revealed the rows of rose-pink bricks lying beneath like ribs. There was a whole landscape

581

on this wall if you peered closely enough to see it; the roofs of a hundred tiny toadstools, red, yellow, and brown, showed in patches like villages on the damper portions; mountains of bottle-green moss grew in tuffets so symmetrical that they might have been planted and trimmed; forests of small ferns sprouted from cracks in the shady places, dropping languidly like little green fountains. The top of the wall was a desert land, too dry for anything except a few rust-red mosses to live in it, too hot for anything except sunbathing by the dragonflies. At the base of the wall grew a mass of plants, cyclamen, crocus, asphodel, thrusting their leaves among the piles of broken and chipped roof-tiles that lay there. This whole strip was guarded by a labyrinth of blackberry hung, in season, with fruit that was plump and juicy and black as ebony.

The inhabitants of the wall were a mixed lot, and they were divided into day and night workers, the hunters and the hunted. At night, the hunters were the toads that lived among the brambles, and the geckos, pale, translucent, with bulging eyes, that lived in the cracks higher up the wall. Their prey was the population of stupid, absentminded craneflies that zoomed and barged their way among the leaves; moths of all sizes and shapes, moths striped, tessellated, checked, spotted, and blotched, that fluttered in soft clouds along the withered plaster; the beetles rotund and neatly clad as businessmen, hurrying with portly efficiency about their night's work. When the last glow-worm had dragged his frosty emerald lantern to bed over the hills of moss, and the sun rose, the wall was taken over by the next set of inhabitants. Here it was more difficult to differentiate between the prey and the predators, for everything seemed to feed indiscriminately off everything else. Thus the hunting wasps searched out caterpillars and spiders; the spiders hunted for flies; the dragonflies, big, brittle, and hunting-pink, fed off spiders and the flies; and the swift, lithe, and multicolored wall lizards fed off everything.

582

Subtopic 3: the scorpions, the most interesting creatures of this small world

But the shyest and most self-effacing of the wall community were the most dangerous; you hardly ever saw one unless you looked for it, and yet there must have been several hundred living in the cracks in the wall. Slide a knife-blade carefully under a piece of the loose plaster and lever it gently away from the brick, and there, crouching beneath it, would be a little black scorpion an inch long, looking as though he were made out of polished chocolate. They were weird-looking things, with their flattened, oval bodies, their neat, crooked legs, the enormous crablike claws, bulbous and neatly jointed as armor, and the tail like a string of brown beads ending in a sting like a rose-thorn. The scorpion would lie there quite quietly as you examined him, only raising his tail in an almost apologetic gesture of warning if you breathed too hard on him. If you kept him in the sun too long he would simply turn his back on you and walk away, and then slide slowly but firmly under another section of plaster.

I grew very fond of these scorpions. I found them to be pleasant, unassuming creatures with, on the whole, the most charming habits. Provided you did nothing silly or clumsy (like putting your hand on one) the scorpions treated you with respect, their one desire being to get away and hide as quickly as possible. They must have found me rather a trial, for I was always ripping sections of the plaster away so that I could watch them, or capturing them and making them walk about in jam-jars so that I could see the way their feet moved. By means of my sudden and unexpected assaults of the wall I discovered quite a bit about the scorpions. I found that they would eat bluebottles (though how they caught them was a mystery I never solved), grasshoppers, moths, and lacewing flies. Several times I found them eating each other, a habit I found most distressing in a creature otherwise so impeccable.

By crouching under the wall at night with a torch, I managed to catch some brief glimpses of the scorpions' wonderful courtship dances. I saw them stand-

583

ing, claws clasped, their bodies raised to the skies, their tails lovingly entwined; I saw them waltzing slowly in circles among the moss cushions, claw in claw. But my view of these performances was all too short, for almost as soon as I switched on the torch the partners would stop, pause for a moment and then, seeing that I was not going to extinguish the light, they would turn round and walk firmly away,

Closing remarks

claw in claw, side by side. They were definitely beasts that believed in keeping themselves to themselves. If I could have kept a colony in captivity I would probably have been able to see the whole of the courtship, but the family had forbidden scorpions in the house, despite my arguments in favor of them.—Gerald Durrell

1. Is the title of the essay fanciful? Why or why not?
2. What is the purpose of the opening lines?
3. Is there a distinct thesis statement? Explain.
4. What is the author's controlling idea?
5. Tell some ways in which he achieves unity and coherence.
6. Relate the three subtopics as you understand them.
7. Is this essay more personal than others you have read? If so, how?
8. Select words or phrases that reinforce the controlling idea.
9. How would you describe the author's style in the essay?
10. What does the final paragraph contribute to coherence and tone?

EXERCISE F: Analyzing Structures of Informal Essays.
Look in books and magazines for essays by the following writers or others. Identify introductions, development, and conclusions in three of them. Try to explain why each writer chose the organization used. Imagine the essay in more traditional form and tell how it would be changed.

Francis Bacon	Nora Ephron	George Orwell
James Baldwin	Jean Kerr	Susan Sontag
Erma Bombeck	Charles Lamb	E. B. White
Joan Didion	Montaigne	George F. Will

EXERCISE G: Writing Informal Essays. Find a topic for an informal essay by drawing on your experience, convictions, memory, or imagination. Select a controlling idea (which you can state or imply) and gather ideas for developing your controlling idea. As you plan, experiment with structure and order. Try blending the introduction and body, or the body and the conclusion. Maintain a consistent tone; link ideas smoothly and subtly. Finally, revise for clarity, unity, and coherence.

DEVELOPING WRITING SKILLS: Focusing on Purpose. The topics below could be used for expository, persuasive, or informal essays. Choose one of the topics and write an essay. Have a classmate read your essay and write two or three sentences about whether or not you achieved your purpose. Revise and copy your essay in final form.

Changing electoral law	Propagating houseplants
Value of the United Nations	South American neighbors
The best U.S. President	The advantages of cross-
Tennis as a spectator sport	country skiing

Writing Workshop: Essays

ASSIGNMENT 1

Topic An Editorial: An Examination of a Stereotype

Form and Purpose An essay that persuades an audience

Audience Readers of a local newspaper

Length Four to six paragraphs

Focus Your thesis statement should introduce the stereotype and state an opinion. The body should develop subtopics that support your opinion. Conclude with a restatement of your opinion and a clincher statement.

Sources Books, magazines, ads, cartoons, films, television shows, personal experiences

Prewriting Select one stereotype and develop a thesis statement. Research and brainstorm for support. Organize your ideas and information in a logical, convincing order.

Writing Use a serious, formal tone as you write a first draft.

Revising Review and revise your draft by using the checklist on page 569. Write a corrected final draft.

ASSIGNMENT 2

Topic   Clothing Style Changes

Form and Purpose   An expository essay that both informs and entertains in a humorous tone

Audience   A group of parents who have teenage children

Length   Four to six paragraphs

Focus   Adopt a humorous tone and attitude toward your subject. Limit your subject to an examination of only two or three aspects of clothing styles; for example, formal clothes or school clothes. Develop specific examples of those subtopics in the body of your essay.

Sources   Old and recent magazines, television shows, movies, and personal observations

Prewriting   Narrow your topic and develop a thesis statement that includes the two or three subtopics you will examine. Research and brainstorm for supporting information. Then develop an outline.

Writing   Using your outline, write a first draft of your essay.

Revising   Use the checklist on page 569 to help you revise. Then prepare a final copy.

Topics for Writing: Essays

George Washington	James K. Polk	Chester A. Arthur	Herbert C. Hoover
John Adams	Zachary Taylor	Grover Cleveland	Franklin D. Roosevelt
Thomas Jefferson	Milard Fillmore	Benjamin Harrison	Harry S. Truman
James Madison	Franklin Pierce	Grover Cleveland	Dwight D. Eisenhower
James Monroe	James Buchanan	William McKinley	John F. Kennedy
John Quincy Adams	Abraham Lincoln	Theodore Roosevelt	Lyndon B. Johnson
Andrew Jackson	Andrew Johnson	William H. Taft	Richard M. Nixon
Martin Van Buren	Ulysses S. Grant	Woodrow Wilson	Gerald F. Ford
William H. Harrison	Rutherford B. Hayes	Warren G. Harding	James E. Carter, Jr.
John Tyler	James A. Garfield	Calvin Coolidge	Ronald W. Reagan

The photograph above and list of Presidents may stimulate a writing idea. Plan and write an expository, persuasive, or informal essay about that idea. If you wish, choose one of the following topics for an essay.

1. The Powers of the President
2. An Abuse of Presidential Power
3. A Presidential Crisis
4. The Most Effective President
5. An Ineffective President
6. A Conflict of Power: President vs. Congress
7. A Conflict of Power: President vs. Supreme Court
8. The Electoral Process: Should It Be Changed?
9. The Balance of Power in the Federal Government: Has It Changed?
10. President of the United States: An Impossible Job?

20

Research Papers

This chapter examines the features of research papers, particularly methods of documenting and incorporating research. It will also show you how to plan, organize, write, and revise a research paper so that it is coherent and unified.

Understanding Research Papers   20.1

Research papers differ from standard essays in that they draw heavily on material gathered through research. They integrate ideas developed through reading and thinking about a topic with information found in research sources.

Sources of Information

While researching your topic in books, magazines, and other similar sources, you need to know how to document information you use, how to give credit to other people for their ideas. Documentation also includes preparing a bibliography.

Documentation of Sources. Whenever you use quotations or ideas found through research, you must *document* the source.

589

Research papers include documented information from outside sources with footnotes at the bottom of the pages or at the end of the paper.

To write footnotes, place a small number above the line immediately following the borrowed information. Each succeeding footnote on the page should be given a higher number. Then, at the bottom of the page, the same number appears with the source documented: the author's name, the title of the work, publishing information, and the page number of the borrowed information. Notice that a second reference to the same work is abbreviated.

Passage with footnotes

> The buffoon, clown, or fool, a dramatic figure popular since the Golden Age of Greece, has rarely been used to such an extent or with such great success as in the plays of William Shakespeare. The fool is a "nearly indispensable personage ... with a many-sided social, theatrical, and literary tradition behind him."[1] Shakespeare's buffoon plays a major role in both comedy and tragedy, serving as entertainer, explainer, and illuminator of the truth, as well as providing the audience with a temporary escape from reality.[2]

> ---
> [1]Leo Salinger, *Shakespeare and the Traditions of Comedy* (London: Cambridge University Press, 1974), p. 15.
> [2]Salinger, *Shakespeare and the Traditions of Comedy,* pp. 15–16.

Footnotes can sometimes be placed on one footnote page following the last page of the research paper, immediately before the bibliography. List sources according to the raised numbers in the text of the paper.

The chart on the next page will show you how to cite a number of different kinds of sources. The most common sources are at the beginning, but take time to study them all so you will be prepared to handle such things as collections and translations. Note also that some works, particularly magazine articles and newspaper articles, will not always have an author listed. Whenever there is no author (or editor), just list the same information beginning with the title of the work.

590

FORMS FOR CITING SOURCES	
Kind of Source	**Footnote**
Book	¹Olga Connolly, *The Rings of Destiny* (New York: David McKay Company, Inc., 1968), p. 63.
Book (with two authors)	¹Martin Maloney and Paul Max Rubenstein, *Writing for the Media* (Englewood Cliffs, N.J.: Prentice-Hall, Inc., 1980), pp. 67–70.
Magazine Article	¹Richard Wolkomir, "Hypnosis: Peephole into the Mind," *Kiwanis,* September 1980, p. 30.
Encyclopedia Article	¹*The Jewish Encyclopedia,* 1902 ed., "Bannaah, Bannay, Bannayah," by Louise Ginsberg.
Newspaper Article	¹Ann Crittenden, "Growers' Power in Marketing Under Attack." *The New York Times,* March 25, 1981, p. A1.
Collection (of one author)	¹Mark Twain, *The Complete Humorous Sketches and Tales of Mark Twain,* ed. Charles Neider (Garden City, N.Y.: Doubleday and Company, Inc., 1961), p. 312.
Collection (of several authors)	¹John W. Bachman and E. Martin Browne, eds., *Better Plays for Today's Churches* (New York: Association Press, 1964), p. 21.
Translation	¹Françoise Sagan, *Sunlight on Cold Water,* trans. Joanna Kilmartin (Harmondsworth, Middlesex, England: Penguin, 1978), p. 82.
Work in Several Volumes	¹Thomas Paine, *The Writings of Thomas Paine,* vol. 1, ed. Moncure Daniel Conway (New York: AMS Press, Inc., 1967), p. 33.

NOTE ABOUT THE MODERN LANGUAGE ASSOCIATION (MLA) SYSTEM FOR CITING RESOURCES: The MLA has recently endorsed a system that is becoming more and more popular, especially in colleges and universities. It calls for in-text citations rather than footnotes. Each citation gives a very limited amount of information, listed

591

in parentheses right after the quotation, fact, or idea that is being cited at the point in the research paper. For the book by Olga Connolly on page 591, for example, the citation would be (Connolly 63).

The following chart shows the information that would be given using the MLA system for some of the items shown in the chart on page 591. Little information is given because all research papers, including those with footnotes, must also have a bibliography that lists all sources in detail at the very end of the paper. Readers can find information they may need there.

MLA CITATIONS	
Kinds of Sources	**Citations**
Book	(Maloney and Rubenstein 67–70)
Magazine Article	(Wolkomir 30)
Encyclopedia Article	(Ginzberg)
Newspaper Article	(Crittenden A1)
Collection	(Twain 312)
Translation	(Sagan 82)
Work in Several Volumes	(Paine 33)

If a book or an article does not have an author, the MLA system would list just the title and page number.

Correct Use of Sources. Using another writer's words or ideas—either directly or by rephrasing—without documenting the source is a form of theft called *plagiarism.* Plagiarism should always be avoided. Only when an idea or fact is well known or included without a citation in many books is it unnecessary to provide a footnote.

Avoid plagiarism by clearly identifying any words, special ideas, or little-known facts that have been found in specific sources.

The passage below is from an article in *Archeology* magazine. Following it are two passages in which writers used it as a source. The first contains plagiarism; the second does not.

Passage from a magazine article   Salt has always played a curious role in the history of human affairs. Widely available to people, salt can be transported easily and requires relatively little energy for its exploitation. Accessible at low cost in most world markets, it is hardly surprising that societies, past and present, have always taken this resource for granted—ironic because a salt scarcity can threaten the very life of a community and disrupt the affairs of an entire nation.

At the bare minimum, people need two grams of salt a day. Failure to maintain this level for a relatively short span of time is fatal. In very humid tropical regions, where laboring people require a great deal more than two grams a day, consumption levels of up to 30 grams daily have been reported. Today in Middle America—the ancient home of the Maya—an individual needs a minimum daily intake of approximately eight grams of salt. A community of 50,000 people requires at least 400 kilograms a day or 146 tons of salt a year. Most communities, however, consume several times the minimum requirement of salt for both dietary and other purposes. When the supply is reduced or cut off, there can be drastic repercussions. It is at this point that salt becomes a critical factor in human affairs.

A sudden shift in supply or demand can create havoc within the trading networks of empires. Competition to obtain salt can even lead to wars. There are many regions in the world where salt has played a crucial role in the history of human events: None is more famous that the great Maya empire. For over 2,000 years, salt was a major trade item throughout the Maya area of southern Mexico and northern Central America. Salt trade figures prominently in both the development and demise of Maya civilization. —Anthony P. Andrews

In the passage at the top of the next page, the writer used some of the material from the preceding article incorrectly. The writer has borrowed word for word in some instances and has rephrased some of the ideas without giving the source of each quotation, idea, and fact in other instances. The plagiarized material in the passage at the top of the next page is underlined.

Passage from an unaccept-able research paper	Of all the economic causes of wars, competition for salt is perhaps one of the least known, but <u>salt has played a curious role in the history of human affairs.</u> People's health has always demanded a daily dosage of salt—anywhere from <u>two grams of salt a day up to thirty grams daily. Accessible at low cost in most world markets, it is hardly surprising that so-</u>
Plagiarism	<u>cieties, past and present, have always taken this resource for granted.</u> When societies have suffered from shortages or cuts in trade supplies of salt, this <u>sudden shift in supply or demand has created havoc within the trading network of empires. Competition for salt has even been the cause of wars.</u>

In the passage above, plagiarism could have been avoided by using quotation marks and footnotes or by rephrasing the ideas, giving credit to the source as in the passage below.

Passage from an acceptable research paper	Of all the economic causes of wars, competition for salt is perhaps the least known. Humans have always needed salt—anywhere from two grams to thirty grams a day. Because salt is a necessity for human life, many societies suffered when faced with shortages or cuts in trade supplies of salt. For example, "salt trade figures prominently in both the development and demise of the Maya civilization"
Quotation cited	(Andrews 24).

Preparing a Bibliography. Sources used in the preparation of the research paper and within the paper itself must also be acknowledged in a formal list called a *bibliography.*

A research paper must contain a bibliography that reflects all of the sources you consulted during the research and planning steps of your paper.

Sources should be listed alphabetically, according to the last name of the author. List the title of the work if no author is given. Entries should give the name of the author, title of the work, name of the publisher, and the place and date of publication. Page numbers are not necessary unless the source is a magazine or newspaper article.

The chart below illustrates entries for a bibliography, covering the kinds of sources you are likely to use.

FORMS OF BIBLIOGRAPHIES

Kind of Source	Bibliographic Entry
Book	Connolly, Olga. *The Rings of Destiny.* New York: David McKay Company, Inc., 1968.
Book (with two authors	Maloney, Martin and Paul Max Rubenstein. *Writing for the Media.* Englewood Cliffs, N.J.: Prentice-Hall, Inc. 1980.
Magazine Article (signed)	Wolkomir, Richard. "Hypnosis: Peephole into the Mind." *Kiwanis,* September 1980, pp. 30–38.
Magazine Article (unsigned)	"Why More Bureaucrats Are Being Sued." *U.S. News and World Report,* September 8, 1980, pp. 44–45.
Encyclopedia Article (signed)	Louis Ginzberg. "Bannah, Bannay, Bannayah." *The Jewish Encyclopedia.* 1902 ed.
Encyclopedia Article (unsigned)	"Religion." *The New Columbia Encyclopedia.* 1975 ed.
Newspaper Article (signed)	Crittenden, Ann. "Growers' Power in Marketing Under Attack." *The New York Times,* March 25, 1981, p. A1.
Newspaper Article (unsigned)	"Drought Slows Mozambique's Recovery Program." *The New York Times,* October 26, 1980, p. 13.
Collection (selected works of a single author)	Twain, Mark. *The Complete Humorous Sketches and Tales of Mark Twain.* Edited by Charles Neider. Garden City, N.Y.: Doubleday and Company, Inc., 1961.
Collection (selected works of several authors)	Bachman, John W. and E. Martin Browne, eds. *Better Plays for Today's Churches.* New York: Association Press, 1964.
Translation	Sagan, Françoise. *Sunlight on Cold Water.* Translated by Joanna Kilmartin. Harmondsworth, Middlesex, England: Penguin, 1978.

Work in Several Volumes	Paine, Thomas. *The Writings of Thomas Paine*, vol. 1. Edited by Moncure Daniel Conway. New York: AMS Press, Inc., 1967.

EXERCISE A: Preparing Citations and Footnotes. Choose one of the following topics or think of one of your own. Then find five different kinds of sources on your topic in the library (for example, a book with two authors, an unsigned magazine article, a signed encyclopedia article, a work in several volumes, and a collected works of a single author). Then, for each source, prepare both a footnote and an MLA citation.

A famous artist or athlete	Child labor in the
One of the world's major	nineteenth century
religions	The Alaskan pipeline
An archaeological discovery	New Zealand's mountains
A history of a game or sport	The history of trains

EXERCISE B: Using Information from Sources Correctly. Read a short magazine article on a topic you know well. Write down the complete publishing information you need to cite this source in a research paper: the author, title of the article, title of the magazine, date of the magazine, and page number. Then write an expository, persuasive, or descriptive paragraph combining your knowledge of this topic with information you learned from the article. In your paragraph use (1) a direct quotation from the article, (2) an idea from the article, and (3) a little-known fact from the article. Be sure to place all quoted material in quotation marks and to give the source for each quotation and piece of information you include from the article.

EXERCISE C: Preparing a Bibliography. List the five sources you located in Exercise A in a bibliography, using correct form.

Structure and Features

While a research paper follows the introduction-body-conclusion structure used for standard essays, it is usually longer than an essay. It will often have at least five or six paragraphs, frequently more, depending on the amount of information necessary to cover the topic.

A research paper must have a title, an introduction with a thesis statement, a body, a conclusion, citation of sources throughout, and a bibliography.

The *title* and *introduction* capture the readers' interest, reveal the topic, and present the purpose of your research paper. The introduction's opening remarks and background information should lead to a thesis statement, often the last sentence of the paragraph. Usually, the introduction to a research paper is only one paragraph long, but sometimes two or more paragraphs are necessary to prepare the reader for the discussion of the topic. In this event, the thesis statement usually comes at the end of the final introductory paragraph.

The *body* of the research paper supports and develops the thesis statement with any relevant examples, facts, details, and other information, much of it taken from research sources. The body may contain any number of paragraphs, and these should develop ideas in a logical sequence for coherence. If the body is long, subtopic headings can be used to guide the reader.

The research paper's *conclusion* summarizes the main point and any subtopics. It brings all of the information presented in the body to a logical close, and it can refer to ideas in the introduction or end the paper smoothly in some other way.

Throughout the research paper, informal citations or *footnotes* identify the sources used, and a *bibliography* at the end lists all of the works read and used in preparing the paper.

The research paper below uses the three-part essay structure and includes the documentation and proper use of sources.

Picasso's Turning Point

Pablo Picasso, probably the greatest artist of our century, enjoyed an extremely long and fruitful career until his death in 1973 at the age of ninety-one. He contributed an unequalled number of masterpieces to the art of the modern period. But perhaps his greatest work is one that he produced relatively early in his career at the age of thirty-six.[1] *Les Demoiselles d'Avignon,* painted in 1907, offered a startling new way of looking at "reality." It was new to Picasso's own work and to the world of painting in general. A look at the work of Picasso that led up to this masterpiece shows both how *Les Demoiselles d'Avignon* grew from his work and how it grew beyond it.

Picasso began his career, like most artists, by imitating others. Copying at first the large, realistic, and sentimental paintings popular at the end of the nineteenth century, Picasso moved in his late teens to Paris, where he began to imitate the more original masters of the time—Cézanne, Gauguin, and Toulouse-Lautrec.[2] In a relatively short period, he absorbed these influences and began to develop his own style, the first of many styles that he would discover for himself. He took the blue line that Gauguin had used to define his figures and began to color whole paintings of pathetic figures with it.[3] But these images of poverty and melancholy in Picasso's so-called "Blue Period" changed within a few years to the happier mood paintings of his "Rose Period." While the figures of the "Blue Period" were thin and starved, those of the "Rose Period" were tremendous and very solid, almost like pieces of sculpture.

This early phase of his career came to a close when Picasso began to be influenced by ancient African and Iberian (Spanish) art. His portrait of Gertrude Stein, which looks more like a statue than like a portrait, has a blank face that resembles a mask. In the portrait, one can see his growing interest in the bold and more abstract art of these ancient cultures.[4]

These influences led to a breakthrough in Picasso's art and opened up an entirely new channel in his imagination. Following ancient models, his new works tended to flatten three-dimensional reality as it has been pictured in Western art for centuries.[5] Even more important, Picasso's interest in ancient masks introduced new images into Western paintings, images that distorted the human form and imposed animal faces on human bodies. This influence appears most dramatically in Picasso's 1907 painting *Les Demoiselles d'Avignon.*

Les Demoiselles depicts five women. Three of them are painted in highly simplified and distorted, but still recognizably human, terms. But the other two are grotesquely contorted and have frightening animal faces. The whole painting looks as if it is made up of angular blocks and wedges, all jammed together. Its effect is that of a bad dream or nightmare. The painting is a very powerful expression of the unknown side of life, with its subjects changing, almost disintegrating, from human beings into twisted geometrical figures.

598

Les Demoiselles d'Avignon produced a strange reception among Picasso's colleagues in the art world. Henri Matisse hated the painting.[6] Picasso's own friends thought he had gone mad.[7] Picasso had not gone mad, but he had broken through to a mad vision of human life. He had used his various influences, but changed them to produce a distinct and revolutionary style, painting "reality" as no one had ever done before.

---

[1]John Ashbery, "Picasso: The Art," *New York*, May 12, 1980, p. 29.

[2]Robert Hughes, "The Show of Shows," *Time*, May 26, 1980, p. 70.

[3]Hughes, "The Show of Shows," p. 71.

[4]*Encyclopedia Britannica*, 1971 ed., "Picasso, Pablo Ruiz." p. 85.

[5]Mark Stevens, "Picasso's Imperial Eye," *Newsweek*, May 19, 1980, p. 85.

[6]H.W. Janson, *History of Art* (Englewood Cliffs, N.J.: Prentice-Hall, 1962), p. 522.

[7]Hughes, "The Show of Shows," p. 73.

Bibliography

Ashbery, John. "Picasso: The Art." *New York*, May 12, 1980, pp. 28–31.

"Picasso, Pablo Ruiz." *Encyclopedia Britannica*. 1971 ed.

Gedo, Mary M. *Picasso: Art as Autobiography*. Chicago: University of Chicago Press, 1980.

Hamill, Pete. "Picasso: The Man." *New York*, May 12, 1980, pp. 34–38.

Hughes, Robert. "The Show of Shows." *Time*, May 26, 1980, pp. 70–78.

Janson, H.W. *History of Art*. Englewood Cliffs, N.J.: Prentice-Hall, Inc., 1962.

Smith, Margaret. *Pablo Picasso*. Minneapolis, Minn.: Creative Education, Inc., 1975.

Stevens, Mark. "Picasso's Imperial Eye." *Newsweek*, May 19, 1980, pp. 80–85.

NOTE ABOUT OTHER FEATURES: A research paper usually begins with a title page that lists the title of the paper, writer's name, date, and class for which the paper is written.

EXERCISE D: Recognizing the Structure of a Research Paper. Answer the following questions about the paper on Picasso.

1. How does the title suit the paper?
2. How does the introduction lead the reader into the body of the paper? What are the tone and purpose of the paper?
3. What are the thesis statement and its subtopics?
4. How many body paragraphs does the paper have? What is the topic sentence of each?
5. How is the supporting information in the body organized?
6. How does the conclusion refer to the main point of the paper? What other closing ideas help to end the paper?

Unity and Coherence in Research Papers

Good writing reflects unity and coherence.

Achieving Unity. To achieve unity in your papers, make sure that each paragraph reflects your thesis statement.

To achieve unity in research papers, reflect and develop your thesis statement in every paragraph.

The paper about Picasso contains an introduction, a body, and a conclusion. Furthermore, the thesis statement, which is summarized in the title, creates the division of topics: the influences on Picasso's work, the development of his own styles, the breakthrough that led to the masterpiece *Les Demoiselles d'Avignon,* and the reaction of the art world to his work.

Achieving Coherence. Use your thesis statement to achieve coherence, and use transitions to maintain it.

To achieve coherence in research papers, use your thesis statement to suggest a logical order for the body paragraphs; to maintain coherence use transitions to combine research with your own ideas.

Topics in the thesis statement of the Picasso paper suggest that chronological order will be used in the body. Transitions within paragraphs help combine research with the writer's ideas.

Two examples of transitions include "Picasso began his ca-

600

reer, like most artists, imitating others" at the beginning of the second paragraph and "In a relatively short period" in the middle of the second paragraph.

EXERCISE E: Understanding Unity and Coherence in Research Papers. Answer the questions below about the paper on Picasso after reviewing your answers to Exercise D.

1. How does each body paragraph develop the thesis statement?
2. How do the facts in each body paragraph work together?
3. How might this paper be different if chronological order had not been chosen as the logical means of organization?
4. Find at least three transitions. What sort of connection does each one make?

DEVELOPING WRITING SKILLS: Analyzing the Features of a Research Paper. Answer the following questions about the use of research material in the paper on Picasso.

1. Which method of documenting sources was used?
2. How many different sources does the writer cite?
3. What kinds of information are incorporated in the paper? Quotations? Ideas? Little-known facts?
4. How varied are the sources which the writer has cited?
5. How many sources are listed in the bibliography? Which of these were not cited in the paper?
6. In a library, locate four additional sources for a research paper on Picasso. List them alphabetically.

Writing a Research Paper 20.2

Preparing a research paper includes research steps, such as locating sources, taking notes, incorporating and documenting ideas, writing footnotes, and preparing a bibliography.

PREWRITING: Planning a Research Paper

The preliminary steps of selecting a topic and locating sources are crucial.

601

Select and Refine a Topic. Choose an appropriate, interesting, manageable research paper topic.

Select a topic that is relevant to your studies and covered adequately in available sources. Then refine it to be sure it is narrow enough for one paper.

One way to choose a topic is to think of several areas of interest and then check out the library's resources on these. Look through the card catalog, *The Readers' Guide to Periodical Literature,* and other indexes for sources—books, magazines, and newspapers.

If few sources are available on a topic, you should probably avoid it. On the other hand, if numerous sources are available you may have to choose a smaller category of the topic so that it suits the length of the paper. For example, if a general topic was dolphins, you might discover this topic to be too broad. You might list more specific topics, such as those in the chart.

NARROWING A GENERAL TOPIC	
General Topic:	**Dolphins**
More Specific Topics:	The intelligence of dolphins How dolphins communicate Feeding and migration patterns Anatomy and physiology

Direct Your Research. Before you read your sources, you should think about your topic enough to have some ideas you want to verify and one main point to concentrate on.

Prepare some key questions and a rough version of your thesis statement to guide your research.

If your topic were on dolphins' intelligence and communication, you might pose questions like those that follow.

SAMPLE QUESTIONS TO DIRECT RESEARCH
1. How intelligent do scientists think dolphins are?
2. What tests have scientists made of dolphins' intelligence?

602

3. How do dolphins communicate with each other?
4. What specific behavior of dolphins indicates their intelligence or communication abilities?

Think about your audience and purpose and use your knowledge and interests to choose a tentative main point. Express it in a preliminary thesis statement. Throughout your actual note-taking and planning, you may change this thesis statement. For now, however, it can focus your research. For the topic on dolphins' intelligence and communication, you might use the following rough version of a thesis statement.

PRELIMINARY THESIS STATEMENT: Dolphins have remarkable intelligence and methods of communicating.

Prepare Bibliography Cards. After selecting and narrowing a topic, list on note cards all the sources you plan to consult.

Record on notecards the bibliographic information of all sources you consult about your specific topic.

Following are suggestions for making bibliography cards.

PREPARING BIBLIOGRAPHY CARDS

1. Write each source on a separate card or piece of paper.
2. Write all the information that you need to include in a bibliography entry. For the exact form for various kinds of sources, see the chart on pages 595–596.
3. Note the location symbol or call number and any illustrations, maps, charts, or tables that the source contains.

Take Notes. Guide your reading and note-taking with your preliminary thesis statement and the questions you devised.

Using modified outlines, summaries, and quotations, take accurate notes from all your sources, remembering to record the page numbers on which the information appears.

This chart explains how to prepare well-labeled note cards so your notes will be effective, well organized, and easy to use.

603

TAKING NOTES
1. Use a different note card for each different source. Also, use a different note card for each new subject or major idea on your topic.
2. In the upper right-hand corner of each note card, write a subject heading to show what information the card covers.
3. In the upper left-hand corner of each note card, write the information necessary for citing the source: author, title, and publishing information. If you have many cards for the same source, you may want to abbreviate this information and just write the author and title on the second, third, and later cards.
4. Keep track of the page numbers from which you record each fact, idea, and quotation.

The actual notes on your note cards can be in several different forms: modified outlines, summaries, and direct quotations. For detailed examples, case histories, and thorough explanations, take notes in modified outline form, paraphrasing the important ideas from the source and indicating the pages that your notes cover. For sources that have information that is either lengthy or interesting but not specific, take notes in summary form, again rephrasing the ideas in your own words and noting the pages covered. For ideas or facts that are particularly useful or well stated, copy the quotation word for word, enclosing the material in quotation marks and indicating the page of the source. From one source, on one note card, you might use several or all three of these forms.

If the same information appears in several sources, take notes on it only once. If most sources do not relate to your thesis statement, write a new one that reflects the information you are finding. Or if all your information centers on one part of your topic, locate and take notes on additional sources.

On the next page, sample note cards about dolphins' intelligence show some of the methods of recording information.

Revise Your Thesis Statement. Once you have thoroughly researched your topic, consider revising your thesis statement.

Revise your thesis statement so that it states your main point precisely.

Subject heading ──────────────────────────────

Author, title, publishing information ──────

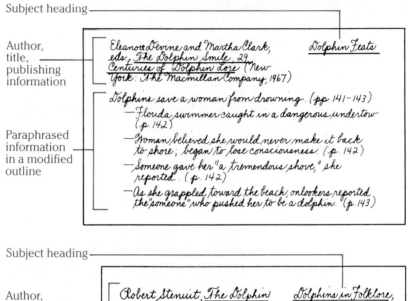

Eleanor Devine and Martha Clark, eds., *The Dolphin Smile: 29 Centuries of Dolphin Lore* (New York: The Macmillan Company, 1967)

Dolphin Feats

Paraphrased information in a modified outline ──────

Dolphins save a woman from drowning. (pp. 141–143)
— Florida swimmer caught in a dangerous undertow (p. 142)
— Woman believed she would never make it back to shore; began to lose consciousness. (p. 142)
— Someone gave her "a tremendous shove," she reported. (p. 142)
— As she grappled toward the beach, onlookers reported the "someone" who pushed her to be a dolphin. (p. 143)

Subject heading ──────────────────────────────

Author, title, publishing information ──────

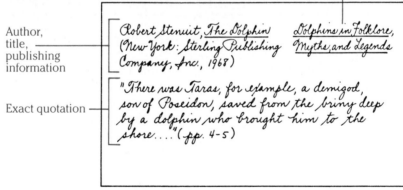

Robert Stenuit, *The Dolphin* (New York: Sterling Publishing Company, Inc., 1968)

Dolphins in Folklore, Myths, and Legends

Exact quotation ──────

"There was Taras, for example, a demigod, son of Poseidon, saved from the briny deep by a dolphin who brought him to the shore...." (pp. 4–5)

Reword your thesis statement to reflect any important information you uncovered during your note-taking. It should clarify your purpose, address the audience you have in mind, and introduce the information you researched.

After researching the topic of dolphins' intelligence and ability to communicate, you might decide to include another subtopic about their accomplishments.

REVISED THESIS STATEMENT: Dolphins have remarkable intelligence and ability to communicate as well as a natural capacity to learn tricks and perform other amazing feats independently.

605

Write an Outline. Prepare a sentence or topic outline to help you build your research paper.

Develop your thesis statement by arranging your own ideas and the information in your notes in a topic or sentence outline.

STEPS FOR ORGANIZING A RESEARCH PAPER
1. If your thesis statement does not include subtopics, determine two or more smaller divisions of your main point from your thoughts and your notes.
2. Group your note cards according to subtopics. Put aside any that do not seem to fit naturally under any subtopics.
3. Choose a logical order for the subtopics in the body of the paper. Then decide on the order of supporting information under each subtopic. Arrange your note cards according to this order. (See Section 17.1 for a discussion of various orders.)

When you have completed these steps, write your outline. Beginning with the introduction, list all introductory ideas as well as your revised thesis statement. Then, to outline the body of the report, write down each subtopic, listing under each the appropriate information you have selected and ordered from your notes. Finally, outline the conclusion, including anything from your research that might help bring your paper to a close.

The following shows a skeleton topic outline.

I. Introduction
   A. }
   B. } Introductory ideas and background information
   C. } *Thesis Statement:* Dolphins have remarkable intelligence and ability to communicate as well as a natural capacity to learn tricks and to perform other amazing feats independently.
II. Subtopic 1: Dolphin intelligence and ability to communicate
   A. }
   B. }
   C. } Information—facts, details—about dolphins'
   D. } intelligence and ability to communicate
   E. }

III. Subtopic 2: Dolphin feats
  A. ⎫
  B. ⎪ Information—examples, facts, details—about tricks
  C. ⎬ that dolphins can perform as well as special feats
  D. ⎪ credited to them
  E. ⎭
IV. Conclusion
  A. ⎫
  B. ⎬ Reference to the thesis statement and closing
  C. ⎭ remarks

Review your outline to see if there are places where your research could be stronger or places where you might add or eliminate details or change the order of the information.

EXERCISE A: Finding and Narrowing a Topic. List four or five general topics. In the library, check the resources available for each topic. Then choose one topic and narrow it down into smaller ones. When you have a list of smaller topics, choose the one that interests you most and that has five or more different sources. Make a bibliography card for each source.

EXERCISE B: Researching Your Paper. Using the topic you just selected, follow these directions.

1. Develop a preliminary thesis statement and five key questions to guide you as you consult your sources.
2. From the sources listed on your bibliography cards, decide which ones are the most useful to read and take notes on.
3. Take notes from your sources. Record relevant information accurately. Include all necessary information on each card, especially page numbers.

EXERCISE C: Revising Your Thesis Statement. Revise your thesis statement so that it expresses a main point your material can support. Consider your audience and purpose as you make changes.

EXERCISE D: Organizing Your Report. Using your revised thesis statement and your notes, follow the steps in the chart on page 606 to write a topic outline of your paper.

WRITING: Creating a First Draft

When you are satisfied with your information and the organization of your outline, write a complete first draft.

Refer to your outline and note cards as you write a first draft.

As you write the paper, use your outline and the grouping and order of your note cards as a guide. Be open to new ideas, better arrangements, or other refinements. Use transitions and other connecting devices to help you combine smoothly your own ideas with material gathered from research. Place quoted material in quotation marks and use one method of citing sources. Finally, close your paper with an effective conclusion.

Decide on a title for your paper and write or type it centered on a title page, a separate page that will be the first page of your research paper. Include your name, the name of the course, and the date you are submitting the paper. However, your teacher may ask for a different format, so check beforehand.

Finally, add a bibliography to the end of the paper. List all the sources you used, even if you did not cite them all in the paper.

If you write rather than type the paper, use every other line to leave room for revisions, corrections, and alterations later on. If you type your first draft, double-space.

A model of a research paper follows.

Those Amazing Dolphins

Introduction	For at least 2,500 years, the dolphin has appeared in folklore, myth, and legend. "There was Taras, for
Background ideas	example, a demigod, son of Poseidon, saved from the briny deep by a dolphin who brought him to
Raised number indicates the use of footnotes	shore. . . . It went without saying: If a castaway is struggling in the water, and suddenly a dolphin appears, the castaway is brought to land, safe and sound, by the dolphin."[1] Why have dolphins caught people's fancy for centuries?
More background information	Today dolphins and humans have been brought together by marine life centers and scientific advancements in techniques of study. In the past twenty years

many scientists and other people have been captivated by tales of dolphins and their abilities.

Now, with results of close observations and studies of dolphins, we can dispel some of the myths and legends—but only some. Old tales of dolphin heroism may well have bases in fact. As we learn more about dolphins, we uncover more evidence of their extraordinary capabilities. Dolphins have remarkable intelligence and ability to communicate and a natural capacity to "learn" tricks and to perform other amazing feats independently.

Thesis statement with two subtopics

Optional heading introduces first subtopic

Dolphin Intelligence and Communication Abilities

The first studies of dolphins' intelligence were examinations of their brains. The French scientist Cuvier revealed in his "Leçons d'anatomie comparée" that "the ratio between the weight of the (dolphin's) brain and that of the body is some 25 to 1."[2] Many scientists believe that such a ratio indicates dolphins' capacity for advanced thinking.[3] An American scientist, Dr. John C. Lilly, showed that the structure of the dolphin's brain is complex, containing a density of cells and folds and convolutions that indicate a high degree of intelligence.[4]

Since dolphins cannot take IQ tests, scientists use other means of measurement to determine how intelligent dolphins really are. Close observation is one method of investigation. One extraordinary example of dolphin ingenuity was observed at Marineland of the Pacific. Two fun-loving dolphins tried in vain to dislodge a stubborn moray eel from its hiding place. One dolphin pulled its tail while the other attempted to snare it from the other end of the hole. One of the dolphins then killed a spine fish with its beak, and stung the eel with the spines. As the eel attempted to flee, the dolphins caught it and played with it until they lost interest.[5]

As a result of these and other observations, scientists have noted the adeptness with which dolphins communicate with one another. By using a type of sonar, dolphins are able to differentiate objects by the sound waves that they send and receive. Then, to communicate discovery of the object to another dolphin, a dolphin reproduces the original echo.[6] This ability to differentiate between sound waves reveals the complexity of the dolphin's brain. Scientists believe dolphins use a "Doppler effect" system for describing complicated movements to other dolphins; that is, dolphins can recreate sounds rising and falling in pitch to communicate messages to other dolphins.[7] In effect, "dolphins may use their sonar sounds to project images into other dolphins' brains."[8]

An experiment conducted by Dr. Jarvis Bastieu at the University of California offers concrete evidence of dolphins' ability to communicate. Using a male and a female dolphin, Dr. Bastieu began by showing each how to push levers in sequence. When the levers were pushed accurately, a reward of small fish would reach the dolphins. Only by seeing flashing or continuous light could the dolphins know how to push the levers. After both dolphins were able to use the lights to figure out the device, a curtain was placed between them so only one dolphin would be able to see the light. With the curtain between them, the first dolphin could be heard sending a sound signal to the second dolphin who then pushed the proper lever. Bastieu repeated the experiment fifty times; the dolphins communicated successfully forty-eight times, earning a 96 percent competency rating.[9]

Heading introduces second subtopic

Dolphin Feats

In addition to their use of a sound system to communicate with each other, dolphins are known for their ability to master complex tricks and for their untaught feats. They shake hands (flippers), catch footballs, race, dive through rings of fire, solve puzzles, and have rescued humans in trouble at sea, earning them distinction as a kind of underwater Red Cross.

For many years, people have harnessed the intelligence of the dolphin for their own entertainment. Dolphins have been trained by experts to perform the most amazing stunts. One such expert is André Cowan at Marineland in St. Augustine, Florida. Cowan uses the "food-technique" method, in which an audible signal tells the dolphin to receive a reward when the trick has been successfully completed. Other methods include loudspeakers and flashing lights. In some cases, dolphins are trained to respond to a rap on the side of the tank. The dolphin's memory enables it to associate a certain learned behavior with a certain sound.[10]

While we can marvel at the performances of dolphins in captivity, their activities in the wild have fostered accounts—some questionable, other documented—of heroic dolphin rescues of drowning swimmers and persons imperiled at sea. In one documented case, six American airmen were shot down over the Pacific Ocean during World War II. They were drifting aimlessly at sea, vulnerable to storms or enemy ships and planes when a dolphin appeared and saved them from possible death by towing their raft onto the sand of a tiny island.[11] In another documented case, a woman was caught in a dangerous undertow while swimming off the coast of Florida. Just as she began to lose consciousness, someone gave her "a tremendous shove," enabling her to reach the beach. That "someone" was a dolphin, according to a witness on the shore.[12]

Reference to main point

Summary of the paper's ideas

Conclusion

Dolphins continue to impress scientists, trainers, and other observers with their ability to decipher and transmit information, to learn, and to act intelligently. It is their potential—still unmeasured, still the source of speculation—that remains for scientists to gauge. Just the dolphins' ability to use a form of sonar to project mental images is still beyond scientists' full understanding. Scientists continue to study dolphins, not just to train them for performing tricks. In the future, who knows what secrets will be learned about dolphins?

---

[1]Robert Stenuit, *The Dolphin* (New York: Sterling Publishing Company, Inc., 1968), pp. 4–5.

611

[2]Stenuit, *The Dolphin*, p. 60.

[3]Michael Parfit, "Are Dolphins Trying to Say Something, or Is It All Much Ado About Nothing?" *Smithsonian*, October 1980, p. 74.

[4]Stenuit, *The Dolphin*, p. 62.

[5]Stenuit, *The Dolphin*, p. 132.

[6]Karl-Erik Fichtelius and Sverre Sjolander, *Smarter Than Man?* (New York: Pantheon Books, 1972), p. 72.

[7]Fichtelius and Sjolander, *Smarter Than Man?* pp. 72–73.

[8]Parfit, "Are Dolphins Trying to Say Something, or Is It All Much Ado About Nothing?" p. 76.

[9]Stenuit, *The Dolphin*, pp. 56–57.

[10]John C. Lilly, M.D., *Man and Dolphin* (New York: Doubleday and Company, Inc., 1961), p. 114.

[11]Stenuit, *The Dolphin*, p. 11.

[12]Eleanore Devine and Martha Clark, eds., *The Dolphin Smile, 29 Centuries of Dolphin Lore* (New York: The Macmillan Company, 1967), p. 142.

Bibliography

Cousteau, Jacques-Yves. *Dolphins*. New York: Doubleday and Company, Inc., 1975.

Devine, Eleanore and Clark, Martha, eds., *The Dolphin Smile, 29 Centuries of Dolphin Lore*. New York: The MacMillan Company, 1967.

Fichtelius, Karl-Erik and Sjolander, Sverre. *Smarter than Man?* New York: Pantheon Books, 1972.

Lilly, John C., M.D. *Communication Between Man and Dolphin*. New York: Crown Publishers, Inc., 1978.

McIntyre, Joan. *Mind in the Waters*. New York: Charles Scribner's Sons, 1975.

Nayman, Jacqueline. *Whales, Dolphins, and Man*. London: Hamlyn, 1973.

Parfit, Michael. "Are Dolphins Trying to Say Something, or Is It All Much Ado About Nothing?" *Smithsonian*, October 1980, pp. 73–80.

Stenuit, Robert. *The Dolphin*. New York: Sterling Publishing Company, Inc., 1968.

EXERCISE E: Writing a First Draft. Use your outline from Exercise D and your notes to write a first draft of a paper. Be sure to use a consistent form for citing sources.

REVISING: Polishing Your Paper

Check your research paper for weaknesses.

Reread your first draft, looking for ways to improve and refine it. Use a checklist to examine all parts of the paper.

Use the following checklist to help you make revisions or corrections and to rewrite parts to improve clarity or style.

CHECKING YOUR RESEARCH PAPER

1. Have you included enough background information and other opening statements to acquaint your reader with the topic and to lead into the thesis statement?
2. Does the thesis statement clearly present the paper's main point and suggest the paper's purpose?
3. Does the information in the body thoroughly support and develop the subtopics of the main point?
4. Is the main idea of each body paragraph clear?
5. Do the body paragraphs develop your main point and subtopics in a logical order? Is all the information logically arranged within each paragraph?
6. Do transitions and other connecting devices link ideas within and between paragraphs?
7. Does the conclusion contain a summary of the paper's main point and subtopics? Does it complete the paper?
8. Have you used complete citations for each fact, idea, or quotation from a source?
9. Are direct quotations exact and punctuated correctly?
10. Is your method of citing sources consistent throughout?
11. Do word choices throughout the paper suit your audience and purpose? Are sentences varied in length and structure?
12. Can you find any errors in grammar, usage, punctuation, or spelling?

EXERCISE F: Revising Your Paper and Writing a Final Copy. Reread the first draft you wrote in Exercise E. Using the checklist above as a guide, make all necessary revisions and corrections on your draft. Then write a neat final copy, adding a title page and a bibliography.

DEVELOPING WRITING SKILLS: Planning, Writing, and Revising a Paper. Think about the paper you completed in the preceding exercises as you answer the following questions. Then choose a new topic for a paper. Follow the planning, writing, and revising steps provided in this section to complete a new paper.

1. What topics did you consider before you chose the one you used? What problems did you have in selecting a topic?
2. To what extent did your questions and preliminary thesis statement help you while you were taking notes?
3. How closely did your revised thesis statement resemble your preliminary thesis statement? How closely did your final report follow your outline?
4. Describe *three* specific ways in which you could improve your approach to writing a research paper.

Writing Workshop: Research Papers

"Now for all the news that lends itself to one-sentence coverage."

ASSIGNMENT 1

Topic   An Original Research Project on Television News

Form and Purpose   A research paper that informs and persuades

Audience   A panel of television news journalists

Length   Seven to ten paragraphs

Focus   Your paper should explore the expanding role of television news. Compare television news coverage with magazine and newspaper coverage. Your conclusion should include an evaluation of television news coverage.

Sources   Newspapers, magazines, television news programs

Prewriting   Compare television news coverage with magazine and newspaper coverage. Take notes on bibliography cards. Also conduct research about television news. Develop a thesis, subtopics, and an outline.

Writing   Using your notes and outline, write a first draft of your research paper. Include footnotes and a bibliography.

Revising   Revise your paper, using the checklist on page 613.

ASSIGNMENT 2

Topic   Contributions to the Development of the United States by One Ethnic Group

Form and Purpose   A research paper that informs and evaluates

Audience   An ethnic organization that is publishing an almanac entitled *Our People*

Length   Seven to ten paragraphs

Focus   Focus on one ethnic group's contributions in such areas as government, science, and the arts. Stress the variety, value, and effects of such contributions.

Sources   Books, magazines, special reference texts, documentaries, ethnic organizations

Prewriting   Narrow your topic; write questions to focus your research. Then research sources and take notes on bibliography cards. Prepare an outline with a thesis statement, subtopics with details, and a conclusion.

Writing   Follow your outline and prepare a final draft.

Revising   Use the checklist on page 613 to revise and prepare a final copy of your paper.

Topics for Writing: Research Papers

The above photo focuses on the subject of money. If it suggests a writing topic to you, then plan and write a research paper on that topic. As an alternative, use one of the topics below for a research paper. You may have to narrow the topic first.

1. Forms of Money in Ancient Civilizations
2. The History of Money in China
3. How Fortunes Are Made or Lost in the Stock Market
4. Toward a Moneyless Society: The Plastic Credit Card
5. The Importance of the Federal Reserve Board
6. Tax Money and Elementary/Secondary Education
7. Inflation in the 20th Century: Roots and Effects
8. The Swiss Banking Industry
9. Helping the Destitute: An Analysis of How Charity Contributions Are Spent
10. Corporations and Taxes

21

Writing About Literature

Often you may be asked to read works of literature and to write about them. Your writing usually takes the form of a *book report* or a *literary analysis*. This chapter guides you through planning, writing, and revising both of these forms.

21.1 Book Reports

In a book report, a writer interprets or gives opinions about a work of fiction or nonfiction. This section focuses on the elements of literature that you can write about in a book report.

Understanding Book Reports

Book reports vary in structure depending on the book being discussed, but they generally share some basic features. Typically they summarize a work of fiction or nonfiction, comment on one or two elements in the work, and present an opinion that either does or does not recommend it to others.

A book report gives an informed overview of a work of fiction or nonfiction and presents a positive or negative opinion of it.

The parts of a book report appear in the following chart.

THE PARTS OF A BOOK REPORT

Introduction	Gives the book's title, author, and a brief summary of its contents.
Body	Explores one or two of the book's literary elements, such as theme or character.
Conclusion	Offers an opinion of the book and advises the reader to read it or to avoid it.

Literature contains elements that resemble threads of different colors which an author weaves into a tapestry. These elements mingle and blend, but you can separate them and concentrate on one or two to understand the entire work better.

RECOGNIZING LITERARY ELEMENTS

Element	Explanation
Theme	A central idea or general truth that the author dramatizes or implies. For example, a theme may be that love of money can destroy a person's humanity. A work can have more than one theme.
Character	A person in a story, poem, or play. Writers reveal characters through actions, dialogue, effects of one character on others, and comments of other characters or the narrator.
Conflict	A struggle between opposing forces or characters. Conflict can be external—between two characters, or between a character and society, nature, God, or fate. Conflict can also be internal—between forces within one character—torn by a wish and a disapproving conscience, for example.
Plot	The planned ordering of events as action grows out of character and conflict. Plot builds to a crisis or climax that resolves the conflict.
Setting	The time, place (physical location), and general background of a story. *Atmosphere* is the mood that the author creates by communicating sensory impressions drawn from the surroundings.

Point of View	The voice or consciousness telling the story; the narrator. A first person narrator tells the story using *I* and takes a role in the events. A third person objective narrator tells the story from the outside, telling only what an observer can see. A third person partially omniscient narrator is outside the story, but can see into the mind of one character; for this reason the reader comes to know that character best. A third person omniscient narrator, while outside the story, can see into the minds of all the characters.
Imagery	Words that appeal to the senses. They may include figures of speech, such as similes and metaphors, and descriptions of scenes, moods, impressions, and actions.
Symbols	Things that stand for themselves and at the same time for deeper and more universal things beyond themselves.
Tone	The author's attitude toward the subject and the audience.

The paper below uses the basic book-report format to describe the literary elements of setting and point of view in the novel *David Copperfield* by Charles Dickens. The numbers of pages in the novel where the direct quotes can be found are given in parentheses.

Report on *David Copperfield*

Introduction

David Copperfield, a novel by Charles Dickens, traces the life of the title character as he grows into manhood in Victorian England. This lengthy novel, told in the first person, interweaves numerous subplots as it follows David from a poor and lonely childhood to a personally and professionally rewarding adult life.

Body paragraph 1: first element described

Dickens' novel depends heavily upon the interaction of its many subplots. The basic plot is rather simple: A young boy, David, has an unhappy childhood, becomes orphaned, is taken in

620

by an aunt, and works hard to make something of himself. Along the way, he meets a series of fascinating characters whose lives create the many subplots of the novel. One subplot involves David's friend Mr. Wickfield, whose assistant, Uriah Heep, schemes to take over his employer's law practice. Uriah's designs on Wickfield's daughter, Agnes, and his attempt to control the law firm, are finally revealed by Mr. Micawber, another old friend of David's. This is typical of the many subplots in *David Copperfield*—a character involved in one subplot meets a character in a second one, and both are involved in David's life.

In another subplot David introduces Steerforth, a college friend, to Little Em'ly, orphaned niece of Mrs. Copperfield's former housekeeper. Steerforth betrays his friendship by running away with Em'ly, thus continuing the subplot until its resolution near the end of the novel.

Body paragraph 2: second element described

The many subplots give Dickens a chance to introduce fantastic, exaggerated characters for which he is best known. Uriah Heep, for example, may be the most physically distasteful villain in English literature. His physical appearance suggests his evil personality. When he first appears in the story, David describes him: ". . . I saw a cadaverous face appear at a small window . . . in the grain of it there was the tinge of red which is sometimes to be observed in the skins of red-haired people. It belonged to a red-haired person—a youth of fifteen as I take it now, but looking much older—whose hair was cropped as close as the closest stubble; who had hardly any eyebrows, and no eyelashes, and eyes of a red-brown, so unsheltered and unshaded, that I remember wondering how he went to sleep. He was high-shouldered and bony; dressed in decent black, with a white wisp of a neckcloth; buttoned up to the throat; and had a long, lank, skeleton hand. . . ." (page 211) His repulsive appearance matches his behavior. Hiding behind a mask of

621

humility and duty, Heep develops complete control over Wickfield, who complains: ". . . look at my torturer. . . . Before him I have step by step abandoned my name and reputation, peace and quiet, house and home." (page 556) Not all characters are evil. One making a pleasant and lasting impression is Mr. Wilkins Micawber, an eccentric whose good intentions do not always meet with success and who often faces bankruptcy. Mr. Micawber is a humorous character with whom the reader sympathizes. An outstanding trait is his habit of giving long-winded speeches and writing flowery letters. This is seen in a letter in which Mr. Micawber asks David for a mysterious meeting. He does not come right to the point but writes, as he talks, in grandiose style: "If your more important avocations should admit of your ever tracing these imperfect characters thus far—which may be, or may not be, as the circumstances arise—you will naturally inquire by what object I am influenced, then in editing the present missive?" (page 676) Characters such as Mr. Micawber and Uriah Heep add interest and humor and contribute to the novel's plot and theme; for in Dickens' story, the good are rewarded and the evil punished.

Conclusion with overall evaluation and recommendation

David Copperfield is a lengthy narrative that involves many subplots woven carefully together to support the main plot. The author's ability to create fascinating and memorable characters to sustain these plots helps make this novel a pleasure to read.

EXERCISE A: Understanding a Book Report. Answer the following questions about the book report on *David Copperfield*.

1. What information does the writer give in the introduction of the book report?
2. How does the introduction of the book report summarize the novel's plot?
3. What element does the first body paragraph discuss?

4. What supporting information does the first body paragraph give?
5. What element does the second body paragraph of the book report discuss?
6. How might you break the second body paragraph into three shorter ones?
7. What supporting information does the second body paragraph give?
8. How does the report clarify the distinctive features of the novel?
9. What is the writer's overall opinion of the book? How do you know? Where did you find it?
10. Based on this book report, would you like to read the book? Why or why not?

PREWRITING, WRITING, AND REVISING: Preparing a Book Report

The steps that you have used to plan, draft, and revise other essays will serve you equally well as you prepare your book report.

Prewriting. In your reading you will find that some authors use one or two literary elements in particularly skillful ways. As you report on their books, you will want to focus on those elements.

Select one or two elements to discuss in your report and illustrate them using information from the book.

In your report you should handle each literary element separately, grouping supporting information under the element that it supports. Then, you should decide on an introduction for your book report that will prepare the reader for the literary elements to follow and a conclusion that will tie the elements together.

The information that appears in the chart at the top of the next page comes from Jane Austen's novel *Pride and Prejudice*. The writer who planned the report decided that two of the novel's noteworthy literary elements are setting and theme.

623

LIST OF SUPPORTING INFORMATION FOR A BOOK REPORT
Book: *Pride and Prejudice,* by Jane Austen
Setting: the English upper classes in Jane Austen's day —the rigid customs of the early 1800's in England —the accepted gulf between aristocrats and others —leisure among the upper-class gentry, including domestic accomplishments and genteel entertainments —the typically comfortable home life of Fitzwilliam Darcy, the novel's aristocratic hero
Theme: the universality of human failings —hypocrisy and self-delusion afflict not only those in the novel's place and time, but all human beings —the good, sensible heroine, Elizabeth, learns that even she is guilty of both pride and prejudice —her father, Mr. Bennet, sees that his prejudice and irresponsible behavior caused his daughter to run off

An outline which organizes supporting information can make it easier to write a book report. The outline below orders the supporting information about *Pride and Prejudice*.

I. Introduction
   A. Author—Jane Austen
   B. Title—*Pride and Prejudice*
   C. Overview—The importance of class difference in Jane Austen's day
      1. Fitzwilliam Darcy is a proud, rich gentleman.
      2. Elizabeth Bennet comes from a simple rural family but has beauty, common sense, and a strong will.
      3. Social differences complicate their relationship.
II. First element—Setting: the English aristocracy in the early nineteenth century
   A. Rigid social customs
   B. Acceptance of class divisions
   C. The indulgent leisure of the upper classes
   D. Ease and comfort in the aristocratic country estate
III. Second element—Theme: The universality of the pride
   A. Austen's England symbolizes a world of fallible people.
   B. Not even common sense and basic goodness are proof against pride.

C. Mr. Bennet is wise enough to admit his error.
IV. Conclusion
   A. Austen's characters display universal faults.
   B. Novel is timeless and worth reading.

Writing. Using an outline of your book report like the one above, prepare a first draft. Be sure to use all the information from your list of supporting material.

Follow an outline and list of supporting information to write the first draft of your book report.

As you work, try to connect ideas logically; use transitions and other linking devices, such as repeating main words and phrases. Order the information in this first draft. Once it is complete, you can revise it for strength and clarity.

The following draft of a book report on *Pride and Prejudice* has been revised and polished a bit. Nevertheless, you can use it as a model for structuring your report.

Book Report on *Pride and Prejudice*

Introduction with brief overview

Jane Austen's novel, *Pride and Prejudice*, vividly depicts early nineteenth century English gentry life. By following the stormy relationship of the proud and wealthy Fitzwilliam Darcy and the beautiful yet prejudiced Elizabeth Bennet, Miss Austen presents a detailed picture of the strictly defined society of her day. Darcy, a handsome gentleman of considerable means, first meets Elizabeth, the second of five daughters, at a ball near her home in the country. Although Elizabeth is from an unsophisticated country family, Darcy is impressed with her beauty and common sense. The novel follows these two main characters through family troubles, misunderstandings, separations, and finally reconciliation.

Body paragraph 1: first element described— setting

Pride and Prejudice is believable because of the author's detailed description of the customs and manners of the time in which she lived. The setting is an important backdrop against which the characters and plot develop. The novel gives an

625

excellent description of evenings spent in the drawing-room of a country estate. Gentlemen and ladies are shown after dinner playing cards, reading, writing letters, and conversing. A gentleman, Charles Bingley, further reveals customs when he defines accomplished ladies: "They all paint tables, even screens, and net purses" (page 35). At another point: "Mr. Bennet was glad to take his guest into the drawing-room again, and when tea was over, glad to invite him to read aloud to the ladies" (page 65).

The homes and food of the period are also detailed. Darcy's estate, Pemberley, is described: "Its windows, opening to the ground, admitted a most refreshing view of the high woody hills behind the house and of the beautiful oaks and Spanish chestnuts which were scattered over the intermediate lawn" (page 249). Servants bring in "cold meat, cake and a variety of all the fresh fruit in season . . . pyramids of grapes, nectarines, and peaches" (page 250).

Body paragraph 2: second element described— theme

Although the novel focuses on nineteenth-century English society, it deals with universal weakness in human nature. It is a moral commentary against pride and prejudice as shown in self-deception, irresponsibility, and hypocrisy. In the course of the novel, several characters begin to realize their faults and question their actions. Elizabeth, who prides herself on being open and a good judge of character, admits that prejudice clouded her opinion of Darcy. "She grew absolutely ashamed of herself. Of neither Darcy nor Wickham could she think without feeling that she had been blind, partial, prejudiced, absurd" (page 176).

Mr. Bennet also admits his weakness. He has behaved irresponsibly and when he learns of his youngest daughter's elopement, he accepts the blame: ". . . let me once in my life feel how much I have been to blame. I am not afraid of being overpowered by the impression" (page 280).

Being aware of one's faults is something people in all societies must learn.

Conclusion   Jane Austen skillfully conveyed the life style and values of her day. She accurately portrayed a time and a people who frequently acted unwisely, with pride and prejudice. Because her characters display the same faults people of all ages exhibit, the novel is timeless and well worth reading.

Revising. When your first draft is complete, reread it carefully, evaluating its content and organization.

Use a checklist in revising your book report.

The following suggestions will help you revise your report.

CHECKLIST FOR REVISING A BOOK REPORT
1. Are the author and the title of the book identified in the introduction?
2. Does the introduction of the book report give an overview of the book?
3. Do the literary elements discussed in the report represent the book accurately?
4. Have you given enough supporting information to make your ideas clear to the reader?
5. Is better support available in the book?
6. Is any information irrelevant? If so, remove it.
7. Have you used quotation marks correctly and given page numbers following any direct quotation from the book?
8. Does your conclusion contain a definite recommendation?
9. Should you rewrite parts so the paper reads more smoothly?
10. Are there errors in grammar, usage, mechanics, or spelling?

After reviewing your report against the checklist, make any improvements and recopy it neatly, proofreading your final copy.

EXERCISE B: Planning a Book Report. Select two elements that you wish to discuss from a book you have enjoyed recently. Support the elements you select by listing specific information from the book, and prepare an outline for your report.

627

EXERCISE C: Writing a Book Report. Using the list of supporting information and the outline you created for Exercise B, write a first draft of a book report.

EXERCISE D: Revising a Book Report. Evaluate the first draft that you wrote for Exercise C using the checklist on page 627. Rework your report as necessary and prepare a clean final copy.

DEVELOPING WRITING SKILLS: Planning, Writing, and Revising a Book Report. Working alone and then with another student, prepare and evaluate a second book report. Follow these steps.

1. Choose a work of fiction or nonfiction that you will enjoy writing about. Then, using the steps presented in this chapter, plan and write a first draft of a book report about the work you have chosen.
2. Exchange first drafts with another student in your class.
3. Evaluate the other student's paper, using the questions in the checklist on page 627. Write a few sentences evaluating the overall paper and offering suggestions for improvement. Then, return the paper you have evaluated to the student who wrote it.
4. Revise your paper, according to the comments written on it. Finally, rewrite and proofread a final copy of your report.

21.2 Literary Analyses

A literary analysis paper interprets a work of literature—a short story, novel, poem, play, or piece of nonfiction—and gives an opinion of it. This section explains the parts of a literary analysis and how to prepare, write, and revise one.

Understanding Literary Analyses

Both book reports and literary analyses evaluate the effectiveness with which an author uses the elements of literature.

628

Readers of book reports often know nothing about the book, but readers of literary analyses papers usually do and thus read to deepen their understanding of the work.

A literary analysis broadens readers' understanding of a work by explaining and interpreting it.

The following chart clarifies the parts of a literary analysis paper.

PARTS OF A LITERARY ANALYSIS PAPER
Title
1. The title often suggests an aspect of the paper's main point.   2. It may or may not contain the title of the work of literature.
Introduction
1. The introduction names the title of the work and its author; it presents any background necessary to the reader's understanding of the main point.   2. The introduction names the form of the work to be analyzed, such as a tragedy, short story, or sonnet.   3. It states clearly the main point which the paper will make, and which will be based on analysis of one or more elements in the work.
Body
1. The body explores subtopics of the main point, using one or more paragraphs for each subtopic.   2. Its uses supporting information from the work of literature to present the main point in a logical order, such as chronological, spatial, or developmental order.   3. The body presents enough material to convince readers that the main point was covered thoroughly.
Conclusion
1. The conclusion restates or summarizes the main point made in the introduction of the paper.   2. It explains how the main point relates to the whole work.   3. It pulls the paper together with satisfying closing remarks.

The following literary analysis paper is based on Henrik Ibsen's play *A Doll's House*. Read the writer's interpretations and supporting information carefully so that you understand how the paper was structured.

The Doll's Dance

Henrik Ibsen's play *A Doll's House* presents the conflict of a woman who has been treated like a child for nearly thirty years and who both longs for and fears full adulthood. The heroine, Nora Helmer, an apparently frivolous and childlike woman, is married to a rather overbearing and overprotective banker. Torvald Helmer treats his wife as an adorable but irresponsible pet and calls her his little squirrel, his skylark. He does not know that ten years earlier, when he had been very ill, Nora bravely, if foolishly, forged her father's signature on a promissory note to finance a rest-cure for him. Over the course of the play, the man who lent Nora the money tries to blackmail her. Nora tries desperately to prevent Torvald from learning the truth, but at the same time she imagines fondly that he will step forward heroically and save her when he does learn it. In a crucial scene at the end of the second act, Nora dances the tarantella for Torvald, to prevent him from opening their mailbox and discovering a letter from the blackmailer. This dance represents the play's most powerful expression of Nora's conflict, her dread of and desire for Torvald's recognition of her one independent act.

Throughout most of *A Doll's House,* Nora behaves like a dependent child-woman. She is always the butterfly, the frivolous one among a group of rather sober adults. And yet, at the same time, she expresses admiration and even envy for her schoolfriend, Mrs. Linde, a widow who has been bowed down by many cares and responsibilities. Nora is also very proud of her secret debt—proud that she *"had the wit to be a little bit clever"*[1] and save her husband's life. One part of Nora *wants* the truth to be known, and it is this part that is released in the turbulence of the tarantella.

The tarantella is a dance that supposedly resembles the violent attempt of a person bitten by a tarantula to rid the poison from his or her system. In the plot of *A Doll's House,* Nora's performance of the tarantella has a clear and simple function. Planning to dance at a party the following night, Nora deliber-

630

ately does a wild and inaccurate rehearsal of the tarantella for Torvald to distract him from opening his mail and to persuade him to direct her performance. Nora dances in a frenzy, which Torvald finds inappropriate and unsettling. He says to her afterward, "Come, come, don't be so wild and nervous. Be my own little skylark, as you used to be."[2] While she is dancing, he tells her, "My dear darling Nora, you are dancing as if your life depended on it." Nora replies, "So it does!"[3]

But although Nora may regard her tarantella as a desperate ploy to buy time for herself, it is clear from her feverish performance that much more is going on in her than either she or her husband is aware of. The dance is her outlet for emotion that has been building up in her ever since she learned of the blackmail threat. In this sense, Nora's situation is like that of a person stricken by a tarantula's poison: She too has been infected with something like poison, and she dances feverishly for release. Dancing the tarantella allows her to express a wildness that would otherwise not be appropriate for a middle-class wife and mother. As the dance gives her a day's reprieve from Torvald's discovery of her wrong-doing, so its fury allows her to escape from herself, her present troubles, and the boundaries and conventions she has accepted all her life.

Even more important, however, is the function of the scene within Nora's development in the play. Just before she dances, she tries to get the damaging letter out of the mailbox before Torvald can see it. She sends her friend Mrs. Linde to beg the blackmailer to withdraw his letter and continues to fight against her husband's discovery of her action. Even the dance itself is one more strategy to prevent the inevitable. But after the dance, Nora seems to have changed. Calmly, she accepts Mrs. Linde's report that she has failed to reach Krogstad:

Mrs. Linde: Gone out of town.

Nora: I could tell from your face.

Mrs. Linde: He is coming tomorrow evening. I wrote a note for him.

Nora: You should have let it alone; you must prevent nothing. After all, it is splendid to be waiting for a wonderful thing to happen.

Mrs. Linde: What is it that you are waiting for?

Nora: Oh, you wouldn't understand. Go in to them, I will come in a moment.[4]

In other words, the tarantella leaves Nora in a new frame of mind. Still fearing what will happen to her when Torvald learns the truth, she has begun to be fascinated with it. She even begins to look forward to it. Romantically, Nora expects that Torvald will take the responsibility for her action and that he will repay her risk with a selfless act of his own.

What happens is actually quite different. When Torvald eventually reads the letter, he turns on Nora angrily and seems concerned only with the effect of her action on his reputation. He forgives her when the blackmailer repents and returns the incriminating evidence to them. But Nora, shocked and disappointed by Torvald's first reaction, packs a suitcase and leaves their home. The "wonderful thing" that she both dreaded and longed for after her tarantella takes a form quite different from what she expected. Belatedly, she realizes that she has been a child for decades, living in a doll's house, playing at life. This tragic recognition has lain underneath her action throughout the play, beneath her envy of Mrs. Linde's maturity and her pride in her own single act of courage. This recognition is the fate that has awaited her, the fate that she both avoided and embraced when she danced the tarantella.

---

[1]Henrik Ibsen, *A Doll's House,* trans. R. Farquharson Sharp in *Four Great Plays by Ibsen,* with an Introduction by John Gassner (New York: Bantam Books, Inc., 1959), act 1, p. 12.

[2]Ibsen, *A Doll's House,* act 2, p. 48.

[3]Ibsen, *A Doll's House,* act 2, p. 47.

[4]Ibsen, *A Doll's House,* act 2, p. 48.

EXERCISE A: Understanding Literary Analysis Papers.

Answer these questions about the literary analysis of *A Doll's House.*

1. What is the main point presented in the introduction?
2. What aspect of the main point does the title suggest?
3. According to the introduction, which elements will the paper discuss?
4. What other information appears in the introduction?
5. How do the subtopics relate to the main point?
6. How does the evidence support each subtopic?
7. Is the evidence adequate? How is it presented?

8. How does the conclusion restate the main point?
9. How does the conclusion pull the paper together?
10. What devices have been used to make the ideas blend together smoothly?

PREWRITING, WRITING, AND REVISING: Preparing a Literary Analysis

A literary analysis paper should be carefully developed.

Prewriting. When you have read a work, understand its general meaning, and recognize some of the elements the author used, skim the work again, jotting down important passages, events, and character traits. Then decide which elements to write about. Those elements will suggest a main point for your paper.

After determining your main point, organize support for it, dividing supporting information under subtopics.

Next, decide which information in your notes will support each subtopic convincingly. If you do not have material for each subtopic, go back to the work to find the missing support.

Writing. Now you are ready to draft your paper. An outline of your main point, subtopics, supporting information, introduction, and conclusion will help you to get started.

Consider your audience as you write. Remember that they will read your paper for interpretation, not merely for a description of bare facts or plot.

Interpret the work for your reader, using your outline and notes, and providing an introduction, a body, and a conclusion.

As you write, use transitions to help readers follow your ideas. Put all direct quotations in quotation marks; give the source of each quotation (Section 20.1).

Be sure that your conclusion rounds out your analysis and leaves the reader with a sense of completion. Finally, choose a title that indicates the topic of the paper, reflects your main point, and arouses reader curiosity.

Revising. When you have completed your first draft, reread it carefully, looking for any weaknesses you can improve.

The following checklist can help you reexamine your paper and focus on key features that should be part of a literary analysis paper.

CHECKLIST FOR REVISING YOUR LITERARY ANALYSIS PAPER

1. Have you chosen the best title for your paper?
2. Do introductory statements in your paper provide enough background and summary information about the work to suit the audience?
3. Does the thesis statement present the main point and the paper's purpose—to report, to explain, or to persuade?
4. Do subtopics develop the main point with sufficient examples, details, and direct quotations as well as your ideas about the work, if appropriate?
5. Have you identified and provided pages for all direct quotations? Have you used one method for citing sources consistently throughout the paper?
6. Does your conclusion include a reminder of the main point and then bring the paper to a satisfying close?
7. Have you used transitions and other devices for coherence?
8. Throughout the paper, is your analysis centered on the work and presented clearly for the audience's understanding?
9. Are sentences varied in length and structure, using a mature, smooth style?
10. Can you find errors in grammar, spelling, usage, or mechanics?

After you proofread and check your first draft, you might have another person read it to make constructive suggestions. Then you should prepare a final copy.

In the literary analysis paper which follows, notice the development of the subtopic that focuses on setting, and the one that treats the character Marian. Notice also that the topic sentences and ideas throughout link setting and character to theme. Short, direct quotations give the flavor of the work and support the main point. Quotation marks and page numbers in footnotes identify these quotations for the reader.

Title   A Scarcity of Charity

Introduction   In the short story "A Visit of Charity" by Eudora Welty, a fourteen-year-old girl visits two women in a home for the elderly to bring them a plant and to earn points for Campfire Girls. Welty implies through this story, however, that neither the society that supports the home nor the girl, Marian, knows the meaning of the word "charity." The dictionary defines "charity" as "the love of man for his fellow men: an act of good will or affection." But instead

Thesis statement with two subtopics   of love, good will, and affection, self-interest, callousness, and dehumanization prevail in this story. Welty's depiction of the setting and her portrayal of Marian dramatize the theme that people's selfishness and insensitivity can blind them to the humanity and needs of others.

Subtopic 1: setting   Many features of the setting, a winter's day at a home for elderly women, suggests coldness, neglect, and dehumanization. Instead of evergreens or other vegetation that might lend softness or beauty to the place, the city has landscaped it with "prickly dark shrubs."[1] Behind the shrubs the whitewashed walls of the Old Ladies' Home reflect "the winter sunlight like a block of ice."[2] Welty also implies that the cold appearance of the nurse is due to the coolness in the building as well as to the stark, impersonal, white uniform she is wearing. In the inner parts of the building, the "loose, bulging linoleum on the floor"[3] indicates that the place is cheaply built and poorly cared for. The halls that "smell like the interior of a clock"[4] suggest a used, unfeeling machine. Perhaps the clearest evidence of dehumanization is the small, crowded rooms, each inhabited by two older women. The room that Marian visits is dark, with a drawn shade and too much furniture. No colors, decorations, or beauty brighten this room, which is packed with beds, a chair, a wardrobe, a washstand, a rocker, and a bed table. The wet smell of everything and the wet appearance of the bare floor suggests that this cramped room is more like a stall in a barn, a place for animals, than

635

that it might be a home fit for use by human beings.

Transitional paragraph
The character Marian represents the society that has confined old women to this dismal, neglected home. Specifically through Marian's thoughts, words, and actions, revealed by the third person partially omniscient narrator, Welty shows how selfishness and indifference can obscure the needs of the less fortunate.

Subtopic 2A: Marian: her thoughts
Throughout her so-called visit of charity, Marian perceives the old women she meets sometimes as things and sometimes as animals. She refers to an old woman as an object to be used and discarded when she announces the purpose of her visit: "I'm a Campfire Girl . . . I have to pay a visit to some old lady."[5] These words and her frequent thoughts about the points she will get for the visit reveal her real reason for coming: self-gain. An old woman—"any of them will do"[6] she says—is an impersonal thing with no identity or personality. Clearly, her concern is focused on her progress in Campfire Girls. During her brief stay at the Home, Marian thinks of the first old woman as a bird and the second as a sheep. In her eyes, the first woman moves in "short, gradual jerks"[7] like a bird, has "a hand quick as a bird claw,"[8] and grabs her with the grip of a talon. The other woman, bundled up in bed with a quilt, appears to Marian to resemble a sheep. When Marian first sees her, she describes her mentally as having "a bunchy white forehead and red eyes like a sheep."[9] When this second woman clears her throat or talks, she sounds to Marian like a sheep bleating or a lamb whimpering. Marian's unconscious dehumanization of the women, her reduction of them to objects and creatures, reveals her own insensitivity.

Subtopic 2B: Marian: her words to the women
Welty also dramatizes the blinding power of self-interest through Marian's lack of preparation for her visit and her inability to talk with or listen to the old women. Marian is so preoccupied with the points she is earning that she never thinks beyond her task to deliver the potted plant to some old woman. When the first woman takes the plant, Marian real-

636

izes that she has not even looked at it. Nor has she thought that during her visit she would be interacting with human beings in need of warmth, concern, and cheer. From the moment she finds herself in the dark, tiny room, her uppermost thought is escape. She is so stunned by her surroundings and the strange, lonely women that she cannot remember her own name or answer the questions that the first woman asks her. She identifies herself only as a Campfire Girl and never learns the names or histories of the women. A few of the remarks Marian blurts out do not even make sense, and the one question she asks, "How old are you?"[10] only serves to remind the bedridden woman of her helplessness and age. If Marian had had a different purpose or had let herself become involved in the lives of these women, she might have seen beyond their squabbling. She might have realized that emptiness and despair led the one to contradict and deny her roommate's identity, past, and meager memories while it led the other to give away her roommate's birthday secret. But Marian only hears and does not understand. Her flash of interest in the old woman's age quickly fades when the woman refuses to answer the question.

Subtopic 2C: Marian: her actions

Finally, Welty illustrates the theme of self-interest and callousness through Marian's actions, particularly at the end of the story. Even before her visit she was thinking about herself when she hid her apple under a bush before entering the building. Marian came to give a thing, a potted plant, not herself. She even gave less time than another Campfire Girl who read the Bible to the old women. Throughout her visit she is uncomfortable, until finally her desire to escape overwhelms her. When the first old woman begs Marian for a penny or a nickel to buy something of her own, Marian does not even speak to her. Instead, she exerts all her strength to free herself from the woman's grasp and run away. Marian is stylishly dressed, indicating her social standing. She could have given the old woman something,

something for the woman's sake and not just something to buy herself points. Even after her rude departure, she is untouched by the raw needs and emotional vacuum revealed to her. As she yells for the bus to wait, leaps on, and chomps on her apple, she shows her untouched feelings and undisturbed ignorance. She is young, vigorous, and free. She has her points; nothing else matters.

Reminder of the thesis statement

Conclusion

Neither the maintenance of the Old Ladies' Home nor Marian's delivery of a potted plant qualify as an act of charity. In fact, as an analysis of the setting reveals, the Home is inhumane in many ways. Marian indicates in her thoughts, words, and deeds that she is opportunistic and indifferent to the needs and feelings of the aging women. Welty further suggests in this story that pseudo-charity can destroy the very humanity it pretends to acknowledge and uphold. People like Marian acting either out of duty or for personal advantage have created the Home and the conditions that have made the inhabitants cranky, clutching, and unlovable. Marian left the women more lonely and distraught than she found them. This kind of charity is uncharitable indeed.

Footnotes credit source; shorter subsequent references

[1]Eudora Welty, "A Visit of Charity" in *Modern Satiric Stories: The Impropriety Principle,* ed. Gregory Fitzgerald (Glenview, Illinois: Scott, Foresman and Company, 1971), p. 245.

[2]Welty, "A Visit of Charity," p. 245.

[3]Welty, "A Visit of Charity," p. 246.

[4]Welty, "A Visit of Charity," p. 246.

[5]Welty, "A Visit of Charity," p. 245.

[6]Welty, "A Visit of Charity," p. 246.

[7]Welty, "A Visit of Charity," p. 246.

[8]Welty, "A Visit of Charity," p. 247.

[9]Welty, "A Visit of Charity," p. 248.

[10]Welty, "A Visit of Charity," p. 251.

EXERCISE B: Writing a Literary Analysis. Write a literary analysis with an introduction, a conclusion, and a title. Include smooth transitions. Cite the sources of all direct quotations.

EXERCISE C: Revising a Literary Analysis. Put the paper you wrote in Exercise B aside for ten minutes. Then reread it. Using the checklist on page 634, revise and recopy the paper neatly.

DEVELOPING WRITING SKILLS: Using Analytical and Writing Skills. Choose a work unlike the one you used in the exercises above. Analyze it using some questions in this section and five of your own. Follow the planning and writing steps in this section. Before you revise, find someone who will read it and suggest changes. Then revise, make any changes, and recopy.

Writing Workshop: Writing About Literature

ALIENATION the TRAGEDY of WAR
STRUGGLE FOR SURVIVAL The Good Life
Individual vs. SOCIETY
EVIL vs. GOOD
LOVE LOSS OF
the Primitive INNOCENCE DEATH
& the Civilized The FORCES of NATURE

ASSIGNMENT

Topic Two Writers from Different Countries and Centuries and Their Treatment of the Same Theme

Form and Purpose A literary analysis paper that informs

Audience Publisher and users of a world literature textbook

Length Six to eight paragraphs

Focus Your paper should be a point-by-point analysis of how the two writers develop a major literary theme. Examine similarities and differences. In your conclusion focus on how each work reflects the culture and attitudes of its time.

Sources Novels, short stories, poems, or plays

Prewriting Read and analyze two works that treat the same major theme, taking notes that compare and contrast each writer's development of the theme. Prepare an outline.

Writing Use your outline to write a first draft of your paper.

Revising Revise your paper using the checklist on page 634.

640

22

Personal Writing

As you gather personal experiences through life, you gain insights that you can share with others. Often, you will choose writing as your way of sharing. In this chapter, you will learn more about forms of personal writings: the journal, personal anecdote, first-person narrative, and autobiography.

Journals   22.1

A *journal* is a private record of a person's life. It retells events as they happened and often includes the personal interests, insights, observations, and feelings of the writer. Some writers keep their journals private, while others expect people to read them.

Understanding Journals

In a journal, a writer responds to life by writing about it. If the journal is intended for others to enjoy, the writer provides details that allow readers to share and respond to the experiences related.

A journal is a personal record of events, feelings, insights, and observations; often, the journal reflects its writer's special interests.

The candor and personal tone of journals make them one of the most popular forms of personal writing.

Kinds of Journals. Journal writers have a variety of objectives. Some may want to record an important chain of events in their lives. Others may simply want to gain skill at expressing themselves in writing. Others may want to keep track of developments in a hobby or other special interest.

The chart below distinguishes four kinds of journals.

KINDS OF JOURNALS		
Kind of Journal	Purpose of Journal	Probable Writing Time
Daily Summary	To keep track of everyday events	Daily
Journal of Personal Feelings	To express candid feelings and insights	Daily or several times a week
Journal of Important Events	To record key events or moments in life	Weekly
Special-Interest Journal	To record experiences in an area of special interest	As each occasion arises

Journal Entries. A journal is a series of individual entries. They vary in length, tone, and detail, as the writer's experiences change. Typically, they include observations about people, places, and things as well as the writer's reactions to them. Skillful journal entries contain vivid, colorful details.

Following is an entry from a journal written more than one hundred years ago. It retells events and includes details about them, but the thing that makes the journal memorable is the writer's personality, as shown in her feelings and impressions.

The Adirondacks, July 22, 1878

Setting   Night before last there came up a violent thunderstorm just at bedtime, most unexpectedly, and we had everything lying around. Such a time we had! There were 2 or 3 parties out in boats, and I had

642

Descriptive
details

made up a great big camp fire on the rocks to guide
them home, and when the wind blew up it began to
blow the sparks all over the dry grass and towards the
tents. There were several fires already burning in the
mountain and I was afraid we should soon have one
in our camp if prompt measures were not taken, so I
had to scatter the burning brands as fast as possible
down the rocks into the water below. Then having no
possible light except matches, there was no hope of
finding anything, and we just had to grapple our way
through, regardless of every consideration of comfort
or propriety.

At last we got settled in our tents, when Mary felt
her pillow heave up and down as though some live
creature underneath were trying to make its way out.
We *thought* it was a snake, and I had to march out in
the dark and the rain through bush and briar to call
one of the guides out of the birch bark shanty to

Personal
observations

come and catch the thing. So much for the outward.
And now for the inward. How do I like this sort of
life? I do not like it at all. I can't sleep comfortably
anywhere off of a spring bed with good bolsters and
pillows . . . I do not care for boating, nor fishing, nor
hunting, and sitting on a log does become monotonous after a while.—Hannah Whitall Smith

EXERCISE A: Understanding a Journal. Reread the preceding journal excerpt and answer the following questions.

1. How do you know this writer did not keep a daily
   summary?
2. What kind of journal did Ms. Smith keep? Why do you think
   so?
3. What were her two major concerns in this entry?
4. What descriptive details did she use? List five.
5. What personal feelings did she share?

EXERCISE B: Looking at Different Journal Entries. Locate three or four published journals and read several entries
in each. Choose one entry that appeals to you and answer
these questions.

1. From what kind of journal does the entry come?
2. What is the focus of this entry?
3. How much time does the entry cover?
4. List three descriptive details that the writer includes.
5. What personal impressions, feelings, or insights does the writer share?

Keeping a Journal

While your journal is your own creation, you should keep certain guidelines in mind while planning and writing.

Decide on the purpose of your journal, plan your entries by brainstorming and making notes, and continue to brainstorm for details as you write.

Identify the purpose of your journal. Knowing why you are keeping it will help you decide on a frequency for making entries and help you choose information to write about.

Planning a Journal. As you plan your journal, keep yourself and your experiences in mind and think also about your readers. Include enough to make sure any reader will understand your ideas and feelings.

As you prewrite and plan, use the following checklist.

PLANNING A JOURNAL

1. Review the kinds of journals listed on page 642, and identify the kind you will keep.
2. Decide how frequently you will make entries.
3. Prewrite each entry by making notes answering the questions: "Who?" "What?" "Where?" "When?" "Why?" and "How?"
4. Brainstorm for descriptive details and pertinent information, and include them in your notes.
5. Include personal observations, insights, and feelings that will make your journal a reflection of yourself.
6. Make a list of ideas or an outline of your entry, making sure that all events follow chronologically.

After completing the steps, you can see what kind of journal you mean to write and some information that will go into it.

The chart shows how a student planned a journal entry.

PREPARING TO WRITE A JOURNAL ENTRY	
When?	Last August
Where?	In Vermont
Who?	Me, my family, the innkeeper
What?	My first visit to a country inn
	—a 19th century farmhouse
	—pleasant atmosphere
	—comfortable lodgings
	—interesting furnishings
	—good food

Writing a Journal Entry. Now, with all the information in hand, you are ready to write your journal entry. You should write so that readers can follow your ideas easily; be sure to connect details or incidents with clear transitions.

Notice that the following entry uses the information gathered in response to the questions above, but adds more details which occurred to the writer in the process of drafting the entry.

Subject of entry

August, 1984

    I had not wanted to go to an old inn at all, much preferring to spend my vacation at the shore. But here I am this evening, with my parents and my sister, pulling off one of Vermont's highways and turning into a long driveway. At the end is the Closter Inn.

    We fall in love with the charm of the restored nineteenth-century farmhouse before we are in it for five minutes. The innkeeper, Cal, and his wife and two pre-teen children are so friendly that we feel at home and welcome.

Descriptive details

    First Cal shows us around the cozy first floor sitting rooms full of interesting country antiques. Then he takes us upstairs to bedrooms so simple and comfortable that they remind us of Grandma's old house in Mason City—quilts, rag rugs, and all.

    Cal doesn't serve dinners, so we drive into town

645

to eat, then return to Closter for a tough game of Scrabble before calling it a night.

Chronological order   We sleep like Rip Van Winkle in the big four-poster beds. In the morning, Cal's wife, Myra, cooks a huge breakfast of sausage and pancakes with homemade syrup and preserves. By eleven o'clock we are back on the road. We all feel so rested, well fed, and content that we know we will visit country inns whenever we get the chance.

EXERCISE C: Planning Your Journal. From the chart on page 642, select a kind of journal to write. Gather notes for entries, collecting information appropriate to the kind you chose.

EXERCISE D: Writing a Journal Entry. Write the first entry for the journal you planned in Exercise C, giving as much detail and as many impressions as you can.

DEVELOPING WRITING SKILLS: Keeping a Journal. Continue writing entries for the journal you started in Exercises C and D. At the end of three or four weeks, reevaluate your journal. Decide whether you will continue or will change the kind of journal in order to suit your purpose better.

22.2 Writing from Personal Experience

In addition to the journal, personal writing includes the anecdote, the first-person narrative, and the autobiography.

Writing an Anecdote

One enjoyable form of personal writing is the anecdote. Like a journal, it contains personal experience, impressions, and feelings, but usually it focuses on an event. A writer typically uses an anecdote to elicit a certain response from a reader.

Understanding Anecdotes. In one sense, an anecdote is a very short story which a writer tells in order to amuse a reader.

An anecdote is a brief entertaining account of a personal experience.

Although an anecdote can be any length, usually it is no longer than a few paragraphs and is amusing in the style of a lively joke. Often speakers tell anecdotes to illustrate key points in a speech or to refresh listeners after a heavy discussion.

As with any other story, the anecdote must present a clear setting and characters in a few words. Its brief series of incidents must lead to a logical conclusion. Often the conclusion is humorous.

Following is an example of an anecdote. It was written by a popular news personality, the late Jessica Savitch, to illustrate the perils and frustrations of news reporting. This anecdote, taken from her autobiography, reveals the writer's sense of humor about herself and her work.

> At a rally that was staged for Senator Muskie during his campaign for the presidency, I competed with a multitude of other reporters to get close enough to ask a few questions for the evening newscast. I was stuck in the body-to-body mob several yards away from him until a rangy, broad-shouldered Texan, crying "Why, it's that cute li'l ole gal from Channel 11!," picked me up, literally held me above his head, and barreled his way through the throng. He deposited me directly in front of the senator. Triumphantly, I looked across the sea of faces to make sure my cameraman was rolling. He was waving something wildly back and forth. My heart sank. It was disconnected microphone cable.—Jessica Savitch

Prewriting, Writing, and Revising. Whether your anecdote will be brief like the one above, or part of a longer composition, such as a speech or autobiographical essay, you should follow certain prewriting and planning steps.

Choose a specific event for an anecdote, and tell the incidents in clear chronological order.

Your anecdote will have a beginning, a development, and a conclusion. You will find it easy to order the material in this way if you first identify the event, your reason for sharing it, and the readers who will see it. As you prewrite, list all the important incidents that you will use. This list becomes an outline for the anecdote. Arrange the incidents in chronological order so that readers can follow the action easily.

Using the outline, begin writing, always brainstorming for pertinent details that you may have missed in the outline. Think again about each incident, and search your mind for descriptive information that will make the anecdote more interesting. Add these to your list, and consider other elements that would improve the anecdote, such as dialogue or figurative language.

As you write, keep in mind the special characteristics of the anecdote, and use the following checklist to help you revise.

CHECKLIST FOR REVISING AN ANECDOTE

1. Is this anecdote complete in itself or part of a longer composition? Is that fact clear?
2. Does it focus on one major incident?
3. Do the incidents follow chronological order with a clear beginning, middle, and conclusion?
4. Will readers understand why you have shared this event with them? Does the conclusion make that clear?
5. Do descriptive details and dialogue enliven the anecdote?
6. Is the point of view consistent? Is it first-person?

EXERCISE A: Planning an Anecdote. Think of an anecdote you can write, perhaps an event from your recent past. Write down the event and your reason for sharing it with others.

EXAMPLE: The time I found an anonymous gift in my locker—
five gallons of water (event)
To illustrate the satisfactions of tutoring upperclass students (reason for sharing)

EXERCISE B: Writing an Anecdote. Write the anecdote you sketched in Exercise A. Check to see that the incidents follow chronological order. Add any new information, descriptive details, or humorous insights that you can think of. Use the checklist to revise the anecdote. Then make a final copy and proofread it.

648

Writing a First-Person Narrative

Like a descriptive essay, a first-person narrative focuses on a person, place, thing, or incident. A key feature of this form of personal writing, however, is its point of view. In first-person narratives, the writer and the narrator are one and the same.

Understanding First-Person Narratives. First-person narratives relate information about a specific person, place, or thing from the writer's vantage point.

> **A first-person narrative relates significant observations about persons, things, or events in the writer's life. It uses an "I" and "we" point of view.**

Sometimes the focus of first-person narrative is fairly simple, relating few details and requiring only a paragraph or two. Other narratives are longer, depending on the complexity of the subject and the writer's technique.

In the following excerpt from a longer first-person narrative, a writer recalls his youthful career as a newspaperman. The account uses people, places, and details, but also the writer's own feelings and aspirations.

Reason for sharing

I first realized that the act of writing was about to enter a new era five years ago when I went to see an editor at *The New York Times*. As I was ushered through the vast city room I felt that I had strayed into the wrong office. The place was clean and carpeted and quiet. As I passed long rows of desks I saw that almost every desk had its own computer terminal and its own solemn occupant—a man or a woman typing at the computer keyboard or reading what was on the terminal screen. I saw no typewriters, no paper, no mess. It was a cool and sterile environment; the drones at their machines could have been processing insurance claims or tracking a spacecraft in orbit. What they didn't look like were newspaper people, and what the place didn't look like was a newspaper office.

Setting

I knew how a newspaper office should look and sound and smell—I worked in one for thirteen years.

649

| Descriptive details | The paper was the *New York Herald Tribune,* and its city room, wide as a city block, was dirty and disheveled. Reporters wrote on <u>ancient typewriters that filled the air with clatter;</u> copy editors labored on <u>coffee-stained desks</u> over what the reporters had written. <u>Crumpled balls of paper littered the floor and filled the wastebaskets</u>—failed efforts to write a good lead or a decent sentence. The <u>walls were grimy</u>—every few years they were <u>painted over in a less restful shade of eye-rest green</u>—and <u>the atmosphere was hazy with the smoke of cigarettes and cigars.</u> At the very center <u>the city editor, a giant named L. L. Engelking,</u> bellowed his displeasure with the day's work, <u>his voice a rumbling volcano</u> in our lives. I thought it was the most beautiful place in the world.—William Zinsser |
| Writer's feelings | |

Prewriting, Writing, and Revising. In prewriting, outline the incidents, arrange them in chronological order, and think of any other information that your reader will need.

Choose a topic for your narrative, then order the incidents and observations chronologically.

Remember to answer the basic questions for the reader: "Who?" "What?" "Where?" "When?" "Why?" and "How?"

Use your prewriting notes to help you write a draft. As you write, continue to add details—consider dialogue, for instance—that will enhance the narrative. As you revise and prepare final copy, use the following checklist.

CHECKLIST FOR REVISING A FIRST-PERSON NARRATIVE

1. Does your narrative keep to its subject without straying?
2. Do the events follow chronological order with transitions to connect ideas?
3. Does the narrative have a clear beginning, a logical development, and a satisfying conclusion?
4. Do descriptive details and dialogue enliven the work?
5. Have you decided to include personal observations or feelings about the subject?
6. Do you maintain your use of first-person point of view throughout your narrative?

650

EXERCISE C: Understanding First-Person Narratives.
Answer the questions below about the first-person narrative on
pages 649–650.

1. What specific details does the author include?
2. What personal observations does he make about the newspaper office?
3. How does he contrast the two offices?
4. Where might the writer have used dialogue?
5. Write a line or two of dialogue to insert in that place.
6. Select some language that the writer used especially well.
7. Which details make the scene seem real to the reader? Select two or three details.
8. Is the last sentence effective? Why or why not?
9. What is the "new era" the writer sees?
10. Do you think he will be content in the changed environ-
    ment? Why or why not?

EXERCISE D: Writing a First-Person Narrative. Follow
these steps to plan, write, and revise a first-person narrative.

1. Select a topic from your personal experience.
2. Brainstorm for important events, information, and details
   that you can include.
3. Make a prewriting list, or outline, of the events, details, and
   other elements that you will use. Arrange them in chronological order.
4. Write a first draft.
5. Revise using the checklist on page 650, write a final version, and proofread it.

Writing an Autobiography

An autobiography resembles a first-person narrative because
both forms use the first-person point of view and focus on
something from the writer's personal experience.

Understanding Autobiographies. While other people, as
well as incidents and settings, will appear in an autobiography,
the emphasis is on the author.

**Your autobiography tells a true story about all
or part of your life.**

651

Usually an autobiography covers more of the writer's life than an anecdote or a first-person narrative does. Therefore, it is often longer and more like a short story. The autobiographies of well-known people, such as presidents and movie stars, are usually book-length.

They may contain many elements which you will recognize from short stories: dialogue, description, and incidents developed in chronological order.

In the following autobiographical composition, a writer tells about a short span in his life. Notice that the excerpt focuses on the writer, even though it includes other people.

Opening incident

So in the spring of 1934 we set off with one of London Films' best cameramen, Borrodaile, all the apparatus for filming, and tents and stores for a fortnight, including a barrel of fresh water, for there was none on the island.

Everything went well. Lockley arranged for an RAF plane to take the cameraman up to film the approach to the island—first a blur of white gradually resolving itself into thousands of separate white dots—the birds on their nests; we obtained close-ups of the feeding of the young and even of a fledgling throwing itself off the grassy cliff into the sea.

Descriptive details

And we captured all their display habits. Whenever a bird rejoined its mate, it would present seaweed as nest material, and the pair went through an elaborate mutual ceremony, bowing their heads, preening themselves under the wing, . . . sometimes even intertwining their necks, cackling loudly and clappering their beaks. Occasionally a bird alone on the nest would be so overcome by emotion that it would perform a display all by itself.

Thanks to the constant sunshine which we were lucky to have all through our stay, the birds' dazzling whiteness shone with an almost sculptural beauty, and enormously added to the impact of our film. It had a long run in cinemas all over England and America, as well as proving useful to departments of Zoology by illustrating the breeding biology, the strange mutual displays of the birds, and their aerodynamic skill. The end of the film was supplied by my old friend John

Grierson, 'father' of documentary films, who chartered a herring-boat to take close-ups of a swarm of gannets diving for fish—a beautiful sequence in slow motion.

Personal observation and conclusion

Our enterprise was crowned with the award of an Oscar for the best documentary film of the year, which gave us a great deal of satisfaction. In any case, I had thoroughly enjoyed the making of this film. . . .
—Julian Huxley

Prewriting, Writing, and Revising. To plan your auto-biography, you should first identify a time span to cover. Deciding about the period of time will also help you determine the length of your autobiography.

Choose a time span to cover in your autobiography, take notes about that period of your life, and present your memories in clear chronological order.

You may, for example, want to write about your first experience of driving a car in a paragraph or two. If you decide to cover all your teen years to date, you may need to write several pages.

Once you have an idea of your focus and length, you can begin prewriting. Think about this period of your life; write notes about it. List pertinent people, events, settings, and any other details that you consider important.

As you write, make sure the events follow chronologically. Use dialogue if you think readers will find it interesting. Keep the point of view consistent throughout, and include personal feelings and observations.

Finally, revise with the help of the checklist below.

CHECKLIST FOR REVISING AN AUTOBIOGRAPHY

1. Is the time span of your autobiography clear?
2. Do the events follow chronological order? Are settings clear?
3. Do you maintain a first-person point of view?
4. Have you included vivid descriptions?
5. Do you need to add dialogue for interest?
6. Have you included personal feelings and observations?
7. Does your autobiography reach a satisfying conclusion?

EXERCISE E: Understanding an Autobiography. Reread the excerpt from Julian Huxley's autobiography on pages 652–653. Then answer the following questions.

1. What is the main incident recounted in this excerpt?
2. List at least three descriptive details the author uses.
3. Would this excerpt have been effective without those details?
4. Why do you think the writer included this incident?
5. Is the ending of this excerpt satisfying? Why or why not?

EXERCISE F: Writing Your Autobiography. Choose a time span or event in your life to write about. Then follow these steps to plan, draft, and revise the work.

1. Prewrite by making notes about setting, incidents, and people who were involved.
2. Make a chronological informal outline of the incidents.
3. As you draft the autobiography, add any new ideas and descriptions that occur to you.
4. Use the checklist as you revise, and write a final version of your autobiography. Proofread it.

DEVELOPING WRITING SKILLS: Writing from Personal Experience. Think about the last five years of your life. List three events that you consider memorable. Select one of these and write it on your paper. Then decide how you will handle an account of the event or time span: as an anecdote, a first-person narrative, or an autobiography. Follow the guidelines in this chapter to plan, prewrite, draft, and revise your composition.

Writing Workshop: Personal Writing

ASSIGNMENT 1

Topic   A Journal of Self-Evaluation: How Independent Am I?

Form and Purpose   Journal entries that help you evaluate one aspect of yourself

Audience   Yourself

Length   At least one entry every other day over a three-week period; you decide the lengths

Focus   Each entry should reflect the above topic by recording an experience, behavior, or event that demonstrates dependence or independence.

Sources   Personal experiences

Prewriting   For each entry, think about one experience, behavior, or event and how it shows dependence or independence. If you wish, write notes.

Writing   Write about the experience, behavior, or event. Also write a summary of what it means about yourself.

Revising   After a week or two, review your journal entries and evaluate your independence.

ASSIGNMENT 2

Topic An Experience I Would Like to Forget!

Form and Purpose A brief anecdote that entertains readers

Audience Yourself or, if you wish, friends

Length One paragraph or longer if you include dialogue

Focus Write about an embarrassing or humorous experience that you have had with a pet, car, or another person. Adopt a humorous tone and style and tell the details of the experience in chronological order.

Sources Personal experiences

Prewriting After selecting the experience, write notes about it. Arrange them in chronological order.

Writing Use your notes to write a first draft.

Revising Review the draft to be sure that it contains a beginning, a development, and a conclusion. Use the checklist on page 648 and prepare a final version.

Topics for Writing: Personal Writing

The photos above may suggest a personal experience. If so, write about that experience in a journal entry, anecdote, first-person narrative, or autobiography. If you prefer, choose one of the following topics.

1. Victory Snatched from the Jaws of Defeat
2. A Crushing Loss in Baseball, Basketball, Football, or Soccer
3. A Coach I Will Never Forget
4. A Coach I Would Like to Forget
5. A Sport That I Cannot Play Well
6. What Competition Means to Me
7. A View from the Bench
8. My Most Embarrassing Moment in Sports
9. Is There Life after High-School Sports?
10. My First Experience with _____ (you name a sport)

Chapter 23

Short Stories

Although short stories are written about almost every field of human interest and in a rich variety of styles, certain characteristics remain the same. They all have a single conflict, a small group of characters, and a point of view.

23.1 Understanding Short Stories

A narrative relating imaginary events that happen to imaginary people and lead to a single climax is a *short story.*

Character and Plot

Characters are the people who appear in stories. *Plots* are the chains of events that affect their lives. A skillful writer of short stories uses these elements almost as one, making plot show character and characters influence plot.

Character. Short-story writers do not enjoy the luxury of building characters slowly; they must sketch their characters quickly and economically. To do this, they try to give a *dominant impression* of each important character, especially of main ones. They leave the rest to the reader's imagination.

In a short story, a writer tries to establish one clear, dominant impression about each important character.

Plot. A plot is not merely a chain of events. For forward motion and reader interest, a plot needs *conflict.*

The plot of a story is a chain of events which flow from a central conflict.

The conflict that drives the plot can be internal or external. Sometimes a main character struggles with an outside force, such as another character, the elements of nature, or society. In other stories, the struggle is inside the character. Often the character is torn by conscience, loyalty, or compassion and must choose between painful alternatives.

Unlike a novel, a short story has only one plot, with rising action, a climax, and a resolution. It has no room for subplots or ideas that do not move the plot forward.

The chart below lists the stages of a short-story plot and tells what happens in each stage.

PLOT OF A SHORT STORY	
Stages	**Functions**
Exposition	Introduces the characters and places them in an appropriate setting
	Establishes a point of view
	Fills in the background information
Opening incident	Creates a central conflict
	Starts the plot moving
Rising action	Adds new incidents or insights that build the conflict to greater intensity
Climax	Raises the conflict to greatest intensity
	Changes the course of events or the way that the reader understands the story
Falling action (not always used)	Relaxes the conflict to prepare readers for the conclusion
Conclusion	Resolves the conflict
	Carries the plot to an end; often interprets the story or gives a final insight

Review a short story you have read, and answer the questions.

1. Who is the main character?
2. What dominant impression does the character create?
3. Is the conflict internal or external? Explain your answer.
4. How do other characters relate to the central conflict?
5. What information does the writer give in the exposition?
6. What is the opening incident? How does it launch the plot?
7. What is the rising action that intensifies the plot?
8. Identify the climax. Is it an insight or an event?
9. Does the story have a falling action? If so, what is it?
10. How does the conclusion resolve the conflict? How does it make you feel about the whole story?

Point of View

All the events in a traditional short story are seen from one vantage point, called the *point of view.*

The point of view must be unified and consistent in a well-structured short story.

The person who tells the story from the single vantage point is the narrator. The narrator tells the story from one of these points of view: first person, limited third person, or omniscient third person. The chart explains the points of view.

KINDS OF NARRATORS	
Narrators	**Functions**
First person	The narrator tells the story as he or she saw it, using first-person pronouns *I* and *me.* The narrator can be the author or a character who takes part in the events.
Limited third person	This narrator is not a participant in the story, cannot read the characters' minds, and uses third-person pronouns *he* and *she.*
Omniscient third person	This narrator uses *he* and *she* and is outside the story but has access to the characters' thoughts.

Study these versions of a story. Ask yourself what each narrator sees and understands. The first narrator tells a story about an experience he had.

First-person   We flew together for almost a year. Every Sunday,
narrator   we took off with Mick in the back seat and me up
               front. I never forgot that he was the instructor and I
               was only a cub, but we became friends, too. If I did
               something dumb, Mick would chew me out. That was
               okay. He was getting me ready to be on my own up
               there.

In the next example, a limited third-person narrator tells the story from a vantage point a bit farther from the action.

Limited   Mick was Jack's instructor for almost a year. Every
third-person   Sunday the pair would take off with Mick in the back
narrator   seat, Jack up front. Jack never forgot that Mick was
               the instructor and he was the cub, but they became
               friends, too. If Jack did something careless, Mick lec-
               tured him, always preparing him to fly alone.

Finally, a narrator tells the story from outside the events or from an omniscient third-person point of view. This narrator knows the characters' thoughts and feelings and comments on them.

Omniscient   Every Sunday, as the pair took off, Jack felt a surge
third-person   of pride. Here he was, practically flying the plane
narrator   alone. Meanwhile, in the back seat, Mick was alert,
               ready to step in if his student made a mistake. When
               Jack did something unwise, Mick lectured him
               sharply. This kid would solo soon. He had to know
               how to handle situations. It was up to him, Mick, to
               be sure of that.

EXERCISE B: Understanding Point of View. Using the story you analyzed in Exercise A, answer these questions.

1. Who is the narrator? Is he or she a participant in the story?
2. Which point of view does the narrator represent?
3. How can you tell which point of view is used?
4. How would a different point of view change the story?
5. Why do you think the author chose this point of view?

Dialogue

Dialogue is conversation between characters in a story. It can also be used to show characters talking to themsleves. Dialogue should help the reader know the characters' thoughts.

Dialogue helps a short story writer to make characters believable and to advance the plot.

We all tell a great deal about our thoughts, feelings, and attitudes by the way we talk. In stories, speech habits such as slang, dialects, and unconventional word choice help to paint pictures of characters. As characters relate events and express opinions, they move the plot forward, too.

Often sections of dialogue are the most memorable parts of a story. Notice how the following dialogue reveals more about the characters with each statement.

Passage with dialogue

"All set, Jack?" The instructor checked the instrument panel quickly.

"Yep." The younger man peered down the runway ahead of them. "Right as rain, Mick."

Jack pulled back on the throttle and the little plane lifted eagerly, without a wobble.

"Nice work, Jack. Now hold 'er in this line until you reach three hundred feet. Then a 90° left bank and on up to five hundred."

"Aye-aye, sir." Jack concentrated on his plane until it completed the take-off pattern, then sat back and relaxed.

This was the best part of the lesson. Jack loved the quiet and the feeling that he had left all his troubles on the ground.

"You're doing fine, kid. I'd say you ought to try it by yourself in a week or so."

EXERCISE C: Understanding Dialogue. Answer the questions, using the story you examined in Exercises A and B.

1. How much dialogue is in the story? How many characters speak?

2. How does the dialogue help you to picture the speakers?
3. Does the dialogue differ from one character to another? How?
4. How do the sections of dialogue advance the plot?
5. If there were no dialogue, how would the story be different?

Language and Tone

In order to write a convincing story with no false notes that startle a reader, a writer must choose words carefully. Throughout a short story, a writer can use language as an artist uses paint, to create a world, people it, and share a conflict that affects it.

A writer must choose language and create a tone that is both appropriate and consistent.

When readers begin a short story, they want to enjoy the illusion of reality. They hope to enter situations they can believe in. Language that destroys illusion deprives them of that literary pleasure. To satisfy readers, choose words that build and preserve the imaginary world you are writing about.

Following are some elements of language to use for effects.

Simple, Direct Language. Everyday language is generally more effective than euphemisms or complicated language. You recall that euphemisms create a flowery tone. They can cause a reader to question your sincerity.

FLOWERY: The funeral procession wound its way to the interment.

SIMPLE: The cars drove in a line to the burial.

FLOWERY: The cook conveyed applesauce from the metal container.

SIMPLE: The cook ladled applesauce from the tin can.

Complicated, flowery, or lengthy words that call attention to themselves can destroy a story's tone. In narrative, fancy language destroys tone because narrators should direct attention to the characters and not to themselves. In dialogue, self-important language should be used only by arrogant or snobbish characters.

OVERLY FORMAL:	Each of the boys who owned a two-wheeled gasoline-driven vehicle was required to submit a registration form to the proper authorities before sixty days had elapsed since the acquisition of the vehicle.
SIMPLE:	Each motorcycle and motorbike owner had to register it with the police within sixty days of buying it.

Use euphemisms and very formal language in narrative only to achieve a certain effect. Use them in dialogue only to depict characters who would talk in a stilted, evasive way.

Readily Understandable Language. Short-story writers must be sure readers will understand the words they choose. Slang and jargon, which vary from place to place and change quickly, are likely to cause confusion. The slang term below, current a few years ago, today sounds so old-fashioned that it might distract readers if it occurs in the narrative part of a story.

SLANG:	The band was hep to the new musical score.
REVISED:	The band understood the new musical score.

Obviously, a writer can use slang to help depict a character who would logically talk in this fashion or to set a scene during the time when the slang was current.

The language of specialized groups, called jargon, can also confuse readers and destroy a story's tone if used carelessly.

SPECIALIZED:	Environmental engineers were measuring the trajectories of plumes from the stacks.
UNDERSTANDABLE:	Environmental engineers were measuring the direction of smoke rising from the smokestacks.

One example of jargon is the language of computer use, which is creeping into everyday use. The following example, which could help to sketch a character who works with computers, would destroy tone when used by a narrator who has nothing to do with computers.

SPECIALIZED:	Input this data to the Long-Range Plan.
UNDERSTANDABLE:	Add this information to the Long-Range Plan.

664

Be sure that any foreign terms you use strengthen a characterization or help to establish an overall tone. Unnecessary foreign words or phrases distract readers. Generally, it is best to use English. Notice the following.

FOREIGN PHRASE: The Mayor presented the award to Detective Maryann Collins in absentia.

ENGLISH PHRASE: The Mayor presented the award to Detective Maryann Collins in her absence.

Precise Connotation. You know that many words have both denotations and connotations, or emotional overtones. To help you select the right words for your short stories, some dictionaries and other books give both kinds of meanings.

Careful writers refer to the thesaurus or dictionary of synonyms, as well as to the standard dictionary, to find words most appropriate to their stories. Notice how the synonyms below, though close in meaning, create different impressions.

SYNONYMS: Mia smiled *sedately* at her prize-winning painting.
Mia smiled *coolly* at her prize-winning painting.
Mia smiled *smugly* at her prize-winning painting.
Mia smiled *priggishly* at her prize-winning painting.

EXERCISE D: Understanding Language and Tone. Rewrite and improve each of the sentences, following the direction preceding it.

1. (Simplify flowery language.) "A superfluity of kitchen workers complicates the preparation of a hot liquid food product," Jack opined.
2. (Simplify overly formal language.) Edna found that a dearth of employment opportunities in her discipline would prevent her from locating a position commensurate with her skills.
3. (Remove the euphemism.) Becky got home on Sunday night only to find that the cat had passed away.
4. (Replace the foreign phrase.) As we reached the top of the hill, we spied a charming antebellum house.
5. (Remove the outdated slang.) Cathy thought the swim club party was the cat's pajamas.

6. (Remove the foreign phrase.) The astronomy club voted to keep the plans status quo.
7. (Select the verb with a connotation that fits the sentence.) Angrily, Zeke (flung/delivered) the huge fish into the trawler's hold.
8. (Simplify the language.) As we pulled up at the corner, the electronically timed, color-coded vehicular traffic regulator device changed color.
9. (Remove the flowery language.) "It is with profound regret," the professor wrote, "that I am obliged to decline your most gracious invitation to deliver an address at the luncheon gathering of your esteemed association."
10. (Remove the overly formal language.) Human beings who reside in domiciles made of vitreous transparent material are well advised to avoid propelling in the air mineral fragments.

DEVELOPING WRITING SKILLS: Understanding Short Stories. Read two published short stories and write a comparison. Include all the elements of the short story which you studied in this chapter: character, plot, point of view, dialogue, language and tone.

23.2 Writing a Short Story

In this section, you will develop all the elements of a short story by following the steps you have used in other forms of writing.

PREWRITING: Planning Your Short Story

By planning carefully, you can combine all the elements you studied in Section 23.1 to produce a complete story.

Organize the details about character, conflict, and setting into a plot outline for a short story.

A character whom you find interesting may provide a good starting point for your planning. It can be someone you know, someone you merely saw on the street, or a totally imaginary human being. In any case, the following questions will help you to develop the character fully.

QUESTIONS FOR DEVELOPING A CHARACTER
1. What is the character's identity (name, age, sex, nationality, era, and so on)?
2. What are the character's principal traits? Main strengths and weaknesses?
3. How does the character speak? How does he or she look?
4. What dominant impression do you want to create for your main character?
5. Describe the character's friends and family. How does he or she relate to them? Will they figure in your story?

Though you may not include in your short story all the ideas that the above list generated, they will all help you to understand your character. This knowledge will show you how the character will act in conflict.

Continue your planning by answering the questions listed in the chart below.

QUESTIONS FOR DEVELOPING CONFLICT
1. Will the conflict in your story be internal or external?
2. Will it explore the main character's feelings, or ideas, or both?
3. Will opposition come from other characters or outside forces?
4. Will dialogue or narration about events convey the conflict? Which will present the climax?
5. Which character is right, and which is wrong or mistaken? Will that fact change during the story?

The answers to the above questions should help you to state the conflict in one sentence, and to sketch a plot that reveals the conflict. Remember that there is only one climax in a short story, which will be either an event or an insight. One way to plot is to decide how the climax will occur, then write the plot with that stage in mind. The chart on page 659 will help you to organize the plot so that the climax has impact.

Now review your plot outline to see which point of view will be best for this story. Does the reader need to know the main character's inner thoughts and feelings? If so, you must make the character the narrator or use an omniscient third-person narrator, who can see into the character. If the character's actions are more important than his or her thoughts, a limited third-person narrator can serve as narrator.

EXERCISE A: Planning a Short Story. Review the notes you made from the two lists in this section. What speech traits might help you to make your main character seem real? What parts of the story should be narration? What parts should have dialogue? Will dialogue or narration be more effective for the climax? Why?

WRITING: Creating a First Draft

In drafting your story for the first time, do not worry about details of description or dialogue. Your first task is to get all the events in order and to start developing your characters.

Follow your plot outline as you draft the story, keeping the point of view consistent.

Connect the events like links in a chain, using transitions and repetitions to keep the reader moving forward with the plot. Sketch as much dialogue as occurs to you, but do not stop to polish it. In both dialogue and narration, consider tone and the words that establish it. Be sure that the narrator you chose relates only facts that he or she would logically know.

The story which follows is the work of a student. Notice that the margin notes outline the structure, by labeling the stages as listed in the chart on page 659.

A Doomed Voyage

Exposition   It was pouring in torrents, but Captain John was still on board the *Intrepid,* preparing it for his voyage. The big, muscular man finished his work and went into the Anchors Away Luncheonette.

There was smoke in the air. In the background, harsh music was being played. Empty mugs stood on the counter. The faint smell of soap and ammonia drifted through the air.

"One tall, cold glass of cranberry juice," he said.

"Comin' right up, Cap'n." When the glass was half empty, John spoke.

"Well, Joey, my ship and I are ready for a trip around the world. Still need a crew member, though. Know anybody who wants to take a little ride with me?"

A man who had been sitting at the end of the counter stood up and walked toward the captain.

"I'd like to join your little boat ride, mister."

The Captain studied the man. He was strongly built, about six feet two. On his right arm was a tattoo of a snake and an anchor. He had not shaved in days, and looked as if he had not slept in weeks.

"What's your name?" Tenny asked.

"Sam. Sam Whitmore."

"Know how to swim and sail a thirty-foot schooner?"

"Yessir, I do. My family had a boat on the Sound."

"All right, then. You're hired. I'm Captain John Tenny of the *Intrepid*. We'll sail Monday at 6:30 a.m."

"OK, Captain. I'll be there at six, with my gear."

Sam arrived at the dock at six sharp on Monday.

"Come on board, Sam, and we'll shove off. Got all your stuff?"

"Yup, I do. Let's get going."

Opening incident

A few days later, John turned the wheel over to Sam, so that he could get some rest.

"Take over for a while, Sam, so I can sleep."

"All right, Cap'n. Pleasant dreams, sir."

About half an hour later, John woke with a start, because the boat had crashed. While trying to figure out what had happened, he heard Sam thrashing in the water on the other side of the wreck.

"Help me! I can't swim! Help!"

Rising action

John swam to the struggling man and gave him a piece of the broken hull to hang on to.

"You said you could swim and sail this boat. Who are you, anyway?"

"I—I'm Amos Proctor. I've escaped from jail and I was gonna hop off your boat in Europe, free from the law with a brand new, clean life. I thought it was

669

gonna work. That is until you asked me to sail the boat alone. I really am sorry for causing you so much trouble, John."

Climax   While looking around, wondering what to do, John spotted a boat in the distance. He had to decide between staying with Amos until help arrived or swimming to safety and then returning for Amos. If he stayed with Amos, help might not come for days, so he decided to swim for it. After what seemed an eternity, but was only a few hours, he arrived at the anchored boat.

"Come on aboard," shouted the captain of the luxurious yacht that John had seen. Once aboard, he told the captain who he was, and why he was swimming in the middle of the ocean.

"My boat rammed a coral reef about two miles east of here. I was wondering if you would be kind enough to radio the Coast Guard for help. My crewman is at the wreck."

"I'll radio for help right away."

Conclusion   About an hour and a half later, the Coast Guard arrived with Amos safely in their custody. They had recognized him and arrested him for the jail break. John thanked the captain of the vessel, and they were on their way.

When they got back to shore, John had a chance to talk to Amos one last time.

"Amos," he said, "When you get out of jail legally, look me up. I'll give you some sailing lessons, and then we will really sail around the world."

EXERCISE B: Drafting a Short Story. Write a draft of your story, based on the notes you gathered in Exercise A. Include exposition, opening incident, rising action, climax, and conclusion. Use dialogue when it is appropriate.

REVISING: Polishing Your Short Story

Remember that a first draft is only a practice copy. Feel free to experiment with it.

Check your short story carefully to make any needed improvements before you make your final copy.

Revise your short story using the ten questions in the checklist below.

CHECKLIST FOR REVISING A SHORT STORY

1. What kind of point of view did you use? Is it consistent?
2. Does the narrator sound consistent? Appropriate? Does he or she relate only what is logical from that vantage point?
3. How would you describe the mood? How did you create it?
4. Is the conflict internal or external? Is it clear?
5. Is the development of the plot logical throughout?
6. How does the rising action advance the plot?
7. Could your climax be more effective? Will it satisfy your readers?
8. Do your characters talk the way such people would talk?
9. What language helps to set the tone you want?
10. Are your grammar, spelling, usage, and mechanics correct?

EXERCISE C: Revising a Short Story. Using the checklist above, revise your story from Exercise B. Recopy and proofread it.

Finding Your Own Approach

Now that you understand the standard steps in planning, writing, and revising a short story, you can adapt the steps to suit your own work habits and your particular story.

Varying the Prewriting Steps. The process of selecting story elements is not necessary if you know your characters and plot.

Vary prewriting steps when you are clear about the characters and plot you will use.

In cases of this kind, you can simply brainstorm to gather ideas about the elements of your story, as in the following.

BRAINSTORMING SHEET
—seven men in a squad —assigned to finding missing men —searching in a forest —uncertain about their location

The notes you gather by brainstorming will help you to see your story as a whole.

Varying the Writing Steps. It is possible to write a short story from notes like the ones you made for Exercise A. Some writers work this way, knowing that they will need to write a second draft to smooth the rough parts of the first draft.

Try writing a first draft of your short story without sketching out a plot outline.

By writing without an outline, you may get fresh ideas. As long as you write a second draft later, this is one way to work.

Rough first draft
> The sun was shining on the fields. The day was dry and hot. The forest was dark and cold and wet. They knew they were someplace north of the border near Lao Cho, but not exactly where. They struggled through underbrush that smelled musty and wet. There were seven men in the detail.

The student writer of this story opening did not organize them logically or supply transitions. The writer knew that this was a practice draft. In the second, more polished draft, the writer revised the work by reorganizing the details for logic and impact, and choosing words that make the details convincing.

Compare this better and smoother version with the first one.

Improved second draft
> The open countryside lay sweltering under a merciless Asian sun, but the forest was dark, cold, and wet. The weary squad of seven men struggled through the dank-smelling thickets of dense underbrush, their rifles snagging in the vines.
>
> They knew that they were somewhere near the border at Lao Cho, but none of them could have said just where. Somewhere, maybe five miles away, the enemy waited.

672

Varying the Revising Steps. The section above shows the value of revising, whether early or late in the process of writing. Revision is especially important when you are working without an outline.

> **Revise early and often when you write without an outline; do not wait until you complete the story.**

Careful writers revise freely and constantly during the writing. They reread frequently, evaluating the story's believability, clarity, and correctness.

EXERCISE D: Varying the Prewriting, Writing, and Revising Steps. Choose a character that you know well and about whom you could devise a plot. Brainstorm to gather further ideas about the character and the action you will plot. Try writing a practice draft, using only the notes and covering just the opening scene of the story. Then revise the scene to eliminate the roughness of the spontaneous draft.

DEVELOPING WRITING SKILLS: Finding Your Own Approach. Write a paragraph describing the steps you used in Exercise D. In a second paragraph, tell whether standard methods or an adapted method seems better to you as a short-story writer.

Writing Workshop: Short Stories

ASSIGNMENT 1

Topic Altering the Clichéd Ending

Form and Purpose A short story that entertains readers

Audience Young children who cannot read

Length Four to six pages

Focus Many stories conclude with an expected ending. Develop a story that is based on a well-known legend, tale, or standard plot. Provide an ending that differs from the original and is surprising and unexpected.

Sources Collections, myths, legends, and fairy tales

Prewriting Select a well-known story. Brainstorm for ideas about changing the characters, plot, and ending.

Writing/Revising Write a first draft without using an outline. Revise at various stages of the story. Review the completed story by following the checklist on page 671. Prepare a final, complete version.

"Then the dragon gobbled up the handsome young prince and his lovely young bride and lived happily ever after."

ASSIGNMENT 2

Topic   Developing a Theme

Form and Purpose   A short story that both entertains and instructs by focusing on an important theme

Audience   Students in a literature class

Length   Five to seven pages

Focus   Select a theme from a story or novel that interests you. Write a story that focuses on that theme.

Sources   Novels and stories that you have read and studied

Prewriting   After selecting your theme, plan your story's setting, characters, and plot. Use questions like those in the checklists on page 667. Prepare a plot outline.

Writing   Follow your outline and write a first draft. Use dialogue to help make your characters believable and to advance the plot's action.

Revising   Using the checklist on page 671, revise your draft and prepare a final copy of your short story.

Topics for Writing: Short Stories

The above illustration may suggest an idea for a science-fiction short story. Plan and write that story, or choose one of the science-fiction topics below.

1. The Invasion of Robots from Thor
2. Colonizing the Planet Saturn
3. Caught in a Reversal of Time or a Time Warp
4. Discovering the Planet Earth
5. Discovering an Exact Replica of the Planet Earth
6. Rebellion of the Crew During an Intergalactic Voyage
7. Lost in a Black Hole
8. The Sun Is Extinguished and Dies
9. A Planet Ruled by Intelligent Animals
10. The Discovery of an Advanced Civilization That Has Conquered Death

Chapter 24

Letters and Applications

At various times you will need to write letters for college and job applications. You may correspond with friends and relatives, respond to invitations, or order merchandise. This chapter provides some guidelines for these types of writing.

Personal Letters 24.1

Probably many of the letters you write are personal; others relate to business. In order to write confidently, you should know the styles and features of both personal and business letters, and you should understand the purpose of each type.

Understanding Personal Letters

In personal letters you correspond with distant friends, invite people to social gatherings, and so forth. Such letters have a simple but helpful format.

The Parts of the Friendly Letter and the Social Note. Usually personal letters have five basic parts arranged in an orderly way.

The five basic parts of a personal letter are heading, salutation, body, closing, and signature.

Place a *heading* in the upper right-hand corner of your letter. Include your street address on the first line, your town or city, state, and ZIP code on the second line, and the date on the third. (If the letter is going abroad, add your country on the second line.) This information enables the receiver to write back to you.

The *salutation* or greeting belongs at the left-hand margin, below the heading. It varies with the nature of the letter and your relationship with the recipient. A comma always follows the salutation.

FORMAL	Dear Steve,	Dear Miss Lynch,
	Dear Aunt Greta,	Dear Mrs. Hopper,
	Dear Dr. Gray,	Dear Ms. Assali,
INFORMAL:	Hi, Pal,	Howdy, Bruce,
	Hey, Cora,	Greetings,

The *body* of your letter starts two or three lines below the salutation. It contains as many sentences and paragraphs as you like and all the ideas, feelings, and personal information you wish to communicate.

A *closing,* placed in the lower right-hand portion below the body, signals the end of the letter. Capitalize only the first word, and place a comma after the last word, as in the examples below. The closing you choose should suit the tone of the letter.

FORMAL:	Very truly yours,	Sincerely,
INFORMAL:	So long for now,	Love,

Your *signature,* placed directly beneath the closing, ends the letter. Use the name which the receiver of the letter uses in addressing you, and write it in ink, even if you have typed the letter.

An *R.S.V.P.* added to an invitation tells the reader to respond by accepting or declining. It appears in the lower left-hand corner.

Different Styles for Friendly Letters and Social Notes. Arrange the five basic parts of a personal letter in one of two styles.

Use either indented or semiblock style for your personal letters.

The *indented style* indents the heading, closing and signature, as well as each body paragraph. The *semiblock style* indents only the first line of each paragraph.

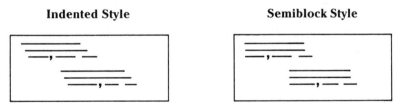

Address your envelope following the same style, either indented or semiblock, that you used in preparing your letter.

The checklist below will also help you address envelopes.

WRITING YOUR ENVELOPE
1. Be consistent. If you type the letter, type the envelope; if you handwrite the letter, handwrite the envelope.
2. Do not use titles such as Mr., Mrs., or Ms. in your own name.
3. Be sure the address of the person to whom you are writing is complete. Include such data as apartment or route number and ZIP code.
4. In addresses, avoid abbreviations that will not be immediately clear to anyone reading the envelope.

Fold letters according to the size of the paper and the envelope. Fold small sheets once; fold large sheets in thirds, as shown below.

Letter	Letter Folded Once	Letter Folded Twice

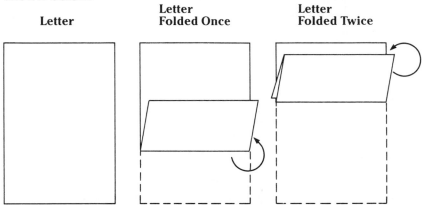

EXERCISE A: Practicing with the Parts of Friendly Letters and Social Notes. Prepare two skeleton letters, using lines instead of words. Follow indented style for one, semiblock for the other. Fill in all five basic parts of each letter, except for the body, using real or fictitious names and addresses.

EXERCISE B: Mailing Personal Letters and Social Notes. Prepare envelopes for the skeleton letters from Exercise A, matching styles from letter to envelope.

Writing Personal Letters

Consider your audience when writing personal letters.

Friendly Letters. When writing to friends or family members, use an engaging opening, relate the personal information you want to share, and end with a suitable conclusion.

Organize the information you want to share in a friendly letter.

The following suggestions will help you to organize your ideas before writing a friendly letter.

SUGGESTIONS FOR WRITING FRIENDLY LETTERS

1. Be sure to answer questions the recipient asked in his or her last letter to you.
2. Mention previous letters, visits, or phone calls if any of these contacts warrant consideration.
3. Use facts and details about people, places, and events that will make them come to life for your readers.
4. Proofread your letter carefully. Did you present ideas clearly enough for your reader to understand them? Do any mechanical errors need correction?
5. Rewrite the letter, if necessary. Make any corrections and additions that will improve it.

Social Notes. Generally, you will find that social notes are shorter and a bit more formal than friendly letters and have a specific purpose.

Focus on your purpose when writing a social note.

An *invitation* has the same five basic parts as a friendly letter. It includes all necessary details about the event to which you are inviting the recipient, and asks for that person's response. The chart below shows the essential elements of an invitation.

WRITING A LETTER OF INVITATION

1. Be specific about the time, date, and place of the event, as well as clarifying the kind of event it will be.
2. If circumstances require it, tell the reader what to wear or bring.
3. Mail early enough to allow ample time for the recipient to respond.
4. Add an R.S.V.P. if you need an advance response.

Reply to an invitation by writing a *letter of acceptance* or a *letter of regret,* using the five parts of a personal letter and

681

including the specific details about the event. If the invitation included a phone number, you can telephone your response.

WRITING A LETTER OF ACCEPTANCE OR REGRET

1. When accepting an invitation, repeat the time, date, and place to avoid misunderstanding.
2. When refusing an invitation, offer a reason for not attending.
3. Always express your appreciation for the invitation.

This model shows the five basic parts of an acceptance.

> 6 Carole Circle
> Mt. Vernon, N.Y. 10550
> September 5, 1986
>
> Dear Lester,
>   I will be happy to attend your party for the exchange students from Spain on December 13. I know I will find it interesting to share information about our school and other activities, and I welcome a chance to practice my Spanish.
>   I plan to arrive at 6:30 p.m. Thank you for inviting me.
>
>   Sincerely,
>   Leona Lewis

A *thank-you note or letter* is appropriate when you receive hospitality or a gift. A *letter of congratulations* or a *letter of condolence* should express joy or sorrow sincerely. All four types should be written promptly.

EXERCISE C: Getting Ideas for a Friendly Letter. List ideas that you might include in a friendly letter to a real or imaginary person.

682

EXERCISE D: Writing Invitations and Letters of Acceptance or Regret. Imagine that you are planning a social event. Write an invitation. Include all necessary information: *who* you are, *what* the event will be, *when* and *where* it will take place, and any other information your guest might need. Then exchange your letter with one written by a classmate and write a letter of acceptance or regret to your classmate's invitation.

DEVELOPING WRITING SKILLS: Writing Different Types of Personal Letters. Write a personal letter suitable to any one of the following situations. Be sure to include all five parts of the personal letter. Use your own name and address for the heading, and someone else's name for the salutation. Make up necessary details. Keep your audience and the purpose of the letter in mind as you write. When you complete the letter, proofread it and, if necessary, recopy it. Prepare an envelope.

1. Your cousin in another state has won a scholarship to a highly respected college. Write a letter expressing your reaction to this news.
2. You have been invited to the wedding of your best friend's brother in a nearby city. Accept or decline the invitation.
3. You are planning an after-prom party at your home. Write a letter of invitation and address it to a classmate.
4. Write a letter sharing information with a good friend or close relative who lives in a distant city and whom you visited last summer.
5. A relative is in the hospital recovering from an operation. Write an appropriate letter.

Business Letters 24.2

Business letters have basic parts, styles, and purposes which distinguish them from friendly letters and social notes.

Understanding Business Letters

Whether its purpose is to order merchandise, apply for a job, or express a complaint, a business letter follows certain rules.

The Parts of a Business Letter. A correct business letter has six basic parts arranged in a unique format on plain paper or business stationery.

Your business letter should include six basic parts arranged as follows: a heading, inside address, salutation, body, closing, and signature.

Present your complete address and the date at least one inch below the top of the paper in the *heading.*

Place the *inside address* two or three spaces beneath the heading, at the left margin. Include the complete address of the person or company to whom you are writing, and a title if this is appropriate.

EXAMPLES: Mr. John Hanson, President
Hanson Motors, Inc.
1550 States Avenue
Milwaukee, Wisconsin 53233

Richardson Furniture Store
1400 Kings Road
Pittsburg, Kansas 66764

Your *salutation,* placed two or three lines beneath the inside address, should be formal, as in the following examples. Notice that a colon follows each salutation.

EXAMPLES: Dear Sir: Gentlemen:

Dear Sir or Madam: Dear Mrs. Simon:

The *body* of your letter, beginning two lines below the salutation, presents all the information you wish to include.

The *closing,* which ends the communication, appears two or three lines beneath the body, begins with a capital, and ends with a comma.

EXAMPLES: Sincerely yours,   Cordially,

Very truly yours,   Respectfully,

Your *signature* follows a few lines beneath the closing. If you typed your letter, type your full name beneath the signature. Women sometimes show the title by which they prefer to be addressed by adding *Mrs., Miss, Ms.,* or *Dr.* in parentheses before their names.

Different Styles for Business Letters. Your business letter can follow one of three styles.

Use block style, modified block style, or semiblock style for your business letter.

In *block style,* the simplest of the three, all parts of the letter are aligned at the left margin. No lines are indented, not even the first line of a paragraph. Spacing sets off the six parts and each paragraph in the body.

In *modified block style,* the heading appears at the upper right margin, and the closing and signature at the lower right margin. The inside address, salutation, and body paragraphs begin at the left margin. *Semiblock style* is similar, but the first line of each body paragraph is indented.

Block Style   **Modified Block Style**

Heading

Inside
address

Salutation

Body
paragraphs

Closing
Signature
Name

Heading

Inside
address

Salutation

Body
paragraphs

Closing
Signature
Name

Semiblock Style

Heading

Inside
address

Salutation

Body
paragraphs

Closing
Signature
Name

The following rules will help you to prepare business letters.

SPECIAL RULES FOR BUSINESS LETTERS
1. Use 8½×11-inch white bond paper and standard matching envelopes for all business correspondence.
2. Handwrite business letters only when you have no alternative.
3. Follow one of the three formats consistently in your letter.
4. Leave a one-inch margin on all sides of your paper.
5. If your business letter has a second page, place the recipient's name at the top, along with the page number and the date.

Use standard business-sized envelopes that match your stationery and address them as in the diagram below.

Fold your letter in thirds, as shown on page 680.

EXERCISE A: Practicing with the Parts of Business Letters. Sketch two different styles of skeleton business letters. Label each letter with the style you are using. Draw lines to represent the body paragraphs. Use your own address for the heading and a local business address for the inside address and salutation.

EXERCISE B: Addressing Business Envelopes. Prepare an envelope for each of the skeleton letters in Exercise A.

Writing Business Letters

State your purpose clearly in business letters.

Write business letters that explain your purpose quickly and directly.

Request and *order letters* ask for information or order merchandise. The following guidelines tell what they include.

WRITING REQUEST AND ORDER LETTERS

1. Be sure the letter contains all six structural parts.
2. State clearly that (a) you are requesting information or (b) you are ordering merchandise.
3. When asking for information, give a reason for the request.
4. When placing an order, specify the items you want, and include order numbers.
5. When an order requires payment, state (a) the amount of the order and (b) whether you will pay by check, money order, charge account, or COD.

Notice how the following order letter meets these guidelines.

310 Monterey Avenue
Los Angeles, California 90007
March 27, 1985

Order Department
Fresh and Salt—Fish and Tackle, Inc.
Whittier, California 90054

Dear Sir:

   I would like to order the following items from your 1984/85 *Outdoorsman* catalogue. To complete my order, I have enclosed a money order for $45.00, including postage and handling costs.

Amount	Item	Price
1	Deluxe Golden Rod fishing pole Order Number: 037	$23.00
15	Pack sets of assorted lures Order Number: 050	22.00
		$45.00

Sincerely,

Phyllis Porter

A *letter of complaint* seeks to solve a business problem, such as faulty merchandise, undelivered order, or overcharge. Present your complaint clearly at the beginning of your letter and give information to help the reader see the problem.

A *letter of opinion* expresses your views, perhaps to an editor of a newspaper. Be sure to begin with a main point, state your view objectively, and support it with facts. Use some of the techniques for persuasive essays.

EXERCISE C: Writing a Request or Order Letter. Write a letter based on one of the following suggestions.

1. Order merchandise from a department store. Give enough information for the reader to fill your order. Choose something practical or something you dream of owning.
2. Ask a state senator for information about environmental protection in your area for use in a class paper.
3. Order tickets for an event, specifying the event, date, time, place, and the payment method you will use.

EXERCISE D: Writing a Letter of Complaint or Opinion. Use one of the following suggestions to write a business letter.

1. Complain to a music club about a record that you ordered and that never arrived.
2. Tell a newspaper editor your feelings about an event that has been making headlines.
3. Tell a television station manager your views on a recent television special which he produced.

DEVELOPING WRITING SKILLS: Writing a Business Letter. Think of a real purpose you might have for writing a business letter. Determine the type of letter you want to write. Review the guidelines, write the letter, and prepare an envelope.

24.3 Applications

Essay questions on college or job application forms may present you with challenging and diverse topics. Your first step is to understand the requirements of each question. Then your writing skills will help you to make a good impression by presenting yourself and your ideas clearly.

Interpreting the Questions

To begin any response on a college or job application, examine the question and try to envision the length and form (paragraph or essay) of your answer. Decide what elements you will need in answering the question and what ideas you will express.

Determine the specific requirements of an essay question on an application.

The purpose of almost any application question is to find out several important things: (1) the quality of your ideas about certain topics, (2) special knowledge that you may possess, or (3) personal information about you. *All* applications seek to determine how well you express yourself in writing.

Let the quality of your ideas shine through, and give any specific knowledge you can apply to the question. The chart lists three common types of questions found on job applications.

QUESTIONS ON JOB APPLICATIONS	
Type of Question	**Sample Question**
1. *Specialized* questions ask what specific knowledge or skills you have that can be applied to a job.	Describe three different business machines often used in a secretarial office, and explain how each is operated.
2. *Problem-solving* questions present a difficult situation that you might encounter on the job.	As a social worker, you might be asked to help an impoverished family of four budget their small income. How would you proceed?
3. *Personal* questions ask for background information, seeking proof of your suitability.	Describe experiences that you feel qualify you for work with the Recreation Commission.

Depending on the amount of information requested and the complexity of the question, you may write a paragraph answer or an essay answer. The preceding *specialized* question might be answered in an essay having a brief introduction, three body paragraphs (one for each business machine), and a brief conclusion. The *personal* question, on the other hand, might be answered in a single paragraph, as in the following model. Often, businesses require complete but short answers.

Paragraph answer on a job application	I seek employment as an assistant recreation director because of my experiences in the field. I have been working in local recreation departments for the past two years, or since my sophomore year in high school. I started as a playground supervisor, and by the time I was a junior, I was working with the local director on programming and planning. I helped to initiate new programs, such as our Apple Cider Field Day, in which townspeople picked apples and made cider. I also helped update the old programs, making them more suitable to the people they were serving. For example, I supervised the reconditioning of an old horseshoe field. In addition, I have taken courses in first aid, health, sociology, psychology, music, art, and physical education, which have prepared me to perform any recreational responsibilities that I may encounter.

Like job applications, questions on college applications measure knowledge and skills, but they may be somewhat broader in scope. College admissions officers want to know how well applicants write, as well as about their extracurricular activities and their educational goals. College applications may contain any of the three types of questions listed in the chart below.

QUESTIONS ON COLLEGE APPLICATIONS	
1. *Topical* questions ask for your understanding, interpretation, or stand on some idea of general interest.	Discuss a problem that faces your country, state, city, home, or school. Include the origin of and possible solutions to the problem.

2. *Goal* questions ask for specific ideas about your future, as a college student and after graduation.	Describe at least one educational objective, interest, or professional goal that has led you to apply to this school.
3. *Personal* questions ask for background information about your school and personal life.	Tell about one or more of your interests or skills—in or out of high school— explaining how you acquired and developed them.

The sample below—an answer to the topical question— gives an idea of a longer piece of writing on a college application.

Essay answer on a college application

Introductory remarks (origin of the problem) Thesis statement

First body paragraph (solutions to the problem)

Because my home town is near a large city, many people drive there for work, activities, and recreation. So our town is often a boring place. Senior citizens have nothing to do, and most young people cannot wait to leave. Yet residents who use their ideas, energy, and money elsewhere could change our town. If they and local officials would turn their talents toward this community, they could give it a new identity.

Homeowners, the school board, and merchants could create cultural, creative, and athletic activities. Working through the schools, residents could organize an acting group, art shows featuring local talent, "white elephant" sales, performances by local musicians, and community courses. Courses could feature exercise, auto mechanics, dancing, guitar, yoga, gourmet cooking, creative writing, and many other subjects. Adults could become involved in athletic activities such as a soccer, softball, or bowling team or a yearly golf or tennis tournament. With merchants' cooperation, the empty warehouse could become a roller skating rink. By coordinating picnics and bazaars with varsity football or baseball games, residents could draw larger crowds to games and activities.

691

Second body paragraph (solutions to the problem)	With planning and publicity, officials could initiate a Founders' Day celebration featuring barbecues and a band. The town could plan a spring or autumn carnival of activities, rides, game booths, and refreshment stands. The town board could encourage merchants to donate prizes, advertise "specials," and display products of interest. School and religious groups would gladly become involved.
Reminder of the thesis statement Conclusion	If our town decided to develop and expand, the results could only be positive. A sleepy suburban town could become a lively, energetic community full of people who enjoy living here and who have fun together.

EXERCISE A: Finding Application Questions. Find five applications for college admission, scholarship, or employment. List any five questions from them that require answers of either paragraph or essay length.

EXERCISE B: Recognizing the Requirements of Application Questions. For each question you found in Exercise A, identify the type (topical, specialized, and so forth), the requirements, the best length for an answer, and the best organization. If necessary, use the sample questions below.

1. (College) What experience had a significant impact on you?
2. (College) What special interests and achievements influenced your life?
3. (Scholarship) Discuss Daniel Webster's statement:"Liberty exists in proportion to wholesome restraint."
4. (Job) What jobs or work-related experience have you had in the last two years?
5. (Job) How would you describe this job to someone else?

PREWRITING, WRITING, and REVISING: Preparing Your Answers

Once you understand an application question and the length and form of your answer, begin your writing preparation.

Follow the steps for planning, writing, and revising a paragraph or essay.

Prewriting. Questions on applications are often broad and open-ended. You must focus your response to an idea that you can cover well in the space allowed. Consider the complexity and scope of the question and your own ideas, then zero in on a manageable topic and main idea. For a paragraph answer, shape your main idea into a topic sentence. For an essay response, shape your slightly larger main idea into a thesis statement, possibly with subtopics. Your topic sentence or thesis statement should give your basic response to the application question and indicate your expository or persuasive purpose.

The following diagram shows the thinking process you can follow, using the initial planning of the topical question essay on pages 691–692 as an example.

FROM ANALYZING A QUESTION TO FOCUSING AN ANSWER	
Analyze question	Discuss a problem that faces your country, state, city, home, or school. In your answer, include the origin and some possible solutions to the problem.
↓	↓
Decide on length	Essay length
Write thesis statement	If *interested residents* and local *officials*
	Subtopic A Subtopic B
—include	would turn their talents toward this
subtopics	community, *they could give our town a new*
—indicate	*identity.*
purpose	(statement of opinion indicates a persuasive purpose)
↓	↓
Think about	What can interested residents do?
support	What can local government officials do?

Writing and Revising Your Answer. Write out a first draft, then make additions, deletions, or alterations. Stick to the point and connect ideas smoothly. State your ideas clearly and directly. Write on every other line, so that you can revise your answer.

Finally, check and polish your answer. Reread it carefully, using a checklist such as the ones in Section 17.2, page 514, and Section 19.2, page 569.

When you are satisfied with the revised draft, write a good final copy. If the application provides space, write your answer on it. If it does not fit, add a sheet of paper and indicate on the application that you have added it.

If possible, type your answer. Anyone who reads many applications will appreciate one that is typed and will often think more highly of a typed application.

EXERCISE C: Prewriting an Answer to a Question on an Application. On the top of your paper, write one of the questions that you worked on in Exercise B. Beneath it, indicate whether you will write a paragraph- or essay-length answer. Then write a thesis statement or topic sentence to express your basic answer. Be sure to focus your purpose and clarify any subtopics for a thesis statement.

EXERCISE D: Writing an Answer to a Question on an Application. Write a rough draft of the answer to the question you chose in Exercise C, following the supporting evidence which you can think of and an outline which you think is appropriate. After you complete the draft, put it aside for a few days.

EXERCISE E: Revising an Answer to a Question on an Application. Reread the draft from Exercise D, making any changes that clarify your prose. Then use a checklist to reveal any additional corrections or improvements you can make. Copy your final draft on a fresh sheet of paper and proofread it carefully.

DEVELOPING WRITING SKILLS: Planning and Writing a Response to a Question on an Application. Choose another question from a college or job application. Follow the steps in this section for planning, writing, and revising a response. If you wrote a paragraph for Exercise E, write an essay this time.

Writing Workshop: Letters and Applications

ASSIGNMENT 1

Topic   Congratulating a Successful Friend

Form and Purpose   A friendly letter of congratulations

Audience   A friend

Length   One to two paragraphs

Focus   Adopt a friendly tone and informal writing style as you congratulate a friend on his or her recent success in acquiring a specific job.

Sources   Personal experiences—real or imaginary

Prewriting   Carefully plan both what you will say and how you will say it. You might mention specific reasons why you think your friend will be successful at the job.

Writing   Complete a first draft of your letter.

Revising   Check capitalization, punctuation, and position of all letter parts. Write a final copy.

ASSIGNMENT 2

Topic   Criticizing the Critic

Form and Purpose   A business letter that expresses a contrary opinion

Audience   The original reviewer or critic

Length   Two to three paragraphs

Focus   Select a movie review that expresses a viewpoint contrary to yours. State your own opinion of the movie. Then choose two or three major points in the review to rebut with specific facts, examples, and reasons.

Sources   A movie, a newspaper or magazine review of that movie

Prewriting   Identify two or three main points in the review that you disagree with and note facts, examples, and reasons that support your viewpoint. Prepare an outline that presents your argument in the order of least important to most important.

Writing   Use your notes and outline to write a first draft.

Revising   Correct any errors in capitalization, punctuation, spelling, and letter parts placement. Then write a clean, final copy, address an envelope, and send your letter.

696

Topics for Writing: Letters and Applications

★ WANTED ★

PRESIDENT of UNITED STATES

A new position with great potential for career growth. This job opportunity was recently created by the Continental Congress. Qualified applicants must possess leadership qualities and have experience dealing with obstinate politicians. Submit essay explaining why you are qualified.

The classified ad above may suggest an idea for writing a letter of application, or one of the topics below may interest you. Plan and write a business letter applying for the position. Adopt the role of the specified applicant and include in your letter a brief essay explaining why you are qualified for the position.

Applicant	Position
1. George Washington	President of the United States
2. Amelia Earhart	Space Shuttle Pilot
3. Bob Dylan	Advertising Lyrics Writer
4. Michael Jackson	Aerobics Instructor
5. Billy Martin	Corporate Personnel Manager

Chapter 25

Essay Exams and Précis

As you take exams, you will often be asked to write paragraph- and essay-length answers to questions. You may also need to write précis of articles or stories. This section will give you practice in adapting your writing skills to these two tasks.

25.1 Essay Exams

Essay questions on examinations call for skills you have already learned. But writing with a time limit adds pressure. In addition, different kinds of essay questions call for specific types of answers, as you will see in this section.

Getting Started

You must learn to budget time so that you can finish all parts of an exam, especially time-consuming essay questions.

Allot time for the parts of an exam, recognizing that essay questions take several planning and writing steps.

First, skim the exam to see how many and what kinds of questions you must answer. Determine the difficulty of each one and the amount of time it might take. Sketch a time schedule for yourself. The following chart offers an example.

SAMPLE SCHEDULE FOR ONE-HOUR EXAM (10:00–11:00)		
Activity	**Time**	**Breakdown**
20 multiple-choice questions	20 minutes —finished by 10:20	1 min. for each
1 essay	40 minutes —be ready to write by 10:30 —stop writing at 10:55 to check	10 min.: plan and outline 25 min.: write 5 min.: check and revise

Next, determine the specific requirements of an essay question. Different essay questions make different demands. Look for word clues to the information each question requires. The chart below explains some common kinds of questions and gives word clues to the types of support each kind calls for.

WORD CLUES IN ESSAY-EXAM QUESTIONS		
Kind of Question	**Word Clues**	**Support Needed**
Compare	compare, similarities, resemblances, likenesses	Specific examples and details that show similarities
Contrast	contrast, differ, differences	Specific examples and details that show differences
Definition	define, explain	Examples and details to explain what something is or means
Description	describe	Specific examples and details to present the main features of something
Diagram	draw, chart, diagram, plot	A drawing or chart with labels and explanations

Discussion	discuss, explain	One or more general statements and supporting facts, examples, details
Explanation	explain why, what, how, to what extent, in what ways	Examples, details, and facts that show how something happens, what it is, why it is so
Illustration	illustrate, draw	Concrete examples with explanations to demonstrate the significance or truth of an idea
Opinion	assess the validity, what do you think, defend your idea, state your opinion	A clear statement of your opinion supported by facts, examples, reasons
Interpretation	significance, meaning of (quotations or events), influence, analyze	Your idea about the overall meaning of something, with examples, facts, reasons to support your idea
Prediction	if . . . then what . . . if	Your prediction or other statement of the logical outcome; information and arguments in support

EXERCISE A: Getting Started. Follow each directive on page 701 as if you were writing an exam.

1. Plan your time for ten multiple-choice questions and two essays in a sixty-minute exam.
2. Schedule your time for a forty-minute test containing ten true-false questions and one short essay.
3. Identify the kind of question this is and the kind of support it requires: What are the principal differences between the Articles of Confederation and the Constitution?
4. Tell what kind of question this is and how you would support your answer: Describe a method of producing gasoline from crude oil.

Planning, Writing, and Checking Your Answer

Your understanding of the essay question will enable you to plan an effective answer. Whatever the length of the essay, you can follow certain planning and organizing steps.

Determining Your Main Idea and Developing Support for It. Try to answer the question in a sentence which becomes the main idea of your answer. With a main idea, you can plan support.

State a main idea in one sentence, and then list supporting ideas and information.

A topic sentence for a paragraph or a thesis statement for an essay offers focus. It should respond to the question as fully as possible. The following chart gives a sample of each main idea.

STATING A MAIN IDEA OR MAIN POINT FOR A PARAGRAPH OR ESSAY ANSWER	
Question	**Answer**
1. Explain the cause of the Northern Lights or Aurora Borealis.	The flickering, multicolored lights known as the Aurora Borealis are believed to result from the collision of atomic particles from the sun with particles in the earth's atmosphere. (Topic sentence)

2. Discuss the economic conditions that enabled the Industrial Revolution to take place in England between 1780 and 1840.	Between 1780 and 1840, England had the money, the labor, the markets, the government's encouragement, and the engineering ideas needed to launch the Industrial Revolution. (Thesis statement)
3. Is Hamlet sane or insane? Defend your opinion.	Hamlet is not insane; rather, his statements and actions reveal a rationality that is both cunning and determined. (Thesis statement)

Now brainstorm for facts and details you have studied on the subject and for your own ideas. Write ideas as they occur to you, but relate them to your one-sentence answer.

Group your items of support into a modified outline. A logical order will make your answer sound more authoritative and will simplify the writing process. Jot a few thoughts about your conclusion, too. Study the modified outlines below, one for each type of answer.

SAMPLE MODIFIED OUTLINES

Paragraph Answer	Essay Answer
Topic Sentence: Hamlet's actions indicate that he is both rational and determined. —Behavior toward Ophelia to make her think he is overcome with love, thereby disguising his real anguish —Feigning insanity helps him gather clues and find a means to seek revenge —His plot to face his uncle with the crime is clever	*Thesis Statement:* Hamlet is not insane; his statements and actions reveal a rationality that is both cunning and determined. *Hamlet's Statements* —Tells his friends Horatio and Marcellus that he will feign madness —Admits in a soliloquy that he must find a way to prove his uncle's guilt

Concluding Idea: Even with his heavy burden of grief, Hamlet's mind remains sharp enough to plan his actions and to manipulate other characters.

Hamlet's Actions
—Chooses to appear insane to disguise his grief while finding answers
—Manipulates Ophelia and her father
—Masterminds a plot to face his uncle with the crime

Conclusion: Hamlet's behavior is coherent, even ingenious; although burdened by grief, he can weigh his options, manipulate other characters, and plot and execute a course of action.

Writing and Checking Your Answer. With two thirds of your time remaining, you can begin to write quickly, fleshing out your outline and making your ideas flow logically.

Fill out the ideas in your outline with complete sentences. Transitions and other connecting words will help you to establish a logical and focused train of thought under pressure. Repeating main words or phrases from your topic sentence or thesis statement will also help you to focus on the question.

Try to keep your writing legible. Leave wide margins or skip lines to allow for your last-minute changes and corrections. When you have completed your answer, reread it carefully. Ask yourself questions such as those in the following chart.

CHECKING YOUR ANSWER

1. Does the paragraph or essay have a clear topic sentence or thesis statement presenting a basic answer to the question?
2. Have you answered the question fully and provided the right kinds of supporting examples, facts, details, and reasons?
3. Do you still need to add specific support?
4. Does your answer end clearly and logically?
5. Can you find any errors in grammar, usage, mechanics, or spelling?
6. Is your paper legible?

Notice that the following essay-length answer to a question about Hamlet's sanity follows the modified outline on pages 702–703. The writer has fleshed out ideas and added new ones.

Essay-length answer to an essay question

A central problem of Shakespeare's *Hamlet* is the question of the main character's sanity. Is Hamlet driven insane by the message of a ghost that his Uncle Claudius has killed his father in order to usurp the throne and marry Hamlet's mother? Hamlet is understandably upset by the ghost's accusation and confused for a time about the wisest course of action. But he is not insane: His statements and actions reveal a rationality that is both cunning and determined.

Hamlet's behavior often appears wild and tortured throughout the play. But it is important to recognize that he is torn by conflicting feelings. He is by nature gentle and fair, and yet he is bound by his love for his father and by honor and duty to avenge his father's murder. Furthermore, if the ghost's message is true, Hamlet's own life is probably in danger. And Hamlet cannot even be certain that the ghost's message is true. Given his painful and difficult situation, Hamlet's behavior in the play is the intelligent attempt of a sensitive man to deal with a heartbreaking and confusing set of circumstances. He decides to seem mad to the rest of the court in order to buy himself time to decide what to do.

Hamlet's own statements indicate his rationality. Early in the play, Hamlet tells his friends Horatio and Marcellus that he will feign madness, and he makes them promise not to break their oath of silence even if they see him act strangely. Shortly afterward, Hamlet admits in a soliloquy that he cannot simply act on the ghost's accusation. He needs to prove his uncle's guilt before avenging his father's death.

Throughout the rest of the play, in almost every case of irrational behavior. Hamlet chooses to appear insane for a reason. He wants to confirm what the ghost has told him without arousing his uncle's or the court's suspicion. His behavior to Ophelia allows her father, Polonius, to believe that Hamlet has been driven mad by unrequited love. Knowing that word of his lovesickness will reach his uncle, Hamlet can disguise the real cause of his suffering from his enemy, and thereby remain free to investigate the truth of the ghost's statements. In addition, if others at the court believe him insane, Hamlet may be able to gather clues to help him confirm his uncle's guilt. For example, he convinces his former friends Rosencrantz and Guildenstern of his insanity and is able to use them to uncover more evidence of his uncle's treachery. Finally, Hamlet's shrewdness and clarity of mind are most evident in the plot that he eventually develops to prove his uncle's guilt. He directs a band of traveling actors to recreate his father's murder in a play. Hamlet knows what he is doing: It is his purpose to confront his uncle with a reenactment of his crime in order to "catch the conscience of the king." He can then prove to himself that the ghost's horrible message is true.

Although Hamlet's actions appear erratic and irrational when viewed separately, his behavior is coherent, and, in some instances, ingenious. Any sane person would be deeply grieved and confused in Hamlet's situation. His burden is heavy, but his mind is not overwhelmed by his grief. He can weigh his options, manipulate other characters, and plot and execute a course of action. Hamlet is brokenhearted, but he is not insane.—Richard Supple

EXERCISE B: Planning Your Answer. Find an essay question from one of your classes, consult the study questions at the ends of chapters in a textbook, or use one that your teacher provides. Choose a question that you have not answered before. Give yourself about ten minutes to plan an essay-length answer. Prepare a modified outline.

EXERCISE C: Writing and Checking Your Answer. Using your outline from Exercise B, take forty minutes to write an essay response. Then use five minutes to revise the essay using the checklist on page 703.

DEVELOPING WRITING SKILLS: Essay Exams. Take another question from a recent examination or use a question that your teacher supplies. Follow the steps and suggestions in this section for planning and writing the answer. Budget your time wisely, and allow a few minutes for checking and revising your essay. After revising, make a clean final copy of the work.

25.2 Précis

A *précis* is a synopsis or summary of an essay, article, book chapter, or other piece of writing. Written in your own words, it condenses the main ideas and major details into a short but accurate version of the original.

Teachers may test your comprehension of written material by assigning a précis. You may use it as an aid to recalling information for a speech or a paper. For these reasons, learning to recognize, plan, write, and revise a précis can be a useful skill, which is presented in this section.

Understanding Précis

A précis is a summary of another piece of writing. It contains none of your own opinions or ideas.

A précis preserves the main ideas, details, purpose, organization, and tone of an original work, using different words.

The following example illustrates the relationship between an original article and a précis. The précis is shorter because the writer omitted minor details and compressed main ideas. But the précis writer preserved the tone and basic organization of the original, while expressing the content in new words.

Article: Locked in the steamy Guatemalan jungle, the three huge mounds had long intrigued archaeologists. But it was not until 1978 that a major expedition began excavating the swampy site known as El Mirador. Experts are now convinced that their findings will dramatically rewrite the history of Mayan civilization.

In the first two digging seasons, teams from Brigham Young University in Provo, Utah, and Washington's Catholic University of America turned up pottery shards older than the earliest known cities in the New World. These fragments showed that El Mirador flourished in the three centuries before Christ—one thousand years before the rest of the Mayan empire reached its zenith. The scientists also began to uncover extensive reservoirs, public plazas, and clusters of residential buildings. This suggested that El Mirador supported diverse political, social, and economic activities.

Archaeologists didn't understand the full extent of El Mirador's lost glory until this season. The most spectacular discovery was the great stone pyramid. It rises twenty stories high from a base 1,000 feet across, making it one of the largest buildings of antiquity. Such immense size means that someone had authority to order thousands of workers to quarry and carry great stone blocks. "It requires the organization of a state," says Raymond Matheny of Brigham Young. Most experts had doubted that Mayan civilization in 300 B.C. was so advanced.

The latest expedition unearthed other examples of sophistication. At the top of a staircase, archaeologists found a perfectly preserved stucco figure of a jaguar—a 20-foot-long, anthropomorphic cat that is probably a deity. The early inhabitants of El Mirador also were skilled scientists. The structures radiating from the great pyramid seem to provide a kind of celestial compass, pinpointing such events as the summer solstice. And there are hints of Mayan class structure: Some homes, outfitted with built-in beds and separate kitchens, undoubtedly belonged to the Mayan elite.

The great mystery of El Mirador remains its collapse. After sampling soil for clues to past climates, Catholic University's Bruce Dahlin now suspects that a severe drop in rainfall—combined with a booming population—may have doomed the metropolis. Ironically, drought may also have triggered the birth of El Mirador: A dry spell coincided with its founding, perhaps forcing the Mayans to band together to build reservoirs to store water. But after the population growth, not even the reservoirs could prevent the disaster.
—*Newsweek*

Précis: Long a source of mystery to archaeologists, three large

707

mounds in the Guatemalan jungle called El Mirador have been discovered to be the remnants of an advanced Mayan civilization dating from 300 B.C. This dramatic revelation suggests that Mayan civilization reached a high level of sophistication at an earlier date than had previously been supposed.

Archaeologists from Brigham Young University and Catholic University were especially impressed with a stone pyramid twenty stories high and one thousand feet across, a building whose monumental proportions imply the surprisingly early existence of a state with the authority to complete such a massive undertaking. In addition, reservoirs, plazas, and elaborate residences imply the existence of a complex and organized society, one which probably had a distinct class structure.

Archaeologists are still puzzled over the fall of this advanced civilization, speculating that drought combined with overpopulation may have brought an end to El Mirador. In an ironic parallel, some experts believe that an earlier drought had caused Mayans to found the city in the first place, as a means of conserving water.

The précis is about two fifths the length of the original. Its writer omitted less important details and combined ideas from several sentences into one. The précis does, however, give the most important details. It keeps the content, purpose, and tone of the original. It also keeps the order of the original.

In writing a précis, you may repeat some words from the original, but use new words where you can. Your précis should be a coherent, well-written composition that makes sense on its own, not a disjointed list of points in the original.

EXERCISE A: Understanding a Précis. Read the following article and précis, and answer the questions.

Article: We rarely see most of them, but they are all around us, day and night: the animals that belong to the order Rodentia. We know them as rats and mice, squirrels and chipmunks, woodchucks and prairie dogs. In numbers of individuals and species, this order is the largest group of mammals in North America—and on earth.

How many are there: We do not know. We can only guess that of the 4,200 living species of animals, nearly 40 percent belong to the order Rodentia. Even though we may know of some of them by their common names, they are all rodents (from the Latin word "rodere"—to gnaw). For gnaw is what they all do to stay alive.

They live in more land areas than any other order—in forest and in desert, on farm and in city. Some places have more rodents than other places. California, Oregon, and Washington, for instance, have about twice as many species as are found in all of western Europe. And, though we think of them as small, they do come in many sizes. The South American capybara—a giant relative of the guinea pig—weighs about 100 pounds. Some mice weigh less than an ounce. In North America, the largest rodent is the beaver. The smallest is the pygmy mouse, whose body is only two inches long.

Rodents are of considerable economic importance to every one of us—particularly as they are pests that feed on our crops, stored grains, and trees. Some rodents serve as hosts for fleas, lice, and other parasites that transmit disease to people or to domestic animals. The classic example is bubonic plague, or "black death," which is transmitted by a flea that lives on the black rat. A similar plague is harbored in the western United States by ground squirrels, prairie dogs, and some voles. The disease, which is often fatal, has been transmitted to humans, probably by fleas.

On the positive side, the native beaver and muskrat, along with the introduced nutria, annually yield furs worth millions of dollars. Laboratory rats and mice have been used extensively in medical research on human diseases and in studies of basic biology. Hunters derive enjoyment from hunting squirrels, which, early in our history, were a valuable food resource.—*Wild Animals of North America.*

Précis: Although we are hardly aware of them, members of the order Rodentia, or rodents, which includes rats, mice, squirrels, chipmunks, and woodchucks, are populous and pervasive. Nearly 40 percent of all living mammals on earth are classified as rodents—which makes them the largest class of mammals.

709

In addition to their large numbers, rodents inhabit more areas of land than any other species. Rodents are found in just about any habitable place, although their numbers may be highly concentrated in certain areas such as the Pacific Coast states.

The sizes of rodents also vary widely. In South America, the capybara, a relative of the guinea pig, can weigh as much as 100 pounds, while some mice can weigh less than an ounce.

Rodents can be dangerous, but also valuable for many reasons. While some carry parasites that cause diseases and plagues, others provide economic benefits. Beaver and muskrat are valuable for clothing and provide breeders with ample profits. In medicine, rats and mice are useful to scientists studying diseases and biology.

1. By how much does the précis reduce the original?
2. What main ideas from the original are included? What details support them? Would you have added any other details?
3. How well does the précis represent the ideas and intent of the original? What other ideas might have been concluded from the original?
4. Compare the order in the original and the précis. Where has it been altered?

PREWRITING, WRITING, AND REVISING: Preparing a Précis

Précis writing demands reading and note-taking skills as well as writing skills.

Planning a Précis. Your first step in planning a précis is to read the original carefully. As you read, take accurate and complete notes.

Read the original several times to learn content, purpose, and tone; take notes on the main ideas and major details.

The chart on page 711 lists the steps you may take in planning your précis.

PLANNING THE PRÉCIS

1. Determine the main point, purpose, tone, and organization. Note subtopics, other important ideas, and major details.
2. Use a dictionary to check unfamiliar words in the original.
3. For a short précis, mention only prominent ideas. If the original has a great many facts, write a longer précis.
4. Decide which information you can summarize or omit. Note main words you must use and those needed to keep the tone.

Writing and Revising a Précis. As you write, be faithful to the original while you create a well-written, shorter version.

Group your notes into smooth sentences that reflect the content, purpose, tone, and organization of the original.

The following checklist gives guidelines for revision.

CHECKING AND REVISING YOUR PRÉCIS

1. Did you reduce the original to a desirable length?
2. Did you include all the main ideas and major details?
3. Did you give the ideas and purpose without adding opinions?
4. Do your words reflect the purpose and tone of the original?
5. Have you followed the organization of the original writing?
6. Does your language maintain the writer's shades of meaning?
7. Will readers understand your précis without the original?
8. Are your grammar, usage, mechanics, and spelling correct?

EXERCISE B: Planning a Précis. Decide the length for a précis of the article below. Read it and take notes in your own words.

Article: Two thirds of the Atlantic's commercially valuable fish and shellfish rely on the salt marsh for food. Crabs and mussels make the creeks a permanent home. Flounder are winter residents, coming into the marsh to feed and to spawn. Bass and menhaden use the warm tidal waters as a summer nursery. For others—smelt, alewives, and shad—the marsh is an important way station on the route to fresh-water spawning grounds.

The ebbing and flowing tides are the farmers of the marsh, watering the grasses, feeding the fish and shellfish, and cleaning away the waste.

The salt marsh is one of our country's most fertile resources, more productive than fields of wheat and hay. Each year, the salt marsh produces up to ten tons of organic material per acre. During the same time, an acre of hay produces only four tons; an acre of wheat, two tons. Wheat and hay require extensive cultivation, expensive fertilizers, and deliberate pest control. The salt marsh yields its bountiful harvest year after year, without depleting its resources or reducing its productivity.

The rhythm of life on the marsh is constant, tuned to the nourishing tides. The harvest, begun in autumn as the grasses die, continues all year. By the end of winter, most of the marsh hay will have disappeared. Anything left by the insects or bacteria sinks into the marsh as a rich peat, ready to fertilize the new grass in the spring.

Many years ago, the salt marsh was a barren ice field. When the glacier melted and the ocean rose, the wind blew in the first seeds of marsh grass. Over six million acres of salt marsh grew behind the newly formed barrier beaches and tidal rivers. Today, fewer than two million acres of salt marsh remain on the Atlantic coast. The rest have been lost to development—to housing, marinas, causeways, and dump sites. What we have thrown away through ignorance and selfishness is not only an aesthetic pleasure, a reassuring contrast to our congested highways and polluted cities, but also an invaluable resource, critical to our food supply. We have the means to protect our salt marshes—through local conservation commissions, state wetlands-protection laws, and Federal coastal-zone management policies. All we need is the will.—Adapted from Deborah Cramer

EXERCISE C: Writing the First Draft of a Précis. Using your notes from Exercise B, write a first draft of a précis. Write varied sentences that condense and join the information. Try to match the length you decided on. Preserve the main ideas and major details, use your own words, and avoid adding your own opinions.

712

EXERCISE D: Revising the Précis. Compare your précis to the original and use the checklist on page 711 to improve your draft. When you are satisfied, write a good final copy.

DEVELOPING WRITING SKILLS: Writing a Précis. Look through magazines, essays, and other works to find an article—about one page long—for which you could write a précis. Then write it, following the planning, writing, and revising steps you learned.

Writing Workshop: Essay Exams and Précis

ASSIGNMENT

Topic Achieving World Peace

Form and Purpose A précis that summarizes and informs readers of an original article on the topic

Audience Participants in a conference on world peace

Length One paragraph

Focus Your précis should summarize the main idea(s) and major details of the original article. Present that information in the order and tone of the original work.

Sources Magazine and newspaper articles and editorials

Prewriting Select a one- or two-page article on the topic. Use the checklist on page 711 to plan your précis.

Writing Complete a first draft that reflects the information, organization, and tone of the original.

Revising Use the checklist on page 711 to revise. Then write a final draft.

Vocabulary and Spelling

26

Vocabulary Building

You are probably aware of how important a good vocabulary is to success in school. At your present stage in life, a good vocabulary is an important asset outside school as well, since job, college, or vocational school interviews are in your near future. With a good vocabulary at your command, you can express yourself clearly and communicate exactly the meaning you intend.

The techniques discussed in this chapter should help you to expand your reading and your speaking vocabulary. Section 26.1 presents methods you can use to recall the meaning of new words. The second and third sections show in more detail how to use two of these methods. Section 26.2 discusses how to use context clues to determine the meaning of a word. Section 26.3 discusses how to analyze parts of words to determine their meaning.

26.1 Techniques for Building Vocabulary

Building a vocabulary is not just a question of acquiring a collection of long, impressive-sounding words. The keys to real vocabulary development are extensive reading and use of proper reference sources, plus whatever memory techniques suit you best. This section will present a variety of methods for making new words a part of your regular vocabulary.

Making Good Use of Resource Material

You can increase your vocabulary through regular use of two valuable resources: a dictionary and a thesaurus.

Using a Dictionary. It is a good idea to consult a dictionary any time you come across an unfamiliar word. For convenience, you should always have a pocket dictionary close at hand, both at home and at school.

Use a dictionary to find the meaning, spelling, and pronunciation of words.

Study the pronunciation of each word you look up. This is given in parentheses right after the word. If you can pronounce a word you are more likely to make it a part of your working vocabulary.

Study the information about the word's origins. This usually appears in brackets.

Note the varied meanings a word can have, depending on how it is used in a sentence or on its parts of speech. For example, the verb *secure* means "defend." It can also mean "to procure or to obtain possession of." When used as an adjective, it can also mean "safe or confident."

Note whether the word is used as part of an idiom. An idiom is a phrase that means something different from the literal meanings of the words in the phrase or sentence. Students from other countries have great trouble understanding idioms in the English language because idioms can't be translated from one language to another. One example of an idiom is, "Your suggestion is *out of the question*."

Using a Thesaurus. A thesaurus is a valuable reference tool when you are writing since it provides lists of words that have meanings the same as, or similar to words you look up. It may also provide contrasting words or entries reflecting the slight differences in meaning between similar words.

Use a thesaurus to find information about words that are similar in meaning.

Words listed in a thesaurus may have different shades of meaning. Some are more vivid and expressive than others; some may be more formal or informal than the meaning you are seeking; and some are not suitable for all-purpose use. If

717

you are looking for a word to replace *temerity*, you might decide that "assurance," a synonym, does not quite express the meaning you intend to convey. You may find the word "audacity" more suitable. On the other hand, "assurance" is a more general word that could be used in a variety of situations, whereas "audacity" conveys too strong a meaning to be used as an all-purpose word. If you are not sure whether a specific word is a satisfactory substitute for another, look it up in the dictionary to pinpoint its exact meaning.

EXERCISE A: Using the Dictionary to Increase Your Vocabulary. Look up each word in your dictionary and write the definition for the part of speech indicated in parentheses.

EXAMPLE: influence (noun)

               power exerted over the minds of others

1. humor (noun)	5. mean (verb)	9. rebel (verb)
2. lacerated (verb)	6. reactionary (noun)	10. recruit (noun)
3. human (adjective)	7. fanatic (adjective)	
4. jail (verb)	8. effect (verb)	

EXERCISE B: Using the Thesaurus to Increase Your Vocabulary. Find a word similar in meaning to each of the following words. Use each word you find in a sentence.

EXAMPLE: terse

               concise

               He gave a concise summary of the repetitious report.

1. inquisitive	5. rancor	9. lethargy
2. derogatory	6. vacuous	10. ingenuous
3. insidious	7. pall	
4. spurious	8. levity	

Recognizing Related Words

You can increase your vocabulary by recognizing words that are related to each other. They may be either similar or opposite in meaning, or they may sound the same.

Words similar in meaning are called synonyms.

As you have learned, a thesaurus provides lists of synonyms. A dictionary, too, may give synonyms. It is easier to remember a one-word synonym than a long definition. For example, you may be more likely to remember the meaning of *evocative* if you associate it with its synonym "suggestive."

Knowing words that are opposite in meaning is also a useful technique to remember the definitions of words.

Words that are opposite in meaning are called antonyms.

If, for example, you want to recall that the word *pungent* means "sharp and stimulating to the mind and senses," you could note that its antonym is "bland."

To use vocabulary words accurately, you should learn about words that sound alike but have different meanings.

Words that sound alike but have different meanings and spellings are called homonyms.

You might, for example, have to choose between *principal* and *principle* or *site* and *sight* when writing.

EXERCISE C: Recognizing Synonyms, Antonyms, and Homonyms. Identify each pair of words as *synonyms, antonyms,* or *homonyms.*

EXAMPLE: thyme/time

            homonyms

1. fatuous/sensible
2. red/read
3. stationary/stationery
4. veracity/falsehood
5. sent/scent

6. insinuate/suggest
7. prosaic/poetic
8. venal/corrupt
9. sullen/gloomy
10. raffish/wild

Remembering Vocabulary Words

Words that you rarely come across in your reading will be more difficult to remember than others. A number of techniques can be used to remember the meanings of such words.

Use one or more review techniques to remember the meanings of new words.

Using a Vocabulary Notebook. For each of your school subjects, keep a vocabulary section in your notebook. In recording words in this section, one of the best arrangements is a three-column format. List the new words in the first column and their definitions in the third column. The middle column should be used for *bridge words*, clues or hints that will remind you of the word's meaning. If, for example, you want to remember that *noisome* means "unwholesome or offensive" you might use a bridge word such as *gross*. To review your entries, simply fold the paper to cover either the definitions or the words themselves.

Using Flash Cards or a Tape Recorder. To make it convenient for you to study your vocabulary words regularly, you may want to use index cards with the words listed on one side and the definitions on the other. You can carry a few of these cards with you at all times so that when you have a few spare minutes you can flip through them. This kind of review is essential for continuing vocabulary growth.

Some people learn more effectively through their ears than through their eyes. If you are such a person, a tape recorder might be a good choice for learning new words. If you have access to one, you can dictate onto the tape a group of words you want to learn. After each word, pause for about ten seconds and then read its definition. Replay the tape, trying to insert the definition in the ten-second pause. Repeat the exercise until you know all of the definitions by heart. Listening to your tape several times a week can help you make new words a permanent part of your vocabulary.

Working with a Partner. Reviewing vocabulary words with another person provides the opportunity for oral drill and mutual encouragement. You can use flash cards, pages from the vocabulary section of your notebook, or any list of new words you may have from other sources. In the first round, one person can read the words and the other can define them. If the definer's memory needs to be jogged, the reader should provide a bridge word. When the definer has supplied the correct meaning for each word and used it in a sentence, the partners can switch roles.

720

Grouping Words. One technique that can be used to remember the meanings of words in your notebook is to break up the material into smaller units. For example, it is easier to remember a ten-digit number such as 2035552527 if you separate it, as you would a telephone number, into 203-555-2527. The same trick works for vocabulary study. Group a list of twenty words into five sets of four words each and study each group separately. You may also find it possible to group together words that have similar meanings or words that can be categorized in some logical way. For example, in the vocabulary section of your history notebook, you may have listed these words: *brutalize; militia; fascism; emperor; century; bellicose; martial; era; socialism; premier; arrogate; jingoism; corrupt; age; democracy; chancellor; decade; czar; communism;* and *commandeer*. The chart shows a logical way to divide these words into smaller groups for study purposes.

Military Words	Time Divisions	Ideologies	Leaders	Aggressive Acts
militia	century	fascism	emperor	arrogate
martial	era	communism	czar	corrupt
bellicose	decade	socialism	premier	brutalize
jingoism	age	democracy	chancellor	commandeer

Setting Daily or Weekly Goals. As you continue your courses and increase your outside reading, you will add more words to your vocabulary lists. If you try to learn the meanings of many words at once, you may become discouraged. It is easier to break down your lists into manageable size, either through the grouping technique described above or by studying a few words each day or week. Make it a practice to learn those few words within the allotted time period. Learning two or three new words a day or ten or fifteen a week can make a difference in the size of your vocabulary after a few months.

EXERCISE D: Adding New Words to Your Vocabulary.
List twenty words from one of your courses. Look up the definition of each word in a dictionary. Then group the words into categories, as shown in the chart above. Learn the words in two weeks, using the methods on pages 717–718.

DEVELOPING WRITING SKILLS: Putting New Words to Use. Choose ten words from the list you made in Exercise D. Write a sentence with each of these words that clearly illustrates its meaning.

26.2 Using Context

This section will show you how to use different types of context clues to determine the meaning of new words. As mentioned in Section 26.1, the information in the sentence in which the word occurs gives a clue to its meaning.

Recognizing Context Clues

Sometimes writers deliberately supply clues to help the reader understand the thought.

Use context clues in all of your reading to improve both your vocabulary and your general reading comprehension.

The following chart gives examples of the types of context clues writers use. You may find it useful whenever you come across a new word in your reading.

TYPES OF CONTEXT CLUES		
Clue	**Example**	**Method**
Formal definition	Many plant *rhizomes*, underground stems or root systems, offer an excellent source of nutritious food.	The reader is given a definition of the word *rhizome*, which means "an underground stem."
Familiar words	The loud, shrill cries of the bluejays broke the early morning silence as they *raucously* called other jays to the bird feeder.	The use of the familiar words *loud* and *shrill* coupled with *cries* alerts the reader to the meaning of *raucously*: "loudly," or "rough-sounding."

Comparison	The *monsignor*, like a village priest, blessed the pilgrims at the shrine with gentleness and compassion.	The comparison of the *monsignor* with a village *priest* shows the reader that the former is connected in some way with the Catholic Church. *Monsignor* is a title of honor given to certain priests.
Contrast	His English students were more *tractable* than he had anticipated; in fact, only his obstinate fifth-period class resisted an appeal to participate in some choral reading.	*Only* used with the words *obstinate* and *resisted* indicates contrast. *Tractable* means "easily led."
Synonyms	Jack's *ignominious* behavior was shameful and disgraceful.	*Shameful* and *disgraceful* are synonyms for *ignominious*.
Antonyms	His sisters reacted to Jack's behavior differently. Angie spoke of Jack with *acerbity* and anger, while Jessica spoke with sweetness and love.	*Acerbity* and *anger* contrasted with *sweetness* and *love* indicate that *acerbity* is an antonym of *sweetness*. *Acerbity* means "bitterness."
Summary	Shane was completely *distraught*. She could not find her glasses; her papers were all over; she did not know how to get to the vet's office; but she had to get the injured puppy to the doctor.	The actions described in the second sentence are summed up in the word *distraught*, which means "mentally confused" or "extremely troubled."

Previous knowledge of an associated word	San Francisco, California, is located in an active *seismic* area.	Previous contact with the word *seismograph* (an instrument that records the severity of the earth's tremors) coupled with an awareness of the famous San Francisco earthquake should alert the reader to the meaning of the word *seismic*, which means "of or having to do with or caused by earthquakes."

In addition to recognizing certain types of context clues, it also helps to have an orderly way of using them. The following chart lists steps that you can take to use context clues effectively.

STEPS FOR USING CONTEXT CLUES

1. Read the sentence, leaving out the unfamiliar word.
2. Examine the surrounding words and note the type of clues they provide.
3. Guess at the meaning of the word.
4. Read the sentence again, substituting your guess for the unfamiliar word.
5. Check your guess in the dictionary; write the word and the definition in the vocabulary section of your notebook or include it in your personal vocabulary list.

Newspaper and magazine articles about developments in the field of medicine often require knowledge of some rather difficult terms. As you read the paragraphs in the following example, use your context skills to guess at the meaning of the underlined words. You might find it helpful to refer to the charts on pages 722–724. Jot down your guesses on a piece of paper.

EXAMPLE: Dr. Rosalyn Yalow received a Nobel Prize for her work in medicine in 1977. The fifty-nine-year old <u>laureate</u> works at the Bronx Veterans Administration Hospital in New York where she has been chief of <u>nuclear</u> medicine since 1970.

The test for which Dr. Yalow received the prize is used to measure the <u>concentrations</u> of various substances in the blood to determine changes that take place in diseased bodies. Her work in this area began when she and her <u>colleague</u> used the test to measure the amount of <u>insulin</u> in the blood of diabetes patients. The scientists discovered that when diabetics were injected with insulin, their blood produced <u>antibodies</u> against the insulin. These antibodies acted as <u>foreign</u> proteins in the body.

The test developed by Dr. Yalow and her colleague is being used today by blood banks to detect the <u>hepatitis</u> virus in blood intended for use in transfusions. Dr. Yalow predicts that her work will have as great an <u>impact</u> on <u>infectious</u> disease control as it has had on the treatment of hormonal disorders.

EXERCISE A: Recognizing Context Clues. Use your list of guesses from the preceding paragraphs for this exercise. For each of the following words, choose the definition that most closely matches the meaning of the word as it was used in the paragraphs. Then check your answer in a dictionary.

1. laureate
   (a) girl's name
   (b) evergreen shrub
   (c) honored person
   (d) rope for a horse

2. nuclear
   (a) relating to atomic nuclei
   (b) energy
   (c) hard to understand
   (d) physics

3. concentration
   (a) strength
   (b) meeting
   (c) meditation
   (d) granting an argument

4. colleague
   (a) inventor
   (b) scientist
   (c) fellow worker
   (d) college graduate

5. insulin
   (a) to keep heat or cold out
   (b) like an island
   (c) hormone that helps the body use sugar
   (d) isolated

6. antibody   (a) penicillin   (c) political group
               (b) puritanical   (d) a protein produced in the body

7. foreign   (a) not domestic   (c) outside the country
             (b) imported   (d) not natural to the body

8. hepatitis   (a) seven-sided figure   (c) inflammation of the joints
              (b) infection of the hip   (d) inflammation of the liver

9. impact   (a) agreement   (c) lodged in the jaw
             (b) power to produce change   (d) taking little space

10. infectious   (a) without end   (c) of a lower order
              (b) tender and loving   (d) tending to spread

Using Context Clues in Textbook Reading

Material in textbooks often includes technical words.

Use context clues to determine the meaning of unfamiliar words in your textbook reading.

The following passage is similar to material you might find in a history textbook. As you read the passage, try to determine the meaning of each underlined word by studying its context. Write down what you think each underlined word means.

EXAMPLE: The New Englander was a product of <u>glaciation</u>, rugged climate, and <u>Calvinism</u>. Glaciers had <u>scored</u> the country into a land of narrow valleys, swiftly flowing streams, and thin soil. The endless stone fences of New England demonstrate the <u>toil</u> involved in scratching a living from such a land. It was difficult for one family to care for many backbreaking acres, so the individual farms tended to be small. In the South, where broad rivers drained wide <u>savannahs</u>, people lived more spaciously. It is <u>significant</u> that here the gatherings were usually social events. Southerners met to enjoy themselves. New England-ers, however, met to improve themselves and others.

It was fortunate for later <u>generations</u> of Americans that New England settlers had great appreciation for property, especially in the form of land. For <u>genera-tions</u>, land had been the symbol of prestige in England. The decline of <u>feudalism</u> and the emergence of the <u>capitalist</u> class brought many landless British farmers to America. In America they could not only work the land, but they could also <u>acquire</u> property, which was considered the mark of a superior person.

EXERCISE B: Using Context Clues in Textbook Reading.

Choose the meaning that most closely matches the meaning of the word as it was used in the passage you just read.

1. glaciation
   - (a) flooding
   - (b) icing process
   - (c) snow
   - (d) sleet
2. Calvinism
   - (a) hedonism
   - (b) religious doctrine
   - (c) atheism
   - (d) agnostic
3. scored
   - (a) multitude
   - (b) tallied
   - (c) notched
   - (d) billed
4. toil
   - (a) pleasure
   - (b) work
   - (c) drudge
   - (d) earth
5. savannahs
   - (a) grassy plains
   - (b) deserts
   - (c) mountains
   - (d) beaches
6. significant
   - (a) inconsequential
   - (b) important
   - (c) illustrious
   - (d) warning
7. generations
   - (a) age groups
   - (b) procreation
   - (c) 30 years
   - (d) growth
8. feudalism
   - (a) European economic system
   - (b) fascism
   - (c) wars
   - (d) equality
9. capitalist
   - (a) business investor
   - (b) cooperative ownership
   - (c) state-owned
   - (d) worker
10. acquire
    - (a) forfeit
    - (b) convey
    - (c) obtain
    - (d) cultivate

The paragraph on the next page represents material you might read describing a lawyer at work. Read the paragraph to get the overall meaning. Then, using the steps in the chart on page 724, guess and write down the meaning of each underlined word.

Using Context Clues in Other Kinds of Reading

Articles about food and its preparation often include words borrowed from other languages. The following paragraph has a number of words borrowed from French. Through the use of context clues, try to guess the meaning of the underlined words. Jot your guesses down on a piece of paper.

EXAMPLE: Jon, who regarded himself as a <u>perspicacious</u> <u>gourmet</u>, read the menu carefully before placing an order with the hovering waiter. He decided to begin with a small cup of <u>consommé</u>. He wavered between the chicken milanese and the lobster. After deciding on the chicken, he ordered <u>lyonnaise</u> potatoes, mushrooms <u>sautéed</u> in butter, carrots <u>julienne</u>, and the spinach <u>soufflé</u> served in an individual <u>ramekin</u>. Finally, he selected chocolate <u>mousse</u> and <u>espresso</u> to complete the meal.

EXERCISE C: Using Context Clues to Complete Sentences. Use your list of guesses from the preceding paragraph for this exercise. For each of the following sentences, choose the word from the paragraph that best completes each sentence. Then check your answer in a dictionary.

1. The true _____ selects food carefully and eats sparingly but with much pleasure.
   (a) gourmet   (b) julienne   (c) soufflé
2. The cook must be careful not to jar the container when removing a(n) _____ from the oven.
   (a) espresso   (b) gourmet   (c) soufflé
3. The chef will _____ the mushrooms very quickly in a special pan.
   (a) soufflé   (b) sauté   (c) julienne
4. A _____ shopper chooses ingredients for a special dish carefully.
   (a) soufflé   (b) lyonnaise   (c) perspicacious
5. Italian coffee, called _____ , is a full-bodied, strong drink.
   (a) mousse   (b) espresso   (c) ramekin

6. The doctor recommended that Sarah have a small cup of
   _____ before trying to eat any solid food.
   (a) julienne   (b) consommé   (c) sauté
7. Many brides consider themselves lucky if they receive a set
   of _____ for a wedding present.
   (a) gourmets   (b) espressos   (c) ramekins
8. Food processors make preparing vegetables _____ extremely simple.
   (a) julienne   (b) ramekin   (c) gourmet
9. French cooks prepare a delicious dessert called _____
   using egg whites, whipped cream, and often, chocolate.
   (a) ramekin   (b) gourmet   (c) mousse
10. _____ potatoes please those people who like the flavor
   of fried onions.
   (a) Perspicacious   (b) Lyonnaise   (c) Julienne

EXERCISE D: Defining Words. For each word choose the
definition that most closely matches the meaning of the word
as it was used in the passage.

1. soufflé	a. Italian-style coffee
2. julienne	b. small baking dish
3. gourmet	c. baked dish made fluffy by the addition of egg whites
4. ramekin	
5. perspicacious	d. having keen judgment
6. mousse	e. prepared with onions
7. espresso	f. clear soup
8. consommé	g. to fry quickly in butter
9. lyonnaise	h. light, chilled dessert
10. sauté	i. cut into strips
	j. excellent judge of good food

**DEVELOPING WRITING SKILLS: Using New Words in
Context.** Choose any one of the following activities to use new
words.

1. Imagine that you are either a very wealthy person or a person with just a few precious possessions. Write a short will
   in which you leave your possessions to family members or

729

friends. Use at least five of the vocabulary words from this section. Try to use them in such a way that someone who is not a lawyer would be able to understand your will.

2. Write a short letter to a friend describing a delicious meal you just enjoyed. Use at least five of the words from this section in such a way that your friend will know exactly what you had to eat.

3. Imagine you are a newspaper reporter. Write a few paragraphs as if they were a part of a longer article describing an achievement in the field of medicine. Use at least five words from this section in such a way that the average reader would be able to understand your article.

26.3 Using Structure

The context in which you find a word provides external clues to its meaning. This section discusses internal clues to the meaning of words. The internal clues are the parts of words—prefixes, roots, and suffixes.

The main part of a word, the part that carries its basic meaning, is the root. Roots can sometimes stand alone (for example, the root *act*). Often, however, they must be completed with a prefix or a suffix (for example, the root *-ven-*). A prefix is a word part added at the beginning of a word that changes its meaning (happy/*un*happy). A suffix is a word part added at the end of a word that changes the meaning or part of speech of the word (act/act*or*).

If you master the prefixes, roots, and suffixes in this section, you should be able to determine the meanings of hundreds of words simply by analyzing them in terms of their structure. Of course, a dictionary check is necessary, since many words acquire special meanings over the years, sometimes changing their original meaning entirely.

Prefixes

Thirty prefixes with their origins appear in the chart on the following page. (The abbreviations *L.*, *Gr.*, and *O.E.* stand for Latin, Greek, and Old English.)

Learn the meanings of common prefixes to improve your vocabulary and reading comprehension.

The additional forms of prefixes whose spelling varies according to the root word to which they are added are listed in parentheses. (For example, the prefix *in-* changes to *im-* in the word *immortal.*)

THIRTY COMMON PREFIXES		
Prefix	**Meaning**	**Examples**
ab- (a-, abs-) [L.]	away, from	abrasive, amorphous, absent
ad- (ac-, af-, al-, ap-, as-, at-) [L.]	to, toward	adhere, accede, affect, alloy, apply, aspect, attend
anti- [Gr.]	against	antiwar
circum- [L.]	around, about, surrounding, on all sides	circumvent
com- (co-, col-, con-, cor-) [L.]	with, together	comrade, coordinate, collapse, confer, correlate
de- [L.]	away from, off, down	decentralize
dis- (di-,dif-) [L.]	away, apart, cause to be opposite of	discomfort, divide, differ
epi- [Gr.]	upon, over, on the outside	epidemic
ex- (e-, ec-, ef-) [L.]	forth, from, out	express, eject, ecstatic, effort
extra- [L.]	outside, beyond	extraterritorial
hyper- [Gr.]	over, above, excessive	hyperbole
in- (il-, im-, ir-) [L.]	not, "un"	ineffectual, illimitable, immaculate, irregular

731

in- (il-, im-, ir-) [L.]	in, into, within, on, toward	intrude, illustrate, impress, irradiate
inter- [L.]	between	interfere
mal- [L.]	bad, wrongful, ill	malfunction
mis- [O.E.]	wrong	mistrial
mono- [Gr.]	alone, one	monotone
non- [L.]	not	nonprofit
ob- (o-, oc-, of-, op-) [L.]	toward, against	observe, omission, occupy, offend, oppose
over- [O.E.]	above, over the limit, in excess	overload
post- [L.]	after	postscript
pre- [L.]	before	predate
pro- [L.]	forward, forth, favoring, in place of	provide
re- [L.]	back, again	review
semi- [L.]	half, partly	semifinal
sub- (suc-, suf-, sup-) [L.]	beneath, under, below	subconscious, succession, suffer, support
super- [L.]	above, beyond, on top	superhuman
syn- (syl-, sym-, sys-) [Gr.]	with, together with, at the same time	synthesis, syllable, sympathy, system
trans- [L.]	across	transfer
un- [O.E.]	not	ungrateful

EXERCISE A: Defining Words with Prefixes. For each of the following words, select the definition that most closely matches the meaning of the word. Be sure to check your guesses in a dictionary.

732

1. supervise   (a) overcome   (c) oversee
                 (b) overhaul   (d) succeed
2. hypercritical   (a) imaginary   (c) extremely
                     illness   active
                     (b) hard to please   (d) excessive
                                           publicity
3. malice   (a) active ill will   (c) hateful
              (b) harmful   (d) long-handled hammer
4. extraneous   (a) extraordinary   (c) not
                 (b) an outgoing   essential
                     person   (d) costing or
                                       spending
                                       too much
5. synchronize   (a) sympathize   (c) to be a
                 (b) rhythmic   symbol
                                   (d) cause to
                                       move or
                                       occur at
                                       the same time
6. avert   (a) turn away   (c) return
            (b) eliminate   (d) straight
7. discern   (a) divide   (c) perceive
              (b) throw away   clearly
                                   (d) dissect
8. proficient   (a) professed   (c) recipient
               (b) lacking   (d) skilled
9. defraud   (a) distort   (c) cheat
            (b) put off   (d) disagree
10. semiconscious   (a) ill at ease   (c) half awake
                    (b) fully awake   (d) inattentive

Roots

The root carries the basic meaning of the word.

Learn the meanings of common roots to improve your vocabulary and reading comprehension.

Adding various prefixes and suffixes to a root can form whole families of related words. For example, the root *-puls-* (also spelled *-pel-*) is the base for *impulse, repel, propeller, ex-*

pel, appellate, repulsion, and others. The spelling of a root can change depending on the letters surrounding it. For example, can you find the three words that have the same root in the sentence *I need a powerful motor to move my mobile home?*

The chart that follows lists thirty roots, their origins, meanings, and forms as well as words containing each root.

THIRTY COMMON ROOTS		
Root	Meaning	Examples
-ama- (-ami-) [L.]	to love	amiable
-cap- (-capt-, -cept-, -ceipt-, -ceive-, -cip-) [L.]	to take, seize	capacity, captive, receptive, receipt, deceive, incipient
-ced- (-ceed-, -cess-) [L.]	to go, yield	intercede, proceed, process
-dic- (-dict-) [L.]	to say, point out in words	predicate, dictatorial
-duc- (-duce-, -duct-) [L.]	to lead	introduce, abduct
-fac- (-fact-, -fec-, [L.]	to do, make	faculty, factory confection, perfect
-fer- [L.]	to bring, carry	conference
-graph- [Gr.]	to write	biography
-ject- [L.]	to throw	eject
-leg- (-log-) [Gr.]	to say, speak, reason	legible, logical
-manu- [L.]	hand	manuscript
-mit- (-mis-) [L.]	to send	transmit, permission
-mov- (-mob-, -mot-) [L.]	to move	movable, mobile, motor
-plic- (-pli-, -ploy-, [L.]	to fold	explicate, pliant, employer, reply
-pon- (-pos-) [L.]	to put, place	postpone, impose

-port- [L.]	to carry	transport
-puls- (pel-) [L.]	to drive	impulse, expel
-quir- (-ques-, -quis-) [L.]	to ask, say	require, request, inquisition
-sci- [L.]	to know	conscience
-scrib- (-script-) [L.]	to write	inscribe, postscript
-sens- (-sent-, -senti-) [L.]	to feel	sensible, sentiment
-sist- [L.]	to stand	persist
-spec- (-spect-) [L.]	to see	speculate, respect
-string- (-strict-) [L.]	to bind, tighten	stringency, restrict
-ten- (-tain-, -tin-) [L.]	to hold, contain	tenement, retain, pertinent
-tend- (-tens-, -tent-) [L.]	to stretch	pretend, tense, extent
-vad- (-vas-) [L.]	to go	pervade, evasive
-ven- (-vent-) [L.]	to come	intervene, prevent
-vert- (-vers-) [L.]	to turn	convert, diversion
-vid- (-vis-) [L.]	to see	evidence, visual

EXERCISE B: Using Roots to Define Words. Write the words in the first column and underline each root. Then write the letter of the correct definition next to the word.

1. conscience
2. portable
3. facilitate
4. consensus
5. complicate
6. manual
7. inducement
8. amicable
9. constriction
10. tenet

a. an opinion held by all or most people
b. operated by hand, pertaining to the hand
c. friendly, showing good will
d. motive, incentive
e. a tightness or inward pressure
f. a sense of what is right or wrong
g. to make easier
h. capable of being carried
i. a doctrine or opinion held as true
j. to make difficult or involved

735

Suffixes

The third word part is the suffix—a syllable or group of syllables added to the end of a word to form a new word.

Learn the meaning of common suffixes to improve your vocabulary and reading comprehension.

Some suffixes, called inflectional suffixes, have a number of functions: to make nouns plural (toy, toy*s*), to show degrees of comparison in modifiers (sleepy, sleepi*er*, sleepi*est*), or to show changes in verb form (skate, skat*ed*, skat*ing*).

The suffixes presented in this section, however, are those that change the meaning and, often, the part of speech of a word. For example, if you add the suffix *-tion* to the verb *predict*, you will have the noun *prediction*. If you add the suffix *-able*, you will have the adjective *predictable*. If you add the suffix *-ly* to the adjective *predictable*, you will have the adverb *predictably*. The chart that follows lists twenty-five suffixes with their various forms, origins, and parts of speech when a particular suffix is added to a word.

TWENTY-FIVE COMMON SUFFIXES			
Suffix	**Meaning**	**Examples**	**Part of Speech**
-able (-ible) [L.]	capable of being; tending to	believable, divisible	adjective
-ac (-ic) [Gr.]	characteristic of; relating to	hypochondriac, prosaic	noun or adjective
-al [L.]	like; suitable for	comical	adjective
-ance (-ence) [L.]	act of; quality or state of being	defiance, diffidence	noun
-ant (-ent) [L.]	that shows, has, or does; a person or thing that shows, has, or does	compliant, occupant, inherent, superintendent	adjective or noun

-ary (-ery) [L.]	pertaining to; connected with	honorary, surgery	adjective or noun
-ate [L.]	making, applying, or operating on	animate	verb
-cy (-acy) [Gr.]	quality; condition; state	hesitancy, fallacy	noun
-esque [L.]	in the style of	picturesque	adjective
-ful [O.E.]	full of; characterized by; having the ability or tendency to	spoonful; beautiful	noun or adjective
-fy [L.]	to make; to cause to become; to cause to have	magnify	verb
-ish [O.E.]	of or belonging to; rather; tending to	stylish	adjective
-ism [Gr.]	the act, practice, or result of; characteristic of the theory of	pacifism	noun
-ist [Gr.]	a person who does or makes; a person skilled in; a believer in	pianist	noun
-ity [L.]	state of being; character; condition of	charity	noun
-ive [L.]	tending to; a person who	declarative, detective	adjective or noun
-ize (-ise) [Gr.]	to make	characterize, improvise	verb
-less [O.E.]	without; lacking	humorless	adjective
-ly [O.E.]	in a certain way	deliberately, locally	adjective or adverb

-ment [L.]	result or product of	statement	noun
-ness [L.]	state of being	promptness	noun
-or [L.]	a person or thing that; a quality or condition that	inventor, horror	noun
-ous (-ious) [L.]	marked by; given to	dangerous, gracious	adjective
-tion (-ion, -sion,-ation, -ition) [L.]	the action of; the state of being	friction, invasion, preparation, condition	noun
-ure [L.]	act or result of; instrument of; state of being	tenure, pleasure	noun

EXERCISE C: Using Suffixes to Form New Words. Add a suffix to each of the following roots to form a word that fits the definition given at the right. Write each new word and its part of speech on your paper. Then check your answers in a dictionary.

1. graph-   a. relating to handwriting
2. amic-   b. tending to be friendly
3. mot-   c. a reason for tending to
4. vent-   d. a risky or dangerous undertaking
5. puls-   e. to beat rhythmically
6. sens-   f. without feeling
7. cap-   g. the act of seizing
8. string-   h. that does bind or tighten
9. port-   i. capable of being carried
10. sci-   j. the act of knowing

DEVELOPING WRITING SKILLS: Using Structure to Determine Meaning. Use your knowledge of the meanings of word parts in analyzing the following words. First, write each word on your paper and circle the root. Then underline any prefix once and any suffix twice. Jot down what you think the word means and then check your guess in a dictionary. Finally, use each word in a sentence.

1. requisition
2. conjecture
3. malediction
4. deductive
5. inversion
6. precedence
7. contentious
8. supplication
9. deference
10. sufferance

Exploring Etymologies 26.4

Etymology is the study of a word's history from its earliest recorded use until its present-day use. Knowing a word's etymology can often help you to understand its present meaning. Some dictionaries provide this information in brackets, using both symbols and abbreviations. You may have to check the key that appears at the front of the dictionary for explanations of these terms.

In this section, you will learn about words that have been borrowed from other languages, words that have changed their meanings over the years, and words that have been created for a variety of reasons.

Borrowed Words

For many centuries, speakers of English in its earlier and modern versions have been borrowing words from other languages. Today, modern English contains over one million words.

Loanwords are words in the English language that have been borrowed from other languages.

Most of the loanwords in English have come from Greek, Latin, and French. When the Normans of France attacked England in 1066 A.D. and conquered the Anglo-Saxons, they brought their own language, which was strongly influenced by classical Greek and Latin. As a result of the Norman conquest, French became the language of the rulers and the upper classes until about 1200 A.D. Thus, many English words borrowed from the French are words connected with government, legal and military matters, or with leisure, the arts, and food.

Most Latin words entered the English language directly in their original forms. Examples are *climax, appendix, epitome, exterior, delirium,* and *axis.* Other Latin words were shortened or otherwise modified. Thus, *consultare* became *consult,* and *absentia* became *absence.* In addition, Latin has provided many prefixes, suffixes, and roots from which new English words have been constructed.

The Greek language has contributed many scientific and technological words to the English language, especially compound words, such as *microscope, astrology, television,* and *agoraphobia.*

To a lesser extent, English has borrowed words from other languages as well, including *balcony, canto, duet, granite,* and *opera* from Italian; *alligator, cargo, contraband,* and *vanilla* from Spanish; *vodka* and *ruble* from Russian; and *caravan, divan,* and *khaki* from Persian.

Many Spanish words entered the English language from Mexico, including *alfalfa, mesquite, pompano, pronto,* and *vamoose.*

The words *chipmunk, hominy, moose, raccoon,* and *skunk* all came from Native American languages.

It is important to be aware that while a word may have entered the English language from another language, its earliest origin may reach further back in time. For example, many words had been part of a very old and now extinct language called Indo-European, and later entered the Latin or Greek language, became part of the French language, and eventually found their way into English. Therefore, when you check the dictionary, look for both the earliest origin of a word and the source language that is closest to its English meaning.

EXERCISE A: Discovering the Sources of Loanwords. In a dictionary that provides etymologies, look up each word below and write the earliest language of origin.

EXAMPLE: cruller

          Dutch

1. piano	3. urban	5. scant	7. umbrella
2. enemy	4. stone	6. cloak	8. felony

9. jasmine	12. awkward	15. etching	18. fire
10. intellect	13. abject	16. paradise	19. conspiracy
11. pugnacious	14. remit	17. wife	20. encyclopedia

EXERCISE B: Finding Loanwords in the Dictionary. In a dictionary that provides etymologies, find at least one word from each of the following languages.

EXAMPLE: Japanese

   sushi

1. Latin	11. Persian
2. French	12. Chinese
3. German	13. Greek
4. Dutch	14. Japanese
5. Spanish	15. Hebrew
6. Old English	16. Old Norse
7. Middle English	17. Arabic
8. Italian	18. Portuguese
9. Native American	19. Hindi
10. Russian	20. Indo-European

Words with New Meanings

English-speaking people are always giving new meanings to words already in the language. Thus, the English language continues to grow and expand.

The English language grows by giving new meaning to old words.

During the Middle Ages, the word *havoc* was an order telling an army to begin plundering. In Shakespeare's time, four centuries ago, the word *communicate* meant "to share or make common to many," a meaning closer to its original Latin meaning.

Some words change by taking on new meanings while in many instances retaining their original meanings as well. This illustrates the idea that words mean what their speakers intend them to mean, and do not have a fixed definition in accordance with their original usage. The word *proposition*, for example, primarily means "a statement set forth for purposes of discussion." Today it also means "an offer," as in "We made him a proposition." It also means "an issue or matter," as in "That's a different proposition."

Words often take on new meaning through *compounding*, joining two words together to form a new word. Thus, we have words like *stopover, hitchhike, sidetrack,* and *soap opera,* whose separate parts have very different meanings from the newly formed word.

Words can often change in meaning when they are used as different parts of speech. Thus, the word *park*, when used as a noun, as in "They had a picnic in the park" has a different meaning than in "We will park the car in the garage," where *park* is used as a verb.

EXERCISE C: Discovering New Meanings of Words. Write a definition for each of the following words as the part of speech indicated in parentheses. Then write a sentence using the word.

EXAMPLE: brave (verb)

to face with courage; to defy; to dare

They braved the snowstorm to find help for the stranded passengers.

1. record (verb)
2. deal (noun)
3. barbecue (verb)
4. blue (adjective)
5. filibuster (verb)
6. comb (verb)
7. back (verb)
8. consummate (adjective)
9. probe (noun)
10. contact (noun)

Coined Words

The English language continues to grow through the spontaneous creation of new words. Some new words are created in response to developments in science and technology. Other words are invented during periods of war or to name new products, ideas, or activities. Some words are created just for fun.

Newly created words are known as coinages.

New words are coined in a variety of ways.

Clipped Words. Some everyday words are shortened versions of words that are no longer in use. Thus, today, people commonly say *bus* and *curio* when they used to say *omnibus* and *curiosity*.

Blends. Sometimes new words are created by combining parts of other words. These words may be called *blends* or *portmanteau words*. Such words may be playful or serious. Thus, we have formal words, such as *dictaphone (dictate + telephone) travelogue (travel + dialogue),* and whimsical words, such as *chortle (snort + chuckle)* and *twiddle (twist + fiddle).*

Words from Proper Nouns. Many English words are based on the names of people and places. Some examples are *Tabasco* from the name of the Tabasco River in Mexico, *Camembert* from the French village that exported this cheese, and *Charleston* (a dance step popular during the 1920's) from the name of the city in South Carolina.

Brand Names. Some words start out as brand names of products or services, but people begin using these names for all similar items. Thus, any clear plastic adhesive tape is often referred to as *scotch tape*, any brand of refrigerator may be called a *frigidaire*, and any photocopy may be referred to as a *xerox* copy.

EXERCISE D: Finding the Origins of Words from Proper Nouns and Blended Words. Use a dictionary that has etymologies, and write a definition for each word that includes the origin of the word.

EXAMPLE: boycott

Boycott—to coerce by refusing to have any dealings with and by preventing others from having any dealings with. It is from the name of a 19th century Irish landowner Captain Boycott, who was threatened in a dispute with tenants.

1. scotch	6. wisteria
2. shrapnel	7. raglan
3. snark	8. lynch
4. mackintosh	9. colt
5. roquefort	10. quisling

EXERCISE E: Finding the Origins of Clipped Words and Brand Names. Use a dictionary that provides etymologies, and write a definition of each word that includes its origin.

EXAMPLE: mod (clipped word for modern)

Pertaining to style of dress that is characterized by bold colors, patterns, and stripes. The word formerly referred to a British teenager who attempted to attain a sophisticated, aloof personality and affected an ultramodern version of Edwardian dress and manners.

1. condo
2. nylon
3. kleenex
4. limo
5. zipper
6. combo
7. demo
8. rep
9. simonize
10. novocaine

DEVELOPING WRITING SKILLS: Determining the Origins of Words. In a dictionary that provides etymologies, look up each of the following words and write a sentence explaining the meaning and etymology of the word.

EXAMPLE: eradicate

Eradicate, which is from the Latin word *eradicare* that means "to root out," means to remove or destroy utterly.

1. diabolical
2. culpable
3. liberty
4. chaos
5. shirt
6. boomerang
7. mood
8. bush
9. treason
10. anonymous

Skills Review and Writing Workshop

Vocabulary Building

CHECKING YOUR SKILLS

Use context clues to write a definition of each underlined word in the following paragraph.

(1) Benedict Arnold was a great hero as well as a disreputable traitor. (2) An intrepid leader, Arnold never shrank from engaging the enemy in battle. (3) In the winter of 1775, he led a brilliant, if unsuccessful, foray against the British, at Quebec. (4) At the battle of Saratoga, Arnold played an integral role in the victory over the British. (5) However, Arnold never received the accolades for his achievements that he felt were due him. (6) His desire for recognition as well as his monetary greed were major reasons why Arnold turned traitor. (7) In 1780, Arnold agreed to surrender to the British the important post at West Point, strategically located on the Hudson River. (8) However, the plot was foiled, and Arnold barely escaped with his life. (9) Later he conducted military maneuvers for the British in Virginia. (10) For his treasonous activities Arnold's name will always be covered with opprobrium.

USING VOCABULARY SKILLS IN WRITING
Writing Autobiographical Material

A rich vocabulary can make your writing more lively and interesting. Write an autobiographical account titled: *My Most Important Achievement*. Follow the steps below in your writing.

Prewriting: Outline the specific details of your accomplishment. What was its significance in your life at the time? Has it had any effect on your life since?

Writing: Begin with an interesting introduction. Then present the details of your accomplishment.

Revising: Change any words that could be more vivid and more powerful. After you have revised, proofread carefully.

Chapter 27

Spelling Improvement

One of the reasons spelling is an important skill is that poor spelling is so noticeable. A reader's response to your writing, whether in school or out, will be affected by spelling errors. People often feel that poor spelling is a sign of carelessness and will judge a writer who makes spelling errors accordingly.

If you have problems with spelling, it is encouraging to know that the great majority of words in the English language are spelled according to a few definite rules. A knowledge of these rules, then, will give you the key to the correct spelling of most words. It is even more encouraging to know that there are proven techniques to help overcome spelling problems. The first section of this chapter explains some of these techniques and gives you an opportunity to practice them. The second section summarizes the basic rules.

27.1 Techniques for Improving Spelling

Whether your spelling skills are excellent, adequate, or in need of improvement, a dictionary is a big help. When you proofread written work, use a dictionary to check a doubtful spelling or to learn the spelling of a difficult word. If you find that you are consistently misspelling certain words, the techniques in this section will be especially helpful.

746

Proofreading Carefully

It is a good idea to get into the habit of proofreading everything you write for spelling errors. This will help you to eliminate misspellings caused by hasty writing and allow you to pinpoint words that always present a spelling problem for you.

Proofread everything you write.

Proofreading is a specialized skill. It is different from revising your thoughts or changing your writing style to suit a specific assignment. When you proofread, focus only on the spelling of each word, not on form or content. Keep a dictionary close by so that you can look up every word you suspect may be spelled incorrectly. After a while, you will have to rely on the dictionary less and less often.

EXERCISE A: Proofreading Carefully. Each sentence below contains one incorrectly spelled word. Write the correct spelling of each word, using a dictionary when necessary.

EXAMPLE: He arrived in New York as an immagrint early in the twentieth century.

immigrant

1. The clinic staff will anoculate the children against polio.
2. John returned to school after a long abcense.
3. He wrote many books under a seudonim.
4. The rythem of the music was infectious.
5. The graduating class will assend the staircase.
6. Incorragible juveniles are sent to a state facililty.
7. Please give me a reciept for that purchase.
8. The pacifist was a disiple of Ghandi.
9. He studied pycology at college.
10. The archeologists were lost in the underground labarinth.

EXERCISE B: More Work with Proofreading. Each sentence in the following paragraph contains one or more misspelled words. Write the correct spelling of each misspelled word.

(1) Whenever a mass of people has been neglected to long by the established orgens of communication, agencies eventu-

ally have been deviced to supply that want. (2) Invariably this press of the masses is greeted with scorn by the sophisticated reader because the content of such a press is likely to be elamental and emotionel. (3) Such scorn is not always desurved. (4) Just as the child ordnarily starts his reading with Mother Goose and fairy storys before graduating to more serious study, so the public first reached by a new agency is likley to prefer what the critics call "sensationalism," which is the emphasis on emotioun for its own sake. (5) This pattirn can be seen in the periads when the most noteworthy developments in populer journelism were apparant. (6) In 1620, 1833, the 1890's, or 1920, this tapping of a new, much-neglected public started with a waive of sensationelism. (7) In 1833, for example, the first sucessfull penny newspaper tapped a resevior of readers collectively desegnated "the common man." (8) The first offerrings of this poor person's newspaper tended to be highly sensationel. (9) This was only a developmentel phase, however. (10) Very quickly the penny newspapers began to attract readers from other sociel and economic brackits.

Studying Spelling Demons

You are probably familiar with the lists of words commonly referred to as spelling demons. Some of these words follow basic spelling rules. Others follow no rules. All may be words that cause problems for you now. Often the best way to learn how to spell such words is simply to memorize them.

Review a list of spelling demons to identify words you may have problems spelling correctly.

Look over the list of common spellings demons and note the words you think might present spelling problems for you.

COMMON SPELLING DEMONS			
abbreviate	accumulate	aggravate	ambassador
absence	adjective	aggressive	analysis
accidentally	admittance	aisle	analyze
achieve	adolescence	allowance	anecdote
acquaintance	aerial	all right	anniversary
accommodate	aerosol	amateur	annual

anonymous	clothes	disappear	guarantee
anxiety	colonel	disastrous	guidance
apostrophe	column	discern	handerchief
apparatus	committee	disciple	height
apparent	comparative	dissatisfied	hygiene
appearance	competitor	distinction	hypnotic
apprentice	concede	distinguish	immigrant
appropriate	condemn	doubt	immobile
argument	congratulate	earnest	incorrigible
ascend	conscience	economical	independence
assassinate	conscientious	efficient	indigestion
association	conscious	eighth	infinite
athletic	contemporary	eligible	inflammable
attendance	continuous	embarrass	inoculate
audience	controversial	emergency	interfere
awkward	convenience	eminent	irrelevant
banquet	coolly	enemy	journal
behavior	cordially	envelope	judicial
believe	correspondence	environment	knowledge
beneficial	counterfeit	equipped	laboratory
benefit	courageous	equivalent	labyrinth
bicycle	courtesy	erroneous	legitimate
bookkeeper	criticism	essential	library
bulletin	criticize	exaggerate	license
bureau	curiosity	exceed	lieutenant
business	curious	exercise	loneliness
cafeteria	cylinder	exhaust	maintenance
calendar	deceive	exhibit	mathematics
cancel	decision	exhilarate	meanness
capital	defendant	existence	mediocre
capitol	defiance	explanation	merchandise
captain	deficient	extension	meteor
career	delinquent	extraordinary	mileage
carriage	descendant	familiar	millionaire
category	description	fantasy	miniature
cemetery	desert	fascinate	mischievous
census	despair	February	misspell
cereal	desperate	financial	mortgage
changeable	dessert	foreign	naturally
chauffeur	dining	grammar	necessary

749

neighbor	physician	receipt	surprise
nickel	pigeon	recognize	suspicious
ninety	pneumonia	recommend	syllable
nuclear	political	reference	symmetrical
nuisance	pollution	rehearse	technique
obsolete	possess	reliance	technology
obstacle	possession	religious	temperament
occasion	prairie	repetition	temperature
occasionally	precede	restaurant	temporary
occur	precision	rhythm	tenant
occurred	preferable	ridiculous	thorough
odyssey	prejudice	schedule	tomatoes
omitted	preparation	scissors	tomorrow
opinion	principal	secretary	tragedy
optimistic	principle	separate	truly
outrageous	privilege	sergeant	twelfth
pamphlet	probably	similar	unanimous
parallel	procedure	sincerely	unforgettable
paralyze	proceed	sophomore	unnecessary
particularly	prompt	souvenir	vaccine
pastime	pronunciation	spaghetti	vacuum
permanent	protein	spiritual	vegetable
permissible	pseudonym	straight	villain
personally	psychology	substitute	vitamin
perspiration	punctuation	succeed	Wednesday
persuasive	really	superintendent	weird
phantom	recede	supersede	whether

EXERCISE C: Working with Spelling Demons.
Write the following spelling demons, filling in the missing letters.

EXAMPLE: congra __ ulate

   congratulate

1. fanta __ y
2. gramm __ r
3. a __ quaintance
4. exten __ ion
5. audi __ nce
6. od __ ssey

7. caf __ teria
8. ab __ ence
9. opt __ mistic
10. attend __ nce
11. prom __ t
12. cool __ y
13. libr __ ry

14. mil __ age
15. im __ obile
16. awkw __ rd
17. b __ cycle
18. __ neumonia
19. condem __
20. vacu __ m

EXERCISE D: More Work with Spelling Demons. Write the correct spelling for the misspelled spelling demon in each sentence.

EXAMPLE: The children's behavor at school was beyond reproach.

behavior

1. All the employees had lunch in the company cafateria.
2. He was in the eigth grade in junior high school.
3. We learned about paralel lines in our geometry class.
4. The class went on a skiing trip last Febuary.
5. Your plan of action is outragious.
6. He considered oil painting a pleasant pasttime.
7. There was a high level of air polutioun in the area.
8. If you want to go it is alright with me.
9. Be sure to put the apostrafe in the correct place.
10. The performance of the dancers was mediocer at best.
11. He knows nothing about meal preperation.
12. People in poor countries often do not eat enough proteen.
13. They traveled west to see the dessert.
14. Our parents celebrated their twenty-fifth anniversery.
15. The article appeared in a medical journel.
16. She is an aquaintance of Mrs. Green, the principal.
17. It will not be nesessary to take them to a restaurant.
18. The association plans to serve spagetti at the dinner.
19. My neighbors love to discuss controvercial subjects.
20. The superintendent of the building helps the tenents.

Studying Problem Words

Although you may misspell some words through simple carelessness, there are other words that may present real spelling problems for you. These may include new words, words that have confusing endings, words that sound like other words, and the inevitable demons.

Use a dictionary to correct spelling errors and record problem words in a personal spelling list.

You can, of course, solve these spelling problems temporarily by referring to the dictionary. For long-term spelling improvement, however, you will need other methods as well.

Using a Dictionary. A dictionary is one of the most useful reference tools you can have. You can use it not only for checking the spelling of words, but to find other information about words that can help you to remember how they are spelled. For example, a dictionary can show you how to break words into syllables so that you will not overlook a syllable when spelling a word. It can show you how to pronounce a word so that you will not omit or add letters that are part of the word. Also, some words can be spelled in more than one way. This is called a *variant* spelling. The dictionary shows you the preferred spelling of the word so you can tell if you have been using a variant, less preferable spelling. In checking the spelling of a word you may find you have confused it with another word that sounds similar but has a different meaning. All of this information can help make you a better speller.

Recording Problem Words. Perhaps the most important technique for improving your spelling is recording in a special section of your notebook the correct spelling of any difficult words.

Whenever a teacher returns a corrected composition or test, check it for spelling errors. In a dictionary, look up the correct spelling of those words. Then set up a personal spelling list in any way that is helpful for you. You may, for example, choose to divide a page into two columns, labeling the first, "Misspelled Words." Here you can enter the words exactly as you misspelled them. The second column can be headed "Correct Spelling." Fill it in after you have looked up the word in a dictionary. Some students also find it helpful to record in a third column hints for remembering correct spellings.

The chart that follows explains an efficient way to commit the spelling of your problem words to memory.

MEMORIZING THE SPELLING OF PROBLEM WORDS

1. Observe each word on your list carefully, noticing the arrangement of letters. Try to visualize the word. For example, observe the word *accommodate*, noticing that there are two *c*'s and two *m*'s.

2. Pronounce the word to yourself in syllables. For example, if you remember that *lightning* has only two syllables, you will have no trouble with the spelling. (If you mispronounce it as *light-en-ing*, you will probably misspell it.)
3. Write the correct spelling of the word on a separate piece of paper and then check to see if you have spelled it correctly.
4. Review your list until you have mastered each word.

EXERCISE E: Selecting Words for a Personal Spelling List. Look over all the work you have done in the last month, including personal writing and school assignments. Record any words you have misspelled on a personal spelling list.

Developing Memory Aids

Words that do not follow any spelling rules are especially hard to learn to spell correctly. The best way to master these words is through the use of memory aids. A memory aid is sometimes called a mnemonic device. The word *mnemonic* is derived from a Greek word meaning "to remember."

Use memory aids to improve your spelling.

One trick is to look for one or more familiar words within a problem word.

EXAMPLES: earnest   Put your *ear* to the *nest* for *earnest*.

          nuclear   Are the arguments concerning nu*clear* plants *clear*?

          prairie   Is there fresh *air* on the pr*air*ie?

Another spelling mnemonic device is to associate the spelling of a problem word with a related idea.

EXAMPLES: parallel   Think of the two *l*'s as parallel lines.

          separate   To separate something you break it apart. Both *separate* and *apart* have two *a*'s.

Try to make up your own memory aids, add them to your spelling list, and you will probably see an improvement in your spelling skills.

753

EXERCISE F: Using Memory Aids to Master Problem Words. Write the words, filling in the missing letters. Then check each word in a dictionary and record on your spelling list any words you missed. Finally, devise a memory aid for each misspelled word. The example below shows a memory aid for the word *vegetable*.

EXAMPLE: veg __ table

vegetable

Please <u>get</u> me more ve<u>get</u>ables.

1. barr __ l	8. spiritu __ l	15. p __ ysician
2. bel __ eve	9. We __ nesday	16. un __ ecessary
3. cere __ l	10. ten __ nt	17. li __ utenant
4. competit __ r	11. tec __ nology	18. refer __ nce
5. cem __ tery	12. s __ mmetrical	19. misch __ evous
6. exag __ erate	13. unanim __ us	20. court __ sy
7. obst __ cle	14. tomato __ s	

Diagnosing Problem Areas

In working with spelling demons, you probably have noticed that many of them do not follow any specific rule. They must simply be memorized. Other hard-to-spell words, such as those in the test below and on page 755, are spelled according to definite rules. After taking this test, correcting it, and analyzing your errors, you should be able to zero in on the rules you need to study. You may, for example, have no difficulty spelling the plural forms of words and yet have trouble with the *ie/ei* words.

Analyze your spelling errors to determine your areas of weakness and then study the rules that will help you.

To take the following diagnostic test, read each sentence and then jot down the word that correctly completes the sentence. Exercise G will then show you how to analyze your errors.

1. Is your new winter jacket _____ ? (Other Confusing Endings)

    (a) reversble   (b) reversible   (c) reservable

2. I consulted a _____ book in the library. (Other Confusing Endings)
   (a) reference   (b) referance   (c) referrence
3. We are _____ a letter to the mayor today. (Suffixes)
   (a) writting   (b) writing   (c) writeing
4. We put plenty of _____ in the stew. (Plurals)
   (a) tomatoes   (b) tomatos   (c) tomato's
5. I was _____ in the election results. (Prefixes)
   (a) disappointed   (b) dissappointed   (c) disapointed
6. The _____ train blocked the crossing. (*ie/ei* Words)
   (a) fraight   (b) frieght   (c) freight
7. We are _____ our papers today. (Suffixes)
   (a) editting   (b) edditing   (c) editing
8. If you have no errors on this test, you are an _____ speller. (Other Confusing Endings)
   (a) excellent   (b) excelant   (c) excellant
9. The color of the autumn _____ is beautiful. (Plurals)
   (a) leafs   (b) leaves   (c) leavs
10. Because he had _____ his return address, Ed received no response to his letter. (Suffixes)
    (a) omitted   (b) ommitted   (c) omited

EXERCISE G: Analyzing Your Spelling Errors. After your test has been corrected, look at each of your errors and note the item in parentheses after each sentence. Then look up the rules in Section 27.2 and study the examples, exceptions, and any charts provided.

Setting Goals for Improvement

Spelling improvement is a long-term goal that cannot be rushed. Instead of trying to learn dozens of new words at one sitting, you will accomplish more if you set achievable goals.

Record all problem words on a personal spelling list and memorize them a few at a time.

By following the above suggestion, you can eliminate five or ten words from the list every week. By setting realistic short-term goals, you'll continue making progress toward your long-term goal of improved spelling skill.

EXERCISE H: Reaching Your Spelling Goals. Record the words you misspelled on the diagnostic test in your personal spelling list. Then choose ten words from the list as your weekly goal. Study these words as suggested in the chart on pages 752–753 and in the section on memory aids.

DEVELOPING WRITING SKILLS: Mastering Your Problem Words. Choose twenty words from your personal spelling list. Use them in a book review describing your reaction to a book you have read recently or in a one-page report discussing a sports event you have read about or attended.

27.2 A Catalog of Spelling Rules

This section catalogs the basic rules governing the spelling of most of the words in the English language. If you spend some time studying these rules, you should be able to spell many words almost automatically. You might want to concentrate on the rules you diagnosed in the previous section as being problem areas for you.

Plurals

The plurals of most nouns are formed by adding *-s* or *-es*.

Add *-s* or *-es* to form the plural of most nouns.

Which addition to add is determined by the noun ending. For these and for spelling changes that result, see the chart.

ADDITIONS AND SPELLING CHANGES WHEN FORMING PLURALS			
Noun Ending	**Rule**	**Examples**	**Exceptions**
s,x,z,sh,ch	Add *-es.*	businesses, boxes, waltzes, dishes, churches	
o preceded by a consonant	Add *-es.*	heroes, potatoes	Musical terms: pianos, sopranos

o preceded by a vowel	Just add -s.	patios, rodeos	
y preceded by a consonant	Change y to i and add -es.	colonies, cities	
y preceded by a vowel	Just add -s.	journeys, holidays	
f, ff, fe	Add -s.	proofs, cliffs	Change -f to -v and add -s or -es: wives, loaves

The plurals of some nouns are formed in irregular ways. In addition to the familiar change from *mouse* to *mice* and from *goose* to *geese*, there are nouns such as *datum*, which becomes *data, medium,* which becomes *media,* and *radius,* which becomes *radii.* The singular forms of some nouns are used to denote the plural (*sheep, moose*) while there are only plural forms (*politics, mathematics*) for some other nouns.

To form the plurals of compound nouns written as separate or hyphenated words, make the modified nouns plural.

EXAMPLES: passer-by   passers-by

bucket seat   bucket seats

If no plural form is given for a word in the dictionary, simply add -s or -es to the singular form.

NOTE ABOUT OTHER SPECIAL PLURALS: As explained in Section 12.6, an apostrophe is used to form the plurals of letters (*a*'s, *b*'s, and *c*'s), numbers (the *1950*'s), symbols (*&*'s), and words used to name themselves (*and*'s).

EXERCISE A: Forming Plurals. Write the plural form of each of the following words. Check your answers in a dictionary.

1. leaf
2. tomato
3. circus
4. fly
5. pen pal
6. roof
7. lunch
8. datum
9. radio
10. salmon
11. alumnus
12. jelly
13. memorandum
14. waltz
15. echo
16. solo
17. enemy
18. loaf
19. mouse
20. attorney-at-law

Prefixes and Suffixes

Adding a prefix does not affect the spelling of a root. Adding a suffix may require a spelling change in some words or roots.

Prefixes. Use the following rule when adding prefixes.

When a prefix is added to a word, the spelling of the root word remains the same.

EXAMPLES: dis + satisfy = dissatisfy

mis + spell = misspell

re + consider = reconsider

For more examples of roots with prefixes added, refer to the chart that begins on page 731. The chart also indicates how the spelling of certain prefixes is changed when they are joined to certain roots. Notice, however, that the rule still applies—the spelling of the root word remains the same. The spelling of the prefix is changed to make pronunciation easier.

EXAMPLES: ad- becomes ap- before prove: approve

in- becomes ir- before reverent: irreverent

sub- becomes sup- before press: suppress

Suffixes. When spelling a word to which a suffix has been added, there are two things you should look at: (1) the ending of the root word and (2) the beginning letter of the suffix.

Before adding a suffix, notice the last letters of the root and the first letter of the suffix.

The following chart details the spelling changes that are necessary when suffixes are added to roots.

SPELLING CHANGES BEFORE SUFFIXES			
Word Ending	Suffix Added	Rule	Exceptions
consonant + *y* (mercy, defy)	most suffixes (ful, ance)	Change *y* to *i*. merciful, defiance	Most suffixes beginning with *i: hurry* becomes *hurrying; defy* becomes *defying*

758

vowel + *y* (convey, employ)	most suffixes (or, ment)	Make no change. conveyor, employment	A few short words: *day* becomes *daily*; *gay* becomes *gaiety*
any word ending in *e* (prove, strive)	suffix beginning with a vowel (able, ing)	Drop the final *e*. provable, striving	1. Words ending in *ce* or *ge* with suffixes beginning in *a* or *o*: *notice* becomes *noticeable*; *courage* becomes *courageous* 2. Words ending in *ee* or *oe*: *see* becomes *seeing*; *toe* becomes *toeing* 3. A few special words: *dye* becomes *dyeing*; *be* becomes *being*
any word ending in *e* (care, love)	suffix beginning with a consonant (ful, ly)	Make no change. careful, lovely	A few special words: *true* becomes *truly*; *argue* becomes *argument*; *judge* becomes *judgment*
consonant + vowel + consonant and a stressed syllable (forbid', permit') (forbid', permit')	suffix beginning with a vowel (en, ed)	Double the final consonant.	1. Words ending in *w* or *x*: *draw* becomes *drawing*; *box* becomes *boxed* 2. Words in which the stress changes after the suffix is added: *prefer* + *ing* becomes *prefer'ring* BUT *prefer* + *ence* becomes *pref'erence*

consonant + vowel + consonant and an unstressed syllable (budget, deposit)	suffix beginning with a vowel (ed, or)	Make no change. budg′eted, depos′itor	No major exceptions
1 vowel + consonant in one-syllable word (step, run)	suffix beginning with a vowel (ing, er)	Double the final consonant. stepping, runner	Words ending in *w* or *x*: *draw* becomes *drawing*; *box* becomes *boxed*
2 vowels + consonant in one-syllable word (pour, heat)	suffix beginning with a vowel (ed, ing)	Make no change. poured, heating	No major exceptions

EXERCISE B: Spelling Words with Prefixes. Form new words by adding one of the following seven prefixes to each of the numbered roots. You will have to use some of the prefixes more than once. You may also have to change the form of the prefix.

com-, de-, dis-, ex-, in-, mis-, sub-

1. -pose	6. -appear	11. -pare	16. -pute
2. -interpret	7. -literate	12. -pel	17. -patriot
3. -pound	8. -migrate	13. -sist	18. -passionate
4. -respond	9. -appropriate	14. -let	19. -missive
5. -marine	10. -press	15. -act	20. -rogate

EXERCISE C: Spelling Words with Suffixes. Spell each of the following items correctly.

1. propel + -er	6. confine + -ing
2. wrap + -ing	7. repeal + -ed
3. peace + -ful	8. compel + -ed
4. arrive + -ing	9. hinder + -ance
5. extreme + -ity	10. classify + -ed

11. tour + -ing
12. request + -ed
13. final + -ist
14. annoy + -ance
15. happy + -ness

16. whimsy + -cal
17. dainty + -ness
18. hate + -ful
19. judge + -ment
20. blaze + -ing

ie and *ei* Words

If you were to ask a group of people, young, old, and in-between, what spelling rule stands out in their mind, they would probably give the following rule.

Write *i* before *e*
Except after *c*,
Or when sounded like *a*
As in *neighbor* and *weigh*.

Helpful as this rule is for many words, such as *chief, ceiling, reindeer,* and *freight*, it has exceptions. For example, the following words do not have a *c*, nor do they have a long *a* sound, yet they use the *ei* spelling.

EXCEPTIONS: either   leisure   sheik
             foreign   neither   their
             height   seize   weird

For another group of *ie/ei* words, another rule may be used.

When *c* is pronounced *sh*, write *i* before *e*.

EXAMPLES: ancient   efficient
           conscience   sufficient

EXERCISE D: Spelling *ie* and *ei* Words. Copy the following *ie/ei* words, filling in the missing letters in the correct order.

Conscious of the fact that I had studied my (1) anc ____ nt history assignment only (2) br ____ fly, I was understandably nervous when I took the exam. When I (3) rec ____ ved the corrected test the next day, I was afraid to look at it. When I finally looked, I couldn't (4) bel ____ ve my eyes! I had (5) n ____ ther failed nor squeaked by with a C. At the top of the paper was a beautiful A! I almost (6) shr ____ ked with joy.

However, my (7) ch ____ f emotion was not (8) conc ____ t but sheer (9) rel ____ f. Next week, I'll plan to set aside (10) suffic ____ nt time to study instead of trusting to luck.

Words Ending in *-cede,* *-ceed,* and *-sede*

A few words with unusual endings may cause spelling problems. These are words that end in *-cede, -ceed,* and *-sede.* There is one good way to master these words.

Memorize the spellings of words thát end in *-cede, -ceed,* and *-sede.*

It will not be difficult for you to memorize these words as there are only a few of them. Only one word ends in *-sede.* Only three words end in *-ceed.* The rest end in *-cede.* The following chart summarizes this information.

Words Ending in *-cede*	Words Ending in *-ceed*	Words Ending in *-sede*
accede	exceed	supersede
concede	proceed	
intercede	succeed	
precede		
recede		
secede		

EXERCISE E: Spelling Words Ending in *-cede, -ceed,* and *-sede.* Write the incomplete word for each sentence, filling in the blanks with *-cede, -ceed,* or *-sede.* Then write a new sentence for each of the ten words in the chart above.

EXAMPLE: We cannot return home until the flood waters
re _____.

recede

1. The candidate refused to con _____ defeat on the basis of the popular vote.
2. We agreed to inter _____ with the the landlord.
3. The provisions of this law super _____ the old statute.

762

4. I would prefer to pre _____ you down the staircase.
5. The family refused to ac _____ to the child's demands.
6. Most new employees are anxious to suc _____ on the job.
7. When you see the yellow light, pro _____ with caution.
8. The final results will ex _____ all expectations.
9. As the plane gained altitude, we saw the airport re _____ in the distance.
10. A group of dissidents threatened to se _____ from the association.

Other Confusing Endings

Although the rules in the preceding chart can help you add most suffixes, you should also become familiar with certain groups of suffixes that are often confused with one another.

Learn to distinguish between confusing groups of suffixes.

-able, -ible. The rules governing the use of this pair of suffixes depend on a knowledge of Latin verbs. You can learn the spelling of some words with these endings, however, by studying the following chart. For words not included, check a dictionary.

Common Words Ending in *-able*		Common Words Ending in *-ible*	
acceptable	imaginable	accessible	irresistible
advisable	irritable	convertible	permissible
available	memorable	digestible	possible
believable	peaceable	edible	responsible
comfortable	predictable	eligible	reversible
considerable	reasonable	flexible	sensible
durable	taxable	horrible	terrible

-ance (-ancy, -ant) **and** *-ence (-ency, -ent).* If a noun takes the *a* spelling of this suffix (*defiance*) the corresponding adjective will also take the *a* spelling (*defiant*). The same applies to the *e* spelling (*eloquence, eloquent*). It is not easy to determine which spelling to use, but there is one rule that

763

helps. Words with a hard *c* or *g* sound usually take the *a* spelling (*significance, arrogant*). Those with a soft *c* or *g* sound usually take the *e* spelling (*deficiency, efficient*). There are many *-ance* and *-ence* words, however, without *c* or *g* sounds. The most common of these words follow.

Common Words Ending in *-ance*		Common Words Ending in *-ence*	
abundance	entrance	absence	experience
acquaintance	guidance	coherence	independence
appearance	importance	coincidence	lenience
assistance	maintenance	conference	opulence
brilliance	radiance	consequence	patience
clearance	tolerance	convenience	presence
		correspondence	residence
		excellence	violence

-ary, -ery. People are often confused about whether to end a word with *-ary* or *-ery*. Fortunately, very few words end in *-ery*. Once you learn these words, you will know that most other words with an ending that sounds similar will take the *-ary* spelling. The following chart will help you decide, in most cases, whether to use *-ary* or *-ery*.

Common Words Ending in *-ary*		Common Words Ending in *-ery*	
auxiliary	secretary	cemetery	scenery
boundary	secondary	distillery	stationery
elementary	stationary	millinery	(note paper)
February	(not moving)	monastery	winery
honorary	temporary	nursery	
imaginary	vocabulary		
library	voluntary		
military			
momentary			
necessary			

-cy, -sy. Another confusing pair of suffixes is *-cy* and *-sy*. Again, only a few words end in *-sy*. If you learn the words in the following chart, you can be fairly sure that other words end in -*cy*. If you are not sure of a spelling, always consult a dictionary.

COMMON WORDS ENDING IN -*sy*			
autopsy	curtsy	epilepsy	hypocrisy
biopsy	ecstasy	fantasy	idiosyncrasy
courtesy	embassy	heresy	pleurisy

-eous, -ious, -ous, -uous. Confusion may arise over the spelling of words ending in -*eous* -*ious*, -*ous*, and -*uous*. Some of this confusion can be resolved by paying strict attention to the pronunciation of the word. Words ending in -*uous*, for example, can be easily distinguished from the others if they are pronounced carefully. The following are the most common of the -*uous* words.

COMMON WORDS ENDING IN -*uous*			
ambiguous	continuous	ingenuous	sumptuous
conspicuous	fatuous	strenuous	

Deciding whether to use -*eous* or -*ious* is more difficult, since pronunciation does not help you. With these endings, it may be more helpful to memorize the spelling of the most common words in these two groups. Fortunately, the lists are not long.

Common Words Ending in -*eous*		Common Words Ending in -*ious*	
advantageous	gorgeous	anxious	harmonious
beauteous	miscellaneous	atrocious	ingenious
courageous	outrageous	cautious	laborious
courteous	righteous	conscientious	officious
erroneous	simultaneous	conscious	precious
		contagious	rebellious
		curious	religious
		delicious	repetitious
		fictitious	superstitious
		furious	suspicious
		gracious	

Careful pronunciation is the key to the correct spelling of words ending in *-ous*. There are many *-ous* words, so learn the words in the preceding lists. If a word does not appear in one of the lists, remember that it probably takes the *-ous* ending.

-efy and -ify. Here again your choices are simplified because one of this pair is rarely used. Of common English words, only the words in the following chart end in *-efy*.

WORDS ENDING IN *-efy*			
liquefy	putrefy	rarefy	stupefy

-sion, -tion. Some of the confusion over the use of this pair of suffixes can be resolved by using the following chart to learn the spelling of some of the most commonly used words that have these suffixes. However, the chart includes just a sampling. If you are not sure of a word that does not appear in the following chart, look it up in a dictionary. It may help you to remember that if a word has the *zh* sound, as in *confusion*, the suffix is *-sion*.

Common Words Ending in *-sion*		Common Words Ending in *-tion*	
abrasion	extension	affirmation	contradiction
aggression	fission	alteration	corruption
allusion	fusion	appreciation	distraction
apprehension	illusion	civilization	flirtation
confusion	immersion	competition	gratification
conversion	intercession	completion	justification
discussion	intrusion	connection	multiplication
dissension	mission	constriction	portion
	version	contention	satisfaction

EXERCISE F: Spelling Words with Confusing Endings. Write the correctly spelled word from each of the following pairs.

    1. Do not include any (miscellaneous, miscellanious) information.

766

2. They're building an (extention, extension) on the old factory.
3. The physics test was (impossibly, impossably) difficult.
4. Only a student with a (brillient, brilliant) mind could hope to pass it.
5. Coming late to rehearsal is (unacceptible, unacceptable).
6. She had an (excellent, excellant) chance of making the team.
7. Have you ever visited a (monastery, monastary)?
8. At least he had the (courtecy, courtesy) to return my call.
9. What (elementery, elementary) school did you attend?
10. The doctor thought it (advisible, advisable) to exercise the injured arm.

DEVELOPING WRITING SKILLS: Using Spelling Rules in Writing Sentences. Write original sentences, following spelling rules.

1. Write five original sentences, each containing a word spelled with *ei* or *ie*. Three of these sentences should also contain plural nouns.
2. Write five original sentences, each containing a word with a prefix. Two of these sentences should also contain plural nouns.
3. Write four original sentences, each containing one of the following:
   (a)   a word ending in *y* with a suffix added
   (b)   a word ending in *e* with a suffix added
   (c)   a one-syllable word ending in a consonant with a suffix added
   (d)   a multisyllable word ending in a consonant with a suffix added
4. Write six original sentences, each containing a word ending in one of the confusing groups of suffixes.

Skills Review and Writing Workshop

Spelling Improvement

CHECKING YOUR SKILLS

Find all the misspelled words in the following paragraph and write them correctly.

(1) A large variety of truely remarkible plants can be found in warm, coastal enviroments. (2) The plants obtain little or no nitrogen from thier soil. (3) They must obtain nitrogen by devourring insects. (4) Perhaps the best-known speceis is Venus's fly trap. (5) This plant has large leafs which contain brisling spikes and tiny hairs. (6) If an unwarry insect touches two of the hairs, the flexable edges of the leavs close, thus traping the insect. (7) The animal is renderred imobile and is slowly digested by the plant's enzimes. (8) The pitcher plant uses brightly colored flowers and sweet necter to lure passerbys. (9) The slipery rim of the plant propells the insect downward into the plant's base which holds rain water. (10) Here the insects drown and are disolved.

USING SPELLING SKILLS IN WRITING
Writing a Proposal

If words are misspelled, your writing will lose some of its impact. Write a proposal to improve your neighborhood. Follow the steps below to write the proposal and avoid spelling errors.

Prewriting: Think of a proposal that would be beneficial and relatively easy to implement. List three reasons why the project should be undertaken.

Writing: In the introduction, briefly describe your proposal. Then discuss the reasons to implement it, beginning with the most important reason.

Revising: Look over your work and rewrite any sentences that could be more effective. After you have revised, proofread carefully for spelling and other errors.

UNIT **VII**

Study and Research Skills

28

Basic Study Skills

Your last year in high school is a transitional one in which you prepare yourself for additional schooling, work, or both. At this point in your school career you should know which study skills you have mastered and which ones you still need to master. In this chapter you will assess your present study skills and make improvements that can enhance your ability to learn in college or on the job.

28.1 Evaluating Your Study Habits

Acquiring good study habits can make you a more effective, active learner in school and in a job. This section provides practice in developing a systematic approach to studying so that you can organize your time better to get everything done and still have leisure time.

Developing a Study Plan

You may find that more demands are being placed on your time. The aim of your developing a study plan is to enable you to make the best use of the time available to you for studying.

Develop a study plan in order to manage your time most efficiently.

An effective study plan includes setting up a study area, establishing a study schedule, and using an assignment book. The chart below is a guide to help you develop your study plan.

DEVELOPING A STUDY PLAN	
Study Area	1. Set up a study area that you associate only with studying. It should be well lighted and free of distractions.
	2. Equip your study area with all the materials you need to work, such as pens, pencils, paper, ruler, eraser, books, and a clock.
Study Schedule	1. Block out areas of time in which you have activities such as the regular school day, after-school clubs, dinner, and so on.
	2. Block out study periods of no longer than forty-five minutes each. Take a ten-minute break between each study period.
	3. Schedule study periods for times when you are most alert.
	4. Study your most difficult subject first.
	5. Make use of study hall and free time at school to complete some assignments.
Assignment Book	1. Divide your assignment book page into four columns. Use one column for the subject, one for a description of the assignment, one for the due date, and one for a check when the assignment is completed.
	2. Record short-term assignments such as homework.
	3. Record long-term assignments such as a research paper. Divide the assignment into short-term goals that must be met in order to complete the assignment.

EXERCISE A: Evaluating Your Study Plan. Identify which parts of your study plan need improvement. Using the features in the chart above, outline an improved study plan.

Setting Goals

Setting goals is a conscious way for you to decide what you want to accomplish. As a student, one long-term goal is to improve your study habits. To help you reach this goal, you need to set short-term goals that you can accomplish in several weeks.

Set long- and short-term goals to improve your general study habits.

One way that can help you reach your goals is to prepare and follow a chart like the one below. By putting your goals in writing you are also making a commitment, a contract with yourself to reach those goals.

SETTING LONG- AND SHORT-TERM GOALS		
Long-Term Goal: To make good use of time for studying		
Short-Term Goals	**Timetable**	**Comments**
Use free period to get math help.	4 weeks (by Dec. 10)	Successfully completed
Extend study blocks to 45 minutes each.	4 weeks (by Dec. 10)	Successfully completed
Review for tests second-period study hall.	2 months (by Jan. 7)	More practice needed; work on skill through end of semester

EXERCISE B: Setting Goals for Study Skills. Using the part of your study plan that you identified in Exercise A as needing improvement, set long- and short-term goals for improving that study habit. Then make a chart, using the one above as a model.

DEVELOPING WRITING SKILLS: Evaluating Your Study Goals. After working for several weeks on improving the study habit you chose for Exercise B, evaluate your progress toward meeting your long-term goal. Write a paragraph that describes the chart you prepared and which of the short-term goals you have completed and which need further practice.

Methods of Taking Notes 28.2

Note-taking can take different forms and styles depending on the needs and personality of the note-taker. If done properly, note-taking can clarify learning, summarize it, and act as a reinforcement mechanism. It is important to keep notes in a notebook that is organized, easy to follow, and up-to-date.

This section provides practice using two methods for taking notes: *outlines* and *summaries.*

Making Outlines

An *outline* is a method of taking notes that organizes information according to main ideas, major details, and lesser details. There are three basic outline forms: *modified, formal,* and *free-form* outlines.

Modified Outlines. In a modified outline, main ideas are used as headings and important details are listed under each heading. The heading is capitalized, underlined, or circled to emphasize it. The details are numbered, lettered, or marked with dashes and indented under the heading. When you take notes in modified outline form, you simply record each major topic as a heading when it is introduced; then list related details under the heading, using numbers, letters, or dashes. You will find a modified outline most useful for quick note-taking from spoken or written material and for organizing ideas for questions on essay tests.

Use a modified outline to take notes while listening or reading.

Read the following part of a modified outline about the functions of the two hemispheres of the human brain. Notice the uses of capitalization, underlining, and numbers to organize information.

MODIFIED OUTLINE:

Left Brain	Right Brain
1. logical	1. creative
2. organized	2. artistic
3. mathematical	3. poetic
4. grammatical	4. musical

773

Formal Outlines. A formal outline not only places information under major headings, but also shows the relative importance of the information and its relation to other information. You will find a formal outline useful for taking detailed notes from textbooks or reference books, to revise a first set of notes, and to prepare papers and speeches.

Use a formal outline to arrange ideas when preparing major written and oral assignments.

The chart below lists the rules for making a formal outline.

RULES TO FOLLOW FOR FORMAL OUTLINES
1. Use Roman numerals for main ideas. Use capital letters for major details. Use arabic numerals for minor details. Use small letters for items under minor details.
2. Place a period after each numeral or letter.
3. Capitalize the first word in each line.
4. Use indentation to indicate importance. Main ideas begin at the left; less important ideas begin farther to the right.
5. Always place two or more items under a heading.

Formal outlines can be either *topic* outlines or *sentence* outlines. A topic outline lists information in words and phrases; a sentence outline uses complete sentences. Notice the use of phrases in the following topic outline.

TOPIC OUTLINE:

The Human Brain and How It Functions
  I. Skills divided by hemispheres
      A. Left Brain
          1. Logical
          2. Organized
          3. Mathematical
          4. Grammatical
      B. Right Brain
          1. Creative
          2. Artistic
          3. Poetic
          4. Musical

II. Crossover between two hemispheres
    A. Hemispheres connected by nerve bundles
        1. Allows hemispheres to communicate
        2. Can be cut without ill effects
    B. One hemisphere usually stronger than other
        1. Can be changed through education
        2. Left brain excellence encouraged more often

Most of the formal outlining you do will take the form of a topic outline. Occasionally, you may be asked to prepare a sentence outline. A sentence outline lists information in complete thoughts and is useful when you are preparing to give a speech or write a paper directly from your outline.

Free-Form Outlines. Unlike other outline forms, the free-form outline is not written and organized from top to bottom. Instead, the main idea is placed in the center, with related information branching off from it. The visual impact of the notes makes information in this form easy for you to recall. You will find a free-form outline useful when you are taking notes from loosely structured material in which the highlights are important.

Use a free-form outline to take notes from loosely organized material or when you need to recall only highlights.

The following free-form outline shows notes from the modified outline on the brain functions from page 773. Notice that the format is loose and only brief notes are taken.

One Form of a Free Form Outline

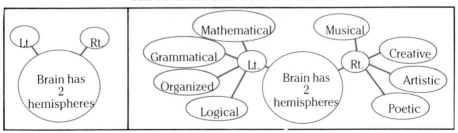

EXERCISE A: Making a Modified Outline. Using an assigned chapter take notes on one section using modified outline form.

EXERCISE B: Making a Formal Topic Outline. Read the passage below. Then take notes on the information as a topic outline.

The planets revolve around the sun in elliptical orbits that in general are nearly circular. Each planet's orbit is determined by the force of gravity exerted on it by the sun. When a planet is closest to the sun it moves fastest; when it is farthest from the sun, it moves slowest. The time that it takes a planet to make one complete orbit around the sun is called its period of revolution, or its year. As each planet revolves around the sun it rotates, or spins, on its axis. The time that it takes for a planet to make one rotation on its axis is called its period of rotation, or its day.

EXERCISE C: Making a Formal Sentence Outline. Rewrite the topic outline on page 774 as a sentence outline.

EXERCISE D: Making a Free-Form Outline. Rewrite the topic outline you made in Exercise B as a free-form outline.

Writing Summaries

A summary is a condensation of the most important points of a reading or lecture. Preparing a summary encourages you to determine the essential information that needs to be remembered, and to internalize the information in your own words.

Use summaries to take notes when you need to remember only the main ideas.

The chart below offers suggestions for summarizing.

WRITING SUMMARIES
1. Listen or read for main ideas.
2. Write down the main ideas using your own words.
3. Shape these main ideas into sentences that express the purpose and point of view of the speaker or writer.
4. Write the summary in paragraph form. The final material should be no more than one third of its original length.

EXERCISE E: Writing a Summary. Below each of the three outlines you have made in Exercises A, B, and C, write a two- or three-sentence summary of the information in the outline.

Developing a Personal Shorthand

When you are taking notes in a lecture, an audio-visual presentation, or at a meeting, writing speed can be an important factor. Using abbreviations and symbols in place of words can make your note-taking more efficient and accurate.

Develop a shorthand for efficient note-taking.

Until you become comfortable with your shorthand, review your notes shortly after you take them. Use the suggestions in the chart below to help you develop your personal shorthand.

DEVELOPING A PERSONAL SHORTHAND	
Suggestions	**Examples**
1. Use only one abbreviation for each word.	Decide whether lk means *like* or *look*
2. Use capital letters to stand for some words and small letters for others.	P (paragraph), p (page) Q (question), w (with)
3. Use only the first two or three letters of a word.	ch (chapter), ex (example), ea (each), dif (different)
4. Use only the first and last letters of a word.	rt (right), wd (word), hr (hour), vs (versus)
5. Use slashes, letters, and symbols for certain words.	w/o (without), b/4 (before), b/c (because), c/o (care of)
6. Use standard symbols to stand for words.	i.e. (that is), # (number), ∴(therefore), = (equals)

EXERCISE F: Using Your Shorthand to Take Notes. Take a page from your notebook. Revise the page using at least ten abbreviations from the chart above and ones of your own.

DEVELOPING WRITING SKILLS. Evaluating Your Note-Taking Skills. Write a paragraph noting which methods work best for you and which need further work.

Skills Review and Writing Workshop

Basic Study Skills

CHECKING YOUR SKILLS

Write a summary of the following paragraph.

The Shakers are a religious sect that arose in England during the eighteenth century. They were named for the emotional shaking that formed part of their religious services. Led by Ann Lee, a small group of Shakers emigrated to America. By 1840, they had established nineteen communities from Maine to Kentucky consisting of approximately 6000 members. The Shakers dedicated themselves to their religious beliefs and to the goal of creating a perfect society, or utopia, on earth. They believed in pacifism, feminism, celibacy, and sharing of property and goods. Shakers invented the clothespin and probably the circular saw. However, they are most widely known for their simple, elegant furniture. Following the Civil War, many Shakers were drawn by the Industrial Revolution to work and live in the large cities. The sect also declined because members did not believe in marriage or having children. Today only two Shaker communities remain in Maine and New Hampshire.

USING STUDY SKILLS IN WRITING
Writing an Outline of a Newspaper Article

Writing clear, effective outlines is an important study skill. Write a modified outline of a newspaper article by following these steps.

Prewriting: Select an article that interests you. Read the article at least twice and identify the main ideas and major details.

Writing: Write down the main ideas and major details in the form of a modified outline.

Revising: Look over your outline and make sure that all the important information has been included. After you have revised, proofread carefully.

Chapter 29

Critical- Thinking Skills

Every day you are called upon to make decisions in many different situations. Learning to think critically—to analyze, apply, and evaluate information—will help you to think clearly to make better decisions in school and in later life. In this chapter, you will learn and practice the skills involved in critical thinking.

Forms of Reasoning 29.1

There are two important skills you must use in critical thinking. First, you must determine if the information that you are analyzing is *reliable*. Second, you must analyze the way the information is presented by distinguishing between *valid* and *invalid* forms of reasoning.

Using Fact and Opinion

The first step in critical thinking is to analyze a statement to decide how *reliable* the information is. Information that is not reliable will only confuse your thinking.

Analyze material first to decide if it is reliable.

In order to determine whether or not the material is reliable, you must distinguish between *fact* and *opinion*.

Fact. A fact is the most reliable type of information because it can be *verified,* or proved true by objective means.

A fact can be verified in any one of several ways: records, experimentation, and personal observation. The method you choose will depend on the type of statement made.

FACT: The longer the mouse is deprived of food the more frantically it makes its way through the maze.

In attempting to verify a factual statement, you may find out that it is *not* true. For instance, even though the statement above is factual, you may find out that in your experiment the mouse becomes lethargic. Therefore, it is important actually to verify factual statements rather than assume they are true.

Opinion. Some statements cannot be proved true or false by objective means. However, these opinions may be *valid,* or reliable, even though they cannot be verified. Because opinions are subjective, that is, influenced by personal experiences and beliefs, listeners and readers must be especially critical in analyzing such statements. Here are three types of opinions.

PERSONAL FEELING: Surely there is life on Planet X.

JUDGMENT: Planet X is probably capable of sustaining human life because of the oxygen levels in its atmosphere.

PREDICTION: Within our lifetime, specimens brought back from the surface of Planet X will prove that life existed there.

The first opinion expresses a personal belief or feeling without offering any support and is therefore invalid. However, a reader or listener might give more weight to such an opinion, depending on the source. If the source were a person long involved in space science, the opinion might be more believable than if it came from a science-fiction writer. However, you should still look beyond the opinion—even the opinion of an expert—for some supporting evidence of its validity.

The second opinion, expressing a judgment, gives a reason for the opinion. Moreover, the reason is a fact that can be verified. When an opinion is supported by fact, it can be taken as valid, although in some cases (as in this one) more than one fact may be required in support.

The prediction can be proved true only if the future events mentioned come about. A prediction made by an authority may be given more weight than one made by an ordinary person, but you must suspend judgment until the evidence is in.

780

EXERCISE A: Analyzing Fact and Opinion Statements.
Identify each statement below as *fact* or *opinion*. For each fact,
list a source or method you could use to verify it. For each
opinion, write whether it is *valid* or *invalid* and why.

1. At sea level, water freezes at 0°C.
2. *Hamlet* is Shakespeare's longest play.
3. The information gathered by space-shuttle missions does
   not justify the high expenditures of the program.
4. The leaves on that maple tree turn red in the fall.
5. The Secretary of State has just resigned.
6. Children today are subject to greater stress than those in
   earlier times because fewer live with both natural parents.
7. Ingrid Bergman's finest role was as Elsa in *Casablanca*.
8. Katharine Hepburn, Henry Fonda, and Jane Fonda co-
   starred in *On Golden Pond*.
9. All of the houses on this street are too expensive.
10. Napoleon was born on the island of Corsica.

EXERCISE B: Evaluating Statements in Writing. Read the
editorial below and list the facts and opinions it contains. In
addition, note whether each opinion is valid or invalid.

> The little girl who had the spontaneity and spunk to ask the
> question that all of us want the answer to is gone. Samantha
> Smith, invited to visit Russia after she wrote a letter to Yuri An-
> dropov demanding to know what he was going to do to help
> keep peace in the world, is now beyond the fears of nuclear
> war.
>
> Samantha asked her question at the age of 10. She died at
> the age of thirteen in an airplane crash not really having an an-
> swer, but, at least, having discovered that mothers, fathers, and
> children in Russia feel just as threatened by the idea of nuclear
> war as we here do. Nevertheless Samantha Smith came to sym-
> bolize what every person wants: a world free from the threat of
> total devastation and destruction.

Using Valid Reasoning

Once you have verified facts and determined that opinions
are valid, the second skill you use in critical thinking is to analyze the way the information is presented. When you think crit-

ically, you think logically, or use valid reasoning, in order to draw valid conclusions from the material given.

Think logically to draw valid conclusions.

Reasoning is the process of putting facts together in a way that will lead to or support a conclusion. There are two main kinds of formal reasoning, *inductive* and *deductive*. Each is capable of producing valid conclusions when properly used and invalid ones when misused.

Inductive Reasoning. Inductive reasoning proceeds from specific facts to a conclusion, or generalization, based on those facts. A *valid generalization* is a statement supported by evidence and holds true in a large number of cases.

Suppose, for example, that you want to find out whether a basket contains sweet apples for eating or very tart ones for cooking. All of the apples look quite similar. You sample one and find it to be sweet and juicy. Your friend samples another with the same result. You try one more apple, and it tastes as good as the others. Reasoning inductively, you draw the conclusion that the apples in the basket are eating apples, not cooking apples. Of course, biting into one more apple could prove your generalization wrong, for you have sampled only three of many apples; but chances are, you are right. You could make your generalization more reliable by taking more samples. When you reason inductively, the more evidence you have, the sounder your generalization will be.

A generalization based on only a few facts or samples is not valid and is a type of logical fallacy called *hasty generalization*. For example, a motorist driving at fifty-five miles an hour is passed by several trucks. He concludes that truck drivers pay no heed to speed limits. The motorist's conclusion, based on only a few cases, is an example of hasty generalization. It does not take into account the many truck drivers on the same highway who may be observing the speed limit. The motorist may be correct but cannot be sure on the basis of only a few samples.

Besides being sufficiently numerous, samples for an inductive generalization should also be *typical*. For example, a traveler notices that all the Italians she meets at the Rome airport and later at her hotel speak English. She concludes that all Italians speak some English. Even though her generalization is based on a number of different examples, the people she observed are not typical of all Italians. People who work at airports and large hotels are more likely to speak other languages than people living in rural areas, who rarely meet foreigners. To find out the percentage of Italians who speak English would require the taking of a very large sample.

In inductive reasoning, evidence should lead clearly and unmistakably to the conclusion. A *non sequitur* (Latin for "it does not follow") is a logical fallacy that draws a conclusion that does not follow from the evidence given.

NON SEQUITUR: Congressmen are elected by the people. They make laws in Washington, D.C. They know what is best for the country.

The fact that congressmen are elected by the people to make laws does not mean that they always know or do what is right. The conclusion does not follow from the evidence that is given.

Deductive Reasoning. Induction starts with facts and proceeds to a general statement. *Deduction* starts with a general statement that is assumed to be true and applies that statement to a particular case. Examples of deductive reasoning appear in the axioms of geometry:

AXIOM: If A is equal to C and B is equal to C, then A is equal to B.

In deductive reasoning, the generalization does not have to be proved true; it is assumed to be true. The purpose of deduction is to determine whether a particular case fits the general rule. A deductive argument is typically stated in a three-part formula called a *syllogism* as shown in the following example.

SYLLOGISM: All mammals are warm-blooded.   (major premise)
Whales are mammals.   (minor premise)
Therefore, whales are warm-blooded.   (conclusion)

The first statement is the generalization called the *major premise*. The second statement, called the *minor premise,* relates the major premise to a specific case. The third statement is the conclusion, which should logically follow from the two premises. If the premises of a syllogism are true and properly worded, the conclusion is sound.

783

1. Is the major premise true? (Could it have been arrived at inductively through studying enough examples?)
2. Is the fact stated in the minor premise true?
3. Does the conclusion follow logically from the premises?

A logical fallacy that sometimes occurs in deductive reasoning is called *begging the question,* also called circular reasoning. A person commits this error by restating the major premise as the conclusion without supplying facts or evidence.

BEGGING THE QUESTION: Michelle is popular because she is well liked.

The major premise, "Michelle is popular," is merely restated in different words, "she is well liked," while appearing to explain it. There is no minor premise given such as "Popular people are leaders" that leads to the conclusion, "Michelle is popular because she is a leader."

Other Forms of Reasoning. In addition to induction and deduction, there are two other forms of reasoning used to draw valid conclusions: *cause and effect* and *analogy.*

Cause and Effect. A cause-and-effect sequence is one in which something is caused by one or more events that happened previously. False cause-and-effect reasoning makes a connection between two unrelated events.

FALSE CAUSE: Mr. Ruiz won a million dollars in the lottery. A week later he won two thousand dollars. His good luck the first time made him lucky again.

The cause-and-effect sequence in this statement is false because there is no evidence that anything other than luck made Mr. Ruiz win money the second time.

Analogy. An analogy is a comparison of two things that are alike in a number of important ways. A good analogy can promote understanding of something unfamiliar by comparing it with something familiar. A false analogy ignores obvious and important differences between the things compared.

FALSE ANALOGY: A high school principal compares his daily routine to the function of a circus ringmaster.

784

EXERCISE C: Analyzing Forms of Reasoning. Identify the form of reasoning (inductive or deductive reasoning, cause and effect, analogy) found in each of the following statements and explain whether it is valid or invalid.

1. America in the 1930's was like the Roman Empire whose economic conditions brought about its collapse.
2. The Roman Empire collapsed after a period of great prosperity. We must guard against too much prosperity in this country or risk suffering a similar fate.
3. This looks like an aspirin bottle, and the pills in it look like aspirin. I guess I can take two for my headache.
4. All of the houses on Maple Street were damaged by the hurricane. The Brodys' house is on Maple Street. Their house must have been damaged.
5. It has been below freezing for three nights in a row, but the water in this pail beside the garage hasn't frozen. It must have antifreeze or alcohol in it.
6. When I visited Wilmington, Delaware, last summer, I heard several people pronounce *greasy* to rhyme with *easy*. I guess that is part of the Wilmington dialect.
7. All tigers are carnivores. Most humans are carnivores. Therefore, most humans are tigers.
8. The importing of inexpensive foreign products costs thousands of American jobs and should be stopped by imposing high tariffs.
9. All of the teachers at our school are college graduates. Mrs. Speare teaches at our school. Mrs. Speare must be a college graduate.
10. All humans are bipeds. An ostrich is a biped. An ostrich is a human.

DEVELOPING WRITING SKILLS: Analyzing and Evaluating Writing. Carefully read the following passage. Analyze each statement and decide whether the information is reliable and the author's reasoning valid. Then evaluate how objectively and logically the author has presented the information.

Early in this century, the trumpeter swan had become an emblem of our vanishing wilderness. Only fifty years ago biologists feared the worst for *Cygnus buccinator*—imminent extinction.

Centuries of hunting the majestic bird for its skin and pure white feathers apparently had reduced the once widespread population, found only in North America, to small pockets of survivors. A 1932 horseback census found sixty-nine birds, believed at the time to be all that remained in the United States.

But a swan song was premature. By 1980, its status had registered a significant turnabout. Former supervisor of waterfowl for the United States, wildlife biologist Jim King, observed a trumpeter population past all expectation. Estimates place its numbers today at about ten thousand.

29.2 Language and Thinking

In addition to evaluating the validity of information and analyzing the reasoning behind the author's presentation, a critical thinker must also be attentive to the ways speakers and writers use language to convey their thoughts.

Uses of Language

Critical thinking demands that you distinguish between language that presents material clearly and honestly and language that intentionally attempts to misrepresent ideas and manipulate emotions.

Learn to identify different uses of language.

Denotation and Connotation. Speakers or writers interested simply in conveying information usually have a neutral attitude toward their subject and will use language in its *denotative,* or literal sense. A speaker or writer who wants subtly to influence the audience's attitude will use more *connotative* language, or words with negative or positive associations surrounding them.

DENOTATION: The speaker offered moderate criticism of the President's policy.

CONNOTATIONS: The speaker offered gentle criticism of the President's policy.

The speaker offered bland criticism of the President's policy.

786

In the first example, *moderate* has the denotative meaning of "temperate; neither too strong nor too weak." *Gentle* has a slightly positive connotation, suggesting that the speaker was using intentional restraint. *Bland,* on the other hand, has a somewhat negative connotation and suggests that the speaker was too timid and therefore ineffectual. Being alert to connotations can help you analyze and evaluate a message more effectively.

Special Uses of Language. Careful language choices ensure that a message will be clear and forceful. Certain choices also are used to emphasize ideas or to set the tone of the message.

Irony. Irony occurs when the literal, or denotative, meaning of a word or a statement is opposite to the intended meaning. In using irony, the author does not intend to deceive the audience. Rather, irony uses language to make totally clear the discrepancy between what is said and what is really meant. Irony is revealed in the tone of the material and can vary from great subtlety to bitter sarcasm.

EXAMPLE: The directions he gave us were so clear that we were
            lost for three hours.

The example of irony above is an overstatement since clearly given directions would not make people get lost. The word *clear* is used to emphasize how unclear the directions were.

Understatement. Opposite to irony is the technique of understating what is really meant. Understatement usually involves the use of opposites to emphasize a statement—either by using an opposite word from what is expected or by denying the opposite of a statement.

EXAMPLE: The newlyweds hired professionals to landscape the
            grounds and clean all thirty-five rooms before they
            moved into their cottage.

The writer establishes the idea of wealthy people moving into a mansion and then mocks the statement by using an understated word—*cottage*.

Misuses of Language. Occasionally, a speaker or writer intentionally makes language choices that lead the audience to an illogical, unreasonable, or overly emotional response. A thoughtful, critical reader will be alert to such misuses and will question the user's motives and credibility.

Jargon. Specialized and technical language is important, in certain technical areas, professions, and hobbies. Sometimes, though, speakers or writers introduce jargon—technical and specialized vocabulary—into ordinary situations in an attempt to impress or intimidate the audience.

Restating jargon in direct, simple language is the first step in finding the real meaning of a statement.

JARGON: The company is finalizing a game plan to facilitate employee feedback to its supervisory personnel.

DIRECT LANGUAGE: The company has planned a way for employees to share ideas with their supervisors.

The audience must take such a statement in overall context to decide whether the author is trying intentionally to confuse or inflate his or her own position or whether the jargon is simply part of the author's normal use of language.

Euphemism. A speaker or writer sometimes uses an indirect expression or one thought to be more polite to avoid the chance of offending an audience. Euphemisms that overly inflate or intentionally mislead are inappropriate.

EUPHEMISM: The governor's passing caused much sorrow.

PLAIN LANGUAGE: The governor's death caused much sorrow.

The euphemism "passing" is appropriate when trying to spare the feelings of a family member of the dead governor; in a lecture on "The Reality of Death," it would be quite out of place.

EXERCISE A: Analyzing Uses of Language. Identify each use of language below as *denotation, connotation, irony, understatement, jargon,* or *euphemism.*

1. The acting and dialogue have all the sparks of a damp match, and the sets and costumes are as colorful as a root cellar.
2. Such aberrant behaviors are symptomatic of severe personality disturbance and require treatment in a residential facility.
3. Dr. Harley was laid to rest in the family plot.
4. Jesse found three fried chicken legs, a quart of milk, two apples, and half a box of cookies a satisfying snack.

788

5. The director assembled the entire staff to tell them she was being put out to graze.
6. The penniless widow, alone and dying in her shabby, one-room apartment, felt her life was not without its difficulties.
7. Rabble-rousers incited the crowd to storm the embassy in protest.
8. Having polled his constituents and conferred with staff, the senator announced that he would seek another term.
9. Helpless infants and puppies will thrive in a warm, secure, loving home.
10. Consistent application of preventive measures would obviate expensive and time-consuming rehabilitation.

EXERCISE B: Evaluating and Improving Uses of Language. Carefully read the following passage, analyzing uses of connotation, jargon, or euphemism. Then rewrite it in clear, honest language.

Improved health care, better nutrition, and changes in life style have led to a national problem approaching crisis proportions: a dramatic increase in the aged population. At the same time that many seniors live in isolation, with decreasing financial resources and increasingly physical limitations, residential-care facilities are bulging with others no longer able to care for themselves. Families and counselors alike are baffled by the dilemma of balancing the need of independence with the need for assistance. Programs must be implemented to assimilate this segment of society and utilize their not inconsiderable experience and expertise rather than isolate them and relegate them to personal diminishment and deterioration. Creative and cooperative programs involving families, social-service agencies, and health-care providers are essential if our aging parents and grandparents are to have in their declining years the quality of life they have earned throughout their lives.

DEVELOPING WRITING SKILLS: Eliminating Misuses of Language. Choose an advertisement from a current magazine and identify any instances of inappropriate connotation, jargon, euphemism, and other misuses of language. Rewrite the advertisement in clear, honest language.

Skills Review and Writing Workshop

Critical-Thinking Skills

CHECKING YOUR SKILLS

Rewrite the passage for correcting examples of unreliable information, invalid reasoning, and misuses of language.

Advertising seems to offer facts about products, but it usually speaks mainly to our hidden feelings. Everybody wants to feel superior to someone. Advertising hints that Product X will set you apart from the common herd. Do you dread being lonely? Cynical copywriters try to con you into believing that you have only to pop the cap off a bottle of Festa Cola to be surrounded by attractive, fun-loving companions. Feel a bit insecure in the kitchen? Advertisers (who have spent megabucks to find out) know that you do. They urge you to choose their mix instead of baking your cake from scratch. They let you console yourself that you are saving time, but they know their glib promise of a "perfect cake every time" is what moved you at the point of purchase. Advertisements appear to speak to our good sense and taste; but they really whisper to our hidden desires and fears.

USING CRITICAL-THINKING SKILLS IN WRITING
Writing a Review of a Movie or a Television Program

Write a critical review of a movie or television program.

Prewriting. Make notes on the main points you want to comment on in your review. Make lists of all aspects you need to cover: theme, characters, plot, costumes, and sets.

Writing. Open your review with a topic sentence introducing your feelings about the show. Use denotation and facts to describe the show objectively. Use connotation and valid opinion to convey your feelings and judgments. Close your review with a sentence to evaluate the show.

Revising. Rework your review to eliminate unsupported opinions, invalid arguments, and inappropriate use of language. After you have revised, proofread carefully.

30

Reading and Test-Taking Skills

After high school, you may never be required to write a summary of a textbook chapter or identify the tone of a newspaper editorial. However, the skills that you use to perform these tasks are ones that you will continue to draw on throughout your life. In this chapter you will practice skills to help you read more effectively and more critically. You will also practice skills to improve your performance on standardized tests.

Reading Skills 30.1

Reading skills are ones that you will continue to use in college and on the job. In college, you will apply your reading skills to textbooks. On the job, the reading matter may be a manual or a handbook, but it is still your basic text. Reading will require a mastery of information and the ability to think and read critically and to use various reading speeds.

Reading Textbooks

Textbooks are organized so that you can learn the information they contain with ease and efficiency. Textbooks are divided into segments that contain reading and study aids that help you understand and remember the information they contain.

Use textbook reading and study aids to help you understand and remember what you read.

Reading Aids. The organization of a textbook allows you to find the information you need quickly and easily. Listed below are the reading aids that most textbooks contain and the information each provides. Not all textbooks contain all of the reading aids below, nor will you need to use all of them regularly.

TEXTBOOK READING AIDS	
Table of Contents	Located at the beginning of a book. Shows how the book is organized by listing units and chapters with their page numbers. Offers a quick overview of the book.
Preface or Introduction	Located at the beginning of a book before or after the table of contents. States the author's purpose in writing the book and may give suggestions for using it.
Index	Located at the back of a book. Lists alphabetically all topics covered in the book and the pages on which they can be found. Makes it possible to locate any information quickly.
Glossary	Located at the back of a book. Gives an alphabetical list of all the specialized terms used in the book and defines them. Can be used for quick definitions.
Appendix	Located at the back of a book. Includes such things as charts, lists, documents, or other materials related to the subject of the book. Acts as a reference source.
Bibliography	Located at the back of a book. Includes lists of books and articles that the author has used or referred to in writing the book. Many of the entries may be useful in follow-up study or for research projects.

Study Aids. Having a strategy for reading your textbooks will allow you to use them most efficiently. You can best use the organization of your textbooks in your studying by mastering the following six skills: *S*urvey, *Q*uestion, *R*ead, *R*ecord, *R*ecite, and *R*eview abbreviated as SQ4R. By using the SQ4R method, you are making use of all the textbook reading aids. You are structuring your learning for increased comprehension. The following chart summarizes the SQ4R method.

USING THE SQ4R METHOD	
Survey	Preview the material you are going to read. Notice these features: chapter title, headings, subheadings, introduction, summary, and questions or exercises.
Question	Turn each heading into a question to help you think about what will be covered under that heading. Ask the questions *who, what, when, where,* and *why* about it.
Read	Search for the answers to the questions that have been posed in the step above.
Recite	Orally or mentally recall the questions and their related answers.
Record	Take notes to further reinforce information. List the main ideas and the major details.
Review	Review the material on a regular basis using some or all of the steps above.

EXERCISE A: Designing a Textbook. Using the reading selection from Exercise B on page 794, make a preliminary design for a biology or an anatomy textbook that could contain that material. Include at least five of the textbook reading aids listed on page 792 in the textbook you design.

EXERCISE B: Using the SQ4R Method. Using the SQ4R method, study the part of a chapter on the following page from a biology textbook. Then evaluate which of the six steps you have mastered and which you need to improve.

Chapter 26 THE NERVOUS SYSTEM

All living things must be able to respond to the external environment in order to survive. The nervous system is the process that allows living things to inform them of their environment and to respond to it. The nervous system is like a complex mission control center that receives and relays messages very quickly.

The Senses

Human beings respond to their environment by means of the five sense organs. They are the *ears, eyes, nose, skin,* and *tongue.* The sense organs are constantly receiving information from the environment and sending it to the brain.

26.1 The Ear

The ear is a complicated mechanism. It can distinguish between various pitches and qualities of sound. The ear is sensitive to vibrations within the 20- to 20,000-movements-per-second range.

The ear is divided into three parts: the *outer ear,* the *middle ear,* and the *inner ear.* The bones in these sections of the ear transmit the sound vibrations from the eardrum to the membrane-window covering the inner ear.

It is important that humans have two ears instead of one. Because of this we can tell the directions from which sound comes. A sound actually enters one ear a split second sooner than the other ear. The brain picks up this split second difference and from it tells us the direction the sound is coming from.

In addition to detecting sound, the ear also helps us to keep our balance. This balance function is attributed to the semicircular canals of the ear.

Varying Your Reading Style

By the time you are a senior in high school your reading style should be fairly well established. *Phrase reading, skimming,* and *scanning* are individual reading skills that fit together to make your reading style. Knowledge of your reading style is as important as understanding your learning style or style of communication. You need to know which reading style is appropriate to use depending on your purpose in reading. In this way no time or effort is wasted and comprehension remains high.

Change your reading style whenever your purpose in reading changes.

In order to adjust your reading style, you need to know how to use each of the styles explained in the chart below.

TYPES OF READING STYLES			
Style	**Definition**	**Purpose**	**Comprehension**
Phrase Reading	Reading groups of words in order to understand all the material	For studying, solving problems, and following directions	Lowest acceptable rate: 70–80%
Skimming	Skipping words in order to read rapidly and get a quick overview	For previewing, reviewing, and locating information	Lowest acceptable rate: 40–50%
Scanning	Reading in order to locate a particular piece of information	For research, reviewing, and finding information	Lowest acceptable rate: 100% (for item found)

EXERCISE C: Evaluating Your Reading Style. After one week of using the reading styles in the chart on this page, answer the questions below.

1. Do you consciously change your reading rate and style when there is a change in your purpose for reading?
2. Do you regularly skim newspapers and magazines in order to locate the articles you want to read more carefully?
3. Do you skim to get an overview prior to a careful reading?
4. Do you know when you need to reread a particular passage?
5. Can you maintain interest in reading for at least a sustained thirty-minute period?

Reading Critically

There are several levels of reading comprehension. On the first level you read to understand main ideas and details. On the next levels you read critically to analyze, apply, and evaluate the ideas. Critical reading is really critical thinking, a process of searching for and creating meaning. It is the ability to ask relevant questions, analyze, and make judgments about what you read.

Read critically in order to question, analyze, and evaluate what you read.

Reading critically is part of a process in which you put together the earlier-learned skills of comprehension and knowledge of material in order to ask questions and attempt to answer them to get below the surface meaning. The chart below lists skills you need to read critically.

SKILLS FOR READING CRITICALLY
1. The willingness to *suspend judgment* about the meaning of what you read until enough facts are gathered to make an informed decision
2. The ability to *ask questions* in order to determine the meaning of what you read
3. The ability to *test the questions* about meaning using methods of logic and reasoned thinking
4. The ability to *evaluate* the meaning of what you read based on reasoned thinking and personal experience

Suspend Judgment. When you come to a new experience you apply your past experience to help you understand the new. It is difficult to suspend your judgment when someone's viewpoint is different from yours. However, when you read critically you need to refrain from evaluating an author's meaning until you have more information. You adopt a questioning attitude so that you can find out more about what an author means. After you have more information, your earlier ideas may be reinforced, or you may decide to revise them. You may agree or disagree with the writer, but your judgment will be an informed one.

Ask Questions. Every author chooses words with a context in mind, that is a *purpose* and an *audience*. Often the author's purpose is not directly stated, and you must infer it from clues found in the reading. After you suspend judgment about meaning, you need to ask questions about how an author chooses words to present ideas to you, the audience.

The following chart gives questions to help you uncover meaning. A full discussion of the terms used below can be found in Chapter 29, Critical-Thinking Skills.

ASKING CRITICAL-READING QUESTIONS

1. Who is the *audience* the author is addressing? Does knowing the audience tell you the author's purpose in writing?

2. What is the author's *purpose* in writing? Is it to entertain, to inform, to persuade?

3. Does the author *directly state* the purpose in writing or is the purpose *implied*?

4. If the author's purpose is *implied,* how does he or she use the following to help you uncover meaning?

   a. Does the author use *connotation,* or suggested meaning of words, to make you feel a certain way? What are the words, and what response do you have to them?

   b. Does the author distinguish between *fact and opinion?* Are opinions backed up by relevant facts? Is opinion disguised as fact?

   c. Does the author use *understatement* or *irony* to imply another meaning from the one stated and expect you to understand the intended meaning?

   d. Does the author use *jargon, slanted words,* or *euphemism* to conceal the real meaning behind words?

   e. Does the author present ideas in a *reasoned, logical manner?* Do conclusions follow from the facts presented? Are like things being compared? Is emotion rather than reason being used to persuade you?

When you become more adept at asking questions about what you read, you have a larger number of questions and your questions have a direction that help you find answers quickly.

Test Questions. After you have asked yourself questions about the way an author uses words to reveal meaning, you can test your questions to come to a conclusion about their validity. If you decide that the author's purpose in writing is to explain or to persuade, you have asked questions about the logical way that the author has presented ideas. The main way to test your questions is to analyze the author's ideas using *inductive* or *deductive* reasoning. The two methods of reasoning are explained in Chapter 29, *Critical-Thinking Skills.*

Evaluate. The final part of the process of critical reading is to evaluate or make judgments about the worth of what you read. You can make judgments based on two criteria, or standards for judgment. The first is an external criterion: How well does the author accomplish his or her purpose? You use the answers to the questions you have asked to determine this. The second is an internal criterion: How relevant is the work based on your personal response? After suspending judgment and asking questions to help uncover meaning, you now look at the work as a whole and evaluate what it means to you.

CRITERIA FOR EVALUATING READING

1. Does the author accomplish his or her purpose? Is there an honest use of language to reveal meaning or does the author use techniques to distort meaning? (Use the answers to the questions on page 797 to help you evaluate.)

2. Does the author have something of value to say? What are the implications of the author's ideas? How are they related to other ideas?

3. Does the author have something valuable to say to you? How do the author's ideas increase your understanding or change your way of looking at things?

EXERCISE D: Applying Critical Reading Skills. Read the passage on the following page using the four critical-reading skills you studied in this section: *suspend judgment, ask questions, test questions,* and *evaluate.* Write your answers to the questions listed in the charts on page 797 and the one above.

Contemporary astronomy is ordinarily at least as much of an observational as a theoretical science. Sooner or later on the basis of observation and analysis, what astronomers detect finds its way into theory, or the theory is modified to accept it.

Neutrino astronomy doesn't fit this pattern. Its highly developed body of theory grew thirty years without any possibility of verification. And despite the construction, finally, of a string of elaborate observatories, some buried in the earth from southern India to Utah to South Africa, the last five years as well have produced not a single, validated observation of an extraterrestrial neutrino.

It is a testament to the persistence of the neutrino astronomers and to the strength of their theoretical base that their intensive search for these ghost particles still goes on.

The neutrino is a particle with a vanishingly small mass and no charge. Having no charge, it does not interact with the fields around which most particle detection experiments are built; it can be detected only inferentially, by identification of the debris left following its rare interaction with matter.

Even such indirect observations need elaborate and highly sensitive equipment which didn't begin to go into place until about five years ago. But the goal is worth the effort: once detected, extraterrestrial neutrinos will provide solid, first-hand information on the sources and conditions that spawned them.

Scientists are sure of this because of the sophistication of experiments on neutrino reactions in particle accelerators and other earth-bound apparatus. These experiments have been refined rigorously over the years, and neutrino theory based on them is an integral part of modern physics.

The existence of neutrinos was first postulated in the early 1930s, in order to explain a form of radioactive decay in which a beta particle—an electron—is emitted. Certain quantities that physicists insist should be the same after an interaction as before—momentum, energy, and angular momentum—could only be conserved if another particle of zero charge and negligible mass were emitted.

DEVELOPING WRITING SKILLS: Evaluating Your Reading Skills. After a week of practice, write a paragraph about your reading skills. Answer the following questions.

1. In which of your textbooks have you found the most helpful reading aids? Which aids have you found helpful?
2. How successful are you at using the SQ4R method?
3. How do you adjust your reading style depending on your purpose in reading?
4. What materials have you recently read where critical reading was a necessity?
5. How successful are you at asking critical reading questions? Which questions do you have least difficulty asking and answering? Which do you have most difficulty?

30.2 Standardized Tests

Taking tests does not end with school but occurs in many situations in later life as well. Sometimes the test may be as insignificant as a test for a driver's license (which can always be taken over at a later time). Sometimes it may be as crucial as a test to get into college or an employment test for a job that you need. Such tests are generally standardized and consist of multiple-choice questions.

Taking Standardized Tests

You cannot prepare for standardized tests by studying specific content. Instead, you must learn and practice basic skills, techniques, and approaches to understanding and answering the types of questions generally included on such tests.

Prepare for standardized tests by studying consistently and reading widely.

In educational and employment situations, the standardized tests you are most likely to encounter from now on will be one of three types. Achievement tests, such as the California Achievement Tests or the English Composition Test, are designed to determine the level of proficiency the test-taker has achieved in a given subject area. Aptitude tests, such as the

SAT and ACT, are intended to compare one test-taker's skill in reading, writing, vocabulary, and mathematics with the skills of others across the country. Employment tests are designed to determine the test-taker's suitability for a particular job.

Since all types of standardized tests follow basically the same format, learning how to take one type should help you to take them all. The following suggested strategies will help you use your time most efficiently to preview the test and to answer the test questions.

STANDARDIZED TEST-TAKING STRATEGIES

Preview the Test	1. Write your name on each sheet of paper you will hand in.
	2. Before beginning each section of the test, skim through the section and figure out how much time you can give to each set of questions. Questions that are worth more points or are more difficult require more time. On the SAT and ACT, each question is of equal value.
Answer the Questions	1. If you are allowed to use scratch paper, jot down any information you want to remember.
	2. Unless you are penalized for guessing, answer all questions on the test. The ACT does not penalize for guessing. The SAT takes off one-quarter of a point for each incorrect answer in order to discourage random guessing.
	3. Answer the easy questions first. *Lightly* mark any questions you have difficulty with and come back to them later.
	4. Unless specifically directed, give only one answer to each question. Choose the *best* answer of those given.
	5. Go with your first response to a question unless you have a good reason to change it.
Proofread	1. If you finish before time is called, check to see if you have followed directions completely.
	2. Reread questions and answers. Make sure that you have answered all the questions.

801

Answering Vocabulary Questions

Most standardized tests for employment or college entrance include a separate and extensive section focusing exclusively on vocabulary. Employers and college admissions officers place a great deal of emphasis on such tests because research has shown a high correlation between vocabulary test results and the potential for success on the job and in school. Typical questions call for the identification of antonyms and the completion of sentences and analogies. Becoming familiar with the types of questions included in standardized vocabulary tests can greatly enhance your chances of success—both in achieving a good score on the tests and in reaching the goals that have led you to take the test.

Learn the types of vocabulary questions and the strategies for answering them.

Antonym Questions. An antonym is a word with a meaning opposite that of a given word. Antonym questions test your knowledge of word meanings. You are asked to choose a word or phrase that is most opposite in meaning to that of a given word. The chart below gives suggested strategies to use when you answer antonym questions.

ANSWERING ANTONYM QUESTIONS
1. If you know the meaning of the given word, think of a word that is opposite in meaning *before* you look at the choices.
2. Look for a word among the answer choices that is as opposite as possible and matches the word you have in mind.
3. Look for a word that is the same part of speech as the given word.
4. Give a different antonym for each possible choice if you are having difficulty eliminating choices.

EXAMPLE: Select the word whose meaning is most opposite to that of the capitalized word.

     1. EXONERATE (A) onerous (B) acquit (C) arrest
                             (D) condemn (E) accuse

    Answer: (D) condemn

Analogy Questions. A verbal analogy is an expression of a relationship between two words. Analogy questions ask you to select two words that are related in the same way as a given pair. Below are strategies to use with analogy questions.

ANSWERING ANALOGY QUESTIONS
1. Define both words in the initial pair. If you cannot define both words, skip the question and go on to the next one.
2. Define how the initial pair of words are related to each other. See the following chart for analogy patterns.
3. Make certain that you keep each pair of words in the order given. If you reverse the order you will come up with an incorrect answer.
4. Make certain that the relationship of the parts of speech are the same for the pair you choose as they are in the initial pair.

EXAMPLE: Choose the pair of words whose relationship is most similar to that expressed by the capitalized pair.

2. BONES : LIGAMENT : :

(A) break : stretch   (B) muscle : tendon
(C) fat : cell   (D) knuckle : finger
(E) knee : joint

Answer: (B) knee : joint

Identifying the relationship between the established pair is the most important part of solving analogy problems. The following chart lists the most common relationships.

COMMON ANALOGY PATTERNS	
Relationship	**Examples**
Synonyms	calm : tranquil : : last : final
Antonyms	quiet : noisy : : innocent : guilty
Similar categories	carrot : potato : : hemlock : spruce
Main and subcategories	tuber : potato : : conifer : hemlock
Sub- and main categories	potato : tuber : : hemlock : conifer

Whole to part	wheel : rim : : tree : branch
Part to whole	rim : wheel : : branch : tree
Product and substance	cheese : milk : : wine : grapes
Using categories	surgeon : scalpel : : writer : pen
Different forms of the same word	ring : rung : : choose : chosen
Grammatical combination	man : woman : : masculine : feminine

Sentence Completion Questions. Sentence completion questions test your vocabulary and your reading comprehension. One or more words in a statement are left blank. You then fill in the word or words that best complete the statement.

The chart below provides strategies you can use for sentence completion questions.

ANSWERING SENTENCE COMPLETION QUESTIONS

1. Read the sentence and try to fill in the blank(s) before you look at the choices.
2. Make use of signal words such as *however, also, because, as a result, instead, before* to predict the correct answer.
3. Make certain that each word or pair of words you choose follows the part of speech required in the statement.
4. Watch for "a" or "an" before a blank to give you a clue whether or not to look for a word beginning with a vowel.
5. Read all possible answers in the sentence blank(s) to see if they make sense.

EXAMPLE: Choose the word or pair of words that best completes the meaning of each sentence.

3. Unable to confirm any of his symptoms, Greg's parents suspected that their shy son was _____ illness to avoid performing in the school play.

(A) developing   (B) fainting   (C) feigning
(D) camouflaging   (E) having

Answer: (C) feigning

EXERCISE A: Locating Antonyms. Use the chart on page 802 to help you find the word opposite in meaning.

1. MALIGN   (A) criticize (B) tumorous (C) attack (D) praise (E) assist
2. INDIGENOUS   (A) indigent (B) native (C) alien (D) lazy (E) whole
3. PRECIPITOUS   (A) rainy (B) level (C) steep (D) dry (E) sloped
4. SECULAR   (A) clerical (B) tomb (C) laic (D) round (E) spiritual
5. DEPRAVITY   (A) loss (B) corruption (C) honor (D) innocence (E) mortality
6. TACITURN   (A) silent (B) calm (C) talkative (D) tactful (E) late
7. RUDDY   (A) healthy (B) rugged (C) rosy (D) pale (E) round
8. FORTUITOUS   (A) incidentally (B) planned (C) fortified (D) accidental (E) frank
9. BLANDISHMENT   (A) insult (B) mildness (C) flattery (D) blemish (E) blandness
10. AMORPHOUS   (A) formless (B) simple (C) incoherent (D) rudimentary (E) well-defined

EXERCISE B: Completing Analogies. Use the chart on page 803 to help you complete the following analogies.

1. ARCHIPELAGO : ISLAND : :
   (A) constellation : star (B) symphony : orchestra
   (C) mountain : hill (D) chapter : book (E) lions : pride
2. GUITAR : PICK : :
   (A) bow : violin (B) keys : piano (C) clarinet : reed
   (D) drum : drumsticks (E) puck : hockey
3. IMPOVERISHED : AFFLUENT : :
   (A) poverty : fluency (B) poor : honest (C) rich : wealth
   (D) wholesale : retail (E) depleted : enriched
4. ARROW : ARCHER : :
   (A) choir : organ (B) sea : sailor (C) needle : tailor
   (D) actor : stage (E) song : singer
5. SPEECH : INTRODUCTION : :
   (A) gun : race (B) overture : act (C) book : preface
   (D) preamble : Constitution (E) speaker : audience

6. WOMEN : WOMAN : :
   (A) boys : men   (B) deer : doe   (C) mouse : mice
   (D) oxen : ox   (E) potatoes : potato
7. PAINTER : STUDIO : :
   (A) lawyer : court   (B) office : secretary   (C) brush : oil
   (D) sculpture : museum   (E) teacher : chalkboard
8. PECAN : NUT : :
   (A) apple : fruit   (B) house : domicile   (C) bean : coffee
   (D) clarinet : reed   (E) meat : sandwich
9. AVARICE : GREED : :
   (A) candor : honesty   (B) thrifty : frugal   (C) grim : lurid
   (D) precaution : accident   (E) valor : cowardice
10. ALGEBRA : GEOMETRY : :
    (A) plane : solid   (B) shape : number   (C) botany : zo-
    ology   (D) theorem : equation   (E) school : subject

EXERCISE C: Completing Sentences. Use the chart on page 804 to help you complete each of the sentences below.

1. After the bloody battle, the troops were _____ and retreated to their homeland.
   (A) victorious   (B) vanquished   (C) cremated
   (D) jubilant   (E) honored
2. The community objected that the proposed highway would
   be a _____ rather than a boon for the area.
   (A) favor   (B) panacea   (C) disaster   (D) help
   (E) courtesy
3. The increased use of rayon, nylon, and other _____ fab-
   rics created a need for new laundry products.
   (A) magic   (B) delicate   (C) new   (D) natural
   (E) synthetic
4. The suspect's alibi would not stand up in court because
   there was no one to _____ it.
   (A) challenge   (B) avow   (C) refute   (D) arrest
   (E) corroborate
5. The reporter's _____ hostility to the President's plan angered the White House staff.
   (A) overt   (B) occasional   (C) subtle   (D) covert
   (E) tired
6. Since neither side would concede on any issue, a federal
   _____ panel will attempt to avert a strike.

(A) arbitration (B) judiciary (C) election (D) social
(E) injunction
7. Each invitation was hand-lettered by a _____.
   (A) graphologist (B) printing press (C) calligrapher
   (D) colophon (E) typist
8. The actor was _____ in his portrayal of Abraham Lincoln.
   (A) convinced (B) obvious (C) credulous (D) identical (E) credible
9. A spoonerism is a _____ of the initial sounds of two
   words, as in "a weaky squeal" for "a squeaky wheel."
   (A) combination (B) transposition (C) confusion
   (D) omission (E) change
10. Perkins accepted the loss as one of life's _____ and
    hoped for better luck tomorrow.
    (A) vicissitudes (B) vestiges (C) holidays (D) out-
    rages (E) whimsies

Answering Reading Comprehension Questions

Reading comprehension questions test how carefully you read and how well you interpret what you read. Such questions generally fall into one of five basic categories: main-idea questions, detail questions, inference questions, definition questions, and questions about tone, purpose, and form.

Learn to identify and answer the six types of reading comprehension questions.

Before examining the specific types of questions found on reading tests, read the following passage carefully as if you were taking a test. You will use this passage in working with the comprehension questions.

Speed Skiing

Downhill skiing and speed skiing involve many of the same skills: balance, reflexes, a deft touch, and nerve. But downhill skiers make turns that keep their speed down to about 80 mph while speed skiers can attain speeds up to 124 mph. Since speed skiers just go straight down a mountain as fast as possible, speed skiing can certainly be considered one of the world's most thrilling sports.

807

The speed skier reaches high speeds quickly because of the pitch of the mountains being skied. However, to get to these speeds, the skier must be able to withstand vibrations that start in the tips of the skis. These vibrations grow more violent with acceleration, move back to the boots, and then up to the legs. Soon the skier's entire body is being severely rattled. The skis twist and bend insanely, and the air rips at the skier's arms. At about 110 mph, though, the vibration stops, and the howling moves behind the skier. It is as though he or she has broken the sound barrier.

After passing through a timing trap, where speed is measured, skiers must worry about slowing down at the end of the course. Gravitational forces on the body are enormous there, because the pitch of the course changes from steep to nearly flat in a short distance. The best speed skiers reach this so-called "transition" at about 110 mph, and they feel as though steel bands are strapped across their chests, trying to pull them down and back. To avoid falls in transition, skiers have to keep their skis as straight as possible and then do a sit-up when they slow down to about 100 mph. If they use too much pressure on the ski tips, they can go headfirst into the deadliest type of fall in speed skiing. A somersault at 100 mph can snap a spinal cord.

Because of the high speed being traveled by speed skiers, they need specially designed gear. The gear consists of an aerodynamic helmet and a slippery wet suit to cut wind resistance. The suit is sealed to the skier's boots and has airfoils from knee to heel. The suit is also nonporous and made with attached hand coverings. This suit would be illegal to wear in downhill skiing because it would have little braking effect on a downed skier who is sliding.

Since the present speed skiing record is 124 mph, several competitors are trying to break it by attaining speeds in the 130-mph range.—Adapted from Michael McRae

The key to finding the best answer to a question on a reading comprehension test is similar to the method of finding the correct answer on standardized vocabulary tests. Often the best procedure is to eliminate some answers by looking for answers that are clearly unrelated, illogical, or incorrect. Keep in mind the general strategies for eliminating incorrect answers listed in the chart on the following page.

GENERAL STRATEGY FOR ANSWERING QUESTIONS

Type of Answer	Reason to Eliminate
Too narrow	Answer covers too small a portion of the reading.
Too wide	Answer covers a wider area than the reading.
Irrelevant	Answer has nothing to do with the reading or is relevant to the reading but not to the particular question.
Incorrect	Answer distorts or disputes the facts in the reading.
Illogical	Answer is not backed up by the facts in the reading.
Similar form of answer	At a quick glance, the answer looks similar to the true answer.
Opposite form of answer	Through the use of such words as *not* or *untrue*, the answer is made the reverse of the true answer.

Main-Idea Questions. A main-idea question asks you to determine the subject of an entire passage. A main-idea question may require you to retitle the passage, to state the topic, to choose a topic sentence, or to select the sentence that best tells what the passage is about. You may find it helpful to skim the first and last paragraphs of the passage before answering this type of question since writers frequently state their topic at the beginning or at the end of a passage.

EXAMPLE: 1. Another title for the passage about speed skiing might be

 (A) Types of Skiing
 (B) Survival of the Fastest in Winter Sports
 (C) The Dangers of Speed Skiing
 (D) Training to Be a Speed Skier
 (E) Winter Sports

Answers: (A) Too wide (B) Too Narrow
 (C) Irrelevant (D) Correct (E) Too broad

809

Detail Questions. Detail questions are ones that you can generally count on getting right because the answer is actually in the selection and does not involve a personal judgment. However, in order to answer a detail question, you may sometimes need to put together information from two different sentences, or you may need to use comparison and contrast or do simple arithmetic.

EXAMPLE: 2. The difference in speeds obtained by an expert speed skier and an expert downhill skier is

(A) 10 mph   (B) 40 mph   (C) 44 mph
(D) 80 mph   (E) 124 mph

Answer: (C) 44 mph (The difference between 80 mph and 124 mph = 44 mph.)

Inference Questions. These are probably the most difficult questions to answer because you can never find the answer directly in the passage. Instead, you must piece together a number of facts and make a generalization based on these facts. Most inference questions include one of these key words: *think, predict, indicate, feel, probably, seem, imply, suggest, assume, infer,* and *most likely.* When you come upon a question that contains one of these words, look back at the selection to find the specific sentences that the question refers to. Then look there for factual clues that you can use to make a sound generalization. Remember, in answering an inference question you are really making a guess, but your guess must be based on facts from the passage you have read, not on your own opinions.

EXAMPLE: 3. The author's view of speed skiers is that they seem to be

(A) angry at the world   (B) fearless
(C) foolish   (D) overly ambitious
(E) fearsome

Answer: (B) fearless

Definition Questions. These are basically vocabulary questions about difficult words in a passage or about ordinary words that are used with a special meaning in the passage. Most often you will be able to arrive at the meaning of a word by examining its context, the words that surround it.

810

To answer a definition question, first locate the word to be defined in the passage. Carefully reread the sentence in which the word appears and try to determine the word's meaning. Then try substituting each of the possible answers in the sentence to see which is closest in meaning. Avoid choosing a word that looks or sounds like the word to be defined unless you have tested it in context.

EXAMPLE: 4. The word *nonporous* in the fourth paragraph means

        (A) tight (B) waterproof (C) slippery
        (D) green (E) loose

    Answer: (B) waterproof

Tone/Purpose Questions. This type of question asks you to determine how or why the writer wrote the passage. The tone of a passage reflects the writer's attitude toward both the subject and the audience. The purpose defines the effect the writer wishes to have on the audience. Understanding the tone of a passage can help you understand the author's purpose. Few writers have a neutral attitude toward their subjects, and most will convey to the reader—through their choice of words and the impression they create—one or more of the following tones.

SOME POSSIBLE TONES		
indifference	disappointment	indignation
appreciation	respect	hostility
admiration	approval	doubt
adoration	surprise	suspicion
optimism	anger	rage
pride	regret	pessimism
contempt	restraint	rejection
objectivity	irony	amusement

EXAMPLE: 5. The author's attitude toward speed skiers is one of

        (A) surprise (B) regret (C) admiration
        (D) irony (E) amusement

    Answer: (C) admiration

811

Form Questions. The form is the method of organization that a writer uses. As you read a passage, try to observe which of the following common patterns of organization the author has used. Some writers will use only one of the patterns, while others may use a combination.

COMMON ORGANIZATIONAL PATTERNS	
Logical sequence of events	Cause and effect
Comparison and contrast	Series of examples
Problem and solution	Order of importance
	Spatial order

EXAMPLE: 6. The speed skiing passage is organized by

      (A) spatial order (B) order of importance

      (C) problem and solution (D) cause and effect

      (E) series of examples

    Answer: (E) series of examples

The chart below lists strategies you can use for answering reading comprehension questions. Follow the steps listed in the chart to help you read the passage and answer the questions for Exercise D below and on page 813.

ANSWERING READING COMPREHENSION QUESTIONS
1. Preview the questions before reading the passage. Do not read answer choices.
2. Skim the passage to get a general idea of the main idea and the author's purpose in writing.
3. Read the passage carefully keeping in mind the questions you have read. As soon as you believe you have found an answer, stop reading, go to the question, and answer it.
4. Read and answer one question at a time. Scan to check your answers or to find information needed to answer a question.

EXERCISE D: Answering Reading Comprehension Questions. Read the following passage and answer the accompanying questions, basing your answers on what is stated or implied in the passage.

812

There is evidence that the usual variety of high blood pressure is, in part, a familial disease. Since families have similar genes as well as similar environment, familial diseases could be due to shared genetic influences, to shared environmental factors, or to both. For some years, the role of one environmental factor commonly shared by families, namely dietary salt (i.e., sodium chloride), has been studied at Brookhaven National Laboratory. These studies suggest that chronic excess salt ingestion can lead to high blood pressure in man and animals. Some individuals, however, and some rats consume large amounts of salt without developing high blood pressure. No matter how strictly all environmental factors were controlled in these experiments, some salt-fed animals never developed hypertension whereas a few rapidly developed very severe hypertension followed by early death. These marked variations were interpreted to result from differences in genetic constitution.

By mating in successive generations only those animals that failed to develop hypertension from salt ingestion, a resistant strain (the "R" strain) has been evolved in which consumption of large quantities of salt fails to influence the blood pressure significantly. In contrast, by mating only animals that quickly develop hypertension from salt, a sensitive strain ("S" strain) has also been developed.

The availability of these two strains permits investigations not heretofore possible. They provide a plausible laboratory model on which to investigate some clinical aspects of the human prototypes of hypertension. More important, there might be the possibility of developing methods by which genetic susceptibility of human beings to high blood pressure can be defined without waiting for its appearance. Radioactive Sodium 22 was an important "tool" in working out the characteristics of the sodium chloride metabolism.

1. The statement that best relates the main idea is
   (A) When salt is added to their diets, rats and humans react in much the same way.
   (B) The near future will see a cure for high blood pressure.
   (C) The medical field is desperately in need of research.
   (D) Modern research has shown that high blood pressure is a result of salt in the diet.
   (E) A tendency toward high blood pressure may be a hereditary factor.

2. The study of the effects of salt on high blood pressure was carried out
   (A) because members of the same family tend to use similar amounts of salt
   (B) to explore the long-term use of a sodium-based substance
   (C) because it was proven that salt caused high blood pressure
   (D) because of the availability of chemically pure salt and its derivatives
   (E) because studies show an increase in the human consumption of salt
3. It can be implied that the main difference between "S" and "R" rats is their
   (A) need for Sodium 22
   (B) rate of mating
   (C) reaction to salt
   (D) type of blood
   (E) general health condition
4. The reader can infer from the passage that Sodium 22 can be used to
   (A) cure high blood pressure caused by salt
   (B) tell the "S" rats from the "R" rats
   (C) determine what a sodium chloride metabolism is like
   (D) put high blood pressure under control
   (E) determine the amount of salt needed to improve our metabolism
5. Among the results of the research discussed in this passage, the most beneficial might be
   (A) the early identification of potential high blood pressure victims
   (B) development of diets free of salt
   (C) an early cure for high blood pressure
   (D) control of genetic agents that cause high blood pressure
   (E) improved laboratory breeding methods

Tests of Standard Written English

The written expression portions of the SAT, ACT, and the English Achievement Test measure your ability to separate standard written English that is used in formal writing from informal or nonstandard English that is often used in speech. These tests measure skills that you will need to use when writing the standard written English required in college. Each test format may differ but each includes questions about punctuation, grammar, usage, and sentence structure.

Learn to identify the grammar, usage, and mechanics for standard written English.

The chart below lists written-expression test strategies.

TAKING STANDARDIZED WRITTEN-EXPRESSION TESTS

1. Read a sentence or passage through twice before making any decision about answers.

2. Look for errors according to difficulty. First look for capitalization, spelling, and punctuation errors; then for grammar and syntax errors; then for usage, sequence of tenses, parallel structure, redundancy, and other errors.

3. Identify the subject and predicate of each sentence to help you find errors in usage, redundancy, and relevance.

Usage Questions. Usage questions test your ability to identify usage errors in standard written English. The format for the SAT and English Achievement Test usage questions is shown in the sample below.

EXAMPLE: The sentence below may contain errors in grammar, usage, word choice, and idiom. Decide which underlined part contains the error and circle its letter. If the sentence is correct as it stands, circle (E). The sentence does not contain more than one error.

1. The spread of literacy in China <u>has long been</u>
                                         A

hampered by the vast differences <u>of</u> regional dia-
   B   C

lects, <u>as well as</u> by the lack of a simple standard-
        D

ized writing system. <u>No error</u>.
                       E

Answer: (C)

815

The usage section of the ACT consists of prose reading passages with portions underlined as shown in the example below.

EXAMPLE: In the passage, some portions are underlined and numbered. Corresponding to each numbered portion are alternative ways of saying the same thing. Read through the passage, then return to the underlined portions. If you feel an underlined portion is correct, mark NO CHANGE. If you feel there is an error in grammar, sentence structure, punctuation, or word usage, choose the correct answer.

Human beings are born with a desire to <u>communi-</u>
1

<u>cate with</u> other human <u>beings, they</u> satisfy this de-
2

sire in many ways. A smile communicates a <u>friendly</u>
3

<u>feeling</u>, a clenched <u>fist, anger</u>: tears, sorrow.
4

1. A. NO CHANGE   B. communicate to
   C. communicate   D. communicate
2. A. NO CHANGE   B. beings. They   C. beings, who   D. beings which
3. A. NO CHANGE   B. a friendly, feeling:
   C. friendship,   D. a friendly feeling;
4. A. NO CHANGE   B. fist an angry feeling,
   C. fist, anger;   D. fist, angriness

Answers: 1. (A)   2. (B)   3. (D)   4. (C)

Sentence Correction Questions. The sentence correction part of the SAT and the English Achievement Test asks you to choose the best wording for a sentence in standard written English.

EXAMPLE: The following sentence may contain problems in grammar, sentence construction, word choice, and punctuation. Part or all of the sentence is underlined. Select the lettered answer that contains the best version of the underlined section. Answer (A) always repeats the original underlined section exactly. If the sentence is correct as stands, select (A).

816

EXAMPLE: 1. Geronimo, a leader of the Apache people, lived to
the age of eighty years old.

    (A) the age of eighty years old
    (B) the old and ripe age of eighty
    (C) the ripe old age of eighty years old
    (D) be eighty years old
    (E) be a ripe and eighty years old

   Answer: (D)

EXERCISE E: Answering Usage Questions. The sentences
below contain errors in grammar, usage, word choice, and idiom. Parts of the sentences are underlined and lettered. Decide
which underlined part contains the error and write its letter. If
the sentence is correct as it stands, write (E). No sentence contains more than one error.

1. <u>Let</u> me say once and for all that between you and <u>I</u> <u>there</u>
   A   B   C

   can be no <u>further</u> friendship. <u>No error</u>.
             D   E

2. He <u>proved</u> to his own <u>satisfaction</u> that he was <u>as shrewd</u>
       A   B   C

   <u>as</u>, if not <u>shrewder than</u>, she. <u>No error</u>.
             D   E

3. We <u>insist</u> upon <u>your</u> telling us <u>who else's</u> signature ap-
      A   B   C

   peared on this petition <u>besides</u> yours. <u>No error</u>.
                   D   E

4. The student organization <u>would appreciate</u> <u>hearing from</u>
                         A   B

   anyone <u>which is</u> interested <u>in</u> organizing a theater club. <u>No</u>
           C   D

   <u>error</u>.
   E

5. English people of the Renaissance <u>were accustomed</u> to <u>re-</u>
                                A

   <u>sorting</u> to wizards and astrologers for help in <u>alleviating</u>
    B   C

   disease, identifying thieves, and <u>to locate</u> lost property. <u>No</u>
                           D

   <u>error</u>.
   E

817

EXERCISE F: Answering Sentence Correction Questions. The sentences below contain problems in grammar, sentence construction, word choice, and punctuation. Select the lettered answer that contains the best version of the underlined section. Answer (A) repeats the original underlined section exactly. If the sentence is correct as it stands, select (A).

1. George served <u>soup to the hungry campers in large mugs</u>.
   (A) soup to the hungry campers in large mugs
   (B) soup, to the hungry campers in large mugs
   (C) soup to the hungry campers, in large mugs
   (D) soup in large mugs, to the hungry campers
   (E) soup in large mugs to the hungry campers
2. <u>Regardless of</u> the danger that the roof might collapse, the fireman entered the building.
   (A) Regardless of (B) Irrespective of (C) Disregarding of (D) Irregardless of (E) Irregardless to
3. I met five soldiers <u>whom, I believe</u>, were members of the 82nd Airborne Division.
   (A) whom, I believe, (B) whom I believe, (C) who, I believe, (D) who I believe (E) who, I believe
4. When Renaldo <u>began to give us advise</u>, we listened.
   (A) began to give us advise (B) begun to give us advise
   (C) begin to give us advise (D) began to give us advice
   (E) began to give us advisement
5. Every student in the whole class understood the assignment <u>except I</u>, and that is why I feel so stupid.
   (A) except I (B) excepting I (C) outside of me
   (D) excepting me (E) except me

DEVELOPING WRITING SKILLS: Evaluating Your Test-Taking Skills. After one month of using the test-taking strategies in this section, write answers to the following questions.

1. How successful have you been in the past on the verbal part of standardized tests? Which areas need improvement?
2. What three things could you do to improve your scores?
3. Which standardized tests will you take this year?
4. Have you developed a final vocabulary review to help you with the verbal section of tests you will have to take?
5. What process have you developed for successfully handling reading comprehension questions?

Skills Review and Writing Workshop

Reading and Test-Taking Skills

CHECKING YOUR SKILLS

Read the following paragraph first by skimming then by phrase reading. Write a summary of the paragraph.

Pearls are produced by oysters and mussels, animals known as mollusks. If a piece of shell, sand, or similar foreign object lodges in the body of an oyster, it will cover the object with layers of *nacre*. This substance, which also forms the mollusk's shell, consists primarily of calcium carbonate. For centuries, natural pearls have been considered extremely valuable. Pearl necklaces were highly prized by Roman women. In America, pearls have also been unearthed in the cities of ancient Indians. People not only used pearls for adornment but also believed that they possessed the power to cure disease. Today most pearls are cultured, not natural. Cultured pearls are created by inserting a bead in an oyster which then surrounds it with nacre. At large mollusk farms located in the world's tropical regions, vast quantities of cultured pearls are produced each year.

USING STUDY SKILLS IN WRITING
Writing Reading Comprehension Questions

Reading comprehension questions are found on many standardized tests. These questions test your ability to recall and interpret information. Write several reading comprehension questions by following these steps.

Prewriting: Select a topic in science or social studies and outline several ideas that relate to it.

Writing: Present your ideas clearly and logically. Then develop three or four reading-comprehension questions based on what you have written. Use the information on pages 793–796 to help you develop your questions.

Revising: Change any phrases or sentences that could be more effective. After you have revised, proofread carefully.

819

31

Library and Reference Skills

A modern library is a valuable information center. The purpose of the first two sections of this chapter is to show you how to get the most out of a library. The first section will concentrate on ways of using the library's resources to find the books you need for research, study, and general reading. The second section will show you how to use the major reference tools in the library. The final section is devoted to the dictionary, perhaps the most important reference tool of all.

31.1 Library Skills

To use the library efficiently, you must plan your research and know how to find the material available in your library. These skills are the subject of this section.

Planning Your Research

Although the library has many uses, you may find it most useful at this point for research. Even before you go to the library, you should take time to plan your research so that you can spend your time in the library wisely.

Begin your research by knowing basic facts about your topic.

To find information about anything, you must know enough about your topic to place it in some sort of context. You must also know where to look for basic information and what kind of information will be useful when you start your research.

Sources of Basic Information. Before you go to the library, you have a twofold job: (1) to pick a topic (unless the topic is assigned) and (2) to find basic information about the topic. The best place to start may be with your class notes and your textbook. If you already have a topic, you can use your notes and textbook to uncover basic information. If you do not have a topic, you can use your notes and textbook to help you focus on what you have learned and what has interested you.

If you have difficulty choosing a topic or find that your topic is not clearly covered in your notes or textbook, the library should be your next stop. Libraries usually contain books with ideas for term papers on various subjects. You can also go to an encyclopedia and read a general article covering the material in your course to find some ideas to pursue.

Types of Basic Information. The first thing you need to know in order to find further information on your topic is the general subject area under which your topic will be found. If you are doing research in science, for example, you will need to know if your general subject falls into the area of biology, chemistry, or biochemistry. If you are looking for information about an author, you will need to know if the writer is a novelist, an essayist, a poet, a dramatist, or a historian.

You may also find the following types of information helpful when you begin your actual research.

INFORMATION NEEDED FOR EFFICIENT RESEARCH WORK

1. What synonyms can be used to describe your topic?
2. What are some related subject areas?
3. What is the time period associated with your topic?
4. What is the geographical area associated with your topic?

Thinking along these lines can often lead to just the sources you need.

Finding General Information About a Topic.
Using your textbook, notes, or an encyclopedia, pick a topic
and list the following information about it.

1. The correct name of your topic
2. The general subject or subjects it comes under
3. Some related subjects
4. The time frame involved, if any
5. The geographical area involved, if any

Using the Card Catalog

To use the card catalog of a library efficiently, you need to
know what kinds of cards are in the catalog, what kind of information is found on the cards, and how the cards are
arranged.

Kinds of Catalog Cards. The card catalog allows you to
zero in on the books you need from many different directions.

**Use the card catalog to find information about
a library's books and other materials.**

Every fiction book in the library has at least a *title card* and
an *author card.* Every nonfiction book has, in addition, at least
one *subject card.* In the following example, the title is *Computers and Their Uses.* The card is alphabetized under *Computers.* Note the various kinds of information found on the
card.

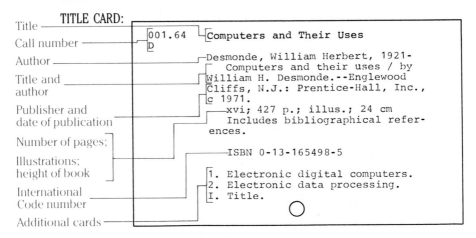

TITLE CARD:

Title ———————

Call number ———————

Author ———————

Title and
author

Publisher and
date of publication

Number of pages;

Illustrations;
height of book

International
Code number

Additional cards ———————

```
001.64    Computers and Their Uses
D
          Desmonde, William Herbert, 1921-
             Computers and their uses / by
          William H. Desmonde.--Englewood
          Cliffs, N.J.: Prentice-Hall, Inc.,
          c 1971.
             xvi; 427 p.; illus.; 24 cm
             Includes bibliographical refer-
          ences.

             ISBN 0-13-165498-5

          1. Electronic digital computers.
          2. Electronic data processing.
          I. Title.
```

If you are unsure of the exact title of a book but know the author, go to the catalog and look at the books listed by that author. For the book on computers, you will find an author card like the one in the following example. It will be alphabetized by the last name of the author, *Desmonde.*

AUTHOR
CARD:

```
001.64      Desmonde, William Herbert, 1921-
D               Computers and Their Uses / by
            William H. Desmonde.--Englewood
            Cliffs, N.J.: Prentice-Hall, Inc.,
            c 1971.
                xvi; 427 p.; illus.; 24 cm
                Includes bibliographical refer-
            ences.

                ISBN 0-13-165498-5

            1. Electronic digital computers.
            2. Electronic data processing.
            3. Title
                        O
```

When a book has more than one author, you should be able to find it by looking up either author.

Sometimes you may be searching for information about a certain subject. In such a case, go to the card catalog and look for a subject card. It will be filed alphabetically according to the subject. Notice in the following example that the subject is written across the top of the card in capital letters.

SUBJECT
CARD:

```
001.64      COMPUTERS
D
            Desmonde, William Herbert, 1921-
                Computers and Their Uses / by
            William H. Desmonde.--Englewood
            Cliffs, N.J.: Prentice-Hall, Inc.,
            c 1971.
                xvi; 427 p.; illus.; 24 cm
                Includes bibliographical refer-
            ences.

                ISBN 0-13-165498-5

            1. Electronic digital computers.
            2. Electronic data processing.
            3. Title
                        O
```

823

Although title, author, and subject cards are the most important cards in a catalog, they are not the only ones. You may also find an *analytic card* in the card catalog. This kind of card refers you to *parts* of books.

If you were looking up information about Albert Einstein, for example, you might find the following card. The card tells you that part of the book *Contemporary Immortals* by Archibald Henderson discusses Albert Einstein.

ANALYTIC CARD:

```
920        Albert Einstein, 1879-1955, in
H
       Henderson, Archibald, 1877-
           Contemporary immortals / by Archibald
       Henderson.--New York, London: D. Appleton
       and Co., c 1930.
           xii; 208 p.; illus.; 21 cm

       Contents: Albert Einstein.--Mahatma
       Gandhi.--Thomas Alva Edison.--Benito Mus-
       solini.--George Bernard Shaw.--Guglielmo
       Marconi.--Jane Addams.--Orville Wright.--
       Ignace Jan Paderewski.--Marie Sklodowska
       Curie.--Henry Ford.--Rudyard Kipling.

           ISBN 0-8369-0533-4

       1. Biography.  I. Title.
                    O
```

Another kind of card found in a card catalog is called a *cross-reference card.* A cross-reference card may be either a *see* card or a *see also* card.

A *see* card tells you that the subject heading you have chosen is not used by the library; the *see* card will, therefore, refer you to the subject heading used by the library. If, for example, you looked up the subject *Solar power* in a card catalog, you might find a cross-reference card referring you to *Solar energy* similar to the one at the top left of the next page.

A *see also* card refers you to additional subject headings that are related to the one you have chosen to look up. This kind of card can be useful when you are doing research because it can suggest related subjects that you may not have thought of. If you were looking for books about American art, you might find a card like the one at the top right of the next page.

824

CROSS-REFERENCE CARDS:

```
       SOLAR POWER                           ART, AMERICAN

          See                                  See also

       Solar Energy                       Afro-American Art
                                          Architecture, American
                                          Architecture, Colonial
                                          Painting, American


              O                                   O
```

Arrangement of the Cards. Most small libraries have a single catalog with all of the cards arranged in continuous alphabetical order. Larger libraries have catalogs divided into at least two separate alphabets. For example, one catalog may contain subject cards and another title and author cards.

Libraries may use a "COM" catalog, a computer-generated catalog with listings available on microfilm or microfiche. A "COM" catalog may include books that are not in that library but are in another library that is part of the same system.

Whatever the type of catalog you are using, you need to know the system of alphabetizing used. There are two different ways of alphabetizing: *letter by letter* and *word by word.*

Letter-by-letter alphabetizing is found in most dictionaries and in some encyclopedias. In letter-by-letter alphabetizing, the order of entries is determined by the order of the letters in the entire entry, even if the entry consists of more than one word. In word-by-word alphabetizing, the order of the entries is determined by the order of letters in the first word and then by the order in the next word.

TWO METHODS OF ALPHABETIZING	
Library's Method: By Word	Other Method: By Letter
New Jersey	newest
New Paltz	New Jersey
New York	New Paltz
newest	newspaper
newspaper	New York

In addition to learning the general rule for alphabetizing in a card catalog, you should learn a few more specialized rules.

CARD CATALOG FILING RULES

1. Ignore *a*, *an*, and *the* when they are the first words of a title. *The Dred Scott Case* is filed alphabetically under *D* for *Dred*.

2. Treat *Mc*, and *M'* as if they were spelled *Mac* and alphabetize accordingly. The following are in correct order: *McBrien*, *M'Coy*, *MacDonald*, *machine*, and *Macmillan*.

3. Treat abbreviations and numbers as if they were spelled out. *Dr.* is filed as if it were *Doctor* and *Mr.* as if it were *Mister*; and *45* as if it were *Forty-five*.

4. Books *by* an author are filed before books *about* an author. *Death Comes to the Archbishop* by Willa Cather comes before a biography of Willa Cather.

5. Subdivisions of a subject are filed before longer terms beginning with the subject name. NEW YORK—HISTORY is filed before NEW YORK STOCK EXCHANGE

EXERCISE B: Interpreting Information on a Catalog Card. Use the following author card to answer the questions.

```
613.71      Kuntzleman, Beth A.
K                 The complete guide to aerobic danc-
            ing / by Beth A. Kuntzleman and the
            Editors of Consumer guide.--Skokie,
            Ill.:Publications International, c 1979.
                  96 p.; illus.; 28 cm

                  ISBN 0-449-80001-6

            1. Aerobic exercises. 2. Dancing.
            I. Title.



                              ◯
```

1. What is the call number?
2. Who is the author?
3. What is the title?
4. What is the copyright date?
5. Who is the publisher?
6. Where is the place of publication?

7. How many pages are in the book?
8. Are there any pictures or photographs in the book?
9. Is there a bibliography?
10. Under what other subjects is this book also filed?

EXERCISE C: Writing Catalog Cards. Using the information below, write an author card, title card, and subject card.

Folk and Festival Costumes of the World, by R. Turner Wilcox, published by Scribner's in New York, in 1969. The book is unpaged, contains illustrations, and has a height of 28 cm. The call number is 391 W and the ISBN number is 0-684-15379-3. The book is filed under COSTUME.

EXERCISE D: Alphabetizing Catalog Cards. Alphabetize the following sets of cards using word-by-word alphabetizing.

1. Hong Kong, Human Genetics, Homework, Home Wiring
2. *New Year's Day, Newark's Future, News Breaks,* New Zealand
3. *Color Television, Collective Bargaining, Colorado Camping*
4. *Press Time, Press and America, Presidential Character*
5. Carbon dioxide, Carnivores, Carbon-oxygen cycle, Carver

EXERCISE E: Using Special Catalog Filing Rules. List the following sets of cards in the correct alphabetical order.

1. *1986 Money Book, 9 to 5, Nine Men's Morris, Ninety Years*
2. *Macintosh, Macbeth,* McCall, *Machine Language,* McNeil
3. U.S.—CIVIL RIGHTS, U.S. CONSTITUTION, U.S.—CRIME
4. *The Scarlet Letter* by Nathaniel Hawthorne, *Nathaniel Hawthorne: A Critical Biography* by Mark Van Doren
5. *The American Man, Animal Behavior, An Introduction to Music*

Going from Catalog to Shelf

In order to locate books on the shelves you use the *location symbol* found at the top left corner of catalog cards.

Use the catalog card location symbol to locate materials on library shelves.

Locating Fiction. Many libraries shelve works of fiction in a separate section. The books are arranged in alphabetical order according to the author's last name. If there is more than one book by an author, they are arranged alphabetically by title.

The card you find in the card catalog for a work of fiction will usually have the location symbol F or Fic. Sometimes, the F or Fic will be followed by the first letter or letters of the author's last name.

Locating Nonfiction. Nonfiction books are arranged on library shelves according to call number. The call number in the upper left-hand corner of the catalog card also appears on the spine of the corresponding book. Usually labels at the ends of the rows of shelves will tell you which call numbers (for example, 300-499) can be found in each row.

The call number is simply a way of classifying books according to one of two systems—the *Dewey Decimal System* or the *Library of Congress System*. The Dewey Decimal System is older and is the one used in most public and school libraries.

The Dewey Decimal System is a numerical system in which knowledge is classified hierarchically. All knowledge is divided into ten main classes, each of which is further divided into 10 divisions. These divisions can be subdivided even further.

MAIN CLASS:	300-399	Social sciences
DIVISION:	320-329	Political science
SUBDIVISION:	324	The political process
FURTHER DIVISION:	324.1	International organizations

Each call number has, in addition to a number, a letter under the number. This letter normally stands for the first initial of the last name of the author. When books have the same number, the arrangement on the shelf is alphabetical by the letters under the numbers.

The Library of Congress System, often used in larger libraries, is an alphanumeric system. The call numbers begin with letters, thus reversing the Dewey Decimal System. The main classes are designated by a single letter; combinations of two letters designate the subclasses. The letter designations are followed by a numerical notation, from 1 to 9999, which can be further subdivided to indicate divisions and subdivisions.

MAIN CLASS: H   Social sciences

SUBCLASS: HA   Statistics

DIVISION: HA
               29   Theory and method

As in the Dewey system, there can also be a letter for the author as well as additional numbers. Although the Library of Congress System differs in many ways from the Dewey Decimal System, the method for finding books on the shelves is similar. With the Library of Congress System, simply start with letters rather than numbers.

Finding Biographies and Special Materials. Libraries using the Dewey Decimal System often shelve biographies in a separate section. The location symbol for a biography shelved separately will generally be B (for Biography) or 92 (short for 920, the Dewey number for biography).

Reference books are commonly marked with the letters R or Ref in front of the call number. This marking usually means that the books are shelved separately and may not be removed from the library.

Most libraries use other location symbols as well. You may find such symbols as M for mysteries, SF for science fiction, LP for books with large printing, YA for books meant for young adults, LH for a local history collection, and so on. If the card catalog uses a location symbol you do not understand, do not hesitate to ask the librarian for help.

EXERCISE F: Locating Fiction. Arrange the following works of fiction in the order in which you would find them on the library shelves.

1. Kurt Vonnegut, *Player Piano*
2. George McCutcheon, *The Merivales*
3. Ernest Hemingway, *The Old Man and the Sea*
4. William MacLeod Raine, *Under Northern Stars*
5. Jane Austen, *Pride and Prejudice*
6. Kurt Vonnegut, *Jailbird*
7. Elizabeth Pope, *The Perilous Guard*
8. Jane Austen, *Sense and Sensibility*
9. Rose Macaulay, *Dangerous Ages*
10. Ernest Hemingway, *For Whom the Bell Tolls*

EXERCISE G: Locating Nonfiction Arranged by the Dewey Decimal System. Arrange the call numbers below in the order in which you would find them on the shelves using the Dewey Decimal System.

016	973.7	973.47	629.2	070
B	C	D	G	M
131.3	305.8	312.6	371.93	324.3
O	J	M	D	J

EXERCISE H: Locating Nonfiction Arranged by the Library of Congress System. Arrange the call numbers below in the order you would find them on the shelves of a library using the Library of Congress System.

LD	AY	HA	HD	HA
531	204	31	803	31
B	M	F	M	G

EXERCISE I: Locating Biographies. Go to the biography section of a library and find biographies of a literary figure, a sports figure, and a political leader. Write the location symbol, the title, and the author for each biography.

DEVELOPING WRITING SKILLS: Using Your Library Skills. Following the steps below, prepare a list of materials on a topic of your choice. Then write a paragraph about your library skills, indicating which library skills you have mastered and which you still need to work on.

1. Choose a topic for a paper and find out as much as you can about your topic in the initial research stage.
2. Using the card catalog, find eight to ten books about your subject. Remember to use cross-reference cards.
3. Copy the essential information from the catalog cards: title, author, and location symbol or call number.
4. Go to the library shelves and see if the books you have found contain the information you need. Choose new books from the card catalog if any books are missing from the shelves.
5. List the books and other materials you have chosen. If they are not directly related, explain why you chose them.

Reference Skills 31.2

Knowing how to make the most of the reference materials that a library usually keeps in a separate section or room can be of great help in quickly finding the information you need.

In this section you will have a chance to review the uses of general and specialized reference materials as well as periodicals such as magazines and newspapers.

General Reference Books

General reference books are among the most useful books in a library. Among them are dictionaries, encyclopedias, almanacs, atlases, and gazetteers. Because dictionaries will be discussed at length in Section 32.3, in this section the discussion will center on other types of general works.

Use general reference books to check basic facts or to explore the range of a topic.

Encyclopedias. A general encyclopedia is usually a multivolume set arranged alphabetically. One volume, usually the first or last, is an index, which will refer you both to subjects for which there are complete articles and to subjects that are contained within articles. Many of the articles themselves will refer you to related articles elsewhere in the encyclopedia.

The example below is from the index to the *Encyclopedia Americana.* The first reference, to Volume 20, page 1, is to the main article on the subject. The other references are to other articles with additional information on the same subject.

NAVAJO (Navaho) (Amerind)
  20–1; 15–6; 22–774; 27–690
Arizona 2–306, 309
Athapaskan Languages 2–603
blankets 15–12
dance 15–22
diet 15–11
Ghost 12–724
homes 15–12
Indian wars 15–30
irrigation project 20–209
Monument Valley Navajo Tribal Park 19–427
Music 19–662; 15–24
rugs 23–858
Weaving 28–550
Illus. 2–ARIZONA; 2–300; 15–INDIAN, AMERICAN; 15–12; rug 23–853; sand

831

In order to be useful, an encyclopedia must be current. Most publishers of encyclopedias follow a policy of continuous revision. This means that each time a new edition of the encyclopedia is published some articles are revised, usually those on subjects in which the information has been most affected by the passage of time. In addition, many encyclopedias publish yearbooks. An encyclopedia yearbook has a twofold purpose: It brings together information about the events of the year, often in a chronological arrangement, and it presents information about new or expanding areas of knowledge.

The following chart lists some popular encyclopedias.

POPULAR ENCYCLOPEDIAS
Collier's Encyclopedia, in 24 volumes *Compton's Pictured Encyclopedia,* in 15 volumes *Encyclopaedia Britannica,* in 29 volumes *Encyclopedia Americana,* in 30 volumes *Encyclopedia International,* in 20 volumes *The World Book Encyclopedia,* in 22 volumes

Almanacs and Other Yearbooks. An almanac contains geographic, political, statistical, historical, and other miscellaneous information. If you want to know the date of an earthquake in Alaska or the winner of the 1954 World Series, you can find it easily in an almanac. Unlike an encyclopedia, however, an almanac seldom provides useful background information. Nor is it arranged alphabetically. Because the arrangement is by broad subject areas, the best way to find the information you need is through the index. Some well-known almanacs include *The World Almanac and Book of Facts, Information Please Almanac, Hammond's Almanac,* and *Reader's Digest Almanac and Yearbook.*

Other annually published references are *Facts on File,* the *Statesman's Yearbook,* and *Europa Yearbook: A World Statesman's Yearbook. Facts on File* is a current events digest. The *Statesman's Yearbook* provides basic information on the countries of the world. *Europa* gives information about the history, government, economy, press, and colleges of each country.

Atlases and Gazetteers. Atlases and gazetteers are similar but not identical. The essential difference between the two is that gazetteers contain no maps. Gazetteers are geographical dictionaries with factual descriptions arranged alphabetically by place name. Useful gazetteers include *Columbia-Lippincott Gazetteer* and *Webster's New Geographical Dictionary.*

You probably have used the maps in atlases from time to time. The type of atlas you may be most familiar with is a general atlas, which consists primarily of political maps showing the boundaries of countries and states and the locations of cities, towns, rivers, and oceans. A general atlas may also include topographic maps showing the physical characteristics of the land. In addition, some general atlases include maps covering such topics as industry, climate, and population density.

The historical atlas is another important type of reference book. In an historical atlas, maps are arranged to show changes over time.

The economic atlas is a type of atlas with which you may not be familiar. It contains maps designed to give economic information: that is, information about energy, industry, population, agriculture, and so on.

POPULAR ATLASES	
Atlas of American History	*The Oxford Regional Economic Atlas of Western Europe*
Goode's World Atlas	
National Atlas of the United States	*Shepherd's Historical Atlas*
	West Point Atlas of American Wars
The Oxford Economic Atlas of the World	
	World Book Atlas

EXERCISE A: Selecting General Reference Books. Write *encyclopedia, almanac,* or *atlas* to identify the types of reference books you would use to find the following.

1. Landforms of the world
2. Three books with information about Libya
3. A biography of former President Gerald Ford
4. How the letter *K* is expressed in Morse Code
5. The principal mountain range of Peru
6. Distribution of rainfall in the United States
7. The political boundaries of France in the sixteenth century
8. The first Secretary of State

9. The winner of the NBA Most Valuable Player in 1985
10. Two United States cities on the Gulf of Mexico

EXERCISE B: Using General Reference Books. Use general reference books to find answers to the following questions. After each answer, write the name of the book you used.

1. What is the largest island in the world?
2. What causes a black hole in space?
3. Where did a major earthquake occur on July 28, 1976?
4. What countries border Nigeria?
5. When was the jazz trumpeter Miles Davis born?
6. How does the process of photosynthesis take place?
7. What are the physical boundaries of Mexico?
8. Who won the Nobel Prize for Fiction in 1961?
9. How do soap and detergent work to remove dirt?
10. What were four major events of 1985?

Specialized Reference Books

Although general reference books have many uses, specialized reference books may be more useful for certain assignments.

Use specialized reference books to find in-depth information about a particular field.

Many specialized reference works are similar to the more general reference works. A number of specialized dictionaries and encyclopedias provide more detail in their special areas than the more general reference works provide.

Specialized Dictionaries. Specialized dictionaries often provide more detailed information about words than do general dictionaries. They are also likely to be devoted to particular fields, such as politics, mathematics, art, music, biology, and many other fields.

One particularly useful specialized dictionary is the dictionary of synonyms. There may be times when you need very fine distinctions between words that are closely related in meaning. For example, if you were writing a paper on the general topic of *magic,* you may need to make precise use of related words such as *sorcery* and *wizardry.*

Two very good dictionaries of synonyms that would make these distinctions in detail are *Webster's New Dictionary of Synonyms* and *Funk and Wagnall's Modern Guide to Synonyms.*

A *thesaurus* is also a specialized dictionary that you may find useful when you are writing, but a thesaurus does not generally provide a detailed discussion of words. Instead, it usually gives simply a list of words that are synonymous or nearly synonymous with the word you look up. *Roget's International Thesaurus* and *Webster's Collegiate Thesaurus* are two popular examples that you may find useful in your writing.

Specialized Encyclopedias. Specialized encyclopedias are valuable reference books for background, bibliographies, and quick reference. The organization of specialized encyclopedias usually follows the format of general encyclopedias, but the specialized encyclopedias will provide more depth because their scope is limited to a specific field. They range from one-volume encyclopedias to multi-volume sets.

The following chart lists just a few of the many specialized encyclopedias that are commonly available in many libraries.

SPECIALIZED ENCYCLOPEDIAS	
Encyclopedia Judaica	*Encyclopedia of the Social Sciences*
Encyclopedia of Chemical Technology	*McGraw-Hill Encyclopedia of Science and Technology*
Encyclopedia of Oceanography	*New Catholic Encyclopedia*
Encyclopedia of Philosophy	

Biographical Reference Books. There are many biographical reference books that are available in most libraries. When you use a biographical reference book, the first thing you should check is the scope of the book. Often, books will be devoted either to people in a certain profession or to famous people of a particular nationality. Some biographical reference books will be limited either to people who are still living or to people no longer living. If the title of the book does not make clear the scope of the book, check the introductory pages.

The chart on the next page provides a sample list indicating the variety of biographical reference books.

BIOGRAPHICAL REFERENCE BOOKS	
American Authors 1600–1900	McGraw-Hill Encyclopedia of World Biography
Composers Since 1900	
Congressional Directory	Modern Men of Science
Contemporary Authors	Notable American Women
Current Biography	Webster's Biographical Dictionary
Dictionary of American Biography	Who's Who in America
Dictionary of National Biography (British)	Who's Who in Finance and Industry
	Who's Who in the East
Dictionary of Scientific Biography	Who Was Who in America

One of the most useful biographical reference books is *Current Biography*, a work that is published each month and then bound annually. The series contains long articles about important people in all fields. Except for the obituary listings, only people living at the time of publication are included.

Two indexes are also valuable when you are trying to obtain biographical information. The first, *Biography Index*, indexes material in periodicals and books. The other, *The New York Times Obituary Index*, indexes obituaries in *The New York Times* from 1858 through 1968. This, together with the entries under *Deaths* in the main index of *The New York Times*, can be an excellent source for information.

Literary Reference Books. In addition to biographical material about authors, you may sometimes need more specific information about the particular works of an author.

One useful literary reference book is the *handbook*, which contains brief articles about authors and their works as well as literary movements. Two notable series are *The Oxford Companion Series* and *The Penguin Companion Series*. Each series contains volumes covering several different types of literature, including American, English, French, Spanish, Oriental, and African. Two other good handbooks are *The Cambridge History of English Literature* and the *McGraw-Hill Encyclopedia of World Drama*. A related tool is a dictionary of literary terms, an example of which is the *Dictionary of World Literary Terms*.

When you need to find a poem, a short story, or a play that has not been published separately, you should consult one of the many indexes of literary works that are usually available in libraries.

LITERARY INDEXES	
Essay and General Literature Index	*Index to Full Length Plays*
Fiction Catalog	*Ottemiller's Index to Plays in Collections*
Granger's Index to Poetry	*Play Index*
Historical Fiction	*Short Story Index*

Indexes of various kinds are also very helpful when your most pressing need is for a critical review of an author or for criticism of a specific work. An excellent source for this kind of information is the *Book Review Digest,* which will direct you to book reviews found in various magazines and journals. Published several times a year and then collected in an annual yearbook, the volumes in this series are arranged alphabetically by author, with subject and title indexes in each volume. The entries in each volume are made up of a series of summaries, or digests, of book reviews, with a reference to the periodical in which the full review appears. A similar publication, *Book Review Index,* is only an index. There are no summaries of the reviews, just references to the periodicals in which the reviews are found.

There are also several indexes that offer in-depth literary criticism. A particularly useful series is the *Library of Literary Criticism,* which contains volumes covering British, American, German, French, and Slavic literature. Each author entry consists of a digest of information about criticism of the author's works and a reference to original sources, which will be found either in books or in periodicals. Other useful literary series are *Twentieth Century Literary Criticism,* covering authors from 1900 to 1960, and *Contemporary Literary Criticism,* covering contemporary authors since 1960. Once again, there are excerpts of criticism of a work and references to the sources of the criticism. In both of these series, the excerpts are long enough to be useful.

Books of quotations can also be very useful when you are doing literary research or when you simply need an appropriate quotation to incorporate into your own writing. The following chart lists some of the numerous books of quotations that are available in many libraries.

BOOKS OF QUOTATIONS	
Bartlett's Familiar Quotations	Stevenson's Home Books of Proverbs, Maxims, and Familiar Phrases
Dictionary of Quotations	
Dictionary of Thoughts	
Hoyt's New Cyclopedia of Practical Quotations	Stevenson's Home Book of Quotations

Social Studies Reference Books. Social studies is an extremely large field with many different types of reference books. Besides the specialized encyclopedias already mentioned *(Encyclopedia of the Social Sciences* and *Encyclopedia of Philosophy),* there are a number of other reference books. Notable are *Dictionary of American History, Safire's Political Dictionary,* and *Dictionary of the Social Sciences.*

There are also useful indexes in the social studies field. The *Social Science Index* is a good index of periodical articles; *PAIS* indexes both periodicals and government documents. A related work, not quite an index, is the *Harvard Guide to American History,* which acts as a comprehensive bibliographical source to material on American history.

The most complete reference work for the kind of statistical information often needed in social studies is probably the *Statistical Abstract of the United States.* Especially useful are the footnotes that appear after each table to guide you to the original source of the information when you need greater detail.

EXERCISE C: Selecting Specialized Reference Books.
Give the title of the specialized reference book that you would use to find each of the following.

1. Reviews of Mary Gordon's novel *Final Payments*
2. Two synonyms for the word *imperil*
3. The scientific meaning of *occultation*

838

4. The achievements of Sigmund Freud
5. What happened at the Diet of Worms in 1521
6. The importance of Fort Sumter in American history
7. The difference in meaning between *letter* and *epistle*
8. A quotation about the meaning of silence
9. How digital computers use the binary system of numbers
10. The early career of film director Alfred Hitchcock

EXERCISE D: Using Specialized Reference Books. Use specialized reference books to answer the following questions. After each answer, write the name of the book you used.

1. What are *continental shelves?*
2. What was Emmeline Pankhurst famous for?
3. Where was Bob Bergland born? What schools did he attend?
4. What books did Belva Plain write?
5. What two books contain John Donne's poem "The Bait"?
6. How many bills did President Carter veto in 1978?
7. How did your own United States senators vote on a recent bill of interest to you? What was the bill?
8. What type of operatic music did Giuseppe Verdi compose?
9. Which synonym for the word *dirty* has the most unpleasant connotation? Explain your reason.
10. What is the importance of the Supreme Court case of *Miranda vs. Arizona?*

Periodicals and Pamphlets

Along with the other types of material in the library's reference section, you are likely to find a number of periodicals and pamphlets. These can be very useful for finding some types of information.

Use magazines, journals, newspapers, and pamphlets for current material about a subject.

Periodical is a general term for anything that is published at intervals during a year. The term usually refers to magazines and journals, but it can also refer to newspapers.

Magazines and Journals. *Magazine* is the term generally used for the more popular weekly and monthly periodicals. *Journal* is the term used for the more scholarly monthly and quarterly periodicals. There are many periodicals of both types, some general and some very specialized. They all share the general characteristic of being good for current, concise information. Almost every library has some periodicals; larger libraries will usually have a good-sized collection.

In order to find information in periodicals, you need to use periodical indexes. There are many types of indexes, some for journals, some for magazines, some general, and some specialized. For everyday use, however, the most valuable is probably *The Readers' Guide to Periodical Literature,* an alphabetically arranged subject and author guide to articles in most of the more common periodicals. Another index, the *Popular Periodical Index,* covers mainly popular magazines and is often the first index to pick up a new magazine. Your library may also subscribe to a new index called the *Magazine Index,* which is a computer-generated index to most of the periodicals in *The Readers' Guide* as well as several others. The references in the *Magazine Index* are displayed on a screen, and since the index is computer generated, entries are always found within a single alphabetical grouping, thereby eliminating the need to look through several volumes.

Although there are slight differences in format among the various indexes, they are sufficiently alike so that if you learn to use one of them you should be able to use any of them. The labels added to the following example from *The Readers' Guide* should help you interpret the various entries.

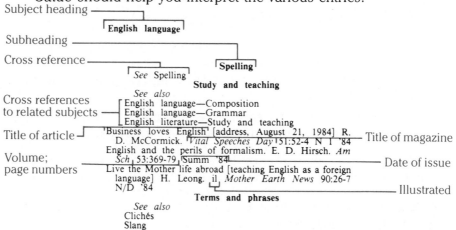

Newspapers. Newspapers, like other periodicals are good for finding current and concise information. However, except for a few special articles, the information tends to be limited. A newspaper generally gives only the basics of a news story, while a magazine or journal will usually give you additional explanation and background information. Although there are many newspapers, your library probably has very few, possibly only your local newspaper and *The New York Times*, which is considered a newspaper of record.

Although several newspapers have indexes, the index to *The New York Times* is one of the most complete, both in terms of time (it goes back to 1851) and in terms of general coverage. This index, published annually, is arranged alphabetically by subject. Each volume covers only the year indicated on the spine of the book; thus, the dates supplied in the index entry do not include the year. The subject heading for many entries is often followed by cross-references. Perhaps most important is the fact that each reference includes a good abstract of the basic facts in an article so that the index alone is often all you need. The following example from a recent volume, with labels for the various parts, should make the system clear.

Subject heading —— **OIL (Petroleum) and Gasoline** –

Ecuador plans to spend $2.24 billion over five years to develop its oil industry (S), F 20,IV,2:6

Article abstract —— McDermott International Inc says two units have received multibillion contracts from Arabian American Oil Co and affiliate to build and install offshore drilling platforms off Saudi Arabia's eastern province (S), F 21,IV,5:2

Short article —— Trading is halted, Toronto, in stock of Dome Petroleum and its affiliate Dome Canada after reports from Japan cast doubt on financing of Beaufort Sea drilling program; Dome says any decision by its Japanese partners will not affect its exploration program or its refinancing talks (S), F 22,IV,6:6

Date; section; page; column

Editorial says ban on export of Alaskan oil should be repealed; says shipment to logical buyers such as Japan, South Korea and Taiwan, would be cheaper than present cost of transporting oil to Virgin Islands; claims amendment to Export Administration Act proposed by Alaska's Senators Frank Murkowski and Ted Stevens, although flawed, offers only hope for reducing harm of current protectionist politics, F 23,I,22:1

Staff of Canada's Restrictive Trade Practices Commission accuses American oil companies of overpricing oil they buy abroad for their Canadian units in order to reduce their Canadian and US tax liability; estimates amount of overcharge at $3.2 billion (Canadian) between 1958 and 1973;

Some libraries subscribe to a service called *Newsbank*. *Newsbank* uses microfiche to reprint articles from many newspapers around the country. The service also provides paper indexes that act as guide to the information on the microfiche.

Pamphlets. Pamphlets, small paperbound texts issued by many groups from private agencies to government, are also useful for finding current information. Unlike periodicals, however, pamphlets do not assume any prior knowledge and usually give a concise background for the subjects they cover. Thus, they may be especially useful for subjects with which you are not very familiar.

Pamphlets are usually arranged alphabetically by subject in what is called a *vertical file.* Because each library uses its own subject headings, you should consult a librarian if you have any trouble finding the pamphlets you need.

EXERCISE E: Using *The Readers' Guide to Periodical Literature.* Look up material about the American hostages held in Iran in 1984 in *The Readers' Guide.* Make a list of at least five articles on this subject. Also, write the issue of the guide and page or pages you used.

EXERCISE F: Using *The New York Times Index.* Follow the instructions for Exercise E, this time using *The New York Times Index* instead of *The Readers' Guide.* After you have completed the exercise, compare your new list with the list you made for Exercise E and note any differences in the number and types of articles in the two sources.

Other Ways of Obtaining Reference Materials

Although your library is likely to have most if not all of the reference works discussed in this section, you still may not always have everything you need. In such a case, there are a number of additional steps that you can take.

For information unavailable in your library, consult national and local organizations, whose addresses may be obtained in your library.

If your library has a copy of Gale's *Directory of Associations,* you can use it to find the name and address of a national organization that is directly concerned with your topic.

842

If you do not have time for a mailing, or if your library has no such directory, you might check with the librarian to see if there is a local organization that might be able to give you similar information or, possibly, an interview. You might also want to check to see if your library has records of such local associations.

When you need information on a local topic, the information is much less likely to be in printed form. Once again, a local association may be willing to help you. If you need the most current population estimate for your town or city, you can call the local planning department. If you need information about the number of new houses built in a certain period, you can call the local building department. In such cases, however, your best bet may be to check first with the librarian to see if the library has records covering this information. If it does not, the librarian may be willing to help you find the necessary organization to contact.

EXERCISE G: Obtaining Additional Reference Materials. Follow the three steps below, listing the sources of your information.

1. Find the addresses of two national organizations concerned with mental health.
2. See if the library can supply you with a local address for an organization concerned with mental health.
3. See if the library has any records from the local health department. If not, obtain the telephone number of the health department.

DEVELOPING WRITING SKILLS: Applying Your Knowledge of Reference Materials. Choose a subject of interest to you and write a short report, using information from at least three of the following sources. Include a list of the reference materials you used to find your information.

1. A general encyclopedia
2. A biographical reference book
3. A magazine
4. A newspaper
5. A pamphlet

31.3 Dictionary Skills

A good dictionary is a valuable resource. In the past, you may have used your dictionary primarily to check the meaning or spelling of words, but dictionaries contain much other valuable information. This section will discuss some of the different kinds of general dictionaries and what they contain.

Recognizing Kinds of General Dictionaries

Lexicographers, the people who make dictionaries, always have a particular audience in mind when they prepare a new edition of a dictionary. Thus, if you were to shop for a dictionary at your local bookstore, you would probably find several shelves of dictionaries representing the work of different teams of lexicographers and publishers. There would be picture-book dictionaries for children just learning to read and dictionaries for students and adults. There might also be very detailed dictionaries for scholars. With such a variety of dictionaries available, it is important that you use one that is right for you.

Use the dictionary that best suits your needs.

The dictionary you use should be neither too easy nor too difficult for you. It should contain all of the words you are likely to encounter in your studies, on a job, or in your general reading. The words should be explained to your satisfaction in language you can understand.

There are two main kinds of general dictionaries: complete *unabridged* and shorter *abridged* dictionaries.

Unabridged Dictionaries. *Unabridged* means "not shortened." A dictionary is unabridged if it is not a shortened version of some larger dictionary. An unabridged dictionary does *not* contain every word in a language. Unabridged dictionaries generally contain 250,000 to 500,000 words, while it is estimated that the English language contains at least 600,000 words.

Some new words and some new meanings of old words may be intentionally excluded because lexicographers cannot find enough evidence to warrant their inclusion in the dictionary. Other words may be excluded because they are no longer used or because they are considered foreign. Most lexicographers do not include the new Latin names of plants and animals and the names of rare chemical compounds.

Two well-known unabridged dictionaries found on special stands in most libraries are *Webster's Third New International Dictionary of the English Language* (published in 1966) and *The Random House Dictionary of the English Language, Unabridged Edition* (published in 1967). You should consult these books whenever you need very specific definitions and extremely detailed information about words, particularly obsolete words that you may find in old literature. Notice in the following example the detail and thoroughness of an unabridged dictionary's definitions.

UNABRIDGED ENTRY:

> ¹ob·serve \əb'zərv, -zōv, -zəiv\ *vb* -ED/-ING/-S [ME *observen*, fr. MF *observer*, fr. L *observare* to watch, guard, observe, fr. *ob-* to, over, completely + *servare* to keep, guard, observe — more at OB-, CONSERVE] *vt* **1 :** to take notice of by appropriate conduct **:** conform one's action or practice to **:** HEED, OBEY ⟨∼ rules⟩ ⟨*observing* common decencies⟩ **2** *obs* **:** to give heed to (as in deference) **:** WORSHIP, HONOR **3 :** to inspect or take note of as an augury, omen, or presage ⟨*observed* the sacred geese⟩ ⟨*observed* the stumble of his horse and turned back⟩ **4 :** to celebrate or solemnize (as a ceremony, rite, or festival) after a customary or accepted form ⟨we always *observed* birthdays at home⟩ ⟨∼ the Sabbath⟩ **5 :** to see or sense esp. through directed, careful, analytic attention ⟨in order to get fresh light on this subject, I have *observed* my own children carefully —Bertrand Russell⟩ ⟨keeping an ear pricked to ∼ the movements of the viceroy —Victoria Sackville-West⟩ **6 :** to come to realize or know esp. through consideration of noted facts ⟨have *observed* that profane men living in ships . . . develop traits of profound resemblance —Joseph Conrad⟩ ⟨as we trace . . . the development of the Greek mind, we can ∼ their intellect and their moral sense expanding —G.L.Dickinson⟩ **7 :** to express as a result of observation **:** utter as a remark **:** say in a casual or incidental way **:** REMARK **8 :** to make an observation on or of **:** ascertain by scientific observation ⟨∼ phenomena⟩ ⟨*observed* the height of the sun⟩ ∼ *vi* **1 a :** to take notice **:** be attentive **b :** to make observations **:** WATCH **2 :** REMARK, COMMENT — usu. used with *on* or *upon* **syn** see KEEP, SEE

Another well-known unabridged dictionary, the *Oxford English Dictionary* (commonly known as the O.E.D.), fills twelve volumes and several supplements. Probably the most ambitious dictionary ever produced, the O.E.D. differs from the two mentioned above in that it is an historical dictionary. It organizes a word's meanings by dates. This organization allows you to determine when a word first appeared in written English, what it meant at a particular time, and how its meanings have changed over the years. Each meaning is followed by dates and examples of the word in use. In the excerpt at the top of the next page from the O.E.D.'s coverage for *eye-witness*, notice how the word was first used in the early sixteenth century. Compare this use with later meanings of the word.

O.E.D. ENTRY:

Eye'-witness. [f. EYE *sb.*¹ + WITNESS.]
† **1.** One who gives testimony to what he has
seen with his own eyes. *Obs.*

  1539 TAVERNER *Erasm. Prov.* (1552) 43 One Eye wytnesse,
is of more value, than tenne eare wytnesses. **1591** SPENSER
M. Hubberd 1278 Which yet to prove more true, he meant
to see, And an ey-witnes of each thing to bee.

  2. One who can give testimony from his own
observation; one who has seen a thing done or
happen.

  1590 SIR J. SMYTH in *Lett. Lit. Men* (Camden) 57, I do
not write the same of mine owne certaine knowledge, as a
eye wittness. **1611** BIBLE 2 *Pet.* i. 16 Wee..were eye wit-
nesses of his Maiestie. **1615** W. HULL *Mirrour of Maiestie*
89 The death of such a sonne .. whereof shee was an eyed
witnesse. **1694** LD. MOLESWORTH *Acc. Denmark* 44 Received not only from eye-witnesses, but also from some of the
principal..Actors. **1744** BERKELEY *Siris* § 17 Leo Africanus
..describes, as an eye-witness, the making of tar in Mount
Atlas. **1798** FERRIAR *Illustr. Sterne* i. 17 Brantome, an
eye-witness .. informs us. **1855** MACAULAY *Hist. Eng.* IV.
93 Different estimates were formed even by eyewitnesses.
1878 *N. Amer. Rev.* CXXVI. 180 It is the narration, by
an eye-witness, of the memorable *coup d'etat* of 1851.

  † **3.** The result of actual observation; a report
made by one who was present. *Obs.*

  1627 HAKEWILL *Apol.* i. i. § 5. 9 By the eye-witnesse of
Ioachimus Rheticus, and others, it hath been proved. **1671**
MILTON *Samson* 1594 Give us .. Eye-witness of what first
or last was done.

  Hence **Eyewi'tnessing** *vbl. sb.*

  1857 H. MILLER *Test. Rocks* iv. 154 Had they been revealed
by vision as a piece of eye-witnessing.

Abridged Dictionaries. Several companies publish shorter
dictionaries especially suited to the needs of the general public
and of students in particular. Unless you want special information about a word or need the meaning of a rare word, you
will probably find all you need to know in an abridged dictionary. Often called college or school dictionaries, these books
are designed for everyday use at home, in the office, and in the
classroom.

DICTIONARIES RECOMMENDED FOR STUDENTS

Webster's New World Dictionary, Second College Edition

The American Heritage Dictionary

The Oxford American Dictionary

Webster's New Collegiate Dictionary

Considerably smaller and less expensive than unabridged
dictionaries, abridged dictionaries usually list between 150,000
and 200,000 words. In addition to containing fewer words,
abridged dictionaries also usually list fewer definitions for a
word than unabridged dictionaries do.

846

EXERCISE A: Comparing Unabridged and Abridged Dictionaries. In a library, compare an unabridged and abridged dictionary by completing the following steps.

1. Write the complete title of each dictionary.
2. Write the most recent publication date of each dictionary.
3. Write the number of pages contained in each book.
4. Look up a common word in both dictionaries. How does the coverage differ? Be specific.
5. Find five words that are entered in the unabridged dictionary that are not in the abridged.

Knowing What Dictionaries Contain

When you read and write, you should have a good abridged dictionary within easy reach for quick reference. By consulting your dictionary often, you can increase both your knowledge of words and the precision with which you use them. The rest of this section will describe the features found in most abridged dictionaries. As you read the following descriptions, keep in mind that all dictionaries are not the same. Apply what you learn here to your own dictionary.

Learn to recognize and use the various features of your own dictionary.

Front Matter. A good dictionary contains an introduction that explains how to use it efficiently. Here, in addition to a description of all of the book's features, you will usually find instructions on how to look up a word, how to find words whose spelling you are unsure of, and how to interpret the pronunciation symbols. A complete pronunciation key and a list of all of the abbreviations used throughout the dictionary will also be found in this part of the book.

Back Matter. Many dictionaries contain helpful charts and lists at the back of the book. Look here for tables of weights and measures; metric conversion tables; guides to punctuation, manuscript form, and business-letter style; proofreaders' marks; explanations of special signs and symbols; and lists of colleges and universities. Some dictionaries also list foreign terms, biographical names, and geographical names separately at the back of the book rather than alphabetically within the main part of the dictionary.

847

Main Entries. Each word in a dictionary, along with the information about it, is called a *main entry*. The word itself is called the *entry word*. All of the entry words are listed in strict alphabetical order, letter by letter, right to the end of the entry. An entry word may be a single word, a compound word (two or more words acting as a single word), an abbreviation, a prefix or suffix, or the name of a person, place, or event. Some dictionaries may also include foreign terms.

KINDS OF ENTRY WORDS	
Single Word	dra·ma·tics
Compound Word	dress rehearsal
Abbreviation	D.A.
Prefix	dem·i-
Suffix	-dom
Person	De·moc·ri·tus
Place	Den·mark
Event	Decoration Day
Foreign Term	do·lo·ro·so

Preferred and Variant Spellings. A dictionary is an authority for the spelling of words. Most English words have only one correct spelling, as shown by the entry word. Some words, however, can be spelled in more than one way. The spelling most commonly used is called the *preferred spelling*. Less commonly used spellings are called *variant spellings*. If the form you are looking up is a variant spelling, the entry will refer you to the entry that begins with the preferred spelling. Here you will also find the definition of the word.

VARIANT SPELLING: **Doomsday Book** *same as* DOMESDAY BOOK

PREFERRED
SPELLING: **Domesday Book** [said to be so named because it judged all men without bias, like the Last Judgment] the record of a survey of England made under William the Conqueror in 1086, listing all landowners and showing the value and extent of their holdings

If a main entry shows two entry words, the form listed first is usually more commonly used and thus the preferred spelling.

ALTERNATE
SPELLINGS: **dé·cor, de·cor** (dā kôr′, dā′kôr) *n.* [Fr. < L. *decor*, beauty, elegance < *decere*, to befit, be suitable: see ff.] **1.** decoration **2.** the decorative scheme of a room, stage set, etc.

848

Syllabification. Centered dots, spaces, or slashes in an entry word indicate how words are divided into syllables. If words are already hyphenated, hyphens will take the place of these symbols. The word *short-tempered*, for example, has three syllables: short-tem·pered. Most, but not all, of these divisions can be used for word breaks at the end of a line of writing. (See Section 12.6 for specific rules about breaking words into syllables at the ends of lines of writing.)

Pronunciation. Pronunciations appear after most entry words, usually in parentheses or between diagonal lines. Pronunciations usually do not accompany entries that are not full words, such as abbreviations, prefixes, and suffixes. Nor are they usually found for entries that are compound words when the individual words are main entries themselves.

A dictionary indicates how to pronounce words by respelling them using a *phonetic alphabet,* a set of letters and special symbols. Each letter and symbol is assigned one sound. Since phonetic alphabets may vary from one dictionary to another, it is important that you become familiar with the one in the dictionary you use. You should consult the *pronunciation key* at the front or back of your dictionary for an explanation of the pronunciation symbols. Most dictionaries also provide short pronunciation keys on every other page to help you pronounce the words.

In addition to helping you pronounce the sounds correctly, the dictionary shows you which syllables are stressed. The syllable that gets the most emphasis has a *primary stress,* usually indicated by a heavy mark after the syllable ('). Words of more than one syllable may have a *secondary stress,* indicated by a shorter, lighter mark after the syllable ('). Unstressed syllables have no stress marks.

When two or more pronunciations for a word are shown, the preferred pronunciation is given first. Following are some entry words with their pronunciations. Notice not only the stress marks but also how additional pronunciations are indicated in abbreviated form.

PRIMARY STRESS ONLY: **drag·on** (drag′ən)

PRIMARY AND SECONDARY STRESSES: **drag·on·fly** (drag′ən flī′)

MORE THAN ONE PRONUNCIATION: **div·i·dend** (div′ə dend′, -dənd)

849

Part-of-Speech Labels and Inflected Forms. The dictionary also indicates how a word can be used in a sentence— whether it functions as a noun, a verb, or some other part of speech. This information is given in abbreviated form, usually after the pronunciation of a word but sometimes at the end of the entry. Entries of two or more separate words, such as *kidney bean,* have no part-of-speech labels because they are always nouns. Some dictionaries omit part-of-speech labels for people and places since these, too, are always nouns.

When necessary, the dictionary shows inflected forms after the part-of-speech label. An inflected form may be the plural form of a noun, the different forms of an adjective or adverb, or the principal parts of a verb. Notice in the following example that inflected forms are sometimes abbreviated.

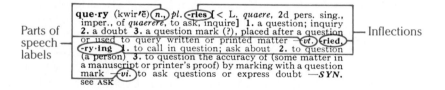

Parts of speech labels — / Inflections

que·ry (kwir′ē) *n.,* *pl.* **-ries** [< L. *quaere,* 2d pers. sing., imper., of *quaerere,* to ask, inquire] **1.** a question; inquiry **2.** a doubt **3.** a question mark (?), placed after a question or used to query written or printed matter *vt.* **-ried,** **-ry·ing** **1.** to call in question; ask about **2.** to question (a person) **3.** to question the accuracy of (some matter in a manuscript or printer's proof) by marking with a question mark *vi.* to ask questions or express doubt —*SYN.* see ASK

Etymologies. The origin and history of a word is called its *etymology* or *derivation.* In dictionaries the etymology of an entry word usually appears in brackets soon after the pronunciation or part-of-speech label. In some dictionaries, the etymology is placed at the end of a main entry.

The historical information in an etymology is arranged from the most recent to the least recent. This information is written in a code made up of symbols, abbreviations, and different kinds of type. One kind of type may indicate, for example, a cross reference to another etymology. Since the codes for etymologies vary from one dictionary to another, it is best to study the introduction in your particular dictionary to understand the code. The following example, however, should give you the basic idea.

al·pha·bet (al′fa bet′) *n.* [LL. *alphabetum* < LGr. *alpha-bētos* < Gr. *alpha* + *bēta,* the first two letters of the Greek alphabet] **1.** the letters of a language, arranged in a traditional order **2.** a system of characters, signs, or symbols used to indicate letters or speech sounds **3.** the first elements or principles, as of a branch of knowledge —*vt.* **-bet′ed** **-bet′ing** to alphabetize

850

The etymology can be translated to read "*Alphabet* comes from the Late Latin word *alphabetum,* which came from the Late Greek word *alphabetos,* which came from the two Greek words *alpha* and *beta,* the first two letters of the Greek alphabet."

Definitions. Many words in English have multiple meanings. These meanings, or senses, are called *definitions.* All meanings for the same part of speech are grouped together in the dictionary and numbered consecutively. Sometimes a definition will be broken into parts to show different shades of meaning. In such a case, the different parts will be arranged by letters: a, b, c, and so on. Most dictionaries help clarify the different meanings of an entry word with a phrase or sentence showing the word in use.

Definition with two parts —

Examples of word in use —

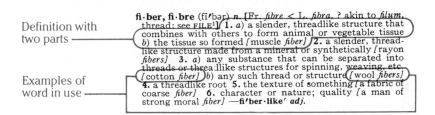

fi·ber, fi·bre (fī′bər) *n.* [Fr. *fibre* < L. *fibra,* ? akin to *filum,* thread: see FILE¹] **1.** *a*) a slender, threadlike structure that combines with others to form animal or vegetable tissue *b*) the tissue so formed [muscle *fiber*] **2.** a slender, threadlike structure made from a mineral or synthetically [rayon *fibers*] **3.** *a*) any substance that can be separated into threads or threadlike structures for spinning, weaving, etc. [cotton *fiber*] *b*) any such thread or structure [wool *fibers*] **4.** a threadlike root **5.** the texture of something [a fabric of coarse *fiber*] **6.** character or nature; quality [a man of strong moral *fiber*] —**fi′ber·like′** *adj.*

When you are checking a word that has more than one meaning, read each definition carefully to find the one that matches the context of the word in the sentence you are reading or writing. You should be able to substitute the correct definition for the word in the sentence. Which definition of *fiber,* for example, can be substituted in the following sentence?

SENTENCE: After two days a small *fiber* emerged from the seed.

As you can see when the sentence is rewritten, only the fourth definition makes sense when substituted.

SUBSTITUTION: After two days a small *threadlike root* emerged from the seed.

Usage and Field Labels. Words and meanings used the way most people in the United States use them are considered standard English and have no special labels. Words and meanings used in an uncommon way will usually be accompanied by *usage labels* such as *Slang, Informal* (or *Colloquial*), *Dialect,* and *British.* Sometimes usage labels are also used to in-

851

dicate whether a word in a particular meaning is usually plural or capitalized.

Other words or meanings may be restricted to a particular occupation, activity, or branch of knowledge. Dictionaries indicate this restricted usage with *field labels* such as *Medicine, Soccer,* or *Mathematics.*

Both usage labels and field labels usually appear before the definitions to which they apply.

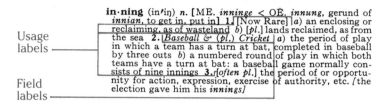

Usage labels ——

Field labels ——

in·ning (in′iŋ) *n.* [ME. *inninge* < OE. *innung,* gerund of *innian,* to get in, put in] **1.** [Now Rare] *a*) an enclosing or reclaiming, as of wasteland *b*) [*pl.*] lands reclaimed, as from the sea **2.** [*Baseball & (pl.) Cricket*] *a*) the period of play in which a team has a turn at bat, completed in baseball by three outs *b*) a numbered round of play in which both teams have a turn at bat: a baseball game normally consists of nine innings **3.** [often *pl.*] the period of or opportunity for action, expression, exercise of authority, etc. [the election gave him his *innings*]

Idioms. An *idiom* is an expression that has a meaning different from that which the words would literally suggest. Expressions such as "take stock in," "cast the first stone," and "up and around" are idioms.

Idioms are usually listed in alphabetical order near the end of a main entry or at the end of the definitions for a particular part of speech. The key word in the expression usually determines the main entry under which the idiom appears. If the idiom seems to have two or more key words, as in "take stock in," you should generally look under the noun first *(stock).* If there are no nouns in the idiom, as in "up and around," you should look under the first key word *(up).*

Idioms ——

shame (shām) *n.* [ME. < OE. *scamu,* akin to G. *scham*] **1.** a painful feeling of having lost the respect of others because of the improper behavior, incompetence, etc. of oneself or another **2.** a tendency to have feelings of this kind, or a capacity for such feeling **3.** dishonor or disgrace [to bring *shame* to one's family] **4.** a person or thing that brings shame, dishonor, or disgrace **5.** something regrettable, unfortunate, or outrageous [it's a *shame* that he wasn't told] —*vt.* **shamed, sham′ing 1.** to cause to feel shame; make ashamed **2.** to dishonor or disgrace **3.** to drive, force, or impel by a sense of shame [*shamed* into apologizing] —*SYN.* see DISGRACE —**for shame!** you ought to be ashamed!; here is cause for shame! —**put to shame 1.** to cause to feel shame **2.** to do much better than; surpass; outdo —**shame on** shame should be felt by; this is shameful of

Derived Words and Run-on Entries. Words that are formed by the addition of a suffix, such as *-ly* or *-ness,* to an entry word are called *derived words* or *run-on entries.* The suf-

852

fixes are added to change words from one part of speech to another part of speech. Derived words are found at the end of a main entry and generally are not defined. They simply appear with their part-of-speech labels and sometimes with pronunciations. If you are not sure of the meaning of a derived word, look up the meaning of the suffix and combine that with the meaning of the entry word.

Derived words

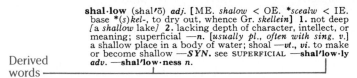

shal·low (shal'ō) *adj.* [ME. *shalow* < OE. **scealw* < IE. base **(s)kel-*, to dry out, whence Gr. *skellein*] **1.** not deep [a *shallow* lake] **2.** lacking depth of character, intellect, or meaning; superficial —*n.* [*usually pl., often with sing. v.*] a shallow place in a body of water; shoal —*vt., vi.* to make or become shallow —*SYN.* see SUPERFICIAL —**shal'low·ly** *adv.* —**shal'low·ness** *n.*

Synonymies. A *synonym* is a word closely related but not identical in meaning to another word. In some dictionaries you will see below the entry a block of words after the heading *SYN.* Here the differences in meaning among synonyms are explained. These explanations are called synonymies. *Antonyms,* or words opposite in meaning, are sometimes found here, too.

Synonymy

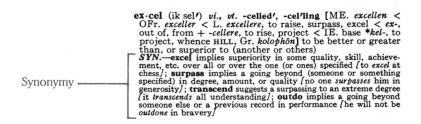

ex·cel (ik sel') *vi., vt.* **-celled', -cel'ling** [ME. *excellen* < OFr. *exceller* < L. *excellere,* to raise, surpass, excel < *ex-,* out of, from + *-cellere,* to rise, project < IE. base **kel-*, to project, whence HILL, Gr. *kolophōn*] to be better or greater than, or superior to (another or others)
SYN.—**excel** implies superiority in some quality, skill, achievement, etc. over all or over the one (or ones) specified [to *excel* at chess]; **surpass** implies a going beyond (someone or something specified) in degree, amount, or quality [no one *surpasses* him in generosity]; **transcend** suggests a surpassing to an extreme degree [it *transcends* all understanding]; **outdo** implies a going beyond someone else or a previous record in performance [he will not be *outdone* in bravery]

EXERCISE B: Using Front and Back Matter. Use a college dictionary to answer the following questions. Be sure to include the name of the dictionary you use.

1. On what page of the front matter does a list appear showing all abbreviations used in the dictionary?
2. What are the meanings of the following: ME., OFr., pp., vt.?
3. Where is Wellesley College and when was it founded?
4. What are the meanings of the following symbols: ⊕ (in astronomy), ♂ and ♀ (in biology), ⇄ (in chemistry), ∞ (in mathematics), & c. (in miscellaneous situations)?
5. Write words that contain the following phonetic sounds: [ä], [ā], [yoo], [yoͦo], [ə], [zħ].

EXERCISE C: Determining Preferred Spellings. Use your dictionary to determine whether the following are preferred or variant spellings. If the spelling is preferred, write *preferred* on your paper; if it is a variant spelling of the word, write the preferred spelling.

1. acknowledgement
2. lichee
3. ax
4. highjack
5. judgment

6. catalog
7. theatre
8. towards
9. monologue
10. esthetic

EXERCISE D: Understanding Pronunciations. Copy from your dictionary the preferred pronunciations for the following words. Be prepared to pronounce them aloud in class.

1. beauteous
2. lissome
3. Upanishad
4. egalitarian
5. porphyry

6. expatiate
7. nucleic
8. cuneiform
9. incunabula
10. litotes

EXERCISE E: Finding Part-of-Speech Labels. Use your dictionary to determine the part-of-speech labels for each of the following entry words. After each label, record the number of definitions listed for that part of speech.

1. inside
2. catch
3. rule
4. prompt
5. remedy

6. beam
7. needle
8. canine
9. only
10. render

EXERCISE F: Interpreting Etymologies. Find the etymologies for the following words in your dictionary. Write a sentence describing the origin and history of each.

1. catamaran
2. manifest
3. queue
4. California
5. mercurial

6. valediction
7. Topeka
8. penny
9. derrick
10. calisthenics

854

EXERCISE G: Applying Definitions to Words in Context.
Look up the word *credit* in your dictionary. Then write the definition of the word that applies in each sentence.

1. We must give him *credit* for his honesty.
2. The couple applied for *credit* to buy a new sofa.
3. The overpayment has been *credited* to your account.
4. Her name was not listed in the film's *credits*.
5. You can take that course for either two or three *credits*.

EXERCISE H: Finding Usage Labels and Field Labels.
Use your dictionary to answer the following questions.

1. What meanings of *upon* are now obsolete?
2. What does *quotation* mean in business or commerce?
3. What does *block* mean in medicine?
4. What does *overplay* mean to a card player?
5. In what sport is an inning also called a "frame"?

EXERCISE I: Finding the Meaning of Idioms. Use your dictionary to find the meaning of each of the following idioms.

1. hole in the wall
2. beat the drum for
3. other fish to fry
4. up to scratch
5. in the red
6. get off the ground
7. burn the candle at both ends
8. change hands
9. lie in one's teeth
10. from the horse's mouth

EXERCISE J: Finding Derived Words. Write the words your dictionary lists as derived words for each word below.

1. jealous
2. spicy
3. literal
4. lip
5. artificial
6. desirable
7. pirate
8. consul
9. slick
10. redeem

DEVELOPING WRITING SKILLS: Using Your Dictionary Efficiently. After completing Exercises B–J, write a paragraph about your skills in using the dictionary. Be specific about which skills you have mastered and those that need more work.

Skills Review and Writing Workshop

Library and Reference Skills

CHECKING YOUR SKILLS

Take notes on this selection.

Libraries originated in the ancient world. The first large reference library arose at Alexandria, Egypt, almost twenty-three centuries ago. This library was founded by the Egyptian ruler Ptolemy, who had been a general in the army of Alexander the Great. At the library in Alexandria, scholars conducted research and produced important works. For instance, Zenodotus of Ephesus compiled a forerunner of the modern dictionary. Another scholar wrote one of the world's earliest guides to the culinary arts. It was called a *Glossary of Cooking Terms*. Sometime later Pliny, the Roman author, carried out the enormous task of single-handedly writing an encyclopedia. One of the earliest works of its kind, the encyclopedia contained information on topics such as geography, botany, and mineralogy. For centuries, Alexandria remained an important center of learning, attracting scholars from many parts of the ancient world.

USING STUDY SKILLS FOR WRITING
Writing a Library Research Project

Library and reference skills are valuable tools that can help you achieve success in school. Using the materials available in your library, write a research report on a scientific subject.

Prewriting: Select a topic that you have studied recently. Find resources in the library that relate to your topic. Read these sources carefully, take notes, and make an outline.

Writing: State your general purpose in the introduction. Then present your main ideas as simply and effectively as possible. Summarize your ideas in the conclusion of the paper.

Revising: Make sure you have presented all the information from your outline. Rewrite any sentences that could be clearer. After you have revised, proofread carefully.

32

Getting a Job

A potential employer has only a limited knowledge of your qualifications for a particular job. A decision about which applicant to hire will generally be based on résumés, job applications, interviews, and references submitted by a number of applicants. Therefore, it is important that you make the most of each step in getting a job so that you can convince the potential employer that you should be hired.

First Steps 32.1

The first step in getting a job is to analyze your skills, interests, and goals. The next step is to find out what jobs are available that might be suitable for you.

Writing a Résumé

The word *résumé* means "summary." The résumé that you prepare for potential employers is a formal summary of your background and interests as they relate to employment. A résumé serves two purposes, one for you and one for the employer. First, it helps you sort out your experiences and organize those that make you a good job candidate. Second, a résumé helps a potential employer see the kinds of experience and interests you have and how your experience fits a particular job opening.

Keep an updated résumé ready to send to potential employers.

Since your objective in preparing a résumé is to get a job, emphasize only the positive things in your background. However, it is important that the information you do include in the résumé is truthful. You need not mention a course that you failed to complete or your reasons for leaving a previous job. On the other hand, you should not make it sound as if your experience is more extensive than it really is. The following suggestions should help you prepare a good résumé.

SUGGESTIONS FOR WRITING A RÉSUMÉ

1. Keep your résumé short, possibly limited to one page.
2. Allow space between items so your résumé is easy to read.
3. Be sure that your résumé is neatly typed.
4. Emphasize information for the kind of job you want.
5. Update your résumé every six months or each year.
6. Keep multiple copies of your résumé.

Heading. The heading at the top of the résumé should include your name, address, and phone number. If you are presently employed and can receive calls on the job, you may want to list both residence and business phone numbers.

Position Desired. Include the specific title of a job you have seen advertised or a simple description of the type of work you would like. If you have a long-range career goal, your entry after this category might read: "Entry level position as . . . with possibility for advancement leading to. . . ."

Education. Begin with your most recent educational experience and work backward. After each listing give the dates of attendance, as well as the city and state of each school. Do not overlook any special courses taken outside school that are particularly relevant to the type of employment you seek.

Work Experience. Begin with your most recent employment and again work backward. Include the name of the employer (company or individual), the address, the dates of employment, and a brief description of your responsibilities. In this category include both paid and volunteer work.

Interests. Briefly describe what you enjoy doing with your leisure time. Such information provides an interviewer with topics for follow-up questions and may suggest how your interests may be compatible with certain aspects of the job.

Activities. Describe clubs and organizations to which you belong, listing the roles you play in each. Also mention any awards or honors you have received for such activities.

References. Obtain permission from three responsible adults to use their names as references. Include former employers, teachers, guidance counselors, coaches, club advisors, religious leaders, or adult friends. Do not use relatives as references unless they have also been employers. Along with the name of each reference, include the person's relationship to you, the person's address, and the person's phone number.

EXERCISE A: Developing a Résumé. Using the format described on pages 857–858, compose a résumé of your own. Have a particular job in mind as you compose the résumé.

Reading Classified Want Ads

Frequently people hear about jobs through friends or go to an employment agency for help. However, reading want ads in newspapers or in professional publications is probably the most common way of learning about job opportunities.

Learn to interpret classified want ads.

Classified ads use a fairly standard set of abbreviations for terms that occur frequently. Once you become familiar with the terms and abbreviations, you can easily interpret classified ads. Compare the following ad and a translation of the ad.

INTERPRETING A CLASSIFIED WANT AD	
SECRETARY to assist VP/ investment. M/F. Min. 55 wpm w/wo steno. Will consider secy. school grads, secy. w/ any exper. Bnfts incl. med., tuition. EOE.	Wanted: A Secretary to assist the Vice President of investment. Male or female. Minimum 55 words a minute typing, with or without stenography. Will consider secretarial school graduates or secretary with any experience. Benefits include medical and tuition. We are an equal opportunity employer.

EXERCISE B: Examining Classified Want Ads. On a separate sheet of paper, write out the following classified ad for computer word processors. Add any necessary words, and write out all abbreviations.

WORD PROCESSING. Int'l law firm. F/PT and Wknds. AM/PM shfts. Trnee. prgm. Excel. sal. and lib. med. bnfts. EOE. M/F. Call personnel 821-6580.

Filling Out a Job Application

Whether you are answering a classified ad or following up on a reply to an inquiry you have sent through the mail, your next step toward getting a job will probably be filling out the company's application form. This part of the employment process is usually done in the personnel or employment office before you meet your potential employer.

Fill out a job application form accurately, completely, and honestly.

Job application forms require your social security number, jobs you have held and dates of employment, names and addresses of schools you have attended and dates of attendance, and the names and addresses of references. You may find it helpful to write out this information in advance and bring it with you to the personnel or employment office. The following suggestions can be useful in filling out job applications.

FILLING OUT JOB APPLICATIONS
1. Type or neatly print all information.
2. Check your spelling carefully.
3. Leave no blanks, unless you have explained why.
4. Be truthful in answering all questions.
5. Use additional paper to answer questions more fully.
6. Include any information that may be job-related.
7. Start with the most recent job and school experiences and then work backward.
8. Include a cover letter with applications that are mailed.

If you are giving your application directly to an employer, you will not need a cover letter. If you are sending your application through the mail, however, do enclose a cover letter with it. The cover letter should include information on the job opportunity you are applying for and times when you are available for an interview. If you have not heard from the employer within two weeks, write again or telephone to ask courteously whether or not your application was received.

EXERCISE C: Filling Out an Application. Obtain an actual job application form from a local employer or from your school's guidance or placement office. For practice, fill it out neatly and carefully, just as if you were applying for a job.

DEVELOPING WRITING SKILLS: Writing a Cover Letter. Using the information at the top of this page, write a cover letter to the employer you listed in Exercise C.

Next Steps 32.2

The last step—the interview itself—is often the most difficult for many people. However, if you prepare your presentation and your follow-up for the interview in advance, you will act more confidently in the interview and improve your chances of getting the job.

Preparing for a Job Interview

When you prepare for an interview, you need to find out all you can about the prospective employer before going into the interview. You should also review your résumé to see if it is current and relevant to the job for which you are interviewing.

Prepare for a job interview by learning about the job and by reviewing your résumé.

A valuable way to prepare for an interview is to go through a mock job interview. Ask an adult who has experience interviewing people for jobs or one who has been interviewed for jobs several times to go over your résumé and play the interviewer by asking you questions a potential employer may ask.

The following chart gives valuable suggestions to help you prepare for an interview.

PREPARING FOR AN INTERVIEW

1. Learn something about the job and employer by either getting brochures from the company or talking with local residents who know something about the company.
2. Plan to be neatly dressed and well-groomed.
3. Be prepared to follow up on information in your résumé or on the application form.
4. Prepare to ask questions about the job that may not arise in the course of the interview.
5. Be prepared to take an employment test or to be interviewed by more than one person.

EXERCISE A: Preparing for an Interview. Prepare a list of ten to twelve questions that you could ask a job interviewer. Include questions about such areas as job responsibility, employee benefits, and possible promotions.

Interviewing for a Job

If you have taken the time to prepare for the job interview, you will have more self-confidence, which your interviewer will sense. In addition to self-confidence, the interviewer will also be evaluating your aptitude, enthusiasm, and sincerity.

Present a positive image to a potential employer.

Allow plenty of time to get to the interview. When you have been introduced, wait for the interviewer to shake your hand and invite you to be seated. Sit erect and maintain eye contact with the interviewer. Avoid criticizing past job situations or making excuses for past mistakes. Take time to answer each question fully and as honestly as you can. Feel free to show enthusiasm and to say that you are qualified for the job.

The following chart lists some of the questions you may be asked during an interview.

862

COMMONLY ASKED INTERVIEW QUESTIONS
1. Why are you interested in the job you are applying for?
2. What skills would you bring to this job?
3. Are there any areas in your personal life (health problems, continuing education, family obligations, transportation problems) that would conflict with the demands of the job?
4. What are your career goals?
5. What would you do if . . . ? (In this type of question, the interviewer gives you a particular job-related problem.)
6. What were your responsibilities in your last job?
7. What are your greatest strengths?
8. How do you think other people would describe you?
9. What do you like to do in your spare time?
10. What are your reading habits? What are you reading now?

Some employers call selected job candidates back for a second interview after screening a number of applicants. A second interview usually includes more probing questions and may include a test or a trial assignment. Once again, a confident attitude will give you an edge over other contenders.

EXERCISE B: Answering an Interviewer's Questions. Select a job that you would like to apply for. Then study the interview questions at the top of this page. Ask an adult to conduct a mock interview using your résumé and the interview questions.

DEVELOPING WRITING SKILLS: Evaluating Your Skills in Getting a Job. Answer the following questions to evaluate your skills in getting a job.

1. Do you check the classified ads on a regular basis?
2. Can you write a résumé that will interest an employer?
3. Can you list three people who would agree to give a written or oral reference to a potential employer?
4. Can you answer the commonly asked interview questions?
5. Do you know the form for writing business letters, and can you write a good follow-up letter?

Skills Review and Writing Workshops

Getting a Job

CHECKING YOUR SKILLS

Put this information in the form of a résumé.

My name is Harold Rogers, and I live at 401 Main Street in Hartford, Connecticut. My home telephone number is 203-525-1878. I am presently interested in obtaining a position as a teller in a bank. This year, I will be graduating from Central High School in Hartford, which I have attended for the past four years. Previously, I attended Carlton Junior High School and Fielding Elementary School, both of them located in Chicago, Illinois. In high school my courses have included mathematics, accounting, and computer literacy. I have also been a member of the school debating team. During the last two summers, I have worked as a clerk at Harrison's Department Store at 1430 Elm Street in Hartford. My responsibilities consisted of stocking shelves, waiting on customers, and operating one of the cash registers. My major interests are tennis, boating, and stamp collecting.

USING STUDY SKILLS IN WRITING
Writing a Cover Letter

Whenever you send an application to an employer, it should be accompanied by a cover letter. Write an effective cover letter by following these steps.

Prewriting: What is the position for which you are applying? When could you be interviewed for it?

Writing: Describe the position for which you are applying. You might also briefly mention that your application is enclosed with the letter. Explain when you can be interviewed for the position.

Revising: Read your letter and change any sentences that could be written more effectively. After you have revised, proofread carefully.

864

Speaking and Listening

Chapter 33

Speaking and Listening Skills

Communication is a two-way process. It involves both the ability to speak and the ability to listen. Communication is also a complex process. Whether you are involved in communication with one other person, with a group, or with larger numbers of people, you need to master certain skills in order to communicate effectively.

In this chapter you will practice one-to-one communication skills needed in interviews. You will also practice group communication skills needed in group discussions, meetings, public-speaking situations, and debates.

Interviews 33.1

An interview is a formal kind of communication in which one person has a definite purpose for speaking with another person. One person, the interviewer, speaks to another, the interviewee, for the purpose of obtaining information. In this section you will practice skills to use when you interview someone.

Conducting an Interview

When you are preparing a speech or a report, speaking with someone who is an expert can be a good source of information about your topic. As the interviewer you need to be in charge of the interview. You will need to prepare for, manage, and follow up the interview.

Conducting an interview requires careful preparation, management, and follow-up.

The following chart lists the steps to follow when you conduct an interview.

CONDUCTING AN INTERVIEW	
Preparing	1. Research the topic that you need information about.
	2. Learn about the interviewee's background and expertise. This will help determine what questions to ask.
	3. List the questions you want to ask the interviewee. Ask only those questions that cannot be answered from other sources.
Managing	1. Come prepared to the interview with paper and pencil and/or tape recorder to record the interviewee's responses.
	2. Arrive promptly and greet the interviewee by introducing yourself and explaining the purpose of the interview.
	3. Encourage the interviewee to express his or her ideas freely, but keep the conversation related to the interview topic.
	4. End the interview when your questions have been answered and you have the information you need. Thank the person.
Following Up	1. If you conducted the interview as part of your research for a school report or speech, send a copy of your report or speech to the interviewee.
	2. Include a letter that shares the outcome of the interview such as favorable comments by the audience. Close the letter by expressing your thanks for the person's assistance.

EXERCISE: Conducting an Interview. Interview a person who now holds the kind of job you might like to hold in the future. Follow the steps listed in the first two sections of the chart on page 868 to prepare and manage your interview.

DEVELOPING WRITING SKILLS: Writing a Follow-Up Letter. After conducting the interview for Exercise A, write a follow-up letter to the person you interviewed. Make sure you thank the person for granting you the interview.

Group Discussion and 33.2 Parliamentary Procedure

Group discussion takes place when three or more people meet to work together for a specific purpose or to achieve a common goal. Large groups often use parliamentary procedure to conduct meetings in a direct and democratic manner.

Recognizing Different Kinds of Group Discussions

The members of all groups work together to reach a common, group goal rather than that of any particular individual.

A group discussion is formed to achieve a specific common goal.

Discussion groups can be organized in several different ways. Described below are the four major kinds of discussion groups that have been developed to achieve different goals.

A *round-table discussion* involves a small group whose goal is to share information or to inform those taking part.

A *committee* is a small group of a larger organization whose goal is to discuss specific ideas and perform certain tasks. A leader keeps the discussion on track. A secretary or recorder takes notes from which a report is made to the organization.

A *panel* is a group of several informed people whose goal is to share ideas with an audience. Members may meet before the discussion to work out each speaker's strategy, the amount of time each can speak, and whether the audience will participate.

A *symposium* is a group of people each of whom delivers a short prepared speech on the topic under discussion. Each member is an authority on a particular aspect of the topic. There may be a discussion among members after the speeches are given. Audience participation may follow.

EXERCISE A: Outlining a Topic for Group Discussions. Choose one of the four kinds of discussion groups. Review the characteristics of the kind of group you have chosen. Using the topic *lowering the voting age,* write a purpose your type of group might have for meeting. Then write a brief description of the people that might make up such a group.

Holding a Group Discussion

For a group discussion to be productive the topic must be appropriate. First, the topic must be one that is of mutual interest to all the members. Second, the topic must be one that is timely, interesting, and one that the group can manage within the discussion time. Third, the topic must be researched thoroughly by each member so that the discussion is informed.

A group discussion should focus on a topic that is timely, interesting, and one the members are involved with and prepared to discuss.

Planning. Most good group discussions are the result of careful planning. The following chart can help you to plan one.

PLANNING A GROUP DISCUSSION
1. Hold a prediscussion meeting to determine the discussion topic. The topic should be timely and interesting.
2. Define the topic precisely. After it is defined, phrase the topic as a question, not a statement.
3. Make an outline of points to be discussed. Include a history of the problem, alternatives or solutions, and possible action to be taken.
4. Research the topic by reading, thinking, and getting as much information as possible before the discussion.

Leading. In less formal group discussions, such as a round-table discussion, the leadership roles can be assumed by several of the members. In more formal groups, such as a committee, a panel, or a symposium, leadership roles are assigned to a chairperson. The chart below lists the duties of a discussion leader.

LEADING A DISCUSSION

1. Introduce members of the group to each other and to the audience if one is present.
2. Introduce the topic. Phrase it as a question.
3. Invite and encourage all members to speak freely, especially a member who is silent.
4. Keep participation balanced by tactfully diverting discussion from a member who is talking too much to one who has said less.
5. Keep the discussion on track. Summarize for the group after they have completed major parts of the discussion.
6. Watch the time limit. Move on to a major point not yet covered to speed things up.
7. Conclude the discussion by summarizing main ideas. Allow time for any member to add summary points or opinions.

Participating. Members of a discussion group should remember the following. First, do not monopolize the discussion. Be brief in your statements and stay on track. Second, keep the discussion goal in mind even if you are opposed to it.

EXERCISE B: Planning a Symposium. Form a group of four or five students. Choose a discussion leader. Plan a symposium, consulting the chart on page 870 and the information on symposiums above. Choose a topic that the members are already familiar with so that no research will be needed.

EXERCISE C: Holding a Symposium. Using the plan your group completed for Exercise B, conduct a symposium on your topic. Limit each speech to five minutes and the discussion among members and the audience to twenty minutes.

Using Parliamentary Procedure

When a meeting of more than ten members is held, it is difficult for each member to be recognized and heard. Using parliamentary procedure makes orderly discussion possible.

Parliamentary procedure guarantees that the rights of the majority and minority are respected and that a meeting is conducted in an orderly way.

Basic Principles. Parliamentary procedure is based on five basic democratic principles that provide for rule by the majority while at the same time guaranteeing the rights of the minority. The following chart lists the five basic principles.

PRINCIPLES OF PARLIAMENTARY PROCEDURE
1. One issue at a time can be debated and voted on. If an issue is not voted on, it must be disposed of in some way before members can consider another issue.
2. The decision of the majority rules. A simple majority consists of more than one half of the people voting on an issue.
3. Minority rights are protected in part by allowing those in the minority to present their views and to change the minds of those in the majority.
4. Every member has a right to speak or remain silent, to vote or not to vote.
5. Open discussion of every issue is protected so that members can vote in an informed way on every issue. A two-thirds vote is needed to limit debate or to end it completely.

Rules of Order. Parliamentary rules of order specify the way the business of a meeting is conducted and also the duties of the chairperson. The rules are fully outlined in a book called *Robert's Rules of Order,* but the main rules are given here.

First, the chairperson or presiding officer must decide if a *quorum* is present. A quorum is the agreed-upon number of persons that must be present to hold the meeting, say one-third of the active membership of the group.

Second, the meeting follows certain steps called the *order of business.* The order of business is listed in an *agenda* that the presiding officer has prepared. The chairperson brings up each item on the agenda at the meeting. The chairperson also helps to maintain order during the meeting and sees that the members are heard impartially. The chart shows the steps for conducting a meeting in the correct order.

STEPS FOR CONDUCTING A MEETING

1. Call to order
2. Roll call
3. Reading and approval of minutes from last meetings
4. Reading of reports of officers
5. Reading of reports of committees
6. Consideration of old (unfinished) business
7. Consideration of new business
8. Adjournment

Third, the business of a meeting is conducted through the making of *motions.* A motion is a formal suggestion or proposal by a member that something be discussed and acted upon. There are eight steps involved in introducing a motion, discussing a motion, and then voting on it, as is shown in the following chart.

STEPS FOR CARRYING OUT A MOTION

1. A member asks to be recognized by the chairperson and introduces the motion by saying, "I move _____."
2. Some other member must second the motion, that is, agree to its introduction for discussion.
3. The chairperson restates the motion so that all members will clearly know what has been proposed for discussion.
4. Discussion of the motion begins; members may agree, disagree, explain, or attempt to change the motion.
5. When the chairperson feels that the motion has been thoroughly discussed, he or she asks the members if they are ready to vote. If two-thirds of the members agree, discussion is ended.

---

6. The chairperson restates the motion which may now include an amendment, a change in the original motion; such an amendment would be included only if a majority present had voted to include it during the discussion.
7. The chairperson asks the members to vote.
8. The chairperson announces the result of the vote by saying, "The motion carried" if the majority favored the motion or "The motion is lost" if the majority was against the motion.

EXERCISE D: Using Parliamentary Procedure. Using parliamentary procedure, conduct a meeting of a club or an organization you belong to. After the meeting, evaluate whether using parliamentary procedure made the meeting effective.

DEVELOPING WRITING SKILLS: Organizing a Club. Obtain a copy of *Robert's Rules of Order.* Write a set of rules and bylaws for a real or imaginary club you would like to organize.

33.3 Public Speaking

Many people feel less confident when speaking alone in front of an audience than they do when speaking in a group discussion. As you practice and improve your public speaking skills, you will be able to communicate your ideas more effectively and confidently.

Recognizing Different Kinds of Speeches

Once you think about the purpose of a speech you want to give and the audience who will listen to your speech, you can then decide on the kind of speech to prepare.

Choose the kind of speech you will give by considering both the purpose of the speech and your audience.

You can choose among four main kinds of speeches depending on your purpose and your audience. An *expository* speech uses facts to explain an idea, a process, or an object. A *persuasive* speech uses opinions supported by facts to per-

874

suade the audience to agree with the speaker's position or to take some action. An *entertaining* speech offers the audience something to enjoy. Humor can offer variety or emphasis when it is part of another kind of speech. An *extemporaneous* speech requires the speaker to rely on knowledge and speaking skills to speak without a formally prepared manuscript.

EXERCISE A: Determining Purpose and Audience. Using the descriptions of the kinds of speeches you have read, give an example of a purpose and an audience that might determine when you would give each kind of speech.

Giving a Speech

After you have decided on the kind of speech you will give and an appropriate topic, you can go through the steps that lead to giving your speech. The chart below lists suggestions for ways to gather information, outline your speech, prepare note cards, practice, and deliver your speech.

GATHERING INFORMATION
1. Research the subject using the library or other sources, especially if the speech is expository or persuasive.
2. Consider interviewing authorities on the topic.
PREPARING AN OUTLINE
1. Begin with any necessary background material.
2. Arrange information in a logical sequence.
3. Include major points and supporting details.
PREPARING NOTE CARDS
1. Use only a few small index cards.
2. Print all information in the order used in the outline.
3. Write beginning and ending statements.
4. Rely mainly on key words and phrases to jog your memory.
5. Letter and indent all details under the ideas they support.
6. Use underlining and capital letters to make important information stand out.

PRACTICING YOUR SPEECH
1. Study outline and note cards until you know the material.
2. Be aware of the *verbal* form of language you are using, such as the *pitch* and *loudness* of your voice, the *rate* at which you speak, and *pronunciation* of words.
3. Be aware of the *nonverbal* forms of language you are using, such as the way you move, posture, facial expressions, gestures, and appearance.

DELIVERING YOUR SPEECH
1. As you stand in front of your audience, try to establish eye contact with several people.
2. Look over your note cards to refresh your mind before speaking, and refer to them only if needed as you speak.

EXERCISE B: Giving a Speech. Choose an *expository, persuasive,* or *entertaining* speech. Use the chart on page 875 and above, to prepare and deliver an eight- to ten-minute speech.

Evaluating a Speech

The main purpose of evaluation is to let the speaker know which public speaking skills were successful and which skills need more work. A secondary purpose is to apply the successful skills to your own speaking.

Evaluate a speech in a way that offers benefits to the speaker and to yourself.

Make a copy of this checklist to use for evaluating a speech.

CHECKLIST FOR EVALUATING A SPEECH
What Was Said?
1. What type of speech was given—expository, persuasive, entertaining, or extemporaneous?
2. Did the speaker introduce the topic clearly, develop it well, and end in a conclusive fashion?
3. Did the speaker support main ideas with appropriate details?

How Was It Said?
1. Did the speaker approach the platform confidently and establish eye contact with the audience?
2. Did the speaker's gestures and movements confirm or contradict his or her words? Where? How?
3. Did the speaker project his or her voice loudly enough?
4. Did the speaker vary the pitch of his or her voice?
5. Did the speaker vary the rate of his or her speaking?
6. Did the speaker pronounce all words clearly and correctly?

EXERCISE C: Evaluating a Speech. Using the checklist on page 876 and above, evaluate a speech given in class. Make note of the speaking skills the person used effectively and plan to use them in a speech you will give. Then give a copy of the evaluation to the person who gave the speech to use for improvement of his or her speaking skills.

DEVELOPING WRITING SKILLS: Evaluating Your Speaking Skills. Write a paragraph discussing the skill you are developing giving public speeches. Mention those parts of the process you find particularly easy as well as those you find difficult. Then note the one skill you plan to work on in the future.

Public Debate 33.4

You probably have engaged in informal debate with one or more people. If you have ever taken a stand on or defended an issue, you have informally debated. Similarly, in a formal debate people argue ideas and issues in open competition.

The Nature of Debate

A debate is similar to other formal group discussions, such as panel discussions and symposiums, in that it is planned and held before an audience. Unlike other kinds of discussion, however, the purpose of a debate is not to arrive at a group decision. Instead, debate is a contest between opposing teams.

The purpose is to use reasoned argument to win the contest.

Debate is a formal public discussion in which opposing sides use reasoned argument to arrive at a decision with one side the winner.

State the Proposition. In a debate the two sides of the issue under debate are stated in the form of a proposition. A formal debate proposition is worded as a positive statement. It should be clearly worded so that it can be answered by *yes* and *no.* It demands that certain action be taken or not taken.

EXAMPLE: Resolved, that the current ten-month school year be lengthened to eleven months.

The two sides of the debate are called the *affirmative* and the *negative.* Both sides take turns presenting their arguments.

Affirmative. The affirmative upholds the proposition by demanding that the *status quo,* the present situation, be changed. The affirmative has the responsibility of proving that a problem exists and that its plan will work better than any other to solve the problem. This responsibility for proving the proposition is true is called the affirmative's *burden of proof.*

Negative. The negative presents arguments to disprove or *refute* the attacks on the *status quo* made by the affirmative. The negative has the responsibility of proving that the present system or *status quo* is satisfactory or that the plan the affirmative proposes is not workable.

EXERCISE A: Stating a Proposition. Using the description of propositions above, state a debate proposition in writing.

Preparing to Debate

Careful preparation is needed to ensure a lively, thoughtful, and interesting debate. First, you must analyze the debate proposition. Then you must prepare sound evidence and reasoning to construct your case. Finally, you must work with your debate partner to plan how you will present your case.

Prepare to debate by analyzing the proposition, preparing sound evidence and reasoning, and working with your partner to build the case.

878

e two important tasks. First, you must present your case in
best manner possible. Second, you must successfully re-
te all of your opponents' arguments.

**In a debate each team must present a strong
case and refute the oppositions' arguments as
well.**

There are several ways to proceed in a debate. One way is
to use different strategies depending whether you are on the
affirmative or on the negative side. The chart lists strategies
each team member should use for his or her first speech.

DEBATE STRATEGIES
First Affirmative Speaker
1. States the debate proposition
2. Defines key terms
3. Shows the need for change in the *status quo*
Second Affirmative Speaker
1. Presents the affirmative side's plan for change
2. Shows advantages of the plan
3. Summarizes the affirmative's case
First Negative Speaker
1. Confirms or redefines the affirmative's definitions
2. Refutes the affirmative's argument about a need for change
Second Negative Speaker
1. Attacks the affirmative's plan
2. Refutes the advantages of the affirmative's plan

After the affirmative and negative sides have presented their
arguments, they begin *rebuttals*. Rebuttals give each side a
chance to refute the opposition's arguments and to answer objections to its own case. During this part of a debate, the order
of the speakers is reversed so that the negative speaks first.
This is done so that the affirmative has an opportunity to make
both the opening and the closing remarks.

After each side has argued its evidence to the best of its ability, a judge decides which side has presented the best persuasive argument for its case.

EXERCISE C: Holding a Classroom Debate. Using the cases developed in Exercise B, hold a classroom debate with two members on each team. Limit the constructive speeches to ten minutes each. Limit the rebuttals to five minutes each. Choose someone to act as judge and to determine the winning team.

DEVELOPING WRITING SKILLS: Evaluating Your Debate. After you have held your debate, write two paragraphs evaluating how both sides presented their cases. Mention logical and faulty uses of reasoning, effective strategies, and reasons why you agree or disagree with the judge's decision.

33.5 Listening Skills

Listening skills are important in every communication situation. Whether you are listening to a teacher in class or to several people in a debate, you need to give the speaker your undivided attention to understand the information you hear. Once you understand the literal or exact message the speaker gives, you can then interpret and evaluate what you hear.

Improving Your Listening Skills

One of the reasons for learning to become a better listener is to acquire new ideas and information. Remembering and taking notes on the main ideas and major details can help you separate important from irrelevant information.

Learn to take mental and written notes on main ideas and major details as you listen.

Main Ideas. It is not always easy to decide what the main ideas are when you are listening to material presented orally. You must force yourself to analyze what you are hearing. Some of the information will be more important than other informa-

tion. The following chart gives steps to follow to help you listen for main ideas.

LISTENING FOR MAIN IDEAS
1. Listen carefully to the beginning statements of the speaker and to the points the speaker emphasizes, repeats, and enumerates.
2. Visualize the main ideas. Restate them in your own words.
3. Decide whether the speaker's examples, definitions, facts, and statistics support the main ideas you have in mind.

Major Details. In order to determine how details are related to main ideas, you must again analyze what you hear. The next chart gives suggestions that can help you.

LISTENING FOR MAJOR DETAILS
1. As you listen, ask yourself what makes each main idea true. Keep the details that answer that question in mind.
2. Try to predict details the speaker will mention.
3. Try to link the main ideas and supporting details into some sort of visual pattern.

Verbal Signals. Speakers often use verbal signals to alert you to important ideas or to the way the ideas are organized. The following chart contains a sample of the verbal signals you should listen for.

VERBAL SIGNALS	
Introduction	
we will discuss	open your books to
today's lecture covers	let's look first at
Main Ideas	
a point to be made	of major importance
make note of	remember that
let me repeat	I want to stress

Change in Direction	
next	turning now to
let us move on to	however
on the other hand	even though
Major Details	
for instance	the following reasons
for example	in support of
namely	that is to say
Conclusion	
finally	in conclusion
the last point	in summation
in brief	all in all

Nonverbal Language. In addition to verbal signals, a speaker may alert you to main ideas, changes in direction, and the conclusion by movements and gestures. A speaker often reinforces words by speaking more loudly, raising an arm, approaching the audience, slowing down, or speeding up.

Taking Notes. The best way to remember information that you hear is to take notes while you are listening. Taking notes forces you to listen actively and concentrate on what you are trying to learn. The chart below offers suggestions to help you take notes from spoken material.

NOTE-TAKING AIDS

1. Have your notebook and pen or pencil ready. Label the top of each page with the date, subject, and topic.
2. Write down only main ideas and supporting details in your own words. Underline main ideas.
3. Write down anything that the speaker says is important or is something you will need to know.
4. Write notes in short phrases, using abbreviations and symbols. See page 777 for ways to develop a shorthand.
5. Summarize sections of notes with a main idea statement. Box the statement to make it easy to find when you review.

Following Directions. You are often required to follow directions that are given orally such as homework assignments or test directions. The chart below lists steps to follow.

STEPS TO HELP YOU UNDERSTAND DIRECTIONS
1. Prepare to concentrate.
2. Visualize each step in the directions. Ask yourself questions about how you would follow the directions.
3. After hearing the directions, repeat them mentally.
4. Ask to have the directions repeated if they are unclear.
5. Take notes if the directions are long or complicated.

EXERCISE A: Listening for Main Ideas and Major Details. Work with a partner on this exercise. While one person reads aloud the following portion from a social studies lecture, the other listens for main ideas and major details, taking written notes while listening. Then compare both sets of notes for accuracy in identifying main ideas and major details.

Today's lecture will cover the powers that the President of the United States holds as chief executive. The powers that the President holds are extensive but not unlimited because the United States Constitution has established a system of checks and balances. Let me repeat and define the term *checks and balances* because it is an important one for you to know. A system of checks and balances is one in which each branch of government can check the power of the others. Thus, no one branch can exceed its authority.

Let's discuss the major powers the President holds and how the system of checks and balances works. First, the President is Commander-in-Chief of the army and navy. He has power to call the state militia into national service; for example, Presidents have called up the National Guard to maintain order during riots. A second power that the President has is to make treaties with foreign nations. However, he must obtain the advice and consent of two-thirds of the Senate to make a treaty. Third, the President has the power to appoint federal judges, cabinet officers, and ambassadors. However, he must obtain approval from the Senate for these appointments.

EXERCISE B: Practicing Your Listening Skills. Make a tape recording of one of the following speech situations while you listen. Take written notes on the main ideas and major details as you listen. Then replay the tape recording and check the accuracy of your notes.

1. A classroom or school debate
2. A teacher's lecture
3. Another student's oral report
4. A classroom discussion
5. An editorial on a national news program

EXERCISE C: Evaluating Your Following Directions Skills. For one week, keep a written list of each error you make in following directions because you failed to listen. Using the chart on page 885, identify the source of each problem. Then, make a note next to each error about how you will work on correcting it during the next week.

Listening Critically

In addition to listening actively so you can understand important information, you also have to listen critically so you can analyze and then evaluate that information. You must listen critically so that you can make decisions about the appropriateness and validity of a speaker's words. Critical listening is really critical or logical thinking in that you use reason to make judgments about what you hear.

Listen critically in order to interpret and evaluate a speaker's words.

A fuller discussion of critical thinking is found in Chapter 29.

Inappropriate Tone. Tone is the effect that a speaker's words have on you. The words provide clues about the speaker's attitude toward the topic and the way you are expected to respond to the topic. Tone is inappropriate if a speaker uses words to mislead or confuse you about the real meaning of what he or she means.

A speaker or writer uses certain techniques that convey the attitude toward and establish the tone of the message. The following chart explains some of these techniques.

LISTENING FOR INAPPROPRIATE TONE

Fact and Opinion

A fact is something that can be verified as true or as something that has actually happened. An opinion is something that can not be proven. Speakers must support opinions with pertinent facts before the opinions can be accepted as valid.

FACT: Mars is a planet in our solar system that is fourth in distance from the sun.

OPINION: Mars is a planet that we could live on if Earth became too crowded.

Denotation and Connotation

The denotation of a word is its literal or exact meaning. The connotation is its suggested or implied meaning. Speakers may choose words with unfavorable connotations to present someone or something unfavorably.

NEUTRAL DENOTATION: That man acts in a *childlike* way.

UNFAVORABLE CONNOTATION: That man acts in a *childish* way.

Euphemism

Euphemisms are words or phrases used in place of others that are considered unpleasant or offensive. A speaker may use a euphemism to soften the meaning that a direct word would convey.

EUPHEMISM: Mr. Carlin *passed on* at the age of 84.

DIRECT WORD: Mr. Carlin *died* at the age of 84.

Self-Important Language

Self-important or inflated language consists of flowery or unnecessarily long words or phrases. A speaker may use it to try to impress listeners. *Jargon,* the specialized vocabulary of a profession or other group, can also be a type of inflated language. Inflated language conceals rather than reveals the ideas behind the words.

SELF-IMPORTANT LANGUAGE: Upon completion of the form, affix signature to the bottom.

DIRECT LANGUAGE: After you fill out the form, sign it at the bottom.

Logical Fallacies. If the rules for logical reasoning are not followed, the result is a logical fallacy. Most logical fallacies occur when a speaker is trying to persuade you about something. Debates, political speeches, or commercials may contain logical fallacies. Following is a discussion of fallacies.

A *hasty generalization* is a statement that offers conclusions based on a few examples without taking into account exceptions or qualifying factors. It fails to follow the rules for *inductive* reasoning since conclusions should be supported by valid references, research, or evidence. Hasty generalizations usually apply to a wide segment of the population or to a controversial issue. They tend to sound highly reliable. However, they are usually being used to exert influence for a particular cause.

EXAMPLE: Many teenagers have reading problems. Some teenagers would rather watch television than read. Television is the reason why teenagers have reading problems.

Begging the question, also called circular reasoning, is a logical fallacy that violates the rules of *deductive* reasoning. A speaker who "begs the question" may start with a definition or a general principle but does not take any further steps to provide proof for the statements. The validity of the conclusion is taken for granted.

EXAMPLE: A movie becomes a classic when it says something new to each generation. This movie says something to me and it came out thirty years ago, so it is a classic.

A *non sequitur* is a logical fallacy that violates the rules of *inductive* reasoning. A *non sequitur* is a conclusion that does not follow logically from the preceding evidence.

EXAMPLE: A man running for the office of treasurer says you should vote for him because his father is wealthy.

A *testimonial* is the use of a famous person to endorse a product or a service so the general public will believe in it. The person, however famous, may not be an authority on the particular subject at all.

EXAMPLE: A movie star who appeared in westerns endorses a brand of jeans.

888

The *bandwagon* technique is used by a speaker to urge people to "jump on the bandwagon" and be part of the group that buys a product, supports a candidate, or holds a point of view.

EXAMPLE: A soft drink commercial urges you to drink their soda to become part of the "now" generation.

Card stacking is a technique in which the speaker emphasizes only the positive points that support his or her position. Any negative aspects or alternatives are not mentioned.

EXAMPLE: A politician makes a speech to outline his plan for increasing the school budget but fails to mention that taxes would be raised.

A *false comparison* is one that compares unlike objects or events in order to gain credibility as evidence for a particular argument or cause.

EXAMPLE: A science writer explains that just as machines need oil so do humans need fat in their diet.

A speaker uses an *emotional appeal* to persuade listeners by arousing their feelings rather than their reasoning abilities. Facts needed to make informed decisions are often omitted.

EXAMPLE: A boy persuades his father to raise his allowance so that he will have more money to save for the father's birthday present.

EXERCISE D: Listening Critically. Watch a television commercial for soft drinks. Record words or phrases from the program that are examples of inappropriate tone and logical fallacies. Draw some generalizations of your own from the material you have gathered.

DEVELOPING WRITING SKILLS: Evaluating Your Listening Skills. Choose one listening skill that you want to practice, such as mentally summarizing a speaker's main ideas or listening for inappropriate tone and logical fallacies. Then choose one class in which to work on this skill. After a week of practice, write an evaluation of your progress in developing the skill.

889

Skills Review and Writing Workshop

Speaking and Listening Skills

CHECKING YOUR SKILLS

Write down the main ideas and important details in the following short speech.

In the eighteenth century, artists began to produce enormous panoramic paintings called cycloramas. Spectators were encircled by the cyclorama and felt as if they were part of the painting. Cycloramas were often used to depict large battle scenes. One early painting portrays the victory of Horatio Nelson at the Battle of the Nile in 1798. Another famous cyclorama presents Pickett's Charge at the Battle of Gettysburg in 1863. This painting can be viewed by visitors to the Gettysburg battlefield in Pennsylvania. Further south in Georgia, travelers can stop and see a cyclorama that portrays the fierce battle for Atlanta in 1864. Cycloramas also depicted popular tourist attractions, such as the Palace at Versailles or Pompeii. The popularity of cycloramas began to decline with the introduction of motion pictures. People could now watch soldiers move across a large screen, an experience that seemed more exciting than looking at static figures in a painting.

USING SPEAKING AND LISTENING SKILLS IN WRITING
Writing a Speech

Imagine that you are to speak at your high school graduation. Write a speech by following these steps.

Prewriting: Select a few main ideas that you want to present and organize them into an outline.

Writing: Prepare note cards based on your outline. Develop an effective introduction, and state your ideas clearly in a logical way.

Revising: Rewrite any phrases or sentences that could be more powerful. After you have revised, proofread your notes carefully.

Manuscript Preparation

The following pages give suggestions for basic manuscript preparation, for dealing with a number of technical aspects of writing, for giving credit to your sources, and for understanding and using correction symbols.

Basic Preparation

Whether handwritten or typed, your manuscript should follow certain basic rules. The following chart shows the suggested procedures for each style.

PREPARING A MANUSCRIPT	
Handwritten	**Typed**
1. Use white 8 1/2 × 11 inch lined paper, but never pages ripped from a spiral binder.	1. Use white 8 1/2 × 11 inch paper.
2. Use black or blue ink only.	2. Use a clear black ribbon.
3. Leave a margin of 1 inch on the right, using the paper's own rules as your margin on other sides.	3. Leave a margin of at least 1 inch on all sides.
4. Indent each paragraph.	4. Double space all lines and indent each paragraph.
5. Use only one side of each sheet of paper.	5. Use only one side of each sheet of paper.
6. Recopy if necessary to make your final copy neat.	6. Retype if necessary to make your final copy neat.

You must also identify your manuscript. For long and important papers, such as research papers, you will probably want an elaborate title page, as shown on page 892. The next page and all the other pages should carry only your name and the page number, beginning with page one.

With Title Page

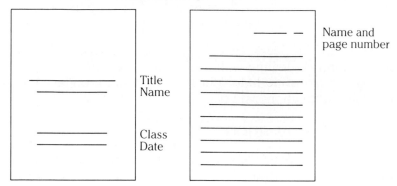

For shorter papers, use a simpler style. Basic identification appears on the first page. The second page carries your name and the page number, beginning with page two.

Without Title Page

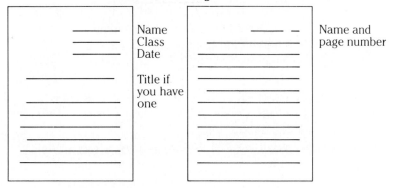

Checking Technical Matters

When preparing any manuscript, you must always check each sentence for correctness. Look for sentence errors—fragments, run-ons, and problem modifiers. Review Chapter 4, pages 132–141, if necessary. Also check the agreement of subjects and verbs. In addition, you may find it helpful to refer to the list of one hundred common usage problems on pages 259–276.

Once you have checked your sentences, look for mechanical

errors such as incorrect punctuation. The following chart offers basic guidelines for using punctuation marks and other mechanical items that seem to cause most manuscript problems.

CHECKING TECHNICAL MATTERS		
Items	**Basic Guidelines**	**References**
Capitalization	Capitalize proper nouns, proper adjectives and first words.	Section 11.1, pages 288–304
Abbreviations	Avoid most abbreviations in formal writing. Feel free, however, to use abbreviations such as Mr. and Mrs., a.m. and p.m., and well-known abbreviations for organizations such as NATO.	Section 11.2, pages 304–320
Commas	Take care not to overuse commas. Also check to make sure you are not dividing compound verbs with commas.	Section 12.2, pages 326–340
Hyphens	Check compound words in the dictionary. Hyphenate at the end of the line only when absolutely necessary and only at a syllable break.	Section 12.6, pages 365–368
Apostrophes	Avoid using apostrophes incorrectly in personal pronouns such as *its* and *theirs*.	Section 12.6, pages 369–373
Numbers	Spell out one- and two-word numbers and all numbers that begin sentences. Use numerals for lengthy numbers, dates, and addresses.	Section 11.2, pages 311–315
Spelling	Use a dictionary when in doubt.	Section 27.2, 756–767

Giving Credit to Sources

Whenever you are quoting the words or using the ideas of another writer, make sure you have given credit to that person. The chart in Section 20.1 on page 591 shows the different forms for these kinds of citations.

Using Correction Symbols

The following chart shows the basic correction symbols used by writers and editors. You may find these symbols very useful when you are proofreading your own manuscript. Your teacher may also choose to use these or similar marks when grading your papers.

USING CORRECTION SYMBOLS		
Symbols	**Meaning**	**Examples**
ᴔ	delete	The colors is red.
C	close up	The color is r ed.
∧	insert	The color is red.
#	add space	The colois red.
∿	transpose	The coolr is red.
TP	new paragraph	*TP* The color is red.
no TP	no paragraph	*no TP* The color is red.
Cap	capitalize	the color is red.
lc	use small letter	The Color is red.
Sp	spelling	The colar is red.
us	usage	The colors is red.
frag	fragment	The red color and the blue.
RO	run-on	The color is red the house is blue.
mod	problem modifier	Newly painted, I saw the house.
awk	awkward	The color is, I think, kind of red.

894

Index

Bold numbers show pages on which basic definitions and rules can be found.

899

900

L, o, d, contractions with, 372
Labels, colon with, 344
Language
   choice of, **663**–666
   emotional, **413**–415
   self-important, **412**, 414–415, 887
   uses, **786**–789
   verbal and nonverbal, 883–884
   see also Clichés; English; Etymology;
     Jargon; Nonstandard English; Standard
     English; Tone; Vocabulary; Words
Languages, capitalization, **294**–295,
   296–297
Latin expressions, 157, **315**–316, **364**
Latter, former, **267**
Lay, lie, **270**
Learn, teach, **270**
Leave, let, **270**
Less, fewer, **267**
Less and *least*, comparisons with, **245**
Letters (correspondence), 677–697
   applications, 688–694
   business, 683–688
   capitalization in, **302**–303
   envelope, 679–680
   friendly, **677**–681, 683
   personal, 677–683
   punctuation in, **337**, 339–340
   social notes, **677**–680, **681**–683
   see also Addresses
Letters of alphabet
   apostrophe with plurals, **373**, 757
   underlining, **356**, 357–359
   see also Alphabetization
Library of Congress System, 828–829, 830
Library skills, 820–830
   biography, finding, 829, 830
   card catalog, **822**–827
   classification systems, 828–829
   fiction, finding, 828, 829
   nonfiction, finding, 828–829, 830
   see also Reference skills
Like, as
   in simile, **421**, 423
   usage, **270**
Linking verb, **32**–33
   be, 32
   listed, 33
   sentence patterns with, 83–85
   subject agreement with, **223**–224,
     226–227
   subject complements after, 76, **81**–82
Listening skills, **882**–889
Lists, colon before, **343**, 345–346
Literary reference books, 836–839
Literature, writing about, 618–640
   analysis, **628**–639
   book reports, **618**–628
Loanwords, **739**–741
Logic
   to connect ideas, **460**–463
   errors in, **468**–473
   fallacies, 888–889
   order to show, **491**–492

   patterns of, **463**–468
   using models for, 473–475
   words to show, 493
   see also Reasoning
Loose, lose, **270**–271
Lovely, nice, good, **268**
-ly ending
   adjective or adverb, 43
   comparison forms with, 244
   no hyphen with, **366**, 368

Mad, **271**
Magazines. *See* Periodicals
Main clause, 119
Main entries, dictionary, 848
Main idea. *See* Idea, main
Manuscript preparation, 891–894
Maps. *See* Atlases
Masculine pronoun use, 229–**230**
May, can, **265**
Maybe, may be, **271**
Meanings, new word, **741**–742
Measurements. *See* Amounts and
   measurements
Meetings. *See* Parliamentary procedure
Memory aids, spelling, **753**–754
Metaphors, **421**–422, 423, 529
   submerged, 421–422
   see also Analogy; Clichés; Similes
Middle English, 158–159, 161
Misplaced modifiers, 137, **138**–139
Miss, 305
Models, for writing, **425**–427, **447**–448,
   473–475
Modern English, 159–160
Modern Language Association (MLA)
   system, 591–592
Modifiers, **37**–45
   absolute, in comparisons, **252**–253
   adjective, **37**–42
   adverb, **42**–45
   dangling, 137, **139**–141
   dash with nonessential, **360**–361
   diagraming, 88–89
   misplaced, 137, **138**–139
   squinting, **138**
   see also Clauses; Comparison; Phrases
Months. *See* Dates, days and months
Mood, **424**–425
More and *most*, comparisons with, 244
Motions, making of, 873–874
Ms., 305

Names
   abbreviations, **305**, 308
   capitalization, **292**–297
   events and times, **294**, 296–297
   geographical and place, **292**–293,
     296–297

902

Polishing writing. *See* Revisions
Political parties, capitalization, **294**–295, 296–297
Poorly, **272**
Portmanteau words. *See* Blends
Positive degree, **242**–248
Possessive
  adjectives and pronouns, 39, 206, **371**, 373
  amounts, **370**, 373
  apostrophe with, 369–**371**, 373
  nouns, **369**, 373
  ownership, joint or individual, **370**, 373
  pronouns before gerund, 105, **206**
  of *sake*, **370**, 373
  of time, **370**, 373
Possessive case, **200**–202, **206**–207, **371**
Precede, proceed, **272**
Précis, **706**–713
Predicate
  complement types, **75**–82
  complete, **61**–62
  simple, **64**–67
  see also Verb (part of sentence)
Predicate adjective, **81**–82, 91
Predicate nominative, **81**–82
  diagraming, 91
  nominative case, **202**–204
Preface, **792**
Prefixes
  capitalization, **298**
  common, 731–732
  hyphen with, **298**, 299, **366**, 368
  spelling with, 758, 760
  for word meaning, 730, **731**–732
Preposition, **46**–49
  common, listed, 46–47
  compound, **46**–47
  object of, **47**
  object of distinguished from indirect object, 78–79
Prepositional phrases, **47**, 48, 49, 95–97
  comma use after introductory, **331**–332
  diagraming, 112–123
  differing from infinitive, 107
  see also Adjective phrase; Adverb
Present, principal part, **165**–166
Present infinitive, 107
Present participle, 101, **165**, 166
Present tense
  forms, **163**, 164
  uses, **177**–179, 182–183
Prewriting, 376–382, 390–392
  book reports, **623**–625, 627
  essay, 555–566
  literary analysis, **633**
  paragraph, 504–512
  research paper, 601–607
  short story, **666**–668, **671**–672
Principal, principle, **273**
Principal parts, verb, **165**–173
  irregular, **167**–173
  regular, **166**–167

Procedure, parliamentary. *See* Parliamentary procedure
Progressive form, verb, **163**, 164, 165, 174–175, 179, 181, 182
Pronoun, **24**–30
  as adjective, 39, 41
  antecendent agreement, **228**–234
  antecendents, **25**, 29
  deity reference, capitalization of, **295**
  demonstrative, **26**–27, 29–30
  gender, **228**, **229**, 230–231
  indefinite, **28**–30, **231**–233, **371**, 373
  indefinite, verb agreement, **225**–226, 226–227
  intensive, **26**, 29–30
  interrogative, **28**, 29–30
  number, **215**–217, **228**
  person, **228**, **229**, 230–231
  personal, **25**–26, 29–30
  possessive, 39
  as predicate nominative, **81**–82
  problems of agreement, **234**–240
  reflexive, **26**, 29–30, **233**–234
  relative, **27**, 29–30
  singular and plural forms, 25, 26, 27
  see also Pronoun usage
Pronoun usage, 200–213
  cases, **200**–207
  for coherence, **494**, 497
  in elliptical clauses, **211**–213
  generic *he*, 229–**230**
  informal, 202–203
  who, whom, **207**–211
Pronunciation, 849, 854
Proofreading
  correction symbols, 894
  for spelling, 388–389, 746–748
Proper adjectives, **38**, **297**–299, **366**, **368**
Proper nouns, **23**–24
  capitalization, **23**, **291**–297
  dividing, **366**, **368**
  words from, 743
  see also Proper adjectives
Proposition, debate, 878
Publications. *See* Newspapers; Periodicals; Titles (of works)
Punctuation, 322–373
  see also specific types

Question, begging the. *See* Begging the question
Question mark
  with direct quotation, **348**–349
  as end punctuation, **68**, **323**, 324
  with quotation mark, **350**–351
  to show uncertainty, **325**–326
Questions
  direct object in, 76
  end punctuation of, **323**, 324
  incomplete, capitalization, **289**, 291
  inverted, patterns, **85**–86, 87
  sentence subject, placement in, 72
  see also Interrogative adjective; Interrogative pronoun; Interrogative sentence; Test-taking skills

Acknowledgments

The authors and editors have made every effort to trace the ownership of all copyrighted selections found in this book and to make full acknowledgment of their use.

The dictionary of record for this book is *Webster's New World Dictionary*, Second College Edition, Revised School Printing, copyright © 1983 by Simon & Schuster, Inc. The basis for the selection of vocabulary words appropriate for this grade level is *Living Word Vocabulary: A 43,000 Word Vocabulary Inventory* by Edgar Dale and Joseph O'Rourke, copyright © 1979.

Citations follow, arranged by unit and page for easy reference.

Usage. **Page 154** Flannery O'Connor. Reprinted by permission of Farrar, Straus and Giroux, Inc. Excerpt from *The Habit of Being: Letters by Flannery O'Connor*, edited with an Introduction by Sally Fitzgerald. Copyright © 1979 by Regina O'Connor.

Mechanics. **Pages 352-353** John McPhee. Reprinted by permission of Farrar, Straus and Giroux, Inc. Excerpt from "The Keel of Lake Dickey" from *Giving Good Weight* by John McPhee. Copyright 1975, 1976, 1978, 1979 by John McPhee. This material first appeared in *The New Yorker*. **353** Suzanne Charlé. From an article in *Travel and Leisure* Magazine.

Composition: The Writer's Techniques. **Pages 426** Katherine Anne Porter, "Flowering Judas," in *Flowering Judas and Other Stories* by Katherine Anne Porter. Harcourt Brace Jovanovich, Inc. **447** Luigi Pirandello, adapted from "A Breath of Air," from *Short Stories by Pirandello*. Copyright © 1959 by Gli Eredi Di Luigi Pirandello, copyright renewed © 1987 by Lily Duplaix. Reprinted by permission of Simon & Schuster, Inc. **473-474** Viktor E. Frankl, *Man's Search for Meaning* (New York: Washington Square Press, 1963), pp. 89-90, 120.

Composition: Forms and Process of Writing. **Pages 479** Josephine Johnson, *The Inland Island*, Copyright © 1969 by Josephine Johnson. Reprinted by permission of Simon & Schuster. **480** Adapted from Carol Simons, "Everyone Figures in the Greatest U.S. Enumeration," *Smithsonian* (March 1980), pp. 94-95. **480** *American Literature* (Houghton Mifflin Literature Series). Boston, Mass: Houghton Mifflin, 1965, p. 413. **481** Adapted from Peter Muller, "Preposterous Pets Have Always Been Our Status Symbols," *Smithsonian* (September 1980), pp. 83-84. **483** Adapted from Maureen Green, "A Tough People in a Tough Time, the Vikings Also Had a Gentler Side," *Smithsonian* (September 1980), p. 62. **483-484** J.A.C. Brown, *Techniques of Persuasion* (Baltimore, MD: Penguin Books, 1963), pp. 16-17. Copyright © Estate of J.A.C. Brown, 1963. Reprinted by permission of Penguin Books, Ltd. **488** Adapted from Emily and Per Ola d'Aulaire, "Meet the Sea Snake: Cautiously," Copyright 1980 by the National Wildlife Federation. From the May-June issue of *International Wildlife* Magazine. **494** Rosamond Bernier, "The Painter Miro, This Month 87, Is As Lively As Ever," *Smithsonian* (April 1980), p. 102. **499, 500** Stefan Kanfar, "80's Babble: Untidy Treasure," *Time* Magazine (January 28, 1980), p. 90. Reprinted by permission from TIME, The Weekly Newsmagazine; copyright Time, Inc., 1980. **501** Noel Grove, "Nigeria Struggles With Boom Times," *National Geographic* Magazine (March 1979), p. 413. **502-503** Robert Wernick, "A Quiet American Painter Whose Art Is Now Being Heard," *Smithsonian* (October 1982), p. 111. **520** "When Hail Breaks Loose," by John Hallett, *Natural History*, Vol. 89, No. 6, June 1980, p. 55. Excerpted and reprinted by permission. Copyright the American Museum of Natural History, 1980. **521** Adapted from Peggy Sealfon, "Holography," *Horizon* (July 1979), p. 33. **522** Adapted from Uta Hagen, *Respect for Acting* (New York: Macmillan, 1973), p. 54. **522** *Scientific American*, "Science and the Citizen" (July, 1980), p. 72. By permission of W.H. Freeman and Company for *Scientific American*. **524** Barbara Tuchman, "The Decline of Quality," *The New York Times Magazine* (November 2, 1980), p. 40. © 1980 by Barbara Tuchman. Reprinted by permission of Russell & Volkening as agents for the author. **527** Thomas L. Kimball, "The Problem That Simply Can't Wait: Dirty Air!" Copyright 1980 by the National Wildlife Federation. Reprinted from the July-August issue of *International Wildlife* Magazine. **530** Joan Didion, *The White Album*. Copyright 1979 by Joan Didion. Reprinted by permission of Simon & Schuster, Inc. **531** Adapted from Archie Carr, "In Praise of Snakes," in *The Audubon Wildlife Treasury*, ed. Les Line (Philadelphia: J.B. Lippincott, Co., 1967), p. 169. **532-533** From "A Tin Butterfly" in *Memories of a Catholic Girlhood* by Mary McCarthy. Copyright 1951, 1979 by Mary McCarthy. Reprinted by permission of Harcourt Brace Jovanovich, Inc. **534-535** Arthur L. Campa, "The Cell of Heavenly Justice." First published in *New Mexico Quarterly*, August 1934, University of New Mexico Press, pp. 219-230. **535-536** Adapted from Dorothy Canfield, "How 'Flint and Fire' Started and Grew" in *Americans All*, ed., Benjamin A. Heydrick, 1920. **537** (first item) Specified excerpt from "Death of a Pig" (p. 19) in *Essays of E.B. White*. Copyright 1947 by E.B. White. Reprinted by permission of Harper & Row, Publishers, Inc. **537** (second item) Specified excerpt from p. 74 in *The Habit of Loving* by Doris Lessing (Thomas Y. Crowell) Copyright © 1957 by Doris Lessing. Reprinted by permission of Harper & Row, Publishers, Inc. **581-584** "The World in a Wall," from *My Family and Other Animals* by Gerald M. Durrell, Copyright © 1956 by Gerald M. Durrell. Renewed © 1984 by Gerald M. Durrell. Reprinted by permission of Viking Penguin Inc. **593** Anthony P. Andrews, "The Salt Trade of the Ancient Maya." Reprinted from *Archaeology* Magazine, Vol. 33, No. 4. Copyright Archaeological Institute of America, 1980, **649-650** Excerpt from *Writing with a Word Processor*, by William Zinsser. Copyright 1983 by William Zinsser. Reprinted by permission of the author. **652-653** Specified excerpt from *Memories* by Julian Huxley, p. 220. Copyright © 1970 by George Allen & Unwin Ltd. Reprinted by permission of Harper & Row, Publishers, Inc. **706-707** *Newsweek*, "The Lost Glory of El Mirador" (December 1, 1980), p. 15. Copyright 1980 by Newsweek, Inc. All Rights Reserved. Reprinted by Permission of Newsweek. **708-709** *Wild Animals of North America* (Washington, DC: The National Geographic Society, 1979), pp. 99-101. **711-712** Adapted from Deborah Cramer, "The Salt Marsh—More Productive Than Wheat and Hay Fields" *The New York Times* (November 22, 1980) © 1980 by The New York Times Company. Reprinted by permission.

Study and Research Skills. **Pages 799** From *College Entrance Examination Board*, selection on "Early Humanoids" from Reading Comprehension section of an SAT examination. **802-818** From *Preparation for the SAT; Verbal Abilities* by Gabriel Freedman and, *Test of Standard Writers English* by Margaret Haller, used by permission of Arco Publishing Inc., New York © 1984, 5th edition, 6th printing. **807-808** Adapted from Michael McRae, "Survival of the Fastest," *Outside* (September 1980). **816** From *American College Testing Program* (ACT) by Eve P. Steinberg, passage V, p. 27 for English Usage, used by permission of Arco Publishing, Inc., New York © 1984. **831** *The Encyclopedia Americana* 1980, Vol. 30, p. 560. Reprinted with permission of The Encyclopedia Americana, copyright 1980, The Americana Corporation. **840** *Readers' Guide to Periodical Literature*, Copyright © 1985 by The H.W. Wilson Company, material reproduced by permission of the publisher. **841** *The New York Times Index*, 1984 Volume, by The New York Times Company. Reprinted by permission. **845** By permission. From *Webster's Third New International Dictionary* © 1981 by Merriam-Webster Inc., publisher of the Merriam-Webster® Dictionaries. **846** *Oxford English Dictionary*, 1979. (Oxford, England: Oxford University Press). **848, 850, 851, 852, 853** with permission. From *Webster's New Collegiate Dictionary* © 1980 by the G. & C. Merriam Co., Publishers of the Merriam-Webster Dictionaries.

Art Acknowledgments. **Pages 403** Robert A. Isaacs, Photo Researchers. **516** NASA. **517** Douglas Corry, DPI. **518** Frank Siteman, Taurus Photos; B. Anderson, Monkmeyer Press. **539** Laura Riley, Bruce Coleman. **540** Bob Adelman, Woodfin Camp. **541** Oldenburg, Claes, Giant Hamburger, 1962, Art Gallery of Ontario. **586** Courtesy of Good Housekeeping. **587** Culver Pictures; Cary Wolinsky, Stock Boston. **588** Edith Reichman, Monkmeyer Press. **615** Lawrence Lariar, 1966, Crown Publishers, Inc. **616** Culver Pictures, Inc. **617** Ed Carlin, The Picture Cube. **655** United Feature Syndicate, Inc., © 1960. **656** Dean Abramson, Stock Boston; Al Kaplan, DPI: Clifford Hausner, Leo de Wys, Inc. **657** Ira Berger, Woodfin Camp; Michael Hayman, Stock Boston. **674** Charles Addams, *The New Yorker*, 1979. **675** Homer, The Metropolitan Museum of Art, Harris Brisbane Dick Fund, 1941. **676** Culver Pictures. **714** Wide World Photos.

GRAMMAR USAGE MECHANICS